Kenosha News 7/23/75

Van Dahm author financial textbook

A new textbook introduction to the financial system titled 'Money and Banking' by Dr. Thomas Van Dahm, Professor of Economics at Carthage College, has been published by the D.C. Heath Co. of Lexington, Mass., and is now on sale.

The needs, abilities and reading level of undergraduate students are Dr. Van Dahm's prime consideration in his new book which blends an institutional approach with appropriate theoretical analysis and a treatment of public policy issues. Institutional aspects of the financial system, the roles of non-bank intermediaries and the financial markets in the entire process of monetary policy are discussed extensively by Dr. Van Dahm.

"I've taken a broad financial system approach in this book," said Prof. Van Dahm, "emphasizing the interrelatedness of all parts of our financial system in the United States — both the monetary and non-monetary segments. The main emphasis is on showing readers how our financial system affects and is affected by the goods and services sector of the economy. I've tried to address myself to the students rather than my peers. Too many texts seem to leave the undergraduate reader, majoring in business administration or economics, out of consideration," he added.

Dr. Thomas Van Dahm

Dr. Van Dahm, who is chairman of the Business and Economics Division at Carthage, is a graduate of Hope (Mich.) College and received both his Master's and Ph. D. degrees from the University of Michigan. In 1959 he was the recipient of a Ford Foundation Fellowship for post-doctoral study at the University of Indiana.

MONEY AND BANKING
AN INTRODUCTION TO THE FINANCIAL SYSTEM

*To my good friend Harold Carlson:
Sincere best wishes to you & Anatel!*

Tom Van Dahm

MONEY AND BANKING

AN INTRODUCTION TO THE FINANCIAL SYSTEM

Thomas E. Van Dahm
Carthage College

D. C. HEATH AND COMPANY
Lexington, Massachusetts Toronto London

To Lois *my helpmeet*

Copyright © 1975 by D. C. Heath and Company.

All rights reserved. No part of this publication may be reproduced or transmitted in any form or by any means, electronic or mechanical, including photocopy, recording, or any information storage or retrieval system, without permission in writing from the publisher.

Published simultaneously in Canada.

Printed in the United States of America.

International Standard Book Number: 0-669-91132-1

Library of Congress Catalog Card Number: 74-10020

PREFACE

As the reader may have surmised (the title is a dead giveaway), this textbook is intended for the basic undergraduate economics course usually labeled "Money and Banking" or something similar. The subtitle, *An Introduction to the Financial System,* indicates the approach of the book. While recognizing the centrality of money and monetary institutions in the financial system, I have tried to place them in the broader context of the system as a whole. This approach is consistent with recent developments in macroeconomic theory and econometrics, notably the tendency to incorporate far more detailed financial sectors in macromodels than had been the case until recently. Moreover, monetary and regulatory authorities of government are giving increasing attention to nonmonetary and nonbanking elements of the financial system and, in fact, are gradually coming around to the view that the financial system must be analyzed and evaluated as a whole, with individual components—for example, the savings and loan industry—analyzed in relation to the system.

The aim of this book, accordingly, is *to guide the student toward an understanding of our financial system: its institutional structure, its interactions with the "real" economy, and its role as a vehicle of government economic policy.* No single aspect of the field—institutions, theory, or policy—is singled out as *the* primary focus of the text. The diverse interests of students, in my experience, are best served by this balanced approach.

In writing the book I have attempted to keep constantly in mind my primary audience: undergraduate students, most of whom are taking the course in conjunction with a major in business administration or economics. The choice of topics, the relative emphasis placed on them, and the level at which they are developed—all these were influenced by this factor. Since nearly all my teaching experience has been centered around undergraduates, I feel reasonably confident of my ability to hit this target.

The student should have completed an introductory course in economics prior to this point, if possible. However, he/she should be able to overcome any deficiencies in background by diligent study and by consulting appropriate sections of any standard text on the principles of economics.

The length of the text will permit the instructor to supplement it in any of a number of ways, if time permits. Excellent books of readings are available, as are paperback treatments of one or another aspect of the subject.

As to the content of the text, the instructor will find that most of the standard topics are included, though not always in familiar settings. Here is a brief catalog of features of content, emphasis, and organization which call for some highlighting:

1. The opening chapter presents an overview of the financial system instead of the customary "introduction to money."
2. Chapter 2 contains, along with the usual mechanics of the money supply process, a brief sketch of the economics of this process. A more comprehensive discussion of this latter topic appears in chapter 17.
3. Also in chapter 2 there is a discussion of our payments system. Recent actions by the Federal Reserve System in this area, plus the prospect of fundamental changes in our methods of handling payments (with implications for the financial system that challenge our imaginations) amply justify inclusion for this topic.
4. A brief history of American financial intermediaries, which opens chapter 3, introduces a full treatment of financial institutions—commercial bank, central bank, and nonbank—which makes up chapters 3 through 9. In view of the approach of this text, the broader scope of this historical treatment seemed more appropriate than the still-common "history of the American banking system."
5. A general survey of central banking precedes the discussion of the structure and functions of the Federal Reserve System in chapters 6 and 7, in order to place our own central bank in proper perspective.
6. Chapters 8 and 9 not only contain descriptions of each major type of nonbank financial institution but also (and perhaps more importantly) stresses significant competitive and complementary relations of each type with other types of financial institutions.
7. There is no separate unit on international finance. Rather, international aspects are incorporated in the discussion at a number of points: institutional relationships in chapter 12, macroeconomic aspects in chapters 15 through 18, and policy implications in chapter 22. This scheme reduces the likelihood that, because of time pressures, international finance will be omitted entirely from the course—as often happens.
8. An entire chapter—13—is devoted to the activities of government in relation to the financial system, as intermediary and regulator, along with the rationale for such activities.

9. In the section on monetary theory (chapters 15 through 18), financial determinants of aggregate expenditures are highlighted. Also, the elementary algebra of the theory is confined to chapter appendixes, carefully keyed to the related sections of the chapter text.
10. Monetary policy is discussed, in chapters 21 and 22, *after* other elements of macroeconomic policy—fiscal policy, debt management, and incomes policy—in recognition of the fact that monetary policy has, in effect, been assigned the task of "policy of last resort."
11. Certain controversies and unsettled points in monetary economics and policy—the monetarist issue and the problem of incidence of monetary policy come immediately to mind—receive due attention but are not emphasized. I believe that an introductory treatment should concentrate on what we can be reasonably certain about, with just enough controversy brought in to demonstrate our humility and to whet the appetite for further investigation.

In writing a textbook one realizes the extent to which one is intellectually indebted to others. I could not begin to list the names of my intellectual creditors: former teachers, present and former colleagues, and writers whose thoughts have become my thoughts; but I must single out as especially influential (though they may not want to admit it!) several men who were on the economics faculty of the University of Michigan during my graduate-school days: Gardner Ackley, Kenneth Boulding, Richard Musgrave, and Leonard Watkins.

A variety of other people have left their mark on the book in one way or another, including (1) the administration of Carthage College, which granted me a sabbatical leave to finish the book; (2) Professors Don C. Bridenstine, Jerry W. Johnson, and Jon Harkness who read the entire manuscript and made many perceptive comments and suggestions; and (3) Mrs. Hsiao-Mei Wiedmeyer, my supertypist, who prepared the final draft of the manuscript. I gratefully acknowledge their contributions.

Finally, less tangible but no less important to the long process of bringing this book to completion has been the understanding and inspiration, expressed in so many ways, of my wife, Lois.

THOMAS E. VAN DAHM

CONTENTS

An Overview   1
 Nature and Necessity of Finance   2
 Elements of the Financial System   3
 The Financial System and the "Real" System   8
 Plan of the Book   13

PART I
MONEY IN THE FINANCIAL SYSTEM   17

1 Money and the Monetary System   19
 The Concept of Money   19
 Evolution of Money: From Pure Commodity
  to Pure Claim   21
 The Monetary System   26
 Summary   44

2 Monetary Role of the Banking System   47
 The Commercial Bank   47
 The Banking System   50
 The Process of Demand-Deposit Creation   55
 The Payments System   73
 Summary   77

PART II
INSTITUTIONAL FRAMEWORK: MONETARY INSTITUTIONS   81

3 Intermediaries and the Process of Intermediation   83
 Intermediation and the Intermediaries   84
 Evolution of American Financial Intermediaries   86
 The Financial Institutions: A Survey   93
 The Nature of the Financial Intermediary   98
 Summary   101

4 Commercial Banks: Sources of Financing   104
 The Combined Balance Sheet   105
 Sources of Financing: The Capital Accounts   109
 Deposits   111
 Demand Deposits   113
 Time Deposits   115
 Other Obligations   123

5 Commercial Banks: The Asset-Mix 126
- Reserves 126
- Earning Assets 132
- Government Influences on the Asset Structure 136
- Application of Balance-Sheet Management Criteria 137
- Summary of Chapters 4 and 5 142

6 Central Banking and the Federal Reserve System 144
- Central Banking 145
- Background of the Federal Reserve System 149
- Structure of the Federal Reserve System 150
- Summary 162

7 The Federal Reserve System and Monetary Control 165
- Member-Bank Reserves and the Federal Reserve Balance Sheet 166
- The Federal Reserve and Member-Bank Reserves 168
- Summary 186

PART III
INSTITUTIONAL FRAMEWORK: OTHER ELEMENTS 189

8 Nonbank Financial Intermediaries: The Savings Institutions 191
- The Depository Savings Intermediaries 193
- The Contractual Savings Intermediaries 201
- Investment Companies 213

9 The Borrowing Intermediaries and Nonintermediary Financial Firms 218
- The Borrowing Intermediaries 218
- Nonintermediary Financial Firms 223
- Intermediation by Nonintermediaries 227
- Summary of Chapters 8 and 9 229

10 The Financial Markets: Money Markets 232
- The Money Markets 234
- Money-Market Instruments 238

11 The Financial Markets: Capital Markets and Interest Rates 252
- Capital-Market Instruments 252
- The Structure of Interest Rates 258
- Summary of Chapters 10 and 11 266

12 The International Context 269
- Monetary Relations 270
- Financial Market Relations 276
- Summary 286

13 The Role of Government in the Financial System 288
- Government as Intermediary 292
- Government Influences on Private Intermediaries 303
- Summary 313

PART IV
MONETARY THEORY: THE FINANCIAL SYSTEM AND THE ECONOMY 317

14 The Accounting Framework of Macroeconomic Theory 319
  The Problem 320
  The Accounting Framework: The National Income and Product Accounts 321
  Summary 329

15 The Building Blocks of Macroeconomic Theory 331
  Consumption and Its Determination 333
  Investment 344
  Government Expenditures 357
  The Rest-of-the-World Sector 357

16 The Structure of Macroeconomic Theory 360
  A Macroeconomic Model 360
  The Multiplier 363
  Summary of Chapters 15 and 16 368
  Appendix: An Algebraic Formulation 370

17 The Financial Sector in Macroeconomic Theory 375
  The Concept of Liquidity 376
  Demand for Liquidity 380
  Demand for, and Supply of, Money 383
  Money Demand and Supply, Income, and the Interest Rate 391
  Equilibrium in the Financial System 394
  Summary 396
  Appendix 398

18 The Real and Financial Systems: Inflation and Growth 400
  A Real/Financial Model of the Economy 401
  Aggregate Economic Activity and the Price Level 409
  Economic Growth and the Macroeconomy 417
  The Model World and the Real World: Final Comments 418
  Summary 419
  Appendix 420

PART V
MACROECONOMIC POLICY: GOALS, MEANS, AND CURRENT ISSUES 425

19 Macroeconomic Policy: Goals and Means 427
  The Goals of Macroeconomic Policy 430
  Summary 440

20 The Means: Fiscal Policy, Debt Management, and Incomes Policy 442
  Monetary Policy 443
  Fiscal Policy 444
  Debt Management 453
  Macroeconomic Role of Incomes Policy 463
  Summary 468

21 **The Means: Monetary Policy** 471
    Monetary Policy Formation 472
    Federal Reserve Actions: Alternatives and Evaluation 477
    Federal Reserve Actions and the Economy's Response 490
    Summary 498

22 **Monetary Policy: Further Considerations** 501
    International Aspects of Monetary Policy 501
    The Incidence of Monetary Policy 511
    Recapitulation of Macroeconomic Policy 514
    Summary 518

Index 520

FIGURES

1.1 Steps in the evolution of money.
1.2 Components of the United States monetary system, October 31, 1973.
6.1 Boundaries of Federal Reserve districts and their branch territories.
11.1 Growth pattern of a $1,000 claim.
11.2 Growth pattern of a $1,000 claim, purchased for $981.92.
11.3 Bond yields.
11.4 Yield curve, based on U.S. Treasury securities, January 28, 1974.
15.1 Consumption and personal saving functions.
15.2 Consumption and gross national product.
15.3 MEI schedule of the firm.
15.4 MEI schedule of the economy.
15.5 Investment and gross national product.
15.6 MEI and MCF schedules.
15.7 Relationship between gross national product and government expenditures for goods and services.
15.8 Relationship between net exports and gross national product.
16.1 Total expenditure function.
17.1 Relationship between gross national product and the demand for money.
17.2 Relationship between the interest rate and the demand for money.
17.3 The money supply.
17.4 Money demand and supply.
18.1 The interest rate and real-sector equilibrium.
18.2 The interest rate and financial-sector equilibrium.
18.3 Macroeconomic equilibrium.
18.4 Zone of inflation.
18.5 Macroeconomic equilibrium, adjusted for inflation.
19.1 Elements in the policy process.
19.2 Modified Phillips curve.
19.3 The Eckstein-Brinner long-run Phillips curve.
20.1 Effects of fiscal measures.
20.2 Full-employment surplus under alternative fiscal programs.
21.1 Macroeconomic effects of a Federal Reserve open-market purchase.
22.1 Effects of monetary and fiscal policy on aggregate equilibrium.

TABLES

1.1 Currency Outstanding and in Circulation, December 1973
2.1 Size Distribution of Commercial Banks, December 31, 1973
2.2 Classification of Commercial Banks, December 31, 1973
2.3 Unit Banking and Branch Banking, Selected Years, 1900–1973
2.4 Deposit Expansion Process
3.1 The System of Financial Institutions
4.1 Combined Balance Sheet, All Commercial Banks, December 31, 1973
4.2 Commercial Bank Deposits, December 31, 1973
4.3 Maximum Interest Rates Payable on Bank Deposits, as of May 31, 1974
5.1 Reserves of All Commercial Banks in the United States, December 31, 1973
5.2 Commercial Bank Earning-Assets, December 31, 1973
5.3 Market Price of a $100 6 Per Cent Bond
5.4 Commercial Bank Loans and Investments, Selected Years, 1947–1973
6.1 Total Assets of Federal Reserve Banks, December 31, 1973
6.2 Earnings and Expenses of the Federal Reserve Banks, 1973
7.1 Consolidated Federal Reserve Balance Sheet, May 31, 1974
7.2 The Reserve Equation: Determinants of Member-Bank Reserves, May 31, 1974
7.3 Member-Bank Reserve Requirements, in Effect May 31, 1974
7.4 Sources of Changes in Member-Bank Reserves, November 30, 1970–September 30, 1973
8.1 Total Assets of Financial Intermediaries
8.2 Financial Assets and Liabilities of Depository Savings Intermediaries, December 31, 1973
8.3 Structure of the Savings and Loan Industry, December 31, 1973
8.4 Financial Assets and Liabilities of Life Insurance Companies, December 31, 1973
8.5 Financial Assets and Liabilities of Non-Life Insurance Companies, December 31, 1973
8.6 Financial Assets of Private Pension Funds, December 31, 1973
8.7 Financial Assets of State and Local Government Retirement Funds, December 31, 1973
8.8 Financial Assets of Open-End Investment Companies, December 31, 1973
8.9 Financial Assets of Real Estate Investment Trusts, December 31, 1973
9.1 Assets and Liabilities of Finance Companies, June 30, 1970
10.1 Selected Money Market Instruments, Volume Outstanding, March 31, 1974
10.2 Ownership of Short-Term Marketable U.S. Government Securities, March 31, 1974

10.3 Treasury Cash Receipts from, and Payments to, the Public, 1970–1973
11.1 Money and Capital Market Yields, Selected Years and Months, 1950–1973
12.1 Foreign Liquid Asset Holdings in the United States, by Holder and Type of Asset, December 31, 1973
13.1 Federal Credit Programs, June 30, 1962
13.2 Permissibility of Nonbanking Activities for Bank Holding Companies
14.1 Gross National Product Valued in Current and 1958 Prices, Selected Years, 1929–1973
14.2 Gross National Product, Expenditure Approach, 1973
14.3 Gross National Product, Income Approach, 1973
14.4 Relationship Between Disposable Income and Expenditures, 1973
14.5 Net Financial Investment of the Household Sector, 1972
15.1 Net Disposable Personal Income, Consumption, and Personal Savings
15.2 Relationship of Gross National Product, Disposable Income, and Consumption
15.3 The MPI Schedule
15.4 Illustration of the Acceleration Principle
16.1 The Total Expenditure Function and Its Components
16.2 Revised Investment and Total Expenditures Function
16.3 Effects of an Increase in Autonomous Expenditures
16.4 Multiplier: Period Analysis
18.1 Total Expenditures Function
18.2 Relationship of Planned Expenditures (E) to Aggregate Income (Y) and the Rate of Interest (R)
18.3 Relationship Between the Interest Rate and Aggregate Equilibrium
18.4 Relationship of the Demand for Money (L) to Aggregate Income (Y) and the Rate of Interest (R)
18.5 Relationship Between the Interest Rate and Monetary Equilibrium
18.6 Relationship Between the Interest Rate and GNP at Which $E = Y$ and $L = M$
20.1 Relationship of GNP and Federal Budget Position
20.2 Ownership and Maturity Composition of Marketable Treasury Securities, November 30, 1973
20.3 Composition of the Public Debt, Selected Years, 1941–1973
20.4 Effects of Shifts of Government Securities Among Classes of Holders
21.1 Relative Advantages of Various Monetary Tools for Countercyclical Actions
22.1 Balance of Payments of the United States, 1973
22.2 United States Liquid Liabilities to Foreigners, December 31, 1973

Nature and Necessity of Finance

Elements of the Financial System
Financial Claims
Financial Institutions: Intermediaries and Others
Financial Markets
Government Agencies

The Financial System and the "Real" System
A Money Economy
Nonmonetary Claims
Financial Intermediaries
Why Study the Financial System?

Plan of the Book

An Overview

The financial system, like the proverbial well-known speaker, seemingly needs no introduction. So pervasive is this system that nothing short of a hermit's existence can keep us from participating in it. But so complex is the financial system that our acquaintance with it is almost bound to be incomplete and piecemeal. In fact, as a result of this complexity, not only do we almost inevitably carry an inadequate conception of what the system is—its size, scope, and variety of constituent parts—but we also generally lack a framework for viewing the system as a whole and for incorporating what we have already learned and will learn about it.

It is no exaggeration to state that our modern highly developed, dynamic economic system would be impossible without our equally sophisticated financial system. The "real," or goods-and-services, economy and the financial system, interacting in numberless ways, are so completely dependent on each other that we cannot really understand the working of our economic system without a clear comprehension of its financial aspects.

Whether your quest for economic understanding is motivated by interest in economics per se or by a desire to learn more about the socioeconomic environment in which the business enterprise operates, the course on which we are embarking should prove worthwhile and—who knows—maybe even enjoyable.

In this introductory chapter we set the stage by briefly examining three related topics: (1) the nature and necessity of finance, (2) the elements of a financial system, and (3) the economic role of the financial system.

Nature and Necessity of Finance

Probably every economic unit—such as a household, business firm, or unit of government—occasionally or frequently faces this kind of situation: in order to accomplish a particular objective, it must (1) purchase certain services without depleting its cash or other assets or (2) add to its present stock of assets. Either of these kinds of actions would necessarily (barring theft, gift, or a lucky number) involve an increase in the obligations of the economic unit to one or more other economic units.

Illustrations of the first type of action are an advertising campaign (services) financed by a bank loan (the obligation), or a tour of Europe (services) on a "fly now, pay later" (the obligation) basis. A familiar example of the second type of action is the purchase of a television set "on time." In this case the household simultaneously acquires an asset (the TV set) and incurs a debt (the obligation to make a series of monthly payments). The same process is involved when a business firm arranges for a loan from its bank (the obligation), agreeing to repay the loan in installments over a three-year period, in order to acquire the money to purchase a delivery truck (asset). The common element in all of these cases—and probably other examples come readily to mind—is the desire of the economic unit to be *financed* or to obtain financing.

Because this widely used term, finance, along with its variant forms, has come to have such a variety of meanings and is so often accompanied with a qualifying adjective (such as *corporation*, *public*, or *consumer*), we must define it clearly and then adhere to our definition in order to avoid confusion. *To finance (or provide financing to) an economic unit means to accept a claim against it calling for one or more future payments of money, in exchange for a specified item or items of value.* The "future payments" might be specified as to time and amount or dependent on certain contingencies (for example, profits above a given amount, or declaration of a dividend). The "item or items of value" could consist of goods, services, money, or claims to money.

It must be apparent by this time that finance is an extremely general phenomenon in our economy. But does this conclusion also apply to other advanced economies as well? A recent comprehensive study in the area of comparative financial systems reached this broad conclusion:

> In most countries a rough parallelism can be observed between economic and financial development if periods of several decades are considered. As real income and wealth increase, in the aggregate and per head of the population, the size and complexity of the financial superstructure grow.[1]

Note that this conclusion applies regardless of the mode of economic organization, whether capitalist, communist, democratic socialist, or whatever, although the institutional details of the financial systems vary

---

[1] Raymond W. Goldsmith, *Financial Structure and Development* (New Haven: Yale University Press, 1969), p. 48.

widely from country to country. The clear implication is that it is no mere coincidence that economic development and financial development occur together; rather, financial development is an integral part of the broad process of economic development.

Elements of the Financial System

The financial system comprises the network of (1) financial claims, (2) financial institutions, (3) financial markets, and (4) government agencies influencing the behavior of the foregoing, together with (5) the laws, customs, and arrangements affecting their operation and usage. In this section our task will be to clarify some of the key terms in the foregoing sentence.

Financial Claims

Financial claims (we shall call them simply "claims," since we are not going to be directly involved with any nonfinancial kinds) *consist of money and rights to receive money under specified circumstances.* Although usually evidenced by a financial instrument setting forth the terms of the claim, it is the claim itself that is our concern.

If we compare the definition of (financial) claims just given with our earlier definition of financing, we will observe that the issuance of claims is inseparable from the financing process. In fact, "to issue claims" is only another way of saying "to be financed": by definition, an economic unit cannot secure financing without incurring an obligation to another economic unit; and such an obligation is, from the standpoint of the provider of financing, a claim.

The variety of terms and conditions found in claims is virtually limitless, but all such claims can be broken down into two broad categories: debts and equities. The distinction is that equities convey ownership rights; debt claims do not. The "claim" aspect of an equity may not be a dominant consideration in the mind of the holder, who may be more interested in control of the enterprise or in the likelihood that he can sell the asset for a higher price than he paid. Nevertheless, since he is entitled to money payments under specified circumstances, he possesses a claim, so far as we are concerned.

MECHANICS OF CLAIM CREATION   Claim creation and claim destruction are commonly depicted with the aid of an expository device that we shall call the *balance-sheet trace statement*.[2] By means of this device we can show (1) which balance-sheet accounts are affected by a given transaction or set of transactions, (2) the direction of effect, and (3) the mone-

---

[2] Writers often use the term "T-account" to describe this device, but this is apt to be confusing to those who are acquainted with accounting terminology, in which the "T-account" is a ledger account.

tary value involved. The form of this statement follows that of the balance sheet: assets on the left side; liabilities and net worth on the right.

To illustrate, suppose you buy a book at the local bookstore for $9.50, paying cash. Your personal balance sheet would show the following changes: (1) cash and "books" accounts affected; (2) cash decreased, "books" increased; and (3) in each case, by $9.50. The bookstore's balance sheet shows (1) cash and "books" accounts affected; (2) cash increased, books decreased; (3) in both cases, by $9.50. Depicting all of this information on the balance-sheet trace statement gives us this picture: (the titles of the accounts are chosen for simplicity, not for conformity to any used by bookstores or individuals).

TRACE 1

Your Balance Sheet		Bookstore Balance Sheet	
Cash	−$9.50	Cash	+$9.50
Books	+9.50	Books	−9.50

No claims have been created. Money, a type of claim, has changed hands.

If, instead, you "charge" the book, agreeing to pay in thirty days, the balance-sheet trace would be as follows:

TRACE 2

Your Balance Sheet				Bookstore Balance Sheet	
Books	+$9.50	"Payables"	+$9.50	"Receivables"	+$9.50
				Books	−9.50

Note that in this case a claim has been created and is held by the bookstore against you, the "issuer." It is a simple claim, merely specifying an amount of money to be paid to a designated party at or by a certain time. But it fits our definition just as well as a claim evidenced by an engraved document calling for periodic interest payments, protected by a pledge of assets or a guarantee by a third party, and requiring the issuer to adhere to certain practices in his financial affairs. You have received financing from, or have been financed by, the bookstore; and, inevitably, a brand-new claim has been created.

(To test your grasp of the balance-sheet trace statement, show the results of the transaction that takes place thirty days later—if all goes as planned—in which you pay the $9.50 to the bookstore.[3])

Claims come into existence in the course of a variety of kinds of transactions. The above illustration, a purchase "on credit," represents one large class: *exchange of goods and services for a nonmoney claim*.

[3]

Your Balance Sheet				Bookstore Balance Sheet	
Cash	−$9.50	"Payables"	−$9.50	Cash	+$9.50
				"Receivables"	−9.50

Some other common members of this class include the purchase of a home in which the buyer is financed by means of a loan secured by a mortgage against the property involved, and the purchase of equipment on the installment plan by business firms.

A second class of transactions involving the creation of claims is illustrated by loans to businesses and governments and by issues of stock (equities) by corporate businesses. Here there is an *exchange of money for a nonmoney claim.*

MONEY AS A CLASS OF CLAIMS   Money ranks number one on almost everyone's list of claims, in economic importance as well as in most other respects. But perhaps we are a bit hesitant about placing money in the same category as the bookstore claim just discussed, or a business loan, or a school-district bond. Money, after all, is "different," we feel. And so it is: money alone serves as a society's means of making payments. In fact, "money" and "means of payment" are virtual synonyms, a point that will be elaborated on in chapter 1.

For the sake of accuracy we should note that there have been and, in some societies, still are types of money that are *not* financial claims.[4] A unit of such money has intrinsic (commodity) value equal to its value as money. In all modern industrialized economies these pure commodity monies have disappeared or survive only as vestigial remnants from earlier days. So, even though money need not be a claim—and, historically, usually was not—we may avoid much confusion by regarding it as a type of claim in our discussion.

To help us grasp the relation between money and claim, let us look at the dominant type of "means of payment" in the United States today: the checking account or demand deposit. By writing and delivering a check, the owner of a demand deposit transfers a claim on his bank (the face amount of the check) to another party. This claim is not merely "as good as money"; it *is* money because it serves as a "means of payment." This is a very important point because most of us still tend to think of money in terms of physical objects, an appropriate mode of thought for the nineteenth century and earlier but not for today.

But what about our hand-to-hand money: coins and paper currency? Are these "claims"? The answer is "yes": claims against the issuing agency, whether government or private. Even our coins are claims, albeit in rather expensive dress, because there is not full commodity value in any of our present-day coins equal to their "claim" value. So if you go to your bank and make a withdrawal of twenty-five dollars in currency, you have merely given up a claim of that amount against the bank in exchange for an equivalent claim against the issuer of currency, perhaps the United States Treasury. The bank, in turn, owes you twenty-five

---

[4] Anthropologists have discovered a fascinating variety of objects that have been used at various times and places as money. See Paul Einzig, *Primitive Money in Its Ethnological, Historical, and Economic Aspects* (London: Eyre & Spottiswoode, Ltd., 1949).

dollars less than before but holds a correspondingly reduced claim, in currency, against the Treasury.

CLAIMS AND THE "PRICE" OF FINANCING We have noted some reasons why economic units *seek* financing, but we also need to know why economic units *provide* it. Why do they decide to accumulate claims instead of goods? A preliminary (and obvious) answer is that they must anticipate some sort of "return" from financial assets, a return at least sufficient to offset any costs and risks involved.

The return could take any of a variety of forms. In the case of debt securities, the main element in the expected return usually is interest, but the return could include an increase in the price at which the security can be sold. Equity (ownership) securities are expected to yield dividends and increases in market value. Even money must yield some sort of return or it would not be held. Returns on money include convenience and economy in transactions, rapid maneuverability in case of unanticipated opportunity or adversity requiring payment, and "peace of mind."[5]

But what about the furniture store that offers "free" ninety-day financing? In cases like this, the return is the difference between the added (expected) sales attributed to the "easy credit" policy and the added expenses associated with these sales.

Financial Institutions: Intermediaries and Others

A financial institution, as defined here, is a private or governmental organization (1) the assets of which consist primarily of claims or (2) the income of which is primarily derived from dealing in, and/or performing services in connection with, claims.

Institutions in the first category are commonly referred to as *financial intermediaries*. The reason is that these institutions stand between the economic units financing and those being financed: they acquire and hold claims issued by economic units securing financing and, in turn, issue obligations held mainly by economic units that are, in a sense to be explained later, the ultimate suppliers of financing.

Some financial intermediaries are of types familiar to most of us—the commercial bank such as "Valley Heights National Bank" found in most communities, for example, as well as the savings and loan association and finance company. Many others are probably unfamiliar at this point but play important roles in particular sectors of the new financial system. As the chapters roll by, we shall develop at least a nodding acquaintance with the investment company, the development credit corporation, and the small business investment company, among others, if we have not already done so.

---

[5] Chapter 17 discusses these and other elements in the demand for money.

Then there are the financial institutions in the second category, those obtaining most of their income by transacting in, or performing services related to, claims. Some of these firms provide financial information and advice, some actually manage portfolios of financial assets on behalf of other economic units, some buy and sell claims on instructions from clients, and some assist in finding sources for those economic units seeking financing.

There would be no point in introducing a long list of categories of financial institutions here. However, we shall be devoting considerable space to them shortly. First and foremost, the monetary intermediaries will be discussed in detail in chapters 4 through 7. The other intermediaries and nonintermediary financial firms will then be taken up in chapters 8 and 9.

Financial Markets

Financial markets are institutions that facilitate transactions in financial claims. Some of these markets center upon a specific geographical point—the New York Stock Exchange, for example—while others lack a definite center; for example, the New York money market, dealings in which are conducted almost entirely by telephone. In either case, though, the essential characteristic of a financial market is that it serves as the means through which the forces of demand and supply relevant to a specified class of financial claims are brought into contact with each other.

Variety is a dominant quality of financial markets. Some are local in scope; others are worldwide. Some have literally thousands of participants; others have but few, with strong monopoly elements present. Some financial markets deal in standardized types of claims; in others, each claim is different and requires separate negotiation. Some financial markets are strictly regulated; others are relatively free.

In chapters 10 and 11 we turn our attention to this element of the financial system, acquainting ourselves with the institutions participating in these markets, the financial instruments involved, and the factors that determine the structure of interest rates in these markets.

Chapter 12 adds an international dimension to the discussion, demonstrating the interconnections of our domestic financial system with that of the rest of the world and introducing some of the implications of the increasing internationalization of commerce and finance.

Government Agencies

The role of government agencies as influences on the behavior of (intermediaries and markets in) the financial system is pervasive. As mentioned above, some serve as intermediaries. Others insure or guarantee certain financial claims, or regulate certain markets and intermediaries. Moreover, partly through its control over certain aspects of the financial system, the Federal government seeks to regulate the overall behavior of the economy, the level and rate of growth of output and employment, the price level, and, to a lesser extent, the composition of output as well.

Chapter 13 is devoted to an examination of the various avenues of influence of the government, particularly the Federal government, on the organization and functioning of our financial system. However, the pressures exerted by government agencies on the system as part of the economic stabilization program of the government, and issues related thereto, are treated in chapters 21 and 22 under the heading "monetary policy."

The Financial System and the "Real" System[6]

Early in this chapter the assertion was made that the financial system is crucial to the workings of an advanced economy. Now, armed with the terms and concepts introduced over the past few pages, we can back up this assertion.

One way of bringing out the importance of the financial system is to construct in our imagination an economy totally lacking in all elements of a financial system, including money. In such an economy, all exchanges of goods and services[7] would have to be by *barter*, with all the inconvenience, cost, and inefficiencies entailed by this system. A fisherman desiring a haircut, for example, would need to find not just a barber, but one who was willing to accept fish.[8]

While barter has a long history of usage in the more primitive stages of societies, it would be unimaginably difficult to operate on that basis in a modern economy. Think of the problems that would be faced by an automobile manufacturer, with hundreds of suppliers and dealers, or by a large mail-order house, with its thousands of customers and more than a hundred thousand catalog items, were they to try to function on a barter basis. Certainly a large part of our national output would be used up in trying to market the rest of it.

There would be other drawbacks to a barter economy. An economic unit wishing to secure command over more goods than current income

---

[6] This section owes much to the work of John G. Gurley and Edward S. Shaw. See, for example, their *Money in a Theory of Finance* (Washington, D.C.: The Brookings Institution, 1960).

[7] It must not be assumed that economic activity requires an exchange system. In certain tightly organized societies in the past there was, for the most part, no voluntary exchange of goods and services. One's rights and duties, including those of an economic nature, were socially defined. This basis for economic organization requires a very tightly knit social structure.

[8] The barber might conceivably be willing to accept a claim against the fisherman for a certain type and weight of fish, but this would not be a financial claim because it does not call for money payment.

allows—to expand production facilities, say, in order to take advantage of the efficiencies of large-scale production or to be able to utilize a new method that it had devised—would be stymied, except in the rare case of being able to "borrow" the desired goods. A lifetime of frugal living might not be long enough for accumulation of the necessary productive assets. Moreover, saving for one's old age, for children's education, or for other reasons would involve the cumbersome and risky process of storing commodities. Thus, both capital formation and saving would be seriously hampered.

Finally, such capital formation that did take place would very likely not be of the economically most productive kinds because the direction of capital formation would be based on the opportunities perceivable to, *and* within the competence of, the accumulator himself. The poor would-be innovator would not be able to obtain the resources, while the contented rich man might not be interested.

In view of the limiting effects of barter on both the level and the direction of capital investment, it is easy to see that economic progress would be retarded in such a regime.

A Money Economy

If, now, we assume that money has been "invented" in our hypothetical economy,[9] we may expect a great deal of improvement in economic performance. In the first place, now that the barter system is no longer the sole basis for the exchange of goods and services, our fisherman can first *sell* his fish and then *buy* a haircut, holding money in the meantime. Secondly, the economic unit wishing to save can accumulate money rather than goods. Finally, the economic unit desirous of expanding facilities can accumulate, then spend, money.

Along with money there inevitably occurs the phenomenon of *price,* the measuring of the economic value of each good or service in terms of a single standard of value, the unit of account. The advantage of this procedure over barter, which requires that the value of each good, service, and unit of economic resources be specified in relation to every other one, is obvious.

Despite the improvements directly attributable to money, our hypothetical economy is still hampered by the fact that, for each individual economic unit, accumulation must precede expenditure. Neither the businessman desiring to expand productive facilities nor the man with the brilliant idea but limited economic resources is any better off than under a barter system. And for a household desiring to purchase a house or a big-ticket consumer good, the need to accumulate money in advance of acquiring the item presents a problem that, particularly in the case of a house, would frequently make the purchase impossible.

[9] The stages in the evolution of money are taken up in chapter 1.

Nonmonetary Claims

What is needed, of course, is *finance*. For efficient operation, a modern economy requires that the financial system include, in addition to money and related institutions, arrangements whereby economic units that experience surpluses, spending less than current income, can acquire financial claims against those units, such as the would-be innovator or homebuyer, that wish to incur deficits. Such arrangements would enable these latter to make expenditures that would not be possible if an economic unit's expenditures were limited to its current income plus past accumulation of money.

The development of financing exerts a stimulating effect on economic progress in at least two respects: (1) innovations are not dependent on asset accumulation by the economic units desiring to effect them, thus increasing the likelihood that capital projects will be undertaken in order of their productivity; and (2) the ability to earn an income on claims held provides some incentive to save (that is, to abstain from spending all current income on consumer goods and services) and to purchase and hold claims issued by would-be purchasers of new capital goods.

Availability of financing facilities through which a would-be deficit household can acquire financing from a surplus household tends to result in a more satisfactory assortment of consumer goods and services, too, for two reasons: (1) it gives households a more flexible expenditure pattern over time, and, (2) as mentioned earlier, it enables the acquisition of certain items which, because of their high unit price relative to incomes, many households would not be able to acquire at all. True, under a "money-only" financial system there is flexibility, but only in one direction: one can spend a dollar of income when earned or later. With the possibility of finance, the choice is expanded: within limits, one can spend income dollars before they are received.

Financial Intermediaries

The type of financing described above, in which the *surplus economic unit* is financing the *deficit economic unit*, we shall call *direct finance*. Although plainly an advance over a "money-only" financial system, direct finance is nevertheless subject to a major weakness: the terms that would be acceptable to the potential *holders* of claims—the savers or surplus units—may not be suitable in general for the would-be *issuers* of claims, the deficit units. The prospective purchaser of a claim may want to be in a position to exchange it for money on short notice, a desire that the issuer generally is in no position to satisfy, since he requires financing for an extended period of time. Also, many prospective purchasers of claims are reluctant to hold all their financial assets in the form of claims against one or a few issuers because of the risk that an issuer would not be able to meet its payment obligations; yet, the deficit unit cannot issue claims for small amounts to many surplus units because of the marketing costs involved.

It is largely in response to this seeming incompatibility of needs as between seekers and providers of financing that financial intermediaries have appeared, evolved, and grown. In the main, an intermediary participates in *indirect finance*: that is, it *issues* to surplus economic units claims on itself that are (1) relatively safe and (2) often (though not necessarily) easy to exchange for money, and it *purchases* claims issued by deficit units—claims that are (1) relatively risky and (2) scheduled to mature at relatively distant dates.

On the face of it, this smacks of economic suicide; the fact that intermediaries thrive on indirect finance calls for explanation. In the case of the different levels of risk as between the claims issued and claims acquired by an intermediary, the explanation is found in the principle of *diversification:* by holding claims against a substantial number and variety of economic units, the intermediary is less vulnerable to any unfavorable event that might affect an individual issuer. A holder of a claim against this intermediary would scarcely be aware of this event, while, had he held the same sized claim directly against the economic unit suffering the setback, the holder might have been seriously harmed. Spreading the risk, therefore, actually reduces the risk.

The second difference between claims issued and claims acquired by some classes of intermediaries, that is, the difference in average scheduled maturity, also is not so dangerous as it might seem. Of course, if all or a large proportion of the holders of short-term claims against the intermediary were to demand payment when the claim fell due, the intermediary would face disaster because the cash generated by its long-term assets (through interest payments, and so on) amounts to only a small fraction of the total amount of these assets. Experience has shown, however, that the probability of such a development is slight. During a given short time period, relatively few holders of short-notice claims against the intermediary will be likely to want to "cash in" their claims; and, in any case, there will probably be other economic units that will be purchasing short-term claims against the intermediary with cash. And even if its cash inflows from regular operations were insufficient to meet outflow requirements, the intermediary usually has other sources of cash, such as (1) borrowing (obtaining financing) from another financial intermediary, private or governmental, or (2) sale of some of its financial assets.

Indirect finance involves certain costs to the intermediary, naturally. In addition to meeting the kinds of expenses that go along with any business operation requiring physical facilities and utilities, the intermediary must also cover costs associated with the financial assets themselves, such as investigation, negotiation, and collection. The wherewithal to meet these costs is provided mostly by the "spread" between the yields on assets held by the intermediary and the interest rates paid on its obligations.

The economic effects of financial intermediaries result from their success in meeting the deficiencies of a nonintermediary system, in which all financing has to be direct financing. With the availability of intermediaries, saving is encouraged, particularly by the small saver who otherwise would be effectively limited to holding noninterest-bearing money and some low-risk securities issued by deficit units, notably the central government. Capital investment is facilitated as well, since the deficit unit is not limited to those projects that can be financed by claims acceptable to the surplus units directly. And the process of economic growth is advanced, since (1) both saving and capital investment are freed from certain institutional limitations and (2) investment tends to be directed into the most productive projects.[10]

On the other side of the ledger, there is reason to believe that, as the financial system becomes more complex and sophisticated, the natural tendency of a capitalist economy toward instability may increase. We cannot discuss the supporting arguments[11] at this early stage, but their general thrust is this: Economic expectations become increasingly favorable when the economy functions satisfactorily for a period of time. The financial system tends to make it easy for private economic units to get into debt positions that are not justified by any conceivable future state of the economy. The result, when the economy finally levels off or even experiences a slowing down of its rate of growth, is a spreading rash of bankruptcies and other financial catastrophes, as more and more economic units find themselves unable to meet their financial commitments and as these failures undermine the positions of other economic units.

Thus, our evaluation of our sophisticated financial system must be that it is a somewhat mixed blessing, enabling and facilitating economic growth but at the cost of a stronger tendency toward instability. Nevertheless, the Federal government has the weapons and the recognized responsibility to keep economic fluctuations within tolerable limits.

The foregoing discussion should have established the case for the economic importance of the financial system, but it also suggests some significant questions. Granted that the *existence* of money and financial institutions affects the development of the economy, is it also true that the *quantity* of money makes a difference in the way the economy behaves? Does the quantity of claims issued by other intermediaries? Is it possible for the government to determine, or at least influence appreciably, the quantities of such assets with a view of altering the behavior of the economy? If it is possible, is it wise to attempt to do this?

---

[10] The importance for economic development of creating a vigorous financial system is stressed in Ronald I. McKinnon, *Money and Capital in Economic Development* (Washington, D.C., The Brookings Institution, 1973).

[11] See Hyman P. Minsky, "Private Sector Asset Management and the Effectiveness of Monetary Policy: Theory and Practice," *Journal of Finance*, XXIV (May 1961), pp. 223–34.

Questions like these certainly seem worth wrestling with. In order to cope with them successfully, however, we need more than knowledge of financial institutions and markets. We must also have a theoretical framework tying together the various elements of the financial system and relating its behavior to the "real," or goods-and-services, system. This is the task of monetary theory, which we intend to survey in chapters 14 and 18. Then, in the concluding section of the book, chapters 19 through 22, we attempt to apply both institutional and theoretical knowledge to questions of macroeconomic policy, that is, the efforts of government directed toward the accomplishment of such overall economic goals as price-level stability, full employment, and adequate economic growth.

Why Study the Financial System?

For some of you, the fact that the financial system performs a vital function in the economy is in itself sufficient reason to attempt to understand it. Whether you are preparing for a career as an economist—academic, business, government, labor union, or other—or seeking a working knowledge of the economy as a means to some other goal, occupational or otherwise, your knowledge of the financial system is an integral part of your total program in economics.

Some of you are preparing for a career in business. For you, work in economics, including the study of the economic aspects of finance, may sometimes seem rather remote from your major concerns. Yet, you certainly realize that the business firm functions in an environment; it must continually be aware of, and adapt to, external forces: economic, political, social, even moral. The businessman is obliged to understand these forces as well as the internal problems of the firm. It would therefore be extremely short-sighted to design an academic program of business preparation that included little or no work in economics. And within the realm of economics, certainly one of the areas of central concern to the businessman is that encompassed by the term *financial system*—its structure, how it works and interacts with the rest of the economy, and how it is affected by government regulations and other actions.

In organizing and preparing this book every effort has been made to keep your particular long-term needs in mind in this regard. Whatever your primary reason for embarking on a study of the financial system, the odds are favorable that it will prove to be a worthwhile venture.

Plan of the Book

By this point you might have picked up some idea of what the book is all about because included in this Overview was at least one specific reference to each of the next twenty-two chapters. Let us combine these references now in making a quick survey of the terrain we shall be travelling over.

In Part I, chapters 1 and 2, we examine money in detail because of its unique role as means of ultimate payment and because of the economic importance of the quantity of money. Parts II and III constitute an examination of the various financial institutions, private and public, and the financial markets in which they operate, filling out most of the descriptive side of this study. Part II, after an introductory chapter 3, surveys the monetary intermediaries (chapters 4 through 7), and Part III (chapters 8 through 13) takes up the other financial institutions and markets and the role of government in the financial system.

Then in Part IV (chapters 14 through 18) the economic aspects of the financial system are discussed, centering particularly on its influence on the level of economic activity. In Part V (chapters 19 through 22) we bring to bear our knowledge of the institutional aspects of the system and their effects on the behavior of the economy in an attempt to understand and evaluate monetary and other macroeconomic policies as means to accomplish certain socioeconomic goals.

KEY CONCEPTS

Finance
Economic unit
Financial system
Financial claim
Financial institution
Financial market
Balance-sheet trace statement

Financial intermediary
Barter
Surplus economic unit
Deficit economic unit
Direct finance
Indirect finance

QUESTIONS FOR REVIEW

1. What are the major elements of a financial system?
2. Would a share of stock be considered a financial claim? Explain.
3. Is "claim creation" involved in the purchase of a TV set on credit? the borrowing of ten dollars from one's roommate? the promise that one will lend his roommate ten dollars next Friday? Explain.
4. How would you distinguish money from other types of claims?
5. What are the disadvantages of barter as a basis for exchanging goods and services?
6. What economic advantages are enjoyed by an economy with financial intermediaries as compared with one without such institutions? What possible disadvantages might be involved?

SUGGESTIONS FOR FURTHER READING

Books of Readings

Carson, Deane (ed.). *Banking and Monetary Studies.* Homewood, Ill.: R. D. Irwin, 1963.
———. *Money and Finance: Readings in Theory, Policy and Institutions,* 2d ed. New York: John Wiley & Sons, 1972.
Entine, Alan (ed.). *Monetary Economics: Readings.* Belmont, Calif.: Wadsworth Publishing Co., 1968.
Ritter, Lawrence S. (ed.). *Money and Economic Activity,* 3d ed. Boston: Houghton Mifflin Co., 1967.
Smith, Warren L., and R. L. Teigen (eds.). *Readings in Money, National Income and Stabilization Policy,* 3d ed. Homewood, Ill.: R. D. Irwin, 1974.
Ward, Richard A. (ed.). *Monetary Theory and Policy.* Scranton: International Textbook Co., 1966.
Wolf, Harold A., and R. Conrad Doenges (eds.). *Readings in Money and Banking.* New York: Appleton-Century-Crofts, 1968.

Official Publications

Federal Reserve Bulletin (monthly)
Economic Report of the President (annually)
Monthly Review of each of the twelve Federal Reserve banks

MONEY IN THE FINANCIAL SYSTEM

PART I

The Concept of Money

Evolution of Money: From Pure Commodity to Pure Claim
Commodity Money and Coinage
Banking and the Origin of Noncommodity Money
Irredeemable Paper Money
Money as Pure Claim
Future of Money
Monetary Evolution and the Financial System

The Monetary System
The Standard
Other Types of Money: The United States Money-Mix
More on the Definition of Money
Institutions of Money Issuance and Control
Our Monetary System: Performance Criteria

Summary

Money and the Monetary System

The one indispensable element in any financial system is *money*. In fact, money is so important to the functioning of a modern economic system that a whole body of analysis has grown up to examine and explain its behavior and economic role. Also indicative of the significance of money is the fact that one of the chief means by which the Federal government seeks to influence the overall level of economic activity is through "monetary policy." It is certainly appropriate for us, therefore, to single out money for extra attention.

In this chapter we examine various facets of money itself—its nature and functions, the pattern of its evolution—and also the monetary *system*, a subsystem of the financial system. Naturally, our emphasis will be on the present-day United States monetary system, for practical reasons; but we shall note examples from our monetary history and from the monetary systems of other nations as well when they are helpful in illuminating particular principles.

The Concept of Money

The term *money* is so freighted with emotion, symbolism, obsolete associations, and contradictory definitions that we must spend some time at this point in order to acquire a firm grasp of it.

Let us start by defining money. This would seem to be an easy task (everybody knows what money is!), but there are some annoying difficulties involved. One is that any definition seems to leave a rather poorly marked boundary between what is and is not included. Another difficulty is that the definers themselves sometimes disagree over where the boundary should be; that is, what should be regarded as *the* true characteristics of money. This is said by way of warning, because you may encounter usages of the term *money* that differ in important respects from the one we shall be using. Money, as we define it, is *anything that is of fixed value in terms of the unit of account of a given society and is generally acceptable in that society in ultimate settlement of obligations.*

Anything means just that: money can be (1) an object worth as much as a commodity as it is as money, (2) an object (such as a specially engraved piece of paper) having money value in excess of its commodity value, or (3) "pure claim," having no physical properties at all. There are no examples of the first type, sometimes called "full-bodied" money, in the monetary system of the United States today; but gold coins qualified under the gold standard, to which we adhered from 1900 to 1933. All our money in current circulation is either the second type (coins and paper money) or the third (bank demand deposits).

The *unit of account* bears the same relation to our system of measuring value as, say, a unit of weight bears to our system of measuring weight. Just as the pound is a measure of physical weight, so the dollar is our basic measure of "economic weight," or *value*. Our unit of account, obviously, is the dollar, since we measure the economic value of objects, claims, and services in dollars per unit (ton, man-hour, dozen, and so on), referring to this value as the *price*. The price (economic weight) of any of these things will not be constant over time, nor do we expect it to be. Only money has, by definition, a constant price (that is, value) in terms of the unit of account. The price of a dollar bill is always one dollar.[1]

In order to qualify as money under our definition, the candidate must be *generally acceptable* in some society as the means of ultimate settlement. Governments and other issuers of money have employed various devices to enhance acceptability. One such device is *legal tender* status. If a creditor should refuse the debtor's tender of money having this characteristic, the debtor, although not discharged from his debt, is not obligated to pay interest for any additional time during which the debt runs nor can he be successfully sued for damages due to nonpayment. Other common means of improving acceptability are (1) accep-

---

[1] It is not uncommon to find discussions of money in which these two concepts—money and unit of account—are merged, with money being considered both the "debt-paying claim" and the unit of account or, what is the same thing, the "standard of value." To continue the analogy in the text above, this usage is like identifying "pound weight" and "pound," which we seldom do, preferring to regard the *pound* as the standard measure of weight and the pound weight as "anything of fixed weight in terms of the unit of weight called the pound." For the sake of conceptual neatness, then, we take our stand on the side of maintaining a clear distinction between money (the thing itself) and the unit of account (the measure of value to which money is uniquely related).

tance by government for tax payment, (2) provision for redemption in precious-metal money, and (3) avoidance of an excessive quantity of money.

Evolution of Money: From Pure Commodity to Pure Claim

The story of money's evolution is a fascinating one. Oftentimes a great deal of information about a particular society—its religion, its stage of development, its values, its way of life—can be deduced from its money by anthropologists. Historians, too, find monetary events of significance in explaining the course of developments of a nation or region.[2] Our concern here, however, is in tracing the highlights in the evolution of money as a means to a better understanding of modern monetary systems. For the sake of brevity we are forced to stick close to the mainstream of developments, particularly as they have had a bearing on our own monetary evolution. Thus, what follows is in no sense a worldwide survey of the development of money.

Commodity Money and Coinage

Early peoples used (and primitive societies still use) almost every imaginable commodity for money: ornamental objects (beads, rings), tools (hoes, fishhooks), apparel (cloth, skins), food (corn, salt), and so on. However, by the process of natural selection, so to speak, metals emerged victorious as various societies advanced. But not until the seventh century B.C., so far as we know, did coins appear on the scene. The significance of this step in monetary evolution was that metallic money could now circulate by number rather than by weight, since the coin itself attested to the weight and quality of the metal. Thus the tedious process of weighing money for each transaction was eliminated.

Banking and the Origin of Noncommodity Money

The next identifiable stage of monetary development in Europe came with the rise of banking, first in the Italian city-states in the thirteenth and fourteenth centuries, then spreading throughout Western Europe over the following two centuries. In order to understand the meaning and significance of banking in the evolution of money, we must examine the operations of these early banking institutions.

Actually, many of these banks originated as goldsmith and silversmith establishments. As trade and production activity expanded in Europe, the use of money also expanded. Businessmen turned to the

---

[2] The reader interested in some of these other aspects of monetary evolution is referred to Arthur R. Burns, *Money and Monetary Policy in Early Times* (New York: Alfred A. Knopf, 1927); Paul Einzig, *Primitive Money* (London: Eyre & Spottiswoode, 1949); and Melville Herskovits, *Economic Anthropology* (New York: Alfred A. Knopf, 1952), Chapter XI.

smiths for the safekeeping of their precious-metal money because these firms, keeping inventories of precious metals themselves, were equipped to safeguard valuables. So long as the money was merely kept in a locked box with the owner's name on it, no monetary significance attached to the operations of the smiths. But when, later, the practice arose of mingling the money deposits of various businessmen and issuing receipts for specified amounts of (gold or silver) money, the stage was set for a development of profound importance. These receipts were the prototype of the modern bank note. At first mere warehouse receipts, these notes gradually began to be used in making payments, a process greatly facilitated when smiths began to issue receipts in convenient denominations. As their use spread, these "goldsmiths' notes" became generally acceptable as means of payment and, hence, *money*.

Observe that the circulating medium in transactions involving these notes was not commodity but *claim*, evidenced by the smith's written promise to pay the bearer on demand. Now, these bits of paper were not regarded at the time as "money," either at law or in the public's view; but our definition of money, being a purely functional one, would have to include these notes.

But what about the gold coins still in the smith's vault? Are we implying that these coins are no longer money? Exactly. So long as these coins are not in a position to be used in current transactions or in payment of debts, we must omit them from the money supply. Of course, if the holder of a "goldsmiths' note" redeems it and withdraws coins, the coins fill the role of money once again. At that point the note disappears as money.

Perhaps this process can be more readily grasped with the aid of the balance-sheet trace statement introduced in the Overview. Assume a depositor takes £10 of coins to the smith-bank. The result will appear something like this on the books of the bank:

TRACE 1.1

Smith-Bank				Public		
Coins	+£10	Notes issued	+£10	Coins	−£10	
				Bank notes	+ 10	

The notes issued are 100 per cent "backed" by coins. (The withdrawal of £10 will, of course, look the same except that the signs will be reversed.)

So far, then, the activities of the smiths have not really affected the quantity of money in circulation. But the record of history shows that, at some point, a revolutionary innovation occurred. Up to that time, although the smiths often made loans to their customers, they had always utilized their own funds, much as you or I would have to do in order to lend money. Then one day it happened: a smith loaned out, not his own coins but some coins that had been deposited by his customers! This act did no harm to the borrower, who acquired the money he wanted, nor apparently to the person currently holding the notes issued on the basis of the original deposit of coins, since he still had the right to redeem his notes in gold. Certainly the transaction did no harm to the smith-banker, who now found himself in the fantastic position of earning interest on coins belonging to other people!

What is the secret of this apparent magic? The answer is simple: so long as most depositors were content to leave their coins in the hands of the smiths, or so long as the coins withdrawn by some were approximately matched in value by coins deposited by others, there was no need to let all this precious metal lie idle. It appears that this line of reasoning easily convinced the smiths, for the practice of lending out the coins of others quickly spread.

Of course, this sort of thing can be overdone. An extra-large demand for coins could (and at times did) cause bankruptcies among the smith-bankers who had overextended themselves and were therefore not in a position to redeem for coins all the notes submitted by their depositors.

The development described above constituted nothing less than a monetary revolution. Prior to this development, the monetary effect of the smiths' activities was merely to change the *mix* of money: when coins in circulation fell, notes rose, and vice versa. But when the smith made a loan by dipping into his depositors' coins, there was no reduction of notes offsetting the increase in coins in circulation! Put in balance-sheet trace form, if a customer borrowed £10 and the smith-banker gave him this amount in coins deposited by his customers, the result would be:

Smith-Bank		Public			TRACE 1.2
Coins	−£10	Coins	+£10	Debt to bank +£10	
Loans	+ 10				

The coins, having gone into circulation, constituted an addition to the money supply.

Incidentally, if the lending smith had instead simply given the borrower some notes redeemable in coins, the result would have been:

Smith-Bank		Public		TRACE 1.3
Loans	+£10	Notes issued +£10	Bank notes +£10	Debt to bank +£10

In either case, the money supply would have been increased by £10.

Through this process in which the smiths loaned either (1) coins deposited by others or (2) notes redeemable in coins, the evolution of money had reached yet another stage. Perhaps the diagram in Figure 1.1 will point up the significance of this development.

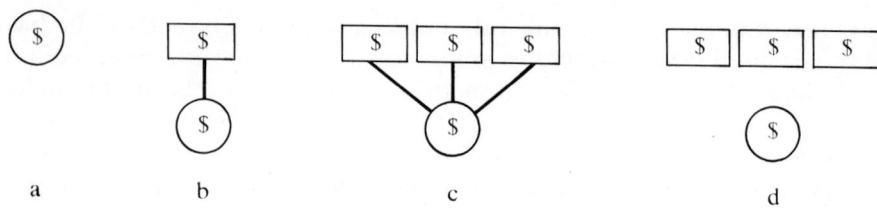

Figure 1.1
Steps in the evolution of money.

In the figure, *a* illustrates the commodity-money situation, in which the money-thing has value in itself; *b* depicts the smiths' original practice of issuing notes in an amount equal in value to that of the coins deposited; and in *c* is represented the later practice of issuing notes in an amount several times the value of the precious-metal "backing" while still maintaining the obligation to redeem the notes in precious metal.

Irredeemable Paper Money

A logical next stage, continuing the gradual reduction in the role of commodity in the monetary system, would seem to be the appearance of circulating paper money completely devoid of any relation to metallic money, as illustrated by *d* in Figure 1.1. This stage appeared frequently (though usually not by design) when the issuing agency—government or bank—was unable to meet demands for redemption. Under such circumstances the paper itself sometimes became unacceptable in settlement of obligations, hence ceasing to be money; but at other times the paper continued to circulate despite its lack of connection with metallic money.

Money as Pure Claim

Does *d* in Figure 1.1 represent the culmination of the process of monetary evolution? No, but the latest stage cannot be represented pictorially since it involves the "appearance"—if that is an appropriate term—of money that has no physical form! First signs of this stage may be traced back to the early days of those same smith-banks just discussed. Sometimes, instead of the notes (receipts) themselves serving as means of transferring claims to coins in the smith's vault, the depositor would write an order directing the smith-banker to pay a designated person out of his (the depositor's) account. This, of course, was the grandfather of the modern check. However, the bank note became the principal nonmetallic method of making payment because this device minimized the risk that the payer might not really have the claim that he purported to be transferring. The bank note, unless counterfeit, was clear evidence of such a claim; a check was not, and in those free-and-easy days this difference was of considerable significance.

With the spread of commerce and industry, developments in transportation and communication, the "normalization" of economic relations, the emergence of stable central governments able and willing to enforce contracts, and the rise of financial institutions, the risks of accepting checks diminished and began to be more than offset by the advantages of this device over bank notes and other forms of money: (1) greater safety in making substantial payments, especially between parties located some distance apart, and (2) convenience and flexibility, as checks can be written in any amount. In practically all advanced countries, demand deposits exceed other forms of money both in quantity and in use.[3]

Future of Money

It is interesting to speculate as to what the next step in monetary evolution might be. Some intriguing possibilities are suggested in this quotation from a recent statement of the Federal Reserve Steering Committee on Improving the Payments Mechanism:

> The Nation's payments mechanism can be expected to evolve in the direction of a system where credit to the payee's account is made at the same time the payor's account is charged. Increasingly, these transfers will be made over a computer-directed communications network. As electronic transfers become technologically and economically superior, checks would be largely displaced. The use of the credit card, or a similar means of activating electronic payments transfers, should expand greatly. Much of today's paper-oriented operation would be displaced by electronic terminals at the point of sale for making direct funds transfers, with the related accounting being done by computers. Significant reductions in the volume of transactions made through the use of paper currency may also take place—by the use of point-of-sale terminals and through other electronic techniques.[4]

Monetary Evolution and the Financial System

It is important that, while we are concentrating on the monetary system, we do not lose sight of the fact that it is indeed a part of the larger financial system. In the following quotation, Sir John Hicks, a distinguished British economist, places monetary evolution in this broader context:

> Throughout the whole time—back before Ricardo, forward after Keynes—money itself has been evolving. The change from metallic money to paper

---

[3] An interesting variant of the system of payment by check is the giro transfer system, which has developed in a number of nations, particularly in continental Western Europe and recently introduced in Great Britain. In contrast to the method of payment by check, in which the deposit holder tenders to the payee an order directing the payer's bank to make payment to the payee or to his order, under the giro mechanism the deposit holder orders the institution holding his account to transfer a specified amount of money directly to the account of the payee and to notify the payee of this action. F. P. Thomson, *Giro Credit Transfer Systems* (Oxford: Pergamon Press, 1964), especially Chapters I and V.

[4] "Evolution of the Payments Mechanism," *Federal Reserve Bulletin,*" (December 1972), p. 1009.

money is obvious; but there are other things which have gone with that change, of even greater importance, which are not so easy to recognize and to assess. Even if we say that metallic money has given place to credit money, we are still not getting to the bottom of what has happened. For credit money is just a part of the whole credit structure that extends outside money; it is closely interwoven with a whole system of debts and credits, of claims and obligations, some of which are money, some of which are not, and some of which are on the edge of being money. The obvious change in the medium, from "full-bodied" coins to notes and bank deposits, is just a part of a wider development, the development of a financial system. This has taken the form of the growth of financial institutions, not just banks, but other "financial intermediaries" as well; it has carried with it a fundamental change in the financial activities of governments. In the course of these changes there has been a change in the whole character of the monetary system. In a world of banks and insurance companies, money markets and stock exchanges, money is quite a different thing from what it was before these institutions came into being. . . .

On the theoretical level—in terms of basic principles—the evolution that was occurring had two aspects. From one of them it was a natural piece of economizing. Metallic money is an expensive way of performing a simple function; why waste resources in digging up gold from the ground when pieces of paper (or mere book entries) which can be provided, and transported, at a fraction of the cost will do as well? That is the reason why the credit system grows: that it provides a medium of exchange at much lower cost. But on the other side there is the penalty that the credit system is an unstable system. It rests upon confidence and trust; when trust is absent it can just shrivel up. It is unstable in the other direction too; when there is too much "confidence" or optimism it can explode in bursts of speculation. Thus in order for a credit system to work smoothly, it needs an institutional framework which shall restrain it on the one hand and shall support it on the other. To find a framework which can be relied on to give support when it is needed, and to impose restraint just when it is needed is very difficult; I do not think it has ever been perfectly solved. Even in this day we do not really know the answer.[5]

The Monetary System

In studying money we must realize that most nations have several kinds of money outstanding, many have several issuing agencies, and there is usually a complex pattern of rules and regulations regarding issue and control of money. In other words, most nations have a monetary *system*. We take up, in this section, the three elements of a monetary system: the standard, the kinds of money and their interrelationships, and the institutional arrangements for issue and control of money.

[5] John Hicks, *Critical Essays in Monetary Theory* (London: Oxford University Press, 1967), pp. 157–58.

The Standard

Monetary systems are often classified on the basis of their standard money. Thus we speak of the United States as having been "on the gold standard" from 1900 to 1933 and France "on the bimetallic standard" from 1803 to 1874. When a nation is on the gold standard, gold is the money of ultimate redemption, and the unit of account is defined as a certain weight of gold. In the case of a bimetallic standard based on gold and silver, the unit of account is defined as a certain weight of gold and, at the same time, a certain weight of silver; the government will redeem other kinds of money in gold or silver, whichever the holder prefers.

The *monetary standard*, we observed, is only one characteristic of the monetary system. Two countries might be on the same standard yet have quite different systems in other respects. In one country, the standard money (that is, full-bodied money minted of the standard metal or metals) might also, at the same time, be the chief type of circulating medium; in the other, the bulk of the standard money might be on deposit in the banks, with other kinds of money circulating but redeemable in the standard money.

In past eras the monetary standard was taken very seriously. Our libraries are filled with learned works on the gold standard, bimetallism, silver standard, and such schemes as symmetallism, the commodity reserve standard, and the like. The tumult and the shouting have very largely died, but the issues are worthy of at least brief examination at this point, not only because of their historical importance but also because they shed light on the behavior of money generally.

Monetary standards are easily divided into two classes: commodity standards and credit standards. By far the most important kind of commodity standard historically is the gold standard; but many countries, including ours, have tried their hand at others. Commodity standards seem to have had their day. Although vestiges remain, no nation is today on a full-fledged commodity standard; and *credit standards* of various sorts completely dominate the monetary scene.

COMMODITY STANDARDS: GOLD To be considered on a full gold standard, a nation's monetary arrangements must meet these requirements: (1) the monetary unit must be defined as a certain weight of gold; (2) there must be a free gold market, both internally and externally; and (3) all money must be redeemable in gold at face value.

Once regarded as the ultimate in standards, the gold standard has been very largely relegated to history books. Why has this fate befallen gold? Certainly the advantages claimed for gold are impressive. Gold, it is said, engenders confidence in the "soundness" of the nation's money. And the discipline imposed by the gold standard's redeemability provision should prevent reckless government spending programs and overexpansion of the money supply. This discipline takes the form of certain developments in the guilty country's domestic economy and international economic position. First, if the ratio of gold to the total stock of money declines, there is danger that the public will become alarmed and turn in their other money for redemption in gold, forcing the treasury to suspend redemption once the gold reserve is exhausted, or nearly so. And, second, overexpansion of the money supply invariably brings inflation; this, in turn, slows the nation's exports and encourages imports, tending to result in a loss of gold to other nations. As a corollary, therefore, the monetary discipline imposed by gold may be expected to prevent inflation.

A different kind of argument for the gold standard (actually, for any commodity standard) is that this is the only "honest" kind of standard: a government that refuses to redeem its paper issues in gold is guilty of fraud and deceit.[6]

Times have changed, however. The traumatic shock of the Great Depression of the 1930s, important developments in economic theory, the increasingly activist role of central governments in economic matters, and the enormous disruptions of World War II have conspired to turn some of the alleged advantages of the gold standard into disadvantages, as the "stability" of gold has turned out to be partly illusory, partly intolerably restrictive. We have learned that, even though yearly gold production is small relative to the total stock of gold (probably less than 2 per cent[7]), there are several good reasons for doubting that an individual nation can be assured of reasonable economic stability if it ties its monetary system to gold. First, the evidence shows that over the long run there have been sizable fluctuations in world gold production. Second, a varying fraction of newly mined gold goes into monetary reserves, the rest going to meet the steadily rising demands of industry and the arts and the fluctuating demands of private hoarders. Third, the monetary gold stock of an individual nation is at the mercy of speculation, rumors, and economic events that occur in other nations as well as within its own borders.

As a matter of fact, the United States had some impressive fluctuations in prices and employment while under the gold standard. Consider these figures: wholesale prices more than doubled from 1914 to 1920, then dropped drastically in the early 1930s. And unemployment as a per cent of the civilian labor force went from below 2 per cent in 1926 to 25 per cent in 1933—all this under the gold standard.

Also, we have had several decades of experience in managing our monetary systems, domestic and international, with reasonable success

---

[6] See, for example, Water Spahr, "A Reply to Mr. Sproul on the Gold Standard," *Commercial and Financial Chronicle*, November 19, 1949; reprinted in Laurence S. Ritter (ed.), *Money and Economic Activity*, 3rd ed. (Boston: Houghton Mifflin Co., 1967), pp. 43–46.

[7] World gold production in 1970 was estimated by the Bank for International Settlements to have been 41.4 million ounces, as reported in the *International Financial News Survey*, XXIII (July 14, 1971), p. 1. According to Barclay's Bank, the total amount of refined gold in the world, as of 1964, was about $2.1 billion ounces. ("The Golden Hoard," *Time*, July 17, 1964, p. 85).

without strict gold-standard conditions. A heavy majority of economists and policy makers are convinced that to return to gold would be to abandon much that we have learned in the past three decades about monetary and fiscal techniques and aggregate economic theory and to repudiate the progress made in integrating our national monetary systems through various international institutions and arrangements.

COMMODITY STANDARDS: BIMETALLISM AND GRESHAM'S LAW To those who think of the gold standard as somehow "normal," at least historically, it may come as a shock to learn that the United States was on a full-fledged gold standard for only thirty-three years, from 1900 to 1933,[8] but on a legal bimetallic standard more than twice as long, from 1792 to 1862. We turn to a brief examination of bimetallism now, mainly within the context of our own monetary history, not only because of its historical importance but also because it illustrates a monetary principle of very broad application: Gresham's law. Named after its discoverer, Sir Thomas Gresham, Chancellor of the Exchequer during the reign of Queen Elizabeth I, this principle is often stated as "bad money drives out good," or words to that effect. However, this way of stating it, though easily memorized, is of little help toward gaining an adequate grasp of the principle. The following statement is a bit broader in scope than Gresham's formulation, but it more adequately conveys the meaning of the law: *Anything in a particular society that has value in both monetary and nonmonetary uses (including use as money in another society) will tend to move into that use in which its value is highest, if it is free to do so.*

As already mentioned, bimetallism exists when the unit of account is defined as a certain weight of gold and also as a certain weight of silver. A full bimetallic standard also requires that there be a free market in both metals and that other types of money be redeemable in either metal, at the option of the holder of the other types. When the unit of account is so defined, the ratio of the monetary value of gold to that of silver is automatically established. For example, the Coinage Act of 1792 defined the dollar as 371.25 grains of silver or 24.75 grains of fine gold. Inevitably, the ratio of the values thus established, called the "mint ratio," was 15:1.

Unfortunately for our bimetallic standard, the "market ratio," the ratio of the values of the two metals on the world's market, was close to 15.5:1. We had *overvalued* silver, had placed a value on it for monetary purposes equal to 1/15 the market value of gold, by weight, whereas the *market* value of silver was only 1/15.5 the market value of gold. A person might legally take, say, 15 ounces of silver to the mint to be coined, demand one ounce in gold coins in exchange (ignoring coinage charges), sell the gold on the market, and buy almost 15.5 ounces of silver for the proceeds. The mint held such a pitiably small quantity of gold, though,

---

[8] Even this reckoning is generous, because from 1917 to 1919 there was an embargo on the export of gold.

that we were, in effect, on a silver standard. As Gresham's law would have predicted, gold, which was more valuable as commodity than as money, moved out of its monetary use since it was "free to do so."

But this was not all! With silver moving to the mint to be coined, one would have expected that our silver coins would be the circulating medium (paper then being of minor importance). For the smaller silver coins, this was the case; but the silver dollars began disappearing from circulation because in the West Indies these shiny new dollars, although lighter than the Spanish dollars, were accepted as their equivalent. Once again, Gresham's law had come into operation: in purchasing power these new dollars were worth more in the West Indies than they were here, so they departed. In fact, President Jefferson in 1806 ordered the mint to stop coining silver dollars, so severe was the drain.

Other examples of Gresham's law in operation can be given. In 1834 our monetary legislation was changed so as to establish a mint ratio of 16:1 by reducing the gold content of the dollar. As we could predict, thanks to the accuracy of hindsight, gold began to flow to the mint since it now took fewer grains of gold to "buy" a dollar. And silver began disappearing until, in 1853, the silver content of fractional coins was reduced by law, thus eliminating the incentive to melt them down for their bullion value since fractional silver coins were no longer more valuable as commodity than as money.

Gresham's law is not limited in application to bimetallism. During the Civil War, Congress authorized the issuance of United States notes (or "greenbacks"), $450 million worth, all told. These notes, although made legal tender, were not redeemable in gold or silver. This large quantity of new money, as might be expected, resulted in substantial increases in the prices of commodities, *including gold and silver*. In line with Gresham's law, gold, having become more valuable as commodity than as money, practically disappeared from circulation.

As our final example of Gresham's law, we may cite the case of silver. The gradual increase in industrial demand for this metal, coupled with production conditions that render silver output rather insensitive to price changes, resulted in a persistent rise in the market price of silver. For a time, the Treasury sold silver from its stockpile in order to keep the market price of silver from rising above the mint price of $1.29 per ounce, but this could not go on forever. In 1965 the Treasury turned off the faucet, terminating the sale of silver from its own stocks and thus allowing the market price to finds its own level.

Predictably, in accordance with Gresham's law, silver coins have disappeared completely, as have silver certificates (paper money redeemable in silver, dollar for dollar). Silver is now just another raw material used in the production of some of our money, as is copper, nickel—and paper![9]

---

[9] Highlights of the story of silver in our monetary history are well summarized in William Burke and Yvonne Levy, *Silver: End of an Era*, rev. ed. (San Francisco: Federal Reserve Bank of San Francisco, 1969).

Bimetallism, as a monetary standard, did not work in the United States. This is not to say that there are no conditions under which it could function successfully. If all or most of the larger nations adopted bimetallism, if they all maintained the same mint ratio, and if all participating nations agreed to subordinate their domestic economic interests to the cause of international monetary stability, then bimetallism would have a strong likelihood of success. But this set of conditions constitutes a very large order—too large, in fact, to justify taking bimetallism seriously as a contender for the position of monetary standard of the future.

Other commodity standards have been suggested and even seriously considered; but further pursuit of this topic would take us too far afield. The future, so far as we can discern now, does not seem to belong to the commodity type of standard. Therefore, we shall turn to the other main category: credit standards.

CREDIT STANDARDS It is difficult to know what to call a monetary system that is not anchored to a particular commodity or pair of commodities. Actually, a monetary system in which the unit of account is not defined in terms of a certain weight of a designated commodity (or commodities), or in which the various types of money are not redeemable in the commodity (-ies) in which the unit of account is defined, really has no standard, only various kinds of money in circulation related to each other in ways prescribed by law and custom. It is certainly misleading to refer to a country in this condition as having a "paper standard," as is often done, because obviously the unit of account is not defined as a certain weight, type, and grade of paper.

Perhaps the term *credit standard*, while not entirely satisfactory, will suffice as a label, since it conveys the idea that no commodity (including paper) really underlies the nation's money, only faith. "Credit" derives from the Latin *credere*, meaning "to believe."

A nation on a credit standard does not necessarily give up *all* ties to precious metal. In most cases the government of such a nation will maintain a gold reserve at home or will hold its "reserve" as balances in a nation or nations that will honor claims against it in gold. The United States, for example, until recently was willing to sell gold at $35 per ounce to foreign monetary authorities and for domestic use in arts and industry; but our circulating money has not since 1935 been redeemable in gold.

Historically, nations have not so much adopted a credit standard as they have found themselves on such a standard as a result of war or other catastrophic event.[10] When the financial demands of waging a war usually proved to be more than the nation's tax system could cope with, the

---

[10] One exception: Sweden and a number of other nonbelligerents suspended free coinage of gold during World War I in order to avoid an inflationary expansion of their money supplies, which would otherwise have resulted from a huge inflow of gold, mainly from the belligerent nations in payment of purchases from the nonbelligerents.

government would resort to printing money to enable it to acquire needed resources. In order to conserve its metallic monetary reserves, it would be forced to suspend the right of citizens to redeem their nonstandard money in gold or whatever was the standard money. At that point the nation was, for all practical purposes, on a credit standard regardless of the phrasing of its monetary statutes.

Such episodes as these were generally considered just that—episodes—and any self-respecting nation that had been forced into credit-standard status would lose no time in attempting to set its monetary house in order by restoring full convertibility of all its money into the metallic-standard money. The economic conditions usually associated with credit-standard situations—inflation, economic dislocations, personal savings wiped out, international trade patterns disrupted, and so on—were enough to convince sound thinkers that the only sensible monetary system was one based on a commodity standard.

Why, then, are not the United States and other economically advanced nations working feverishly toward restoration of the gold standard or some other "sound" standard? Part of the answer has already been given: we are unwilling to entrust our national welfare to the vagaries of gold and/or silver production and distribution. With our more sophisticated economic tools of analysis, our improved statistical data collection and interpretation, our experience in monetary management, we believe that we have outgrown the automatic commodity standards of yesteryear in controlling the quantity of money.[11] Furthermore, it is now clear that neither redeemability nor the expectation of future redeemability is essential to the continued acceptability of money in a nation's internal economic affairs.

The international monetary system appears to be going through the same sort of evolutionary process as that experienced by domestic monetary systems, moving gradually from commodity to claim. For example, as later discussion will explain, nations include in their international monetary reserves their holdings not only of gold but also of short-term, easily sold claims denominated in the units of account of many leading nations and of Special Drawing Rights, which are a type of claim against the International Monetary Fund. For this and other reasons, it seems reasonable to expect that, while gold continues to play

---

[11] A new kind of "automatic" mechanism is currently being vigorously advocated. A number of economists, although differing among themselves on details, are arguing that the money supply should be increased at some regular rate, more or less continuously, since there are certain problems inherent in discretionary monetary management that, in their opinion, render it more likely to destabilize than to stabilize the economy. The proposal, however, is not based on any type of commodity standard. See, for example, Milton Friedman, *A Program for Monetary Stability* (New York: Fordham University Press, 1960), p. 100: "Instruct the Federal Reserve System to use its open market powers to produce a 4 percent per year rate of growth in the total of currency held by the public and adjusted deposits in commercial banks." This doctrine, known as monetarism, will be examined and evaluated in chapter 21.

a role in international monetary relations, it will be one of declining importance.

Other Types of Money: The United States Money-Mix

We recall that the idea of a monetary system includes not only the standard money—the money of ultimate redemption—but other kinds of money as well, together with the institutional arrangements for issuing, retiring, and controlling the stock of money. In this section we examine these nonstandard monies, concentrating on the present-day monetary structure of the United States.

Although at numerous points in the foregoing discussion we have referred to various elements in our past and present money-mix, it is time now to draw together these scattered bits of information, supplementing it with other data, for a clear picture of the kinds of money presently in circulation in the United States, their relative importance, and their interrelations. We plan to examine the components in this order: present domestic monetary role of gold, paper money and coins, and demand deposits. It will be helpful to refer to Table 1.1 as the discussion proceeds.

PRESENT DOMESTIC MONETARY ROLE OF GOLD   Officially there are no gold coins or gold certificates in circulation. Gold certificates, fully backed by gold, were once the most important component of our money supply. However, when we went off gold in 1933, it made no sense to allow gold certificates redeemable in gold to continue to circulate; they were called in along with gold. At present, only the Federal Reserve

TABLE 1.1
Currency Outstanding and in Circulation,
December 1973
(in $millions)

Class of Currency	Amount Outstanding	Less: Held by Treasury and Federal Reserve	Amount in Circulation
Gold	$11,567	$11,567	
Gold certificates	(11,460)	(11,460)	
Federal Reserve notes	68,161	4,031	$64,130
Treasury currency:	8,716	348	8,368
Dollars	767	34	733
Fractional coins	7,338	312	7,026
United States notes	323	1	321
In process of retirement	288		288
	$88,443	$15,946	$72,497

Source: *Federal Reserve Bulletin*, February 1974, p. A15.

banks and to a limited extent, numismatists may legally hold gold certificates. Thus, there are about $11.5 billion in gold certificates *outstanding*, but not in actual circulation.

PAPER MONEY AND COINS   Article I, Section 8, Paragraph 5 of the United States Constitution gives Congress the power "to coin money." This power, in the narrow sense, has never been shared: The Federal government has been and is the sole official supplier of our coinage.[12] Demand deposits, however, are issued by private business enterprises called commercial banks; and paper money is issued both by the Treasury and by twelve quasi-public institutions known as the Federal Reserve banks. In fact, the most important form of paper money by volume is the Federal Reserve note, which currently constitutes nearly 90 per cent of our circulating currency—paper and coins.

Although our money-mix could profit from some judicious streamlining, the present situation presents no real problem. In fact, it is practically ideal in comparison with the monetary conditions that existed during some periods of our history. For example, according to one estimate, in the 1850s there were nearly seven thousand different kinds of bank notes in circulation in the United States. Only 1,500 of these were notes of banks in existence at that time, the remainder being either outright counterfeits or notes of banks that had failed or had never existed as going concerns.[13] Some bank notes circulated "at par," that is, equal in purchasing power, dollar for dollar, with precious-metal money; but most circulated at some discount. As a result, a person whose business required him to take in money from various sources never knew what his cash balance was actually worth! Also, during the Civil War small-denomination notes were issued even by various merchants and local governments.

Federal Reserve notes, as mentioned above, are the dominant form of currency. They are issued by (liabilities of, or claims against) Federal Reserve banks and are placed into circulation through commercial banks. Many people still believe that these notes are somehow "backed by gold." It is true that, prior to 1968, the Federal Reserve had been required by law to maintain a reserve of gold certificates equal in value to at least 25 per cent of outstanding Federal Reserve notes. However, in 1968, when gold losses threatened to reduce the ratio below 25 per cent, Congress authorized the elimination of this requirement. Now, therefore, there is no legal connection whatsoever between the volume of Federal Reserve notes outstanding and the volume of gold certificates that the Federal Reserve happens to hold.

[12] Underline "official"! During several periods in our history fractional coins were so scarce that private economic units issued "paper coins." In fact, as recently as World War II, "pennies were so scarce that Chambers of Commerce issued cardboard tickets redeemable at 1¢ each," according to a news item in *Banking*, July 1965, p. 14.

[13] Leland J. Pritchard, *Money and Banking*, 2d ed. (Boston: Houghton Mifflin Co., 1968), p. 41.

United States notes are prime candidates for retirement. As we observed earlier, these notes were originally issued by the Treasury to help finance the Civil War. At first these notes were irredeemable, but provision was later made whereby any holder could exchange his notes for gold, dollar for dollar, beginning in 1879. Obviously this is no longer permitted; but, through a quirk in our monetary statutes, the Treasury continues to maintain a $156 million reserve in gold against an amount of United States notes that is fixed by law at $347 million. No economic purpose is served through maintenance of this anachronism, but it seems destined to continue mainly because it is rather harmless and its existence generates no pressures toward its elimination.

"In process of retirement" are a number of kinds of money, including one type with the exotic name of Treasury Notes of 1890. They all had their historical justification (or so it seemed at the time), but it would serve no purpose to list and describe them here. Their aggregate amount had been declining steadily until suddenly augmented, in June of 1968, by the addition of the silver certificates still unredeemed. Since that time the decline has resumed.

Coins in circulation exceed, in dollar amount, all circulating Treasury issues of paper by a wide margin. In fact, if Congress were to authorize the retirement of United States notes, the money-issue function of the Federal government would revert to the literal Constitutional mandate quoted earlier; namely, "to coin money."

Until 1964, with the exception of a few periods in our history when metallic money practically dropped out of circulation, silver was the principal metal for coinage. The so-called minor coins, nickels and pennies, are of a copper-nickel alloy and copper respectively. For more than a century the higher-denomination coins, from dime through dollar, consisted of an alloy of nine parts silver and one part copper. In 1965, however, Congress authorized a substantial change in the formula. The new and completely silverless dimes and quarters are minted in a sandwich form. The outer layers consist of a copper-nickel alloy; the inner core is pure copper. The new half-dollars contain 40 per cent silver instead of the previous 90 per cent.

DEMAND DEPOSITS   Most of our money is classified as bank deposits subject to check, or demand deposits. Not all demand deposits, however, are considered money in the official tabulations, so we must spend some time now in examining the process whereby the figure for "demand deposits adjusted," the "money" part, is determined.

Demand deposits are obligations (liabilities) of banks and are owned, or held, by individuals, business firms, nonprofit organizations, governments at all levels, nonbank financial intermediaries, and even by banks themselves as deposits in other banks. Moreover, these various classes of holders, though mainly domestic, also include foreign individuals and organizations. Should we count *all* these holdings in the money supply?

We might argue for this position on grounds that every dollar is considered by its holder as available for immediate spending. Nevertheless, there is good reason to make certain deductions from this gross demand-deposit figure, based on (1) the purpose for which balances are held and (2) the nature of the holder.

One obvious candidate for deduction from gross demand deposits is "domestic interbank balances." These deposits are not held by banks in anticipation of later spending on goods, services, or claims but rather primarily in order to qualify for certain services performed by the depository bank and also as a reserve in case of an unexpectedly large cash drain.

Another item reasonable to deduct from gross demand deposits is something called "cash items in process of collection," thereby eliminating most double counting from our figures. Suppose, for example, you deposited in your bank a five-dollar check from Aunt Martha, who lives in a distant state. The process through which the check finally returns to Aunt Martha's bank need not concern us now,[14] but one incidental result is that you receive credit for the amount of the check from your bank before the amount is officially deducted from Aunt Martha's checking account. (Aunt Martha, we hope, recorded the deduction in her checkbook when she wrote the check.) So, for one or a few days, the money supply is artificially increased by the amount of this check. In place of one five-dollar check, substitute the total number of checks "in process of collection" and dollar amounts involved and you begin to glimpse the magnitude of this double counting. But even the *fact* of the double count is not serious; it is the occurrence of large *fluctuations* in its size day by day, week by week, and month by month that makes imperative the correction of such items in the published figures of demand deposits. Only in this way are the figures usable by government and business analysts concerned with credit conditions and the money supply.

United States government deposits also are widely approved for deduction, and the official figures embody this view.[15] The reason for deduction is this: since the Federal government is a money issuer itself and, besides, has virtually unlimited credit, its holdings of bank demand deposits do not have the same significance as an influence over economic behavior as is the case with deposits of most other holders. State and local deposits are, however, included in the final figures because they are held for essentially the same reasons as those of large private economic units.[16]

Finally, to this net figure is added foreign demand-deposit balances at Federal Reserve banks, since these deposits are, from the standpoint

---

[14] But it will later. See chapter 4.
[15] For a dissenting opinion see Harold Barger, *Money, Banking and Public Policy*, 2d ed. (Chicago: Rand McNally & Co., 1968), p. 53.
[16] For a full explanation of the process of arriving at the demand-deposits component of the money supply, see the *Federal Reserve Bulletin*, November 1971, pp. 880–93.

of their holders, indistinguishable in usage from their demand-deposit holdings at commercial banks.

In summary, "demand deposits, adjusted" is the net figure arrived at after deducting demand balances held by banks in other banks, cash items in process of collection (the double-count component) and demand deposits of the Federal government and adding foreign demand deposits at Federal Reserve banks.

CHECKS VERSUS DEMAND DEPOSITS   This question might have occurred to you: since we formerly regarded the gold certificates themselves, not the gold backing, as money, why not count the checks, rather than the demand deposits, as a component of the money supply? It is the check, after all, that is passed from hand to hand, or that we tender in payment of a debt or to purchase a good or service.

The reason for counting the deposit and not the check may be explained by example. Suppose nobody were to write a check for a week, so that almost all checks would have had a chance to complete their existence from checkbook to the bank on which they were drawn. Would it be sensible to consider that most of the money supply had therefore ceased to exist? Obviously not. The difference in treatment of checks as compared to paper money is due to the fact that, whereas paper money is counted as "in circulation" whether it is in the process of changing hands or is at rest in someone's sugar bowl or mattress, a check, by its very nature, exists only when it is in the process of changing hands, that is, between its transfer from the check writer to another party and its ultimate presentment at the check writer's bank. The only way to include demand deposits "at rest" as well as those "at work" is to count the deposits, not the checks.

CURRENCY VERSUS DEMAND DEPOSITS   Over the course of the preceding pages we have literally "analyzed" our money supply: we have taken it apart and examined the components. While these components are still spread out, so to speak, let us examine the specific uses of each, because in the remainder of this book we shall nearly always find it convenient to speak of "money" without reference to the money-mix.

How can we be sure that, in view of the variety of denominations of coins and paper money, the right quantity of each will be available? And how is the correct ratio of currency to demand deposits maintained? These problems are much simpler than might appear. The provision of the correct denomination-mix is mainly a physical production and distribution problem; and the United States mint, the Bureau of Engraving and Printing, and the Federal Reserve banks have rarely been unable to provide the desired quantities.[17]

The ratio of currency to demand deposits also is automatically ad-

---

[17] An occasional swift and substantial spurt of demand for coins can cause some consternation, as happened in the mid-1960s.

justed to public desires, through the banking system. To illustrate: suppose that, to finance a deficit, the Treasury were authorized to issue several billions of dollars' worth of currency (United States notes) instead of borrowing by means of issuing securities in the conventional manner. Would that not flood the economy with paper money, thus changing the ratio of currency to the total money supply? Initially, yes; but the original or subsequent recipients of this currency would quickly take it to their banks, have the amount credited to their demand deposit accounts, and the money-mix would look much as it did before.[18]

Statistics show clearly that these two major components of the money supply—currency and demand deposits—do not move in lock step. Nor should we expect them to, because their respective amounts are not subject to the same set of determinants. Demand deposits change roughly in accordance with changes in banks' reserves, that is, their cash on hand and on deposit at other banks, particularly at Federal Reserve banks. Thus it sometimes happens that, because the Federal Reserve has added to bank reserves, demand deposits will rise even though the nation has entered a recession and seemingly "needs" less money for transactions purposes. The volume of currency in circulation, on the other hand, is responsive to changes in the dollar volume of business activity, particularly the sales of consumer nondurable goods and services, the kinds of transactions for which currency is more likely to be used.

The ratio of currency to demand deposits has exhibited large fluctuations. Several reasons have been identified, but we have no idea of the relative importance of any of them. Even the experts admit to being somewhat mystified.[19]

Tending to raise the ratio over short periods have been such crises as wars and depressions. Wars increase the volume of black-market and other illegal transactions, best executed with currency, which leaves no "tracks" on bank records. Wars also tend to bring into the labor force many people unacquainted with banks and unaccustomed to dealing with checks. And there seems to be a general increase in the hoarding of currency for security. It takes a considerable time following the end of a war for the economy to work off these accumulations of currency. In depressions the ratio of currency to demand deposits rises because of a decline in confidence in the safety of banks (an attitude with ample historical basis, incidentally). The currency-to-demand-deposits ratio sometimes declines over short periods when bank reserves rise rapidly relative to the rise in economic activity.

Over the long run, other factors may be identified as influencing the currency-to-demand-deposits ratio. Tending to raise it are, first, the

---

[18] This is not the end of the story; such an expansion of bank reserves would probably affect the money supply still further and also tend to bring about an expansion of aggregate demand. See chapters 2 and 18.

[19] Robert D. Laurent, "Strong Rise in Currency in Circulation," *Business Conditions*, Federal Reserve Bank of Chicago (August 1969), pp. 2–6.

gradual increase in the amount of currency lost through destruction, forgetfulness, or other causes. This currency is still counted as "in circulation," though. Thus, the dollar amount of currency in *circulation* must exceed the volume demanded for its economic services by an ever-increasing amount.

Secondly, it seems likely that the increase in foreign travel by United States citizens has for several decades fed the appetite of foreigners for "safe" U.S. currency. Third, the continued rise in the use of vending machines has been a powerful force in the increase in demand for coins, one category of currency. Other factors behind the growth in the volume of coins in circulation have been the rise in the price of silver (stimulating hoarding and illegal melting of silver coins) and the growing popularity of coin collecting.

Then, acting to raise the ratio of currency to demand deposits through decreasing the denominator has been the growing sophistication of business cash-management techniques, enabling business firms to handle increasing volumes of sales with far less than proportionate growth in their checking-account balances.

Exerting a downward pull on the currency/demand deposit ratio have been several influences. First, the rapid rise in credit cards and similar arrangements enabling small items to be purchased on credit has correspondingly reduced the need for currency for these type of transactions. Second, the rising tide of burglaries, purse snatchings, and similar crimes in many areas encourages efforts to economize on currency holdings. Third, an increasing percentage of the population utilizes checking accounts in making payments.

More on the Definition of Money

Our approach to defining money is the customary one: whatever performs a certain designated function or functions *is* money; whatever does not, is not money. The function that we settled on was its use as the asset of ultimate settlement of obligations.[20] Applying this criterion, we discovered that the two classes of assets that qualify in our economy are demand deposits and currency.

If we examine recent monetary literature, though, we discover that some studies define "money" to include all or most classes of *time* deposits at commercial banks in addition to demand deposits and currency. Now, time deposits are not subject to transfer by check and so are not directly spendable. Why, then, do these writers include them as part of the money supply?

The answer is that these authors have adopted a somewhat different criterion: they ask, in effect, "What assets do people regard as readily available for use, directly or indirectly, in ultimate settlement of obliga-

---

[20] Definitions stressing the physical properties or legal status of particular assets as criteria have largely fallen into disuse.

tions?" Since many, but not all, varieties of bank time deposits are, in practice, subject to withdrawal without prior notice, the fact that the holder cannot spend these deposits directly is not considered important; he can legitimately regard them as part of his stock of assets available for spending.

A major issue is where to draw the line. For example, some researchers believe that a broader set of assets should be included as money, such as time deposits in savings and loan associations and mutual savings banks. One writer, on the basis of certain statistical tests, advocates the inclusion of "unutilized trade credit" (that is, the additional amount businesses could accumulate in debt to their suppliers for goods purchased) in the money stock.[21]

Even the Federal Reserve System, the source of our data on the money supply, shares in this uncertainty over definitions. Until well into 1971, the monthly *Federal Reserve Bulletin* recorded "the money supply" as currency plus demand deposits (after certain adjustments). Since that time the same table has been titled "Measures of the Money Stock" and has presented three variations. Take your choice:

M_1—currency plus demand deposits, adjusted.

M_2—M_1 plus time deposits at commercial banks, with certain exceptions.

M_3—M_2 plus deposits at mutual savings banks and savings and loan associations.

The extent of confusion should not be exaggerated. In nearly all "popular" discussions the traditional meaning of money as comprising currency and demand deposits is used. But, as students of the financial system, we need to be aware of developments in the literature and to make certain that when the word *money* is used, we know what concept the user has in mind.

Institutions of Money Issuance and Control

Up to this point we have paid scant attention to the circumstances under which money is issued and the mechanisms through which its quantity is controlled—surely two crucial aspects of the monetary system. This section considers these topics briefly, rounding out our discussion of the elements of the monetary system.

The three kinds of issuing institutions have all been mentioned already: the United States Treasury, the Federal Reserve banks, and the commercial banks. All that need be done here is to pull together the material scattered over the foregoing pages. Of the three issuers, the

[21] Arthur Laffer, "Trade Credit and the Money Market," *Journal of Political Economy,* LXXVIII (March–April 1970), pp. 239–67.

Treasury is of least importance in terms of quantity of money involved. It is the sole issuer of coins, but as a source of paper money it has steadily lost ground to the Federal Reserve banks, whose notes now constitute the only important kind of paper money in circulation. The Treasury is required by law to maintain in circulation $347 million dollars in United States notes; but other kinds of paper money are being retired, including the silver certificate, which until recently was the only type of one-dollar bill and the most common type of five-dollar bill.

Commercial banks, though not usually considered by the man in the street as issuers of money, are actually responsible for the bulk of our money today, in the form of demand deposits.

The interrelations among these issuers can be represented graphically, as is done in Figure 1.2. Observe that all types of money in our system are liabilities of one or the other of the three issuers. The key to the system is seen to be in the circumstances under which each issuer creates money liabilities. Commercial banks create demand deposits in the course of making loans and purchasing other debt claims, a process to be examined in some detail in chapter 2. It turns out that banks are limited in their capacity to create demand claims against themselves by the fact that, just as in the case of the smith-banks of yore, modern-day banks must maintain cash reserves against their deposits. In contrast to the smith-banks, banks today are required by law or administrative regulation to maintain these reserves, the amount being based, in general, on the quantity and mix of deposits. These cash reserves must usually be held in the form of currency and, for most sizable banks, in deposits in the Federal Reserve banks. It is here that we have our first clue as to the manner in which the total stock of money is controlled. The Federal Reserve can take certain actions that have the effect of increasing or decreasing bank deposits held with it. Since banks cannot force the public to give up or take back currency (the other component of bank reserves), these Federal Reserve actions affecting bank reserves also determine the ability of banks to create demand-deposit money.

No effort is made by the Treasury or Federal Reserve to control separately the quantity of currency, as such, or any of its components. The supplying of currency is a service performed by these two money issuers to the public, whose demands are registered as withdrawals from commercial banks. When, for example, banks' customers withdraw currency in anticipation of the Christmas season, banks order reinforcements from the Federal Reserve banks (or from their big-city correspondent banks, which in turn must have their vault cash replenished from Federal Reserve stocks). After Christmas the flow is reversed: currency is redeposited in the banks; they, in turn, send their surplus cash to the Federal Reserve banks for credit to their reserve accounts. In addition to seasonal movements such as the one just described, there is also a fairly regular intramonthly pattern of currency flow, a cyclical pattern, and a

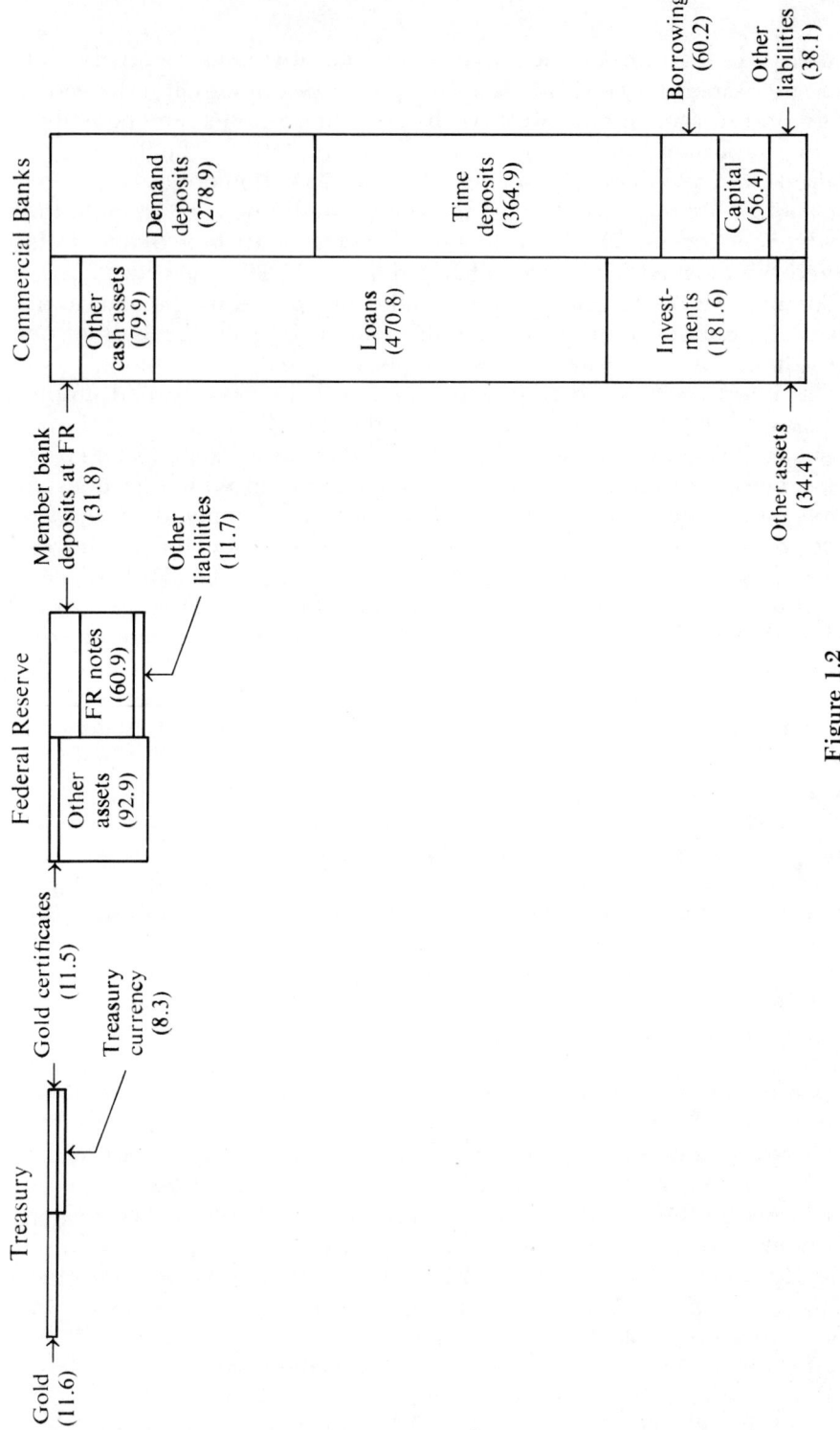

Figure 1.2
Components of the United States monetary system, October 31, 1973 (figures in $ billions).

Source: *Federal Reserve Bulletin*, November 1973, pp. A2, A12, and A18.

long-run rise in demand for currency as the economy grows.[22] All of these needs are met with minimum inconvenience by the issuers of currency: the Treasury and the Federal Reserve banks.

Our Monetary System: Performance Criteria

Having examined, albeit in summary fashion, the elements of the monetary system—standard, types of money, and institutions of issuance and control—we would not be completely satisfied if we did not at least make an attempt to "rate" our system somehow. But what standards should we use? How *should* a monetary system behave? The following standards are suggestive; perhaps you can think of others. In this game, any number can play.

Probably a good starting point is the observation that the monetary system is not working well unless it is working inconspicuously! When money is in excess supply, we become aware of this fact, labeling the resultant condition "inflation." When some kinds of money are less acceptable than others, so that the inferior types circulate at a discount, this malfunction of the monetary system also is painfully evident. These and other kinds of monetary difficulties can all be classified as failures of elasticity or parity or both. Or, expressing this idea in an affirmative manner: a well-functioning monetary system is one that has both parity and elasticity. *Elasticity* is present when the quantity of money adjusts itself to changes in the economy's need for money. *Parity* exists when all the kinds of money in the system circulate without discrimination as to type or denomination.

The test of parity is simple: either a system has it or it does not; deviations are highly visible. We have observed that our own monetary system lacked this quality for decades on end, as a motley and ever-changing mixture of banknotes, government-issued paper money, and hard money circulated through most of our history up to the last quarter of the nineteenth century. At present, however we enjoy virtually complete monetary parity.[23] We do not scrutinize each piece of paper money to ascertain whether it is a United States note, a Federal Reserve note, or a silver certificate, or each coin to see whether it is of the new or old type. To maintain parity we rely mainly on provisions whereby any kind of money is convertible into any other kind.

Elasticity is not so easy to identify and measure. How can we quantify the concept of "need for money"? We cannot get at "need" directly, but we can use certain indirect criteria. If, say, during a seasonal expan-

---

[22] See Irving Auerbach, "Forecasting Currency in Circulation," *Monthly Review*, New York Federal Reserve Bank (February 1964), pp. 36–41.

[23] One minor deviation from parity comes from the practice of some small banks charging a fee to honor checks drawn by their own depositors. People who accept such checks in payment might demand a few cents more than the amount of the obligation to compensate them for this exchange charge. Thus the demand deposits of these banks may circulate at a discount.

sion of business as farmers took their crops to market, banks were unable to expand their loans to aid in financing—with the result that prices fell and interest rates rose sharply—the verdict would be that the system lacked elasticity. Or if, under a gold standard, there were a rapid expansion in the stock of monetary gold from discovery of rich deposits, so that the price level rose rapidly in response to a substantial rise in the money supply, we would say that the rate of rise must have exceeded the rate justified by the normal growth of the economy, that is, the money supply obviously was not adjusting to the needs of the economy.

The monetary system is supposed to contribute not only to stability of prices and to orderly conditions in the financial markets; it is expected, as well, to pull its weight in a program of economic stability at high and rising levels of output. The test of proper monetary elasticity is thus highly complex, even controversial, because one person's evaluation will stress price stability, while another's focuses on growth or on the level of employment. In any event, pursuit of such a multifaceted goal probably calls for conscious operation of the monetary system with a high degree of both economic and political acuity. As this task has been assigned to the Federal Reserve System, our understanding of the financial system obviously requires careful study of this our central bank.

Summary

Money has gone through a gradual process that we might appropriately call "decommoditization," since it has gradually evolved from pure commodity to pure claim. In its early stages the commodity itself, by weight and later (in the form of coins) by number, served as money. Gradually, however, the role of the money commodity changed. Other forms of money—notes and deposits—were found to be easier to handle; while the money commodity served as "backing" for the circulating money, with the circulating money being redeemable in the money commodity at the holder's option. Even this supportive function is no longer performed domestically by the money commodity, although vestiges remain in the international monetary system. All our money at present is currency (coins and paper) and demand deposits, not a trace of a relationship remaining between the quantity of money and gold, or any other money commodity.

The monetary system consists of three basic elements: the standard, the money-mix, and the institutions of money issuance and control. The importance of the standard is considerable, historically; but, along with the general decline in the significance of the "commodity" aspect of money, we have observed the decline in the importance of the monetary standard.

The United States money-mix, too, has changed considerably over time. One of the outstanding features of this evolution has been a movement toward simplification. At one time there were thousands of issues of paper money; now there is only one of any significance: Federal Reserve notes. Another characteristic is the decline in the monetary role of silver. In part this was due to the operation of Gresham's law, the principle that any commodity with a potential money role tends to move toward the use where it is most highly valued. In the case of silver, the rise in value as commodity gradually priced it out of the market for its use as coin. Third, demand deposits have become our dominant form of money.

The major issuers of money in the United States are the United States Treasury (mostly coins), the Federal Reserve System (paper money), and the commercial banks (demand deposits). The *size* of the money stock is essentially under the jurisdiction of the Federal Reserve System, while the *composition* of the money stock is automatically adjusted to public preferences, as people make bank deposits and withdraw currency and vice versa.

KEY CONCEPTS

Money
Unit of account
Legal tender
Monetary standard
Bimetallism
Gresham's law

Credit standard
Federal Reserve notes
M_1, M_2, and M_3
Elasticity of the monetary system
Parity of the monetary system

QUESTIONS FOR REVIEW

1. Can money exist in a society in which there is no unit of account? Can a unit of account exist in a society in which there is no money?
2. During a period in history, "goldsmith's notes" were money, according to our definition. What characteristics of these notes qualified them for this status?
3. Money has moved further and further from its origins as commodity. Why?
4. What are the major elements of a monetary system?
5. What are the advantages of a gold standard? Why, then, has the world gradually grown away from this kind of standard?
6. "Although Gresham's law was originally formulated with reference to bimetallism, this principle has many applications in the monetary field." Discuss.
7. The United States Treasury holds around $10 billion in gold. What purpose or purposes, if any, does this gold serve?
8. Identify the issuing agency of most of the U. S. currency.
9. Are demand deposits (adjusted) part of the money supply? Why or why not?

10. Are checks part of the money supply? Why or why not?
11. Is there a possibility that the money-mix might become chronically out of balance, with too much or too little currency in circulation relative to demand deposits? Explain.
12. In this chapter, two approaches to defining money are discussed. Explain the distinction between them.

SUGGESTIONS FOR FURTHER READING

Einzig, Paul. *Primitive Money in Its Ethnological, Historical, and Economic Aspects.* London: Eyre & Spottiswoode, 1949.

Friedman, Milton, and Anna J. Schwartz. *A Monetary History of the United States: 1876–1960.* Princeton: National Bureau of Economic Research, 1963.

Lash, Nicholas A. "What is Money?" *Business Conditions.* Federal Reserve Bank of Chicago (June 1971), pp. 9–15.

McKinnon, Ronald T. *Money and Capital in Economic Development.* Washington, D. C.: The Brookings Institution, 1973.

Mason, Will E. *Clarification of the Monetary Standard.* University Park: Pennsylvania State University Press, 1963.

Nussbaum, A. *A History of the Dollar.* New York: Columbia University Press, 1957.

Richardson, Dennis W. *Electronic Money: Evolution of an Electronic Funds-Transfer System.* Cambridge: M.I.T. Press, 1970.

Studenski, Paul, and Herman E. Krooss. *Financial History of the United States*, 2d ed. New York: McGraw-Hill Book Co., 1963.

Thomson, F. P. *Giro Credit Transfer Systems.* Oxford: Pergamon Press, 1964.

The Commercial Bank
The Bank and the Nonfinancial Firm

The Banking System
Structure of the System
Interbank Relations

The Process of Demand-Deposit Creation
The Individual Bank
Further Results of the Initial Deposit
Empirical Verification
Refining the Model
The Deposit-Destruction Process
Money Supply and Demand:
A Preliminary Sketch
The Commercial Bank and
Other Financial Firms

The Payments System
Clearing and Collection of Checks
Evaluation of the Payments System

Summary

Monetary Role of the Banking System

The process through which additions to the stock of coins and paper money enter our money supply is quite straightforward; they are simply minted and printed, respectively, and placed in circulation via commercial banks. But the process through which new demand deposits are "created" appears somewhat mysterious. How can banks actually create money through making loans? Don't they merely loan out money deposited with them? And if it is true that they can create money, why aren't all bankers millionaires?

Actually, there is no magic about it, of course. Armed with our knowledge of the mechanics of claims creation (Overview) and further fortified with an understanding of our banking system (the first two sections of this chapter), we shall find the process readily comprehensible if we work at it a bit. And comprehend it we must. Not only are demand deposits by far the largest element of our monetary system, as we have learned, but it is mainly through actions intended primarily to affect demand deposits that the Federal Reserve attempts to influence the economy's course. This chapter is therefore a vital one.

The Commercial Bank

There is a danger that, if we proceed directly into a consideration of demand deposit creation, the process might not seem "real." Our discussion almost necessarily will stress changes that occur in balance sheets, so it would be easy to find ourselves thinking in terms of disembodied, abstract balance sheets, to which things happen and which, in turn, cause things to happen to other balance sheets. To avoid this danger, we begin with some descriptive material concerning banks: first, the individual bank as a business firm; then the interrelations among banks, which makes appropriate the designation *banking system.*

It is impossible to convey in the space of a few paragraphs more than a sketchy impression of the individual bank and the banking system. But if you receive little beyond an impression of variety, this in itself will be helpful because many people have an image of "bank" which simply does not do justice to reality. The following vignette, told by a vice-president of a New York bank, shows that the lack of an adequate image of the bank is not limited to beginners:

> I am reminded of an occasion many years ago when I rode from the Federal Reserve Board building in Washington with a group of Reserve Bank economists who had apparently been discussing all day why excess reserves accumulate in country banks. They still could not understand this uneconomic behavior. The profit-minded economic man will seek to invest excess reserves! I listened for a while and finally asked, "Have any of you ever examined small country banks?" They hadn't, obviously, and I said, "Well, if you had you would understand perfectly why not only excess reserves, but back numbers of banking periodicals, and even instructions from the supervisor, pile up in country banks. You should see the desks of country bankers!"[1]

At the opposite extreme from the small country banks are the giant banks, highly departmentalized, often having numerous branches here and abroad, serving customers throughout the nation and beyond, and performing a wide variety of functions, from consumer and industrial loans to check clearing, from travelers' checks to trust management. It is plain, therefore, that great care is called for in making generalizations that purport to be true of all banks—pygmies, giants, and the whole range between them.

The Bank and the Nonfinancial Firm

The individual commercial bank has much in common with the business firms with which it deals. Like many of them, the bank is a corporation. It has applied for, qualified for, and received a charter from the proper national or state government agency, empowering it to do business as stipulated in the charter. The stockholders (owners) are limited in their liability to the extent of their investment in the corporation, and they are permitted to vote at stockholders' meetings on a one-vote-per-

---

[1] Howard D. Crosse, "Banking Structure and Competition," *Journal of Finance,* XX (May 1965), p. 350.

share basis. The bank performs certain productive activities for which others are willing to pay; and, in so doing, it incurs certain costs. In order to remain a going concern, it must experience a cash inflow from productive services rendered and from other sources that is sufficient for meeting all obligations as they become due, including all costs of doing business. Furthermore, its activities must provide an acceptable rate of return on investment. Usually a large fraction of a bank's income is in the form of interest on the claims it holds, particularly loans; while the two leading classes of bank costs are usually wages and salaries and interest paid on time deposits, that is, deposits not subject to check.

In their behavior, too, banks have much in common with nonfinancial firms. Like many nonfinancial firms, many (but not all) banks are alert for opportunities to introduce potentially profitable new services or products and for signs that existing services or products might profitably be changed, curtailed, or dropped.

Like nonfinancial business firms, banks sometimes form subsidiaries to provide these new services. Some services that banks are eager to provide are not considered appropriate for banks, however, because they are believed to entail a level of risk that is excessive in view of the monetary role of banks; so a large number of banks (including the giants) have formed one-bank holding companies. By means of this device, the holding company becomes, through an exchange of stock, the owner of the bank. Then this holding company can proceed to acquire, by merger and other means, subsidiaries in fields performing these services forbidden to banks as such. The *letter* of the law is followed, since the bank division of the holding company does not carry on these activities; but, as to the *spirit* of the law, the controversy is still bitter.

Finally, like their nonfinancial counterparts, banks have tended to spread geographically as population has expanded and shifted, forming branches at a rapid clip in recent years, though restrained in most states by laws limiting or prohibiting the establishment of branches.

The differences between a bank and an ordinary nonfinancial business are considerable, however. First, as a financial intermediary the bank has an asset structure consisting primarily of claims, not plant, equipment, and inventory. Second, its liabilities are highly volatile. A substantial fraction—sometimes over 50 per cent—of the claims against the bank are legally payable on demand; and most of its other obligations, though in principle due on short notice, are in practice treated by the bank and the claims holders as payable on demand. In the third place, the ratio of claims by owners (equity) to claims by outsiders (debts) is far below that of most nonfinancial firms. In fact, the ratio is usually smaller than 1:10! No wonder, then, that banks must be very careful to maintain both ready sources of funds to borrow and also an asset-mix that is biased toward ease of conversion into cash, just in case.

A fourth characteristic differentiating the bank from most of its business customers is the degree to which its behavior is subject to government regulation. The crucial economic role of banks in providing most of our money, in handling its transfer, and in allocating credit, plus the rather chaotic history of the American banking system, have made close regulation almost inevitable. The bank is restricted in its choice of assets, the interest rates it charges, the interest rates it pays on deposits, its power to merge or establish branches, and in a number of other respects, as we shall be observing in subsequent chapters, particularly 4, 5, and 13.

The type of regulation of closest relevance to the process of demand-deposit creation is the requirement that the bank maintain a specified amount of its assets in the form of *legal reserves*. The exact amount required depends on several factors, including (1) the reserve requirements of the state or Federal authority to which the bank is subject, (2) the amount of its deposit liabilities, and (3) the makeup of deposits, as between demand (checking account) and time. With a given quantity of reserves and time deposits, then, there is an ascertainable limit to the quantity of demand deposits it can maintain, a point of great significance in the process of deposit-money creation, as we shall see.

The Banking System

On December 31, 1973, there were 14,172 corporations organized and operating as commercial banks in the United States. The number of banking locations—banks, branches, and other offices—was nearly three times as large, amounting to 40,626 on that date.[2] These banks, as we observed above, range in size and complexity from the small, nonspecialized, "cluttered-desk" operations to the giant department stores of finance with deposits in the billions of dollars. Nearly half (44.4 per cent) of the commercial banks are at the lower end of the size distribution, with deposits of $10 million or less; but they account for only 4.9 per cent of total deposits, as of year-end 1973, according to Table 2.1. At the opposite extreme, the largest 1.3 per cent of banks, those with deposits of $500 million or more, accounted for 48.7 per cent of commercial bank deposits.

Structure of the System

A bank has a number of options open to it regarding source of charter (state or national), whether or not to become a member of the Federal Reserve System, and whether or not to join in the Federal Deposit Insurance Corporation (FDIC). However, these are not truly *separate* options, since the choice of one option of a pair may eliminate one or two further choices. To illustrate, if a bank chooses (and qualifies for) a national charter, it is required to become a member of the Federal Reserve

[2] Data from *Federal Reserve Bulletin*, April 1974, pp. A88–A89.

TABLE 2.1
Size Distribution of Commercial Banks,*
December 31, 1973

Deposit size (millions)	Banks		Deposits	
	Number	Per cent	Amount (millions)	Per cent
Under $5	3,043	21.4	$ 9,340	1.4
$5–$10	3,260	23.0	23,986	3.5
$10–$25	4,436	31.2	70,530	10.3
$25–$50	1,809	12.7	62,769	9.1
$50–$100	860	6.1	59,077	8.6
$100–$500	614	4.3	126,264	18.4
$500–$1,000	94	0.7	67,915	9.9
$1,000 or more	78	0.6	265,633	38.8
Total	14,194	100.0	$685,514	100.0

Source: Federal Deposit Insurance Corporation, *Annual Report 1973* (Washington: Federal Deposit Insurance Corporation, 1974), p. 182.
* Includes a small number of nondeposit trust companies.

System and the FDIC. And all members of the Federal Reserve System, whether state or national banks, must also be affiliated with the FDIC.

The accompanying chart (Table 2.2) shows the results of past choices. Nearly all banks have decided to protect their depositors (up to $20,000 for each account) by joining the FDIC. Comparatively few banks operating under state charters have elected to join the Federal Reserve System; those that have are mostly the larger state banks. These banks, which generally cater to larger business firms and therefore must provide a greater variety of services, are convinced that the value of the services available to them through the Federal Reserve System more than outweighs the costs of membership. The national banks are those which have decided that the added status that accrues from possession of a national charter more than outweighs the added burdens of stricter supervision and certain restrictions on activities to which national banks are subject.

Most banks are single-office enterprises, sometimes by choice and sometimes because of restrictive state legislation. However, the 4,724 banks maintaining branches or other additional offices as of year-end 1973 had a total of 26,246 such facilities.[3] The trend is strongly toward branch banking, as is evident from Table 2.3. The gradual relaxation of state laws limiting or prohibiting branching, the economies of scale in banking, and the movement of population to the suburbs are among the most important reasons for increased branching. In recent years most new branches have represented net additions to the total of banking offices, but a sizable number have resulted from mergers. Frequently,

[3] *Federal Reserve Bulletin*, April 1974, pp. A88–A89.

TABLE 2.2
Classification of Commercial Banks, December 31, 1973

	National	Member	Insured	Total	State	Nonmember	Noninsured
National	4,661	4,661	4,661	4,661	—	—	—
State member	—	1,076	1,076	1,076	1,076	—	—
Nonmember insured	—	—	8,229	8,229	8,229	8,229	—
Noninsured	—	—	—	206	206	206	206
Total	4,661	5,737	13,966	14,172	9,511	8,435	206

Source: Federal Reserve Bulletin, April 1974, p. A88.

TABLE 2.3
Unit Banking and Branch Banking, Selected Years, 1900–73

Year-end	Branch Banks	Unit Banks	Total Banks	Branch Banks as Per cent of Total Banks	Branches*	Branches as Per cent of Total Banks
1900	87	8,651	8,738	1.0	119	1.4
1920	530	28,129	28,659	1.8	1,281	4.5
1930	750	22,295	23,045	3.3	3,518	15.3
1940	954	13,334	14,288	6.7	3,525	24.7
1945	1,122	12,889	14,021	8.0	3,947	28.2
1950	1,291	12,830	14,121	9.1	4,843	34.3
1955	1,659	12,057	13,716	12.1	6,923	50.5
1960	2,329	11,143	13,472	17.3	10,483	77.9
1965	3,140	10,664	13,804	22.7	15,756	114.1
1970	3,994	9,694	13,688	29.2	21,424	156.5
1973	4,724	9,448	14,172	33.3	26,246	185.2

Source: Board of Governors, Banking Studies (Washington, D.C., 1941), pp. 418, 428; Federal Reserve Bulletin, various issues.
* Includes branches, additional offices, and facilities.

when two banks merge, one becomes a branch and the other is designated the "head office."[4]

In states where branching is prohibited or narrowly restricted (for example, to the head-office city or county) and in cases where it is desired to carry on a banking business with facilities in more than one state, *group banking* systems have been established. Such a system is nothing more than a holding company and its subsidiary banks, each of which is a separately chartered corporation controlled, through stock ownership, by the holding company. Through this device many of the economies of a branch system may be realized, though it is inferior to the branching method in certain respects because each bank must be a separately organized, separately capitalized entity subject to its own reserve requirements, periodic reports, and so on.

Bank groups are far from insignificant. At the end of 1973, the 1,677 groups registered under the Bank Holding Company Act of 1956 controlled 3,097 banks with 15,374 branches, accounting for 45.7 per cent of all banking offices and 67.4 per cent of all deposits of commercial banks in the United States.[5] This compares with 43 groups, 418 banks, and 848 branches as recently as December 1958.

We might also give brief mention to a closely related form, *chain banking*. This relationship exists when two or more separately organized banks are controlled by one person or family or a close-knit group of people.

Interbank Relations

Now, although we have examined a number of aspects of banking—membership, source of charter, and single and multiple-office operations—we still have not really shown why we should speak of the banking *system* rather than merely the banking *industry* or some such designation. It is this topic toward which the discussion thus far has been leading.

THE PAYMENTS SYSTEM Each bank in the United States is related to the other banks in one or more ways. Undoubtedly the most obvious one is through the *payments system*, the designation for the nationwide complex of institutions, facilities, and arrangements through which checks and other financial instruments are submitted by their holders for credit or payment and ultimately collected from the economic units having primary obligation to make payment.[6] The typical bank receives from its own depositors checks drawn on other banks, thus giving it

---

[4] When state laws prohibit branches, the merged banks must combine physically as well as organizationally.
[5] *Federal Reserve Bulletin*, June 1974, p. A83.
[6] Later in this chapter we shall examine this system and its relations with the monetary and banking system.

claims on these other banks. And, of course, other banks are simultaneously acquiring similar claims against it. Through the facilities of the Federal Reserve banks and big-city commercial banks, these checks are returned in a matter of days to the banks on which they are drawn. Without going into detail at this point, we may simply observe that once a particular check has completed its journey, the bank on which that check was drawn will have experienced a loss of reserves equal to the amount of the check; but at the same time its demand-deposit debt to the depositor who wrote the check will have declined by the same amount.

CORRESPONDENT BANKING Another kind of relationship is designated by the term *correspondent banking*. This form of interbank relations arose as a result of certain characteristics of American banking and its legal environment. While other economically advanced nations have developed banking structures composed of national and regional branch systems, the United States, fearful of concentration of financial power, has not permitted this development. Yet banks were compelled, by the very nature of deposit banking in a single, large, politically unified geographical area, to find ways to handle economically and expeditiously claims against each other. One element in a solution was to develop correspondent relations with other banks. Smaller banks would keep funds on deposit with banks in metropolitan areas. These city banks would agree to handle all the checks sent to them by their "country cousins" and drawn against other banks, thereby enabling a smaller bank to send items to only a few banks rather than to all the banks against which it had acquired claims, that is, checks deposited by customers. Even though the Federal Reserve System now provides a nationwide clearing network for its members (for nonmembers, too, if they will maintain a nominal deposit at their district Federal Reserve bank), many smaller banks still clear checks through correspondents because of speed and convenience.

Clearing is only one reason why banks maintain deposits in other banks. Metropolitan banks provide a broad array of other services for their correspondents. Routine aids include (1) currency shipment, (2) wire transfer of funds, (3) facilities for safekeeping of securities, and (4) means for making foreign payments. In addition, expert specialized personnel of the big banks provide credit information, advice on bond investment, and even outlets for temporarily surplus reserves. Often a metropolitan bank will agree to take a participation in (buy a piece of) a loan that is too large for the smaller bank to handle, or even to lend to the smaller bank when the latter is temporarily deficient in reserves.

Thus, smaller banks may receive a number of very useful services in exchange for maintaining deposits in larger banks. But why should the depository banks provide all these services? First, these interest-free deposit claims of other banks provide financing to the big banks, enabling them to acquire claims on businesses and consumers in the form of loans and investments. And, less tangible but often more important, the city bank gains valuable business contacts in outlying areas, some of which may eventually "graduate" into becoming customers of the larger banks.

CLEARING HOUSE   Still another example of interbank relations is the local clearing house. When there are several banks in a community, time and effort is saved by providing a central location to which representatives of each bank report with checks drawn on all the other members of the clearing-house association, where their claims on each other are netted out, and only small residuals are left for ultimate settlement.

COMMON OWNERSHIP   The final form of interbank relations to be mentioned is common ownership and control through group and chain banking. Since we discussed this topic a few paragraphs ago, we need only be aware of the "interbank" aspects of common ownership and control at this point.

It should be evident now that the term *banking system* is no misnomer. Even the smallest bank is connected with the largest banks through this elaborate network of correspondent-clearing relationships. This fact is of central importance to the operation of our monetary system, since it means that impulses received at one point are transmitted (with varying speed and intensity) throughout the entire system. There are no completely isolated financial pockets immune to the events occurring elsewhere in the system.

The Process of Demand-Deposit Creation

With the aid of this institutional background, we are prepared now to examine the mechanics of demand-deposit creation and destruction.

The Individual Bank

As a starting point, we assume that the Federal Reserve Bank of New York has purchased $1 million worth of United States Government securities from a life insurance company[7] and that the insurance company has deposited the check in a commercial bank (Bank 1), a member of the Federal Reserve System.

Banks that are members of the Federal Reserve System—all national banks and some state banks—are subject to its *reserve requirements*. That is, each member bank is required to hold reserves equal to, or greater than, a specified percentage of deposits. Two kinds of claims may be used to meet these requirements: currency on hand and demand claims against a Federal Reserve bank. Nearly all such demand claims

---

[7] We bypass the government securities dealer to simplify the example, keeping in the back of our minds the fact that, in reality, government securities transactions of any substantial size are handled through a small number of such dealers.

are deposits; however, checks such as the one received by the insurance company, which are drawn on a Federal Reserve bank and acquired by member banks, are plainly demand claims, too.

It will be almost impossible to follow the effects of this and subsequent transactions on the balance-sheet positions of the parties involved without using balance-sheet trace statements, as introduced in the Overview. Here, then, are the effects of this set of transactions thus far on the balance sheets of the three parties involved:

TRACE 2.1

Federal Reserve Bank of New York

U.S. government securities	+1,000,000	Member-Bank reserve deposits	+$1,000,000

Bank 1

Reserve with Federal Reserve +$1,000,000	Demand deposits +$1,000,000

Life Insurance Company

Cash in bank U.S. government securities	+$1,000,000 −1,000,000

In the course of these two transactions—the sale of securities and the deposit of the check—several claims were created and/or exchanged.

1. $1 million of claims on the United States Treasury (the securities) were transferred from the insurance company to the Federal Reserve bank.
2. A claim against the Federal Reserve bank (the check) was created in favor of the insurance company, then transferred (by deposit) to the commercial bank.
3. A claim (deposit) against the commercial bank was created in favor of the insurance company by the bank, in exchange for the claim against the Reserve bank.

This might seem like a great deal of busywork about a mere sale of securities, but the fact is that the two claims created are of direct monetary significance: (1) the demand deposit issued by Bank 1 to the insurance company *is* money, newly created at that, and (2) the claim acquired by Bank 1 against the Reserve bank constitutes an addition to bank reserves, not merely for this particular bank but for the banking system as well. And it is the limited availability of this type of asset, bank reserves, that constitutes the main limit to commercial bank "manufacture" of money, whether of bank notes by a goldsmith of old or of demand deposits by the First National Bank of Kenosha, Wisconsin.

Simply by purchasing government securities, therefore, this Federal Reserve bank has actually created additional reserves, thus paving the way for additional demand-deposit creation.[8] But how does the process work? And how much more money can and will be produced?

---

[8] Of course, $1 million of new deposits have already been added, but obviously the bank does not need to keep the entire $1 million in reserves as backing for this deposit.

SIMPLIFYING ASSUMPTIONS Development of an answer to the first question will occupy us for the next few pages. In the course of our discussion it will become clear that the answer to the second question depends on a number of factors. To aid us in analyzing the deposit-creation process, we shall use the framework of a "simplified" United States-type banking system, that is, a system with a large number of separate banking firms but differing in several respects from the actual present-day banking system of the United States.

1. *All banks are members of the Federal Reserve System.* Fewer than half of the commercial banks are member banks currently, but they hold nearly 80 per cent of total deposits. This assumption enables us to treat the banking system as though all banks were subject to the same set of reserve requirements.
2. *Reserve requirements are 20 per cent of demand deposits for all banks.* This figure is somewhat higher than is presently the case in the United States but not seriously so; and it makes computations easier. Our simplified system also ignores the fact that large banks face higher reserve requirements on demand deposits than do smaller banks.
3. *There exists a considerable volume of unsatisfied demand for loan accommodation.* In other words, banks will have no difficulty increasing their loans if enabled to do so by an inflow of new reserves. The inducement to make such loans is, of course, the interest income that they yield.
4. *Banks want to create deposits to the maximum allowed by their reserves.* In other words, we ignore the remote possibility that banks might want to accumulate significant amounts of reserves beyond those necessary to meet legal requirements.
5. *No currency is withdrawn from the banks in consequence of deposit growth.* We learned in chapter 1 that currency in circulation varies with economic activity. Although ultimately the stimulus of an increased money supply will very likely affect prices and incomes, this process is much slower than the money-creation process and therefore can safely be neglected here.
6. *Demand deposits are the only type of bank deposits.* This assumption involves neglect of a significant amount of bank deposits, but it does not affect the deposit-expansion process itself.

DEPOSIT CREATION: STEP 1 Back to Bank 1 now. When we subtract from the total of *new* reserves ($1 million) the amount of additional reserves *required* because of the new deposit (20 per cent of the $1 million or $200,000),[9] we find that the bank has $800,000 of *excess reserves*. How large an amount of additional loans can the bank safely make on the basis of this $800,000? For reasons that will be apparent in a moment, it turns out that the answer is "around $800,000."

For convenience (ours as well as the bank's), let us assume that a credit-worthy business borrower wishes to obtain a loan of $800,000. The loan officer and the applicant discuss the matter and arrive at mutually satisfactory terms, the proper forms are filled out, and the borrower receives his money. Obviously he will not want the cash in the form of currency, so the amount is credited to his demand-deposit account.

This transaction causes certain changes in the bank's balance sheet, which are recorded below. In addition, it will be helpful if we depict the effects of this and subsequent transactions on the consolidated balance sheet of the commercial banking system as a whole so that we can more easily follow the cumulative effects of a sequence of transactions. In a consolidated balance sheet encompassing all banks, by the way, claims of one bank against another cancel out; only claims against, and obligations to, the nonbank would remain.

We plan to record the traces of each new transaction in the sequence in capital letters. The cumulative traces of previous transactions in a particular series are retained for reference but are printed in ordinary lower-case type. Thus, in the figure below, the new loan and its accompanying demand deposit are recorded in capital letters while the original deposit now appears in lower-case type.

TRACE 2.2

Bank 1		Banking System	
Reserve with Federal Reserve bank +$1,000,000 LOANS +800,000	Demand deposits +$1,000,000 DEMAND DEPOSITS +800,000	Reserve with Federal Reserve banks +$1,000,000 LOANS +800,000	Demand deposits +$1,000,000 DEMAND DEPOSITS +800,000

A NECESSARY DIGRESSION Before going on with the main thread of our exposition, we must digress a moment in order to deal with an always bothersome question: "Where did this new money come from?" In the present illustration, specifically, what is the origin of the $800,000 in new deposit money?

There was a day when most bankers would have answered, "From the deposit we received. We took in $1 million and we are able to loan out most of it while putting aside the rest as reserves." This sounds reasonable enough until we ask, "But doesn't the depositor of the original $1 million still have access to that money? How can you say that you have 'loaned out' a part of this deposit when the depositor still has it?"

The point is that bankers cannot "loan out" deposits because de-

---

[9] Recall that, in line with assumption (4), the bank had no excess reserves prior to this transaction.

posits are themselves liabilities of the bank. We get into difficulties when we think of deposits as "things" that are taken into the bank, then loaned out, as were the gold coins of old, instead of thinking of them as claims against the bank. Thus, although banks cannot "loan out" deposits, they can and do create deposit obligations against themselves, in exchange for which they acquire (1) *loans,* that is, claims against borrowing economic units, as in the case being discussed, (2) *other earning assets,* such as government securities, and (3) *cash items,* such as currency and checks drawn on other banks but submitted for deposit credit by bank customers.

Once we become accustomed to regarding money as it really is—as claims rather than things—the source of money will no longer seem mysterious. The original question "Where does the new money come from?" makes no more sense than, say, "Where do newly issued bonds come from?" Bonds are "created" when they are issued, just as is deposit money.

Further Results of the Initial Deposit

Returning once more to the problem of Bank 1 and looking at its balance sheet, we may be tempted to accuse the management of being unduly conservative. After making the $800,000 loan the bank still has $640,000 in excess reserves (the original $1 million in new reserves less the $360,000 required for the $1,800,000 in new deposits). Before writing any memos to the board of directors, however, we had better observe the borrower's activities. He undoubtedly took out the loan in order to spend the proceeds; and, when he does so, the recipients of the checks he writes will probably deposit them elsewhere in the banking system.

Thus Bank 1 stands to lose both reserves and deposits when these checks are presented against it through the clearing process; and other banks, which we designate collectively as Banks 2, experience an increase in reserves and deposits. Nothing has happened to *total* reserves and deposits, however, so the consolidated balance sheet remains the same. To simplify, let us assume that the borrower spends the entire $800,000. When all transactions are complete and all checks written by the borrower have found their way back to Bank 1, the various traces will appear as follows:

Bank 1		Banking System		TRACE 2.3

Reserve with Federal Reserve bank +$1,000,000
Loans +800,000
RESERVE WITH FEDERAL RESERVE BANKS
  −800,000
	Demand deposits +$1,800,000
	DEMAND DEPOSITS
	  −800,000
		Reserve with Federal Reserve banks +$1,000,000
		Loans +800,000
			Demand deposits +$1,800,000	

(continued on next page)

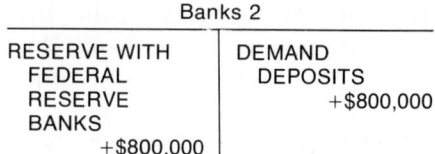

	Banks 2	
RESERVE WITH FEDERAL RESERVE BANKS +$800,000		DEMAND DEPOSITS +$800,000

Having lost $800,000 of reserves, (the amount of its original excess reserves, remember?), Bank 1 is "loaned up." In effect, it has given up $800,000 worth of claims against the Federal Reserve Bank of New York in exchange for an $800,000 claim against a borrower. We have lost interest in Bank 1 now, and our attention shifts to Banks 2.

Banks 2 hold $800,000 in new reserves and "owe" $800,000 more to their depositors. With a 20 per cent reserve requirement, only $160,000 of these reserves are needed in relation to the deposits, so these banks are in a position to make loans equal to the excess reserves, or $640,000; and now they proceed to do just that:

TRACE 2.4

Bank 1 (Final Position)			Banking System		
Reserve with Federal Reserve bank	+$200,000	Demand deposits	+1,000,000	Reserve with Federal Reserve banks	+$1,000,000	Demand deposits	+$1,800,000
Loans	+800,000			Loans	+800,000	DEMAND DEPOSITS	+640,000
				LOANS	+640,000		

Banks 2	
Reserve with Federal Reserve banks |$800,000 LOANS +640,000	Demand deposits +$800,000 DEMAND DEPOSITS +640,000

The above balance-sheet trace records the results: both loans and demand deposits are up by $640,000. And once again the banking system shows an increase in total demand deposits, so additional money evidently has come into existence.

The borrowers then, we assume, spend the proceeds of their loans; and the recipients of these checks deposit them in Banks 3. When all these checks have cleared, the balance sheets of Banks 2 and 3 will have registered these changes:

TRACE 2.5

Banks 2			Banking System	
Reserve with Federal Reserve banks +$800,000 Loans +640,000 RESERVE WITH FEDERAL RESERVE BANKS −640,000	Demand deposits +$1,440,000 DEMAND DEPOSITS −640,000		Reserve with Federal Reserve banks +$1,000,000 Loans +1,440,000	Demand deposits +$2,440,000

Banks 3	
RESERVE WITH FEDERAL RESERVE BANKS +$640,000	DEMAND DEPOSITS +$640,000

This shifting of reserves and demand-deposit claims does not affect the consolidated balance sheet of the banking system, of course.

Banks 3, now in possession of excess reserves, can and will make loans to the extent of their capacity (assumptions 3 and 4). A quick computation shows us that their excess reserves, hence their lending capacity, is $512,000. (You should be able to do the computations.[10]) Completion of the loan transactions will result in these balance-sheet changes (Banks 2 make their final appearance, to show their balance sheet in loaned-up condition):

TRACE 2.6

Banks 2 (final position)	
Reserve with Federal Reserve banks +$160,000 Loans +640,000	Demand deposits +$800,000

Banking System	
Reserve with Federal Reserve banks +$1,000,000 Loans +1,440,000	Demand deposits +$2,440,000

Banks 3	
Reserve with Federal Reserve banks +$640,000 LOANS +512,000	Demand deposits +$640,000 DEMAND DEPOSITS +512,000

LOANS +$512,000	DEMAND DEPOSITS +$512,000

We observe that the money supply has again expanded, in the course of the banks' lending activity.

CHARACTERISTICS OF THE EXPANSION PROCESS By this time the reader can probably predict the next steps: (1) withdrawal of the loan proceeds from Banks 3 as the borrowers write checks, (2) increased lending by Banks 4 on the strength of their new excess reserves, (3) and so on.

Necessary as these details are to our understanding of the deposit-creation process, we have reached the point now where we must step back and examine the process as a whole. Several important aspects of the process should be highlighted: (1) the *rate* of growth in demand deposits slows down as the process continues, (2) total reserves in the banking system are not changing, only shifting about as demand deposits grow, (3) the reserves received by the banking system are gradually converted from excess reserves into required reserves, and (4) the process of demand-deposit expansion is evidently closely tied to the process of bank loan expansion. For a more accurate statement, substitute "earning-asset expansion" for "loan expansion" because, as we shall

---

[10] New reserves ($640,000) less added required reserves, ($128,000, which is 20 per cent of the new deposits of $640,000), leaves excess reserves ($512,000).

next see, bank purchases of securities have the same effect on the money supply as does their loan-making activity.

It will not be necessary to trace further steps individually in such detail. The following Table (2.4) summarizes the sequence of developments of the process.

Reading from left to right, we see, for each set of banks in the sequence (column 1), the initial *stimulus* (col. 2: reserves received for deposit credit), the *response* (col. 3: loans made; deposits created), and the *final position* (cols. 4 and 5: reserves retained, deposits retained) after the loan-related deposits have been withdrawn.

We observe that reserves *not* retained, although lost to the bank or banks involved, are picked up by other banks in the system. This is crucial. If it were not for the fact that reserves lost at one point in the system reappear elsewhere, there could not be any multiple expansion of demand deposits. The whole process would stop dead. Thanks to the almost universal use of bank money in our society, we feel safe in assuming that, in the present case, the "Total Reserves" column (col. 6, under "Banking System") will remain at $1 million. The makeup of these reserves changes, though. As loans (col. 9) and deposits (col. 10) increase in dollar volume, more of the $1 million in reserves becomes *required* reserves (col. 7), less remains *excess* (col. 8). By the tenth step, over 90 per cent of the original $1 million increment in reserves has been put to work. The final outcome, when all reserves have achieved the status of "required," is a $4 million increase in loans and a $5 million increase in deposits.

Why $5 million? Quite simply, since the reserve requirement assumed in this example is 20 per cent, each dollar of reserves can support five dollars of deposits. Thus, at the final position, the $1 million of new reserves must be carrying $5 million of new deposits, $1 million being 20 per cent of $5 million.

AN ALGEBRAIC SUMMARY If we let ΔB be the change in bank reserves; r, the reserve requirement; and ΔD, the change in deposits, then their relationship, when the process has reached its conclusion, can be expressed as

$$\Delta B = r \Delta D$$

A more useful form of this equation is obtained by dividing both sides by r and then switching the sides:

$$\Delta D = \Delta B \left(\frac{1}{r} \right)$$

This version focuses directly on the determinants of ΔD. The expression $(1/r)$ is the *deposit multiplier;* a given change in reserves, multiplied by $(1/r)$, yields the ultimate change in deposits.

Armed with this equation, we can predict the short-run effect of new reserves on demand deposits in our model system under various reserve requirements and with different initial injections of reserves. If, for

TABLE 2.4
Deposit Expansion Process

Banks (1)	Reserves Received for Dep. Credit (2)	Loans Made; Deposits Created (3)	Reserves Retained (4)	Deposits Retained (5)	Banking System			Loans (9)	Deposits (10)
					Total (6)	Reserves Required (7)	Excess (8)		
1	$1,000,000	$800,000	$200,000	$1,000,000	$1,000,000	$360,000	$640,000	$ 800,000	$1,800,000
2	800,000	640,000	160,000	800,000	1,000,000	488,000	512,000	1,440,000	2,440,000
3	640,000	512,000	128,000	640,000	1,000,000	590,400	409,600	1,952,600	2,952,000
4	512,000	409,600	102,400	512,000	1,000,000	672,320	327,680	2,361,600	3,361,600
5	409,600	327,680	81,920	409,600	1,000,000	737,856	262,144	2,689,280	3,689,280
6	327,680	262,144	65,536	327,680	1,000,000	790,285	209,715	2,951,424	3,951,424
7	262,144	209,715	52,429	262,144	1,000,000	832,228	167,772	3,161,139	4,161,139
8	209,715	167,772	41,943	209,715	1,000,000	865,782	134,218	3,328,911	4,328,911
9	167,772	134,218	33,554	167,772	1,000,000	892,626	107,374	3,463,129	4,463,129
10	134,218	107,374	26,844	134,218	1,000,000	914,101	85,899	3,570,503	4,570,503
. . .	. . .	. . .	. . .	. . .	. . .	. . .	. . .	. . .	. . .
∞	0	0	0	0	1,000,000	1,000,000	0	4,000,000	5,000,000

example, the reserve requirement were 15 per cent and the reserve increment were $300,000, what would the increase in deposit money amount to?[11] And we must not forget, either, that this formula cuts both ways. Suppose that the reserve requirements were 18 per cent and the banking system *lost* $540,000 of reserves. By how much would the system need to contract demand deposits, assuming an initial loaned-up position?[12]

Empirical Verification

This explanation of demand-deposit creation, while mathematically neat, makes the whole process appear highly mechanical, does it not? Does the process *really* work this way, or is this another case of "this is how it is *supposed* to work, but *in practice* . . ."?

It is not possible to subject demand-deposit creation to a laboratory experiment, of course, but such evidence as we do have is unanimous in supporting the hypothesis that banks respond, and respond quickly, to changes in their reserve positions. One study, based on data over the period 1953–55, concluded: "The response of bankers to changes in effective reserves was fairly immediate; it usually occurred in an interval which is no greater than a month, and probably much less."[13] Another study, encompassing "three periods since 1951 in which total reserves have been increased markedly for sustained periods," found that during such periods "bank assets, bank deposits, and the money supply have also increased markedly. The increases in total reserves have not been manifested in any considerable measure in increases in excess reserves."[14] And still more recently, a study covering the 1960–63 period concluded that "there is virtually no lag in the response of banks to changes in their unborrowed reserves."[15] (Translation: when banks acquire new reserves, they put them to work quickly.)

Thus, despite the simplifications built into our "first-approximation model" of deposit creation, it yields results that seem to correspond generally with the "real world."

---

[11] $\Delta D = \$300{,}000 \left(\dfrac{1}{.15}\right) = \$2{,}000{,}000$

[12] $\Delta D = -\$540{,}000 \left(\dfrac{1}{.18}\right) = -\$3{,}000{,}000$

[13] George Horwich, "Elements of Timing and Response in the Balance Sheet of Banking, 1953–1955," *Journal of Finance*, XII (May 1957), p. 254.

[14] "Excess Reserves," *Review* of the Federal Reserve Bank of St. Louis, April 1963, pp. 14, 15.

[15] C. Rangarajan and Alan K. Severn, "The Response of Banks to Changes in Aggregate Reserves," *Journal of Finance*, XX (December 1965), p. 664. The most important source of "unborrowed reserves" is Federal Reserve securities purchases, as in our example.

Refining the Model

THE ORIGINAL ASSUMPTIONS The time has come now to try to deal with some of these simplifying assumptions, implicit as well as explicit. First, let us examine the original set of six assumptions on which we based our model.

The first two, concerned with membership in the Federal Reserve System and reserve requirements, need not detain us here. The essential elements of the process are not affected by the ratio of member banks to total banks nor by the size of the reserve requirement. However, the next four are not so easily dismissed. They imply that a given increase in reserves induced by the Federal Reserve authorities will result (given assumptions 1 and 2) in increased demand deposits of $(1/r)$ times the amount of the reserve increase. But if there is no "unsatisfied fringe" (to use Keynes's term) of would-be borrowers, or if the banks decide to hold more excess reserves, a part of all these new reserves will not be put to work. Or, if currency is withdrawn from the banking system, the system's reserves will be reduced by that amount, partially or entirely offsetting the original stimulus, since currency held by banks is included in legal reserves. Finally, if time deposits increase, some of these new reserves will be required as "backing" for them, about 5 cents per dollar of deposits, thus reducing the demand-deposit expansion potential.

Should we, then, build any or all of these factors into our deposit-change formula?[16] If any of them were found to vary systematically and predictably with changes in reserves, following approximately the same time path as do demand-deposit changes, we certainly ought to incorporate such factors into our formula. However, neither currency nor time deposits seem to follow changes in reserves closely. Currency movements tend to be related to movements in aggregate economic activity, as we observed in chapter 1; and time deposits, a heterogeneous collection of different types of deposits, depend in the aggregate on a variety of influences: overall economic activity, money-market interest rates, and government interest rate regulations are among the key ones. All things considered, therefore, the case for a more complex formula is weak, so we shall stay with $\Delta D = \Delta B \, (1/r)$.

IMPLICIT ASSUMPTIONS, POSSIBLE SHORTCOMINGS, AND OTHER COMPLICATIONS Now we must deal with some assumptions that have been more or less hidden as we developed the deposit-expansion model, as well as other aspects of the process that the model does not cover.

In the first place, our model seems to imply a normal sequence like this: (1) a bank acquires excess reserves, (2) it makes a loan (or loans)

---

[16] Some textbook writers do. See, for example, Eli Shapiro et al., *Money and Banking*, 5th ed. (New York: Holt, Rinehart, & Winston, 1968), pp. 140–46; and Harold Barger, *Money, Banking and Public Policy*, 2d ed. (Chicago: Rand McNally & Co., 1968), pp. 134–39.

equal to this amount, and (3) all the proceeds are quickly withdrawn. Now, a bank obviously cannot conduct its business in this fashion ("Good news, Mr. Jones! We have just received a sizable deposit so we can now lend you the $35,281.") Although banks do watch their reserve position (sometimes very closely), this does not mean that a bank would turn down the loan application of a valued customer just because it would thereby incur a reserve deficiency. Rather, the bank would probably make the loan and others like it. Banks have a number of ways of coping with a reserve shortage, as we shall study later, but certainly turning down old customers is last on any list! As one New York banker is quoted as saying: "Sure, we would turn down a loan to a good corporate client who had maintained good balances with us over the years, but not until after we had sold our building and all the furniture."[17] The crucial point to be kept in mind, though, is this: no matter how resourceful an *individual* bank is in obtaining additional reserves, for the most part[18] these reserves must come from elsewhere in the system. Thus, the expansion potential of the entire banking system is not affected by the relative aggressiveness of some banks.

Another shortcoming of the preceding discussion is that it ran entirely on the basis of making loans, whereas banks have other outlets for excess reserves, which are usually lumped together in the term *investments*. Loosely speaking, investments are securities bought and sold through middlemen, while loans are negotiated directly between borrower and lender. We intend to sharpen this definition later (chapter 5), but it will do for now. A bank lacking qualified loan opportunities or feeling the need to diversify can select from a wide assortment of securities of various maturities, issued by the United States government, state and local governments, and large corporations. Banks are especially likely to be purchasers of securities during recessions, when their customers are repaying loans to a greater extent than they are requesting new ones, thus causing the banks to seek other outlets for their surplus reserves.

Although we could go through an entire expansion (or contraction) routine using investments instead of loans, a single-step example will serve to show that these two, loans and investments, are equivalent means of expanding or contracting the money supply. Assume, as we did earlier, that a bank has received a $1 million deposit, but this time it uses the $800,000 in excess reserves to purchase some municipal bonds. The seller deposits the proceeds (perhaps a "cashier's check" drawn by Bank 1 on itself) in another bank, which credits the amount to the account of

---

[17] Quoted in Guy E. Noyes, "Bank Competition and Monetary Policy," *Business Review*, Federal Reserve Bank of Philadelphia, (April 1970), p. 22.

[18] The main exception is reserves "borrowed" from the Federal Reserve. The stringent conditions imposed on such borrowing, plus the fact that the Federal Reserve can take offsetting action to reduce reserves, justify our ignoring this source here. This point is examined fully, though, in chapters 7 and 21.

the depositor. The results of these transactions are recorded below, with the effects of the securities purchase and deposit of the proceeds in capital letters:

TRACE 2.7

Bank 1			
Reserves	+$1,000,000	Demand deposits	+$1,000,000
RESERVES	−800,000		
INVESTMENTS	+800,000		

Bank 2			
RESERVES	+$800,000	DEMAND DEPOSITS	+$800,000

Just as in the loan case, demand deposits have increased by $800,000, this time in consequence of the bank's purchase of securities. The entire expansion process could be traced in this manner, and the ultimate result would be the same expansion as in the loan case. In practice, the result of the banking system's acquiring new reserves would probably be an increase in both loans and investments.

Two other complications might be brought up at this point, now that we have (hopefully) mastered the fundamentals of the deposit-creation mechanism. Both complications affect the results with respect to deposits of *individual* banks but not total deposits, so there will be no need to "unlearn" what we have painfully learned thus far.

First, we have assumed that all the proceeds of a loan (or purchase of securities) are deposited in banks other than the lending (investing) bank. But suppose that some of the proceeds are redeposited in the original bank? What then? No problem: instead of one bank losing reserves equal to the loan (or investment) and other banks acquiring them, the first bank loses less in reserves, and other banks gain correspondingly less, than was the case under our original assumptions. So the first bank still has some excess reserves, but other banks have acquired less than otherwise. The important point is this: Since the total reserves in the *system* are not affected by the fact that some of the proceeds are redeposited in the original bank, the maximum possible increase of deposits must be unaffected as well. It is the size of these categories—total reserves and deposits—that concerns us here, not their distribution within the banking system.

Another assumption we made was that all the proceeds of the loan are utilized by the borrower. But suppose that the bank receiving the initial $1 million deposit has a policy of requiring any borrower to keep on deposit an amount at least equal to 10 per cent of the loan. This is not a farfetched "what if" question; requirements of this type are fairly common, especially for large banks and large borrowers.[19] If we suppose

---

[19] Actually the requirement may be imposed instead against the "line of credit" (that is, the maximum amount of credit the bank has agreed to hold against the borrower at any one time), but the conclusions of our analysis are unaffected by this difference.

further that, in the absence of this requirement, the entire proceeds would be withdrawn, it is clear that the borrower must secure a larger loan in order that the proceeds, net of the amount he must keep on deposits, are sufficient for his desired expenditures.[20]

The individual bank is in the fortunate position of being able to lend an amount in excess of its initial excess reserves because it can count on retaining part of the loan.[21] However, the *system* again runs into the limit imposed on total expansion by the reserve requirement. If all banks were to impose a uniform 10 per cent compensating balance requirement, the *time path* of growth or decline would be different, showing a more rapid rise in the early stages, but the *destination* would be the same as in the non-compensating-balance case. The early-stage banks would be able to retain, and put to work, more of the original reserve increment, each passing on a smaller amount to the next stage.[22] However, this more rapid expansion would use up excess reserves at a correspondingly more rapid pace, leaving less in "raw materials" for subsequent banks to work with.

Finally, you may have an objection that goes something like this: although it is now clear that, when a bank adds to its earnings assets by making a loan or buying securities from the public, the money supply is increased; this increase appears to be only temporary. Eventually any loan or security matures, and the money supply reverts to its previous level.

This objection has some merit. If we examine the mechanics of loan repayment, we can see that the money supply does actually decline by the amount of the repayment. For example, assume that the original borrower from Bank 1 has been adding to his checking account by depositing the proceeds of the sale of goods and services, so that on D-Day (Due-Day), he can simply write a check, hand it to the loan officer, and receive in exchange a canceled note. Ignoring the interest involved, this transaction would affect the bank's balance sheet thus:

---

[20] Let L be the size of the loan; P, the actual proceeds—the amount needed by the borrower; and a, the compensating balance requirement expressed as a per cent of the loan. The amount of the loan must equal the sum of the compensating balance plus the proceeds; therefore

$$L = aL + P$$

solving for L:

$$L - aL = P$$
$$(1 - a)L = P$$
$$L = P\left(\frac{1}{1-a}\right)$$

Therefore, L varies directly with both P and a.

[21] For formula-lovers, $L = E/[1 - a(1 - r)]$, where L is the maximum increase in loans for the individual bank, a is the compensating balance requirement expressed as per cent of the loan, r is the reserve requirement, and E is excess reserves.

[22] For example, in a pure-loan case using a 10 per cent compensating balance requirement, after four steps the banks could have expanded demand deposits by $4,123,353 on the basis of $1,000,000 in excess reserves as compared to $3,361,600 without this requirement.

Bank 1				TRACE 2.8
LOANS	−$800,000	DEMAND DEPOSITS	−$800,000	

The borrower has relinquished a claim against the bank in exchange for the bank's surrender of a claim against him, the borrower. But the money supply (demand-deposit portion) has certainly declined.

At the same time, however, this transaction has provided the bank and the banking system with excess reserves. Based on a 20 per cent reserve requirement, the $800,000 decline in demand deposits has reduced required reserves by $160,000, thereby increasing excess reserves by the same amount, since total reserves are unchanged. This $160,000 of excess reserves can then serve as basis for an expansion of demand deposits equal to five times this amount, or exactly $800,000, which was the size of the original decrease in demand deposits!

Yet all this stress on the results of a single loan repayment is highly artificial. In reality, this single transaction would be lost in a sea of transactions involving loans: new loans, renewals, partial payments, and full payments, not to mention an occasional default. Focusing not on individual transactions but on the ongoing banking process, we realize that this repayment is just one small factor in the reserve position as seen, and adjusted to, by the bank's management.

The Deposit-Destruction Process

Reversing the process now, we take a brief look at the process of demand-deposit destruction. In a formal sense, there is no problem: simply plug in the deposit-change formula, inserting a negative value for ΔB, and a solution pops out. Yet there is enough difference in the actual process to justify separate treatment.

The banking system, we assume, is "loaned up"—has no excess reserves. Now the Federal Reserve sells $1 million of United States government securities to a pension fund, which pays for them by writing a check on its account in a big New York bank, Bank 1 again. The bank finds its reserves and demand deposits diminished by $1 million each, as a result. If the reserve requirement is 20 per cent, the bank is now deficient in reserves by $800,000—not by the whole $1 million because $200,000 of the lost $1 million of reserves had been serving as required reserves for the $1 million of deposits that were extinguished. In terms of balance-sheet traces:

Bank 1		Banking System		TRACE 2.9
RESERVE WITH FEDERAL RESERVE BANK −$1,000,000	DEMAND DEPOSITS −$1,000,000	RESERVE WITH FEDERAL RESERVE BANKS −$1,000,000	DEMAND DEPOSITS −$1,000,000	

What can Bank 1 do about this deficiency? One possibility is to sell securities to depositors of other banks, that is, Banks No. 2:

TRACE 2.10

Bank 1	
Reserve with Federal Reserve bank −$1,000,000 INVESTMENTS −800,000 RESERVE WITH FEDERAL RESERVE BANKS +800,000	Demand deposits −$1,000,000

Banking System	
Reserve with Federal Reserve banks −$1,000,000 INVESTMENTS −800,000	Demand deposits −$1,000,000 DEMAND DEPOSITS −800,000

Banks 2	
RESERVE WITH FEDERAL RESERVE BANKS −$800,000	DEMAND DEPOSITS −$800,000

The result: since the demand deposits of the buyers were extinguished by the amount of the transaction, total *system* demand deposits are reduced by another $800,000, thus reducing the reserve deficit by another 20 per cent of $800,000, or $160,000. Now, however, Banks 2 are suffering a reserve deficiency and must adjust thereto.

Instead of reducing their investment account, these banks could have let their loan accounts decline by, say, making fewer new loans as existing loans matured. In this case, we would simply record a reduction in loans instead of in investments, but the effect on demand deposits would be the same. The main point is that the individual banks would have to take steps to reduce deposits in line with the decline in reserves by reducing their earning assets—loans and investments. Through contraction by *individual* banks, the banking *system* as a whole gradually experiences a reduction of total deposits until, other things equal, the decline in deposits is five times the initial decline in system reserves.

Money Supply and Demand: A Preliminary Sketch

The mechanics of demand-deposit creation and destruction, which we have been examining, leaves us with a rather incomplete view of the whole process. In our model, the banks and other economic units seem to respond completely automatically to certain stimuli. When the Federal Reserve presses a button, creating new reserves, the banking system springs into action, converting these new reserves into bank earning assets and deposits, as other economic units automatically take out loans from, and sell securities to, the banks.

In other words, we have grappled only with the mechanical "how" of the process, not with the behavioral "why," that is, the reasons why banks exchange these new reserves for earning assets or why other economic units decide to borrow from, or to sell securities to, the banks. Later, especially in chapters 17 and 18, we shall give due attention to this and related questions, but a sketch of the topic here may help "humanize" the process.

What is involved, once the Federal Reserve presses that button, is a vast shifting about in portfolios, in response to changes in opportunities. Even the first step—the initial sale of securities to the Federal Reserve by the insurance company—exhibits this. The insurance company, responding to an acceptable offer, agrees to sell. Probably the company, in turn, offers to purchase other financial claims to replace the ones it sold, since keeping large quantities of idle noninterest-earning cash is rarely defensible. The insurance company's offer tends to exert upward pressure on securities prices and downward pressure on interest rates.

Turning our attention now to Bank 1, we note that the deposit by the insurance firm of the original Federal Reserve check pushes the bank's portfolio out of balance: it has (unwanted) excess reserves. In attempting to restore balance, it makes a loan or loans and/or purchases securities. One effect is to shift reserves to other banks, which respond as Bank 1 did. And then on to Banks 3 and 4, and so on. The result of all of this lending and acquisition of securities is to push up prices of existing claims and to push down the yields on claims.

The lower yields (and the accompanying easing in other terms for financing) affect decisions in the "real" economy, increasing the demand for, and possibly the production of, goods and services.

Why do the new demand deposits, once "created," *remain* in circulation, despite the fact that every dollar held in that form involves some sacrifice of potential interest income? Something must change, we realize almost intuitively, in order to induce economic units to be willing to hold more money. Two such changes are a higher level of economic activity and a higher price level, which generate a desire to hold more money for transactions purposes. Moreover, lower interest yields on nonmonetary financial assets (a phenomenon accompanying money creation, other things remaining equal, as we have seen) both (1) reduce the "foregone interest" cost of holding money and (2) may induce the holding of money in expectation that rates will increase shortly, that is, that securities prices will decline.

This is neither the end of the story nor the whole story as far as it goes. But it should impress us with the fact that, though the process of demand-deposit creation seems remote from real economic matters, it actually is intimately related. A bank creates money not because it has excess reserves but because, in view of conditions and opportunities in the financial markets, it serves the bank's interests to shift its portfolio in the direction of a smaller volume of reserves and more earning assets.

Other economic units also respond to changes in their financial environment in ways that are quite understandable, sometimes shifting their portfolios of claims, sometimes increasing or decreasing their total claims and obligations.[23]

The Commercial Bank and Other Financial Firms

The commercial bank shares with other kinds of financial institutions the functions of making loans, holding securities, and supplying a safe, accessible outlet for savings of surplus economic units. Its uniqueness lies, as we have stated before, in its ability to create a type of claim against itself—demand deposits—that serves as money, as it makes loans and purchases securities. When another financial institution, say, a savings and loan association, makes a loan, it acquires one financial claim (the loan) by parting with another (money). When a bank makes a loan, it acquires a financial claim (loan) by creating a money claim (demand deposit) against itself.

The following illustration points up the crucial difference between banks and nonbank intermediaries in the credit-expansion process. First, let us assume that a savings and loan association (which we shall refer to as a S&L) has $1,000 of excess cash reserves, which it lends to a credit-worthy applicant. Since S&L reserves are mostly in the form of demand deposits, we take it for granted that the association would write the borrower a check on its deposit, which check the borrower deposits, let us assume, in the bank on which it was drawn. The effects on the balance sheets of the three parties involved may be depicted as follows:

TRACE 2.11

Savings & Loan Assn.		Bank		Public	
Cash reserve	−$1,000	Demand deposits (public)	+$1,000	Cash	+$1,000	Debt	+$1,000
Loans	+1,000	Demand deposits (S&L)	−1,000				

The consolidated balance sheets of the banking system and the entire financial system are affected as follows:

TRACE 2.12

Banking System			Financial System		
	Demand deposits (public)	+$1,000	Loans (to public)	+$1,000	Demand deposits (public) +$1,000
	Demand deposits (S&L)	−1,000			

Notice that the financial system balance sheet does not show the decline in savings and loan demand deposits or cash reserves since these are internal to the system. Also, so far as the money supply is concerned, there is no change in amount, only a redistribution.

---

[23] James Tobin, "Commercial Banks as Creators of 'Money,'" in Deane Carson (ed.), *Banking and Monetary Studies* (Homewood, Ill.: R. D. Irwin, 1963), pp. 408–19.

This time let us assume that a bank has the $1,000 in excess reserves and that it lends this amount to a worthy customer, who promptly writes checks on the entire amount. After the checks have arrived at the bank, via the clearing process, we have the following balance-sheet traces:

Bank			Public			
Reserves	−$1,000		Cash	+$1,000	Debt	+$1,000
Loans	+1,000					

Banking System			Financial System		
Loans	+$1,000	Demand deposits +$1,000	Loans (to public) +$1,000		Demand deposits (public) +$1,000

TRACE 2.13

Comparing these results with the case involving S&L lending, we note that, so far as the balance sheets of the public and of the financial system are concerned, there is no apparent difference. Also, the balance sheet of the lender in both cases is affected similarly: (cash) reserves down, loans up. When we compare the banking system in the two cases, we observe one difference: the money supply, unchanged in the S&L case, has increased in the bank-lending case.

By far the most important difference, though, is not so clearly visible. To detect it, focus on *reserves*. In the S&L case, reserves lost by one association as a result of lending are lost to the S&L system. There is no reason to expect that the cash withdrawn will turn up in another S&L. In contrast, as we know, reserves lost by one bank will normally be acquired by others. Therefore, the $1,000 of excess reserves of this bank can serve as the basis for an expansion of deposits and credit by the banking system equal to several times this amount, whereas no comparable mechanism exists in the case of the S&L system.

This in no way should be taken to suggest that the nonbank section of the financial system is of only marginal importance. Later we shall see how completely mistaken such an inference would be. Nor, on the other hand, are we justified in concluding that, apart from its money-creating role, the commercial banking system is somehow totally different in economic effects. A proper stance toward commercial banking demands an appreciation of its uniqueness as the main source of money in our economy and, at the same time, of its position as an integral part of the financial system as a whole.

The Payments System

While the circulation of currency is a simple process, usually merely involving delivery by the economic unit making payment to the economic unit receiving payment, the process of making payment by check cannot be described in twenty-five words or less. At the very least, the payment involves three parties: the *drawer* (writer of the check), the *drawee* (bank on which the check is drawn), and the *payee* (designated recipient of payment).

If the payee chooses to have the amount of the check credited to his account with the drawee bank, the result is a transfer of ownership of that dollar amount of demand deposit. If, however, the payee takes the check to a different bank, requesting that the amount be credited to his deposit account, at least one additional party is involved: the payee's bank. Moreover, if the payee's bank has no direct connection with the drawee bank, at least one and probably several more parties will play a role in the processing of this check before its short life span has ended.

The processing of checks, in both physical and bookkeeping aspects, is the most important element in the payments system. We turn now to a consideration of this process, after which we shall briefly look at some of the predicted profound changes in the payments system.

Clearing and Collection of Checks

Each business day the typical bank receives from depositors checks drawn on (1) itself, (2) other local banks (if any), and (3) out-of-town banks. A check of the first type is, of course, handled internally, by reducing the deposit balance of the drawer of the check and increasing the balance of the party submitting it for deposit credit. Checks of the second type are commonly handled through a local *clearing house*. Details of procedure are not our concern here; we simply observe that the process involves the daily mutual exchange of checks by all associated banks at one location rather than bilateral check exchanges between each pair of banks in the locality.

A recent development, which is in its beginning stages but shows considerable promise, is the regional check-clearing center, through which checks from banks in a particular area are processed much as is now done by local clearing houses. The Federal Reserve System is in the process of establishing such centers and expanded clearing-house arrangements in about forty locations. It is possible that "a series of such centers, connected by wire with each other and with their participating banks, could well bridge the gap between the present payments system and the 'checkless society' of the future."[24]

Out-of-town checks may be handled by a particular bank in any of four ways.

    1. A bank may send some or all of its out-of-town checks to one or more of its city correspondent banks, which continues processing them via the next two procedures to be described.

---

[24] H. Lee Boatwright, III, and C. P. Kahler, "The Washington-Baltimore Regional Check Clearing Center," *Monthly Review*, Federal Reserve Bank of Richmond, (May 1970), p. 11

2. A member bank (or nonmember bank maintaining a so-called clearing balance with its district Federal bank) may send some or all of its nonlocal checks to the appropriate Federal Reserve bank or branch.
3. In some cases a bank sends a batch of checks directly to the bank on which they are drawn.
4. In the few locations where a regional check-clearing center is available, a bank sends to this facility checks drawn on participating banks.

Of these methods, the second is the most frequently used. So that we may gain a better understanding of the process, let us follow a single check through the clearing and collection process. The check, in payment for a carload of zilchtrons, is drawn by Kenosha Wholesale, Inc., on its account at Mid-City Bank of Kenosha, Wisconsin, instructing the bank to pay to the order of Rockford Manufacturing Co. the sum of $51,000. Sent by the Kenosha firm and received by the Rockford firm, the check is deposited in Central National Bank of Rockford, Illinois, by the recipient. Next, this check is sent on, just one item in a big batch of items, to the Federal Reserve Bank of Chicago, where it is processed and sent to the Kenosha bank, which eventually returns it to Kenosha Wholesale, Inc.

So much for the actual physical handling. More significant for our purposes are the accounting traces left in the course of this activity on the balance sheets of the participants. After all the dust has settled, we find the following:

TRACE 2.14

Central National Bank		Mid-City Bank	
Reserve with Federal Reserve bank +$51,000	Demand deposits: Rockford Mfg. +$51,000	Reserve with Federal Reserve bank −$51,000	Demand deposits: Kenosha Wholesale −$51,000

Federal Reserve Bank	
Member bank reserve deposits: Central National, Rockford Mid-City, Kenosha	+$51,000 −$51,000

The Federal Reserve bank has credited the reserve account of the bank that submitted the check and reduced correspondingly the account of the bank against which the check was drawn. The Kenosha bank has experienced a loss of reserves (asset) and a decline in demand deposits (liability), while reserves and demand deposits have moved upward for the Rockford bank.

Now, in this example, both banks were in the same Federal Reserve district. There are twelve such districts, each with its own reserve bank.

If our transaction had involved banks in different districts, the procedure would have been somewhat more complex. Physically, the check would probably have passed through two Federal Reserve banks; and the accounting trace also would have been a bit different. If the Kenosha wholesale firm had contracted to purchase zilchtrons from Consolidated Corp. of St. Cloud, Minn., the check would have passed through the Federal Reserve banks of Minneapolis and Chicago. Though there is no need to go into the finer points, we should be aware of the existence of the Interdistrict Settlement Fund, through which the balance maintained by Federal Reserve banks is adjusted in accordance with the volume of claims submitted by, and against, that bank for clearing, in a manner roughly analogous to that in which member-bank balances within a district are handled by the district Federal Reserve banks.

Evaluation of the Payments System

The system for clearing and collecting checks—in fact, the whole system of transferring demand deposits by the use of checks—has been subject to considerable study in the past few years by the Federal Reserve System, the American Bankers Association, and other organizations. The main reason for their concern is that the volume of checks is so large and is growing so rapidly that, according to projections,[25] the system will be increasingly susceptible to more and more serious breakdowns.

In 1970, about 22 billion checks were written. Most checks (around 70 per cent, according to one study)[26] are cleared through the banking system, and over half of these are cleared through the Federal Reserve facilities. The man-hours and time involved in the physical processing of checks have convinced more and more students of the subject that the check is the culprit—that the use of alternative means of transferring demand deposits must be developed and encouraged.

So far we have been fortunate in the timing of innovations, technological and otherwise, in the payments system. Nearly all checks are now sorted automatically by machines that "read" information encoded on the checks in magnetic ink, a development dating from the 1950s. And several "check savers" are now coming into increasing use:

> 1. Arrangements by which the drawer, using only one document, orders the bank to pay specified amounts to a number of payees.

---

[25] For example, Aubrey N. Snellings, "The Evolving Payments System," *Monthly Review*, Federal Reserve Bank of Richmond, (May 1967), pp. 2–6; John J. Clarke, "The Payments System: Problems, Fantasies, and Realities," *Monthly Review*, Federal Reserve Bank of New York, (May 1970), pp. 109–15. These two articles were the main sources of information for this section.

[26] Bank Administration Institute, "An Electronic Network for Interbank Payment Communications," (Park Ridge, Ill., 1969), cited in Clarke, "The Payments System," p. 109.

2. The bank credit card, which enables the debtor to substitute a single payment to the bank for a number of individual payments to various creditors.
3. "Preauthorized payments," which order the bank to pay a designated payee (mortgage holder, utility, or insurance company, for examples) each month.
4. Payroll servicing arrangements, by which the bank is authorized to credit the checking accounts of employees with their take-home pay each payday.
5. Facilities to transfer deposits "by wire," that is, by using teletype facilities to effect the transfer instantly between banks in different cities.

The regional check-clearing center, mentioned earlier, does not reduce the number of checks, but it eliminates certain steps in the clearing route, thus cutting down on both cost and time taken to process checks.

Yet, looking toward the future, there are grounds for doubt that measures like these will suffice to cope with the mounting flood of paper generated by checks. The check has this basic flaw: although the drawer orders the *bank* to pay the payee (actually to his order), the check is sent to the *payee*. Then begins the often roundabout, slow, and costly process of getting the check to the drawee bank. Notice, in contrast, that a characteristic of most of the newer arrangements discussed above is that the party initiating payment communicates directly with the drawee bank. This is also the distinguishing characteristic of the *giro system*, mentioned in a footnote in chapter 1.

While the check method is generally satisfactory when payment is made via mail to one payee, it makes no sense at all when communication takes place by wire. Why send to the payee a message that orders the bank to pay to his (the payee's) order? As we move in the direction of an electronic payments system, the advantages of the giro method over the check method of making payments become ever stronger; and step by step we are moving in this direction. According to experts, the technological know-how for an electronic payments system is available. Any estimate of the timetable for the actual adoption of such a system would be sheer guesswork, though.

Summary

Since most of our money is created by the commercial banking system and most of our money payments are handled through the banks, it is important that we understand the mechanics and process of demand deposit creation (and destruction) and the payments system.

The commercial banking system is made up of a large and diverse collection of approximately 14,000 firms, one-fourth of which have less than $5 million in deposits, while the largest seventy-two hold $1 billion or more. Commercial banks operate well over 24,000 branches and, through holding company affiliates, carry on other activities as well. Banks are related to each other through the payments system, correspondent relations, and ownership links.

Through the process of demand-deposit creation described in this chapter, a given change in bank reserves sets in motion actions in the banking system that result in a change in bank demand deposits several times the size of the initiating reserve change. Although we concentrated on the mechanics of the process, we also recognize that (1) the process itself is not purely mechanical but is "touched by human hands" at all stages and (2) in the course of the change in the money supply, other things happen in the financial system—interest rates, for example, are affected—and the "real" sector also will be influenced. But these matters must be postponed until chapters 14 through 18, on monetary theory.

Important as is the function of demand-deposit creation to the economic system, much of the manpower of the banking system (and of the Federal Reserve System as well) is involved in the process of handling money payments involving checking accounts. The rapidly growing volume of payments has subjected the payments system to increasing strains and has stimulated a great deal of research and some experimentation on means to improve the performance of the system. Some actual and suggested changes involve more efficient handling of checks; others involve finding ways of reducing (or at least slowing the rate of increase in) the volume of checks; while still others call for totally new methods of making payments, through a computer-based network of regional centers and looking forward to a completely electronic payments system in the foreseeable future.

KEY CONCEPTS

Commercial bank
Correspondent banking
Group banking
Chain banking

Clearing house
Payments system
Deposit multiplier
The giro system

QUESTIONS FOR REVIEW

1. What are some of the main similarities of commercial banks to ordinary nonfinancial firms? What are some key differences?
2. How has the structure of the banking system changed over the past decades in number of (a) banks, (b) branches, and (c) holding companies? Why?
3. What are the leading forms of interbank relations?

4. What effect would a reduction in the amount of reserves required per dollar of demand deposits have on the potential increase in demand deposits from a given increase in bank reserves?
5. Is the process of demand-deposit expansion (or contraction) completely "automatic," or is it influenced by the behavior of the participants? Explain.
6. Can banks "loan out" deposits? Explain.
7. Explain, as if to your ignorant roommate, the relation between an increase in bank lending and an increase in the nation's money supply.
8. Since every dollar of demand deposits held by an economic unit represents a sacrifice of potential interest income that could be earned by a dollar's worth of security, what keeps newly created demand deposit dollars in existence?
9. "An individual bank does not increase its demand deposits by a multiple of its new reserves; rather, it reduces its new reserves to a fraction of its new demand deposits." Comment. Does this apply to the banking system as a whole?
10. What is the role of commercial banks in the nation's payments sytem?
11. In what respects would a giro transfer system be superior to the system of paying by means of checks?

SUGGESTIONS FOR FURTHER READING

Alhadeff, David A. *Monopoly and Competition in Banking*. Berkeley: University of California Press, 1954.
Burger, Albert E. *The Money Supply Process*. Belmont, Calif.: Wadsworth Publishing Co., 1971.
Cagan, Phillip. *Determinants and Effects of Changes in the Stock of Money, 1875–1960*. New York: National Bureau of Economic Research, 1965.
Clarke, John J. "The Payments System: Problems, Fantasies, and Realities." *Monthly Review*, Federal Reserve Bank of New York (May 1970), pp. 109–115.
Eastburn, David, "Banking's Widening Limits." *Business Review*, Federal Reserve Bank of Philadelphia (May 1972), pp. 3–22.
Fischer, Gerald C. *American Banking Structure*. New York: Columbia University Press, 1965.
Modern Money Mechanics: A Workbook on Deposits, Currency, and Bank Reserves, rev. ed. Chicago: Federal Reserve Bank of Chicago, 1968.
Tobin, James "Commercial Banks as Creators of 'Money,'" in Deane Carson (ed.), *Banking and Monetary Studies*, Homewood, Ill.: R. D. Irwin, 1963.

INSTITUTIONAL FRAMEWORK: MONETARY INSTITUTIONS

PART

Intermediation and the Intermediaries
Intermediation by Nonintermediaries
Nonintermediation by Intermediaries
Some Dubious Analogies

Evolution of American Financial Intermediaries
Early Commercial Banking
Mutual Savings Banking
Financial Intermediaries in the Developing West
Savings and Loan Associations
Insurance Companies
Consumer Financing
Recent Developments and Emerging Trends

The Financial Institutions: A Survey
Monetary Intermediaries
Depository Savings Intermediaries
Contractual Savings Intermediaries
Investment Companies
Borrowing Intermediaries
Nonintermediary Financial Firms
Government and Quasi-Governmental Intermediaries

The Nature of the Financial Intermediary
Net Income
Safety
Liquidity

Summary

Intermediaries and the Process of Intermediation

With this chapter we begin a fairly detailed study of financial institutions and markets, a study that will occupy us through all of Parts II and III. Much of the material in these parts will be descriptive in character. We can legitimately defend this approach on grounds that, in order to understand the financial system, we need to be familiar with its component parts and their interrelations, as they exist and function in the present-day United Stated economy. In other words, we have to do more than simply come up with a system of equations and announce, "Behold, this is your financial system!"

Our procedure in this introductory chapter will be to look at three general aspects of financial institutions: (1) the nature of *intermediation,* a key function of many classes of financial institutions; (2) the structure of the system of financial institutions, as it has evolved and as it is today; and (3) the nature of the financial intermediary itself, that is, its distinguishing characteristics and behavior.

Intermediation and the Intermediaries

It would be convenient if we could say, "Intermediation is what financial intermediaries do" and leave it at that; but this would be wrong on two counts: (1) intermediation is "done" not only by intermediaries but by other kinds of economic units as well, and (2) intermediaries engage in a number of important activities in addition to intermediation. So we must define the two terms, *intermediation* and *intermediaries*, separately.

Intermediation is the process whereby an economic unit both acquires financial claims against economic units and issues its own obligations to economic units. This definition is general because the phenomenon is general. Intermediation is performed by all classes of economic units: households, nonfinancial corporations, government agencies, and financial intermediaries, to cite a few examples. The *claims* and *obligations* could take any of a million or more combinations of characteristics involving maturity, pattern of payments, priority of payments, and so on. The claims could be acquired and the obligations issued, in exchange for money (usually itself a claim), for other claims, or for goods or services.

It is a simple matter to determine whether intermediation has taken place. If a transaction or sequence of transactions produces *at least* these two changes in the balance sheet of an economic unit,

TRACE 3.1

Claims +	Obligations +

intermediation has occurred. If neither or only one of the two entries is found, there has not been an instance of intermediation. Incidentally, if the two accounts have changed in a negative direction, then *disintermediation* has occurred.

A financial intermediary (as we learned in the Overview) *is an economic unit, public or private, the assets of which are mainly financial.* This definition encompasses only those organizations that are *primarily* involved in intermediation, as defined here. However, there are also classes of firms closely associated with financial markets and with the buying and selling of, or the performance of services in connection with, financial claims. These firms we classify as "nonintermediary financial firms."

Intermediation by Nonintermediaries

With these key definitions in mind, let us go back to the two numbered statements in the first paragraph of this section. First, what sorts of economic units beside financial intermediaries engage in intermediation? We asserted above that *all* classes of economic units do.

Consider, for example, the granting of *trade credit*, whereby a supplier sells goods to a business customer with the understanding that the customer will pay for the goods within a specified time. At first glance this may not appear to be a case of intermediation. The supplier, after all, granted credit *directly*, did he not? No middleman was involved. But if we stand back some distance and concentrate not just on the individual transaction but the whole process, we will see that the supplier, in turn, had to be financed, too. That is, the supplier must have issued claims (equity, and perhaps debt), in order to be in a position to "carry" not only inventory and cash but also receivables. Thus, the supplier has actually participated in intermediation, by issuing claims against itself and acquiring claims against other economic units.

Trade credit is only one among many kinds of interbusiness finance.[1] And in addition to intermediation through interbusiness finance, we should include *consumer credit* granted by business firms directly to consumers, because this, too, requires the credit-granting organization to increase its liabilities to owners or debt holders in order to extend financing to consumers. Besides financing their own business and household customers, a growing number of businesses maintain sizable portfolios of *securities*, corporate and government, mostly in anticipation of tax payment of seasonal increase in inventories and receivables.[2] This, too, is obviously a type of intermediation, since financing is required in order to enable these assets to be held. Households intermediate as well. Many families own homes against which there is a mortgage loan outstanding, requiring monthly payments, while at the same time they hold a savings account, a U.S. savings bond, or other financial assets.

Yet we cannot class all these organizations as financial intermediaries lest the term lose all meaning. For this reason we consider as intermediaries only those organizations whose assets are *mainly* financial.

Nonintermediation by Intermediaries

We have indirectly touched upon the second numbered statement in this section's first paragraph: financial intermediaries evidently do more than intermediate! Some of these other financial functions of intermediaries are closely related to intermediation. Probably the most important of these functions are the creation of money and the administration of the payments system. As we saw in chapter 2, these functions are the responsibility of the commercial banks—which create money (demand claims against themselves) in the process of acquiring claims

---

[1] For a comprehensive list of forms of interbusiness financing, see Robert P. Hungate, *Interbusiness Financing: Implications for Small Business* (Washington, D.C.: Small Business Administration, 1962), pp. 4–5.

[2] To cite a rather extreme example, it was reported a few years ago that General Motors was holding $2.3 *billion* worth of cash and marketable securities. See "Affluent Companies," *Wall Street Journal* (September 9, 1963), p. 1.

against other economic units—and of the Federal Reserve System. Another function closely related to intermediation is the provision of relatively safe, easily "divisible," income-yielding outlets for savings, in the form of claims (for example, savings deposits issued to the public by some intermediaries).

Less closely related to intermediation per se are such financial services as information and advice to holders and issuers of claims, managing portfolios of claims on behalf of their owners, owning and leasing equipment and real estate, and issuing travelers' checks.

Some Dubious Analogies

Sometimes the intermediation process is described in "marketing" terms, as in this quotation: "In general, financial intermediaries stand in the same relation to financial markets that retail merchants and wholesalers do to commodity markets."[3] This analogy must be used with care, because it seems to imply a particular product's moving through the distributive pipeline, while in reality what the intermediary acquires from the issuer (for example, a claim in the form of a loan) is *not* what it, in turn, issues (or sells) to the surplus economic unit (that is, a claim against the intermediary).

Another comparison, also tending to mislead, is that which is sometimes made between intermediation and the manufacturing process. It is said that intermediation generally involves purchasing relatively risky claims as inputs and "converting" them into relatively safe, liquid claims against the issuer. The flaw in this analogy is that the unit purchasing the *input*, so called, still holds it when it creates and sells the *output!* Thus, while resembling both marketing and manufacturing in some respects, intermediation is a process distinguishable from both of them.

Evolution of American Financial Intermediaries

The various classes of financial institutions that have evolved in our nation over the past two centuries will now be introduced in their historical context. This method will also serve the purpose of giving us the feel of the evolutionary process involved, as new types of financial institutions appear, grow, and find their place in the financial system—at least temporarily.[4] We shall concentrate most of our attention on the financial intermediaries here.

[3] C. R. Whittlesey et al., *Money and Banking,* 2d ed. (New York: Macmillan Company, 1968), p. 65.
[4] Helpful sources for this section have been Edward C. Ettin, "The Development of American Financial Intermediaries," *Quarterly Review of Economics and Business,* III (Summer 1963), pp. 51–69; and Karl R. Bopp, "Financial Institutions in a Changing Environment," *Business Review,* Federal Reserve Bank of Philadelphia, (June 1966), pp. 2–8.

The present system of financial intermediaries in the United States is not the product of some master plan but is rather the result of a process of evolution still at work. Many factors have influenced the direction of this process: the pattern of our national economic development, the structure of government regulation, the response of the managements of various intermediaries to particular challenges, the economic advantages and disadvantages of specialization versus diversification, and a miscellany of other factors.[5] In the following paragraphs we shall be observing these factors in action.

Early Commercial Banking

In the beginning was the commercial bank—not, however, the kind of "department store of finance" that we shall study in chapters 4 and 5. The early American ancestors of our modern commercial banks confined their activities mainly to short-term loans to businessmen. The borrowers, however, took the proceeds not in the form we would expect today (demand deposits) but in bank notes issued by the individual banks. Thus, early commercial banking met two pressing needs simultaneously: (1) circulating money and (2) short-term commercial credit.

This rather narrow scope of operations, as judged by modern standards, left unmet in the early nineteenth century a number of financial needs that became increasingly urgent as our country developed. One of these was for suitable outlets for small individual savings. Banks were not interested in providing savings-account arrangements; and, for the great bulk of savers, corporate and government securities were not a feasible form in which to hold small savings. Another unmet need was for housing credit, the financial means to enable housing to be provided in the Eastern cities for their expanding populations, fed by a continuous flow of immigrants.

Mutual Savings Banking

Partly in response to the needs for a depository for small savings that would be safe and would also yield some income, and partly to encourage thrift on the part of the "working poor," some leading public-spirited citizens in the larger cities (beginning in 1816 with Philadelphia) established the first mutual savings banks. The organization of these banks reflected the noble and yet (by our standards) rather paternalistic attitudes of their founders and benefactors: mutual savings banks were, and are, usually controlled by a self-perpetuating board of trustees, the members of which serve with little or no compensation.

---

[5] Marvin Rozen, "The Changing Structure of Financial Institutions," *Quarterly Review of Economics and Business*, II (November 1962), pp. 69–80.

The financial environment was most favorable for rapid growth of this new form of intermediary because of (1) the ready supply of savers willing to hold claims against these institutions, (2) the demand in the real-estate market for home financing, and (3) the lack of competition by commercial banks in both these markets.

Mutual savings banks flourished and spread throughout most of the nineteenth century, but a look at the chartering dates of present-day mutual savings banks brings out a surprising fact:

> Of the 514 mutual savings banks in the continental United States at the end of 1960, approximately two-fifths were established prior to 1860 and four-fifths before 1875. . . . Only thirty-six banks . . . were formed in the period from 1900 to the present, and of these twenty-five were in existence prior to 1920.[6]

Moreover, savings in mutual savings banks as per cent of savings in all private depository savings institutions plus life insurance companies reached its highest point around 1880.

Why, despite the continuing geographic and economic growth of the American nation, did the mutual savings banks not keep pace in numbers and economic size? The answer is found largely in two factors—the influence of regulatory statutes and the activities of old and new competitors—which quite effectively confined mutual savings banking to the older, slower-growing Northeast.

Financial Intermediaries in the Developing West

At first there was little opportunity for savings banking in the newer areas as the nation expanded westward. Financial saving was negligible: economic units accumulating a surplus, that is, an increase in net worth, generally preferred real (capital) assets to financial assests as the form in which to accumulate because of the high rates of return anticipated on the former. There was a chronic shortage of capital in the Western areas, and the financial system was not developed to the point where Eastern institutions could utilize their resources in financing (that is, purchasing claims issued by) Western business and agriculture.

Commercial banks, however, found this new environment to their liking. In these times, the second half of the nineteenth century, it was relatively easy to secure a bank charter; and regulation tended to be quite permissive. These new banks were able to supply some desperately needed financing by indirectly "tapping" unwitting Eastern sources. You recall from the section on early commercial banking that these early banks generally granted credit in the form of bank notes. The

---

[6] National Association of Mutual Savings Banks, *Mutual Savings Banking: Basic Characteristics and Role in the National Economy* (Englewood Cliffs, N.J.: Prentice-Hall, 1962), p. 28.

business borrowers would often spend these notes on goods from the Northeastern states. In this way, the East, as a region, would acquire claims (bank notes) issued in the West in exchange for Eastern goods. As it turned out, banking excesses of inept and sometimes dishonest managements often resulted in the destruction of all or most of the value of these bank-note claims; but the outcome was a more rapid growth and development of the newer regions than would have been possible with more "orthodox" financing.

Another result of these developments was that the commercial banking industry became firmly entrenched in these areas and was able to block any encroachment by the mutual savings banks through a combination of (1) offering savings accounts themselves and (2) exerting pressure against passage of legislation that would have permitted chartering of these banks. Also, it seems probable that the organizational basis of mutual savings banks—the "public-spirited leading citizens" helping the "working poor"—was not compatible with the more egalitarian individualistic philosophy of the early West.

Savings and Loan Associations

During this period another form of financial intermediary was emerging: the savings and loan association. The first of these was established in 1831, using a type of British intermediary as a model. The basic idea took hold so well that, by the 1880s, there were probably associations in every state.[7] Except for the basic purpose—providing financing for home purchases—the modern savings and loan association little resembles one of its early ancestors. These latter usually consisted of a closed association of local people who had agreed to contribute a specified sum monthly into a common pool. As soon as enough had been accumulated, one of the members would be chosen, by lot or by bids; and the lucky winner would be permitted to borrow money from the association up to a certain ceiling to finance the purchase or construction of a home. This process would continue until, if all went well, the last loan was paid, at which time the association would cease existence, its purpose having been fulfilled.

The more modern method of operation dates from 1870 or thereabouts. Associations were established on a permanent basis, without the built-in suicide mechanism. Shares could be bought at any time, and there was (and is) no requirement that the borrower also be a shareholder or depositor.

Savings and loan associations began to assume national importance during the last quarter of the nineteenth century. Supporting this statement is the evidence that, beginning in New York in 1875, states began

---

[7] Leon T. Kendall, *The Savings and Loan Business: Its Purposes, Functions, and Economic Justification* (Englewood Cliffs, N.J.: Prentice-Hall, 1962), p. 5.

to pass legislation to regulate savings and loan associations! By 1900 more than half the states had such statutes on the book.[8]

Growth of the savings and loan industry was significantly aided by two factors. First, in contrast to the mutual savings banks, the savings and loan association form of intermediary was not limited to any particular geographical area. The second factor was the urgent need for new housing and housing finance by a nation expanding both in area and in population. Savings and loans associations were organized specifically *for* the purpose of financing real estate, whereas the savings banks turned to home mortgages only as a suitable outlet for the savings money placed with them. Although at first not able to make substantial inroads in states where savings banks were already well established, the savings and loans had the field pretty much to themselves in the rest of the nation until commercial banks and their regulators awoke to the potentialities of residential real-estate finance.

Insurance Companies

Our economic growth was giving rise to another kind of financial need, which the financial institutions described above were not able or willing to meet: the need for long-term business capital financing. It was in response to the opportunity provided by this "financial gap" and by the growing household demand for a means of providing for future contingencies that a variety of other savings intermediaries arose and flourished beginning in the second half of the nineteenth century: fire, casualty, marine, and life insurance companies; trust companies; and, considerably later, investment companies and private pension funds.

These institutions have two characteristics in common: (1) performance of their particular functions involves the accumulation of large amounts of financial assets, and (2) cash inflows and outflows are regular and can be predicted quite accurately. They therefore need not keep any substantial amount of their assets in liquid form but are free to hold mainly long-term, generally higher-yielding assets—which meant, in practice, claims against business, providing growing business enterprises (railroads, manufacturers, and public utilities) with needed long-term financing.

Consumer Financing

A noteworthy aspect of our developing economy has been the increasing importance of consumer durables: the sewing machine, the icebox and later (wonder of wonders) the electric refrigerator, the "victrola" and its descendants, the radio, and, in particular, the automobile. The growing need for consumer financing was met at first primarily by a

---

[8] Ibid., pp. 5–6.

new kind of financial intermediary, as usual, rather than by existing ones. The decade of the 1920s saw the rise to prominence of the sales finance company. This type of intermediary specialized in consumer installment loans secured by particular durable items.

Why did existing institutions not respond to this need? Savings and loan associations and mutual savings banks were (and are) generally not permitted by law to do so, while commercial banks considered this kind of credit outside the scope of "sound" banking. Besides, banks had neither the staff nor the experience to deal with the special problems involved in this kind of financing.

One final class of formerly unmet needs that deserves mention here is for consumer credit that is not specifically related to purchases of durable consumer goods—credit needed by consumers experiencing a "liquidity crisis" from, say, a sudden economic reverse, or even poor financial planning. There have always been "loan sharks," of course, available to meet this need after their fashion at illegal, sometimes fantastically high, rates of interest. Pawnbrokers, remedial loan societies, and other sources were hopelessly inadequate to fill the gap. A combination of high per-dollar cost of small loans and usury statutes fixing the ceiling interest rate at 6 to 8 per cent on loans blocked the establishment of a consumer finance industry on a business basis.

After the turn of the twentieth century, state legislatures began to pass special small-loan statutes in order to cope with the twin problems of the loan shark and inadequate consumer credit. These statues permitted the establishment of consumer lending firms, provided special maximum interest rates that were economically realistic, in view of the higher costs of consumer lending, and imposed limits on the maximum loan size that such institutions were allowed to grant. As household incomes have increased, this legal limit has had to be periodically raised; but the inevitable lag has tended to hamper the growth of the consumer finance industry.

Another factor curbing somewhat the growth of these institutions has been the rise of the credit union, a unique form of financial intermediary organized on a cooperative basis. As one authority on credit unions has stated, "Credit unions are . . . intended . . . to serve the savings and credit needs of well-defined groups, associated under a 'common bond.' "[9] This "common bond" could be religious, fraternal, or community, but in practice the usual one is an employer or occupation.[10] Often the credit union is, in effect, subsidized by provision of free time by

---

[9] John T. Croteau, *The Economics of the Credit Union* (Detroit: Wayne State University Press, 1963), p. 1.
[10] "Now there are credit unions for grave diggers in Chicago, berry pickers in San Jose, Calif., Gros Ventre Indians in Montana, members of the Philadelphia Orchestra, and White House employees." M. S. Mendelsohn, "Lively Credit Unions," *Wall Street Journal*, XLII (May 3, 1962). Reprinted with the permission of the *Wall Street Journal*, © Dow Jones & Company, Inc. 1962.

members and sometimes free office space and other help by a sponsoring employer. Also helpful to the credit union movement has been its ideological appeal. "Its inspiration is humanitarian; its history is one of service.... It appeals to the idealist.... Credit unions seek to protect the weak, to save them from the exactions of usurers."[11] And, for the nonidealist, the appeal is relatively low interest rates on consumer loans, plus competitive or better rates paid on savings.

Recent Developments and Emerging Trends

At this point one might be tempted to say, "I get the picture: a new financial need arises and, presto, a new type of financial intermediary arises in response." Historically, this generalization would stand up quite well—at least until recently. It would be dangerous to apply it to the present-day situation, let alone to the future, because financial intermediaries themselves have been evolving in two directions: (1) they have been moving closer together, tending to extend their activities into the traditional markets of the others; and (2) they have become more innovative, more aggressive in seeking out financial opportunities not met or inadequately met by other intermediaries.

The reasons for these developments are worth our investigating for the light they shed on the behavior of our financial system.

Consider commercial banks first: they had been doing very well, but the 1920s saw hard times for agriculture and also the rise of internal financing by business, both of these inducing banks to seek other types of earning assets in addition to agricultural and commercial loans. The result was both a rise in bank holdings of securities and, conveniently, the emergence of a rationalization for the change in portfolio policy toward holding these assets.[12]

Then, in the 1930s, after the initial shock of the depression wore off, the banks began to take stock of greatly changed economic circumstances, in both the real and the financial sectors. Among these circumstantial changes were (1) large amounts of excess reserves, (2) the ready availability of government-insured home mortgages, (3) drastically reduced demand for short-term business loans, (4) more permissive regulatory practices, and (5) favorable experience of other types of intermediaries with consumer lending and business term lending. Under pressure of economic circumstances and encouraged by changes in regulatory practices, banks effected drastic shifts in their asset portfolios, expanding into consumer and real-estate lending, purchasing government securities in unprecedented quantities, and adopting the practice of "term lending," that is, making loans to business that were to be repaid on a regular basis over a period exceeding a year.

Banks have learned their lessons well, and in the process they have

---

[11] Croteau, *The Economics of the Credit Union*, p. 3.
[12] This is the "shiftability" theory of liquidity discussed in chapter 4.

gradually transformed themselves from institutions specializing in short-term business finance and providing obligations that serve as our means of payment to their present status as highly diversified "department stores of finance." But other financial intermediaries have been undergoing the same process: they are spreading into new (for them) financial markets where permitted and are pressuring regulatory authorities to change the rules where not permitted. Both mutual savings banks and savings and loan associations are seeking, through their central organizations, to enter the consumer lending field. The savings banks are active in selling life insurance and have begun a mutual fund; some sell travelers' checks and provide other financial services. Savings banks and some savings and loan associations even allow depositors to draw money orders against their accounts—a practice that comes close to a checking-account arrangement. Two states, in fact, have authorized mutual savings banks to offer interest-bearing accounts on which checklike "negotiable orders of withdrawal" may be drawn in making payments.

On the other side of the balance sheet, all these institutions compete fiercely for savings, intensified by the fact that most savers consider the savings obligations of the various intermediaries to be practically identical from the standpoints of safety and liquidity. The so-called "contractual intermediaries," such as insurance companies, also have enlarged the scope of their investment activities in response to both market opportunities and the broadened area of discretion allowed by regulatory authorities.

Numerous innovations, too, have appeared and are appearing. In chapters 4 and 5 we shall examine some of these originated by banks: devices to secure financing (deposit and other) and new loan arrangements. Savings and loans are selling short-term notes; some are opening branches in supermarkets and making loans on urban renewal projects. Life insurance companies not only finance housing projects, they sometimes buy and operate them as well. And their innovations in types of life insurance arrangements seem inexhaustible.

Therefore, while it would be foolish to state that there will probably be no truly new type of financial intermediary appearing in the foreseeable future,[13] it does appear that, in view of the prevailing spirit of aggressive innovation and market interpenetration, the appearance of new and viable types will be rare events.

The Financial Institutions: A Survey

This historical sketch has brought out the fact that the term *financial intermediary* covers a wide assortment of different types of organizations; and, of course, the term *financial institution* is a still broader one.

---

[13] The real-estate investment trust might be considered a genuine new form of intermediary, dating in its present form from 1960, when Congress passed the Real Estate Investment Trust Act. See chapter 8 for details.

Actually, financial institutions differ in ownership (public and private), mode of organization (partnership, corporate, mutual, cooperative), range of activities, outlets for their own obligations (households, other intermediaries, and/or nonfinancial businesses), major types of obligations issued (deposits, bonds, equities), types and range of claims purchased, and so on.

Because of this diversity, one can make but few generalizations about financial institutions that are true of *all* of them, so it seems best to discuss each type individually, noting any characteristics it has in common with other types and any interrelations with other areas of the financial system. The accompanying outline (Table 3.1) may be helpful as a means of giving some order to the large assortment of intermediaries with which we must acquaint ourselves.

TABLE 3.1
The System of Financial Institutions

I. Monetary Intermediaries
    Commercial Banks
    The Federal Reserve System

II. Savings Intermediaries
    A. Depository
        Mutual savings banks
        Savings and loan associations
        Credit unions
    B. Contractual
        Life insurance companies
        Property and casualty insurance companies
        Pension funds
    C. Investment companies (including Real Estate Investment Trusts)

III. Borrowing Intermediaries
    Finance companies
    Small business investment companies
    Development credit corporations

IV. Nonintermediary Financial Firms
    A. Market-contact
        Investment bankers
        Mortgage companies
        Securities brokers and dealers
    B. Portfolio management and advice
        Institutional trustees
        Investment counsel service

V. Government and Quasi-Governmental Intermediaries

In this chapter a brief introduction to each will have to suffice; the remaining chapters of Parts II and III will provide a much fuller acquaintance with them.

Monetary Intermediaries

The most important class of intermediaries by almost any test is commercial banks.[14] While we have studied one aspect of banking, demand deposits, in connection with our analysis of the monetary system, we must examine other characteristics of the bank as a private financial institution in order to appreciate its economic role and that of the banking system. Chapters 4 and 5 are devoted to that task.

The other monetary intermediary, the Federal Reserve System, is the keystone of the entire financial system. Not only is the system the issuer of nearly all of our paper money but it also exercises effective control over the quantity of deposit money by means of its power to determine the volume of bank reserves and their capacity to "support" demand deposits. We examine the structure and functions of the Federal Reserve System in chapters 6 and 7.

Depository Savings Intermediaries

Chapters 8 and 9 are devoted entirely to the nonbank financial intermediaries and the nonintermediary financial firms. For convenience, they are classified under several headings.

There are, first, the *depository savings intermediaries*, which include savings and loan associations, mutual savings banks, and credit unions. In a sense, commercial banks belong in this category too, since they issue interest-bearing time and savings deposits that meet the safety and liquidity tests. But the fact that they also issue demand liabilities puts them, literally, in a class by themselves.

Members of this group of intermediaries have one important characteristic in common: they issue obligations that are purchased primarily by consumers as an outlet for their current savings. These obligations are, by and large, liquid, that is, easily "converted" into (exchanged for) a prearranged quantity of money with little or no advance notice, and earn interest for the holders as well. Along with commercial-bank savings accounts, these obligations are often called "near-money" because they perform one of the functions of money—store of value—almost as well as money itself, though they do not serve as means of payment.[15]

---

[14] Some writers do not classify commercial banks as intermediaries primarily because they hold to a different conception of intermediation. See, for example, Warren F. Smith, "Financial Intermediaries and Monetary Control," *Quarterly Journal of Economics*, LXXIII (November 1959), p. 534; and Leland Pritchard, *Money and Banking*, 2d ed. (Boston: Houghton Mifflin Co. 1964), p. 617.

[15] Mutual savings banks in several states are authorized to offer NOW (negotiable order of withdrawal) accounts, utilized by households in paying bills. Though not included as part of the money supply, they are practically indistinguishable from checking accounts, so far as household use is concerned. See chapter 8.

On the asset side, there are some differences worth noting. Savings and loan associations, as a class, hold nearly 85 per cent of their total assets in the form of mortgage loans, about three-quarters of which are on single-family dwellings. In contrast, credit union assets consist largely of non-real estate loans to members. Mutual savings banks, however, hold a more varied asset-mix. Their largest category of assets is mortgage loans on one- to four-family dwellings, accounting for a little over two-fifths of total assets.[16]

Contractual Savings Intermediaries

Besides the issuers of near-money, there are other types of intermediaries that are major outlets for consumer savings: life insurance companies, property and casualty insurance companies, and pension funds.[17]

Although it may seem odd to classify *life insurance firms* as intermediaries, considering that their main function is providing protection, the "saving" feature of most insurance plans has enabled these firms to accumulate well over $100 billion in assets, mainly in the form of financial claims against government and business. Also, as many policyholders know, most kinds of policies have provisions permitting the policyholder to borrow up to a specified amount against the policy.

Property and casualty insurance companies also hold billions of dollars of financial assets, "financed" in large part by policy-holders, who are required to pay premiums in advance.

Pension funds do not, strictly speaking, constitute a distinct class of intermediary institutions. Some funds are administered by life insurance companies, some by trust companies or trust departments of commercial banks, and some by designated individual trustees. Yet they do constitute a distinct type of intermediary *activity,* a method of building up a claim by regular contributions (one's own and/or one's employer), the claim to come due upon, say, retirement from the employ of a particular firm or unit of government. Most fund assets are in the form of debt and equity claims against private business corporations.

Investment Companies

Investment companies issue claims, usually in the form of equities, and acquire claims, also mostly equities. While this may sound somewhat unnecessary, the purpose of this activity is quite rational: to enable

---

[16] Figures in this paragraph were taken and adapted from *1973 National Fact Book of Mutual Savings Banking* (New York: National Association of Mutual Savings Banks, 1973), pp. 7, 26; and *'74 Savings and Loan Fact Book* (Chicago: United States League of Savings Associations, 1974), pp. 78, 94.

[17] The Old Age, Survivors, Disability, and Health Insurance (OASDHI) program, under the Social Security Administration, is excluded from our list because (1) it is tax-financed, (2) for most participants it is compulsory, and (3) its investments are limited to special United States Government securities.

the purchaser of shares in these companies to reduce the risks characteristic of stock and real estate investment. This is possible because the investment company (1) holds a diversified assortment of securities and/or real estate and (2) utilizes the services of expert portfolio managers and advisers.

Borrowing Intermediaries

Another important category of intermediaries consists of the borrowing intermediaries, so named because their primary source of financing is not the direct savings of households but is rather other intermediaries and large business firms in a position to hold liquid assets in excess of current needs. Dominating this class of intermediaries are the *finance companies* of various kinds, some of which specialize in lending on the security of automobiles and other durable goods, others in making small, unsecured consumer loans.

Other borrowing intermediaries are the *small business investment companies*—the title of which pretty well explains their function—and *development credit corporations,* which have appeared in a number of states.

Nonintermediary Financial Firms

Finally, there is a heterogeneous collection of kinds of institutions the main activities of which involve participation in the financial system in ways other than intermediation. Some we describe as *market-contact institutions,* for want of a better term. Firms in this category perform the function of bringing together buyers and sellers of particular kinds of claims: mortgages, corporate bonds, equities, government securities, and so on. In some cases the seller is also the original issuer; in others, he (or it) simply wants to effect an asset-structure change.

In addition to market-contact institutions, there is the category of nonintermediary financial firms made up of firms that provide *portfolio management and advice* for institutional and individual clients. Firms in this category carry a variety of labels: investment counselors, investment advisers, institutional trustees, and so on.

Government and Quasi-Governmental Intermediaries

It would be possible to classify government agencies that finance private economic units in the categories already discussed. Most of them would then be placed under the heading of *borrowing intermediaries,* the source of their financing being primarily the United States Treasury and various private financial intermediaries. They face many of the same operating problems as private financial firms. Some are quite competitive with one or another class of private financial firms. In fact, almost any kind of relationship, both competitive and complementary, can be found between private and government lenders. Nevertheless, because of differences between these two classes of lenders in terms of goals, standards of success, policies, and other areas, it seems wise to keep them separate for discussion purposes.

As an indication of the scope of government lending, we may note that even a list of such agencies would cover several pages. In chapter 13 we discuss government intermediaries along with other elements of the government's role in the financial system.

We have been no more than introduced now to all the major and most of the minor classes of financial institutions. Parts II and III are designed to move us on to the level of acquaintance. No only shall we observe the distinguishing characteristics of each but, of equal importance, we shall also note the more significant relations of each with other types, underscoring again the point that what we are studying is the financial *system*, not a mere assortment of intermediaries, markets, laws, customs, and what have you, which happen to have something to do with finance.

The Nature of the Financial Intermediary

Our final general topic concerning financial institutions is the behavior—the "theory"—of the financial intermediary. We are deliberately ignoring the nonintermediary financial firms at this point because they are not really "special": they provide services such as information, advice, facilities for buying and selling claims, custodial facilities—services that have their counterpart in other sectors, so their behavior poses no special problems for us.

The case of the financial intermediary, though, is not so simple. What, really, do they "do," in economic terms, to justify their existence? The fact that intermediaries are able to obtain higher rates of return from economic units that they finance than the interest rates that they (the intermediaries) must pay to economic units financing them implies that whatever they do is at least economically viable. Moreover, the rapid growth of intermediaries attests to the continued and increasing demand for "whatever they do." Thus, an examination of the behavior of intermediaries on a general level seems worthwhile.

No intermediaries are 100 per cent pure intermediaries. All of them obtain a fraction of their income, and incur a fraction of their costs, in the performance of nonintermediation activities. To keep it simple, however, we shall ignore these other activities here; our discussion will be in terms of the "pure" intermediary. The income and costs of such a firm will depend on both the total volume and the "mix" of claims it holds, and the obligations it issues. In other words, different balance sheets generate different patterns of income and costs. Alternative balance sheets also differ in other attributes (exposure to various kinds of risk, for example) with which the management of the financial intermediary will naturally be concerned.

Since both the size and composition of the balance sheet are important to the achievement of management's goals, it seems reasonable to use the framework of the balance sheet as the basis on which to organize our discussion of the behavior of the financial intermediary. Let us express it this way: *the task that the intermediary sets for itself is to acquire from among various alternative possible collections of assets and obligations, the collection that comes closest to meeting its objectives.*

Several aspects of this statement may require elaboration. First, the expression "collections of assets and obligations" is used in order to convey the idea that the two sides of the balance sheet are interrelated: for each asset-mix there is an optimum obligations-mix, and vice versa.

Second, the term *collection* includes the characteristic of size as well as composition. In fact, the two aspects—size and mix—may be interrelated.

Third, the statement implies search for *the* optimum collection. This is probably an exaggeration. Yet, it is a characteristic of intermediaries generally that they are seldom satisfied for long with the way that they are doing things but are continually searching for new ways of providing financing and new sources of financing, reevaluating existing policies, and adjusting to changes in their environment. The statement thus seems a good approximation to actual behavior in this respect.

Fourth, and related, we should be aware that "searching," that is, seeking information, itself involves costs; therefore, the intermediary must weigh the possible benefits of more and better information against the added costs of search. This fact limits search efforts, making the movement of the financial intermediary toward the optimum and also the policy response of the intermediary to shifts in economic circumstances slower than would be the case if information were costless.

Finally, the statement does not spell out the criteria for choice among alternative balance sheets. This topic we now take up. Three objectives are usually and rightly singled out as of special importance in the decision making of financial intermediaries: net income, safety, and liquidity.[18]

Net Income

Since most intermediaries are private business firms, the flow of net income (income in excess of costs) is a necessary condition for survival; though, as we shall see in a moment, it is not a *sufficient* condition. Naturally, in making decisions, the management of the financial inter-

---

[18] We are thus ignoring other possible goals that are often present and sometimes of overriding importance. Examples are (1) advancement of the interests of "insiders," a goal not always compatible with the above trio, and (2) attainment of broader socioeconomic goals, a consideration especially important for some government and quasi-government intermediaries.

mediary is concerned with expected income and costs associated with possible collections of assets and obligations.

On first thought, it may seem that the way to achieve the largest possible expected net income is to purchase those securities and to make those loans that carry the highest possible interest rates, net of costs of handling. A quick second thought, though, should convince us of the foolishness of such a policy. If, for example, the intermediary has the opportunity to make a 9 per cent loan to a firm in serious financial difficulties, its "expected" yield from such an asset may well be negative, since it may anticipate that the most likely outcome of the arrangement is that it will receive back 60 cents on the dollar. If, on the other hand, the intermediary has the opportunity to make a 6 per cent loan to a potential new customer—a well-managed firm which, because of expansion, is in need of additional financing—the intermediary would not look solely at the prospective yield and cost associated with *this* loan transaction but would think of this as the possible beginning of a long-term relationship and evaluate it accordingly.

Generalizing, the expected net income associated with a given collection of assets and obligations depends on (1) prices paid for the various assets; (2) costs associated with the acquisition, maintenance, and disposal of these assets; (3) payments the intermediary expects to receive in connection with the assets, including interest, periodic and final repayments, and proceeds from sale; (4) costs of financing the assets, including costs of securing financing, the periodic money payments required, and other costs (for example, record keeping); and (5) the time pattern of all of the in- and out-payments.

Safety

To estimate the net income that *probably* will be realized on the basis of a given collection of assets and obligations is not a sufficient basis for decision. The intermediary must also have some conception of the degree of assurance such an expectation carries. Is there a fair chance that the assets will yield much more? or much less? And what would be the likely consequences of "much less"? Some classes of financial intermediaries—banks and depository savings intermediaries in particular—operate with such thin capital cushions that a substantial decline in recorded asset values could prove highly embarrassing, even disastrous, to the management of a financial intermediary, and to the intermediary itself, experiencing such a problem. At the other extreme, some investment companies have virtually no debt, only shareholders' equity, and have a well-publicized policy of seeking above-average yields even though this means assuming above-average risks.

Safety, as a characteristic of a balance sheet, depends partly on the quality of the individual assets themselves, such as the reputation and expected economic status of the debtor, the characteristics of the financial claim (security, priority, etc.) and the nearness of the claim to maturity. But also important are such factors as the degree of diversification (for example, by geographical area and by industry) of the asset portfolio and the expected state of the economy in the near future.

Safety inevitably has a subjective element. Therefore, if an intermediary is observed to have shifted in the direction of riskier assets, and assuming no change in relative interest rates, we cannot be sure whether this movement resulted from a change in the "safety-preference" of management or from a change in management's evaluation of the relative riskiness of the assets involved, or both.

Liquidity

Finally, a continuing problem for financial intermediaries is *liquidity*, which we defined provisionally[19] as "financial maneuverability."

Liquidity, too, defies precise measurement because it depends not only on such obvious factors as the cash-to-debt ratio but also on the percentage of other assets that could be exchanged for money (through sale or otherwise) without the likelihood of appreciable loss and on the availability of additional financing on short notice.

The "solution" to the balance-sheet problem is a compromise among these (and perhaps other) objectives. As we examine in more detail the various classes of financial intermediaries in chapters 4 through 9, it will be interesting and instructive to contrast them in terms of their economic and regulatory environments and of the ways in which their managements have arrived at solutions believed to be appropriate to their particular situations.

Summary

A major function of financial intermediaries is, of course, intermediation. Although, on the surface, intermediation may appear rather pointless—purchasing claims against other economic units while selling obligations against oneself—it makes perfectly good sense to the intermediaries involved. Moreover, the economic importance of the process is considerable, as we noted in the Overview: through intermediation the need of prospective deficit economic units to issue long-term, relatively risky and illiquid obligations is reconciled with the desires of surplus economic units for claims that are safe and liquid.

The present system of financial intermediaries in the United States is the outcome of a myriad of forces—economic, political, and other—acting and interacting over the past two centuries and more. Beginning with early commercial banking in the colonial era, the system has

---

[19] Chapter 17 will include an extensive discussion of liquidity.

evolved in several dimensions: (1) new forms of financial intermediaries appeared in response to specific needs and opportunities; (2) existing intermediaries have changed, through adaptation to changes in their environment; and (3) government regulation and other types of intervention in the financial system have increased, in response to shortcomings in the structure and behavior of the system.

Today's financial intermediaries are far more sophisticated in their knowledge of, and responses to, changes in the politico-economic environment. A commonly noted characteristic of intermediaries is their increasing innovativeness in the types of obligations they offer, the types of claims they offer to purchase, the markets they attempt to cultivate, and the auxiliary services they offer (or seek authorization to offer), and in other respects.

Although each intermediary class has its own identifying characteristics, they all share certain problems in common, problems involved in attempting to achieve particular objectives through management of their asset portfolios and acquisition of financing: net income, safety, and liquidity. The management of each financial intermediary seeks to reconcile these sometimes conflicting objectives in the light of its perceptions of the economic and regulatory environment and its own preferences.

KEY CONCEPTS

Intermediation
Depository savings intermediaries
Contractual savings intermediaries
Investment companies
Borrowing intermediaries

Nonintermediary financial firms
Trade credit
Safety
Liquidity

QUESTIONS FOR REVIEW

1. Is intermediation actually a kind of marketing activity? Is it really an example of manufacturing? Explain your answer.
2. Why did mutual savings banks emerge before savings and loan associations? In view of the role played by MSB's, why did S&L's emerge at all?
3. Why did S&L's emerge before consumer finance companies?
4. Why are some financial institutions considered "intermediaries" while some are not?
5. What are the three main objectives of a financial intermediary? Are these different from the objectives of other business firms? Explain.

SUGGESTIONS FOR FURTHER READING

Cameron, Rondo. *Banking and Economic Development: Some Lessons of History.* Fair Lawn, N.J.: Oxford University Press, 1972.

Ettin, Edward C. "The Development of American Financial Institutions." *Quarterly Review of Economics and Business,* III (Summer 1963), pp. 51–69.

Goldsmith, Raymond W. *Financial Intermediaries in the American Economy Since 1900.* Princeton: Princeton University Press, 1963.

Hammond, Bray. *Banks and Politics in America from the Revolution to the Civil War.* Princeton: Princeton University Press, 1957.

Hungate, Robert P. *Interbusiness Financing: Implications for Small Business.* Washington, D.C.: Small Business Administration, 1962.

Jacobs, Donald P., et al. *Financial Institutions,* 5th ed. Homewood, Ill.: R. D. Irwin, 1972.

Krooss, Herman E., and Martin R. Blyn. *A History of Financial Intermediaries.* New York: Random House, 1971.

Studenski, Paul, and Herman E. Krooss. *Financial History of the United States,* 2d ed. New York: McGraw-Hill Book Co., 1963.

Trescott, Paul B. *Financing American Enterprise.* New York: Harper & Row, 1963.

The Combined Balance Sheet
Characteristics of the Balance Sheet
The Banking Problem

Sources of Financing:
The Capital Accounts

Deposits

Demand Deposits
Government Deposits
Interbank Deposits
Other Demand Deposits
Service Charges

Time Deposits
Savings Deposits
Certificates of Deposit
Regulation of Deposits:
The "Regulation Q" Issue

Other Obligations

Commercial Banks: Sources of Financing

Because of the central importance of money not only in the financial system but in the "real" economy as well, it is surely appropriate to begin our review of financial intermediaries with those institutions that are primarily responsible for the creation and control of money: the commercial bank[1] and the Federal Reserve System.

From the discussion in chapter 2 we recall that the commercial banking system, although made up of somewhat over 14,000 individual firms operating over 26,000 branches, is truly a system by virtue of the interrelations among banks: interrelations through the Federal Reserve System and a complex network of correspondent relationships, ownership links, and clearing-house memberships. But this system of banks does not exist in isolation. Rather, it is interlinked with the rest of the financial system in a number of important ways.

1. Banks serve as depositories of all other types of private financial institutions, because bank demand deposits are our basic medium of exchange.
2. Banks acquire and hold claims against other financial intermediaries.

---

[1] Following common usage, we use the terms *banks* and *commercial banks* interchangeably. Other kinds of banks (mutual savings, investment, central, and so on) will always be designated by the appropriate adjective.

3. Banks compete with other institutions, for deposits and for many classes of claims.
4. Banks sometimes participate with other financial intermediaries in particular transactions.
5. Banks sell services to other intermediaries.
6. Finally, banks sometimes own, or are owned by, other intermediaries.

These relationships will be discussed further as we go along.

The Combined Balance Sheet

Some indication of the business of banking may be gotten by studying a "stripped-down" version of the combined balance sheet of all United States commercial banks, as of a recent date. (See Table 4.1).

The terminology should present no problems, since we met most of the terms already in discussing deposit creation in chapter 2. *Reserves* comprise (1) demand claims against (that is, deposits held in) Federal Reserve banks and other commercial banks, (2) the banks' holdings of currency for transactions needs, and (3) cash items (checks) in various stages of the clearing and collection process. *Loans* and *securities* (usually called investments) are the banks' earning assets. The main distinction (although somewhat hazy at the boundary) between the two categories of earning assets is that banks *originate* loans, through direct negotiation with the borrowers (issuers of the claims), while the banks *purchase* securities for their investments account, without face-to-face dealings with the issuers of the securities.

On the other side of the balance sheet, the major categories of claims held against the banks are *demand deposits* (checking accounts), *time deposits* (claims having a specified due date or waiting period, which

TABLE 4.1
Combined Balance Sheet,
All Commercial Banks, December 31, 1973
(in $millions)

Assets		Liabilities and Capital	
Cash assets	$118,276	Demand deposits	
Loans	494,947	U.S. government	$ 9,865
Securities		Other	300,206
U.S. Treasury	57,277	Time deposits	371,775
Other	130,574	Borrowings	58,994
Other assets	34,150	Other liabilities	36,256
	$835,224	Total capital accounts	58,128
			$835,224

Source: *Federal Reserve Bulletin*, May 1974, p. A16.

period may be waived), *borrowings*, and *capital* (mostly ownership claims).

Characteristics of the Balance Sheet

Because they are crucial to our understanding of the behavior of banks, several aspects of this balance sheet call for comment:

1. *Relative size of the reserves category.* Banks hold an unusually high percentage of their assets in the form of reserves as compared to other financial and also nonfinancial firms because, as we have already observed, they are required to do so by whatever regulatory authorities are over them; but, even in the absence of requirements, they would hold some reserves (cash) for the same reasons any economic unit holds cash—for ordinary transactions, to meet unforeseen contingencies, to take advantage of unexpected opportunities, and, on occasion, in anticipation of lower securities prices (higher yields) or lower prices of real assets.
2. *Capital-to-assets ratio.* Any nonfinancial firm having a ratio of capital to total assets of 1:14 or thereabouts would be considered to be in a most precarious position. Yet bankers and their regulators seem quite unconcerned with this overall capital ratio. The reasons will be brought out shortly when we examine the question of the adequacy of bank capital.
3. *"Liquidity" of liabilities.* All but a small fraction of the banks' debt obligations are due on demand or within a short time—a year or less. Naturally, this condition exerts some effect on asset-structure decisions on the part of bank managements, as we shall discuss at some length in chapter 5.
4. *Ratio of time deposits to total deposits.* Certain developments that have taken place over the past few years have put strong upward pressure on the ratio of time deposit to total deposits. The rise in this ratio, in turn, has influenced bank asset-mix policy: since time deposits are less volatile than demand deposits, banks feel freer to make intermediate and long-term loans to business firms and home buyers.
5. *Loans-to-assets ratio.* Intense pressure for financing by bank customers in recent years, primarily because of the rapid growth of our economy, has pushed the loan ratio to new postwar highs. At this time, however, we cannot be sure whether ratios this high will be sustained over the years ahead; but the reactions to this development vary from cries of alarm to elaborate defenses of the viewpoint that the banking system was never healthier.

The Banking Problem

The balance sheet of any particular bank will naturally deviate from this consolidated one (and sometimes drastically) in the proportion of its total assets or liabilities-plus-capital in a particular category because, at any point in time, a bank's balance sheet is the result of (1) a myriad of outside influences, some general and some primarily affecting a region or even a locality; and (2) the bank's response to these influences. This response, in turn, is influenced by management's perception of its obligations and opportunities and by the objectives and preferences of management with respect to income, safety, and liquidity.

The bank's need for *net income* is self-evident, since it is a privately owned enterprise. The need for *safety* (a low-risk balance-sheet position) exerts a continuing influence on the bank's asset choices. If the bank should incur losses on loans or experience substantial declines in the market values of its investments, the published balance sheet might not even reveal this fact as a decline in its worth due to a complicated set of "reserve accounts." However, the financial managers of the bank's important business customers would almost certainly be aware of these developments as would the regulatory authorities. Even a hint of trouble might induce its large customers to withdraw their deposits and might damage in other ways, too, the bank's carefully cultivated reputation. Thus, bankers are generally "risk-averters," taking care that the *actual* net income of the bank will probably not deviate sharply up or down from the *expected* net income. This consideration calls for relatively "safe" assets.

LIQUIDITY   Although a matter of concern to all economic units, liquidity is especially crucial for banks because such a large fraction of their obligations are "due" at the whim of the holder, which is the case for demand deposits and (in effect) for passbook savings accounts.

The thinking of bankers and their regulators concerning liquidity as applied to earning assets has evolved considerably over the past century. Traditionally, emphasis was on the purpose and maturity of the asset—in practice, the loan. If the loan is short-term and for the purpose of financing the production, shipment, or storage of goods, then, according to this theory, the subsequent sale of these goods automatically provides the means to repay the loan. A bank concentrating its earning-asset portfolio on such loans, evenly spaced, would have small probability of liquidity problems because, in the unlikely event of a surge of withdrawals, the bank could simply make new loans at a slower rate than the rate of repayment of existing loans until its reserve position was restored. This, in essence, was the so-called *self-liquidating* theory of liquidity.[2] So

---

[2] There is much more to the theory than this; it was advocated as a means for achieving economic stability as well. See, for example, Lloyd W. Mints, *The History of Banking Theory* (Chicago: University of Chicago Press, 1945), chapter 13. This aspect of the theory, however, goes beyond our present concern.

long as business conditions remained stable and the borrowers had no trouble in selling the goods, there should be no great problems. If, however, the economy were to slump and the merchandise had to be sold at a loss, both bank and borrowers could be in trouble.

Changes in methods of business finance away from reliance on the short-term loan and growing bank experience with investments gave rise to the *shiftability* approach to liquidity. Bankers discovered that, when they needed extra cash, all they had to do was sell some of these easily marketable securities. So long as there was a wide market for a particular security, it was potential "instant liquidity." Unfortunately, as the depressed 1930s brought out so vividly, this process works only when the rest of the financial system is not trying to do the same thing! Bankers discovered that, although they could still get rid of their securities, sometimes the sale had to be at ruinously depressed prices.

A third approach (one is tempted to use the term *rationalization*, because in all these cases the "theory" followed the inception of the practice) is called the *anticipated income theory*.[3] Its purpose is to justify the practice of making term loans to business, that is, loans that (1) run for longer than a year, (2) provide financing for expansion and other longer-term business purposes, and (3) are repaid on an installment basis. Like the old self-liquidating theory, this one stresses the regular repayment of loans to the bank, rather than the sale of securities, for liquidity. The difference lies in the *source of repayment:* rather than the sale of goods, this approach relies on the increase in cash generated by the project for which the loan was desired. For example, a store modernization program might be expected to increase sales volume, or construction machinery might be bought in order to reduce costs. Insofar as the particular project is successful, it favorably affects the cash position of the borrowing firm, enabling it to repay the loan gradually and relatively painlessly, that is, without depriving it of cash needed for other purposes. Naturally, the turnover of such loans is much slower than for ordinary short-term loans; and the risk is greater, since the repayment is spread over a longer period. Also, these loans do not furnish "emergency liquidity." Nevertheless, this theory focuses the lender's and borrower's attention on the relationship between the quality of the loan and the source of repayment.

A fourth approach to liquidity seems to have emerged gradually over the past decade or so. In contrast to the three approaches discussed so far, all of which depend on *asset* adjustments—total or partial repayment of loans or sale of securities—to acquire needed reserves, this approach involves reliance on the ability of the bank to issue *liabilities* as a means of obtaining reserves. This new approach, generally called *liability management banking*, was originated in the early 1960s by large met-

---

[3] Harold V. Prochnow, *Term Loans and Theories of Bank Liquidity* (Englewood Cliffs, N.J.: Prentice-Hall, 1949).

ropolitan banks that were coming under strong double pressures at the time: growing demand for loans, as the economy experienced recovery from the 1960–61 recession, plus an inadequate growth of demand deposits at these banks. This slow growth was due primarily to the increasingly sophisticated cash-management practices of the banks' major depositors, the giant corporations, who were able to hold their deposit balances down in the face of rising sales.

The actual liability management techniques utilized by the big banks involved not only innovations and price competition to obtain more deposit financing but also the development and cultivation of nondeposit sources of debt financing. This a far cry from traditional banking, which regards the "banking problem" largely in terms of tailoring the bank's asset-mix to a given volume and mix of deposits.

Bankers and others have gradually learned that the bank's liquidity position is more than a matter of the qualities of the assets themselves, as emphasized in the first and third of the foregoing theories. Also important are the marketability, or shiftability, of assets and the ability to issue acceptable liabilities in providing liquidity when needed, as the second and fourth theories stress. But going even further, the liquidity position depends on factors *outside* the banking system: on the likelihood of need for additional reserves in a hurry and on the presence of a central bank that stands ready to provide reserves in an emergency, not just to one or a few banks but to the system.

This, then, is the banking problem: how to reconcile the needs and desires for income, safety, and liquidity within the limits imposed by government regulation. We turn now to an examination of the manner in which the banks have coped with this problem and are continuing to do so.

Sources of Financing: The Capital Accounts

Banks, in common with other business firms, are financed both through debt obligations and through equity. In the remainder of this chapter we propose to examine the major sources of bank financing, highlighting recent developments and a few current controversies.

The first source of financing for our examination is *capital*. Except for a relatively small amount of long-term borrowings, bank capital represents "net worth," that is, the residual left after the bank's total obligations to depositors and other creditors are subtracted from the value of total assets. Avoiding unnecessary (to us) details and technicalities, we may divide total capital into three major accounts: capital stock, surplus, and undivided profits.

The capital stock account represents the number of shares of stock outstanding multiplied by the par value per share. *Surplus* arises from two sources: (1) the amount paid to the bank for the stock, at time of issue, in excess of par value and (2) the amount of the bank's earnings that have been retained and allocated to this account. *Undivided profits* is, in a sense, an "interim" account, designating retained earnings that have not been allocated to surplus, mainly in order to give management more flexibility. Banks are most reluctant to show a decline in the surplus account due to, say, a bad year; but a similar decline in the undivided profits account would not be regarded with such seriousness since its decline could result from any of a number of causes—payment of dividends in excess of current earnings, allocation to a reserve account, or allocation to surplus.

Under these circumstances, why would a bank ever allocate retained earnings to surplus? The reason is that the amount that a bank may loan to any one borrower on an unsecured basis is usually limited by law to some fraction (for national banks: 10 per cent) of the bank's combined capital stock and surplus. To qualify to serve larger borrowers adequately, then, the bank is under economic pressure to increase its capital stock plus surplus accounts.

ADEQUACY OF BANK CAPITAL   The "right" amount of capital for a given bank at a given time is not susceptible of precise calculation. This is partly due to the conflicting primary interests of stockholders (higher profits), depositors (maximum protection), and the general public (adequate monetary system, efficient allocation of credit); but another reason is that we simply do not know enough about either the capital cushion necessary to cope with a given set of economic circumstances or the kinds of economic conditions we are likely to face in the relevant future. Even if we did know these things, it is obvious that the capital cushion appropriate for a particular bank would depend on the bank's asset structure.

For example, suppose that one year ago a particular bank's capital was deemed barely adequate. If today, as compared to the year-ago situation, (1) its earning assets are, on the average, riskier, (2) its reserve ratio is lower, (3) its deposit-mix is more volatile, (4) its deposits have increased more rapidly than its capital, (5) economic conditions have deteriorated, and (6) standards of evaluating capital have not changed, it is obvious that this bank will be evaluated as deficient in capital. But what if one or two of factors (1)—(5) had moved in the opposite direction, that is, toward a less risky position, what then? Clearly, in large part the evaluation will depend on the judgment of the evaluators: the bank management, the bank examiners, and perhaps the bank's more important customers.

There are many variables actually employed by bank examiners in assessing the adequacy of a particular bank's capital.[4] Crude ratios, like capital-to-assets or capital-to-deposits, are still used. These measure the

---

[4] William F. Staats, "The Adequacy of Bank Capital as Viewed by State Authorities," *Banking* (October 1965), pp. 43–44.

relative *size* of the capital cushion, but they are not very helpful for ascertaining its *adequacy* because they do not take into account the relative degree of vulnerability of the bank's assets to a decline in value. For this reason, examiners are turning increasingly to supplementary ratios: capital-to-risk-assets (total assets less cash and U.S. government securities), loans-to-assets, or loans-to-deposits, and so on. Of course, the process of judging capital adequacy goes beyond mechanical calculation of ratios and comparing the calculated values with benchmark values. Nonquantifiable considerations also enter in, such as the general quality of credit and the quality of the bank's management.

The problem of capital adequacy is of concern at the system level as well as at the level of the individual bank. Over the past several decades the capital-to-deposits and capital-to-assets ratios have declined considerably, yet the banking system is considered less vulnerable to serious trouble now than it was earlier. Why? Three reasons stand out: (1) bank assets are less risky, on the whole; (2) deposits are less volatile, and, most importantly, (3) the economic environment has changed radically. Banking is far more sophisticated in its policies and practices, there are fewer and larger banks now, the Federal Deposit Insurance Corporation (FDIC) insures most bank deposits (up to $40,000 per deposit) and indirectly reduces the likelihood of a "run on the banks," and the Federal government now has both the power and the mandate to prevent a major depression.

Deposits

Although banks have begun to use other types of debt financing in significant amounts recently, their largest source of financing by far is still deposits. The variety of deposit arrangements offered to the public has grown considerably in recent years, too, as part of the overall effort of banks to maintain their position of dominance among financial intermediaries.

From the standpoint of the individual bank (though not of the system: recall chapter 2), most deposits on the books at a particular time result from transactions wherein typically a depositor turns over to the bank one or more of a variety of cash items (currency, checks, and drafts) and other items for collection, in exchange for which the bank acknowledges its deposit obligation to the depositor. The *terms* of a particular obligation constitute the basis by which we classify the deposit. Some deposit arrangements oblige the bank to pay to the depositor or to his order all or a specified portion of the deposit upon demand of the depositor or of any party to whom the deposit has been transferred. These are, of course, the demand deposits. Other deposit arrangements either designate a due date or allow the bank a waiting period between the time a notice of intent to withdraw is given and the time the bank is obligated to make money payment. Within each of these categories, in turn, there is a variety of other terms covering such matters as interest payments, service charges, free services, waiver rights, and so on. Table 4.2 provides a breakdown of demand and time deposit ownership by major classes of holders.

One source of confusion to many students is the dual use of the term *deposit*. On the one hand, we often speak of "making a $500 deposit," that is, of turning over $500 worth of (usually) currency and checks to the teller, for which he gives us credit on the bank's books. The "deposit" here refers to the financial assets transferred to the bank. On the other hand, we speak of deposits to denote a category of bank obligations as described in the preceding paragraph. And, making the matter even more confusing, sometimes the bank is described as "holding deposits,"[5] as though deposits were physical objects stored in a vault, while at the same time the economic unit owning the deposit claim is considered the deposit holder!

We shall consistently use the term *deposit* only in its liabilities sense. The only deposits a bank "holds" are its deposit claims against other commercial banks and a Federal Reserve bank.

DEPOSIT INSURANCE Deposits in nearly all commercial banks are fully insured up to $40,000 per account by the Federal Deposit Insurance Corporation (FDIC), an agency of the Federal government. The FDIC obtains its operating income from assessments on the deposits of insured banks and from income on the financial assets accumulated due to the excellent loss record of the banks.

TABLE 4.2
Commercial Bank Deposits, December 31, 1973
(in $millions)

Class of Deposit	Demand Deposits	Time and Saving Deposits
Individuals, partnerships, and corporations	$233,009	$311,966
U.S. government	9,865	439
States and political subdivisions	18,663	44,385
Foreign governments, central banks, etc.	1,625	9,371
Commercial banks in the U.S.	29,975	5,858
Banks in foreign countries	5,584	263
Certified and officers checks, etc.	11,349	—
	$310,071	$372,282

Source: Adapted from *Federal Reserve Bulletin*, May 1974, p. A19.

[5] For example: "A commercial bank is a profit-seeking institution that (1) receives and holds demand deposits...." Clifton H. Kreps, Jr., *Money, Banking and Monetary Policy* (New York: Ronald Press Co., 1962), p. 218.

The FDIC shares with other regulatory agencies the task of regularly examining and supervising banks. This aspect of its work will be discussed in chapter 13.

Demand Deposits

Although banks compete with a variety of other institutions, public and private, for their financing and for the earning-assets they acquire, they have no important direct competition in issuing and servicing demand-deposit claims.[6] All demand-deposit dollars are essentially alike, but the holders and their motivations and behavior with regard to demand deposits are not. We turn now to a brief examination of some major categories of holders. Table 4.2 gives an indication of the relative importance of each.

Government Deposits

Balances held by the Federal government and its agencies are accumulated through tax receipts, issuance of securities, and certain minor types of receipts. These balances are not, however, used for disbursements to the public. Rather, from time to time the Treasury transfers portions of its bank deposits to the Federal Reserve banks to offset its drawing on these accounts in making payments to the public. Since we plan to discuss the Treasury's management of its cash later (chapters 7 and 20), we shall not elaborate here. One reminder though: these deposits, as we noted in chapter 1, are not included in the money supply figures.

Interbank Deposits

In chapter 2 we looked at correspondent banking as a characteristic of our banking system. Instead of being subject to an elaborate schedule of fees for various services performed by the larger banks, the practice from the beginning has been for the smaller, outlying bank—called the *customer* bank—to maintain deposits in one or more larger, big-city banks, called *correspondent* banks.

Interbank balances have been declining rather steadily as a per cent of total deposits.[7] In 1941, these deposits constituted nearly 15.4 per cent

---

[6] Some mutual savings banks and savings and loan associations allow depositors the privilege of using their savings accounts to buy travelers' checks and money orders and to make regular insurance payments. Recently MSB's in some states have been authorized to offer NOW (negotiable order of withdrawal) accounts, which permit holders to utilize savings accounts to make checklike payments.

[7] This section is largely based on Paul S. Nadler, "The Coming Change in Correspondent Relationships," *Banking* (April 1966), pp. 45–46, 94.

of total commercial bank deposits. By the end of 1973, domestic interbank deposits had declined to 5.3 per cent of total bank deposits.

This trend is easily explained. For the customer banks, higher interest rates on earning assets means that every excess dollar in correspondent balances "costs" more, in terms of interest income foregone, than was the case earlier; and smaller banks are becoming more sophisticated in their asset management. Also, for reasons to be discussed next, time deposits have grown far more rapidly than demand deposits in recent years; and time deposits require far less in correspondent-bank services per dollar than do demand deposits. One continuing incentive for customer banks to maintain deposits with their big-city brothers, though, is the fact that, for nonmember banks in many states, such balances may be counted toward meeting the legal reserve requirement.

Other Demand Deposits

The great bulk of bank demand deposits—about three-quarters of the dollar volume—is held by individuals, partnerships, and corporations.

Perhaps *held* may not seem to be an appropriate word in the last sentence because most demand-deposit balances are acquired to be spent, are they not?[8] Some people, it is true, hold checking balances that are very large relative to their utilization of them, perhaps out of ignorance, inertia, or some irrational fears. Other balances may be relatively idle because the bank has required that they be maintained at a certain (minimum or average) level as part of a loan or credit-line arrangement. We shall take a long look at this matter in chapter 5 when we examine the asset side of the bank's balance sheet. But even beyond this requirement, a business customer may hold a larger deposit balance than would be necessary for transactions purposes alone, despite the fact that banks pay no interest on demand deposits because of a legal prohibition. Why do these depositors behave this way? George Mitchell, member of the Board of Governors of the Federal Reserve System, explains:

> [In] substance, a return is being paid on demand deposits in the form of bank services, and ... these services are being measured, more and more precisely as account balance equivalents, by the electronic capacity for accounting minutiae now becoming available.... [There] is also an implicit loan commitment fee that is, in effect, earned by demand deposits; it is the value attributable to the access to bank credit that goes with a prized demand deposit (one which the customer maintains well above service requirements over the years).[9]

---

[8] The demand for money will be discussed more fully in chapter 17.

[9] George W. Mitchell, "Interest Rates versus Interest Ceilings in the Allocation of Credit Flows," *Journal of Finance*, XXII (May 1967), p. 266

Federal Reserve figures on IPC (individuals, partnerships, and corporations) ownership of demand deposits show that since June 1970 (when the Federal Reserve began its quarterly survey) nonfinancial business firms have held about one-half of these demand deposits, fiinancial businesses one-tenth, households between three-tenths and one-third, foreign economic units and others the small remainder.[10]

Service Charges

All or nearly all banks have a schedule of service charges designed to meet a substantial proportion of the cost of demand-deposit activity. This is a relatively recent innovation. Prior to the Great Depression of the 1930s banks were generally willing to perform the check-handling function for their customers without explicit charge, as part of a total "package"; the depositors would provide cheap financing to the bank by holding no-interest or low-interest demand obligations of the bank, in exchange for which the bank would handle the deposit-transfer bookkeeping. The bank, in turn, was able to use this financing to purchase and hold earning-assets. A combination of low interest rates on earning-assets plus a rise in the use of cost accounting by banks convinced them of the wisdom of imposing explicit service charges on deposit activity.

INTEREST ON DEMAND DEPOSITS Although banks have not been permitted since 1933 to pay interest on their demand deposits, they have developed a number of substitute competitive devices to encourage the holding of demand-deposit balances. The so-called "free checking account," which spread rapidly in the 1960s, is an obviously close substitute for explicit interest. In exchange for "financing" the bank through his checking account (perhaps with the requirement that he maintain a specified minimum balance) the depositor has all his checks and deposits processed without charge. The bank is, in turn, compensated by the interest it earns on the earning assets thus held.

Another method of offering a "yield" on demand deposits is the practice of some banks of varying interest rates charged on loans to large corporate borrowers with the balances maintained in their checking accounts: the larger the balance, the lower the interest rate charged.

Time Deposits

Innovations during the past few years in interest-bearing obligations—nondeposit as well as deposit—of commercial banks have profoundly altered the nature of the banking business. The possible ramifications of these changes for other financial intermediaries and financial markets

[10] *Federal Reserve Bulletin*, May 1974, p. A30.

and for the task of the Federal Reserve are still the subject of much controversy. Study of this section should provide some background for current discussions of this topic.

There are three general classes of time deposits: (1) savings deposits, (2) time certificates of deposit, and (3) time deposits, open account. Not much can be said concerning the third of these classes because it is quite heterogeneous, being made up of such diverse elements as Christmas Club Savings, some interbank and United States government interest-bearing deposits, accounts accumulated for payment of personal loans, and a miscellaneous bag of other items. The other two categories, however, beside being less "assorted," are much more important quantitatively.

Savings Deposits

In the main, savings deposits, or "savings accounts," are used by individuals as a safe, convenient, yet income-yielding form in which to hold some or all of their savings.[11] These accounts involve the use of a passbook, issued to the holder(s) of the deposit, in which deposits and withdrawals are entered by the bank. Although the terms of the agreement between bank and deposit holder specify that the bank has the right to require a thirty-day written notice of any intended withdrawal, this right is so rarely enforced by banks that any attempt to do so would be interpreted as a signal that the bank was having liquidity problems.

Banks are in direct competition not only with each other but also with other financial institutions—the depository savings intermediaries—for savings deposits. These intermediaries were identified in chapter 3 as savings and loan associations, mutual savings banks (in some states), and credit unions. Other savings outlets offering at least some of the characteristics of savings accounts are United States savings bonds and marketable securities, some kinds of life insurance policies, municipal securities, corporate securities, pension funds, and shares in investment companies.

Of course, not all of these are realistic alternatives for each deposit holder; in each instance, the degree of substitutability will depend on such factors as (1) the deposit holder's motives for holding financial claims, (2) the size of his income and total assets, (3) the availability of other savings outlets, (4) the terms currently offered by the bank and the alternative outlets. To illustrate: A family in the lower-middle income and wealth range who live in a small town or rural area and are saving for a vacation trip next summer will very likely not regard municipal securities as a sensible alternative to a bank savings account; whereas an upper-income family, headed by a sophisticated investor making in-

---

[11] Since January 1964 national banks have been permitted to enter into savings-account arrangements with businesses as well.

vestment plans that look ahead twenty or more years, would consider any number of alternatives to a bank savings account as possible outlets for at least a part of the family's savings.

What this means to a bank is that, if its interest rate on savings accounts should decline relative to those of depository savings intermediaries, then, based on past experience, it can expect a decline in its savings deposits relative to those of the competing institutions; *but* the bulk of its savings deposits would probably remain because of (1) lack (or unawareness) of alternatives and (2) the convenience, safety, and other noninterest attributes of bank savings accounts. The same conclusion would apply, although less strongly, if interest rates on savings accounts of banks and depository savings intermediaries would decline relative to those of direct obligations of governments and businesses, as usually happens at the peak of the cycle.[12] And the record shows also that opposite circumstances generate opposite results.[13]

Certificates of Deposit

The rapid rise, in dollar volume and extent of use, of the time certificate of deposit is one of the more striking financial phenomena of recent years. There is nothing particularly novel or sophisticated about the time certificate of deposit, or CD, as it is universally called. A CD is simply a written acknowledgement by the depository bank, duly signed and dated, that "there has been deposited in this bank on [date] $ . . . payable to bearer on [date due] upon surrender of this certificate, with interest at the rate of . . . per cent per annum until maturity," or words to that effect. Usually these certificates are negotiable, a quality that makes them more readily transferrable to parties other than the original deposit holder.

There were two main reasons for the rapid growth of the CD after 1961. The first was the development of a *secondary market* in CD's, that is, an arrangement whereby a holder desiring to sell a CD can be brought into contact with a party desiring to invest in a short-term financial asset. This converted the CD from a private arrangement between banker and depositor to an *open-market instrument*, a financial claim enjoying wide acceptance because of unquestioned soundness of the issuer, ease of transfer, and nearness to maturity.

The second major reason for the rise of the CD was the willingness of issuing banks to compete for CD financing on a price basis, that is, by offering interest rates comparable to those on alternative open-market instruments. Both of these, in turn, resulted from the concern of big New York banks that some important providers of deposit financing to these banks—large businesses, state and local governments, and so on—were

---

[12] Richard G. Davis and Jack M. Guttentag, "Time and Savings Deposits in the Cycle," *Monthly Review*, Federal Reserve Bank of New York (June 1962), pp. 86–91.
[13] Ibid.

beginning to bypass the banks, purchasing short-term, open-market securities instead of holding large demand-deposit balances for nontransactions liquidity purposes.

CD'S AND COMPETITION FOR FINANCING Incidentally, this second reason is frequently expressed in such terms as this: "The [CD] represents an attempt of the commercial banking system to attract corporate funds, with a view to regaining deposits and increasing lending potential."[14] The implication is that, somehow, these deposits have left the banking system. But where could they have gone? Perhaps another writer on CD's can enlighten us: "In the late 1950s and early 1960s the banks saw that they could not keep the large demand deposits from being removed and placed into earning assets."[15]

Could this be the answer, that the lost demand deposits have all been "placed into" earning-assets? How do demand deposits turn into, or become buried in, something else? Perhaps if we recast the situation in terms of balance-sheet traces, we will be enabled to see the light.

First, assume that a bank's worst fears are realized: a large corporate depositor removes $1 million from its demand deposit and "places" this amount into Treasury bills (short-term obligations of the United States Treasury), turning over to a securities dealer a check for this amount. Chances are that the corporation's depository bank will find itself drained of $1 million in reserves as well as "owing" the corporation $1 million less in demand deposits after this check is cleared and collected.

TRACE 4.1

Corporation		Corporation's Bank	
Cash −$1,000,000 (Demand deposit)		Reserves −$1,000,000	Demand deposits −$1,000,000
Securities +1,000,000			

But now we must back up a bit to the point where the securities dealer receives the $1 million check that has been "placed into earning-assets." Does the dealer set the check on a shelf somewhere? We know better: he turns it over to his bank for credit to his account. Quite possibly this bank is the same one as the corporation's depository; if not, the banks are almost certainly two out of a small handful of large money-market banks.

TRACE 4.2

Securities Dealer		Securities Dealer's Bank	
Cash (Demand deposit) +$1,000,000		Reserves +$1,000,000	Demand deposits +$1,000,000
Securities −1,000,000			

[14] *Money Market Investments: The Risk and the Return* (New York: Morgan Guarantee Trust Company, 1964), p. 18.
[15] Paul S. Nadler, "The Use and Mis-use of CD's" *Banking* (July 1965), p. 51.

Has the demand deposit disappeared? From the standpoint of the individual bank, the answer is yes; but from the standpoint of the banking system, no; total demand deposits are unchanged.[16] "Placing" demand deposits into earning-assets does not affect total demand deposits.

TRACE 4.3

Banking System	
Demand deposit (corporation)	−$1,000,000
Demand deposit (securities dealer)	+1,000,000

Now we return to the first quotation, which pictures the CD as a means whereby the banking system seeks to regain those "lost" deposits. Assume that this same corporation has been induced by the bank to sell those Treasury bills and buy a $1 million CD (a common size) instead. The first step is the sale to a securities dealer of the $1 million of Treasury bills (we assume that their price has not changed). So far, no change in total deposits has occurred, merely a transfer from one holder to another (step 1 in Trace 4.4).

TRACE 4.4

Corporation		Corporation's Bank	
(1) Securities	−$1,000,000	(1) Reserves	Demand deposits
Cash	+1,000,000	+$1,000,000	+$1,000,000
(2) Cash	−$1,000,000	(2)	Demand deposits
CD	+1,000,000		−$1,000,000
			Time deposits (CD)
			+1,000,000

Securities Dealer		Securities Dealer's Bank	
(1) Cash	−$1,000,000	(1) Reserves	Demand deposits
Securities	+$1,000,000	−$1,000,000	−$1,000,000

	Banking System	
(1)	Demand deposit (corporation)	+$1,000,000
	Demand deposit (securities dealer)	−$1,000,000
(2)	Demand deposit (corporation)	−$1,000,000
	Time deposit (corporation)	+$1,000,000

Next, the corporation buys a CD from a bank, which custom-builds one to the customer's specification in terms of amount ($1 million) and maturity. The customer thus holds $1 million *less* in cash, $1 million *more* in CD's (step 2).

Result thus far: *no change* in total deposits, a *decrease* in the money supply (demand deposits)! Have the banks regained the demand deposits they had "lost"? No, because they had never lost them! As we saw

---

[16] This sort of transaction, multiplied many times over, very likely will have an impact on the structure of interest rates; but this topic is reserved for chapter 11.

in the previous illustration, when a corporation purchases Treasury bills or any other kind of money-market instrument, demand deposits are not extinguished; they merely change hands. And when the banking system issues CD's, far from regaining any supposedly lost demand deposits, it actually destroys them!

We have, however, neglected one implication of the fact that $1 million worth of CD's have been substituted for a like amount of demand deposits in the liabilities side of the banking system. Since the reserve requirement for time deposits, including CD's, is much lower than the demand-deposit reserve requirement (see chapter 5), the banking system now has excess reserves. To illustrate: assume that the demand-deposit reserve requirement is 15 per cent and the reserve requirement for time deposits is 5 per cent. Since the $1 million demand deposit required $150,000 of reserves while the new CD requires only $50,000, the system now holds $100,000 more in excess reserves, which it can utilize to "back" $666,667 of new demand deposits, as per the process that we studied in chapter 2. For the banking system, the final results of (1) the initial CD purchase and (2) the subsequent expansion on the basis of the increase in excess reserves are as follows:

TRACE 4.5

	Banking System		
Earning-assets	+$666,667	Demand deposits	−$333,333
		Time deposits	+$1,000,000

Demand deposits have recovered all but $333,333 of their initial $1 million reduction, time deposits (CD's) are up by $1 million, and total bank credit (earning-assets) increased by $666,667, without any change in reserves.

To sum it all up, what these writers should have stated is that the CD is a competitive weapon enabling a particular bank to offer terms that induce large economic units to "finance" it by purchasing CD claims against it. This effectively increases the range over which the bank is able to attract deposits and, hence, increases its ability to acquire earning assets.

VARIANTS OF THE CERTIFICATE OF DEPOSIT Although CD's in their 1960s revival were originally designed and viewed as an instrument to be used by the giant banks to serve their big customers, they were quickly adapted for use by other banks. Several hundred banks are now issuing them; and purchasers-holders include not only business corporations but also savings banks, state and local governments, foreign agencies, and other economic units.

Another variant of the CD is a sort of cross between a savings account and a conventional CD, designed for the individual saver and smaller business concerns. In *form,* however, it is a certificate of deposit, with specified maturity date. The American Bankers Association would like the term *savings certificate* to be used to designate these certificates, but numerous local labels have been affixed to them by innovative bankers, so outsiders like us must look to the *nature* of the arrangement, not its label, to understand it.

The CD is an excellent example of "liability management banking," which we described earlier. Banks can increase or decrease the attractiveness of CD's to large-sized investors looking for liquid assets by varying the interest rates that they (the banks) offer on their CD's. Thus they are able to vary their CD financing in accordance with the demand for their loans.

Regulation of Deposits: The "Regulation Q" Issue

Regulatory authorities do not concern themselves with the bank deposit-mix directly, but they often impose ceilings on the "prices" that banks may pay to holders of various categories of deposits. On demand deposits the ceiling price is zero: banks are not permitted to pay *any* interest. However, as we saw earlier, banks perform a number of services for the business demand-deposit holder without charge. Even households receive what amounts to a return on their demand-deposit balances in that banks, in computing their service charge on checking-account activity, commonly allow a certain number of "free" items (checks and deposits), the number depending on the average deposit balance maintained for the computation period.

REGULATION Time and savings deposits also are subject to "price control."[17] Member banks are subject to Federal Reserve Regulation Q, which sets ceilings on interest rates in various categories of interest-bearing deposits (See Table 4.3); and insured nonmember banks are subject to these same rate limitations, imposed by the Federal Deposit Insurance Corporation. From 1936 to 1957 the ceiling rates remained unchanged; but since that time there have been numerous changes, almost invariably upward[18] and in the direction of greater complexity.

The explanation of the upward revisions is simple: each time interest rates on open-market instruments have risen to the Regulation Q ceiling level, the Federal Reserve authorities have faced the choice of either raising the ceiling or inducing a decline in total banking-system assets, which would surely take place as the banks' major sources of time-deposit financing would turn instead to the more lucrative open-market

---

[17] The discussion that follows relies on Charlotte E. Ruebling, "The Administration of Regulation Q," *Review*, Federal Reserve Bank of St. Louis (February 1970), pp. 29–40.

[18] The reduction during 1966 on certain classes of time deposits constituted an attempt to relieve pressure on depository savings intermediaries, which had experienced a substantial loss of big deposits to the commercial banks in response to the higher rates paid on deposits by the latter.

TABLE 4.3
Maximum Interest Rates Payable on Banks Deposits,
(per cent per year)
as of May 31, 1974

Savings deposits	5
Other time deposits	
Less than $100,000	
30–89 days	5
90 days to one year	5½
1 year to 2½ years	6
2½ years and over	6½
4 years and over, in minimum denomination of $1,000	7¼
$100,000 and over	no maximum

Source: *Federal Reserve Bulletin*, June 1974, p. A10.

investments. And each time the Federal Reserve has chosen the first alternative, although there were some dissenting opinions expressed at times on the Board of Governors. One reason for the dissent was the fear that banks would be tempted into paying rates that were too high and would, therefore, be forced to acquire claims that were too risky, in attempting to cover their costs for deposit interest. The other reason for dissent was concern that these higher rates paid by the banks would induce people to reduce their deposits at depository savings intermediaries, causing a drop in the availability of home financing.

The increasing complexity of the structure of regulated rates is the result of gradual recognition of the variety of deposit holders and reasons for holding deposits in the category *time and savings deposits.* A ceiling rate appropriate for passbook savings accounts could be far too low for large CD's, for example.

There is more to the "complexity" story. Since banks are in competition with the depository savings intermediaries for savings-deposit financing, it seems logical that interest rates paid by all these intermediaries should be subject to a ceiling if any should be. So, in September 1966, legislation was enacted by Congress authorizing the Federal Home Loan Bank Board to set ceiling interest rates payable by member savings and loan associations. Immediately the Board imposed ceiling rates, and simultaneously the FDIC set a rate ceiling on deposits in insured mutual savings banks, acting under authority it had had since 1935 but had never used! Now there are three Federal regulatory agencies—Federal Reserve Board of Governors, FHLBB, and FDIC—setting interest-rate ceilings on deposits issued by three types of intermediaries: insured commercial banks, insured mutual savings banks, and savings and loan associations that are members of the Federal Home Loan Banking System. Any change in the *pattern* of ceiling rates will tend to favor one or another class of institutions and, hence, the classes of borrowers typically using that institutional source of credit. And any change in the general level of *all* ceilings on savings rates will tend to affect the allocation of current demand for short-term financial assets, as between financial institutions and open-market instruments.

End of story? Not quite! A rapid rise in short-term open-market rates of interest induced many of the larger savings depositors at these institutions to shift out of intermediary claims into open-market obligations of the Treasury and larger businesses; thus ceiling rates on *all* the depository intermediaries were raised. Again, in 1970, ceilings were raised all around due to higher open-market rates, but only after these intermediaries had gone through months of hardship because of their inability to raise deposit rates in line with market rates. This process was repeated once more, though on a smaller scale, beginning in late 1973. Banks were induced, partly by this kind of experience, to develop nondeposit sources of financing, which we shall discuss in the next section.

Our experience with controls on time and savings deposit interest rates has moved many analysts to advocate abandonment of all such ceilings, relying on the business acumen of the managers of financial institutions to allocate their available resources in the most efficient manner and to refrain from offering uneconomically high deposit interest rates.[19] Others note that, while such managers might *wish* that they could keep or push rates down, they fear that the consequence of being out of step on the low side might be large-scale withdrawals of deposits. As seen by these observers and managers, Regulation Q and similar ceilings offer a logical way to avoid this kind of "ruinous" competition. And so the battle rages.

Other Obligations

In recent years banks have begun to obtain an increasing percentage of their total financing through nondeposit arrangements: "advances" from the Federal Reserve, borrowing from other banks and from foreign branches, and issuing open-market securities. In fact, by October 1973, borrowings exceeded commercial-bank capital, whereas five years previously borrowings were only one-sixth the size of capital.

BORROWING FROM THE FEDERAL RESERVE Just as an individual or business borrows from a commercial bank, so commercial banks that are members of the Federal Reserve System may borrow from their "bank," our central bank. Since this kind of borrowing is intimately connected with central banking and monetary policy, we defer detailed treatment to chapter 7 and Part V.

---

[19] They also point to the futility of the ceilings in controlling credit, but this is another aspect of Regulation Q, which is taken up in Part V.

BORROWING FROM OTHER BANKS Banks sometimes borrow from each other, occasionally from a correspondent, more often in the form of an overnight transfer of Federal funds, that is, deposits held in Federal Reserve banks. By means of this device, a bank acquires needed reserves temporarily from another bank that holds excess reserves. We plan to study this type of arrangment in chapter 5.

OTHER FORMS OF BORROWING A number of other bank borrowing arrangements have emerged, and new ones continue to appear as banks become more adept at "liability management banking" and as other banks join the parade.[20] Some of these arrangements involve direct issues of nondeposit obligations by the banks; some work through bank holding companies. An example of the latter is the issuance by a one-bank holding company of short-term open-market obligations ("commercial paper") to the public and the use of the proceeds to "buy" loans and investments from the affiliated bank. So far as the banking organization *as a whole* (holding company plus bank subsidiary) is concerned, the result is the same as in the case of bank-issued paper.

REGULATION OF BORROWING One important type of government influence on bank borrowing is the policy of the Federal Reserve concerning (1) the rate charged on its discounts and advances to member banks and (2) the circumstances under which member banks may become, and continue to be, indebted to the Federal Reserve. This matter will be dealt with in our later discussion on monetary policy.

Another influence on borrowing is the reserve requirement imposed on borrowing from overseas branches and on bank and bank holding company short-term open-market borrowing. Since such borrowing is a close substitute for the CD as a source of short-term financing for banks, particularly large banks, the Federal Reserve authorities correctly reasoned that to exempt borrowing from the reserve requirement would be an open invitation to the banks to concentrate on this source, thus avoiding the intent of the reserve requirement.

KEY CONCEPTS

Reserves
Loans
Investments
Time deposits
Capital account
Shiftability

Liability-management banking
Surplus account
Interbank deposits
Time certificate of deposit (CD)
Regulation Q

---

[20] See Robert E. Knight, "An Alternative Approach to Liquidity," *Monthly Review*, Federal Reserve Bank of Kansas City (December 1969; February, April, May 1970), for details.

QUESTIONS FOR REVIEW

1. In what ways are banks linked with other elements of the financial system?
2. Why do banks hold so much cash (reserves) and have so little capital, relative to their total assets?
3. Describe the four "theories" of bank liquidity. Are they competitive or complementary? Explain.
4. What are some key determinants of the adequacy of bank capital? Why is it so difficult, then, to decide whether the capital of a given bank is adequate? or, for that matter, the capital of the banking system?
5. In what respects are time deposits similar to demand deposits? In what respects different?
6. Why do banks maintain demand deposits in other banks, even though such deposits earn no interest?
7. Why do business firms often maintain a larger demand-deposit balance than normal transactions purposes would seem to require?
8. What are some of the devices used by banks to "pay" their customers for holding demand deposits?
9. What competition do banks face in their efforts to attract savings depositors?
10. How do certificates of deposit (CD's) differ from savings accounts?
11. Since CD's call for interest payments by the issuing banks while demand deposits do not, why do banks compete vigorously for CD business?
12. "The CD is an example of liability management banking." Explain.
13. Why is it so difficult for the government to control interest rates by imposing ceiling rates on deposits?
14. In what respects are bank borrowings similar to deposits? In what respects different?

SUGGESTIONS FOR FURTHER READING   SEE END OF CHAPTER 5.

Reserves
Rationale for Reserve Requirements
Reserve Policies of Banks

Earning Assets
Loans
Investments
Other Assets

Government Influences on the Asset Structure
Purposes
Means

Application of Balance-Sheet Management Criteria
External Influences
Bank Responses to Changes: Nature and Determining Factors

Summary of Chapters 4 and 5

Commercial Banks: The Asset-Mix

The commercial bank has been aptly described as the department store of finance. In terms of both variety of customers and range of "products," the commercial bank has no close rival. In one respect, though, the bank differs from the usual retail store; through its lending activities it "sells" money and "buys" nonmonetary claims! Its customers include business firms, households, governments, and even other financial institutions. Since these other financial institutions, in turn, buy the claims of other economic units, banks are really doing a wholesale as well as retail business.

Our sequence of topics in considering the bank's asset-mix will follow the order in which classes of assets are listed in the typical condensed bank statement—reserves, loans, investments, and "other assets"—and will also include a brief look at government influences on the asset-mix and, finally, a general recapitulation of bank balance-sheet management.

Reserves

In discussions such as this, the term *reserves* used without any modifiers (other than *commercial bank*) usually means *primary reserves,* that is, currency plus assets convertible to currency on demand. The statistical data published by the Federal Reserve and FDIC follow this practice; however, the phrase "cash and due from banks," used on bank statements of condition, has the same meaning. These reserves may be broken down into vault cash (currency), reserves with the Federal Reserve banks, balances with other banks, domestic and foreign, and cash items in the process of collection, (Table 5.1). Primary reserves make up the first line of defense, so to speak, against demands for settlement by holders of claims on the bank: depositors, recipients of checks against the bank's depositors, and other banks (including the Federal Reserve) that have acquired checks against this bank in connection with our system of check clearing and collection.

To illustrate this last point, suppose that a member bank on a particular day acquires from its depositors, and then sends to its district Federal Reserve bank for collection, $800,000 worth of checks against other banks. Suppose that on the same day the district Federal Reserve bank acquires from other banks $900,000 in checks drawn against this bank by its (the bank's) depositors. The net result of these two events would appear like this:

TRACE 5.1

Member Bank	
Reserves	Demand deposits
−$100,000	−$100,000

Observe that the commercial bank has not really "paid" anything, in the usual sense of the word. What has happened is that the (net) claim of $100,000 by the Federal Reserve bank against this bank has been offset against the bank's claim (reserve deposit) against its Federal Reserve bank.

Beside primary (cash) reserves, banks hold another class of assets called *secondary reserves*, their second line of defense against threats to their liquidity. This classification is not found on the bank's balance sheet, but the concept is important in bankers' thinking. In order to qualify as a member of the secondary reserves, an asset must be convertible quickly into primary reserves through sale of maturity with little

TABLE 5.1
Reserves of all Commercial Banks in the United States, December 31, 1973
(in $millions)

Currency and coin	$10,706
Reserves with Federal Reserve banks	27,816
Balances with domestic banks	34,084
Balances with banks in foreign countries	1,029
Cash items in process of collection	44,641
Total	$118,276

Source: *Federal Reserve Bulletin*, May 1974, p. A18.

likelihood of any significant decline in value. These standards require, in practice, that a secondary reserve asset have (1) high quality, (2) a wide market, and (3) nearness to maturity.

This classificatory scheme for reserves emphasizes their function of protecting depositors or, from a social standpoint, helping to ensure that our monetary system will have *parity,* that is, circulation without discrimination among the components—in this case, currency and demand deposits. There is another method of classifying reserves, however, used both by the Federal Reserve authorities and by state regulatory agencies. Under this method reserves are divided into legal and working reserves. *Legal reserves* are those assets that may be used to meet the requirements of the regulatory authorities. *Working reserves* are primary reserves held for carrying out the routine transactions of banking and consist of (1) excess (legal) reserves and (2) primary reserves in forms not legally usable to meet reserve requirements.

For member banks of the Federal Reserve System, those assets qualifying for legal reserve status are vault cash and reserve deposits at the Federal Reserve banks.[1] Deposits in other banks are excluded, as are cash items (mostly checks) in the possession of the bank or in the process of collection but for which the bank has not yet received reserve credit.

States are generally more easygoing, commonly allowing balances with other banks to be counted as well as the Federal Reserve-approved items. Many states even permit a limited amount of United States government securities and other "safe" earning-assets to be counted as well. For this reason legal reserves were defined in the paragraph above as "those assets . . . " rather than simply as a class of primary reserves.

Rationale for Reserve Requirements

Why are reserve requirements imposed? In the case of the Federal Reserve System, the reason is to aid in the control of money and the regulation of credit. Federal Reserve ability to determine total reserves, plus its power to specify the minimum ratio of reserves to member-bank deposits, gives this agency a powerful influence over the money supply and bank credit. But in the case of state nonmember banks, the reasoning in support of reserve requirements seems quite confused. In decreeing that bank reserves must equal at least x per cent of deposits, the regulatory agency in effect "freezes" this quantity of reserves, making this portion of the bank's assets virtually unavailable for ordinary liquidity purposes! Of course, there is some flexibility in meeting these requirements, in that the bank need not maintain its required reserve position daily; nevertheless, the effect is still quite the opposite from that intended: rather than being the most liquid of assets, these required reserves become practically untouchable.

---

[1] The computation of required reserves will be discussed in chapter 7.

Reserve Policies of Banks

A variety of influences operate on the bank's desired quantity of primary and secondary reserves. Most obvious, of course, is the reserve requirements. Given the bank's total deposits in each category, the quantity of required reserves is not subject to managerial discretion, although the "mix" can be altered as between vault cash and deposits at the Federal Reserve bank. Other influences worth mentioning are (1) the variability of bank's deposits, (2) the need for services of correspondent banks, and (3) the ability of the bank to obtain additional primary reserves when needed.

Developments in this last category have been particularly important in recent years, as we have already observed. In addition to the old standby sources of additional reserves, such as borrowing from the Federal Reserve or from correspondent banks and selling secondary reserve assets (or allowing them to run off without being replaced), three other methods of meeting reserve needs have grown popular: (1) borrowing Federal funds, (2) issuing negotiable certificates of deposit and related forms of time deposits and short-term nondeposit liabilities, as discussed in chapter 4, and (3) borrowing dollar deposits from overseas (Eurodollars).

"Federal funds" is jargon for deposits at Federal Reserve banks. When a member bank "buys" Federal funds, it, in effect, borrows a quantity of reserve balances from another member bank, usually overnight. As far as the Federal Reserve bank involved is concerned, reserves are transferred from the account of one bank to that of another for the designated period, hence contributing toward meeting the reserve requirement of the latter, then transferred back the following day. A very extensive market in Federal funds has developed, with even many of the smaller member banks participating. Thanks largely to the Federal funds market, the big New York money-market banks, which must cope with fluctuations of 20 per cent or more in their reserves over short periods of time,[2] can operate with negligible excess reserves.

The CD has come into prominence even more recently. Banks, particularly the larger ones, are relying much less on secondary reserves as their second line of defense now, feeling that they can attract needed reserves by raising the rate offered on their CD's.

Borrowing dollars from banking offices overseas is an option available almost exclusively to the largest banks. Consider this simplified example. An American corporation has paid a European corporation $100,000 in the form of a check against American Bank B. Wishing to keep this amount in *dollar* form rather than in local money, yet desiring to earn interest on it, the European corporation submits the check to a European branch of U.S. Bank A as a Eurodollar deposit. This transac-

---

[2] Paul Meek and Jack W. Cox, "The Banking System—Its Behavior in the Short Run," *Monthly Review*, Federal Reserve Bank of New York (April 1966), p. 87.

tion is recorded as step 1 below (all figures in the balance-sheet traces are in thousands of dollars).

Now the home office of Bank A, experiencing a reserve deficiency, borrows $100,000 from the European branch (step 2) in the form of a check against U.S. Bank B. When the home office sends this check to its district Federal Reserve bank, its reserve account is credited with this amount and the account of Bank B is correspondingly reduced (step 3).

TRACE 5.2

	European Branch of U.S. Bank A		U.S. Bank A, Home Office	
(1)	Demand deposits in U.S. Bank B +$100	Time deposits (Eurodollars) +$100		
(2)	Demand deposits in U.S. Bank B −$100 Loans to home office +100		Demand deposits in U.S. Bank B +$100	Owed to European bank +$100
(3)			Reserves with Federal Reserve bank +$100 Demand deposits in U.S. Bank B −100	
(1–3)	Loans to home office +$100	Time deposits (Eurodollars) +$100	Reserves with Federal Reserve bank +$100	Owed to European bank +$100

	U.S. Bank B		
(1)		Demand deposits (U.S. Corp.) Demand deposits (European branch of U.S. Bank A)	−$100 +100
(2)			
(3)	Reserves with Federal Reserve bank −$100	Demand deposits (European branch of U.S. Bank A)	−$100
(1–3)	Reserves with Federal Reserve bank −$100	Demand deposits (U.S. Corp.)	−$100

During 1969, when demand for bank credit far outdistanced the ability of banks to supply it, borrowings by U.S. banks from foreign branches rose to nearly $15 billion. However, not only did monetary ease greatly reduce this figure the following year, but also the imposition by the Federal Reserve of reserve requirements on such borrowing has made it unlikely that foreign dollar borrowings will again be an important means of reserve adjustment for American banks.

Although all the foregoing means can be effective in helping individual banks to replenish their reserves, we must not make the mistake of assuming that they can also increase member-bank reserves *as a whole*. In fact, only one of these devices—borrowing from Federal Reserve banks—will increase total member-bank reserves.

To grasp this, we must recall that there are only two categories of assets that can qualify as member-bank reserves: vault cash held by member banks and member-bank deposits at the Federal Reserve. Thus, the only transactions that will increase the total of such reserves are transactions that increase either vault cash or member-bank deposits at the Federal Reserve. None of these devices increases bank holdings of vault cash; and, with the single exception noted above, none of these results in an increase in *total* member-bank deposits at the Federal Reserve. They do, however, tend to reduce the excess reserves held by the system.

One final point: no matter how "tight" reserves are for the banking system as a whole, as evidenced by the data on bank borrowing from the Federal Reserve and the Federal funds rate, there are always substantial excess reserves shown in the published figures. Why? At least three reasons may be advanced, although we cannot evaluate their relative importance:

1. There is an inevitable lag between an increase in reserves initiated or permitted by the Federal Reserve and the banks' utilization of these reserves.
2. In times of recession, low interest rates and reduced demand for loans tend to lessen the incentive to squeeze the last bit of use out of available reserves.
3. Even in tight-money periods, some excess reserves, particularly those of smaller banks, are maintained as "liquidity buffers" to meet unexpected reductions of reserves via the clearing and collection process and cash withdrawals. These banks, lacking expert specialized personnel and/or being remote from the sources of "instant" additional reserves, find it more economical to try to maintain some excess reserves on the average. Yet, they are not immune to outside pressures: over the past fifteen years or so, these banks have reduced their excess reserves considerably, reflecting both higher interest rates on earning assets (rising cost of liquidity) and improved availability of alternative sources of reserves when needed.[3]

---

[3] Hugh Chairnoff, "Country-Style Wizardry: Bankers Are Managing with Less Excess Reserves," *Business Review*, Federal Reserve Bank of Philadelphia (April 1967), pp. 11–14. Also "Some Observations on Excess Reserves of Member Banks," *Business Review*, Federal Reserve Bank of Philadelphia (November 1960), pp. 6–8.

Earning Assets

The bank's earning assets are, as we know, divided into two major categories: loans and investments. It would be convenient if we could define each of these in a neat, mutually exclusive manner, but we cannot do so and still conform to conventional usage. This much we can say: loans are usually negotiated directly between borrower and lender; investments are usually handled through middlemen (investment bankers, securities dealers) who place the securities, evidencing claims against the borrower, in the hands of lenders. Related to these characteristics, it is generally true that loans are usually less readily transferable to another party than are investments and they (loans) are evidenced by less complicated documents.

Banks' adjustments to changes in circumstances take place much more through shifts between and within categories of earning assets than between reserves and earning assets. The factors that initiate the shifts are many: changes in demand for financing by a particular industry; a financial innovation introducing, or changing the characteristics of, a particular type of financial asset; a marketing innovation changing financial arrangements; a technological innovation reducing costs involved in a given class of assets; a change in regulations or in bank examiners' attitudes respecting a particular financial arrangement; a shift in the deposit-mix; and so on. These points should be quite evident: (1) with so many forces that can initiate earning-asset mix changes, change should be regarded as normal, and (2) any given development in the asset structures of banks is likely to be the product of several forces, some pulling in the same direction, some in other directions. It is a sheer impossibility to do justice to all these factors, but, as we move along, we shall observe examples of many of them in action.

Loans

The leading earning asset of commercial banks in the United States until at least a half-century ago was the so-called commercial loan. Since it was short-term and "self-liquidating" (that is, generated the wherewithal for its own repayment), the commercial loan was considered *the* appropriate earning asset for banks, in view of the fact that banks had most of their obligations in the form of deposits or (earlier) bank notes, redeemable on demand.

Little by little, however, the commercial loan was elbowed out of its place of prominence, first by United States government securities beginning in World War I, then by consumer loans, corporate securities, mortgages and securities loans in the 1920s, by the beginnings of term loans and a flood of Treasury securities in the days of World War II, and, more recently, by the rise to prominence of the term loan, a rapid increase in bank holdings of state and local securities, the appearance and spread of bank credit-card lending, and even the beginnings of bank leasing to business (which amounts to lending "productive assets" rather than money).

We would accomplish little by a detailed, exhaustive description of the many lending arrangements used by some or all banks. The accompanying chart (Table 5.2) summarizes the main contours of bank lending activities in the aggregate.

This breakdown hardly begins to suggest the variety encompassed in the word *loan*. Taking bank loans as a whole, we can classify them a number of ways for illustration.

1. *By maturity.* Loans vary from *demand loans*, which continue from day to day only by the mutual consent of the parties, to *term loans*, which may run for ten years, occasionally longer, and call for periodic installment payments.
2. *By sector of borrower.* Banks lend to virtually all sectors: business, consumers, financial institutions, state and local governments, other financial institutions, and to foreign economic units.
3. *By purpose.* Reasons for borrowing include replenishing of reserves (that is, Federal funds loans); financing the purchase of securities or of another firm; financing the purchase of a home, or a shopping center, or a home appliance, or business

TABLE 5.2
Commercial Bank Earning Assets, December 31, 1973
(in $millions)

Category	Amount	
Loans		$460,143
Commercial and industrial	$159,417	
Agricultural	17,327	
For purchasing or carrying securities	11,974	
To financial institutions	40,715	
Real estate	118,032	
Other, to individuals	99,927	
Other	12,751	
Investments		188,852
U.S. Treasury securities	$58,277	
Other U.S. government agencies	29,252	
State and local government securities	95,145	
Other securities	6,177	
Federal funds sold		35,311
		$684,305

Source: Adapted from *Federal Reserve Bulletin*, May 1974, p. A18.

equipment; interim financing until permanent financing can be arranged; enabling a local government to pay its bills until tax receipts flow in; and numerous other reasons.

4. *By security.* The lender may receive some additional protection beyond the borrower's signature. Sometimes the security is simply *another* signature, whereby another person assumes some liability for payment. Or the obligation may be insured or payment guaranteed by a firm or by an agency of the Federal government. A very common arrangement is a pledge by the borrower to the bank of certain assets, such as inventory, accounts receivable, fixed assets, or land and buildings.

This sort of thing could continue for quite a few more paragraphs; we could classify loans by method of negotiation (personal vs. open-market), by interest arrangement (straight loan vs. discount), by withdrawal arrangement (one-time loan, revolving credit, and so on), and any number of other criteria. But we surely have seen enough now to convince us that although some classes of borrowers and loan arrangements are more characteristic than others in bank lending, there is no such thing as a "standard" bank loan or borrower.

Investments

The second major category of bank earning-assets is investments. As is true of loans, investments include a broad array of assets; but the largest components are municipal (state and local) securities and United States government securities, the two categories together accounting for slightly less than 90 per cent of total investments. High-grade corporate securities make up nearly all the remainder.

Since 1960 there has been a drastic shift in the distribution of bank investments. At the beginning of that decade, about 75 per cent of bank investments were in U.S. government securities, about 20 per cent in municipal, the remainder in other securities. Thirteen years later, U.S. Treasury issues were just over 30 per cent, issues of U.S. government agencies accounted for 15 per cent, and municipals had risen to a bit over 50 per cent, with "other securities" category accounting for about 3 per cent (Table 5.2).

Some of the reasons for this rapid and significant change illustrate well the kinds of factors influencing bank portfolio policy:[4] (1) a large increase in state and local borrowing, producing a rise in yields on this category of securities relative to those on Federal securities; (2) pressures on banks to "support" local municipal projects; (3) the rapid rise in bank time and savings deposits relative to demand deposits; and (4)

---

[4] Thomas E. Davis, "Bank Holdings of Municipal Securities," *Monthly Review,* Federal Reserve Bank of Kansas City (December 1970), pp. 3–8.

the spread of "liabilities management banking," which puts less emphasis on holding short-term liquid assets for liquidity purposes.

Bank investments cover a far wider range of maturities than do loans. Most (well over 80 per cent recently) of their holdings of U.S. government securities are in the "five years or less" maturity class; nearly all of the rest are five to ten years, with less than 3 per cent having maturities more than ten years hence.[5] Municipals show a far different maturity distribution. In the case of national banks, for example, less than 50 per cent mature within a year, and about a quarter are in the "over ten years" category, according to a recent survey.[6]

Most of the banks' so-called secondary reserves are found in the investments component of the asset-mix. Because of stringent regulations, bank investments almost invariably meet the secondary reserve criteria of quality and marketability; but, of course, only those investments at the short end of the maturity structure meet the "short-term" criterion as well.

Since U.S. government securities are almost completely certain to be paid at maturity and since they are bought and sold in enormous quantities daily, thus assuring a wide market, you might be tempted to ask why banks should not count all such securities in their secondary reserve account, regardless of maturity. The answer is that prices of government securities, particularly long-term types, can fluctuate over a substantial range as a result of changing market rates of interest.

Suppose that a bank buys at par a $100, 6 per cent bond scheduled to mature in twenty-one years. Suppose that a year later, in response to brisk demand for long-term credit, the interest rate on *newly issued* twenty-year bonds identical in all other respects to the one the bank had bought a year earlier, is 8 per cent. As a result, the original bond, now also twenty years from maturity, will fetch only $80.36 on the market! (See Table 5.3.) Can you see why? A person purchasing for $100 a bond that will pay $8 interest per year for twenty years and $100 at the end of the twenty years will then realize the same actual yield as a person who

TABLE 5.3
Market Price of a $100 6 Per Cent Bond

Years to Maturity	Market price, if yield is:				
	4.0%	5.0%	6.0%	7.0%	8.0%
1	101.92	100.95	100.00	99.07	98.15
5	108.90	104.33	100.00	96.90	92.02
10	116.23	107.72	100.00	92.98	86.58
20	127.18	112.46	100.00	89.50	80.36

[5] Based on *Federal Reserve Bulletin*, May 1974, p. A39.
[6] Jack C. Rothwell, "The Move to Municipals" *Business Review*, Federal Reserve Bank of Philadelphia (September 1966), p. 7.

purchases for $80.36 a bond that pays $6 interest per year for twenty years and $100 at the end of twenty years. If the price of the "old" bond were higher, a prospective purchaser would prefer the new one.

Of course, if interest rates were to drop, the prices of securities already outstanding would rise, thereby conferring on the owners a capital gain. The point is, though, that a bank which loaded up on long-term securities at the wrong time might be financially embarrassed if forced to sell at low prices in response either to withdrawals or to intense customer loan demand. The risk of a fall in price is inherent even in "riskless" securities traded on a free open market. And, although our example featured United States government securities, exactly the same reasoning applies to other types of securities providing fixed periodic interest payments and specified final payment on a designated maturity date. It is for this reason that long-term marketable securities are not appropriate as secondary reserve assets.

Since no class of investments is *exclusively* held by banks, we shall defer a more detailed discussion of the various classes of securities until chapters 10 and 11, on financial markets.

Other Assets

Covered by the label *other assets* is a wide variety of items, such as the bank's own premises, stock in subsidiaries and (for member banks) in the Federal Reserve banks, equipment owned but leased to businesses (a small but growing category), interest earned but not collected, and so on. While important to the particular banks involved, in the aggregate "other assets" constitute but a small fraction of bank assets—seldom over 5 per cent.

Government Influences on the Asset Structure

Because of the pivotal position that commercial banks have always held in our economy, it was inevitable that government would take a strong interest in the kinds of assets that the banks hold. There is a bank regulatory authority in each of the fifty states plus three at the Federal level, so it would be absurd for us to go into all the details of statutory enactments, administrative rules, and examiners' applications. We leave these to the harried managements of the banks involved. Our interest here is in the specific purposes that governments seek to accomplish through influencing bank asset structures and the means used to accomplish these purposes. We treat these topics rather sketchily, though, because chapter 13 is devoted entirely to a broad discussion of the purposes of, and the means employed by, government to influence the performance of the financial system.

Purposes

Historically, the most important reason for government efforts to affect banks' asset-structure decisions has been to limit the risks assumed by banks, in order to protect the status of the money claims—demand deposits and (formerly) bank notes—issued by the banks, which have long been our principal medium of exchange. Another purpose for asset-structure influence is to favor or limit certain groups of borrowers, in order to achieve a different allocation of the nation's resources (for example, more housing construction or, in wartime, less production of consumer durables) or to alter the distribution of income.

Means

We may divide the means used into two categories: (1) measures that have the effect of *reducing* bank holdings of certain categories of claims (for example, loans to a particular class of borrowers or for a particular purpose, or investments containing certain terms) and (2) those that have the effect of *increasing* such holdings. These measures can range from outright prohibition or requirement to subtle influences.

Some illustrations of negative measures are these:

1. Severe restriction on bank holdings of corporate stock.
2. The requirement that member-bank lending on real estate (exclusive of insured loans) not exceed the amount of its capital stock plus surplus or 70 per cent of its time and savings deposits, whichever is larger.
3. A ceiling on the interest rates banks may charge on certain kinds of loans (the so-called "usury laws").
4. The prohibition of lending to bank examiners.

Devices to increase the holding of certain kinds of assets include: (1) reserve requirements, (2) government insurance or guarantees of certain kinds of loans, (3) provision of a secondary market for certain classes of loans and investments, and (4) the grant of favorable tax status to certain kinds of financial claims.

There are many more kinds of policy measures, but these should serve to impress the reader with the variety of means used to influence bank asset behavior in order to advance particular socioeconomic goals.

Application of Balance-Sheet Management Criteria

In chapter 4 we examined the general criteria—net income, safety, and liquidity—that collectively dominate bank management thinking in the area of balance-sheet policy. Following this, we surveyed the sources of bank financing and the kinds of assets found in bank portfolios; and we also considered the influences exerted by government on bank balance sheets. But the job of putting these together remains to be done. We now set ourselves the task of answering, in a general way, this question: given the "menu" of possibilities for the makeup of its balance sheet and the rules and pressures imposed by government agencies, how does the bank management go about applying its selection criteria in making the actual decisions that result in a particular balance sheet?

One school of thought claims that banks set up a system of priorities.[7] For example:

> A bank's loan policy involves questions as to the percentage of assets to be placed in loans and discounts after its primary- and secondary-reserve requirements have been met.... After caring for primary and secondary reserves and meeting demands for acceptable loans, banks place their remaining funds in investments.[8]

This approach, while useful as a rough first approximation, does not jibe with modern portfolio management practices. It seems to say that, regardless of customer pressures for loan accommodation in boom times, banks will turn down any and all requests rather than reduce secondary reserves below the floor set by bank policy. It also implies a completely inelastic supply schedule of loans: regardless of the interest rate on loans, the bank stands ready to accommodate any and all worthy prospective borrowers, up to the absolute limit set by liquidity needs.

A more realistic approach to understanding bank portfolio changes recognizes possible "trade-offs" among asset classes and between subclasses as circumstances change.

> In this approach, an increase in the expected return on loans relative to liquid assets encourages banks to shift funds into loans. Even though this shift of funds reduces the liquidity of the asset portfolio, a bank is willing to accept an increased probability of either unforeseen asset sales or borrowing from its Reserve Bank if it is sufficiently compensated by an increased rate of return on loans.[9]

As we examine these changes, we should bear in mind, though, that this approach, too, is deficient in one respect; it fails to acknowledge the interdependence of the two sides of the balance sheet. It implies that banks take the liabilities side—the deposits and other obligations—as *given* and adjust their asset portfolios to it, which is less and less adequate as a description of bank behavior in view of the spread of liability management banking.

---

[7] For example, Roland I. Robinson, *The Management of Bank Funds*, 2d ed. (New York: McGraw-Hill Book Co., 1962), especially pp. 13–18; and Charles F. Prather, *Money and Banking*, 7th ed. (Homewood, Ill.: R. D. Irwin, 1961), pp. 208–10.

[8] Prather, *Money and Banking*, p. 209.

[9] James L. Pierce, "Commercial Bank Liquidity," *Federal Reserve Bulletin* (August 1966), p. 1098.

In looking back over the post-World War II period, we cannot but be impressed by the striking changes in the makeup of the banks' asset structures as depicted in Table 5.4. Here, indeed, is portfolio policy in action! Let us focus on some of the leading external (to the banking system) forces that have exerted pressure toward asset-mix changes and the internal characteristics and developments in banking that have shaped banks' responses to these forces.

External Influences

One force explaining much of the massive shift from investments to loans is the relative rise in private demand for financing. Federal government debt has continued to move upward, to be sure, but private debt has grown far more rapidly; and, of course, it is private, particularly business, debt that banks traditionally favor. The major reasons for the rise in private demand for financing have been (1) economic growth and (2) rising prices. Much of this growth has been associated with spending for durables and construction by both consumers and business, a fact that is reflected in longer maturities for bank loans and investments in these categories.

Commitment of the Federal government to the goal of stable high-level economic activity and strong evidence of the ability of the government to achieve this goal have reduced the degree of liquidity and safety considered essential for "sound" banking.

Several external developments have had the effect of increasing time deposits as per cent of total deposits. One, changes in Regulation Q, which governs the ceiling rate permitted on these deposits, has already been mentioned. Another is the increasing sophistication of corporate cash management. Instead of keeping excess deposits "just in case," corporations utilize forecasting and cash-budgeting techniques to keep the cash component of liquid assets down to a minimum, placing the remainder in short-term marketable securities, including larger amounts

TABLE 5.4
Commercial Bank Loans and Investments, Selected Years, 1947–73

Earning-Asset Class	Amount (in $millions)			Per cent		
	1947	1966	1973	1947	1966	1973
Loans	$38,057	$217,726	$495,454	32.7	67.5	72.4
U.S. government securities	69,221	56,163	58,277	59.5	17.4	8.5
Other securities	9,006	48,772	130,574	7.8	15.1	19.1
Total	$116,284	$322,661	$684,305	100.0	100.0	100.0

Source: Data from *Federal Reserve Bulletin*, June 1973, p. A20, and May 1974, p. A18.

of bank-issued CD's. This increase in the time-deposit component has encouraged banks to assume a less liquid asset-mix for two reasons: (1) time deposits are generally more predictable, less volatile, and (2) interest costs on time deposits induce banks to look for high-yielding assets.

Bank Responses to Changes: Nature and Determining Factors

The ultimate effects that these outside events and developments have on the asset structures of banks depend on the behavior of the banks themselves, their reactions to these influences. What sorts of factors that bear on banks' responses can we identify?

One important factor is the asset market structure. In acquiring earning assets, banks operate in markets ranging from purely competitive to extremely monopolistic. The securities that the bank purchases for secondary reserve or longer-term investment purposes are traded in markets of the former type: there are many buyers and sellers, and the bank is nearly always a passive "price-taker" in transactions. At the opposite extreme are the dealings between a bank in a one-bank town and its smaller business borrower-customers. With respect to such firms, the bank may be in a virtual monopoly position as source of credit and therefore is likely to have considerable discretion as to rates charged and other terms of the loan agreement. And between these two extremes are other borrowers, such as intermediate-sized firms with several bank and nonbank alternative sources of credit. Here the bank has some control over interest rates and other terms but must be alert to possible responses by close rivals.

Possession of market power means that a bank's area of decision goes beyond choices among different classes of earning assets, each carrying its own characteristics and terms; the bank actually participates in the *determination* of these characteristics and terms. This adds another dimension of uncertainty for the bank; namely, the effects of its own actions on the volume of available assets in certain classes, both because of the possible reactions of borrowers and the possible responses of rivals.

In addition to market-structure considerations, there is a second determinant of banker response to external changes: the ability of bankers to learn. As a result of this human characteristic, the ultimate response of the banking system to a particular change in circumstances may be very different from the immediate response. For example, banks have learned to live happily with loans-to-deposits ratios that would have seemed downright reckless a few years earlier.

Sometimes the learning is based on the experience of other financial institutions. For example, banks entered the field of consumer financing in increasing numbers in the 1930s and 1940s, but only after observing the successful operation of consumer finance companies and the experience of those banks that would stoop low enough to make direct loans to consumers. Now the consumer loans category is an established part of the asset structure, as a glance at Table 5.2 will confirm. Experience of banks with term lending to business went through a similar process. In the 1930s two government agencies—the Reconstruction Finance Corporation and the Federal Reserve System—began making this type of loan to business and inviting banks to participate, as a result of which

> banks became more acutely aware of the fact that the term of loans could often be safely extended beyond the traditional limits if amounts of debts were systematically reduced in accordance with the income and expenditure pattern of the borrower.[10]

According to one observer, writing in late 1965: "Banks undoubtedly have done more innovating in the last five years than in the preceding twenty-five."[11] For the most part, opportunity was the mother of innovation, to paraphrase an old saying. Nevertheless, the fact that banks have been so alert to opportunities and so resourceful in exploiting them is a plus factor in any assessment of our financial system.

Since all these innovations have been discussed in this and the preceding chapter, all we need to do is recall them in the present connection. One innovation, the negotiable certificate of deposit (CD) and its accompanying secondary "resale" market,[12] was the answer of the system to the threatened decline of large business deposits as corporate financial managers developed and refined techniques for economizing on their cash balances. Of course, as we observed in chapter 4, these deposits were not lost to the banking *system*, but this fact was small comfort to the individual banks that found themselves losing ground or felt threatened by the situation. Then adaptations of the CD appeared, which also constituted actual innovations, fitting it for smaller businesses and individual savers.

Even more recently, the rise of the bank credit card is an innovation with implications that can only dimly be foreseen. These cards involve the extension of bank credit to consumers, with the merchant serving, in effect, as a go-between. Almost certainly this innovation will increase consumer credit and will probably involve gradual substitution of consumer credit for trade credit. As customers increasingly "charge it" with their bank instead of with the merchant, the latter needs less financing to carry his receivables.[13]

---

[10] Neil H. Jacoby and Raymond J. Saulnier, *Term Lending to Business* (New York: National Bureau of Economic Research, 1942), p. 25.
[11] A. James Meigs, "Recent Innovations in the Functions of Banks," *American Economic Review* (Papers and Proceedings), LVI (May 1966), p. 167.
[12] For complete accuracy, we should state that the CD is not new; only the secondary market for them is new. But the combining of the two represents a true financial innovation.
[13] See Karl A. Scheld, "Bank Credit Cards," *Business Conditions,* Federal Reserve Bank of Chicago (June 1967), pp. 6–9.

Summary of Chapters 4 and 5

Commercial banks are truly department stores of finance. Their asset structures show the widest possible array of claims, in terms of maturity, sector of borrower, purpose, security arrangement, and other respects. Similarly, their liabilities side reveals a large variety of debt obligations—deposit and nondeposit, ranging from demand to long-term—as well as equities.

Both in their sources and in their asset-mix, banks are subject not only to the usual economic influences but also to an unusual degree of government regulation, due primarily to their position as creators of most of the nation's money.

KEY CONCEPTS

Reserves
Primary reserves
Secondary reserves
Legal reserves
Working reserves

Federal funds
Earning assets
Loans
Investments
Term loans

QUESTIONS FOR REVIEW

1. "The same asset that is included in secondary reserves by a member bank might be considered a part of legal reserves by some nonmember banks." Explain.
2. "Some assets that are classified as primary reserves may not be included among legal reserves by member banks." Explain.
3. What are the sources of reserves for an individual member bank? Which of these are *not* sources of reserves for all member banks taken together?
4. "So long as there are excess reserves in the hands of member banks, we can expect further expansion of bank earning assets and the money supply." Comment.
5. "So long as there are excess reserves in the hands of an individual member bank, we can expect that bank to acquire additional earning assets." Comment.
6. Should a bank include all, some, or none of its holdings of United States government securities in its secondary reserve account? Why?
7. Why does the government single out the banking business for particularly detailed regulation? What means have been, and are, used to influence bank behavior?

8. What forces on the demand side and on the supply side have been influential in increasing the percentage of total bank assets in the form of loans?
9. What are some recent illustrations of bank innovativeness and resourcefulness in responding to changes in the environment of banking?

SUGGESTIONS FOR FURTHER READING FOR CHAPTERS 4 AND 5

American Bankers Association. *The Commercial Banking Industry.* Englewood Cliffs, N.J.: Prentice-Hall, 1962.
Crosse, Howard D. *Management Policies for Commercial Banks.* Englewood Cliffs, N.J.: Prentice-Hall, 1962.
Dill, Arnold. "Liability Management Banking: Its Growth and Impact" *Monthly Review,* Federal Reserve Bank of Atlanta (February 1971), pp. 22–33.
Gies, Thomas G., ed. *Banking Markets and Financial Institutions.* Homewood, Ill.: R. D. Irwin, 1971.
Hayes, Douglas A. *Bank Lending Policies: Domestic and International.* Ann Arbor: Bureau of Business Research, University of Michigan, 1971.
Hodgman, Donald R. *Commercial Bank Loan and Investment Policy.* Champaign: Bureau of Economic and Business Research, University of Illinois, 1963.
Jessup, Paul F., ed. *Innovations in Bank Management.* New York: Holt, Rinehart and Winston, 1969.
Morrison, George R. *Liquidity Preference of Commercial Banks.* Chicago: University of Chicago Press, 1966.
Murphy, Neil G. *A Study of Wholesale Banking Behavior.* Boston: Federal Reserve Bank of Boston, 1969.
Nadler, Paul S. *Commercial Banking in the Economy.* New York: Random House, 1968.
Prochnow, Harold V. *Term Loans and Theories of Bank Liquidity.* Englewood Cliffs, N.J.: Prentice-Hall, 1949.
Robinson, Roland I. *The Management of Bank Funds,* 2d ed. New York: McGraw-Hill Book Co., 1962.

Central Banking
Management of the Money Supply
Bankers' Bank
Fiscal Agency
International Financial Relations
Central Banking and Central Banks

Background of the Federal Reserve System

Structure of the Federal Reserve System
The Board of Governors
Federal Open Market Committee
The Federal Reserve Banks

Summary

Central Banking and the Federal Reserve System

In the foregoing chapters we had the occasion to mention the Federal Reserve a number of times and in a number of connections. We recall (chapter 1) that nearly all our paper money is issued by this institution. Also we observed (chapters 2 and 5) that most of the banking system's reserves are in the form of demand claims against the Federal Reserve. The Federal Reserve banks supply most of these reserves by purchasing United States government securities in the market, a type of transaction discussed in chapter 2. We also noted in chapter 2 that the great bulk of all checks are cleared through the facilities of these Reserve banks. And in chapters 4 and 5 the Federal Reserve appeared in its role of regulator of deposit interest rates and other aspects of bank operations.

There are, moreover, still other important relationships between the Federal Reserve and the banks. In fact, we cannot really understand the behavior of our commercial banking system without a knowledge of the Federal Reserve System, and vice versa. It is time, therefore, to examine this rather unusual institution at close range now.

Although it is the only one of its kind in the United States, the Federal Reserve System is actually a member of a class of financial institutions called *central banks*. We therefore shall precede our study of the Federal Reserve System by a discussion of central banking in general. Then we shall survey briefly the historical background that led to the establishment of our own central bank; and, finally, we shall examine the actual structural details of this institution and its varied service functions.

Central Banking

In a recent address, Louis Rasminsky, former governor of the Bank of Canada, stated well the position of the central bank in a nation's financial system:

> The powers accorded to a central bank, which enable it to influence the rate of expansion of the banking system, to act as lender of last resort to the banking system and the money market, and to act as banker and debt manager of the government, place it at the centre of the financial system.[1]

Details of organization, ownership, relationships with government, powers, and functions vary (sometimes quite widely) among central banks, but "in every major country of the world the central bank is the central arch of the monetary and financial system."[2] In fact, there is hardly a nation today that does not have its own central bank or at least share one with one or more neighboring countries.[3]

The quotation from Governor Rasminsky suggests the characteristic functions of a central bank, which we may restate as: (1) to manage the nation's money supply, (2) to serve as "bankers' bank" to the nation's banking system, (3) to act as fiscal agent for the national government, and (4) to supervise the nation's international financial position.

Management of the Money Supply

A renowned British student of banking has stated: "The essence of central banking is discretionary control of the monetary system."[4] While this statement is not very helpful in informing us of what central banks, in fact, *do*, it does identify the sine qua non of central banking. That is, any institution not charged with this responsibility is not a "central bank" within the accepted usage of this term; and, conversely, any institution having this responsibility *is* a central bank, regardless of its label or its other duties.

Control of the money supply is a supremely important responsibility of the central bank because changes in the nation's stock influence its level of output and employment, its price level, and its balance of international payments. The actions of the central bank, therefore, affect not only the financial system but the real (goods-and-services) system as

---

[1] Louis Rasminsky, "The Role of the Central Banker Today," (Washington, D.C.: The Per Jacobsson Foundation, 1966), p. 18.
[2] B. U. Ratchford and Jimmie Monhollon, "Notes on Central Banks" (Richmond: Federal Reserve Bank of Richmond, 1963), p. 1.
[3] Sharing is done in some of the newer nations of French-speaking West Africa, for example. See J. Keith Horsefield, "Why a Central Bank?" *Finance and Development*, II (September 1965), p. 159.
[4] R. S. Sayers, *Central Banking after Bagehot* (London: Oxford University Press, 1957), p. 1.

well. It is this function, above all others, that gives the central bank its economic significance.

The central bank does not, in practice, control the money supply directly but does so indirectly, usually through its influence over the behavior of the banking system, which is the leading issuer of money in economically advanced nations. Sometimes this influence is exercised rather informally, through communications by the central bank to the nation's commercial banks. But much more commonly the central bank acts to influence the money supply by utilizing its powers of control over bank reserves—their quantity and their legal relationship to deposits. So important is this topic to our understanding of our own financial system that we will devote most of chapter 7 to an examination of the factors that determine bank reserves and the powers of the Federal Reserve to affect them.

In nearly every country the central bank is the sole or dominant issuer of paper currency; however, central banks do not directly regulate the public's holdings of paper money. An attempt to restrict currency in circulation, for example—since it would involve limiting the ability of the public to acquire currency in exchange for their demand deposits—would render the latter less acceptable as a medium of exchange than currency, thus destroying the parity of the money system. An attempt to increase the quantity of currency in circulation, on the other hand, would be thwarted, as the public would simply return currency not desired for transactions to the bank for demand-deposit credit, thus reducing currency in circulation and increasing the demand-deposit component of the money supply. In practice, therefore, the central bank regulates the total supply of money but does not attempt to influence its composition.

Where the central bank is wholly or partly owned by private parties, a possible conflict between public interests and stockholder interests exists. For example, profit maximization considerations would seem to call for the central bank to lend and invest as much as it can, subject to the limits of its own liquidity and safety needs; but this activity might so inflate the money supply that prices would rise at an intolerable rate. Today it is universally recognized that private interests simply must be subordinate to those of the public in this extremely sensitive area.

Bankers' Bank

A second universal function of the central bank is serving as a "bankers' bank" or, more accurately, a bank for banks, that is, performing many of the same functions for banks that banks perform for other economic units. This function overlaps the monetary management function in a number of ways, as we shall see, since it is largely through its relations with banks that the central bank influences the nation's money supply.

PROVISION OF "CHECKING ACCOUNT" SERVICES Just as nonbank economic units hold easily transferable demand-deposit claims on commercial banks, so the banks of a nation hold similar claims on that nation's central bank. This service is often referred to as "holding the reserves" of the nation's banks,[5] but this is not really an appropriate description of the service. It is the commercial banks themselves, after all, that actually "hold" the reserves, in the form of deposit claims against the central bank!

The central bank also clears and collects checks against, and in favor of, each commercial bank maintaining a deposit with it, in much the same fashion as the individual commercial bank services its depositors.

LENDING TO BANKS The central bank invariably has the legal right to extend credit to commercial banks under designated circumstances. In fact, the central bank is frequently characterized as the "lender of last resort," that is, the ultimate provider of liquidity to the financial system.

PROVIDING CURRENCY Also resembling a service of banks to their customers is the provision of currency by the central banks to the commercial banks. Just as the bank's customer reduces his bank deposit by acquiring currency from his bank, so the bank experiences a reduction in its central bank reserve deposit when it receives currency from the central bank. And, conversely, a return flow of currency in either case replenishes the deposit.

SUPERVISION AND EXAMINATION The central bank acts not only as a "service station" to the banks but also as supervisor and examiner. This duty is not, strictly speaking, inherent in the role of central banking and is quite often performed by an agency other than the central bank, or jointly by the central bank and one or more other government agencies.[6]

Fiscal Agency

The third characteristic duty of central banks is acting as financial arm of the national government. This involves performing the usual banking services and, in addition, certain duties in connection with the national debt.

BANKER FOR THE GOVERNMENT The central bank typically handles the checking accounts of the national government and some or all of its agencies. In addition, it is often obligated by statute to make loans to the

---

[5] For example: "The central bank holds much of the reserves of [commercial] banks...." Eli Shapiro et al., *Money and Banking*, 5th ed. (New York: Holt, Rinehart, and Winston, 1968), p. 155; "As a bankers' bank [the central bank] holds the reserves of commercial banks...." Ratchford and Monhollon, "Notes on Central Banks," pp. 2–3.

[6] Hans Aufricht, *Comparative Survey of Central Bank Law* (New York: Frederick A. Praeger, 1965), pp. 173–82.

central government, under specified circumstances and up to a designated maximum amount and maturity. Yet another parallel with the banker-customer relationship is found in the practice of the central bank of serving as financial adviser to the government. Sometimes, in fact, this adviser role is required by law.[7]

DUTIES RELATING TO THE GOVERNMENT DEBT Usually the central bank is designated the agency to handle all the details of issuing, servicing, and redeeming the debt instruments of the national government. Frequently the central bank, especially in the newer nations, is charged with the overall responsibility of managing the national debt.[8]

International Financial Relations

The central bank is frequently the depository of the nation's international reserves, particularly gold; deposits in foreign commercial and central banks; and foreign government securities. Statutes may set certain requirements as to the composition of these reserves and/or their minimum amount relative to (for example) the volume of trade.

On the other side of the balance sheet, the central bank also has deposit obligations to various foreign central banks, to other foreign government entities, and to the International Monetary Fund (in the case of member nations). The Fund Agreement specifies that the central bank shall be the depository of the IMF holdings of the nation's currency.

Finally, central banks have dealings with each other. Relationships among central banks range from informal consultation to veritable "central banks for central banks."

Central Banking and Central Banks

To conclude this brief general introduction to central banking and to smooth the transition from the general to the particular—our own Federal Reserve System—we must bear in mind that the foregoing discussion was not an exposition of the "pure theory of central banking" but rather an attempt to arrive at some generalizations about central banking as it has actually evolved. Also, we should note that, although the generalizations are broadly true, each central bank is a bit different from each of the others in respect to duties, powers, and functions. Thus, just as we found in chapter 3 that the statement "intermediation is what financial intermediaries do" is not correct, so, similarly, we cannot simply assert that "central banking is what central banks do." Central banks do more than this. In some nations they deal directly with the nonbank

---

[7] Ibid., pp. 104–6.
[8] John S. Stockton, "New Central Banks," *Monthly Review*, Federal Reserve Bank of New York (January 1967), p. 17.

public, either as a general practice (particularly in underdeveloped lands) or to fill certain "credit gaps," that is, financial needs with high social priority that the financial system had not been meeting adequately.[9] Moreover, certain of the functions that we have labeled as "central banking" are sometimes performed by agencies other than the central bank or are performed partly by the central bank, partly by other agencies.

Background of the Federal Reserve System

The Federal Reserve Act became law on December 23, 1913; the first Federal Reserve Board took the oath of office on August 10, 1914; and the twelve Federal Reserve banks officially opened for business November 16, 1914. Thus the United States joined the ranks of nations having a true central bank.

We might wonder, now that we have been impressed with the crucial role performed by central banks, how a financial system such as ours could have operated *without* a central bank. In general, the answer is "not very well." Although the functions of a central bank were being carried out, after a fashion, through a variety of institutional arrangements,[10] no single agency was specifically empowered for, or entrusted with, the central banking functions. For example, checks were indeed being cleared and collected, but there were no central regional points through which checks could be channeled. Instead, they would be sent through a network (perhaps *patchwork* would be a better term) of correspondent banks, a process not only slow but also costly, as many banks would levy a charge for handling checks.

Another aspect of the "bankers' bank" function also was being performed to a degree through the correspondent banking system, as depository banks would make loans to their correspondent-bank customers. However, since the larger banks were, after all, themselves profit-seeking firms, they could not reasonably be expected to fill the role of "lender of last resort," supplying currency and other cash items as needed by their bank customers.

Nobody, to put it briefly, was "in charge." No one organization was responsible for seeing that the monetary mechanism behaved as it should. As a result of this and of certain peculiar characteristics of our banking system, small increases in the demand for currency tended to set in motion developments that eventuated in periodic "money panics," characterized by widespread bank and business failures, unemployment, and related woes. Although the economy generally bounced back

---

[9] U.S. Congress, House Committee on Banking and Currency, *Activities by Various Central Banks to Promote Economic and Social Welfare Programs*, Committee Print, 91st Congress, 2d Session, 1970.

[10] William G. Dewald, "The National Monetary Commission: A Look Back," *Journal of Money, Credit and Banking*, IV (November 1972), pp. 935–52.

rapidly, pressures in Congress to "do something" finally resulted in action, following the particularly severe Panic of 1907.

That "something" consisted of the establishment of the National Monetary Commission in 1910 to study the problem—hardly a heroic step, but one that had far-reaching consequences. The studies sponsored by the Commission were quite extensive and provided much background knowledge of our own financial system and those of other nations, helping to shape the Federal Reserve Act of 1913:

> An Act to provide for the establishment of Federal Reserve banks, to furnish an elastic currency, to afford means of rediscounting commercial paper, to establish a more effective supervision of banking in the United States, and for other purposes.[11]

The Federal Reserve Act was, not surprisingly, a child of its times, reflecting (1) belief in the efficiency of an automatic, self-regulating market system, (2) the current state of banking theory, (3) fear of Eastern financial interests ("Wall Street"), and (4) a conviction that regional organization would be beneficial economically and would help avoid the dangers of both Wall Street and government domination. As events and theoretical developments have altered the views of policy makers, the Federal Reserve Act has been amended numerous times, so that today's Federal Reserve System differs significantly both in goals and in methods of operation from its 1914 ancestor.

Rather than attempt a chronicle of these amendments, let us look at the present-day structure and functions of the system, noting some of the more important changes as we go along.

Structure of the Federal Reserve System

Technically, the United States does not have a central *bank*; it has a central banking *system*, consisting of twelve regional Federal Reserve banks coordinated by a Board of Governors. The practical importance of this distinction, however, is no longer great because the discretionary powers of the regional banks have been gradually reduced until today their activities are largely limited to the performance of routine banking functions for member banks, the United States Treasury, and other Federal government agencies.

We need to examine carefully these two components of the System—the Reserve banks and the Board of Governors—and their relations to each other and to the rest of the system. In addition, one other element in the structure must be singled out for special attention: the Federal Open Market Committee. Almost by accident, this committee has come to play a crucial role in the formulation of monetary policy.

---

[11] Preamble, Federal Reserve Act (38 Stat. 251 Ch. 6).

It is common to speak of the member banks as part of the Federal Reserve System; but it seems preferable to refer to these banks as *related* to the system, for two reasons: (1) the relationship of the member banks to the Federal Reserve System (as we shall use the term) is much the same as the relation between customers of a bank and the bank; that of depositor, borrower, recipient of advice, and so on; and (2) whenever the *functions* of the Federal Reserve System are discussed in financial literature, it is obvious that the writer has in mind the system as we shall be using the term, that is, *without* the member banks. We shall try, therefore, to be consistent in referring to the Federal Reserve System as composed of: (1) the Board of Governors, (2) the Federal Open Market Committee, (3) the regional Federal Reserve banks and their branches, (4) advisory committees.

The rest of this chapter will consider the first three of these system elements in order listed, with only incidental reference to advisory committees, since they are peripheral to the functioning of the system.

The Board of Governors

At the pinnacle of the Federal Reserve structure is the Board of Governors. The seven members of the board are chosen by the President of the United States (subject to Senate confirmation) for fourteen-year terms, arranged so that every other year one member's term expires. The president is required to have regard for various interests (financial, agricultural, industrial, and commercial) and geographical areas in making his appointments.

Board membership is a full-time salaried position. As it has been considered vital, from the very beginning, that members not be beholden to the banking community, the Federal Reserve Act stipulates that "no member of the Board of Governors . . . shall be an officer or director of any bank, banking institution, trust company, or Federal Reserve bank or hold stock in any [of these]."[12]

The requirement that the board membership encompass a broad range of "interests" and a variety of geographical areas reflects earlier fear of Eastern financial domination. Many experts today feel that, in view of (1) the national character of our economic and financial system, (2) the fact that some important economic groups (like consumers and educators) are not specifically represented, and (3) the awesome complexity of our financial system and consequent need for expertise in this

---

[12] Incidentally, to placate the banking interests, who had originally conceived of the central bank as a sort of "service station" for banks, President Wilson conceived the idea of a Federal Advisory Council. This body, as established in the act, is made up of one banker (in practice, from one of the largest banks) from each Federal Reserve district, selected annually by the district Federal Reserve bank, to meet at least quarterly with the board to discuss general business conditions and to make such recommendations to the board concerning the affairs of the system as the council may wish; but the board is not obligated to accept these recommendations, of course.

area, it would seem preferable to drop this requirement, substituting a requirement of professional qualification.[13]

The powers and duties of the board range all the way from its authority in the broad area of monetary policy to such mundane matters as requiring bonds of Federal Reserve agents and regulating their safekeeping of money and property. Mostly, though, the board's responsibilities are related to monetary policy, the operations of the regional Federal Reserve banks, and certain operations of member banks. In addition, the board carries on certain public information activities, including the monthly *Federal Reserve Bulletin*, press releases, occasional Staff Economic Studies, the *Annual Report,* and appearances of board members before Congressional committees, conventions, and so on. Rather than list all these items separately, we shall meet them in context, as we consider national financial policy, bank examinations, and other matters in which the Board of Governors is involved.

One member of the Board of Governors is designated by the president as chairman for a four-year term. He tends to be the main (but by no means the only) voice of the Federal Reserve in testimony before Congressional committees and elsewhere.

To whom is the board responsible? Legally, its responsibility is to Congress, its creator; but the fact that the Federal Reserve Board is financially independent from the government budget mechanism (it simply levies a semiannual assessment on the regional Federal Reserve banks to meet its expenses) means that Congress cannot hold the threat of reduced appropriations over the board. Also, Congress has been most reluctant to discipline the board, although there have been, and are, some voices raised in criticism of the board in several influential Congressional committees.[14]

The main issue in this area, though, is whether, and to what extent, the board should be answerable to the president in the conduct of monetary policy. The framers and revisers of the Federal Reserve Act sought to insulate the board from short-run political influences in several ways:

1. With Board of Governors members appointed for long and overlapping terms, a president would seldom have the opportunity to appoint a majority of the board.
2. Board appointments are not renewable, so there is no incentive for a member to make his decisions with a view to improving his chances for reappointment.

---

[13] For a full discussion of this issue see Michael D. Reagan, "The Internal Structure of the Federal Reserve: A Political Analysis," in Commission on Money and Credit, *Monetary Management* (Englewood Cliffs, N.J.: Prentice-Hall, 1963), pp. 380–86.

[14] The Joint Economic Committee, in particular, has become increasingly vigorous and incisive in its criticism of the conduct of Federal Reserve policy making. See, for example, Joint Economic Committee, "Standards for Guiding Monetary Action" (Washington, D.C.: U.S. Government Printing Office, 1968).

3. Removal from the board can only be "for cause"; and in practice no president has ever had the temerity to attempt to remove a board member.
4. The board is financed by assessments levied on the regional banks and is therefore independent of budgetary controls.

The reasoning behind the desire to secure for the Board of Governors independence from political pressures is mainly a conviction that, politics being what it is, the Administration and Congress are likely to undervalue price stability relative to high employment whenever there is a conflict between these two goals. The result is a built-in inflationary bias in economic policy making. Therefore, there is a need for a counterforce that is likely to stress price stability. The central bank is the logical candidate for this task because of its concern with financial, as opposed to goods-and-services, matters and the close association of central bankers with the commercial banking community.

Now, of course, both the Board of Governors and the rest of the government policy makers are bound by the same mandate, the Employment Act of 1946, which states: "It is the continuing responsibility of the federal government to use all practicable means ... to promote maximum employment, production, and purchasing power." The board, in fact, has often explicitly recognized this obligation. But this same act imposes on the president the task of presenting annually to Congress in his Economic Report a program to accomplish the goals of the act; such a program inevitably involves monetary policy as well as fiscal policy. In fact, "the Economic Reports recognize the fallacy of considering each policy [that is, monetary and fiscal] as an independent entity by their usual treatment of both as aspects of total economic policy."[15] The problem, then, is: how can the President formulate and execute economic policy when one agency, Congress, legislates fiscal measures and, in effect, the Federal Reserve Board of Governors "legislates" monetary measures?

Most students agree that the problem looks worse on paper than it really is. Independence does not imply a surly isolation. Rather,

> All major Federal Reserve officials have agreed on the need for close working relationships with the Treasury on monetary, fiscal, and debt policy.... An effective Federal Reserve voice for the stable money point of view can best be assured if the Federal Reserve is an active, continuous participant in the day-to-day process of governmental economic policy formulation.[16]

A variety of informal and semiformal arrangements for coordination have, in fact, evolved, both between the Federal Reserve officials and

---

[15] Reuben E. Slesinger, *National Economic Policy: The Presidential Reports* (Princeton: D. Van Nostrand Co., 1968), p. 183.

[16] G. L. Bach, "Economics, Politics, and the Fed," *Harvard Business Review*, XL (January–February 1962), p. 88.

their counterparts in the Treasury and Council of Economic Advisers and among staff aids working on similar analyses. Perhaps there is need for more formal coordinating machinery, such as a cabinet-level Advisory Board for Economic Growth and Stability, which would include the chairman of the Board of Governors, as recommended for consideration by the Commission on Money and Credit.[17] The dominant (though by no means unanimous[18]) view seems to be that close coordination is needed between the Federal Reserve and the other economic policy branches of the Federal government: in other words, that the Federal Reserve should be independent *within,* not *of,* the government.

Federal Open Market Committee

A vital though controversial element in the Federal Reserve organization is the Federal Open Market Committee. Its membership comprises (1) the seven members of the Board of Governors and (2) five representatives (in practice, presidents) of Federal Reserve banks, one of which must be from the New York bank, the others from the remaining eleven on a specified annual rotating basis. It meets fairly often, approximately once every four weeks, its discussions ranging far beyond matters of open-market operations. It has, in fact, become *the* forum at which monetary policy matters are discussed and decisions made in the light of current and expected economic conditions, as reviewed for the committee by board economists. Meetings of the committee are attended not only by the dozen members but customarily also by the presidents of the seven Federal Reserve banks who are not currently serving on the committee, as well as economists of the board and the banks.

The controversial aspect of the committee is this: although monetary policy is the responsibility of the "public" Board of Governors, somehow the system has gradually evolved into the present anomalous position in which most of the important monetary decisions are made by a committee of which the Board of Governors constitutes a bare majority. Theoretically, if the five Reserve bank presidents were to vote en bloc the board's policy preferences could be thwarted. For example, suppose that an open-market operations program for moving the financial climate toward greater monetary ease came to a committee vote. If a "liberal" board approved it 5–2 while a "conservative" group of Reserve bank presidents opposed it unanimously, the proposal would be defeated despite its approval by the board!

[17] Commission on Money and Credit, *Money and Credit* . . . , pp. 276–77.
[18] For a vigorous statement opposing the idea of an independent central bank, see Harry G. Johnson, "Should There Be an Independent Monetary Authority?" in *The Federal Reserve after Fifty Years,* Hearings before the Subcommittee on Domestic Finance, Committee on Banking and Currency (Washington, D.C.: Government Printing Office, 1964), pp. 970–73; reprinted in Warren L. Smith and Ronald L. Teigen, (eds.), *Readings in Money, National Income, and Stabilization Policy,* rev. ed. (Homewood, Ill.: R. D. Irwin, 1970), pp. 303–306.

When we add the further fact that trading in securities in the open market is the most important means whereby the Federal Reserve seeks to affect the performance of the economy,[19] it would be easy to conclude that the makeup of this committee involves potential serious difficulties for the conduct of monetary policy.

We must not overdramatize the situation. In practice, most committee decisions have been unanimous, with the remainder mainly involving one or two dissenting votes. And there is no evidence of significant cleavage between the two factions, Board of Governors members and Reserve bank presidents. Also, there may be some benefit in considering the views of men who have close contacts with bankers and with regional economic developments.

Suggestions for change have been numerous and wide-ranging.[20] One proposal that attempts to centralize responsibility in the Board and yet to utilize the expertise of the regional Reserve bank presidents is that of the Commission on Money and Credit:

> The determination of open market policies should be vested in the Board. In establishing its open market policy the Board should be required to consult with the twelve Federal Reserve bank presidents.[21]

The Federal Reserve Banks

We finally arrive at the "business end" of the Federal Reserve System, where all the plans, decisions, and policies are translated into action. The central banking functions examined earlier in the chapter are carried out mainly by the twelve regional Federal Reserve banks and their twenty-four branches. (See Figure 6.1.)

Each bank is headed by a nine-man board of directors. The composition of this board was carefully specified in the original Federal Reserve Act and has not been changed since then:

> Three Class A directors, chosen by, and representing, the member banks.
>
> Three Class B directors, elected by the member banks and actively engaged in business, representing the borrowers.
>
> Three Class C directors, chosen by the Board of Governors, representing the public. One of these, who must have had banking experience, is designated by the bank's board of directors as chairman.

---

[19] Open-market operations will be discussed fully in chapter 21.
[20] See Reagan, "The Internal Structure," pp. 387–90.
[21] Commission on Money and Credit, *Money and Credit: Their Influence on Jobs, Prices, and Growth* (Englewood Cliffs, N.J.: Prentice-Hall, 1961), p. 90. This was advocated earlier by G. L. Bach in *Federal Reserve Policy-Making* (New York: Alfred A. Knopf, 1950), pp. 234–35.

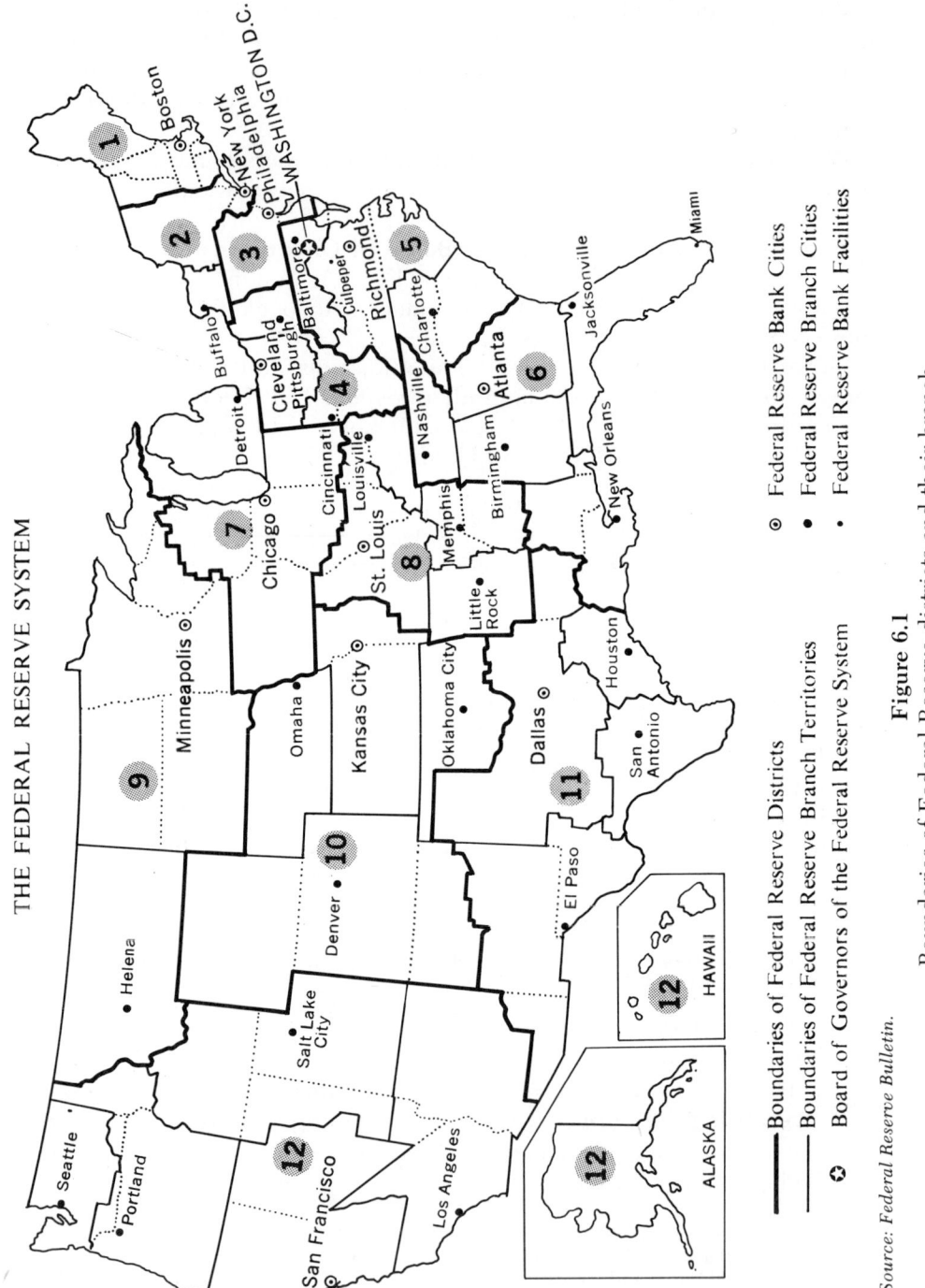

Figure 6.1
Boundaries of Federal Reserve districts and their branch territories.

Source: Federal Reserve Bulletin.

There has been some objection to the way the board is constituted. Some "interests" (for example, organized labor and pensioners) are explicitly omitted, while others (for example, "dirt farmers" and small businessmen) have, in practice, not been included. Suggested remedies have been (1) to enlarge the board to allow representation of more interests and (2) to repeal the whole complex formula. Actually, since the board of directors has little policy power anyway, it is of minor importance which, if any, of the alternative changes is adopted.

Despite a diminished policy role for the regional Reserve bank boards, these boards are far from functionless:

> Now the major tasks [of the boards] are to provide information on regional economic conditions for the OMC and the FRB to take into account in setting national policy, and to serve as a communication and public relations link between the System's policy-making organs and the local communities—both the general community and specific "communities" of commercial banking, industry, merchants, and other financial institutions.[22]

Each bank also has a president, chosen by the board of directors subject to the approval of the Board of Governors. As we noted earlier, the president attends meetings of the Federal Open Market Committee and is periodically a member of this committee, based on the established rotation formula. The route to Reserve bank presidency is typically "through the ranks," most presidents being Federal Reserve career men; but a minority came to the presidency directly from commercial banks.

The "owners" of each Federal Reserve bank are the member banks in its district. Each member bank is required, as a condition of continued membership, to subscribe to stock in its district Reserve bank in an amount equal to 6 per cent of the member bank's capital and surplus. Half of the subscribed amount it must purchase; the other half is subject to call—a remote possibility indeed. The stock pays 6 per cent in dividends annually—no more than this, despite the fact that in recent years the system has had net earnings sufficient to pay dividends of over 300 per cent!

On the surface, it looks bad to have a regulatory agency "owned" by the very institutions it is supposed to regulate. However, as we have observed, this ownership carries scarcely any of the usual advantages of stockholding since dividends are limited to 6 per cent, and the control of the enterprise in any meaningful sense is vested not in the regional bank board of directors but in the Board of Governors of the system. The present arrangement, then, is a virtually useless but harmless anachronism.

The Reserve banks themselves are big business: the smallest bank, Minneapolis, held $2.3 billion in assets; and the largest, New York, $26.8 billion at the end of 1973 (see Table 6.1). Total assets of all Federal

[22] Reagan, "The Internal Structure," p. 374.

Reserve banks, after deductions of interbank claims, amounted to $103.0 billion on that date.[23] Net earnings in 1973 amounted to over $4.5 billion, nearly all of which was turned over to the U. S. Treasury (Table 6.2). Indicative of the flow of business through these institutions is the fact that, in 1972, the banks handled just over nine billion checks, with a dollar value of well over $3.5 trillion.[24]

The Reserve banks perform a wide variety of largely routine services, which, for purposes of discussion, can be classified by recipient: services to banks, to the government, to the Board of Governors, and to others.

SERVICES TO BANKS Each Federal Reserve bank performs the usual nonpolicy central banking functions in its own region: clearing and collecting checks, making loans to banks (the "lender of last resort" function), handling currency issuance and retirement, assisting banks in managing their securities portfolios, and holding securities for safekeeping. The first of these we have already discussed (chapter 2); the second will be treated in chapter 7, since it is closely related to the monetary control function; and the other three, although contributing to the smooth functioning of our financial system, are largely matters of procedure and not of primary concern to us in this text.

Sometimes the "pooling of reserves" is included as a service to banks. One writer, for example, noting that member banks keep the bulk of their reserves on deposit at the Reserve banks, makes this claim:

> As a result of this centralization, reserves can be mobilized and used to help any bank in trouble. That is, any bank in difficulties may borrow reserves from the Federal Reserve. Reserves are no longer useless in an emergency.[25]

This is another instance of the fallacy we analyzed in chapter 2 in connection with bank credit creation: the fallacy of regarding as physical objects items that are essentially claims: "demand deposits" in the earlier case, "reserves" in this one. When a member bank wishes to "borrow reserves," the Reserve bank, in granting its request, does not authorize it to dip into a "pool of reserves." Rather, by making an advance to the borrowing member bank, the Reserve bank creates *new* reserves in the form of a deposit credit on the books of the Reserve bank in favor of the borrowing bank, in exactly the same manner as a commercial bank, in making a loan, creates new money, in the form of a demand-deposit credit to the account of the borrower.

SERVICES TO THE GOVERNMENT Handling the very active checking accounts of the Federal government is one of the major tasks of the regional Reserve banks, in terms of manpower, plant, and equipment

---

[23] *Federal Reserve Bulletin*, (January 1974), p. A13.
[24] Board of Governors of the Federal Reserve System, *Annual Report*, 1972, p. 242.
[25] Walter W. Haines, *Money, Prices, and Policy*, 2d ed. (New York: McGraw-Hill Book Co., 1966), p. 210.

TABLE 6.1
Total Assets of Federal Reserve Banks, December 31, 1973

Bank	Total Assets Amount (in $millions)	Per Cent
New York	$ 26,778	25.2
Chicago	16,497	15.5
San Francisco	14,065	13.4
Richmond	8,486	8.0
Cleveland	7,779	7.3
Atlanta	6,656	6.3
Philadelphia	5,778	5.4
Boston	4,751	4.5
Dallas	4,699	4.4
Kansas City	4,370	4.1
St. Louis	3,979	3.7
Minneapolis	2,325	2.2
Total	$106,163	100.0

Source: Federal Reserve Bulletin, January 1974, p. A13.

TABLE 6.2
Earnings and Expenses of the Federal Reserve Banks, 1973
(in $millions)

Current earnings		
U.S. government securities		$4,897
Other		120
	Total	$5,017
Current expenses		
Salaries and Benefits		$ 274
Other		221
	Total	$ 495
Current net earnings		$4,522
Net deductions		81
Net earnings before payments to U.S. Treasury		$4,441
Less: Dividends		49
Transferred to surplus		51
Payments to U.S. Treasury		$4,341

Source: Adapted from Federal Reserve Bulletin, February 1974, p. A96.

employed. Each year hundreds of millions of government checks (617 million in 1972) are processed by the Federal Reserve banks.

Nearly all disbursements made by the Treasury to the public are in the form of checks drawn against Treasury accounts at the Reserve banks; but receipts of the Treasury from the public are generally deposited in Treasury accounts in virtually all the nation's commercial banks. Then, as the Treasury makes disbursements, reducing its balances at the Federal Reserve, it replenishes these balances by drawing down its deposits at the commercial banks.

Consider this simplified example as it would affect the balance sheets of the banking system, the Federal Reserve system, and the Treasury. Assume that (1) the Treasury initially receives $1 billion in tax payments from the public, leaving the proceeds as deposits with member banks. Later (2) the Treasury makes disbursements to the public totaling $1 billion which, deposited in member banks, increase bank reserves and deposits by $1 billion. Simultaneously, (3) the Treasury calls $1 billion from the member banks, depositing it in the Reserve banks, thus reducing bank reserves and Treasury deposits by $1 billion.

U.S. Treasury		Member Banks	
(1) Deposits in Commercial banks +$1		Treasury deposits +$1 Deposits of public +1	
(2) Deposits in Federal Reserve banks −$1	Reserves +$1	Deposits of public +$1	
(3) Deposits in Commercial banks −$1 Deposits in Federal Reserve banks +1	Reserves −$1	Treasury deposits −$1	

	Federal Reserve Banks
(1)	
(2)	Treasury deposits −$1 Member-bank reserve deposits +1
(3)	Treasury deposits +$1 Member-bank reserve deposits −1

Why does the Treasury resort to this rather roundabout procedure instead of utilizing the Reserve banks as its sole depository? After all, in our example the final net results of all three transactions on all three balance sheets was zero! The answer relates to the *timing* of these transactions. At certain times, particularly on or just prior to tax payment due dates, the Treasury accounts in the nation's banks experience large increases while those of the taxpayers are correspondingly depleted. Were the Treasury to deposit these tax receipts in Federal Reserve banks, the commercial banks would experience a severe famine of reserves, resulting in extreme "tightness" in the financial markets. Then, as the Treasury would draw down its deposits in making disbursements, bank reserves would again rise.

As we saw in the preceding simple illustration, the present arrangement avoids this sort of unsettling activity, since the Treasury can regulate the flow of reserves *from* the banking system as it transfers deposits to the Reserve banks to coincide with the flow of reserves *to* the banking system resulting from its disbursements to the public.

The Reserve banks also provide a variety of services for the Treasury in connection with the government's debt. They publicize new debt issues and handle all the paperwork associated with the issuance, exchange, and retirement of government securities.

"Fiscal agency" functions are also performed by the Federal Reserve banks for a number of government agencies that operate independently of the Treasury, including components of the Federal Farm Credit Administration, the Federal Deposit Insurance Corporation, and others.

SERVICES TO THE BOARD OF GOVERNORS   As the "operating arm" of the Federal Reserve System, the Reserve banks actually serve the Board of Governors through all its activities, in a general sense. But there is a group of functions which, though they are the responsibilities of the board and could be performed by the staff of the board, have been delegated to the regional banks.

The major function in this category is that of supervision and examination of member banks. This task, even as regards member banks, is shared with several agencies; but that portion of the job assigned to the Reserve System has been delegated by the board to the several Reserve banks, each one of which maintains a staff of bank examiners. The staff is also responsible for making analyses of situations involving requests for approval of proposals for bank mergers, new banks, and new branches, and for making recommendations to the agency—the Board of Governors or the Reserve bank—responsible for the final decision.

Open-market operations of the entire system are centralized in one of the banks: the Federal Reserve Bank of New York. The Manager of the System Open-Market Account, an officer of this bank, has general oversight of open-market operations and is responsible for following the instructions of the Federal Open Market Committee as regards open-market operations, a process to be examined in chapter 7.

Since 1962 the Federal Reserve, through the New York bank, has been active in foreign exchange markets, working cooperatively with the United States Treasury in efforts to maintain the stability of the external value of the dollar.

Finally, under legislation passed by Congress in 1966, the board has delegated a number of administrative tasks and decisions to the Reserve banks while, of course, retaining the right of review of such action. The reasoning behind the new law and subsequent board actions delegating authority to the banks was the need of the board for more time to give to broad policy matters.

SERVICES TO OTHER ORGANIZATIONS The Reserve banks, particularly the New York bank, are involved in various international financial relationships, serving as depository of a number of foreign central banks and international financial institutions, including the International Monetary Fund, International Finance Corporation, and World Bank.

Government securities dealers obtain part of their financing from the Reserve banks (see chapter 10). Even private business firms have on occasion been authorized to borrow from the Federal Reserve. This was the case during the Great Depression of the 1930s and again during World War II and the Korean War.

Finally, each of the Reserve banks maintains a research staff, which compiles, analyzes, and publishes data on economic and financial developments in the bank's region and also undertakes studies of broader scope. The research staff carries on activities of an educational nature, too, serving area schools and businesses with speakers, guided tours, literature, and the like.

Individuals and business firms have access to the wire transfer facilities of the Federal Reserve System through the Reserve banks and their branches. This service is available not only to depositors in member banks but, by arrangement, to depositors in nonmember banks as well.

Summary

Although differing among themselves in a number of respects, the central banks of the world share these functions: (1) manager of the nation's money supply, (2) "bankers' bank" to the nation's commercial banks, (3) fiscal agent for the nation's government, and (4) supervisor of the nation's international financial position.

Our own central bank—in reality, a tightly centralized system of regional central banks—is the Federal Reserve System. Main components of the system are:

> *Board of Governors*—the seven-person policy-making apex of the system.
>
> *Federal Open Market Committee*—twelve persons (the seven members of the board plus five representatives of the Federal Reserve banks) responsible for overall Federal Reserve dealings in the open markets.

Federal Reserve Banks—twelve regional banks, owned but not controlled by the member banks of their respective districts. The Federal Reserve banks carry out the policies of the board and perform various services for the board, the member banks, the government, and other organizations.

A number of controversies exist concerning the structure and responsibilities of the Federal Reserve System. Among the current areas of conflict are these:

1. Should the Board of Governors attempt more specific representation of designated groups or stress expertise?
2. Should the Board be answerable to the president in the conduct of monetary policy?
3. What agency should make open market policy: the board only or (as at present) the broader Open Market Committee?
4. Should the board of directors of each Federal Reserve bank be representative of more interests?
5. Should member-bank ownership of Federal Reserve banks be abolished?

KEY CONCEPTS

Central banking
Fiscal agency
Board of Governors,
    Federal Reserve System
Federal Open Market
    Committee
Federal Reserve bank
"Member bank"

QUESTIONS FOR REVIEW

1. What are the characteristic functions of a central bank? Of these, which one is *the* central function?
2. What services to commercial banks does the central bank typically perform? In what other roles does it deal with, or affect, the banking system?
3. "Central banking is what central banks do." Criticize.
4. How were the main functions of a central bank carried out in the United States prior to the creation of the Federal Reserve System?
5. Discuss some of the issues surrounding the makeup, powers, and responsibilities of the Board of Governors and the Federal Open Market Committee.
6. Who owns the Federal Reserve banks? Who controls them? Who manages them?

7. What services do the Federal Reserve Banks perform (*a*) for member banks (*b*) for the government, (*c*) for the Board of Governors, and (*d*) for other organizations.
8. "A member bank experiencing a sudden loss of reserves can dip into the pool of reserves held by the Federal Reserve for temporary relief." Criticize.

SUGGESTIONS FOR FURTHER READING

Aufricht, Hans. *Comparative Survey of Central Banking Law*. New York: Frederick A. Praeger, 1965.

Beckhart, Benjamin H. *The Federal Reserve System*. New York: Columbia University Press, 1972.

Fousek, Peter G. *Foreign Central Banking: The Instruments of Monetary Policy*. New York: Federal Reserve Bank of New York, 1957.

Lash, Nicholas A. "Commentary on Central Bank Activities," *Business Conditions*, Federal Reserve Bank of Chicago (April 1971), pp. 6–11.

Rasminsky, Louis. *The Role of the Central Banker Today*. Washington: The Per Jacobsson Foundation, 1966.

Ratchford, B. U., and Jimmie Monhollon. *Notes on Central Banks*. Richmond: Federal Reserve Bank of Richmond, 1963,

Reagan, Michael D. "The Internal Structure of the Federal Reserve: A Political Analysis," in Commission on Money and Credit, *Monetary Management*. Englewood Cliffs, N.J.: Prentice-Hall, 1963.

Sayers, Richard S. *Central Banking After Bagehot*. London: Oxford University Press, 1958.

Member-Bank Reserves and the
Federal Reserve Balance Sheet
Federal Reserve Balance Sheet

The Federal Reserve and
Member-Bank Reserves
*Non-Federal Reserve Factors
Supplying Reserves
Factors Absorbing Reserves
Federal Reserve Bank Credit
and Member-Bank Reserves
Federal Reserve Control over Reserves
Federal Reserve Control over the Expansion
Power of Reserves
Defensive and Dynamic Aspects
of Reserve Control*

Summary

The Federal Reserve System and Monetary Control

At the beginning of chapter 6 we surveyed the important functions of central banking and later in the chapter observed the manner in which the Federal Reserve System performs a number of these. The most important function, however, the management of the money supply—the "essence of central banking," according to Sayers[1]—we have put off until now. This postponement was deliberate, based on the conviction that, by first becoming acquainted with the structure and service functions of the system, we might more easily understand the rationale of Federal Reserve activities directed toward influencing monetary variables and the machinery through which Federal Reserve actions have their effects.

The Federal Reserve does not control the money supply directly, nor does it control the cost and availability of bank credit—much less the total amount of credit in the economy or the level of interest rates. It does, however, have effective control over *member bank reserves,* both their quantity and their "expansibility," that is, the amount of reserves that the bank must hold per dollar of deposits and (indirectly) earning assets.

The influence of the Federal Reserve on the cost, quantity, and expansibility of bank reserves is one link in a highly important chain of causation, other links of which are (1) the effects of changes in bank reserves on the money supply and on the cost and availability of bank credit, (2) the effect of changes in bank credit and money on overall credit availability, interest rates, and liquidity, and, finally, (3) the effects

[1] R. S. Sayers, *Central Banking after Bagehot* (London: Oxford University Press, 1957), p. 1.

of changes in these latter variables on the prices and outputs of goods and services, on employment, and on our balance of payments. In this chapter we intend to look very closely at the first link, the means used by the Federal Reserve authorities to control member-bank reserves. These other links will be discussed in Part IV: Monetary Theory, except for the relation between bank reserves and the money supply, which we considered in chapter 2.

Member-Bank Reserves and the Federal Reserve Balance Sheet

Member-bank reserves,[2] we recall, consist mainly of deposits of the member banks in the regional Federal Reserve banks. The remainder, not quite one-fifth of the total in recent years, is in the form of vault cash, mostly Federal Reserve notes because practically all United States paper currency today is of this type. Thus, nearly all reserves of member banks—both reserve deposits and vault cash—are claims against the Federal Reserve banks. The question "What determines the volume of member bank reserves?" may legitimately be rephrased as "What kinds of transactions affect the volume of member-bank claims against the Federal Reserve?" (Warning: we are talking now about *total* member-bank claims against the Federal Reserve. Individual member banks, of course, may gain such claims at the expense of other member banks through various means, as discussed in chapters 4 and 5, but the banking system claims are not affected thereby.)

Federal Reserve Balance Sheet

Clearly we are involved in a topic requiring us to become familiar with various balance-sheet accounts of the Federal Reserve System because member-bank reserves, though *assets* of the member banks, are, for the most part, *liabilities* of the Federal Reserve. Table 7.1 contains the accounts in which we are interested.

ASSET ACCOUNTS: GOLD CERTIFICATES Gold certificates are claims against the United States Treasury backed dollar for dollar by gold in possession of the Treasury. Movements in this account closely parallel movements in our monetary gold stock, since the Treasury usually issues gold certificates to the Federal Reserve when gold flows into the Treasury and redeems the certificates when gold flows out.

Until very recently the Reserve banks were required by law to hold gold certificates equal to at least 25 per cent of their Federal Reserve

---

[2] Following standard practice, the term *member-bank reserves* will be used as a synonym of *legal reserves of member banks*. Other forms of cash reserves, notably deposits with other banks, are excluded because they cannot, by law, be used in meeting reserve requirements.

TABLE 7.1
Consolidated Federal Reserve Balance Sheet, May 31, 1974
(in $millions)

Assets		Liabilities and Capital	
Gold certificate account	$11,460	Federal Reserve notes	$64,732
Special Drawing Rights		Deposits:	
Certificate Account	400	Member-bank reserves	30,898
Cash	223	U.S. Treasury	3,133
Reserve bank credit		Foreign	429
Member-bank borrowing	3,298	Other	667
Acceptances	373	Other liabilities	1,160
Federal agency obligations	3,263	Capital accounts	2,219
U.S. government securities	81,395	Total liabilities and capital	$103,238
Float*	1,811		
Other assets	1,015		
Total assets	$103,238		

Source: Adapted from *Federal Reserve Bulletin*, June 1974, p. A12.
* Cash items in process of collection (asset) less deferred availability cash items (liability).

notes outstanding. This requirement was removed by legislation in March 1968, leaving the gold certificate account practically functionless, so far as our domestic monetary system is concerned.

SDR CERTIFICATE ACCOUNT The SDR (Special Drawing Right) is a new form of international reserve, issued by the International Monetary Fund to member nations and utilized internationally much as gold is in settlement of claims among nations arising from international payments imbalances.

"RESERVE BANK CREDIT" ACCOUNTS Most of the assets of the Reserve banks are in the five categories that together are generally labeled Reserve Bank Credit: (1) loans, (2) acceptances, (3) Federal agency obligations, (4) United States government securities, and (5) float.

All, or nearly all, *loans* made by Federal Reserve banks are made to member banks for very short periods and are practically always secured by U.S. government securities. The term *acceptances* refers to bankers' acceptances purchased and held by the Reserve banks. An acceptance is a time draft that has been drawn on a bank by prearrangement and "accepted" by it.[3]

---
[3] Chapter 10 contains an explanation of the nature and uses of bankers' acceptances as money-market instruments.

Federal agency obligations are securities issued by a half-dozen or so quasi-governmental agencies related to, but financially independent of, the Federal Treasury. Acting under a new law, the Federal Reserve began purchasing such securities in limited quantities in 1971. *United States government securities* are issues of the Treasury itself.

Float is not really a separate balance-sheet account; it is arrived at by subtracting "deferred availability cash items" (a liability) from "cash items in process of collection" (an asset). The difference constitutes a form of credit granted by the Federal Reserve to the banking system as a consequence of its practice of granting deposit credit to the bank that submits a check in two days or less after the submission while not charging the check against the deposit account of the bank on which the check is drawn until the item is actually collected. The "float" account measures the extent of this kind of credit in the aggregate as of a given date.

OTHER ASSETS   We lump together the rest of the assets into an "et cetera" category. Most of them are small individually, and they have no special monetary significance.

LIABILITIES   All but a trifling few hundred million dollars of the Federal Reserve banks' liabilities consist of Federal Reserve notes and deposits. The latter category is dominated by member-bank reserve deposits, our primary focus in this chapter. Other important deposit holders are the United States Treasury, a substantial number of foreign governments and central banks, certain government agencies and international organizations, and nonmember banks that keep clearing balances at their regional Reserve banks in order to qualify to have their checks and other items cleared through the Federal Reserve facilities.

CAPITAL ACCOUNTS   The nominal "owners" of each Federal Reserve bank are the member banks of that district, we recall. Each member bank must purchase an amount of Federal Reserve stock equal to 3 per cent of its capital and surplus accounts (another 3 per cent is subject to call), so the size of the Federal Reserve capital stock account bears a fixed relationship to the size of the member banks' aggregate capital stock and surplus accounts. Most of the profit earned by the Reserve banks is turned over to the Treasury each year, only enough being withheld to pay a 6 per cent dividend on the stock and to bring the surplus account into equality with the capital stock account.

The Federal Reserve and Member-Bank Reserves

In analyzing the financial mechanisms through which the quantity of reserves is manipulated, it will be helpful to use a type of financial statement that, though essentially based on the Federal Reserve balance sheet and differing only slightly from it, makes the role of the Treasury more specific. Issued weekly by the Federal Reserve Board and also published monthly (with weekly figures) in the *Federal Reserve Bulletin,* it is generally known as the "reserve equation" (see Table 7.2). The various "factors supplying reserve funds" less the "factors absorbing reserve funds" equals member-bank reserve deposits.

We turn now to the individual items in the equation, stressing in each case how the particular factor exerts its influence on bank reserves. First, in order to demonstrate what the Federal Reserve is "up against" in attempting to provide the quantity of reserves it feels is desirable, we examine the non-Federal Reserve influences on reserves. Then we analyze the reserve-influencing weapons at the disposal of the system.

TABLE 7.2
The Reserve Equation: Determinants of
Member-Bank Reserves, May 31, 1974
(in $millions)

Factors supplying reserves		
Gold stock		$ 11,567
Special Drawing Rights certificate account		400
Treasury currency outstanding		8,859
Reserve bank credit outstanding:		
U.S. government securities*	$84,658	
Loans	3,298	
Acceptances	373	
Float	1,811	
Other Federal Reserve assets	1,015	91,155
		$111,981
Less: Factors absorbing reserves		
Currency in circulation (outside member banks)		$ 73,155
Treasury cash holdings		304
Deposits other than member banks		
Treasury	$ 3,133	
Foreign	429	
Other	667	4,229
Other Federal Reserve liabilities and capital		3,395
		$ 81,083
Equals: Member bank reserves with Federal Reserve		$ 30,898
Plus: Member bank holdings of currency and coin		6,652
Equals: Total member bank reserves		$ 37,608†

Source: *Federal Reserve Bulletin*, June 1974, pp. A4, A5, and A12.
* Includes Federal agency obligations.
† Includes $58 million of reserve deficiencies on which Federal Reserve banks are allowed to waive penalties for a transition period in connection with bank adaptation to a recent change in Federal Reserve Regulation J.

To make the discussion more concrete, we shall use our familiar balance-sheet trace statements in observing the effects on member-bank reserves of hypothetical (but typical) transactions involving changes in the major "factors."

Non-Federal Reserve Factors Supplying Reserves

Any increase in one of the "supplying" factors, unless offset by a corresponding decrease in another "supplying" factor or increase in an "absorbing" factor, will increase member-bank reserves by the same amount. Similarly, a decrease in one of these "supplying" factors, unless offset, will result in a corresponding decrease in member-bank reserves.

GOLD STOCK To demonstrate that a change in the gold stock will (unless offset) actually change member-bank reserves in the same direction, let us assume that a foreign economic unit, a central bank, utilizes some of its deposit balances built up in American commercial banks to purchase $100 of gold from the Treasury. (1) First, since the foreign central bank will be paying for the gold with a check drawn on its account at the Federal Reserve Bank of New York, it builds up its account there in anticipation of the gold transaction by transferring funds from member banks to the Reserve bank. (2) Next, the actual sale of gold is consummated, involving the transfer of $100 on the books of the New York Federal Reserve Bank from the foreign central bank's account to that of the Treasury. (3) The Treasury, having sold the gold that had been serving as "backing" for an equivalent dollar amount of gold certificates, buys back this amount of gold certificates held by the Federal Reserve banks. The combined effect of all three transactions is a $100 reduction in gold, member-bank reserve deposits, and demand deposits:

TRACE 7.1

	Treasury		
(1)			
(2) Gold Deposit with Federal Reserve	−$100 +$100		
(3) Deposit with Federal Reserve	−$100	Gold certificates	−$100
(1–3) Gold	−$100	Gold certificates	−$100

	Federal Reserve Banks		
(1)		Member-bank reserve deposits Foreign deposits	−$100 +$100
(2)		Foreign deposits Treasury deposits	−$100 +$100
(3) Gold certificates	−$100	Treasury deposits	−$100
(1–3) Gold certificates	−$100	Member-bank reserve deposits	−$100

	Member Banks	
(1) Reserves with Federal Reserve −$100	Demand deposits	−$100
(2)		
(3)		
(1–3) Reserves with Federal Reserve −$100	Demand deposits	−$100

An inflow of gold will have opposite effects, of course. The seller of gold to the Treasury normally deposits his check in a bank almost certainly a member bank. This check, drawn on a Federal Reserve bank, is "instant reserves" to the banking system. And the Treasury then completes the set of transactions by tendering gold certificates for deposit credit at the Federal Reserve. (For practice, the student should record these transactions in a manner similar to the gold outflow illustration.)

SDR CERTIFICATE ACCOUNT (1) When the Treasury receives a $1 billion allotment of SDR's from the issuing agency, the International Monetary Fund, it tenders them to the Federal Reserve for deposit credit. The factor of increase (SDR certificates) is thus offset by an increase in Treasury deposits. (2) Only when the Treasury, by making expenditures, reduces its deposit at the Federal Reserve to its previous level does the increase in SDR certificates have its full effect on member bank reserves.

Federal Reserve Banks		Member Banks		
(1) SDR certificate account +$1	Treasury deposits +$1			TRACE 7.2
(2)	Treasury deposits −$1 Member-bank reserve deposits +1	Reserves with Federal Reserve +$1	Demand deposits −$1	
(1–2) SDR certificate account +$1	Member-bank reserve deposits +$1	Reserves with Federal Reserve +$1	Demand deposits +$1	

TREASURY CURRENCY OUTSTANDING (1) When the Treasury issues currency (for example, $1 million in coins to the Federal Reserve for deposit credit), nothing happens to bank reserves, since the increase in the Treasury deposit at the Federal Reserve (an "absorbing" factor) offsets the new currency. (2) However, if we make the very reasonable assumption that the Treasury spends this $1 million, allowing its deposit at the Federal Reserve to revert to its former level, then, considering the combined effects of both transactions, member-bank reserves increase by the amount of the currency issue:

TRACE 7.3

Federal Reserve Banks				Member Banks		
(1) Cash	+$1	Treasury deposits	+$1	(1)		
(2)		Treasury deposits	−$1	(2) Reserves with Federal Reserve	+$1	Demand deposits +$1
		Member-bank reserve deposits	+1			
(1–2) Cash	+$1	Member-bank reserve deposits	+$1	(1–2) Reserves with Federal Reserve	+$1	Demand deposits +$1

Factors Absorbing Reserves

It is probably obvious that, when we speak of "factors absorbing reserves," we really mean "factors *reducing* reserves." An *increase* in one of these factors will, other things equal, *reduce* reserves. Put generally, member-bank reserves move inversely with the "absorbing" factors.

CURRENCY IN CIRCULATION   In the above illustration we left $1 million in newly issued coins in the Federal Reserve banks. Now assume that (1) as the result of increased public demand for coins, people withdraw $1 million in coins from the member banks, and (2) these banks, to avoid running out of coins, secure $1 million of new coins from the Reserve banks.[4] When we depict the balance-sheet changes caused by these transactions, we see clearly the inverse relation between currency in circulation and member-bank reserves:

TRACE 7.4

Federal Reserve Banks				Member Banks		
(1)				(1) Vault cash −$1		Demand deposits −$1
(2) Cash	−$1	Member-bank reserve deposits	−$1	(2) Vault cash +$1 Reserves with Federal Reserve	−1	
(1–2) Cash	−$1	Member-bank reserve deposits	−$1	(1–2) Reserves with Federal Reserve	−$1	Demand deposits −$1

[4] The reserves were lost in step 1, so step 2 was not strictly necessary to the demonstration. It does, however, bring out the role of the Federal Reserve as source of supply of currency to the banking system.

A return flow of currency from circulation back to the banking system, such as occurs after Christmas, would increase member-bank reserves, other things equal.

Although changes in the volume of currency in circulation from month to month and even within a month are substantial, the Federal Reserve has found definite seasonal patterns in these movements. "Of the major operating factors that affect member-bank reserve positions, the periodic changes in the demand for currency are the least difficult to predict."[5] One of the tasks the Federal Reserve performs is countering the effects of these short-run influences on bank reserves.

TREASURY CASH HOLDINGS AND DEPOSITS OTHER THAN MEMBER-BANK DEPOSITS   Treasury cash consists of the Treasury's holdings of (1) Federal Reserve notes, (2) Treasury-issued currency and coins, and (3) "free gold," that is, gold against which the Treasury has not issued certificates. Major deposit holders other than member banks are, as noted earlier, the United State Treasury and other government agencies, nonmember banks, certain international organizations, and foreign central banks.

Each of the accounts in this category has this common characteristic: if the holder were to spend a portion of it, member bank reserves would increase, because the recipients would deposit most or all of the proceeds at member banks, as illustrated below:

Federal Reserve Banks		Member Banks		TRACE 7.5
Other deposits Member-bank reserve deposits	−$100 +100	Reserves with Federal Reserve	Demand deposits	
		+$100	+$100	

Federal Reserve Bank Credit and Member-Bank Reserves

It should be very clear now that there are numerous forces influencing the quantity of member-bank reserves, forces ranging from foreign central banks and international financial organizations to Federal agencies other than the Treasury to ordinary private citizens desiring to increase or decrease their holdings of currency. Yet the Federal Reserve has the obligation to control bank reserves in order to carry out its mandates of (1) stabilizing financial markets and (2) working toward the realization of the goals of the Employment Act of 1946. To fulfill these responsibilities requires a high order of sophistication in collecting and interpreting data and in forecasting future developments, both financial and economic.

---

[5] Irving Auerbach, "Forecasting Currency in Circulation," *Essays in Money and Credit* (New York: Federal Reserve Bank of New York, 1964), p. 13.

We turn now to the "Reserve Bank Credit" portion of the Reserve Equation in order to observe the effects of Federal Reserve activities on the quantity of member-bank reserves. Our purpose will be to gain insight into the nature and potentialities of the tools available to the Federal Reserve to influence the quantity, cost, and expansibility of member-bank reserves.

Earlier in this chapter we were introduced to the four categories of Federal Reserve bank credit; here we examine the mechanism through which Federal Reserve purchases and sales of financial assets actually result in corresponding changes in member-bank reserves. We shall not, at this point, be concerned with such important questions as the relative economic effects of these forms of credit, their interrelations, their limitations, and possible alterations to increase their effectiveness. In Part V, however, we will delve into these and related issues in our discussion of monetary and other macroeconomic policies.

LOANS Virtually the entire amount of credit granted under this heading is in the form of "advances" to member banks; that is, loans secured by financial claims that, by law, qualify as collateral for these loans.[6] In balance-sheet terms, the effects on the two parties involved as a result of a $10 advance is as follows:

TRACE 7.6

Federal Reserve Banks		Member Banks	
Loans +$10	Member-bank reserve deposits +$10	Reserves with Federal Reserve +$10	Bills payable +$10

Observe that the Federal Reserve is not lending the bank "money," which the bank, in turn, "lends out"; rather, it is providing *reserves*, on the basis of which the banking system can expand credit and deposits by an amount several times that of the new reserves, through the process of deposit expansion described in chapter 2. Not surprisingly, therefore, the Federal Reserve authorities have established certain safeguards designed to prevent excessive use of this source of reserves. The Federal Reserve also changes the discount rate (the price of borrowing) from time to time both to indicate changes in its attitude toward bank borrowing (hence, toward economic conditions generally) and to increase or decrease the attractiveness to banks of borrowing from the Federal Reserve versus alternative sources of reserves. In other words, an increase in the discount rate implies that the Federal Reserve authorities (1) feel

---

[6] The Federal Reserve banks are authorized, under certain circumstances, to make advances secured by United States government securities to individuals, partnerships, and corporations (including nonmember banks); but this authority is so rarely utilized that we shall ignore it in our discussion. Also neglected here is the authorization (seldom exercised) to make loans secured by gold to foreign central banks.

that conditions warrant some "tightening" of credit and therefore (2) want to make borrowing from the Federal Reserve banks less profitable.

ACCEPTANCES Bankers' acceptances are purchased under authorization of the Federal Open Market Committee, which specifies (1) a lower limit on the effective rates of return and (2) an upper limit on the quantity, both in absolute amount and in relation to total acceptances outstanding. The acceptances are purchased either outright or under repurchase agreement, by which the seller agrees to buy back the acceptance within fifteen days of the original purchase. The dollar amount of reserves provided in this way is almost infinitesimal.

Purchase of an acceptance by the Federal Reserve will increase member-bank reserves, as can be seen in the following example:

Federal Reserve Banks		Member Banks		TRACE 7.7
Acceptances +$100	Member-bank reserve deposits +$100	(a) Reserves with Federal Reserve +$100	Demand deposits +$100	
		(b) Reserves with Federal Reserve +$100 Loans and discounts −100		

We assume in this illustration that, in case (a), a nonbank holder sells an acceptance to a Reserve bank for $100, turning the check he receives over to a member bank for deposit credit; while, in case (b) a member bank sells an acceptance to its regional Federal Reserve bank for $100 for reserve credit. The effect on reserves is the same in either case: a $100 increase.

UNITED STATES GOVERNMENT SECURITIES Although acceptances as well as U.S. government securities are purchased on the open market, discussions of Federal Reserve open-market operations nearly always concentrate on transactions in the latter. Not only do holdings of such securities dominate the asset side of Federal Reserve bank balance sheets but the Reserve banks themselves likewise dominate the U.S. government securities market by virtue of the size of their holdings, the volume of transactions, and the manner in which the actions of the Reserve banks, as coordinated by the Federal Open Market Committee, influence the decisions of other market participants.

The purchase by the Federal Reserve of U.S. government securities, including securities issued by Federal agencies, results in an increase in member-bank reserves; and the sale of such securities results in a decrease in reserves, regardless of whether the other party to the transaction is a bank, another financial institution, a business corporation, or a private individual.

Taking the bank case first, assume that the Federal Reserve purchases $100 of U.S. government securities from a member bank.[7] The "payment" received by the bank is a claim on the Federal Reserve, which the bank may count immediately as an increase in its reserves. The Reserve bank, in turn, has acquired an asset (U.S. government securities) but has added to its liabilities (member-bank reserve deposits).

TRACE 7.8

Federal Reserve Banks		Member Banks	
U.S. government securities +$100	Member-bank reserve deposits +$100	Reserves with Federal Reserve +$100 U.S. government securities −100	

If, instead, the seller had been some other kind of economic unit, the effect on the balance sheet of the Federal Reserve banks would have been the same; but the balance sheet of the member banks would differ, as follows, from that previously shown:

TRACE 7.9

Federal Reserve Banks		Member Banks	
(1) U.S. government securities +$100	Officers' checks +$100	(1)	
(2)	Officers' checks −$100 Member-bank reserve deposits +100	(2) Reserves with Federal Reserve +$100	Demand deposits +$100
(1–2) U.S. government securities +$100	Member-bank reserve deposits +$100	(1–2) Reserves with Federal Reserve +$100	Demand deposits +$100

Nonbank Economic Unit	
(1) Cash (check on Federal Reserve) U.S. government securities	+$100 −100
(2) Cash (check on Federal Reserve) Cash in bank	−$100 +100
(1–2) Cash in bank U.S. government securities	+$100 −100

---

[7] Strictly speaking, the seller will be one of a small number of government securities dealers, so we are implicitly assuming that the dealer, in turn, purchases the securities from the bank to replenish his inventory.

In the above exhibit, step 1 shows the balance-sheet effects of the purchase by the Federal Reserve of $100 of U.S. government securities from a nonbank seller, payment being made in the form of an officers' check (one of the categories of "other deposits"). In step 2 the check is presented for deposit credit at a member bank, which sends it to the issuing Reserve bank for credit to its reserve account. Net result: an increase in reserves equal in dollar amount to the value of the securities purchased, just as we observed in the immediately preceding case.

The difference in the two cases as they affect the member banks, as you may have noticed, is that only the second case involves an immediate increase in the money supply (demand deposits). However, since both cases involve the same dollar increase in reserves, the *potential* effects of the two cases on the money supply are identical.

A relatively small fraction of total Federal Reserve System holdings of U.S. government securities (though a large fraction of total transactions in these securities) consists of those acquired on a repurchase basis. The chief reason for this practice is to provide temporary "emergency" financing for government securities dealers, as part of the Federal Reserve's overall program of preventing excessive instability in financial markets.

A discerning eye might have observed that purchasing securities under a repurchase agreement is really a thinly disguised form of loan financing. Even though the Reserve banks do not make advances to private enterprises other than member banks, as a rule, the effect of a repurchase arrangement between a dealer and a Reserve bank is precisely the same as that of a short-term loan, secured by government securities, to the dealer by a Reserve bank.

One final point should be added regarding open-market operations in U.S. government securities. In each example so far, we have assumed that the transaction involved one or more *member* banks. Suppose instead that only nonmember banks participate directly in a particular transaction. Take the case of a purchase by the Federal Reserve of U.S. government securities from, say, a business firm that is a customer of a nonmember bank. Step (1) would show the seller depositing the officers' check obtained from the Reserve bank in his own (nonmember) bank. But what is this bank to do with the check? Since nonmembers keep most of their cash reserves in the form of demand deposits in big-city banks, which a e almost invariably member banks, step (2) records the deposit of the officers' check in the depository bank and the ultimate return of the check by the member bank to the Reserve bank for deposit credit. In terms of effects on member-bank reserves, therefore, the final outcome of this case is the same as that of the original case, in which the depositor dealt with a member bank.[8]

---

[8] It may appear that, since the nonmember bank still has "reserves" also, the banking system as a whole has $200 of new reserves! However, the nonmember bank will not wish to keep this "idle deposit" at its big-city depository bank but will purchase earning

TRACE 7.10

Federal Reserve Banks		Nonmember Banks	
(1) U.S. government securities +$100	Officers' checks +$100	(1) Cash items +$100	Demand deposits +$100
(2)	Officers' checks −$100 Member-bank reserve deposits +$100	(2) Cash items −$100 Balance with other banks +100	
(1–2) U.S. government securities +$100	Member-bank reserve deposits +$100	(1–2) Balance with other banks +$100	

Member Banks			
(1)			
(2) Reserves with Federal Reserve +$100		Interbank deposits	+$100
(1–2) Reserves with Federal Reserve +$100		Interbank deposits	+$100

FLOAT The final category of Federal Reserve bank credit to be examined is that designated by the term *float*. Earlier in this chapter we briefly described the nature of this arrangement; now we must examine more closely the effects of float on bank reserves. Consider, for example, a $500 check drawn on an Eastern bank, acquired by a member bank in the West, and sent, for reserve credit, through the clearing facilities of the Federal Reserve System. (1) To the receiving Reserve bank, this check is one of many "cash items in process of collection." It does not, however, give the Western bank immediate reserve-deposit credit, so an entry in the "deferred availability cash items" account is made. (2) A maximum of two days later the check is credited to the Western bank and the "deferred availability" entry is removed. But the check has not completed its cross-country trip to an Eastern Reserve bank and the commercial bank on which it was drawn. Thus, the Federal Reserve has, in effect, granted credit to the Western bank by writing up its reserve-deposit account before reducing the account of the bank against which it

---

assets, thus losing these reserves. In contrast to reserves held with the Federal Reserve, which do not disappear through the clearing process but merely shift owners, these reserves lost in the course of lending or investing by nonmembers are lost to the system. Since they are merely deposit claims on member banks, when they are transferred to nonbank holders they become "just plain deposits"—part of the money supply but no longer bank reserves. Only the increase in interbank deposits retained to meet the state's reserve requirement in connection with the $100 demand deposit is a permanent increase in banking system reserves.

was drawn. Completing the illustration, (3) the reserve account of the Eastern bank is reduced, as is the "cash items in process of collection" account, on the books of the Federal Reserve banks; and the Eastern bank reduces the deposit account of the drawer of the check.

Since millions of checks per day pass through the Federal Reserve banks and branches, this practice of granting reserve credit to the member banks submitting checks before deducting the dollar amounts of these same checks from the reserve accounts of the banks on which they are drawn results in float that has seldom fallen below $2 billion in recent years.

TRACE 7.11

Federal Reserve Banks			
(1) Cash items in process of collection +$500		Deferred availability cash items	+$500
(2)		Deferred availability cash items	−$500
		Member-bank reserve deposits	+500
(3) Cash items in process of collection −$500		Member-bank reserve deposits	−$500
(1–3)			

Western Bank		Eastern Bank	
(1) Cash items in process of collection +$500	Demand deposits +$500		
(2) Reserves with Federal Reserve +$500 Cash items in process of collection −500			
(3)		Reserves with Federal Reserve −$500	Demand deposits −$500
(1–3) Reserves with Federal Reserve +$500	Demand deposits +$500	Reserves with Federal Reserve −$500	Demand deposits +$500

The size of float is affected by a number of factors, some of which can be forecast fairly accurately by the Federal Reserve. Other factors are inherently difficult to forecast accurately while still others—notably the weather—are simply not predictable at all.[9]

[9] See Irving Auerbach, "Forecasting Float," *Monthly Review*, Federal Reserve Bank of New York, (February 1963), pp. 30–35, for a discussion of the methods used and difficulties faced in connection with this task.

> It is not unusual... for the amount of float outstanding to change by as much as $200 million in a single day. In mid-December, moreover, the daily variation in float may be as much as $500 million.[10]

A bad snowstorm, for example, will enlarge the "cash items in process of collection" account by keeping checks "in process" sometimes several days longer than normal; nevertheless, the banks that have submitted these checks still receive deposit credit one or two days following their receipt by the Reserve banks. The result is a temporary but unexpected expansion of member-bank reserves. Since banks generally strive to keep excess reserves to a minimum, the result (unless offset by Federal Reserve action) would be that banks would bid for short-term securities, thus raising their prices and lowering their yields, introducing a wholly artificial easing into the money markets.

Federal Reserve Control over Reserves

It is evident that the degree of Federal Reserve control varies widely among the categories of Reserve bank credit. Although the Federal Reserve has broad powers with respect to each credit category, in some cases the mechanism of control is too clumsy or slow to be useful in short-run situations. For instance, it would be extremely difficult to attempt to influence the size of float by varying the "availability schedule" which specifies the number of days member banks must wait before including in their legal reserves the dollar amounts of particular checks sent to Federal Reserve banks for collection. Therefore, in the short-run sense, the Federal Reserve has no more effective control over float than over gold movements!

In the case of loans to member banks, the Federal Reserve controls the discount rate, changing it periodically; but, again, it would be far more difficult to change other terms of the borrowing agreement—eligibility (collateral) requirements, and so on. So, in this case, too, the Federal Reserve authorities do not really have *control* over this credit category.

Bankers' acceptances, to be sure, are subject to a stated maximum quantity that the Federal Open Market Committee can alter at will, but there is no way to compel holders of acceptances to sell to the Federal Reserve. The total amount of bankers' acceptances outstanding is so small relative to the magnitudes in which the Federal Reserve deals that this market could not be utilized as a major weapon of credit control without completely disrupting it.

Only in the case of U.S. government securities does the Federal Reserve have tight effective control over a particular credit category. It holds the initiative in purchasing and selling. Also, considering its own

---

[10] Ibid, p. 30.

huge portfolio of government securities and the enormous volume of them outstanding, there is little likelihood of its being hampered by unavailability of government securities either to sell or to buy. Not surprisingly, therefore, open-market operations in government securities have become the key Federal Reserve weapon for controlling total reserves.

Referring to chapter 6 for a moment, perhaps we can better understand now the (unanticipated) rise to prominence of the Federal Open Market Committee. As the system leaders came to understand the enormous power of open-market operations, this committee's role gradually, almost inevitably, evolved into its present one: the principal forum for general monetary policy discussions and decisions.

Federal Reserve Control over the Expansion Power of Reserves

At the beginning of this chapter we pointed out that the Federal Reserve authorities exercise control not only over the volume of bank reserves but also over the amount of deposits that each reserve dollar can support. It is time now to look at this second aspect of monetary control: the reserve requirement.

Table 7.3 summarizes the pattern of member-bank reserve requirements as of a recent date:

The quantity of reserves that a given member bank must maintain over a given reserve period evidently depends on the volume of its deposits in each of three categories: demand, savings, and "other time."[11]

A member bank need not maintain its reserves at or above the legal market moment by moment, nor even day by day. It is expected to maintain average reserves during a given week based on average deposits (size and mix) as of two weeks earlier. Any deficiency will result in an assessment on the deficiency at a rate 2 per cent above the existing Federal Reserve discount rate—hardly a drastic punishment, but one that tends to discourage persistent deficiencies.

Changes in member-bank reserve requirements do not, of course, directly affect the total of member-bank reserves, but they do affect the reserve situation of member banks in two ways. First, they affect the expansibility of each reserve dollar. An across-the-board doubling of reserve requirements would double the quantity of reserves needed to support a given deposit level; or, looked at from the opposite side, would

---

[11] There are other complexities, which we need not go into. For instance, the volume of demand deposits actually subject to the reserve requirement is reduced by the amount of cash items in process of collection and also its holdings of demand deposits in other banks. Borrowings of a bank from its foreign branches and commercial paper it has issued also affect total reserves required.

TABLE 7.3
Member-Bank Reserve Requirements, In Effect May 31, 1974

Category of Deposits	Reserve Percentage Applicable
*Net demand deposits**	
First $2 million or less	8
Over $2 million–$10 million	10½
Over $10 million–$100 million	12½
Over $100 million–$400 million	13½
Over $400 million	18
Savings deposits†	3
Other time deposits	
First $5 million or less	3
Over $5 million	5

Source: Federal Reserve Bulletin, June 1974, p. A9.
* Gross demand deposits minus cash items in process of collection and demand balances due from domestic banks.
† Includes Christmas and vacation club account.

cut in half the volume of demand deposits that a given quantity of legal reserves could support.

The second effect of reserve-requirement changes is much like that of a change in the quantity of member-bank reserves. To illustrate, a reduction in reserve requirements increases bank *excess* reserves, as some of the bank's (given) total reserves are reclassified from required to excess. This change increases the ability of the banks to acquire additional earning assets just as surely as does an open-market securities purchase by the FOMC. Similarly, an increase in reserve requirements reduces excess reserves.

Note that the two effects of a change in reserve requirements reinforce each other. A decrease in requirements both (1) increases excess reserves and (2) increases the expansion potential of the banking system's excess reserves. And the same generalization applies, with signs reversed, in the case of an increase in reserve requirements.

The authority to change reserve requirements is a potent weapon. For example, if the demand-deposit reserve requirement were a flat 16 per cent, each reserve dollar could "support" $6.25 in demand deposits. If the reserve requirement were reduced to 15 per cent, each dollar could support $6.667, an increase of 6.67 per cent. A given volume of reserves, therefore, could then support 6.67 per cent more demand deposits, an increase considerably larger than our average *annual* rate of increase in demand deposits. Little wonder, then, that every change but one in demand-deposit reserve requirements since 1958 has been by one-half percentage point.

Defensive and Dynamic Aspects of Reserve Control

In considering the actual activities of the Federal Reserve aimed at regulating bank reserves as a means of accomplishing certain goals, it is useful to distinguish between *defensive* and *dynamic* aspects of these activities. Quoting from Robert V. Roosa, the originator of these concepts:

> Defensively, the System's job might be seen as that of keeping a given volume of reserves in being and helping with the economic distribution of that given total. Dynamically, the job is to vary the quantity of reserves (after allowing for seasonal variations) by such amounts, and through such methods, as to make the banking system, and the money market as well, an active force in the economy—promoting growth, resisting depressions, and limiting inflations.[12]

DEFENSIVE ACTIVITY   The following passage describes one type of defensive operation. The "accounting traces" have been inserted to help us observe the effects of these transactions both the member-bank reserves and on the member-bank reserve position, that is, the relation between actual and required reserves.

> The responsiveness of the banking system to the economy's changing need for cash stems both from operational policies of the Federal Reserve System and from the relative ease with which individual commercial banks are able to adjust their reserve positions in the fact of shifting demands for cash balances and credit . . .
>
> A good illustration of the way the banking system meets the economy's changing need for cash balances is provided by the quarterly dates on which corporations pay their Federal income taxes. On these dates, (1) businesses

TRACE 7.12

Member Banks			
(1) Loans	+	Demand deposits	+

> borrow directly from banks and also (2) exchange maturing negotiable time

(2)		Demand deposits (public)	+
		Time deposits (CD's)	−

> certificates of deposit for demand deposits in order to pay the Treasury. At the same time, (1) the nonbank dealers in Government securities look to the banks to refinance securities returning from maturing repurchase agreements with corporations, and (1) sales finance companies borrow from banks to pay off maturing paper held by tax-paying corporations. The counterpart of this large increase in bank loans is, of course, an expansion in (3) demand de-

---

[12] Robert V. Roosa, *Federal Reserve Operations in the Money and Government Securities Markets* (New York: Federal Reserve Bank of New York, 1956), pp. 13–14.

(3)	Demand deposits (public)	−
	Demand deposits (Treasury)	+

posits that corporations immediately pay over to the Treasury, which leaves them in . . . commercial banks for the time being. With the required reserves of the banking system increasing rapidly because of the rise in deposits, banks step up their collective demand for Federal funds to meet their requirements. (4) The Manager of the System Open Market Account, armed

(4) Reserves with Federal Reserve	+	Demand deposits	+

with forecasts based on past experience, sees that reserve availability rises, but at a rate geared to the demands actually emerging in the Federal funds market.[13] Subsequently, (5) the Treasury draws down its enlarged balances

(5) Reserves with Federal Reserve	−	Demand deposits (Treasury)	−

in the normal course of paying the government's bills. (6) These payments by

(6) Reserves with Federal Reserve	+	Demand deposits (public)	+

the Treasury flow to individuals and to corporations, which are at the same time also acquiring deposits from their sales of goods and services across the nation. (7) Loans at banks tend to be repaid, as some corporations reduce

(7) Loans	−	Demand deposits (public)	−
		Time deposits (CD's)	+

their indebtedness and others rebuild their holdings of short-term earning assets out of corporate cash flow. Declining deposits being reductions in required reserves, the supply-demand balance in the Federal funds market shifts, and (8) the system withdraws reserves to prevent the undue easing

(8) Reserves with Federal Reserve	−	Demand deposits	−

in the money market that would otherwise result from reduction in cash needs.[14, 15]

---

[13] We assume that the securities are purchased from nonbanks.
[14] Paul Meek and Jack W. Cox, "The Banking System—Its Behavior in the Short Run," *Monthly Review*, New York Federal Reserve Bank, (April 1966), pp. 84, 85–86. Numerals in parentheses added.
[15] We assume that the Federal Reserve mops up reserves by selling U.S. government securities to nonbanks.

A DYNAMIC EXAMPLE To take a longer-run look at the role of the Federal Reserve System vis-à-vis member-bank reserves, let us examine the movements in the components of the Reserve Equation between November 1970 and September 1973, a period characterized by economic expansion. Table 7.4 depicts the "before" and "after" Reserve Equation and the change in each component, organizing these changes according to the direction of their effects on reserves.

Over this period of nearly three years, the Federal Reserve "supplied" reserves totaling about $18.5 billion, 90 per cent of this amount through open-market purchases of government securities. Adding to this $18.5 billion the effects of the change in Treasury currency (+$1.5 bil-

TABLE 7.4
Sources of Changes in Member-Bank Reserves,
November 30, 1970–September 30, 1973
(in $millions)

Source of Change	Nov. 30, 1970	Sept. 30, 1973	Effect on Member-Bank Reserve Deposits
Factors supplying reserves			
Gold stock	$11,117	$10,410	−$ 707
SDR certificate account	400	400	
Treasury currency	7,126	8,614	+1,488
Reserve bank credit,			
Total	64,596	83,090	+18,494
U.S. government securities	(61,294)	(77,900)	(+16,606)
Discounts and advances	(300)	(1,558)	(+1,258)
Acceptances	(87)	(145)	(+58)
Float	(1,987)	(2,513)	(+526)
Other Federal			
Reserve assets	(928)	(974)	(+46)
Total	$83,239	$102,514	+$19,275
Factors absorbing reserves			
Currency in circulation	$56,381	$ 68,217	−$11,836
Treasury cash	453	361	+92
Treasury deposits	587	1,624	−1,037
Foreign deposits	136	250	−114
Other deposits	692	798	−106
Other Federal Reserve			
liabilities and capital	2,302	3,021	−719
Total	$60,551	$ 28,271	−$13,720
Member-bank reserves			
with Federal Reserve	$22,689	$28,240	+$5,551

Source: *Federal Reserve Bulletin*, January 1971 and November 1973, pp. A4–A5, A12.

lion) and our gold stock (−$0.7 billion) brings the total of reserves supplied by the so-called "Factors Supplying Reserves" during the period to nearly $19.3 billion. Yet member-bank reserve deposits rose by slightly less than $5.6 billion! What went wrong?

The bulk of the $13.7 billion discrepancy is accounted for by one item: an $11.8 billion increase in currency in circulation, reflecting a rise in demand for currency because of the sustained growth in the level of economic activity and of prices during this period.

We cannot, however, conclude on the basis of these figures alone that, had the Federal Reserve kept its credit outstanding unchanged instead of increasing it by $18.5 billion, member-bank reserve deposits would have declined by $12.9 billion instead of rising by $5.6 billion. These various components are to some degree interdependent. If, for example, the system had purchased only $5 billion of government securities, evenly spaced over this period, the money supply, along with bank loans and investments, would have grown much more slowly; and it seems logical to infer that, with the economy thus "starved" for credit, our average rate of growth of income over the thirty-four months would have been much lower than it, in fact, was. The public's needs for currency would therefore have expanded much more slowly, absorbing a smaller amount of potential reserves. All things considered, then, the actual reduction in reserves would probably be far less than the smaller increase in Federal Reserve bank credit would lead us to believe.

Thus the Federal Reserve System, in attempting to fulfill its statutory responsibilities as our central bank, must keep one figurative eye on the day-to-day behavior of the financial markets and the other on the changing longer-run (cyclical and secular) needs of the banking system for reserves as a means of achieving the proper financial environment for the economic system. Its main "handle" for accomplishing these purposes is a single balance-sheet account—member-bank reserve deposits—which it can influence by a number of actions but has the ability to manipulate largely through buying and selling United States government securities.

Summary

The Federal Reserve System exercises control over the nation's money supply through its influence over the volume and expansibility of member-bank reserves, most of which are in the form of deposit claims on Federal Reserve banks.

Both the link between Federal Reserve actions and member-bank reserves and that between member-bank reserves and the money supply are far from tight. With reference to the former link (the latter we examined in chapter 2), the problem is that a number of factors in addition to the Federal Reserve itself influence bank reserves. The most important non-Federal Reserve factors have been changes in currency in circulation and (until recent years) changes in our gold stock. Nevertheless, the system is able to anticipate some movements in these factors and to take rapid action to offset any unexpected movements, so there is no likelihood of a long-duration deviation of member-bank reserves from the path charted by the Federal Reserve.

The Federal Reserve has several weapons of monetary control, but by far the most important is its *open-market operations:* the purchase and sale of (mainly) United States government securities on the open market. A purchase of such securities by the system, whether from banks or from other economic units, results in the expansion of member-bank reserves; a sale has the opposite effect.

KEY CONCEPTS

Gold certificates
Reserve bank credit
Federal agency obligations
Float
The "Reserve Equation"
Defensive open-market operations
Dynamic open-market operations

QUESTIONS FOR REVIEW

1. Why do the Federal Reserve banks hold such an enormous amount of U.S. government securities?
2. In what respects is the "reserve-creation" process similar to the deposit-creation process described in chapter 2? In what respects different?
3. Does the Federal Reserve have any short-run influence over the size of float? any long-run influence?
4. What influences beside action of the Federal Reserve itself affect total member-bank reserves?
5. Is borrowing by member banks from the Federal Reserve banks a right or a privilege? Explain.
6. "If the Federal Reserve were to sell U.S. government securities from its holdings, member-bank reserves would probably decline." Describe the mechanics of this process.
7. Distinguish between "defensive" and "dynamic" open-market operations.

SUGGESTIONS FOR FURTHER READING

Board of Governors, Federal Reserve System. *Annual Report.*
――― *Open Market Policies and Operating Procedures.* Washington, D.C.: Board of Governors, 1971.

Fousek, Peter G. *Foreign Central Banking: The Instruments of Monetary Policy.* New York: Federal Reserve Bank of New York, 1957.

Maisel, Sherman J. *Managing the Dollar.* New York: W. W. Norton, 1973.

Meek, Paul. *Open Market Operations.* New York: Federal Reserve Bank of New York, 1969.

Modern Money Mechanics: A Workbook on Deposits, Currency, and Bank Reserves, rev. ed. Chicago: Federal Reserve Bank of Chicago, 1968.

Roosa, Robert V. *Federal Reserve Operations in the Money and Government Securities Markets.* New York: Federal Reserve Bank of New York, 1956.

Sayers, Richard S. *Central Banking after Bagehot.* London: Oxford University Press, 1958.

Smith, Warren L. "The Instruments of General Monetary Control." *National Banking* Review, I (September 1963), pp. 47–76.

INSTITUTIONAL FRAMEWORK: OTHER ELEMENTS

PART III

The Depository Savings Intermediaries
Mutual Savings Banks
Savings and Loan Associations
The Federal Home Loan Bank System
Credit Unions

The Contractual Savings Intermediaries
Life Insurance Companies
Property and Liability Insurance Companies
Pension Funds

Investment Companies

Nonbank Financial Intermediaries: The Savings Institutions 8

Chapter 3 introduced us to a number of nonbank financial institutions, intermediary and other. In this and the following chapters we intend to broaden and deepen this acquaintance. Since our purpose in studying the financial system is to gain an understanding of the system, not merely to learn facts about it, we shall continually be attempting to discover *how* and *why* (and even *why not*) as well as *what* in our investigation.

Financial intermediaries, we recall, are economic units the assets of which are primarily financial. While commercial banks constitute the largest class of private intermediaries, in terms of total assets, and perform the crucial function of creating most of our money, the other financial intermediaries also play an important economic role, influencing (1) the rate of economic growth through their impact on the level of saving and the allocation of financing and (2) the working out of efforts by the Federal Reserve to stabilize the economy.

In this chapter we shall be concentrating on institutions that cater to the individual saver, that is, that issue obligations commonly held by households for liquidity, precautionary, and long-term income purposes. Some of these institutions we call *depository intermediaries*, since they issue deposit or depositlike claims, held by households mainly for liquidity or precautionary purposes. Most obligations of these institutions are payable on demand or on short notice, or mature within a comparatively short time. Moreover, these obligations are not generally purchased by households at a highly predictable rate. Depository intermediaries, therefore, need to maintain a more liquid asset structure than do the so-called *contractual intermediaries*, the second category, which have patterns of cash inflow and outflow that can be forecast fairly accurately.

The third category of savings institutions, *investment companies*, shares certain "family resemblances" with the other two; but it is easily distinguished from them in that obligations of institutions in this category (1) are generally in the form of equity and long-term debt and (2) are not typically issued or incurred as part of a contractual arrangement in connection with which other services are provided.

As we focus on each individual class of intermediaries, we naturally shall be stressing ways in which that class differs from the others. At the same time, however, we shall be taking note of similarities among the classes, emphasizing a point made earlier, in chapter 3, that intermediaries are gradually becoming less distinctive as each attempts, whenever feasible, to penetrate markets of others—markets for services, claims, and sources of financing.

The relative size and growth since 1945 of the major and most of the minor intermediary classes can be seen in Table 8.1. We should refer to this table as each financial intermediary is discussed.

TABLE 8.1
Total Assets of Financial Intermediaries
(year-end figures, in $billions)

Intermediary	1945	1955	1960	1965	1970	1973*
Commercial banks	$160.3	$210.7	$257.6	$377.3	$576.2	$806.4
Depository savings Intermediaries:						
Mutual savings banks	17.0	31.3	40.6	58.2	79.0	106.6
Savings and loan associations	8.7	37.7	71.5	129.6	176.2	272.4
Credit unions	0.4	2.7	5.7	10.6	17.9	28.6
Contractual savings Intermediaries:						
Life insurance companies	44.8	90.4	119.6	158.9	207.3	252.1
Private pension funds	2.8	18.3	38.2	73.6	110.8	131.5
State and local pension funds	2.6	10.8	19.6	33.2	57.7	80.2
Investment companies	1.3	7.8	17.0	35.2	47.6	46.5
Finance companies	4.3	18.3	26.9	44.8	62.5	88.3
Total	$242.2	$428.0	$596.7	$921.4	$1,335.1	$1,812.6

Source: United States League of Savings Associations, *'74 Savings and Loan Factbook* (United States League of Savings Associations: 1974) p. 53. See this reference for primary data sources.
* Preliminary.

The Depository Savings Intermediaries

Table 8.2 summarizes the balance sheets of the three classes of depository savings intermediaries. In our discussion we shall have occasion to refer to the distinctive features of each of the classes, as brought out in this table.

Mutual Savings Banks

Small in number—just under five hundred—in comparison with other depository intermediaries, mutual savings banks (MSB's) are far

TABLE 8.2
Financial Assets and Liabilities of Depository Savings Intermediaries, December 31, 1973
(in $billions)

Item	Savings and Loan Associations		Mutual Savings Banks		Credit Unions	
	Amount	Per Cent	Amount	Per Cent	Amount	Per Cent
Assets						
Demand deposits and currency	$ 3.4	1.2	$ 1.2	1.1	$ 1.0	4.1
Time deposits			0.8	0.7	0.4	1.6
Corporate equities			4.0	3.8		
U.S. government securities	22.8	8.4	7.1	6.7	2.6	10.6
State & local government obligations			0.9	0.8		
Corporate & foreign bonds			13.1	12.3		
Home mortgages (net)	188.1	69.0	44.2	41.5	1.0	4.1
Other mortgages	44.1	16.2	29.0	27.2		
Consumer credit	2.6	1.0	1.7	1.6	19.6	79.6
Other loans			2.1	2.0		
Misc. financial assets	11.5	4.2	2.5	2.3		
Total	$272.4	100.0	$106.6	100.0	$24.6	100.0
Liabilities						
Time & savings accounts	$227.3	83.4	$ 96.3	90.4	$24.6	100.0
Other debt obligations	22.0	8.1				
Misc. liabilities	6.0	2.2	2.6	2.4		
Total	$255.3	93.7	$ 98.9	92.8	$24.6	100.0

Source: *Federal Reserve Bulletin*, October 1974, p. A59.25.

larger in average size than any other type. At the end of 1972, the average amount of assets held by an individual MSB was $207.0 million, in comparison with figures of $51.5 million and $44.7 million for commercial banks and savings and loan associations respectively. Over two-thirds of the savings banks operate at least one branch, and the number of branches on December 31, 1972 was 1,354, nearly triple the number of home offices.[1]

ASSET STRUCTURE As we might expect, the asset-mix of MSB's reflects the fact that they require far less liquidity than do commercial banks, primarily because their obligations are much less volatile, being made up almost entirely of savings deposits that turn over very slowly. For the years 1964–68, annual turnover of MSB deposits, that is, the ratio of the year's withdrawals to the average deposit level over the year, ranged from .26 to .30 and averaged .269. In contrast, the turnover rate of demand deposits in 226 urban areas outside leading financial centers over the same period varied between 29.2 and 36.6 times a year, averaging 33.0, or over 120 *times* greater! Providing additional liquidity for some of these institutions are the Savings Bank Trust Company and the Mutual Savings Central Fund, Inc., of New York and Massachusetts, respectively, which perform a number of services for the savings banks in these states, including loans for those savings banks experiencing unusual and large withdrawal demands. Furthermore, because the state usually imposes a ceiling on the size of an individual deposit, there is no likelihood that an individual depositor or small number of depositors could cause a crisis by demanding that the bank "buy back" his (their) deposit for cash.

Safety receives high priority in asset holding—a practice that has paid off in a remarkable survival record. To make sure that the savings banks behave themselves in their selection of assets, most MSB's are obliged to choose most or all of their earning-assets from a *legal list* provided by the state regulatory authority, with ceilings, expressed as per cent of assets or liabilities, on each class of assets held. While the concept of a legal list smacks of a "father knows best" attitude, in practice the area of discretion generally has been broad enough, and the lists updated often enough, that restrictions have seldom hampered the mutuals severely. Also, the recent tendency has been to broaden the legal investment powers of MSB's both by extending the list of permissible categories and, in some states, by granting permission to acquire some assets, up to a given per cent of assets or liabilities, that are not on the list.[2]

[1] Unless otherwise indicated, figures in this section are taken from the National Association of Mutual Savings Banks, *1973 National Fact Book: Mutual Savings Banking* (New York: 1973), passim.

[2] National Association of Mutual Savings Banks, *Mutual Savings Banking: Basic Characteristics and Role in the National Economy* (Englewood Cliffs, N.J.: Prentice-Hall, 1962), pp. 103–7.

In practice, MSB's tend to favor local mortgage loans as an earning asset since they combine favorable yield (and, after all, MSB's must compete with other depository intermediaries) with an acceptable level of safety under most circumstances. The record shows that they have almost always concentrated heavily on home mortgages, except for unusual periods such as the Great Depression of the 1930s and World War II.

In the early decades of this century, they also had large holdings of corporate and municipal securities. However, the importance to MSB's of these two classes of claims has declined relative to that of home mortgage loans, particularly because of these factors:

1. The trend toward direct placement of corporate securities (see chapter 11) has meant relatively fewer suitable corporate securities available to MSB's, and at less attractive yields.
2. The rise of Federal personal and corporate income tax rates caused prices of municipal securities to rise (yields to fall) relative to those of other securities because of their tax-exempt status. Since mutual savings banks were not subject to income taxation until 1951, the relatively low yields were most unattractive; and the savings banks gradually liquidated municipals. Although now subject to income taxation to some extent, these banks still have little incentive to buy municipals for reasons of yield, but they sometimes purchase bonds issued by their particular city or state for "community service" or related reasons.
3. Strong demand for housing financing, plus permission granted (as of the 1950s) to purchase out-of-state mortgages, led MSB's, particularly those in areas with slow housing demand, to purchase mortgage loan contracts originating in the fast-growing regions of the nation, especially the Pacific and Southwestern areas.

SOURCES OF FINANCING   Deposits constitute over 90 per cent of mutual savings banks' financing sources, with "surplus and undivided profits" making up nearly all the rest. Most of the deposit volume is in the form of ordinary passbook savings accounts, but MSB's have sought to compete with other financial intermediaries by offering a variety of special forms of deposits, including savings certificates.

In 1972 a revolutionary new form of deposit was authorized in two states and shows signs of spreading. This is the so-called NOW (negotiable order of withdrawal) account, which permits the depositor to make payments by writing *negotiable orders of withdrawal* (in effect, checks) against his interest-bearing savings account. Since the privilege of offering these accounts is denied to other types of financial intermediaries, MSB's understandably are intrigued with the potentialities of this device, and lobbies for banks and savings and loan associations are working frantically to have this device outlawed—or, at least, authorized for them, too.

OTHER ACTIVITIES OF MUTUAL SAVINGS BANKS   Savings bank life insurance, although permitted in only three states, is a rapidly growing service of mutual savings banking in those states. At the end of 1972 over $5 billion of savings bank life insurance was in force, a figure four times the 1960 total. A mutual fund serving only depositors in participating MSB's began operations in 1969 and is now available through over two hundred savings banks—further evidence of the trend toward expansion in services offered by the savings banks.

Savings and Loan Associations[3]

True financial "specialty shops," savings and loan associations (S&L's)[4] exist to provide housing credit. Their main business is still financing the purchase of homes by granting credit secured by a mortgage against the property, although they are slowly moving in the direction of financing certain other types of expenditures as well.

STRUCTURE OF THE SAVINGS AND LOAN INDUSTRY   From Table 8.3 we can see that about one-third of the S&L's are Federally chartered, the rest being state-chartered. The Federal S&L's account for somewhat over half of the total S&L assets, however. Most associations, accounting for all but 3 per cent of S&L assets, participate in the deposit-insurance program of the *Federal Savings and Loan Insurance Corporation* (FSLIC), which insures deposits to a maximum of $40,000 per account. Strangely, associations need not participate in the FSLIC program in order to qualify for membership in the Federal Home Loan Bank System (FHLBS), the "central bank" of the S&L industry (see the next section).

Organizationally, most S&L's are mutual in form; however, stock associations are strong in several states, notably California, and account for about one-fifth of total association assets.

One characteristic that S&L's share with commercial banks and mutual savings banks is a decline in the number of firms and a rise in the number of total offices, due to branching. The 5,243 associations collectively had a total of 7,100 branches as of the end of 1973, more than triple the number of branches in 1962. Actually, only about one-third of the associations have branches, a far smaller fraction than either mutual

---

[3] The annual *Savings and Loan Factbook*, issued by the United States Savings and Loan League, Chicago, contains a wealth of information about S&L operations and the legal and competitive environment of the industry. The 1974 *Factbook* was the main source of information for this section.

[4] In some states the term *building and loan association* is more common; and in Massachusetts state-chartered associations are called *cooperative banks*.

TABLE 8.3
Structure of the Savings and Loan Industry, December 31, 1973

A. Number of Associations

Class of Association	Federal	Insured Member	Total	State	Noninsured	Nonmember
Federal	2,039	2,039	2,039			
State insured member		2,123	2,123	2,123		
State noninsured member			149	149	149	
State noninsured nonmember			932	932	932	932
Number	2,039	4,162	4,311	5,243	3,204	1,081	932
Per cent	38.9	79.4	82.2	100.0	61.1	20.6	17.8

B. Assets of Associations (in $billions)

Class of Association	Federal	Insured Member	Total	State	Noninsured	Nonmember
Federal	$152.2	$152.2	$152.2			
State insured member		112.6	112.6	112.6	$112.6		
State noninsured member			1.3	1.3	1.3	$1.3	
State noninsured nonmember			6.3	6.3	6.3	$6.3
Amount	$152.2	$264.8	$266.1	$272.4	$120.1	$7.6	$6.3
Per cent	55.9	97.2	97.7	100.0	44.1	2.8	2.3

Source: Derived from Tables 49, 50, 91, and 92, *1973 Savings and Loan Factbook* (Chicago: United States League of Savings Associations, 1974).

savings banks or commercial banks, reflecting the smaller average size and primarily local nature of their operations.

The merger movement seems to have hit S&L's, too. The number of mergers has risen almost yearly, from 23 in 1960 to 132 in 1971, declining slightly to 124 in 1973.

At the end of 1973 the largest 4.4 per cent of S&L's accounted for 42 per cent of the total assets of the industry. By way of comparison, the largest 3 per cent of commercial banks contain about two-thirds of all system assets, and the "big five" life insurance companies account for 45 per cent of all life insurance assets.

SAVINGS AND LOAN ASSET-MIX Throughout the 1950s about 95 per cent of the total loan portfolio of savings and loans consisted of mortgage loans against one- to four-family homes, but this percentage has dropped gradually to just over 80 per cent. About 30 per cent of all mortgage loans made by associations between 1961 and 1969 and 31 per cent of such loans in 1970–73 were for purposes *other than* the construction and purchase of one- to four-family homes. These loans include

> apartment loans, loans on nonresidential income properties, land development loans and loans on building lots. It also embraces advances to home owners on existing loans, advances for taxes and insurance which have been added to loan balances, and loans made to refinance existing loans.[5]

Since 1964 Federal S&L's have been authorized to make loans to finance a college education. The dollar volume is small, but this represents a rather remarkable departure from the policy of limiting S&L's to housing and other real estate-related lending.

The Housing and Urban Development Act of 1968 added further legal encouragement to a wider range of lending. It permitted Federally chartered associations to make loans up to $5,000 for the "equipping" of real property, including vacation homes, and to make loans to help finance the purchase of mobile homes.

This process of broadening the scope of lending is in line with the generalization made a few pages ago, to the effect that intermediaries are increasing market interpenetration. And, just as commercial banks changed their ideas as to "proper" earning assets under pressure of economic circumstances, so savings and loans can be expected to move into markets for other financial assets whenever their traditional types of earning assets are insufficient in quantity and/or attractiveness.

SOURCES OF FINANCING The main source of financing for S&L's is savings accounts. Until recently these accounts were called *shares*, or *share accounts*, in the mutual savings and loan associations, reflecting

---

[5] United States Savings and Loan League, *'74 Savings and Loan Fact Book*. (Chicago: United States League of Savings and Associations, 1974), p. 83.

the fact that this claim in reality represents ownership and voting rights as well as rights to income. Now, however many states and (since 1969) Federally chartered associations are permitted to call these claims *deposits*.

Until a few years ago, nearly all savings accounts were of the passbook variety, that is, the depositor's additions to, and withdrawals from, his account would be recorded in his passbook (and in the association's records, of course). Recent FHLBS regulations have increased the variety of deposit arrangements that member associations may offer, however; and in 1973 for the first time the nonpassbook deposits, mostly in the form of certificate accounts, exceeded in dollar volume the traditional passbook deposits (53.3 per cent of the total, as of the end of 1973). The main reason for the popularity of these new types is that the Federal Home Loan Bank Board permits higher ceiling interest rates on them.

Although most accounts, by number and volume, are held by households, about 3 per cent of the accounts, 6 per cent of the total volume of savings deposits, were held by business, financial, government, and nonprofit organization depositors as of 1968.

Another source of financing has recently (1973) been authorized to members of the Federal Home Loan Bank System. Member associations may now issue debt securities privately to large investors, such as pension funds and insurance companies. The purpose of this authorization is to reduce the liquidity problem of S&L's as well as to enable them to "bid" for financing by offering a type of financial instrument other than a deposit. It is much too early to determine whether S&L's in any significant numbers will take advantage of this new source.

The turnover rate of deposits at savings and loans during the 1964–68 period was 31 per cent annually,[6] very close to that of mutual savings banks. Therefore, S&L's need not keep substantial amounts of liquid assets in relation to shares. Besides, most associations have a supplementary source of liquidity: the Federal Home Loan Bank System (FHLBS).

The Federal Home Loan Bank System

The FHLBS is organized along the lines of the Federal Reserve System—a central board and twelve regional banks—and relations between the savings and loan associations and the FHLBS resemble those between the member banks and the Federal Reserve System. All Federally chartered associations must belong, state-chartered associations may belong, to the FHLBS. Advantages of membership are compelling for institutions of any size, and costs are reasonable. As a result, about 80 per cent of all associations have joined; but they account for 98 per cent of all savings and loan assets.

---

[6] *National Fact Book: Mutual Savings Banking*, 1969, p. 15.

Undoubtedly the chief advantage of membership is access to the credit facilities of the regional Federal Home Loan Bank. In contrast to the "tradition against borrowing," which deters many commercial banks from borrowing from the Federal Reserve, S&L's borrow rather freely. The maturities, too, differ considerably from those available to member-bank borrowers from the Federal Reserve: the FHLBS will make advances with maturities as long as ten years to member associations, although most run for less than a year.

The Home Loan Banks, in turn, obtain the bulk of their financing through the issuance of "consolidated obligations," ranging in maturity from one year to ten years, which are held by a wide variety of institutional investors. Thus the FHLBS is an "intermediaries' intermediary," acquiring claims against local associations, the nondeposit debt obligations of which would have no standing at all in the capital markets, and issuing its own obligations, which, by virtue of the status of the issuer and their ease of resale, are readily accepted in the capital markets.

In exchange for the availability of this liquidity source, member associations must subscribe to stock in their regional Federal Home Loan Bank and adhere to the reserve requirements and certain other standards imposed by the board. Such is the dynamics of government regulation that these stipulations are gradually becoming more detailed and specific. The borrowing privilege is increasingly granted or withheld on the basis of whether the institution applying for an advance or extension has been a "good boy"—has adhered to FHLB Board directives in its lending policies. And the board has the authority to impose minimum reserve requirements for member associations, not merely to "suggest," as was the case prior to 1966.

Credit Unions

From a strictly economic standpoint, the resemblance of the credit union to the other depository intermediaries is strong: like the others, the credit union is financed chiefly by issuing its own liquid claims ("shares") to household savers, it is nonprofit in form, and it purchases claims against (makes loans to) households. But unlike the others, most of these loan-claims are small loans for the purpose of purchasing consumer durables; and loans may be granted only to members, that is, people sharing in the particular "common bond" on which the credit union is based and having purchased one or more shares in the union. These membership shares, in turn, are almost the sole source of credit union financing.

True believers tend to stress the credit union ideology of service and mutuality as reasons for the rapid growth of this type of intermediary, a claim impossible to assess quantitatively. Other contributing factors, though, have been subsidies in kind by sponsors and members (labor and office space chiefly); exemption from income taxation; resultant favorable rates charged to borrowers and paid to savers; and other financial services to members, such as counseling.

Each credit union is separately organized and financed and is chartered and supervised by the National Credit Union Administration or a state agency, depending on whether the union is or is not a Federal Credit Union; but there are various links among them. The local unions are members of their state league, and at the peak is CUNA International,[7] which is an association of *leagues* of credit unions, with affiliated leagues in seventy countries as of 1966. Through their leagues, many credit unions have set up central funds, to which the members contribute, to provide emergency liquidity. There is also a certain amount of "interlending" whereby surplus credit unions make loans to those unions wherein saving falls short of loan demand.

The Contractual Savings Intermediaries

Like the depository intermediaries just discussed, the contractual intermediaries issue claims to (are financed by) households, primarily. The major difference between institutions in these two categories, so far as their obligations are concerned, is in the *form* of obligation: deposits versus claims that "ripen" only when a specified event happens to the claimholder, such as death, sixty-fifth birthday, or disability.

Major classes of contractual intermediaries are life insurance companies, property and liability insurance companies, and pension funds. First we shall briefly note their common features; then we shall focus on each of these classes individually.

There is nothing on the asset side of these intermediaries' balance sheets that will cause us trouble; most of the assets are familiar financial claims of various kinds—debt and, to a far lesser extent, equities. The other side, however, is going to require explanation because of some peculiarities that arise out of the nature of the contract between intermediary and claim holder.

To illustrate: when a person "buys" a life insurance policy for $20,000, payable to his wife upon his death, sealing the contract by paying his first premium, how should the insurance company record this transaction on its balance sheet? "Cash" has increased, obviously; but what about the corresponding liability entry? In a sense, the insurance company "owes" the policyholder $20,000, an obligation that will fall due when the policyholder dies. But it would be foolish to require the company to record the entire face amount of the policy as an obligation *now*. Every insurance company would be hopelessly insolvent were this practice to be followed; total assets of all life insurance companies at the end of 1972 amounted to $239.7 billion—a sizable amount, surely—but total

---

[7] The acronym CUNA originally stood for Credit Union National Association.

life insurance in force was $1.6 trillion.[8] And other contractual intermediaries are in a similar position with respect to the relation between assets and future liabilities.

How, then, can these intermediaries record their liabilities to claim holders in some meaningful way? The solution is based on the fact that, although the intermediary cannot predict the "due date" of each individual liability item, it can predict reasonably accurately the total amount that will fall due to *all* claim holders in a particular class (such as persons of the same age and sex, or buildings having the same type of construction) during a particular period of time. The intermediary then is able to set the "price" of each kind of contractual arrangement so that the receipts from these contracts, plus other income, will be sufficient to cover outpayments based on claims under the contracts, plus other expenditures, leaving at least a "reasonable" return for the owners. Since receipts are scheduled to be in advance of expected claims payments (sometimes many years in advance), the intermediary is able to accumulate substantial amounts of assets—which are the major source of "other income."

Details differ by intermediary and by "program," so we shall not follow this topic any further here. The point is, though, that the intermediary dare not consider these accumulations of earning assets as adding to its net worth because it is anticipated that both the income from these assets and, under certain circumstances, the proceeds from the disposition of the assets themselves will be called upon to meet the claims against the intermediary. Of course, we would be able to observe this process completely only in the case of a company in voluntary liquidation.

Life Insurance Companies

It may seem strange to refer to life insurance companies as *savings* intermediaries because for many policyholders the "savings" element is quite incidental to their major purpose in taking out an insurance policy; namely, to provide an income and asset cushion to the beneficiary in case of the early death or disability of the holder. Nevertheless, the life insurance company is truly a savings intermediary in a number of respects. First, many policies contain a provision whereby the holder, at age sixty-five (or whatever the designated age) will receive a regular monthly payment until death; so in these kinds of policies the savings element is clear. Second, policyholders, especially holders of large-sized policies, are often aware of the fact that (with some exceptions) policies feature a "loan value," indicating the amount they can borrow from the company. Not only is this a right, not subject to company discretion, but, moreover, the policyholders are not obligated to repay the loan; any

---

[8] *Life Insurance Fact Book, 1973* (New York: Institute of Life Insurance, 1974), pp. 25, 71.

unpaid loan is simply offset against the policy amount, when the claim "ripens." Therefore, except for the fact that the policyholder pays interest at a modest rate on the amount outstanding, a policy loan is more like a withdrawal from a savings account than an ordinary loan. Finally, most of the liabilities of the insurance company are "policy reserves," which belong, in a sense, to the policyholder, as we shall see in a few lines.

The life insurance industry is characterized by large firms, in terms of total assets, with an unusually high degree of concentration. As of 1965 the ten biggest life firms held 60 per cent of the industry's total assets; the top hundred, 95 per cent.[9] There are both mutual and stock life insurance companies. Although the latter far outnumber the former, the mutuals tend to be the larger. In fact, as of the end of 1970, mutuals accounted for about 8 per cent of the number of companies but held about two-thirds of all life company assets.[10]

There is an almost fantastic variety of life insurance arrangements. The number of permutations and combinations of face amounts of policy, conditions under which benefits will be paid, rights to earnings of the company, conditions entitling the policyholder to change the amount of insurance or type of policy, conditions under which the company or holder may terminate the contract, and so on, is so large and the jargon of insurance so extensive that we must limit ourselves to the big picture. This will involve an explanation of the manner in which life insurance companies have been able to accumulate vast quantities of assets, an inquiry into determinants of their portfolio policies, and a discussion of the relations between the life insurance industry and the rest of the financial system.

First, then, we must ascertain why the receipts of life insurance companies have exceeded by far their actual expenditures so that they have managed to accumulate huge stores of financial and other assets. Perhaps we can best get to the answer by means of an example. Let us say that you take out a life insurance policy at age twenty-two, calling for a $120 annual premium. The chances that the company will have to pay on that policy during the first year are about one in 500,[11] that is, if the company insures 10,000 men aged twenty-two that year, nineteen will die during that year, or fewer than 0.2 per cent. Thirty years later 8,800 of the original 10,000 will still be around. During the next (or thirty-first) year, 876 of the 8,800 will die—about 10 per cent. Yet the yearly premium is still $120! Obviously it "costs" the insurance company much more per person to insure these people when they are fifty-two year-olds than it did when they were twenty-two. How can the company afford it?

The answer lies in the fact that the premiums in any specified early

---

[9] Raymond W. Goldsmith, *Financial Institutions* (New York: Random House, 1968), p. 66.
[10] *Life Insurance Fact Book, 1973*, pp. 68–90
[11] These and the following figures in this illustration are based on the Commissioners 1958 Standard Ordinary Mortality Table, as printed in *Life Insurance Fact Book, 1973*, pp. 110–11.

year of the policy are far greater than the benefit payments to the surviving beneficiaries plus a pro rata share of all the other costs of running the company. The bulk of this excess in payments is placed in earning-assets. However, the corresponding liabilities-side entry is not in the net worth category but is a liability account, "policy reserves," which the Institute of Life Insurance defines as

> the amounts than an insurance company allocates specifically for the fulfillment of its policy obligations. Reserves are so calculated that, together with future premiums and interest earnings, they will enable the company to pay all future claims.[12]

Life insurance companies are becoming involved in an increasing number of other market areas in response to income opportunities and, in some cases, more permissive legislation. To illustrate, more companies are offering mutual fund shares (see the "Investment Companies" section), health and accident insurance, group pensions, and variable annuities (contracts that provide for future income, with the amount dependent on the market value of securities in which the holder's payments have been invested by the company).

PORTFOLIO POLICY AND MANAGEMENT Asset-structure decisions by the portfolio managers of life insurance companies are influenced, of course, by the same factors that any portfolio manager must consider: liquidity, safety, and earnings, plus regulations of such government agencies as have jurisdiction. However, the peculiar characteristics of the industry and its environment have influenced the manner in which these determinants have worked themselves out. (See Table 8.4).

The long-term nature of life insurance arrangements, coupled with the high degree of predictability of the "maturity" of the obligations (not individually but in total), renders the liquidity problem rather minor as compared to that of commercial banks and even depository savings institutions. Some liquid assets must be held because it is impossible to match cash inflows with outflows exactly. Other than that, life companies can hold most of their assets in long-term form, spacing their maturities so that, for the most part, unexpectedly large cash outflows relative to "normal" inflows can be handled simply by not reinvesting money realized from the redemption of maturing assets.

Unexpected demands for cash can arise, though, because of two characteristics of the usual insurance contract: (1) the policyholder has the right to borrow from the company an amount based on his policy reserve, and (2) the policyholder may terminate his insurance contract at any time. Although this amount in the aggregate does not fluctuate widely, these two sources of instability can hit individual companies hard.

[12] *Life Insurance Fact Book, 1973*, p. 125.

TABLE 8.4
Financial Assets and Liabilities of Life Insurance Companies, December 31, 1973

Item	Amount (in $billions)	Per Cent
Financial assets		
Demand deposits and currency	$ 2.1	0.9
Corporate shares	25.9	10.6
U.S. government securities	4.4	1.8
State and local government securities	3.4	1.4
Corporate and foreign bonds	92.5	37.8
Home mortgages	22.0	9.0
Other mortgages	59.2	24.2
Policy loans	20.2	8.2
Other loans	3.0	1.2
Miscellaneous assets	12.0	4.9
Total	$244.6	100.0
Liabilities		
Life insurance reserves	$142.7	58.3
Pension fund reserves	57.5	23.5
Taxes payable	0.8	0.3
Miscellaneous liabilities	30.5	12.5
Total	$231.5	94.6

Source: *Federal Reserve Bulletin,* October 1974, p. A59.26.

In selecting long-term assets, the companies obviously must pay careful attention to safety needs, both from the policyholder's standpoint and from the standpoint of their own long-term survival drive. State regulatory authorities reinforce the natural caution of life companies: first, by specifying that the total amount in certain asset categories (common stock, for example) may not exceed a given per cent of the total assets; and, second, by laying down quality standards.

Since nearly all the insurers' liabilities are in fixed-dollar amounts, it is logical that the bulk of their assets be debt securities—which they are. About 10 per cent of life insurance company assets are in common stock, with another 3 per cent in real estate.

Life insurance companies, as business firms, are under continual pressure for earnings on assets. This need is reflected in the ever-changing composition of their asset portfolios as circumstances have changed. A few quick illustrations: railroad bonds, once very big in life company portfolios (30 per cent in 1917), are now an insignificant fraction of total assets. United States government bonds, 46 per cent of total life company assets in 1945, are below 2 per cent today. And mortgage investments of these companies have shifted toward income-producing properties: commercial buildings and multifamily housing.

Another response by life companies to income needs is financial innovations. Since World War II these companies have not only financed but also constructed and actively managed large-scale housing projects. They have also been active in so-called *purchase-lease-back* arrangements whereby an office building or shopping center, for example, is purchased by the insurance company and leased back to the former owner on a long-term basis. Perhaps the most significant recent innovation has been the *direct, or private, placement* of entire bond issues with individual insurance companies. Through this arrangement, by "eliminating the middleman" and other costs of a public issue, the borrower is able to get long-term credit more cheaply and the insurance company simultaneously gains a higher return. Also, terms can be "tailored" to the needs of the two parties, whereas a public issue often has to embody customer terms with which investors are familiar. Liberalization of state regulations has been an important enabling factor.

In summary, the present asset structure, as well as past and future changes therein, can be explained largely as the response of the life insurance companies to changes in the economic and legal environment, given their needs for liquidity, safety, and earnings, Thus, liquid asset holdings are minimal, reflecting their fairly predictable cash flows; and most of the assets are presently in mortgages and high-grade corporate bonds, providing reasonably good, safe yields.

RELATION TO THE FINANCIAL SYSTEM   Life insurance companies are connected to the rest of the financial system in a number of ways: competitively with some parts, cooperatively with others.

Life companies must compete both in the sale of their services and in the purchase of assets. Although these firms are dominant in the provision of life insurance, about 5 per cent of such insurance is provided by other sources, mainly the Veterans' Administration and fraternal organizations, with mutual savings banks a small but fast-growing supplier. In the provision of pension plans (to be discussed presently), life companies are an important but minority segment, most pension reserves being managed by bank trust departments or independent trustees.

As an outlet for long-term savings, life insurance companies compete with many kinds of firms: the depository intermediaries and investment companies among intermediaries, plus the direct issuers of securities—governments at all levels and business corporations. Life companies have begun pushing into other markets, too. They play a large role in the health insurance field, particularly group health plans; and very recently have begun to move into the mutual fund field, as we noted above.

In the acquisition of assets we can observe the effects of competition on life insurance company behavior. For example, one reason for their shift toward multifamily residential and commercial mortgages was the increased competition of specialized lenders, notably savings and loans, for one- to four-family housing mortgages. And the trend toward private placements reflects "the growing competition of other institutional investors (first the private pension funds and more recently those administered by local governments) for available investment outlets."[13] But even direct placements involve growing competition with pension funds. And then there is the strange case of "involuntary competition" in which these companies are forced to compete with other lenders for consumer and business loans, often against their will. We refer, of course, to policy loans. As noted earlier, because these loans carry fairly low rates (generally 5 to 7 per cent) and are literally "on tap" to the policyholders, they increase substantially in periods of tight money, thus forcing life companies to keep larger amounts of assets in this low-yield form at the very time yields on other suitable financial assets—bonds and mortgages—are rising.

Several kinds of cooperative relations merit comment. Most obvious is the role of banks as depository for the cash balances of insurance companies and as means of rapid regional transfer of funds. Banks also participate with insurance companies in certain term loan arrangements in which the bank will take installment notes covering the first five or ten years of a loan, and the insurance company the balance, which could extend another five to fifteen years.

Life insurance firms and mortgage bankers (see below) often maintain a cooperative arrangement whereby the latter accumulate batches of mortgages, sell them to the insurance company, and then service the mortgages for the insurance company. With their local-market connections and small resources, mortgage bankers thus neatly complement life insurance companies, which possess huge amounts of resources but lack machinery for maintaining continuous contact with local mortgage markets.

Property and Liability Insurance Companies

Although it would have been convenient for all concerned to incorporate property and liability insurance companies in our discussion of life insurance, we would have found that the differences are simply too great. For one thing, the insurance contract in the fire and casualty area is for a relatively brief time period—one to five years generally—rather than for life or until a (distant) birthday. Related to this difference, no element of saving is involved in these contracts. Also, the policyholder is not assured that he or his survivors will eventually collect, as would be the case in a life policy. From the company's standpoint, the timing and amount of policy claims are far less predictable than they are for life insurance companies. Finally, and not unexpectedly in view of these differences, details of government regulation differ as between these two major categories of insurance companies.

[13] Daniel Brill, "The Role of Financial Intermediaries in U.S. Capital Markets," *Federal Reserve Bulletin,* January 1967, pp. 23–24.

Property and liability insurance companies (we shall refer to them as P&L companies from this point) cover a large variety of risks, including automobile liability, fire, burglary and theft, workmen's compensation, marine, crop and hail, and others. Most companies are mutual in organization, but stock companies are far larger in size, on the average; comprising only one-fifth of the number, the stock companies hold about three-fourths of the industry's assets.[14]

Before looking into the problems of asset-mix, as seen by the P&L companies, we should inquire into the *sources* of these assets. For stock companies, initial financing is, of course, provided by the owners. A substantial fraction, about one-quarter of the total assets held by P&L companies, arises from the fact that premiums are paid in advance. Another quarter, claim reserves, is the estimated value of claims already pending against the companies plus the estimated amount of claims not yet reported. Most of the rest, about two-fifths of the total is classified as policyholders' surplus and represents earnings retained by the firms as a cushion against unusually large claims of policyholders.

PORTFOLIO POLICY AND MANAGEMENT The asset structure of the industry as of December 31, 1973 is given in Table 8.5. In the ensuing paragraphs we look at some of the determinants of this pattern. In interpreting this table, we must bear in mind that totals often obscure differences—an important point in this industry, which is quite heterogeneous in size of firms, organization forms, types and grades of risks assumed, and loss experience.

Liquidity is a rather more pressing consideration for P&L companies than for life insurance firms because of the nature of their risks. Take fires, for example. Not only are the amount and timing of fire damage impossible to predict accurately but also the regional incidence and, of crucial importance, the incidence by insurer. A few excerpts from the 1966 yearbook *Insurance Facts* are enlightening in this regard:

> The property and liability insurance business in 1965 weathered some of the most formidable adversities in its history. . . . Extraordinary strains were placed on the resources of the business by a bumper crop of disasters, both natural and manmade, and by sharp increases in automobile accident claims and fire losses.
>
> Topping the list was Hurricane Betsy, which became history's costliest insurance catastrophe. . . . The riots in the Watts area of Los Angeles [were costly]. . . . In all, 13 major catastrophes ($1 million or more of insured loss) were recorded in 1965.[15]

The passage from which this quotation is taken adds still other woes, including record high fire losses, sharp increase in crime, the tenth

---

[14] Goldsmith, *Financial Institutions*, p. 112.
[15] *Insurance Facts, 1966* (New York: Insurance Information Institute, 1967), p. 7.

TABLE 8.5
Financial Assets and Liabilities of
Non-Life Insurance Companies, December 31, 1973

Item	Amount (in $billions)	Per Cent
Financial Assets		
Demand deposits and currency	$ 1.5	2.2
Corporate shares	19.6	28.5
U.S. government securities	3.4	4.9
State and local obligations	30.4	44.2
Corporate bonds	7.2	10.5
Other assets	6.7	9.7
Total	$68.8	100.0
Liabilities		
Policy payables	$45.8	66.6
Taxes payable	0.3	0.4
Total	$46.1	67.0

Source: Federal Reserve Bulletin, October 1974, p. A59.26.

straight year of underwriting losses on auto insurance, and unusually heavy airline losses.[16]

Liquidity needs are reflected in a higher cash-to-assets ratio and shorter maturities on securities held than is the case for life companies. Maturities are spaced, too, to provide a regular flow of cash for meeting claims, if necessary, but preferably to be reinvested.

Safety considerations (plus prodding by state insurance regulatory agencies in some cases) induce P&L companies to concentrate their portfolios in relatively low-risk securities. Nearly half the total assets are in government bonds: Federal, state, and local. Even their stock holdings lean toward the conservative side, being heavy in utilities, insurance companies, and banks. Safety needs are also met in part through the practice of *reinsurance,* a device that enables risks to be split among several insurance companies.

Earnings, however, are by no means a minor factor in portfolio constructions. The heavy concentration in municipal securities, for instance, is encouraged by their tax-exempt status—an important factor, since it is the after-tax yield that eventually matters.[17] Long-term yield is also the main reason for the substantial holdings of common stock. Legislation is far more permissive, in this regard, than for life companies, which are severely limited in their holdings of common stock.

---

[16] Ibid., p. 8.
[17] Those companies incurring losses, however, are induced to switch out of municipals into common stock, since the tax-exempt status of the former is obviously of no value to them!

RELATION TO THE FINANCIAL SYSTEM Although as an industry P&L insurance is a middleweight among intermediaries, ranking well ahead of credit unions, finance companies, and investment companies, the only category of financial assets in which these companies are a significant market factor is state and local bonds. P&L companies compete with high-income individuals and with commercial banks on the demand side of the markets for these securities, since all three of these classes of economic units are subject to Federal income taxation at potentially high marginal rates. The only important cooperative relation with other parts of the financial system is as demand-deposit holder at commercial banks.

Pension Funds

There are several distinguishing characteristics of pension funds. First, in contrast to all the other intermediaries studied, a pension fund is not a firm but is a collection of assets under separate administration. Contributions to, and withdrawals from, a fund are made in accordance with an agreement between employer (or employers) and a designated group of, or all, employees. Second, participation is generally not voluntary but is a condition of employment. Third, the financial aspects of these funds are by no means the only, or even necessarily the most, important consideration since pensions are part of the total employer-employee relationship, often subject to collective bargaining. Finally, pension funds necessarily involve at least three parties—employer, employees, trustee—plus possibly one or more unions or an association of employers.

Pension funds have grown at a phenomenal rate since World War II because of (1) increased coverage, (2) rising scales of benefits and contributions, and (3) a rather low ratio of pensioners to covered workers (a characteristic of "young" plans). Unions have seized upon pensions as a desirable form of compensation. Indeed, there has been a radical shift in general attitudes toward pensions from regarding them as a form of reward (along with the gold watch) for long service to treating them as a type of deferred compensation.[18]

INVESTMENT POLICIES: PRIVATE FUNDS Most private funds are actually managed by the trust departments of commercial banks; others, by mutual funds and investment advisers; still others, by salaried trustees whose job it is to manage a particular pension fund.[19] In any case, the employers are usually the dominant influence in determining investment policy—hardly surprising, since employers are the major contributors, and often the sole contributors, to the funds!

---

[18] William M. Anderson, "Group Accumulation through Equities for Pensions," *Journal of Finance*, XVII (May 1962), p. 196.

[19] Bear in mind that we are discussing only *noninsured* funds here. The figures given exclude the insured plans, assets and reserves of which are included in the life insurance sector.

Liquidity needs for these funds are minimal, but safety and earnings needs are crucial; so their managers concentrate on the higher-yielding long-term assets with low speculative content. One suitable type of asset, therefore, is corporation bonds (see Table 8.6). Like life insurance companies, the larger funds have been active in direct placement of corporate bond issues.

These funds, however, have one need that is not a pressing one for most other intermediaries: price-level protection.

> Since pension benefits are often tied to salary levels near the date of retirement, the potential liabilities of these funds are very much a function of price level. Higher price levels would increase the liability of these funds greatly.[20]

Therefore, common stock also occupies a very important position in pension fund portfolios, accounting for nearly two-thirds of their total financial assets at year-end 1973.

Public regulation is unimportant as a portfolio determinant. Apart from the common-law requirement applicable to any trustee of property (that he exercise ordinary prudence), there are no legal limitations on management discretion. The Federal government exerts an influence in one respect, however. The tax-exempt status of the earnings of these funds makes state and local securities relatively unattractive to them.

INVESTMENT POLICIES: STATE AND LOCAL GOVERNMENT PENSION FUNDS[21] There are over two thousand state and local pension funds, with roughly 90 per cent of their total assets concentrated in the largest

TABLE 8.6
Financial Assets of Private Pension Funds,
December 31, 1973

Item	Amount (in $billions)	Per Cent
Demand deposits and currency	$ 2.3	1.7
Corporate shares	89.2	66.2
U.S. government securities	4.3	3.2
Corporate bonds	29.8	22.4
Home mortgages	2.7	2.0
Miscellaneous assets	4.9	4.5
Total	$133.3	100.0

Source: Federal Reserve Bulletin, October 1974, p. A59.26.

[20] Roland I. Robinson, *Money and Capital Markets* (New York: McGraw-Hill Book Co., 1964), p. 49.
[21] This discussion excludes the Federal programs. Virtually all the assets of both the Old Age, Survivors, Disability, and Health and the Federal Civil Service funds are simply invested in U.S. Government securities.

hundred funds.[22] Strict rules imposed on most state and local funds prevent their managers from adopting imaginative and resourceful policies in portfolio construction (Table 8.7). Sometimes these rules have been necessary, as when the trustees are elected officials. However, the trend toward the liberalization of investment rules, already observed in our discussion of a number of other intermediaries, has affected these pension funds too. One result has been a rapid increase in corporate bond holdings relative to the "traditional" government securities. A number of states now allow common stock in their pension fund portfolios, a trend expected to spread in response to the favorable experiences of private pension funds with common stock investment and to pressures for higher pension benefits. Common stock holdings of these funds have risen dramatically in the past few years, from 2.7 per cent of total financial assets at year-end 1961 to 22.8 per cent at year-end 1973.[23]

RELATION TO THE FINANCIAL SYSTEM Because of the size and rapid growth of this sector of the financial system, pension funds have been a dominant factor in several markets for financial assets, notably those for corporate securities, directly competing with insurance companies and investment companies in particular for corporate stock and with insurance companies for corporate bonds.

On the opposite side of the balance sheet, it is apparent that life insurance-managed funds are directly competitive, in a general sense, with the noninsured funds. However, it is doubtful that the average employee considers his equity in pension funds as a substitute for his savings placed in depository institutions.

TABLE 8.7
Financial Assets of State and Local Government
Retirement Funds, December 31, 1973

Item	Amount (in $billions)	Per Cent
Demand deposits and currency	$ 1.0	1.2
Corporate shares	18.6	22.8
U.S. government securities	4.6	5.6
State and local obligations	1.4	1.7
Corporate bonds	49.4	60.5
Mortgages	6.7	8.2
Total	$81.6	100.0

Source: *Federal Reserve Bulletin*, October 1974, p. A59.26.

[22] George W. Cloos, "Pension Funds and Capital Markets," *Business Conditions*, Federal Reserve Bank of Chicago (August 1969), p. 8.
[23] *Federal Reserve Bulletin*, September 1973, Table A, p. 71.26.

Investment Companies

A third category of savings intermediaries comprises the investment companies. Although neither depository nor contractual in nature, investment companies somewhat resemble both of these types, as we shall see.

The collective balance sheet of investment companies has this rather strange property: most of the assets are common stock (see Table 8.8[24]), and almost the entire liabilities side also consists of common stock! An explanation of this characteristic is, at the same time, an explanation of the nature of an investment company: a diversified portfolio of securities, financing for the acquisition and maintenance of which is provided mainly by the issuance of common stock. A minority of investment companies are closed-end, that is, they issue stock just as an ordinary business corporation does (once or occasionally) so that the only way the prospective investor can acquire stock in such a company is by purchasing it from another holder.[25] A present stockholder, however, can acquire additional shares periodically by specifying that his proportionate share of the company's realized capital gains over a given period (usually a year) be reinvested in the company rather than paid in cash. Some closed-end companies issue preferred stock or bonds in addition to common stock for the same reason any corporation does—financial leverage: if the return on its additional investment is expected to exceed the added cost associated with debt or preferred-stock financing, the anticipated earnings per share of the fund's capital stock is thereby increased, although the risk also rises.

An *open-end* investment company, or *mutual fund* in common speech, issues common stock in much the same manner as a mutual

TABLE 8.8
Financial Assets of Open-End Investment Companies, December 31, 1973

Item	Amount (in $billions)	Per Cent
Demand deposits and currency	$ 1.2	2.6
Corporate shares	38.3	82.4
U.S. government securities	1.2	2.6
Corporate bonds	4.2	9.0
Open-market paper	1.6	3.4
Total	$46.5	100.0

Source: *Federal Reserve Bulletin,* October 1974, p. A59.27.

---

[24] This table omits certain classes of investment companies, but the percentages are fairly representative of the industry as a whole.
[25] The machinery through which such a purchase usually takes place will be discussed in chapter 11.

savings bank "issues" deposits, except that the former sells only shares, not simply "dollars' worth." The prospective investor buys shares in the mutual fund, paying a price per share (in addition to the broker's commission) consisting of (1) the per share market value of the fund's present assets net of offsetting liabilities plus (2) typically, a "front-end load," amounting to 8 to 9 per cent of the price. The fund then uses the proceeds (net of salesman's commission and so on) to purchase securities on the market, in accordance with its own announced investment objectives.

The shareholder also has the right to redeem (sell back) his shares, at a price at or near the net asset value per share at the time of redemption. This right gives an appearance of "liquidity" to such shares which, in the opinion of some, has helped to sell mutual funds. However, in the case of a general market decline, the net asset value per share of a mutual fund would decline, too.

Mutuals are by far the largest class of investment companies. In mid-1966 there were 380 mutual funds, which held nearly 80 per cent of all investment company assets. The liabilities of mutuals consist almost exclusively of common shares and related equity accounts.[26]

PORTFOLIO POLICIES Investment companies generally hold small amounts of cash and short-term credit instruments relative to their total assets because their liquidity needs are minimal (Table 8.8). At times they hold substantial liquid assets, however, in anticipation of a decline, or a further decline, in stock prices.

As usual, aggregate figures conceal individual differences in earning-asset portfolio makeup and policy. To illustrate, funds may be classified by portfolio composition as follows:[27]

1. Common-stock funds—predominantly or exclusively common stocks.
2. Balanced funds—common and preferred stocks and bonds, the proportion varying from time to time.
3. Speciality funds.
   (a) Exclusively bonds.
   (b) Exclusively preferred stocks.
   (c) Speculative common stocks.
   (d) Single-industry common stocks.
   (e) Foreign securities.

Funds also differ in their investment objectives. The following types may be distinguished, although differences exist even within categories.[28]

[26] Goldsmith, *Financial Institutions*, p. 114.
[27] Donald P. Jacobs et al., *Financial Institutions*, 5th ed. (Homewood, Ill.: R. D. Irwin, 1972), pp. 294–5.
[28] Ibid.

1. Primarily capital appreciation.
2. Emphasis on income.
3. Moderate income and moderate appreciation.
4. Maintenance of principal value and stable income.
5. Unusually promising long-range opportunities, including perhaps a direct management responsibility.

Specific government regulation aimed at fund portfolios is almost nonexistent. The only Federal statute directly concerned is the Investment Company Act of 1940, the relevant provisions of which have been summarized as follows:

> Any security (mortgages are not securities under the Act) may be purchased provided:
> 1. that the shareholders are informed;
> 2. that the security fits into the fund's stated policy;
> 3. that the fund allocates 75 percent of its assets in such a way that within that 75 percent no more than 5 percent of total assets are in one issue and no more than 10 percent of voting securities in one corporation are held. These restrictions do not count for the remaining 25 percent of assets.[29]

REAL ESTATE INVESTMENT TRUSTS[30]   A new type of intermediary has come upon the financial scene in recent years: the real estate investment trust (or REIT, for short). The REIT resembles an ordinary investment company in several respects: (1) it can qualify for exemption of its earnings from Federal corporate income tax by meeting certain requirements, which are essentially those imposed on investment companies; (2) it must be an *investor* (in real estate and financial instruments related thereto) rather than a producer or seller of physical things; (3) its liabilities side consists mainly of equity, rather than debt.

The appearance and rapid growth of REIT's since 1969 can be explained largely by two factors: (1) the Real Estate Investment Act of 1960, which laid down the "ground rules" for this type of financial intermediary, and (2) the tight-money conditions of the late sixties, which, along with deposit interest-rate ceilings, drastically curtailed the financing available for real estate through conventional channels.

The REIT was attractive in this environment both because it was (and is) not subject to interest-rate limitations and because it provided a means to tap new sources of financing. The possible management fees were appealing, too. A number of insurance companies, financial con-

---

[29] Thomas G. Gies et al., "Portfolio Regulation and Policies of Financial Intermediaries," in Commission on Money and Credit, *Private Financial Institutions* (Englewood Cliffs, N.J.: Prentice-Hall, 1963), p. 204.

[30] See Peter A. Schulkin, "Real Estate Investment Trusts: A New Financial Intermediary," and "Recent Developments in the REIT Industry," *New England Economic Review*, Federal Reserve Bank of Boston (November–December 1970), pp. 2–14, and (September–October 1972), pp. 3–12.

glomerates, mortgage companies (see chapter 9), and large banks sponsor REIT's, as do groups of independent entrepreneurs.

Thus far all or nearly all REIT's have taken the "closed-end" form, recognizing the hazard of offering to redeem shares based on their mostly illiquid assets. REIT's obtain financing mainly through equity issues plus, to a limited extent, commercial paper issues and bank borrowing.

On the asset side, some REIT's own real estate outright; others concentrate on mortgage loans or on construction and development loans. In almost all cases, emphasis is on multifamily and nonresidential real estate lending. (See Table 8.9.)

It is far too early to predict the position of REIT's in the financial system, say, ten years from now. Much depends on (1) the management quality of the REIT's, (2) the defensive reactions of other real-estate lenders and investors, and (3) the regulatory environment of the REIT's and of competitive intermediaries.

RELATIONS WITH THE FINANCIAL SYSTEM On the assets side, investment companies obviously compete with other institutional investors in common stock, notably pension funds and property and liability insurance firms, while REIT's compete with numerous classes of financial intermediaries for nonresidential mortgages. In obtaining financing, their main institutional competitors are the providers of long-term outlets for savings; namely, insurance companies and (especially for the smaller savers) the depository intermediaries.

Many REIT's are partially owned by financial intermediaries, as we have noted, which is one type of complementary relation.[31] And, of course, in common with all other classes of financial intermediaries, investment companies and REIT's hold demand deposits in banks and sometimes obtain short-term financing from them.

TABLE 8.9
Financial Assets of Real Estate Investment Trusts,
December 31, 1973

Item	Amount (in $billions)	Per Cent
Home mortgages	$ 4.1	24.0
Multifamily mortgages	3.7	21.6
Commercial mortgages	7.4	43.3
Miscellaneous assets	1.9	11.1
Total	$17.0	100.0

Source: *Federal Reserve Bulletin*, October 1974, p. A59.27.

[31] The relation of REIT and sponsoring bank appears intrinsically susceptible to conflict-of-interest situations. See Schulkin, "Real Estate Investment Trusts," pp. 11–12, for an impressive list.

KEY CONCEPTS

Mutual savings banks (MSB's)
"Legal list" (for MSB's)
Negotiable order of withdrawal
Savings and loan association (S&L)
Federal Savings and Loan Insurance Corporation (FSLIC)
Credit union
Federal Home Loan Bank System (FHLBS)
"Purchase-lease-back" arrangement
Direct (or private) placement
Property and liability insurance company
Pension fund
Investment company
Mutual fund
Real estate investment trust (REIT)

QUESTIONS FOR REVIEW

1. Compare MSB's, S&L's, and credit unions with respect to (a) asset structure, (b) degree of concentration, (c) geographical dispersion, (d) regulation, (e) sources of financing, and (f) extent of branching.
2. What new developments have appeared in the financing of S&L associations?
3. In what respects is the relation between the FHLBS and member S&L's similar to the relation between the Federal Reserve System and member banks? In what respects different?
4. Why are insurance companies classified as "savings intermediaries"? What characteristics of life insurance contracts enable the companies to accumulate huge quantities of assets?
5. Would you expect life insurance companies to have greater liquidity needs or smaller liquidity needs than property and liability insurance companies? Why? Is this difference reflected in their asset structures?
6. What are the major areas of competition between life insurance companies and other financial intermediaries? between property and liability companies and other intermediaries? between pension funds and other intermediaries? between investment companies and other intermediaries?
7. Why have pension funds experienced such a rapid rate of growth?
8. Do investment companies resemble contractual savings intermediaries or depository savings intermediaries more closely? Explain.

SUGGESTIONS FOR FURTHER READING
SEE END OF CHAPTER 9

The Borrowing Intermediaries
Finance Companies
Small Business Investment Companies
State Development Credit Corporations

Nonintermediary Financial Firms
Market-Contact Services
Portfolio Management and Advice Services
Et Cetera

Intermediation by Nonintermediaries
Interbusiness Financing
Consumer Credit Extended by Business

Summary of Chapters 8 and 9

The Borrowing Intermediaries and Nonintermediary Financial Firms

In this chapter we discuss a number of additional financial institutions grouped into two broad classes: the so-called *borrowing intermediaries* and a variety of *nonintermediary financial firms*. As in the last chapter, our approach will be to describe briefly the particular type of institution—focusing on the nature of its business, as seen particularly in its asset-mix and sources of financing—and to indicate its connections with the rest of the financial system. We also will give brief attention to the intermediation activities of firms that are not ordinarily classified as financial intermediaries.

The Borrowing Intermediaries

Included under the heading of "borrowing intermediaries" are *finance companies, small business investment companies,* and *state development credit corporations*. What these types of intermediaries have in common is the fact that financing activities are directed primarily toward particular classes of borrowers, and their obligations are issued mainly to other financial intermediaries and to business corporations. By way of comparison (although we do not want to push the distinction too far), the intermediaries discussed to this point—particularly commercial banks and the depository and contractual intermediaries—concentrate relatively more attention on finding suitable outlets for the financing generated more or less automatically in the course of their functions as depository (for transactions and savings balances) or as provider of insurance and retirement protection, while the borrowing intermediaries are relatively more concerned with finding the financing to meet the credit demands of their customers.

Finance Companies

In common with a number of other types of intermediaries, finance companies finance both households and business firms. As recently as 1965 finance companies were classified as sales finance, personal finance, and business finance companies, according to whether they specialized, respectively, in installment lending on consumer durables and home repairs, personal cash loans, or loans based on accounts receivable or sales of equipment. However, finance companies have diversified so aggressively into each others' territories that these distinctions are no longer meaningful[1]—another example of the phenomenon of interpenetration noted in chapter 3. Wide differences among individual finance companies remain, though; and we need to keep this in mind as we examine the broad aggregate data on the finance company industry.

Between 1960 and 1970 the number of finance companies declined by over 60 per cent. Primary causes seem to have been (1) mergers, (2) failures, and (3) shifts to other fields, financial or nonfinancial; but it is not possible to rank these causes in order of importance. The degree of concentration in the finance company field is considerable. The largest 4.5 per cent of finance companies (measured by gross receivables holdings) accounted for slightly more than 95 per cent of total gross receivables. This degree of concentration may be largely explained by the fact that the "finance company" label is applied not only to huge diversified firms with branches throughout the nation but also to tiny one-office firms with activities limited to small loans to local households.

PORTFOLIO COMPOSITION   As shown in Table 9.1, loans to households accounted for the largest per cent of assets, with loans to business a not-too-distant runner-up, in 1970. "Consumer receivables" include both installment loans, based on automobiles and all sorts of durable goods, and also personal cash loans. "Business receivables" cover installment loans to durable-goods dealers and to business purchasers of equipment, trucks, and so on; financing in the form of leases; loans based on accounts receivable; and a few other categories.

Government regulation, incidentally, has not been an important factor affecting portfolio composition. States frequently establish interest-rate ceilings and maximum maturities on small loans, the main stock-in-trade of many finance companies; but regulations regarding business lending are minimal.

> Legally, . . . finance companies are free to invest in tax-exempt bonds, corporate stock, and real estate mortgages. The fact that they have not generally done so . . . must be attributed to management preference for a specialized role in finance.[2]

---

[1] See Evelyn M. Hurley, "Survey of Finance Companies, 1970," *Federal Reserve Bulletin* (November 1972), pp. 958–67. Much of the information here is based on this article.

[2] Thomas G. Gies et al. "Portfolio Regulations and Policies of Financial Intermediaries," in Commission on Money and Credit, *Private Financial Institutions* (Englewood Cliffs, N.J.: Prentice-Hall, 1963), p. 252.

SOURCE OF FINANCE   Table 9.1 reveals several facts about finance-company sources of finance. First, note the rather high ratio of short-term debt to total debt: about .64 in 1970. The main reason was that finance companies were hesitant to lock themselves into the historically high long-term rates that they faced in 1969–70 and therefore sought short-term financing primarily. Just five years earlier, in mid-1965, this ratio had been .53. Note also the extent to which finance companies rely on commercial paper (promissory notes sold on the open market) rather than on direct loans from banks. With the rapid growth of the commercial paper market (see chapter 10), finance companies have found this source to be relatively lower in cost and more flexible than bank financing in many cases. Many of the larger finance companies market their paper

TABLE 9.1
Assets and Liabilities of Finance Companies,
June 30, 1970
(in $millions)

	Amounts	Per Cent
Assets		
Cash and interest-bearing deposits	$ 2,022	3.3
Consumer receivables	31,773	52.4
Business receivables	22,999	38.0
Other receivables	2,342	3.9
Less: reserves for unearned income and for losses	−6,254	−10.3
Total receivables, net	50,859	84.0
Other loans and investments	6,041	10.0
All other assets	1,655	2.7
Total assets	$60,577	100.0
Liabilities		
Loans and notes payable to banks	$ 7,551	12.5
Commercial paper	22,073	36.4
Other short-term debt	975	1.6
Deposit liabilities and thrift certificates	639	1.1
Other current liabilities	3,468	5.7
Other long-term debt	15,501	25.6
All other liabilities	424	0.7
Total liabilities	$50,630	83.6
Capital, surplus, and undivided profits	$ 9,947	16.4
Total liabilities, capital, and surplus	$60,577	100.0
Short-term debt	29,629	48.9
Long-term debt	16,470	27.2

Source: Evelyn M. Hurley, "Survey of Finance Companies, 1970," *Federal Reserve Bulletin* (November 1972), adapted from Appendix Table 5, p. 966.

directly; in fact, as of mid-1970, 87 per cent of all finance company paper had been placed directly rather than through dealers. Holders of significant amounts included banks, insurance companies, and pension funds, as well as nonfinancial corporations and individuals.

RELATIONS WITH THE FINANCIAL SYSTEM   The foregoing discussion suggests several categories of competitive and complementary relationships. Considering the former first, there is intense competition between finance companies and other classes of intermediaries for consumer installment loan business. Commercial bank holdings of these loans exceeds finance company holdings by about 50 per cent, whereas in 1955 finance companies held a somewhat larger volume than commercial banks. Credit unions, too, are strong competitors for consumer installment loans.

In the case of business financing, finance companies and banks compete for leasing business and for some types of installment lending. There is, however, one class of lending that banks seldom touch but that is suitable for certain specialized finance companies. For example, consider the case of the small or medium-sized business firm with financing needs that entail a level of risk considered excessive by commercial banks, in view of their liquidity and safety standards (not to mention the standards of the bank examiners!). Often a situation of this kind would be quite acceptable to the finance company, because of its larger capital cushion and flexibility in sources of financing.

Competition for this kind of business is closer, though, between finance companies and small business investment companies and state credit development corporations, both of which will be discussed in the next sections.

As we noted earlier, banks are related to finance companies as a source of financing, both through direct lending and through purchase of open-market finance company paper. This relationship creates another layer of claims, interposing a second intermediary between ultimate provider and user of finance.

Small Business Investment Companies

Although small business investment companies (SBIC's) are privately owned, they owe their existence to the Small Business Investment Company Act of 1958, which not only provides for favorable tax treatment to the SBIC and its owners but also set up the machinery whereby an agency of the federal government, the Small Business Administration, could furnish much of the financing. The motivation for the creation of this new class of intermediaries was a long-felt "credit gap": equity and long-term debt finance for small business firms.

Some SBIC's concentrate on a particular industry; others have no such self-imposed limitations and are widely diversified. A number of SBIC's were instituted by particular companies in order to provide long-term or equity financing to customers, as, for example, in the case of a grocery wholesaler using this means to finance food retailers. Commercial banks have been active in sponsoring SBIC's. The banks are permitted by law to invest up to 5 per cent of capital and surplus in SBIC stock, but no bank may own more than 49 per cent of the stock of an individual SBIC.

The SBIC industry is still very young, of course, still in a state of becoming. Experience thus far has given rise to a number of amendments to the original statute, mostly in the direction of greater liberalization. There has occurred, and is occurring, a weeding-out process in which weaker firms have disappeared or merged. Although SBIC's in the aggregate constitute only a tiny element in the financial system, indications are that they are meeting a definite financing need but that, at the same time, they are far from representing a complete solution to the problems of small-business financing.

INVESTMENT POLICIES Thus far SBIC's have not done much financing through direct purchase of common stock. Rather, their most popular means of providing finance have been through term loans and through unsecured bonds that are convertible into common stock at a preestablished ratio of shares per $1,000 of the bonds. In the case of these convertible bonds, if the earnings of the borrower—the issuer of the bonds—increase substantially, the SBIC may elect to convert; if earnings do not seem to justify conversion, the SBIC still has a legal right to periodic interest payments and ultimate (twenty-year maximum) redemption of the bonds. SBIC's also provide management counsel to their business clients, in the manner of business finance companies.

SOURCES OF FINANCE The nucleus of the liabilities side is equity provided by the owners—a minimum of $300,000 by law, at the time of formation. Beyond this, the SBIC may borrow from the Small Business Administration: $2 for every $1 of capital and paid-in surplus up to $1 million, and $3 for every $1 over $1 million, up to a specified limit and upon meeting certain other requirements. They may also borrow additional amounts from private sources. Thus far, SBIC's have utilized only a small fraction of their SBA "credit line."

REGULATION An SBIC is restricted with respect to (1) the maximum amount of financing furnished to one firm and to firms in the same major industry, relative to the SBIC's capital and paid in surplus, (2) the maximum interest rate it may charge, and (3) both minimum and maximum maturity of the debt instrument it acquires. As mentioned above, controls are being eased; however, large SBIC's, less dependent on SBA financing, are finding these controls a high price to pay for financing and tax breaks, and some have given up their SBIC licenses. Thus equilibrium is far from being achieved in this new cooperative venture between Federal government and the private sector.

RELATIONS WITH THE FINANCIAL SYSTEM Commercial banks are very closely involved with SBIC's in a number of ways: (1) as stockholder; (2) as founder or cofounder; (3) referring potential clients to the SBIC; (4) "lending" the bank's staff members' services to the SBIC; (5) becoming its banking connection, as both depository and a source of financing.

Because of differences in types of financing provided and utilized, banks and SBIC's do not compete directly to any extent for assets or for financing. Direct competitors with SBIC's on the asset side are certain finance companies, which offer financing-plus-counseling packages designed for small and medium-sized firms.

State Development Credit Corporations

Another fairly new form of intermediary, state development credit corporations, dates from 1949, when Maine passed an act authorizing the creation of the first such corporation. About half the states have at least one of these now, known by various names but having these common characteristics: (1) chartered by the state, (2) owned primarily by business and financial interests, (3) debt-financed by cooperating financial institutions, (4) lend and lease property to firms with propositions too risky for other financial institutions, (5) operate for profit and to further the development or rehabilitation of a particular state or region.

Still a drop in the financial bucket and likely to remain so, this form of intermediary may nevertheless be considered a success in at least two respects: (1) the developers of these corporations believe them to be successful, and (2) there was recently formed the National Association of Business Development Corporations!

Nonintermediary Financial Firms

A variety of financial firms have evolved in response to demands for certain financial services in connection with intermediation or with transactions in claims that result from the financing process itself. These services may be classified into two groups:

1. *Market contact.* Assistance to prospective buyers and sellers (including issuers) of financial assets in getting together.
2. *Management and advice.* Trustee services and counsel in connection with the management of financial asset portfolios.

Our discussion of nonintermediary financial firms will be built on this framework.

We should note that very often the same financial firm will be found in several of the categories to be discussed. For example, it is highly probable that a given investment banking house will also act as securities broker/dealer and perhaps investment counselor as well. In fact, intermediaries themselves frequently perform some of these services.

Market-Contact Services

INVESTMENT BANKING HOUSES These are the firms that locate buyers (investors) for entire new issues of securities. The *investment banker* is in a position to do this because he has developed contacts with institutional investors and also with other investment banking firms, which, in turn, have still other contacts.

In some cases the investment banker purchases the issue outright, playing the role of merchant and profiting (or losing) on the basis of the spread between purchasing and selling prices. This arrangement, of course, requires temporary financing of the investment banker, usually in the form of bank credit. In other instances the investment banker contracts to sell on a "best efforts" basis, acting only as an agent and receiving a commission. An issue of any size is generally marketed through a *syndicate* consisting of a number of investment banking houses. A syndicate is a short-lived arrangement formed for the express purpose of marketing a particular issue.

Investment bankers also utilize their market contacts in the case of private placements, locating and negotiating with prospective large buyers of bond issues, such as insurance companies, and in advising firms and units of government concerning terms, in cases of securities issues that will be offered on the basis of competitive bidding.

Securities marketing is a closely regulated activity; many aspects of both the issuance and subsequent trading of securities are subject to the scrutiny of the Securities and Exchange Commission.

SECURITIES BROKERS AND DEALERS In the aggregate, securities brokers and dealers hold a larger volume of financial assets than do credit unions. $26.1 billion worth were held by securities firms at the end of 1972, compared with $21.7 billion held by credit unions.[3] Yet we classify the former as *nonintermediary* financial firms. Why?

The reason is that their financing activities are incidental to their main task of buying and selling securities, either on their own accounts (as dealers) or acting as agents for their clients (as brokers). Yet, securities brokers and dealers must be classed as financial firms because they are in the business of handling financial claims, not merchandise.

Somewhat over half of the financial assets of securities firms consist of loans to their customers, with the remainder being in the form of securities held in their own accounts as "inventory." Their major source of financing is commercial bank loans. Customer balances held with securities firms are an important source of financing, too, accounting for between one-sixth to nearly one-third of their total liabilities in recent years.[4]

Some securities firms specialize, or function as dealers, in bankers' acceptances, commercial paper, municipal securities, or United States

---

[3] Flow of funds data recorded in the *Federal Reserve Bulletin* (September 1973), p. A71.27.
[4] *Federal Reserve Bulletin*, June 1972, p. A73.21.

government securities. We shall have more to say about these firms in chapters 10 and 11 on money and capital markets.

MORTGAGE COMPANIES Performing the market-contact function in the real-estate finance market are mortgage companies. In their mode of operation these firms resemble most closely the investment bankers in that mortgage companies, too, act mainly as go-betweens, bringing borrower (issuer) and lender (investor) together, holding title to the financial assets only until this function is completed. The two intermediaries differ in important respects, though, and a look at these differences will tell us much about the operations of mortgage banking firms.

First, the mortgage company represents an investor or investors—for example, a life insurance company, mutual savings bank, or pension fund—while the investment house typically represents the issuer-borrower. Also, the mortgage company performs a *collecting* function, assembling mortgage paper from various sources, whereas the investment company is concerned with *dispersing*. Third, the mortgage company often knows in advance the spread between what it pays in purchasing a mortgage loan and what it will receive from the buyer; the investment banker, on the other hand, is at the mercy of the market in distributing the securities issue. Finally, the mortgage company usually operates locally in behalf of distant large buyers, while the investment company (specifically, the originating house) operates nationally, selling to widely scattered local buyers directly or through other investment bankers.

Several interrelated factors go far toward explaining the position of the mortgage company in our financial system:[5] (1) the high level of construction activity, (2) the rapid growth of large financial intermediaries that do not have extensive networks of contacts with local financial markets, and (3) the existence of Federally insured and guaranteed mortgages, which, "with their standardized mortgage contract, uniform and improved property and borrower appraisal techniques, and minimization of risk, have reduced geographic barriers to mortgage investment and enhanced negotiability of contracts."[6]

A mortgage company requires financing because of the time that elapses between purchase of a mortgage and its ultimate sale to an institutional buyer. Such financing is usually easily obtained from banks because the mortgage company nearly always has a firm commitment from the buyer to purchase the mortgage (assuming that it meets the stipulated conditions). In fact, in a growing number of cases, a mortgage banking firm is a subsidiary of a bank or is controlled by the same holding company that controls a bank—a convenient arrangement for all parties involved.

---

[5] Saul B. Klaman, *The Postwar Rise of Mortgage Companies*, Occasional Paper No. 60 (New York: National Bureau of Economic Research, 1959), p. 1.
[6] Ibid.

Sale of a particular batch of mortgages does not conclude the mortgage company's activities with respect to those mortgages. It continues to "service" them, that is, collect the monthly payment, make sure the taxes are paid, the property kept up, and so on.

Government regulation of mortgage companies is light. Those firms that decide to handle FHA-insured mortgages (and nearly all of them do) submit to examination and audit by this agency; but there are no regulations concerning liquidity ratios or any other asset-mix characteristics.

The small size of the typical mortgage company has made for strong competition both for mortgages and for outlets. Another form of competition is that between mortgage companies and those few insurance companies handling mortgages through their own branch offices. Most of the relations between mortgage companies and other financial firms are of a transactions nature—as borrowers from banks and as sellers to life insurance companies and other intermediaries.

Portfolio Management and Advice Services

We need not concern ourselves about sources of financing of the firms in this section because the financial firms considered here are those dealing with "other people's money" in an advisory or management capacity.

INSTITUTIONAL TRUSTEES There are three parties to a trust arrangement: (1) the *trustee,* an individual or corporation (usually a bank), holds title to certain assets that have been turned over to him (or it) by (2) the individual or corporate *creator* of the trust, with the understanding that the trustee will manage these assets for the benefit of (3) a third party, the *beneficiary,* in accordance with the terms of a trust agreement. Thus, in a sense, we are really discussing not an institution but a legal arrangement in this section. Yet because trust management has become so thoroughly institutionalized and because of the huge amounts of financial assets involved, it is appropriate to consider trust management here, keeping in mind that our discussion is limited to institutional trustees, such as trust companies and bank trust departments.

The dollar magnitudes involved in trusts are impressive. As of the end of 1971 the personal trust fund assets of the largest class of institutional trusts, insured commercial banks,[7] totalled $160 billion, about two-thirds of which consisted of common stock.[8]

Institutional trustees perform in a variety of situations, as executors

---

[7] It should be noted that trust assets of commercial banks are segregated from those of the banking operations and are under separate management.

[8] Edna E. Ehrlich "The Functions and Investment Policies of Personal Trust Departments—Part II," *Monthly Review,* Federal Reserve Bank of New York (October 1972), pp. 18–19.

or administrators of estates, as guardians of property in behalf of a minor child, widow, or other beneficiary (including bondholders and nonprofit foundations), and as managers of pension funds. In some instances the institutional trustee functions much like an investment company. This is the case with a so-called common, or commingled, trust fund, which the trustee manages in behalf of a number of beneficiaries, each of which holds an interest in the fund proportional to his contribution to it. Thus far, however, these funds are a very small fraction of total trusteed assets.

Each trust must be individually managed. The creation of the trust may limit the trustee's role to that of custodian of a bundle of assets or, at the other extreme, give no specific investment instructions at all. Even in the latter case, however, the trustee is held legally liable for prudent management of the assets and, in some states, is wholly or partially limited in his asset choices to "legal lists," as specified by state authorities.

INVESTMENT COUNSELORS AND ADVISORS Like trustees, investment counselors provide services in connection with substantial blocs of financial assets for wealthy individuals and for institutional investors such as banks, insurance companies, pension funds, college endowment funds, etc. They do not, however, hold title to the assets. In some cases they manage the assets, buying and selling on behalf of the owner; in other cases, they merely sell advice, based on the investor's own stated goals and the counselors' analysis of possible investment alternatives.

Et Cetera

We have not yet reached the end of the list of our financial institutions. At least a nod of recognition is merited by such classes as pawnbrokers, legacy lenders, Thrift and Loan (T&L) institutions, and investment development companies—classes of intermediaries of small, often declining, importance. Still others, however, must remain anonymous.

There are some financial institutions of considerable significance in international finance, though, which we are neglecting here. These will receive their due when we consider, in chapter 12, the "international context" within which our domestic financial system operates.

Intermediation by Nonintermediaries

Recall a statement made in chapter 3: "Intermediation is 'done' not only by intermediaries but by other kinds of economic units as well." One important kind of intermediary activity by nonintermediaries is interbusiness financing: the financing of business by other businesses through trade credit, open-market commercial paper, and other activities. Another is the direct financing of households by business. These we shall consider briefly in this section. An additional type—a very important one—is government-granted credit, which we take up in chapter 13.

Interbusiness Financing

Even though interbusiness financing is in a sort of "twilight zone" between the real and financial sectors, we should not ignore it because of the dollar magnitudes involved and because of its implications for the financial system. As as indication of the size of this phenomenon, at the end of 1973, United States nonfinancial corporations held $259.4 billion in receivables against other corporations, noncorporate businesses, and so on; and these corporations owed $256.3 billion in the form of notes and accounts payable, mostly to each other.[9]

TRADE CREDIT   Most interbusiness financing is in the form of trade credit, that is, credit granted by the selling firm to the buying firm as part of a transaction involving the sale of goods. Since cash sales are not the usual practice between firms, the volume of trade credit is understandably large, though we have no accurate information as to how large. In the general case, the obligation is evidenced only by the purchase order and invoice (the "bill"), although sometimes the signature of the buyer on a formal document is also included. Terms of payment—due date, discount allowed, or interest amount, and so on—are generally specified. Thus trade credit does not involve a "pure" financial transaction but is part of a "package" in which goods change hands, credit is granted, and perhaps other matters are involved; for example, services to be provided, return privileges, and so on.

Trade credit is likely to be granted by larger firms to smaller firms for two reasons. First, on the average, manufacturers are larger than the merchandising firms to which they sell; thus the smaller firm is more likely to owe the larger than vice versa. Second, larger firms generally have a much easier time arranging their own financing. For the latter of these reasons, trade credit tends to increase as per cent of sales both during recessions and during tight-money periods.[10]

Sometimes interbusiness financing is based on receivables. The supplier, by prior arrangement, will purchase the receivables in satisfaction of a debt or as credit against future purchases of merchandise. A commonly observed example is the case of oil company credit cards. The purchaser of gasoline on credit initially owes the service station proprietor; he, in turn, transfers these accounts over to his supplier for credit; and the supplier bills the station's customer directly.

Purchase and leasing of equipment provides other examples of inter-

---

[9] *Federal Reserve Bulletin* (May 1974), p. A44.
[10] Richard P. Hungate, *Interbusiness Financing* (Washington, D. C.: Small Business Administration, 1962), pp. 24–31. This work was helpful as background for this section.

business finance. In the case of leasing, the user has possession of the equipment but does not own it. In the case of outright purchase, the user acquires ownership at once or when payment is complete. Both methods involve periodic payments to the firm supplying the equipment.

Consumer Credit Extended by Business

Despite the growth of credit cards of all kinds (the oil company type, bank credit cards, and others) *"charge-account" credit* extended to customers by retailers has continued to grow, although considerably more slowly than other categories of consumer credit. *Service credit*, such as that granted by dentists and physicians, is also a sizable item. In 1972 this class of credit exceeded charge-account credit for the first time; and by March 1974 service credit outstanding was larger than charge-account credit by more than $2.7 billion: $10,677 million as compared to $7,939 million.[11]

Summary of Chapters 8 and 9

This two-chapter account of our major types of financial institutions may have seemed extremely detailed; but, considering the fact that entire volumes (even some multivolume works) have been published about single types of financial institutions (see Suggestions for Further Reading), we realize that these two chapters have hardly given us a decent introduction to them.

Looking at the system as a whole, and recalling the brief historical sketch in chapter 3, we cannot avoid the impression of constant change in response to shifting economic and political pressures. Year-to-year changes are seldom striking, but decade-to-decade changes clearly show the relative rise of some types of financial institutions, the relative decline of others, and even the occasional emergence of new types.

If your mental picture of the whole system of financial institutions is somewhat blurred, this is to be expected. The movements of the system are just too rapid for our slow-speed verbal cameras.

KEY CONCEPTS

Finance companies
Small business investment
  companies (SBIC's)
State development credit
  corporations

Investment bankers
Syndicate
Mortgage companies
Service credit

[11] *Federal Reserve Bulletin* (May 1974), p. A50.

QUESTIONS FOR REVIEW

1. All intermediaries "borrow," that is, incur debt obligations, so why is one group designated as "borrowing intermediaries"?
2. Contrast commercial banks and finance companies with respect to (a) sources of short-term financing, (b) degree of regulation, and (c) relations with other types of financial institutions.
3. "Small business investment companies are really the creation of government." In what sense? In what other ways are they related to government? In what respects are they private businesses?
4. Contrast the functions of investment banking and mortgage banking.

SUGGESTIONS FOR FURTHER READING FOR CHAPTERS 8 AND 9

American Mutual Insurance Alliance, Association of Casualty and Surety Companies, National Board of Fire Underwriters. *Property and Casualty Insurance Companies, Their Role as Financial Intermediaries.* Englewood Cliffs, N.J.: Prentice-Hall, 1962.

Benston, George J. "Savings Banking and the Public Interest." *Journal of Money, Credit and Banking,* IV (February, 1972, Part II), pp. 133–226.

Black, Robert P., and Doris E. Harless. *Nonbank Financial Institutions.* Richmond: Federal Reserve Bank of Richmond, 1969.

Colean, Miles L. *Mortgage Companies: Their Place in the Financial Structure.* Englewood Cliffs, N.J.: Prentice-Hall, 1962.

Commission on Money and Credit. *Private Financial Institutions.* Englewood Cliffs, N.J.: Prentice-Hall, 1963.

Croteau, John T. *The Economics of the Credit Union.* Detroit: Wayne State University, 1963.

Dublin, Jack. *Credit Unions: Theory and Practice.* Detroit: Wayne State University, 1966.

Friend, Irwin, ed. *Study of the Savings and Loan Industry.* 4 vols. Washington, D.C.: Federal Home Loan Bank Board, 1969.

Goldsmith, Raymond W. *Financial Institutions.* New York: Random House, 1968.

———. *Financial Intermediaries in the American Economy Since 1900.* Princeton: Princeton University Press, 1958.

Grebler, Leo. *The Future of Thrift Institutions: A Study of Diversification Versus Specialization.* Danville, Ill.: Joint Savings and Loan and Mutual Savings Bank Exchange Groups, 1969.

Investment Company Institute. *Management Investment Companies.* Englewood Cliffs, N.J.: Prentice-Hall, 1962.

Jacobs, Donald P., et al. *Financial Institutions,* 5th. ed. Homewood, Ill.: R. D. Irwin, 1972.

Kendall, Leon T. *The Savings and Loan Business: Its Purpose, Functions, and Economic Justification.* Englewood Cliffs, N.J.: Prentice-Hall, 1962.

Life Insurance Association of America. *Life Insurance Companies as Financial Institutions.* Englewood Cliffs, N.J.: Prentice-Hall, 1962.

Lindow, Wesley. *Inside the Money Market.* New York: Random House, 1972.

Ludtke, James B. *The American Financial System*, 2d ed. Boston: Allyn and Bacon, 1967.
Murray, Roger F. *Economic Aspects of Pensions: A Summary Report*. New York: National Bureau of Economic Research, 1968.
National Association of Mutual Savings Banks. *Mutual Savings Banking: Basic Characteristics and Role in the National Economy*. Englewood Cliffs, N.J.: Prentice-Hall, 1962.
National Consumer Finance Association. *The Consumer Finance Industry*. Englewood Cliffs, N.J.: Prentice-Hall, 1962.
Polakoff, Murray E., et al. *Financial Institutions and Markets*. Boston: Houghton Mifflin Co., 1970.
Teck, Alan. *Mutual Savings Banks and Savings and Loan Associations: Aspects of Growth*. New York: Columbia University Press, 1968.
Welfling, Weldon. *Mutual Savings Banks*. Cleveland: Case Western Reserve, 1968.

Yearbooks

Credit Union National Association. *International Credit Union Yearbook*. Madison, Wis.
Institute of Life Insurance. *Life Insurance Fact Book*. New York.
National Association of Mutual Savings Banks. *National Fact Book: Mutual Savings Banking*. New York.
United States Savings and Loan League. *Savings and Loan Fact Book*. Chicago.

The Money Markets
The Participants

Money-Market Instruments
*Short-Term Treasury Securities:
Treasury Bills
Agency Securities
State and Local Government
Short-Term Debt
Federal Funds
Certificates of Deposit
Bankers' Acceptances
Commercial Paper
Foreign Money-Market Instruments*

The Financial Markets: Money Markets 10

One important aspect of the financial system to which we have not given much attention so far is the complex of markets for financial claims. True, we have been introduced to most of the participants in the markets—the intermediaries and other financial firms—and to many of the kinds of claims that they issue, hold, service, and exchange. But in order to perceive the financial system as a *system*, we need to examine the markets themselves in more detail, both the mechanism through which transactions in claims take place and (just as importantly) the interconnections among the markets.

Financial markets are no different conceptually from any other kind of market, so let us define a financial market as a set of arrangements through which items in a particular class of financial claims are issued, exchanged, and extinguished. Thus there are at least three elements involved: (1) the transactors, (2) the "stock in trade," and (3) the procedures through which the exchange terms and quantities are determined and the transactions are consummated.

Notice that we did not refer to the market as a "place." The reason is that, while most markets have a focal point wherein the transactors assemble, this is not an inherent characteristic of a market but is rather one convenient (sometimes necessary) means of communication. In a number of financial markets, however, the communication is handled much more expeditiously by telephone, with written confirmation following, making face-to-face contact unnecessary, even inefficient. Markets do tend to have geographical boundaries, though, but they are usually not sharply defined. Thus, we describe the market for home mortgage loans as primarily local and the market for U. S. government securities as national, meaning, in each case, that a single price tends to exist—or, at most, the range of prices is relatively narrow—at any given time in that market.

As might be expected, we find a wide variety of market conditions in financial markets. There are several ways of classifying these markets, two of which we utilize as aids for fitting individual markets into a reasonably small number of categories.

Financial markets, in the first place, can be divided on the basis of *procedures* into two major subclasses: *negotiated markets* and *open markets.* In the former group are the markets in which particular financial claims are issued by the obligors to the purchasers on an individual basis, through direct, usually face-to-face, negotiations. Each item is unique, and generally the initial purchaser expects to hold the claim until maturity. Most loan markets fit into this category. Incidentally, we cannot conclude, merely because "each item is unique," that loan markets must be monopolistic. While numerous small-business borrowers are caught in situations in which their source of loan finance is limited to one or two intermediaries, at the opposite extreme are the large, reputable, profitable, nationally known businesses that have a wide choice of financial firms eager to accommodate them.

In the open-market category are markets in which highly standardized claims are traded, claims that holders usually expect to be able to resell easily. The market for some of these claims is centered in an organized exchange (the New York Stock Exchange, for example); but most are traded on an over-the-counter basis; that is, an economic unit desiring to purchase or sell a particular claim works through a broker or dealer who either holds an inventory of such claims or can contact a broker or dealer who does.

In this chapter our interest will center on the open markets, not because the negotiated markets are not important—they definitely are—but because the open markets are much more "visible," they are generally more responsive to changing financial conditions, and it is through some of them that the Federal Reserve attempts to work its will on the economy. It would be well to keep in mind, though, that the two kinds of markets do not function independently of each other; some economic units operate in both kinds of markets. A large, nationally known corporation, for example, needing financing for a seasonal bulge in its business operations, may choose to borrow from a bank or several banks (negotiated market) or, alternatively, to issue short-term claims to be sold on the open market. And banks, on their part, both make loans and purchase securities. So movements in market yields in one class of markets are closely related to movements in the other class.

The second major basis for classifying financial markets is by maturity of claim traded: *money markets* for short-term claims and *capital markets* for intermediate- and long-terms. Writers differ over where the line should be drawn,[1] but a quick nose-count of authorities would seem

---

[1] Two recent treatments of financial markets appearing in the same year illustrate this difference. Professor Roland I. Robinson seems to vote for one year as the dividing line—see his *Money and Capital Markets* (New York: McGraw-Hill Book Co., 1964) pp.

to support a one-year maturity as the most common dividing line between money-market and capital-market claims.

One reason for the difficulty in deciding where to mark the boundary between these two maturity categories is that, wherever we place it, we find some economic units operating on both sides of the line. Commercial banks, for example, while traditionally specializing in short-term negotiated claims, have become key intermediaries in financing business capital expenditures. On the demand-for-financing side, the U.S. Treasury, large corporations, and the major sales finance companies operate effectively all over the maturity range. Thus, developments in one sector will affect the other as well—a point we return to in the following chapter in connection with our consideration of the term structure of interest rates.

Yet it makes sense to draw a distinction between the two maturity sectors, partly because some intermediaries, surplus economic units, and deficit economic units operate only or mainly in one or the other sector, partly also because the difference in maturity generally imparts a qualitative difference to the claim involved, so that short-term securities are a different *kind* of claim in general from long-term securities, although the distinction is blurred at the boundary.

Our basis of organization for this chapter and chapter 11 will be (1) to discuss the two sectors separately—first the money market and then the capital market—and (2) to organize the discussion in each around "stock in trade," that is, to treat the distinguishing features of the markets for each of several of the major types of open-market claims.

The Money Markets

Perhaps the first point to be made concerning the money market is that it is not the market for *money* as we have been using this term: that is, means of payment. Rather, "money" has long been used in financial circles to refer to short-term, highly liquid, virtually riskless assets. We will simply have to adapt our thinking to this usage of the term *money* in this frame of reference.

Another point is that there is no such thing as *the* money market in the strict microeconomic-theory sense, in which we specify a demand function and a supply function for a particular good or service. Rather, the term *market* is used in this connection in much the same way as we speak of the labor market or the housing market. In other words, what we really have in mind when we use the term *money market* is a set of interrelated markets for short-term financial assets subject to many eco-

---

8, 95, and 109—while Professor G. Walter Woodworth, in his *The Money Market and Monetary Management* (New York: Harper & Row, 1964), p. 3, votes for five years. But both recognize the arbitrariness of any such dividing line.

nomic forces in common and therefore experiencing nearly parallel movements in yields (and prices) of the claims traded therein.

Finally, as stated earlier, our concern is with open markets and their behavior; so we are not considering the markets for short-term business loans, or trade credit, or retail charge accounts, or any other negotiated market.

In order to achieve open-market status (suitability for large-volume national trading), claims must meet these criteria: (1) they must be issued by large economic units, (2) the issuers must be of the highest credit standing, (3) maturities can be up to a year but are usually ninety days or less, and (4) they must be of a type familiar to the clientele trading in that particular market. In practice, this means the claims issued by the U. S. government, by some state and local governments, and by the largest business corporations able to meet criteria (2) through (4) above. Open-market status of a class of claims also requires that its market be assured of an adequate volume of claims and be organized to handle transactions of any volume speedily and at low transactions cost. Only a handful of classes of claims have been able to qualify, but the list is not permanent—some have disappeared; others have only "arrived" during the past decade or so.

As we examine the workings of this sector of the financial system, it may at times seem that the functions of the money market are merely (1) to match large economic units having a temporary surplus of money with similar economic units experiencing a temporary shortage thereof and (2) to enable economic units with large portfolios of liquid assets to shuffle their portfolios smoothly in response to changing conditions in the markets for these types of financial assets. The money market is all of that; and corporate financial managers as well as bankers and other financial institution management executives are appreciative of its efficiency. But the economic significance of this complex of markets goes far beyond this busy surface activity.

For one thing, an efficient money market works in the direction of a higher rate of economic growth. Large corporations feel free to hold a smaller quantity of liquid assets than they otherwise would, due to ready access to short-term financing, and are therefore able to devote more of their total assets to capital resources.[2] Banks, too, feeling less need to "tie up" assets in primary and secondary reserves because of the availability of additional financing through borrowing, are more willing to make business loans than they otherwise would be.

Related to this function of an efficient money market is its contribution to resource allocation.

---

[2] In many cases this additional amount of real capital could have been financed by borrowing. However, corporations are generally less willing to expand capital through external financing than through financing generated internally, that is, by retaining profits rather than distributing them as dividends to stockholders.

By providing diversified, competitive facilities that reach into all other markets for credit and capital, a developed money market helps to assure the channeling of funds into the uses most needed for the expansion of the economy, and facilitates the most efficient utilization of domestic saving.[3]

The money market, since it is the focus of pressures of demand and supply in the market for short-term financing, is an ideal vantage point for the Federal Reserve to observe and assess credit conditions nationally. There have been (and still are) sharp differences of opinion on what certain money-market "signals" really mean (see chapter 21), but the fact that the money market does yield its continual flow of information available for study and analysis over against the behavior of the "real" economy is grounds for confidence that further research will gradually narrow the area of disagreement.

The Participants

The money market of the United States is centered in New York City. It is here that most of the nation's largest banks are headquartered, as well as the largest industrial corporations. The open-market policy decisions of the Federal Reserve are executed by the Federal Reserve Bank of New York. Although New York City is the focal point of the nation's money market, regional money-market centers have developed in a number of major cities as the nation has grown and urbanized. But all these regional centers are closely tied with the New York money market in three ways:

> First, commercial banks located throughout the United States are themselves linked with large commercial banks in money centers and through them to New York by a network of correspondent relationships. . . . Second, the Federal Reserve System and the correspondent banking system together form a nation-wide mechanism for moving funds swiftly throughout the country. Third, the various securities dealers have branch offices in the major cities and banking and business connections across the country, and can use these to seek out available funds.[4]

A small number of firms handle most of the mechanical details of the money market, that is, accommodate those economic units seeking to buy or sell money-market claims by either adding to or reducing their own inventories of claims or by contacting outlets for, or sources of, such claims. These firms consist of the so-called *money-market banks,* of which there are about forty-five nationwide, and brokers and dealers in particular classes of money-market instruments. Most of these latter par-

---

[3] Peter G. Fousek, *Foreign Central Banking: The Instruments of Monetary Policy* (New York: Federal Reserve Bank of New York, 1957), p. 83.
[4] Carl H. Madden, *The Money Side of "The Street"* (New York: Federal Reserve Bank of New York, 1959), p. 17.

ticipate in the markets for several kinds of instruments and deal in stocks and bonds as well. The money-market banks not only transact for others but are also themselves large holders and issuers of money-market instruments.

Regular customers of these banks and specialized money-marketers include some of the nation's largest nonfinancial corporations, the U.S. Treasury, the Federal Reserve, large finance companies, nonmoney-market banks, and foreign central banks. There are other economic groups that are of lesser or only occasional importance. Some of these customers, important and otherwise, mainly seek short-term financing; others are usually looking for short-claims; still others participate actively on both sides of the market.

Commercial banks are major holders of money-market claims, but in recent years they have also become major issuers of such claims; namely, negotiable certificates of deposit and certain other classes of short-term credit instruments.

Large *nonfinancial corporations* also operate on both sides of the market, though primarily on the supply-of-claims side. More sophisticated cash management, however, has resulted in these firms holding less and less money as a per cent of their total liquid assets, thus being better customers for money-market instruments.

The *United States Treasury* participates in the money market almost solely as an issuer of claims. Short-term Treasury securities are far and away the largest component of money-market issues. The *Federal Reserve*, on balance, operates mainly on the opposite side. Over the long pull, the Federal Reserve is a huge net purchaser of U.S. government securities, mainly short-term. As we know, it increases its holdings of these securities in order to increase bank reserves that are used, in turn, to support the amount of growth of our money supply believed by Federal Reserve authorities to be appropriate to our expanding output of goods and services. Occasionally, for short periods of time the Federal Reserve will be a net seller of securities in order to accomplish a tightening, or to reduce an easing, in money-market conditions.

Like the United States Treasury, *large finance companies* are in the money market as issuers of short-term claims. Some of these companies have grown so huge that they not only bypass banks for most of their need for short-term financing but they bypass financial middlemen as well, dealing directly with large institutional investors.

The role of *foreign central banks* and other monetary authorities as holders of United States money-market claims has increased enormously over the past decade, largely as a result of our balance-of-payments deficits, which have resulted in a buildup of dollar claims in the hands of these agencies. Rather than to leave these dollar holdings as noninterest-earning demand deposits in American banks, the foreign holders have for the most part chosen to purchase and hold short-term obligations of the United States Treasury and also CD's issued by the money-market banks.

Money-Market Instruments

Table 10.1 records the volume outstanding of the leading money-market instruments. It hardly requires much study to discover that, in terms of dollar volume, securities of the U.S. government dominate the market. The importance of these securities is also due to the part they play in the implementation of monetary policy. Federal Reserve open-market operations are conducted almost entirely in Treasury securities.

On the other hand, we should note that, of the $145.5 billion total of short-term U.S. government securities outstanding on March 31, 1974, two-thirds, or $96 billion were held by private investors, the remaining $49.5 billion being in the hands of the Federal Reserve ($47.0 billion) and various government agencies ($2.4 billion).[5] Also, in assessing the relative importance of these money-market securities, we should consider not only the dollar volume outstanding of the various kinds but the dollar volume of transactions as well. There are no accurate transactions figures for most of these instruments, but we can illustrate the point by looking at the Federal funds market. In 1966 member-bank reserves at the Federal Reserve never exceeded $20 billion. Yet during that period on an average day $3.5 to $3.8 *billion* of Federal funds were purchased (that is, borrowed) by one bank from another.[6]

Short-Term Treasury Securities: Treasury Bills

The United States Treasury, America's largest debtor, issues securities in every maturity range from three-month Treasury bills to forty-year bonds. However, no matter what their maturity at the time of issue,

TABLE 10.1
Selected Money-Market Instruments,
Volume Outstanding, March 31, 1974
(in $billions)

Treasury bills	$111.9
Other Treasury securities due in one year or less	33.6
Certificates of deposit*	67.8
Bankers' acceptances	10.2
Open-market commercial paper	44.7

Source: *Federal Reserve Bulletin*, May 1974, pp. A24, A27, and A39.
* In demoninations of $100,000 or more; issued by "weekly reporting member banks" as of March 27, 1974.

[5] *Federal Reserve Bulletin*, May 1974, p. A39.
[6] Parker B. Willis, *A Study of the Market for Federal Funds* (Washington, D. C.: Federal Reserve Board of Governors, 1967), p. 10.

almost all of them eventually end up as short-term securities,[7] as we use the term. The importance of this category of money-market instruments is obvious because of its size and monetary-policy role, as mentioned above, but also—and related to these properties—because short-term Treasury securities are the most widely held of all money-market instruments (see Table 10.2). They are ideal nonmonetary liquid assets for temporary holding, being totally free of default risk as well as susceptible to very little price-fluctuation risk and extremely easy for holders of any size to acquire and dispose of.

Treasury bills are issued regularly in several denominations, ranging from $10,000 to $1,000,000, and in maturities of three, six, and nine months, and one year. Each issue is advertised and sold on an auction basis through the Federal Reserve banks in their fiscal-agent capacity. The Treasury does not specify the interest rate that it will pay, only the dollar amount that it will pay for the bill at maturity. The institutions submit bids for particular quantities of specific denominations. The higher the bid price, the lower the yield,[8] of course; the Treasury accepts the most favorable (to it) bids down to the one that just exhausts the amount available of that issue, which is the total to be issued less the

TABLE 10.2
Ownership of Short-Term Marketable U.S. Government Securities, March 31, 1974
(par values, in $billions)

Holders	Total	Treasury Bills	Others Maturing within One Year
U.S. government agencies and trust funds	$ 2.4	$ 0.7	$ 1.7
Federal Reserve banks	47.0	36.9	10.1
Commercial banks	16.7	7.8	8.9
Mutual savings banks	0.5	0.2	0.3
Savings and loan associations	0.6	0.2	0.4
Insurance companies	0.8	0.4	0.4
Nonfinancial corporations	3.5	2.1	1.4
State and local governments	7.0	5.7	1.3
All others	66.8	57.8	9.0
Total	$145.4	$111.8	$33.6

Source: *Federal Reserve Bulletin*, May 1974, p. A39. Based on Treasury Survey of Ownership.

---

[7] The only exceptions are those that are called for redemption before their due date, a process known as "advance refunding."

[8] The formula used to determine the discount rate (d) on three- and six-month bills is:

$$d = \frac{360}{n}(100 - p)$$

where n = number of days to maturity and p = the price paid per hundred dollars of maturity value.

amount for which noncompetitive tenders have been received. These latter are sold at the average price at that day's auction.

Each year the Treasury designates some issues of bills as *tax anticipation bills* because they are mainly issued in the second half of the calendar year and scheduled to mature around dates when the bulk of the corporate income tax payments are due, in the first half of the calendar year (last half of the Treasury's fiscal year). These bills meet the needs of both parties. The need of business corporations is for a type of liquid asset that can be accumulated gradually and that will mature around the time when corporate income tax payments are due. The Treasury's need is to finance a deficit likely to occur in the second half of the year or to be considerably larger during this period (see Table 10.3) since most of the receipts from corporate income tax are relatively light during this half. Thanks to tax anticipation bills, the transfer of billions of dollars to the Treasury in payment of corporation tax liabilities is accomplished every year with a minimum of confusion and churning about in the money markets.

There is a very active secondary market in Treasury bills—in all types of marketable Treasury securities, in fact. A key role in this market is played by the two dozen or so major government securities dealers. These firms carry substantial inventories of various issues of Treasury securities, so that they can fill orders of almost any size on either side of the market at a moment's notice. Competition among the dealers keeps rates highly responsive to market conditions, while the size and flexibility of their inventories—their ability to accommodate sudden surges of buying and selling—keep fluctuations within tolerable limits.

Naturally, operations of this size and variation require substantial yet flexible financing. Government securities dealers, being equal to the

TABLE 10.3
Treasury Cash Receipts from, and Payments to, the Public, 1970–1973
(millions of dollars)

Period	Budget Receipts	Budget Outlays	Surplus (+) or Deficit (−)
1970 January –June	$102,910	$ 97,661	+ 5,249
July–December	87,584	104,216	− 16,632
1971 January–June	100,830	107,242	− 6,412
July–December	93,180	111,557	− 18,377
1972 January–June	115,469	120,319	− 4,850
July–December	106,061	118,586	− 12,525
1973 January–June	126,165	127,940	− 1,775
July–December	124,253	130,360	− 6,107

Source: Federal Reserve Bulletin, Various issues. Based on Treasury data.

task, have developed an extensive network of sources of financing. In recent years business corporations have provided about 40 per cent of outside financing for government securities dealers, with banks, particularly the big New York money-market banks, providing most of the remainder.

The device most commonly used in dealer financing, especially by business corporations, is the *repurchase agreement.* Although in substance a loan, in form it is a contract by which one party (say, a business firm) agrees to purchase certain securities from the other (a dealer) for a designated amount of money; the other party simultaneously agrees to repurchase these securities by a certain future date (or, sometimes, when one of the parties chooses to terminate) for the same amount of money, plus interest at an agreed-upon rate.

Until recently a Treasury bill or other Treasury security had the form of a piece of paper. Purchases and sales of such securities involved a great deal of examining, counting, and transporting of these pieces of paper. Now, however, most of the Treasury's marketable debt securities, like most of our money, have no physical existence but rather take the "form" of magnetic impressions in the memory of Federal Reserve bank computers, under the so-called *book-entry system.* In the case of most transactions, "delivery" consists of bookkeeping entries recording the change of ownership of the securities.

> Securities which are book-entries with the Federal Reserve can be transferred to other book-entry accounts, shipped to other districts by wire transfer, or withdrawn from custody in certificate form. The Reserve banks satisfy requests for certificates by drawing on their stocks of unissued paper securities. Conversely, securities deposited for safekeeping (as book-entries) are added to these unissued stocks. A record of the details of each such transaction is transmitted to the parties involved by way of an "advice of transaction."[9]

The Treasury, not the Federal Reserve, remains the debtor, of course.

Agency Securities

Several agencies of the Federal government are authorized to issue their own securities. Federal Land Banks, Federal Intermediate Credit Banks, Banks for Cooperatives, Federal Home Loan Banks, and Federal National Mortgage Association are the major issuing agencies. The volume of securities issued by these five agencies has expanded sharply over the past few years. At year-end 1954 the total short-term open-market debt of the "big five" agencies listed above was $1282 million. On September 30, 1973, the total had reached $20.2 billion! This rep-

---

[9] Ronald J. Talley, "Phasing Out the Certificate System: New Federal Reserve Methods," *New England Economic Review,* Federal Reserve Bank of Boston, July–August 1970, p. 15.

resented about one-third of the total outstanding issues of these agencies on that date.[10]

These securities are not guaranteed by the Federal government; but they have a somewhat special status in that they are eligible for purchase and sale by the Federal Reserve in connection with open-market operations, and some are eligible as collateral for advances by Federal Reserve banks to member banks. Along with the growth in the volume of these securities outstanding there has developed an active secondary (or resale) market for them, so they are properly included in our section on money-market instruments.

In addition to the "big five" borrowers, a growing number of Federal agencies have been authorized to issue their own securities. The resultant clutter of individual issues, varying in size, method, and frequency of interest payment, tax status, and other characteristics, became a source of confusion and irritation to money-market participants in recent years. Moreover, each agency borrowing separately needs its own staff to carry out this function.

To alleviate this situation, Congress established the Federal Financing Bank (FFB), which began operation in 1974. About 20 agencies that issue their own securities are now authorized (but not required) to borrow directly from the FFB; and the FFB, in turn, raises money by the issuance of its own securities. Early indications are that these securities, backed by the "full faith and credit" of the U.S. government, are achieving ready acceptance as money-market instruments.

State and Local Government Short-Term Debt

State and local units of government also issue short-term obligations, mostly in anticipation of tax receipts and as interim financing, pending a bond issue. As interest on these notes is exempt from Federal personal and corporate income tax, the notes are attractive to, hence held by, commercial banks, business corporations, and other economic units for which this feature is of value.

Several firms and money-market banks in New York carry on secondary-market activities in short-term state and local securities, but not on a large scale; as a result, purchasers generally expect to hold these securities until maturity.

Federal Funds

Next we consider three classes of money-market instruments that are important liabilities of commercial or Federal Reserve banks. One, Federal funds, is a class of liabilities of the Reserve banks; the other two,

---

[10] Figures based on *Federal Reserve Bulletin*, November 1973, p. A39.

certificates of deposit and bankers acceptances, are almost exclusively obligations of commercial banks.

We encountered Federal funds briefly in our chapter 5 discussion of the commercial bank asset-mix, where we learned that "Federal funds" is merely another term for "deposits at Federal Reserve banks." Now we must look at this topic in a money-market context.

Although the literature consistently refers to the *purchase* and *sale* of Federal funds, what is really involved is their *borrowing* and *lending*. The typical transaction consists of an agreement whereby (1) one member bank lends to another member bank a specified amount of the former's deposit in a Federal Reserve bank, and (2) the borrowing bank agrees to return this amount plus interest on the following day.

The mechanics of a transaction in Federal funds would look something like this.

Bank A		Bank B		TRACE 10.1
(1) Reserves with Federal Reserve +$1,000,000	Federal Reserve funds borrowed +$1,000,000	(1) Reserves with Federal Reserve −$1,000,000 Federal Reserve funds loaned +1,000,000		

The next day all these entries would be reversed, but an additional set of entries would be required to show that Bank B has gained $166.67 in reserves (the interest payment[11]) at Bank A's expense.

Generally the reason that the lending bank is willing to enter into this arrangement is that it possesses excess reserves. The borrowing bank is usually suffering a reserve deficiency during the current reserve period. Thus this transaction is beneficial to both parties; the borrowing bank gets needed reserves; the lending bank, some extra income. However, some large banks make it a practice to buy Federal funds from, and sell to, their correspondent banks as a service to them, regardless of their (the big banks') reserve needs. Also, some large banks buy Federal funds when the price is right, as a source of financing—another example of "liability management," discussed in chapter 4.

Although the dominant type of transaction in Federal funds, accounting for about 90 per cent of the total, is between banks, there is another important class of participants in this market: government securities dealers. As transactions in government securities are handled in Federal funds, the dealers must have working balances in this form of claim.

It may seem strange to include the Federal funds market in our treatment of the (open) money market. In fact, a few years ago it would

---

[11] 6 per cent × 1/360 (of a year) × $1,000,000.

have been. Now, however, the market no longer resembles a negotiated market, with face-to-face contact, but rather has taken on more of the character of an impersonal open market, with a standardized commodity and with rates that respond rapidly to changing market conditions. The two developments most responsible for the change have been (1) the increased number and use of firms acting as brokers in bringing together prospective "buyers" and "sellers" of Federal funds, and (2) the emergence of the practice by numerous large banks of "accommodating" smaller country banks in the efforts of the latter to participate in the market.

Like the market for other instruments, the Federal funds market is centered in New York. Here the brokerage firms mentioned above are headquartered; here, too, are most of the largest accommodating banks. The market is truly a national one, however; there are also strong regional centers for Federal funds activity, notably on the West Coast.

The quantitative importance of the market can be glimpsed by recalling the fact, noted a few pages ago, that the daily average of transactions in Federal funds was over $3.5 billion in 1966. Clearly, bankers rely heavily on this market in adjusting their reserve positions. In fact, it was estimated recently that about one-third of the country-bank members of the Federal Reserve System and nearly all reserve-city member banks now participate in the market.[12]

The Federal funds market is also important in relation to monetary policy. Rates on Federal funds are extremely sensitive and serve as indicators of pressure in the money markets. Also, the operation of this market rapidly transmits the effects of open-market actions of the Federal Reserve through the banking and financial system. The initial impact of a Federal Reserve sale of government securities is felt primarily by the New York money-market banks, which, in turn, "mop up" excess reserves throughout the country via the Federal funds market. With reduced excess reserves, these banks are going to be more reluctant lenders, especially to new applicants for credit.

In fact, the integration of the Federal funds market with the correspondent banking system has been one factor in the reduction of the volume of excess reserves held throughout the banking system, thus making the system more responsive to tightening actions by the Federal Reserve.

Certificates of Deposit

Our discussion of the certificate of deposit (or CD) in chapter 4 was mainly from the perspectives of the bank and the banking system. Here, our point of view is the money market: we focus on the issuers and holders of CD's and the market institutions and mechanisms through which transactions take place.

[12] Willis, *A Study of the Market for Federal Funds*, pp. 3–4

The CD is a simple instrument: it is a document that is simultaneously a receipt for money deposited and a promise to repay that amount of money plus interest at an agreed-upon rate on a specified date. Not all CD's are money-market instruments, though. To qualify for that status, a CD must be (1) negotiable, (2) of large denomination, preferably not less than $1 million, (3) issued by a large, well-known bank, and (4) of short maturity, preferably around four months. The interest rate that the issuing bank must pay will vary with conditions in the money market, of course, but in addition it will tend to be higher for smaller-denomination CD's and for less well known banks. Only a handful of banks—one or two dozen—qualify for the "prime" category.

As we discussed in chapter 4, the reason for banks turning to issuing CD's was to secure financing, a particularly acute problem for money-market banks because of heavy demand for loans coupled with a tendency for their big corporate customers to trim their demand deposits as low as possible. Naturally, issuing CD's does not increase total bank reserves—the quantity of these is largely determined by the Federal Reserve—but it does channel reserves to the banks issuing CD's, which banks can utilize the reserves as basis for meeting their customers' loan demands. Then, when loan demand is slack, or the bank is being deluged with offers to purchase its CD's, it merely lowers its posted scale of "base rates" and the potential buyers of CD's melt away, since money-market investors are highly responsive to changes in relative yields.

Large corporations are the major original buyers of CD's. Quite often they will specify a maturity date that coincides with a tax-due date or a date on which a dividend is payable. Such a corporation is likely to hold the CD until maturity; and, in fact, most CD's are not traded at all. But the existence of a secondary market has been an important factor in the growth of this financial instrument, making CD's close competitors with Treasury bills and other instruments for placement in the liquid-asset portfolios of large corporations. Other economic units that purchase CD's both from issuing banks and in the secondary market include savings institutions, units of government, foreign banks, and government securities dealers.

The secondary market for CD's is of respectable size but relatively immature, dating only from 1961. During the period since then, however, the CD has become a key money-market instrument and holds promise of considerable further growth.

An important role is played by a group of firms that are also in the select number of government securities dealers discussed earlier. These dealers hold inventories of CD's, thus giving the secondary market a greater degree of stability and the instruments a higher degree of liquidity, enhancing their attractiveness to potential holders.

Another factor contributing to increased stability in the market for CD's was the decision of the Federal Reserve Board of Governors in mid-1970 to exempt large CD's (those over $100,000), with maturities of thirty to eighty-nine days,[13] from its Regulation Q, which imposes interest rate ceilings on various classes of time and savings deposits of member banks. Prior to that time Regulation Q had been a serious obstacle to the orderly development of the CD as a money-market instrument. Whenever money-market rates would rise to and above this ceiling, the issuing banks could only watch helplessly as holders of CD's redeemed them at maturity and turned to other instruments, as did those who might otherwise have bought CD's.

A case in point was the 1968–70 situation. From December 4, 1968, when large CD's issued by the so-called "weekly reporting member banks" reached a ceiling of $24.3 billion, the amount of the large CD's outstanding had declined steadily to $10.3 billion on February 4, 1970, a drop of well over 50 per cent! A decline of this magnitude (and a similar drop occurred in 1966) is undesirable from the standpoint of the orderly development of the secondary market for CD's, although it may have been defensible from the standpoint of monetary policy.

Bankers' Acceptances

Bankers' acceptances are a pygmy among giants in the open-money markets. Relatively few people are familiar with them, let alone actually work with them. Nevertheless, acceptances are holding their own relative to the money market as a whole; and they are an important instrument in the conduct of international trade.

A bankers' acceptance is one species of the genus *bill of exchange*, or *draft*. Like all drafts, it is an instrument, drawn by one party on another, ordering the second party to pay to the order of a third party (which may be the same as the first party) a certain sum of money on a specified date, or on demand. An ordinary check is the species of draft that is most familiar to the majority of us. Like a check, a bankers' acceptance starts life as a draft drawn on a particular bank. Unlike a check, this draft does not call for immediate payment but rather for payment a specified number of days (usually 30–180) after "sight." However, not until the bank, through the signature of an appropriate officer, signifies its acceptance of the obligation to pay as stated on the face of the draft does the draft become a bankers' acceptance. By accepting the draft, the bank makes itself primarily liable to make payment; and the legal holder of this acceptance has a valid claim against the bank.

But why would the bank agree to accept this draft? To answer this question, it is necessary to look at a stripped-down version of one kind of transaction giving rise to an acceptance.

---

[13] Three years later the board suspended the rate ceiling as applied to maturities from ninety days to one year.

1. A U.S. importer makes an arrangement with his New York bank whereby the bank will "accept" a ninety-day draft of a predetermined dollar amount, to be drawn on it shortly by a foreign exporter. The importer, of course, agrees to reimburse this bank for the amount, plus interest and a fee.
2. The importer sends an order for certain merchandise to the exporter who, informed of the arrangement described in (1), draws the draft on the importer's bank.
3. The exporter sells the draft to his bank for local currency and ships the goods.
4. The exporter's bank sends the draft to the importer's bank, which accepts it.

Let us pause now to catch our breath. Who is actually financing the transaction at this point? Not the exporter; he already has his money (step 3). Not the importer; he is being financed, since he has the goods or will have very shortly (step 4) but will not have to pay for them for nearly three months (step 1). Not the importer's bank; it has signed a paper agreeing to pay the holder of the acceptance—but, again, not for nearly three months (step 1). Evidently, then, it is the exporter's bank that is actually financing the importer since it holds a claim against the importer's bank, which, in turn, holds a claim against the importer. Now, to go on:

5. The exporter's bank can either (a) hold the acceptance until maturity (a very common practice), or (b) sell it to the accepting bank (also very common), or (c) authorize its sale on the market, with the proceeds being credited to its account in its American correspondent bank.
6. At maturity, the importer makes payment to his bank, and his bank—the accepting bank—pays the party holding the acceptance, unless the exporter's bank chose option (b) in step 5.

We have left out many details that are important to the parties involved but not to us at this point. And we have only described the essentials of one use of acceptance credit; namely, financing an import. This is, to be sure, one important use of acceptances; but there are other uses, for example, in connection with the financing of exports and of the storage and shipment of goods within foreign countries. But the nature of the acceptance is the same in all cases.

A rather small number of banks, with a heavy concentration in New York City, account for most of the acceptances issued. The largest class of investors in acceptances is foreign banks, both central and commercial, and foreign nonbank institutions. Among domestic investors, commercial banks are the largest class, with a small per cent of the total outstanding being held by the New York Federal Reserve Bank and a scattered selection of intermediaries and nonfinancial corporations.

It may seem odd that most acceptances in the portfolios of banks are "own bills," that is, issued by their present holders. Why would a bank accept a draft on itself and then immediately buy it? The reason is found in the existence of a secondary market for the instrument. If the bank's reserve position becomes tight, it can simply sell the acceptance out of its portfolio.

The secondary market for acceptances is well developed and functions smoothly. The major facilitating institutions are about a half-dozen firms, for most of which their acceptance business is a sideline operation, their main concern being U.S. government and other securities. They maintain inventories of acceptances, obtaining their income from the narrow spread between the buying and selling prices.

Commercial Paper

"A commercial-paper note is an unsecured, negotiable promissory note made payable to the bearer on a stated maturity date."[14] These notes are nearly always sold on a discount basis, as are Treasury bills. However, open-market commercial paper is not sold at auction but at rates posted by the (would be) seller.

Commercial paper acquires its money-market status by virtue of certain characteristics both of the instrument itself and of the market. The issuers are large, well-known firms with excellent credit standing.[15] The face amount of a commercial-paper note is usually in the $50,000–$1,000,000 range but can be as small as $5,000. Maturity of a note issue will vary from three days to nine months, though most fall in the "under ninety days" category.

In contrast to other money-market instruments, there is no organized secondary market for commercial paper. Most investors therefore expect to hold the paper until maturity. If the holder is genuinely pinched for liquidity, however, he can usually count on the issuer, in the case of direct placements, to repurchase the paper. Even dealers will buy back paper in certain cases. These arrangements serve to increase the liquidity of commercial paper.

ISSUERS The issuers of commercial paper can be grouped into three categories: (1) finance companies, (2) affiliates of large commercial banks, and (3) industrial borrowers and real estate investment trusts.

[14] Nevins D. Baxter, *The Commercial Paper Market* (Boston: Bankers Publishing Co., 1966), p. 28. The following discussion owes much to this source. Also see Frederick C. Schadrack and Frederick S. Breimyer, "Recent Developments in the Commercial Paper Market," *Monthly Review*, Federal Reserve Bank of New York (December 1970), pp. 280–91.

[15] This does not in itself guarantee safety. In 1970 the Penn Central Transportation Company declared bankruptcy, with $82 million of commercial paper outstanding.

By far the largest class of issuers, accounting for well over half the total dollar amount outstanding, is finance companies. Most finance-company issuers work through dealers, who buy outright entire issues and, in turn, peddle them to institutional investors. Some twenty or so finance companies, however, are so huge that they can economically maintain their own sales force, contacting investors directly.

Holders of finance-company paper fill the same role for these intermediaries that depositors, particularly time-deposit holders, fill for banks and other depository intermediaries: suppliers of more or less "permanent," yet short-term, financing. As an issue of commercial paper matures, the finance company generally replaces it with another. When demand for credit provided by finance companies increases, these companies must compete more aggressively for financing. Also, in order to keep their financial structures balanced, they must occasionally go into the market for long-term financing.

For finance-company issuers, bank loans and the commercial-paper market are regarded as alternative sources of short-term financing. One reason that finance companies, particularly the largest ones, have increasingly turned to the open market is their enormous financing needs relative to the capacity of even large banks to supply. It is costly and inconvenient to negotiate with dozens of individual banks. Another reason is that open-market borrowing nearly always costs less—not only because of lower interest rates but also because banks generally impose compensating balance requirements on their finance-company borrowers. After all, these companies are their competitors both in making loans and in acquiring financing (especially since banks have begun issuing CD's), so customer relations are far from intimate between them.

The handful of finance companies selling directly to investors account for somewhat over half of all outstanding commercial paper. These firms offer notes of any maturity (up to 270 days) and of any denomination ($25,000 or over) at their advertised rate.

Over the last few years large commercial banks have become an important factor on the borrowing side of the commercial-paper market, through their corporate affiliates. On March 31, 1974, commercial paper issued by these affiliates amounted to $6 billion, which was about 13 per cent of the $44.7 billion outstanding on that date.[16]

The paper is issued by the nonbank affiliate (often a holding company), which uses the proceeds to purchase loans and securities held by the bank itself. The bank thus acquires reserves in exchange for earning assets, while the earning assets acquired by the affiliate are financed by the holders of the commercial paper.

Considering the bank and its nonbank affiliate as a single entity, the results of the above transactions are (1) an increase in its reserves, financed by (2) an increase in its liabilities, in the form of commercial

---

[16] *Federal Reserve Bulletin* (May 1974), p. A27.

paper. The Federal Reserve Board of Governors, taking this "single entity" approach, has imposed the same reserve requirement on commercial paper issued by bank affiliates of member banks as that on large CD's issued directly by member banks.

The 450 or so companies as of 1968 that utilized dealers in marketing commercial paper included about 100 finance companies, 250 industrial concerns, 90 utilities, and a few firms in other fields. In contrast to the finance companies and utilities, which regard commercial paper as part of their permanent financial structure, the industrial firms use the commercial paper market mainly to finance seasonal needs.

Fewer than a half-dozen dealers market most of the commercial paper that is not placed directly. They carry small inventories of commercial paper, not for secondary-market purposes but only pending its ultimate placement.

HOLDERS Until recently most commercial paper was held, appropriately enough, by commercial banks. However, while still important holders, banks have slipped well behind nonfinancial corporations, which probably hold more than 60 per cent of the dollar volume of paper outstanding, according to a recent estimate.[17] Banks seem to purchase commercial paper mainly to fill the portfolio gap left by insufficient loan demand. In fact, commercial paper is classified as a "loan" on bank balance sheets—an illustration of the ill-defined boundary line between loans and investments, mentioned in chapter 5.

Commercial paper is attractive to business corporations because of its yield and, especially in the case of directly placed paper, its extreme flexibility of amount and maturity, plus the fact that the issuer will repurchase the paper if the investing company experiences a liquidity problem.

Considered together, two trends—the growth in the number of firms issuing commercial paper and the increase in the importance of business corporations as holders of commercial paper—have interesting implications for the financial system, particularly for banks, because the result of these trends is that banks are being bypassed in the financing process. The company purchasing the commercial paper is, in effect, making a direct loan to the issuing company. This new development, of course, forces the banks to watch closely the relation of their loan interest rates to rates on commercial paper.

Foreign Money-Market Instruments

Corporate financial managers and managers of institutional portfolios have begun to look beyond our national borders for money-market investments. Along with certain developments in financial markets in

---

[17] Schadrack and Breimyer, "Recent Developments," p. 282.

other countries, this trend is moving us in the direction of a truly international money market (although we still have a good distance to go). Increasingly, American institutional investors are looking into Canadian Treasury bills and commercial paper and even British Treasury bills and other short-term instruments. The Eurodollar market, while not a true "open" money market, competes directly with domestic and foreign instruments for the dollars of investors aggressively looking for more desirable short-term claims. More on this topic follows in chapter 12.

KEY CONCEPTS

Open markets
Money markets
Capital markets
"Money-market banks"
Treasury bills
"Tax anticipation bill"
Repurchase agreement

"Book-entry system"
 (U.S. government securities)
Federal funds
Certificate of deposit (CD)
Bankers' acceptance
Commercial paper

QUESTIONS FOR REVIEW

1. What is the basis for distinguishing between money markets and capital markets?
2. Is the money market the market for money? Explain why the answer is yes and no.
3. What standards must an asset class meet to qualify for trading in money markets?
4. What are the economic functions of money markets?
5. Compare the money-market roles of large nonfinancial corporations and large finance companies.
6. How is the effective interest rate paid on new issues of Treasury bills determined?
7. Contrast Federal funds, CD's, and open-market commercial paper with respect to (a) issuers, (b) purchasers, (c) maturity, and (d) secondary market.
8. "The issuance of a bankers' acceptance does not provide financing in a transaction but rather provides the basis for financing." Explain.

SUGGESTIONS FOR FURTHER READING See end of chapter 11.

Capital-Market Instruments
Government Securities
Corporate Securities: Bonds
Corporate Securities: Stock
Relationships Among Markets

The Structure of Interest Rates
The Pattern of Yields
Term Structure of Interest Rates

Summary of Chapters 10 and 11

The Financial Markets: Capital Markets and Interest Rates

We now turn to the other major division of the financial markets, the capital markets, continuing to limit ourselves to open markets as we did in chapter 10. Our basis for organization will again be the "stock in trade": we shall consider the markets for government securities, corporate bonds, and corporate stock, in that order.

Capital-Market Instruments

Many of the participants in the capital markets have already been introduced in our money-market discussion. Some borrowers and some lenders, as well as some facilitating institutions, operate in both maturity sectors. However, there are several differences between the two sectors—besides, but related to, the obvious difference in distance to maturity of the claims traded therein—that justify our separate treatment of these sectors.

In the first place, claims traded in the capital markets tend to be more complex. While most short-term open-market instruments are brief and uncluttered, long-term instruments and their supporting documents often specify most or all of the following:

> *Maturity*—date or dates when payment will be made on principal; whether the claim may be paid in advance; and, if so, whether and with what penalty.
>
> *Compensation for holding the claim*—amount(s); when due, or method of determining due date; priority over, or subordination to, other claims.
>
> *Claims on assets of issuer*—general claim or claim against specific assets; priority of claims.
>
> *Promises of issuer*—to do, or refrain from doing, certain acts or maintain certain conditions.
>
> *Other provisions*—convertibility into other securities; voice in management (under what circumstances, if any).

Second, as a corollary to the greater complexity of capital-market instruments, these instruments are much less homogeneous than are money-market instruments. A bankers' acceptance is a bankers' acceptance, after all, and nearly all commercial paper and large CD's are rated "prime"; but corporate bonds vary widely in quality, maturity, collateral, callability, and all the other dimensions.

Third, because of the distance to maturity (which is infinite, in the case of most equities), marketability is of great importance for most capital-market instruments.

And, finally, the purposes for which the economic unit seeks capital-market financing tend to be different from those of economic units seeking money-market financing, although there are important exceptions. Long-term debt and equity financing is usually obtained to carry permanent additions to current assets (cash, receivables, inventory) and for plant and equipment expenditures, whether by business firms, units of state and local government, or nonprofit organizations. Short-term financing, in contrast, is primarily for temporary bulges in current assets or for interim financing of items for which long-term financing will later be obtained. The two major exceptions are (1) many financial institutions—commercial banks, the savings intermediaries, and finance companies in particular—which customarily utilize short-term (even demand) financing to carry longer-term assets and (2) the United States Treasury, which, as we shall see, follows different criteria in deciding upon its debt maturity-mix.

Government Securities

Not much need be added here concerning securities issued by the Federal government: the Treasury and various government agencies. The same dealers and classes of holders, by and large, are present here as were in the short-term market. Some classes of holders, of course, concentrate on a particular range of maturities, in accordance with their portfolio needs and objectives. Commercial banks, for example, held a very small percentage of their U.S. government securities in the "ten years and over" category—only 2.3 per cent at the end of September 1973, while somewhat over half of their holdings are in the "one-to-five years" range. About 70 percent of the U.S. government securities held by nonfinancial corporations had scheduled maturities less than a year away, while over 60 per cent of insurance company holdings were in the "five years and over" range.

On March 31, 1974, somewhat less than half of the Treasury's $172.8 billion of marketable debt held by all private investors was in the "over one year" maturity range, and within this range two-thirds was in the one-to-five year range. This leaves about one-sixth of the total (or one-third of the "over one year" category) in the "five years and over" class.[1]

---

[1] Figures in this section are taken from *Federal Reserve Bulletin*, May 1974, p. A39.

The explanation for this particular maturity distribution is partly economic, partly a matter of legal sanctions. We cannot pause to discuss this topic here but must wait until our discussion of debt management in chapter 20.

The debt structure of state and local government units is quite different from that of the Federal government, since maturities are more evenly spaced over the spectrum. These are the reasons: (1) state and local governments borrow mainly for capital projects and (2) their issues are usually in the form of serial bonds, with maturities in a given issue ranging from short- to long-term.

State and local government bond issues (referred to as "municipals") are generally required by law to be awarded on a competitive-bidding basis, thus minimizing the danger of collusion between issuer and underwriter. The winning syndicate (group of investment banking firms submitting a single bid) then has the task of peddling the issue.

Commercial banks have become important holders of municipals in recent years. Other major investor groups are high-income individuals (directly or through trusts set up in their behalf) and property and casualty insurance companies. In all these cases the main reason for the attractiveness of municipals, of course, is that income from such securities is exempt from Federal taxation. Other intermediaries and nonfinancial firms either are not subject to Federal income taxation or qualify for special tax treatment, or they must concentrate their portfolios in short-term instruments.

The secondary market in these securities is fairly active, no doubt because the characteristics of the major investor groups are such that the securities are not likely to be held to maturity by the original purchasers. Most individual holders are middle-aged or older, people who prefer a nice, safe portfolio. Banks buy relatively heavily when money is easy and loan demand is low; they reduce their holdings of municipals when loan demand is intense. Property and casualty insurance companies find the tax-exempt feature valuable in good years but worthless in bad years, as we noted in chapter 8.

Corporate Securities: Bonds

As a corporation grows in sales, it requires additional assets, not only of the fixed, or plant-and-equipment, variety but current assets as well. Cash and inventories almost necessarily increase in volume, and even accounts receivable expand, in line with increased sales. These additional amounts of assets must be financed. If growth is extremely slow and the earning rate very large, the corporation may be able to generate sufficient financing through retained earnings plus the rise in accounts-payable debt to suppliers that "automatically" accompanies a rise in the volume of purchases.

Often, however, when the pressure for financing is too great to be met by these means, the corporation turns to external sources. If the increase in current assets is expected to be permanent, then both these assets and the additions to plant and equipment will normally be financed ultimately through long-term obligations.

Corporations secure long-term financing in a number of ways. The leading debt-financing arrangements are term loans (primarily from banks) and bonds. Equity financing is obtained partly through issuance of new shares of stock, partly by retaining earnings. The latter method has the ultimate effect of placing more net assets (assets minus liabilities) behind each share of stock.

In line with our procedures followed so far, we are limiting our discussion of instruments of corporate long-term financing to those in which open markets are involved. Accordingly, we concentrate in this section on corporate bonds and, in the next, on stock.

Corporate bonds are negotiable long-term promissory notes. Beyond these three characteristics, which all corporate bonds have in common, there are a large number of features differentiating individual issues. These differences of maturity, risk, and the like give rise to differences in market yields, a point to which we return later in this chapter.

Major holders of bonds are insurance companies and pension funds, both private and state-local, these groups accounting for about three-quarters of the total. Pension funds generally acquire bonds on the open market, while insurance companies rely mainly on "direct placement," a process closely analogous to bank lending.

In a direct placement, one or a group of insurance companies purchase an entire bond issue of a corporation. In fact, the insurance company or companies generally work with the issuer, and often with an investment banker, in setting the terms. Strictly speaking, therefore, this method of issuing bonds belongs in the category of "negotiated markets"; their inclusion here is a matter of custom rather than of principle.

Insurance companies realize certain economies of scale in thus dealing directly with the issuer. Also, there is more flexibility of terms possible than in an open-market issue, where the issuer is never certain as to whether or not the market will respond favorably to an innovation in the bonds' terms. The major drawback is that these bonds are not readily marketable once they are placed; but this is not a vital consideration to most insurance companies, particularly life companies, which have highly predictable liquidity needs and do not anticipate having to sell bonds to meet a sudden cash shortage.

For public issues, the services of an investment banking firm are nearly indispensable. Such a firm, having continuous contact with the financial markets, is in a position to give valuable advice concerning the most advantageous terms of an issue and also proper timing. Then the actual marketing of a new issue is generally performed by an investment banking firm, through negotiation or competitive bidding. This firm, either alone or (for issues of any size) with other firms associated with it for the marketing of this issue, undertakes to place the issue as soon as possible with investors.

The secondary market for corporate bonds is relatively small, chiefly because the bonds tend to stay where they land. However, bond prices are quoted on the major securities exchanges and by dealers, and the market appears to function efficiently.

A comparison of the size of the secondary market for corporate bonds with that for long-term government securities is instructive:

> The daily volume of corporate bonds traded on the registered exchanges averaged $19 million in 1970 and $25 million in 1968, the peak year for bond trading. In each year since 1960, the average volume of trading in government bonds with maturities beyond ten years has substantially exceeded the volume of organized trading in all seasoned bonds.[2]

During the 1961–70 decade the annual average of daily figures of "over ten years" bonds was $38.4 million; the figure for five–ten year government bonds was $106.7 million.

Corporate Securities: Stock

Comparatively few people have ever heard of bankers' acceptances, probably more are somewhat familiar with certificates of deposit, but everybody knows as least a little about the stock market! In popular participation, in coverage by news media, as an element in economic forecasts, and in sheer glamour, "the market" has no serious rivals among financial markets. Yet to us, at this point, the stock market is not the institutional symbol of capitalism; it is merely the name given to the institutional arrangements governing the buying and selling of *corporate stock,* or equities, mundane as it all sounds.

We must distinguish between the stock market and the New York Stock Exchange, or even stock exchanges in general. While in the exchanges the buying and selling of stock is highly visible, the stock of a substantial number of corporations is traded in the so-called *over-the-counter market,* that is, bought from, and sold to, dealers who are known to maintain inventories in certain issues. In addition, the stocks of smaller, locally known corporations usually change hands through more informal channels involving bankers, businessmen, and other members of the local "establishment."

Because shares of stock represent ownership and have no maturity or pattern of money payments set by contract, the market for stocks has certain distinctive features as compared with the other financial markets that we have discussed. In the first place, the secondary market completely overshadows the primary market in importance. New stock is-

---

[2] James L. Cochran, "U.S. Government Bonds as Capital Market Instruments," *Economic Review,* Federal Reserve Bank of Cleveland (August 1971), p. 11.

sues are relatively few. Most companies "raise" new ownership capital gradually by retaining earnings.³ The reasons for corporate preference for providing new financing by issuing bonds rather than stock are (1) the fact that bond interest is treated as an ordinary business expense and is therefore tax deductible while dividends are not so treated and (2) reluctance on the part of management and owners to issue what amounts to corporate "votes" to outsiders, thereby incurring the possibility of loss of control of the corporation by present management.

The other more or less distinctive feature of the stock market is the extent of speculation. This is inevitable, given the variability of profit of most corporations and dependence of common-stock income on profits. But beyond that is the unpredictability of the public's reaction to variations in profits or to any news that might conceivably have a bearing on profits—or a bearing on people's expectations! Keynes compared speculation (or "professional investment") with

> ... those newspaper competitions in which the competitors have to pick out the six prettiest faces from a hundred photographs, the prize being awarded to the competitor whose choice most nearly corresponds to the average preferences of the competitors as a whole; so that each competitor has to pick, not those faces which he himself finds prettiest, but those which he thinks likeliest to catch the fancy of the other competitors, all of whom are looking at the problem from the same point of view. It is not a case of choosing those which, to the best of one's judgment, are really the prettiest, nor even those which average opinion genuinely thinks the prettiest. We have reached the third degree where *we devote our intelligences to anticipating what average opinion expects the average opinion to be.*⁴

The whole process through which a public issue of stocks finally reaches the hands of the public may involve a number of steps and options, a topic that we must treat very briefly here. Investment bankers play the leading role at all stages in the process from preliminary investigation through negotiation and final sale—even sometimes in maintaining the market for a period after the entire issue is placed. Federal legislation, administered by the Securities and Exchange Commission, requires (with certain exceptions) full disclosure of all facts concerning the new issue itself and the issuing corporation that would have a bearing on the quality of the security.

As mentioned above, secondary marketing of stocks is conducted through organized exchanges, through securities dealers on the over-the-counter market, and through informal, mainly local, channels. Both

---

³ The only industry sector that consistently issues significant amounts of stock is public utilities, which have been, and are, caught between heavy demands for more plant and equipment due to our economic growth and limited opportunities to retain earnings because their rates are regulated by governmental commissions.

⁴ J. M. Keynes, *The General Theory of Employment, Interest and Money* (New York: Harcourt, Brace and Co., 1936), p. 156. Emphasis added.

in terms of dollar amount of securities and dollar volume of transactions, the exchanges are far more important than the over-the-counter equities market, according to estimates.[5] And the dollar volume of activity in local stocks is extremely minor in comparison with either.

The exchanges impose certain requirements that a corporation must meet in order to have its stock listed and must continue to meet in order to maintain listing. Because listing requires the disclosure of certain information, some firms (including many banks and insurance companies that could meet the requirements) have chosen to remain unlisted.

Trading on the securities exchanges is done by members only, transacting for their own portfolios and on behalf of customers. Large institutional investors, such as investment companies, pension funds, and insurance companies, are impatient to "eliminate the middleman," however; and trading of sizable blocks of stock directly between pairs of institutions is becoming increasingly common.

Relationships Among Markets

In closing this discussion of the markets for various kinds of financial instruments, we would do well to recollect that these markets are far from airtight compartments. Both issuers and investors have flexibility —some more than others, of course—concerning their capital structures and portfolios, respectively, in terms of maturity and other characteristics of instruments; and the longer the time period, the greater the degree of flexibility. Thus, increased pressure applied in one market, whether from the demand or the supply side, is transmitted quickly, via changes in relative prices (and yields) of the instruments involved, to the markets in which closely substitutable instruments are traded, and less intensely and rapidly to more remotely related financial markets.

This brings us quite logically to the topic of interest rates: what they really are, what forces affect them, and what determines their responsiveness to these forces.

The Structure of Interest Rates

The term *interest rate* (or *yield*) has different meanings in different contexts. Here, we use the term, as applied to a given financial claim, to denote *the annual rate of return that the purchaser of a financial claim will realize on the claim, assuming all contractual payments are met* (or, in the case of common stock, assuming the current dividend rate). In order to bring out key aspects of this concept, let us examine a few illustrations.

---

[5] Roland I. Robinson, *Money and Capital Markets* (New York: McGraw-Hill Book Co., 1964), p. 170.

First, suppose an economic unit purchasing for $1,000 a newly issued financial instrument, embodying the promise of the issuer to pay to the holder $1,060 one year from the date of issue. The additional $60 we call *interest;* and the yield, or implicit interest rate, is evidently 6 per cent, that is, $60 as a per cent of $1,000. No problem here.

Now, suppose the identical circumstances as in the above illustration, except that the issuer has agreed to pay the $1,060 at the end of six months. In this case, the rate of interest is actually 12 per cent, since 6 per cent in a half-year is tantamount to 12 per cent for a full year. Remember, interest rates are expressed as per cents but also *on an annual basis.*

Or suppose the amount of the claim is $1,000 at maturity, one year from today, the date of issue, and the instrument is issued at a discount, as is the case with Treasury bills, open-market commercial paper, and a few other money-market instruments. The purchaser pays $940. The interest is still $60, but this is computed as a per cent of—what? In the two earlier examples we used the amount paid by the purchaser as our base, so, for consistency as well as by tradition, we use $940 and express $60 as a per cent of that figure. Therefore, the rate of interest is nearly 6.4 percent.

Next, consider another complication. Suppose that at the end of six months the original purchaser of the one-year claim in the first illustration sells the claim to a third party for $1,040. Now we suddenly have three interest rates: (1) the rate the issuer pays, (2) the yield obtained by the original purchaser, and (3) the yield obtained by the third party. The first rate presents no problem: the issuer pays 6 per cent, as agreed, regardless of what the instrument sells for subsequently. But what yields are received by the first and second holders?

The original purchaser's yield on this claim is actually 8 per cent: he received $40 more than he paid for it, a gain of 4 per cent *in six months,* which translates into 8 per cent on an annual basis. The second purchaser, however, will earn less than 4 per cent if he holds until maturity. He has paid $1,040 for a claim which, six months from now, will pay him $1,060. The $20 gain is 1.923 per cent of the $1,040 that he paid, or 3.846 on an annual basis.

Which one of these, then, is the relevant one for us in discussing market interest rates? Since we are interested in actual conditions in the financial markets, the third would be our choice. The rate the issuer had to pay was relevant to the conditions that had existed six months earlier. The fact that the original purchaser realized a gain when he sold was no doubt welcomed by him (and the Internal Revenue Service); but, in order to ascertain current market interest rates, we need to know the yields implied in current transactions.

For our final complication we must look at financial instruments that call for more than one payment, as capital market instruments typically do. Suppose that the original transaction involved the issuance of a claim

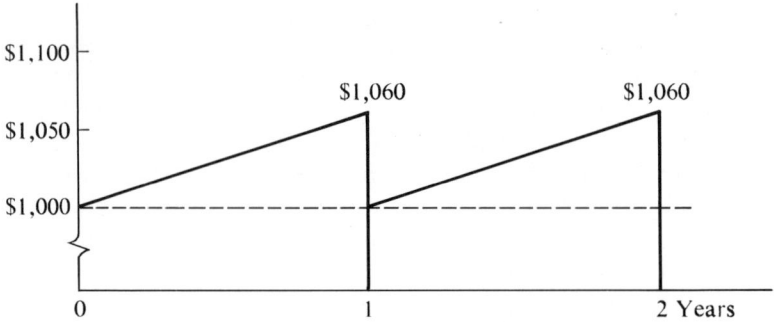

Figure 11.1
Growth pattern of a $1,000 claim.

that promised to pay the holder $60 at the end of the first year and $1,060 at the end of the second year. If the purchaser pays $1,000 for this claim, we know that, if all goes well and he holds until maturity, the claim will yield him 6 per cent. We may think of this claim as "growing" at a 6 per cent rate. At the end of the first year we "harvest" $60, leaving the original $1,000, which then grows another $60 the second year.

But suppose that, instead, this particular instrument had been purchased from the issuer for $981.92. What would its yield be? That is, what rate of growth is involved here, such that this claim grows for a year at that rate, yields a "harvest" of $60, and grows for another year, at the end of which it returns $1,060? Fortunately, there are tables available with answers worked out to such problems. In this case, a 7 per cent growth rate, and only that rate, will produce this result. Observe: $981.92, growing at a 7 per cent rate, becomes $1,050.65 at the end of one year. Harvesting $60 leaves $990.65, which, at a 7 per cent rate, grows to $1,060 at the end of the second year!

This illustration provides only a glimpse of the mathematics of yield determination. In chapter 15 we probe this subject a bit more deeply in our discussion of investment. Hopefully, enough has been said so that

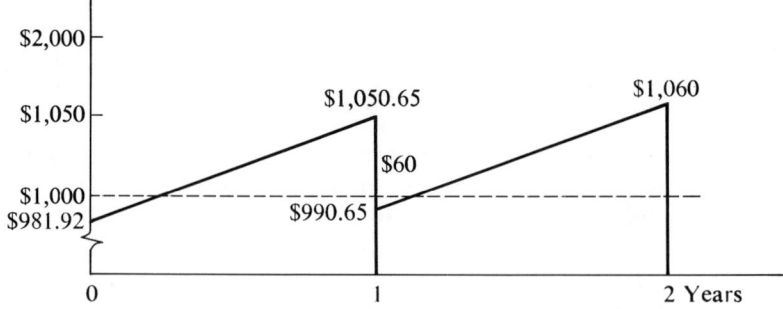

Figure 11.2
Growth pattern of a $1,000 claim, purchased for $981.92.

we can accept this generalization: the yield of a financial claim depends on (1) anticipated future cash receipts, (2) their time distribution, and (3) the price paid for the claim.

The Pattern of Yields

Table 11.1 conveys an impression of both variety and change. At any given time interest rates vary substantially, and over time the differences are even greater. As we study the table, though, we are impressed by certain behavior patterns. Some rates are always lower than others; some fluctuate over a wider range than others; some have changed position relative to one or more others. Let us examine briefly the major forces responsible for these patterns.

A few of these influences are obvious. Differences in *riskiness*, for example, reflect themselves in interest-rate differences.[6] Thus we see in Figure 11.3 that U.S. government bonds, lowest in default risk of all securities, yield less than corporate bonds; and lower-rated (Baa) more than high-rated (Aaa) corporate bonds. This figure also shows the

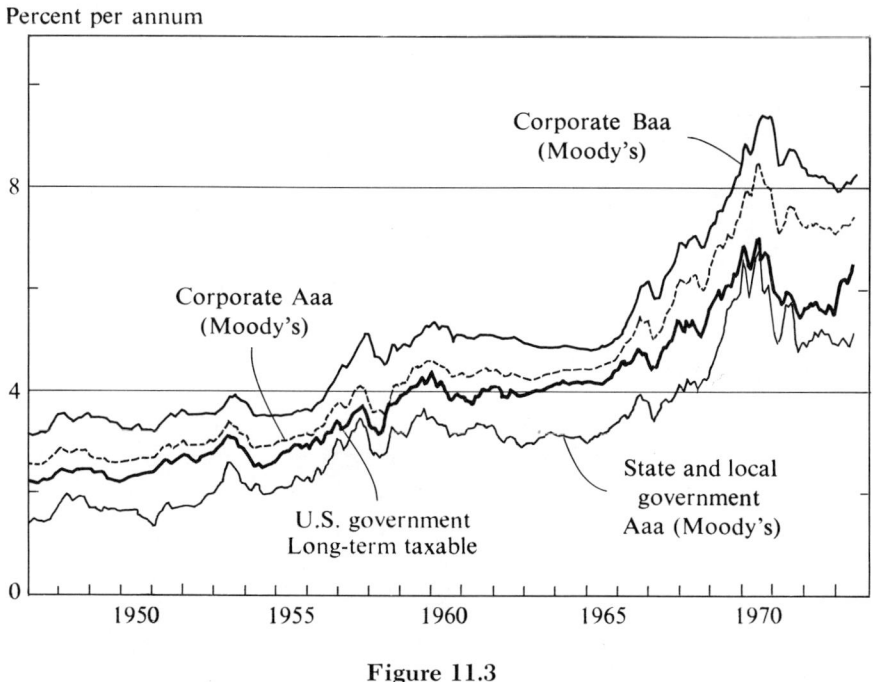

Figure 11.3
Bond yields.

Source: *1973 Historical Chart Book* (Washington, D.C.: Board of Governors of the Federal Reserve System, 1973); p. 31.

[6] See Avery B. Cohan, *The Risk Structure of Interest Rates* (Morristown, N.J.: General Learning Corporation, 1973).

TABLE 11.1
Money- and Capital-Market Yields,
Selected Years and Months, 1950–73
(per cent per annum)

Year or Month	U.S. Treasury Issues		State and Local Bonds	Corporate Bonds		Bank Loans to Business	Prime Commercial Paper	FHA New Home Mortgages
	3-months Bills	Bonds		Aaa	Baa			
Year								
1950	1.218	2.32	1.98	2.62	3.24	2.69	1.45	4.17
1955	1.753	2.84	2.53	3.06	3.53	3.70	2.18	4.64
1960	2.928	4.02	3.73	4.41	5.19	5.16	3.85	6.18
1965	3.954	4.21	3.27	4.49	4.87	5.06	4.38	5.46
1970	6.458	6.58	6.51	8.04	9.11	8.48	7.72	9.05
1971	4.348	5.74	5.70	7.39	8.56	6.32	5.11	7.78
1972	4.071	5.63	5.27	7.21	8.16	5.82	4.69	7.53
1973	7.041	6.30	5.18	7.44	8.24	8.30	8.15	8.08
Month	(1973)							
Feb.	5.558	6.14	5.12	7.22	7.97	6.52	6.22	7.55
May	6.348	6.22	5.12	7.29	8.06	7.35	7.27	7.73
Aug.	8.672	6.81	5.47	7.68	8.53	9.24	10.21	8.19
Nov.	7.866	6.31	5.17	7.67	8.42	10.08	8.94	8.97

Source: *Economic Report of the President, 1974* (Washington, D. C.: U.S. Government Printing Office, 1974), pp. 317–318. Consult these pages for details of each of these series.

influence of *tax status* on market yields: state and local government top-rated issues yield less than the U.S. government issues.

Administrative costs are also a factor, helping to explain the fact that sometimes smaller instruments in a given category will carry higher rates, for instance. And at times differences exist that can be best understood as merely "frictional." The various open markets usually adjust swiftly, but not instantaneously, to shifts in underlying supply and demand conditions.

Term Structure of Interest Rates

Interest rates also vary by the *maturity* of securities that are alike in other relevant respects. The pattern of rates from short- to long-term instruments, given these other characteristics is referred to as the *term structure* of interest rates. A convenient device for depicting the term structure is the "yield curve," in which per cent yield is measured vertically and years to maturity horizontally. By using only Treasury securities, as is done in Figure 11.4, we are able to hold all "other things"—risk, cost, tax treatment, and so on—constant, since the only important difference among these securities is their distance to maturity.[7]

Although the highest rates have usually been carried by long-term securities, sometimes intermediate-term or short-term securities have

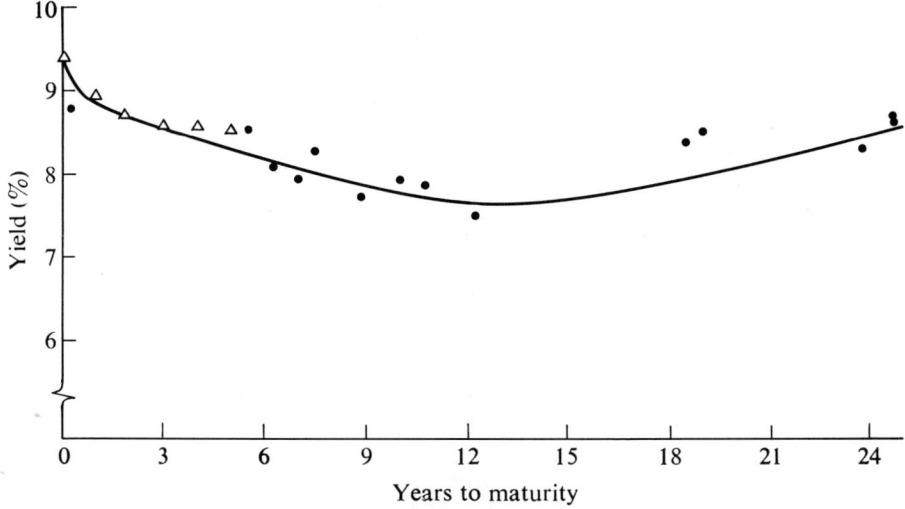

Figure 11.4
Yield curve, based on U.S. Treasury securities
January 28, 1974.

---

[7] Several issues, when part of an estate, are redeemable at par in payment of an estate tax. Since, under current conditions, this feature raises their market value relative to issues that are similar in other respects, we have not included them in drawing the curve.

had the highest rates. Usually, when rates in general are rising, they rise in all maturities; but short-term rates increase more than do long-term rates. When rates are falling, the same is true, with signs reversed. Some observers say that it is "normal" for long-term rates to exceed short-term rates, but even this is disputed.

When we seek to learn why interest rates vary by maturity and, relatedly, what shape a "normal" yield curve would take, we discover that there is profound disagreement among those who have investigated this topic. Three theories have emerged: market-segmentation, expectations, and liquidity preference. Each of these will be sketched now, along with some indications of a possible synthesis.

MARKET SEGMENTATION One theory of the term structure holds that the behavior of the yield curve is mainly due to market segmentation; that is, particular classes of borrowers and lenders largely stick to particular segments of the maturity range because of legal requirements or managerial policies. Sometimes (at cyclical peaks, for example) typically short-term borrowers have unusually large demands, so short-term rates are higher. Or the resources of traditionally long-term lenders may be growing comparatively slowly; then long-term borrowers find market rates in their range higher than usual.

Why, then, do all rates tend to move simultaneously in the same direction? Because, say defenders of this approach, general changes in the economic environment usually influence supply-demand relationships in all maturity ranges. Also, some participants are willing to shift to the next maturity-segment, so to speak. An increase in demand for short-term financing tends to cause short-term rates to rise, inducing some lenders to shift somewhat toward this end of the maturity range and perhaps diverting some borrowers into longer maturities. But the possibilities of this sort of intersegment movement are considered to be rather limited.

EXPECTATIONS Opposed to this type of explanation is the *expectations hypothesis,* which explains the shape and movement of the yield curve in terms of expectations of future short-term interest rates. Suppose, for example, that most participants in financial markets believe that present interest rates are low compared to what they will be in, say, a year. Prospective investors, accordingly, will be unwilling to purchase long-term securities at their present prices but will be inclined to buy short-term securities now, in order to be in a position to acquire long-term securities carrying higher yields in a year or less.

This behavior by investors will tend to shift the yield curve, raising long-term yields relative to short-term yields as sellers and issuers of long-term securities are forced to offer more favorable yields in order to attract buyers.

If interest rates are expected to be lower in the near future, prospective investors will be more inclined to favor long-term securities, and the yield will, of course, respond by a fall in long-term relative to short-term yields.

It would not be correct to infer that, according to this approach, when the yield curve is upsloping, future short-term rates *will* be higher than they are now. The theory claims only that the market *expects* them to be higher. Then suppose that the market is disappointed and short-term rates remain at levels that are low by previous standards? The result may be that the level of rates considered "normal" is itself adjusted downward, as happens numerous times.

LIQUIDITY PREFERENCE Now, suppose that the market expected short-term rates to remain the same over the next twenty years. Would this cause an absolutely flat yield curve? The purists among expectations theorists say, "Yes, since the long-term rate is merely the average of current and expected short-term rates." But others point to the uncertainty surrounding all expectations of future rates as an inducement to the investor to prefer the short, more "liquid," maturities to the longer, despite expectations of constant rates.

To illustrate, suppose that you, as an investor, do not expect future short-term rates to change, but yet you are not certain. You believe that they *might* change, and that the chances are about equal that they will rise by any given per cent or fall by that same per cent. It may seem that the two possibilities of change should cancel each other out; then you should have no preferences as between short- and long-term securities. However, the *consequences* of a change would not be symmetrical. A rise in the long-term rate would involve a reduction in the price of a long-term bond and, in case of a need to sell the asset, could ruin the holder financially. A fall of the same magnitude in the long-term rate would involve a rise in the price of a long-term bond, but no accompanying bonanza is likely to occur, offsetting the possible evil consequence of a rise in rates.

Generalizing, the "pure" liquidity-preference theorist will assert that, over the long run, the yield curve will tend to be upsloping in the long run, reflecting the risks inherent in holding long-term securities.

A SYNTHESIS These three approaches are not diametrically opposed, except in the hands of their most fervid apostles. It is possible to combine them into a broader picture of the determination of the interest rate structure; and most recent empirical work in this area would support this approach.[8] Investor *expectations* appear to be highly important in the

---

[8] Two useful recent summaries of work in this area are Burton G. Malkiel, *The Term Structure of Interest Rates: Theory, Empirical Evidence, and Applications* (New York: McCaleb-Seiler Publishing Company, 1970), pp. 14–22; and James C. Van Horne, *Functions and Analysis of Capital Market Rates* (Englewood Cliffs, N. J.: Prentice-Hall, 1970), Chapter IV.

process. However, the fact that the yield curve is usually upsloping cannot be shrugged off as mere coincidence but seems to point to the existence of *liquidity preference* on the part of investors, that is, of the need for some inducement to take the risk of holding longer-term securities than they would really prefer. And these preferences on the part of investors and issuers, in some cases for short-term securities and in others for long-terms, give rise to a degree of *market segmentation,* raising the possibility that differences in relative supplies of securities in various maturities could alter the shape of the yield curve, at least marginally.

Summary of Chapters 10 and 11

Financial firms are linked with each other and with other economic units through a complex system of financial markets. For discussion purposes, we divided these markets into two classes on the basis of maturity of the financial instruments traded: money markets, where short-term instruments are traded; and capital markets, for intermediate- and long-term financial instruments.

This does not imply a wall of separation between the two classes of markets, however, but a recognition of a general tendency for long- and intermediate-term instruments to be more complex, less homogeneous, and often more dependent on secondary markets than are short-term instruments. Moreover, the purposes for which capital-market claims are issued tend to differ (though with important exceptions) from those that induce short-term issues, the former being more likely to be issued to finance plant and equipment expenditures and permanent additions to current assets, the latter to provide for short-duration financing needs.

Within each of the two categories, there are several major classes of financial instruments that are traded on the open markets and are reasonably close substitutes from the standpoint of asset holders. There is some substitutability among maturity classes as well as within each class. United States Treasury bills are the largest category of money-market instruments by volume, followed by certificates of deposit, open-market commercial paper, Treasury securities other than bills, and bankers' acceptances. The major categories of capital-market instruments are securities (other than short-term) issued by the United States government and its agencies and by state and local governments, and bonds and stock issued by corporations.

Financial instruments differ among themselves in a number of respects—including maturity, riskiness, administrative cost, and tax status—that have a bearing on their attractiveness to investors. We can observe some of these effects statistically: other things equal, the riskier, or more costly to handle, or less favored for tax purposes is the security, the higher the yield it must offer relative to securities similar in other respects, in order to attract investors. But the relation between maturity and yield has proven to be considerably more complex and has given rise to several competing explanations—market segmentation, expectations, and liquidity preference—and attempts to reconcile them.

KEY CONCEPTS

"Municipals"
Corporate bonds
Corporate stock
Over-the-counter market
Term structure of interest rates
Yield

QUESTIONS FOR REVIEW

1. "The only difference between instruments traded in capital markets and those traded in money markets is that the former are long-term and the latter are short-term." Comment.
2. Compare corporate stock and corporate bonds with respect to (a) major classes of holders, (b) importance of secondary markets, and (c) rights of holders.
3. Compare U.S. government bonds and municipal bonds with respect to (a) major classes of holders, (b) importance of secondary markets, and (c) method of issuance.
4. Why is the coupon rate of a bond potentially misleading as an indicator of its "true" yield?
5. "A rise in market interest rates would make existing securities more valuable, this causing their prices to rise." Evaluate.
6. What are some factors that might explain why security X yields more than security Y.
7. Is it possible to reconcile the market segmentation and expectations explanations of the yield curve? Explain.

SUGGESTIONS FOR FURTHER READING FOR CHAPTERS 10 AND 11

Baxter, Nevins D. *The Commercial Paper Market.* Boston: Bankers Publishing Co., 1966.

Commission on Money and Credit. *Private Capital Markets.* Englewood Cliffs, N.J.: Prentice-Hall, 1964.

Dougall, Herbert E. *Capital Markets and Institutions.* Englewood Cliffs, N.J.: Prentice-Hall, 1970.

Federal Reserve Bank of Cleveland. *Money Market Instruments,* 3d ed. Cleveland: Federal Reserve Bank of Cleveland, 1970.

Federal Reserve Bank of New York. *Essays in Money and Credit.* New York: Federal Reserve Bank of New York, 1964.

Homer, Sidney. *A History of Interest Rates.* New Brunswick, N.J.: Rutgers University Press, 1963.

Hungate, Richard D. *Interbusiness Financing.* Washington, D.C.: Small Business Administration, 1962.

Lindow, Wesley. *Inside the Money Market.* New York: Random House, 1972.

Madden, Carl. *The Money Side of "The Street."* New York; Federal Reserve Bank of New York, 1959.

Malkiel, Burton G. *The Term Structure of Interest Rates: Theory, Empirical Evidence, and Applications.* New York: McCaleb-Seiler Publishing Co., 1970.

Meiselman, David. *The Term Structure of Interest Rates.* Englewood Cliffs, N.J.: Prentice-Hall, 1962.

Nichols, Dorothy M. *Trading in Federal Funds.* Washington, D.C.: Board of Governors, Federal Reserve System, 1965.

Polakoff, Murray, et al. *Financial Institutions and Markets.* Boston: Houghton Mifflin Co., 1970.

Robinson, Roland I. *Money and Capital Markets.* New York: McGraw-Hill Book Co., 1964.

Scott, Ira O., Jr. *The Government Securities Market.* New York: McGraw-Hill Book Co., 1965.

Stone, R. W. "The Changing Structure of the Money Market." *Journal of Finance* XX (May 1965), pp. 229–38.

Struble, Frederick M. "Current Debate on the Term Structure of Interest Rates," *Monthly Review.* Federal Reserve Bank of Kansas City (January–February, 1966), pp. 10–16.

Treasury–Federal Reserve Study of the U.S. Government Securities Market. Washington, D.C.: U.S. Government Printing Office, 1969.

Van Horne, James C. *The Function and Analysis of Capital Market Rates.* Englewood Cliffs, N.J.: Prentice-Hall, 1970.

Willis, Parker B. *The Federal Funds Market—Its Origin and Development*, rev. ed. Boston: Federal Reserve Bank of Boston, 1964.

———. *The Secondary Market for Negotiable Certificates of Deposit.* Washington, D.C.: Board of Governors, Federal Reserve System, 1967.

———. *A Study of the Market for Federal Funds.* Washington, D.C.: Board of Governors, Federal Reserve System, 1967.

Woodworth, G. Walter. *The Monetary Market and Monetary Management.* 2d ed. New York: Harper & Row, 1972.

Monetary Relations
The International Payments System
Foreign Exchange Market:
International Payments Facilities
Foreign Exchange Market: Other Functions
The Dollar in World Finance

Financial Market Relations
Private Institutions in International
Financial Markets
The Export-Import Bank
Government-Sponsored International
Intermediaries
Money Markets: Eurodollars
Money Markets: Other Instruments
Capital Markets

Summary

The International Context 12

The economies of the world are gradually evolving into a world economy. We are observing the emergence of truly international companies—international not only in markets but also in production facilities, in management facilities, and in financing. In fact, for some companies the national location of the home office is more a matter of historical accident than of importance in terms of production, marketing, or financing.

Paralleling the "internationalization" (as it is often called) of business enterprise are similar developments in financial institutions and markets. It would probably be an exaggeration to speak of a "world financial system," yet there is no doubt that the world is moving in that direction. Through numerous kinds of relationships—of ownership, debtor-creditor, partnership, and less formal cooperation—the financial systems of the United States and the other nations of planet Earth are becoming ever more closely linked together. There is no question but that, in our quest for an understanding of our own financial system, we must take explicit account of this development as it relates to all three aspects of the system: institutions, economics, and policy.

In this chapter we deal mainly with the institutional aspect of our international financial relationships. The implications of these relationships for the behavior of our economy will be explored in Part IV in the course of our examination of monetary theory; and in Part V we investigate the influence of our international financial relationships on the conduct of aggregate economic policy.

Monetary Relations

Whenever economic units in different nations, each nation having its own monetary system, regularly engage in economic transactions with each other, two related problems must be solved: (1) the development of an *international payments system,* that is, a set of arrangements whereby the money of each nation can be exchanged for that of the other, since the seller generally has little use for the buyer's alien money and the buyer seldom maintains an inventory of the seller's type of money; and (2) the establishment of an institutional basis for the determination of the *rate of exchange,* the price of the monetary unit of one nation in terms of that of the other. The ways in which these problems are solved to a large extent determines the nature of the *international monetary system,* "a rather loose set of relationships among separate and independent parts," which has been well defined as the "institutions, arrangements, and practices through which international payments are made."[1]

The International Payments System

Various arrangements for exchange rate determination have existed in the past, adequate discussion of which would require far more space than would be justifiable here. So in our discussion of the second international-transactions problem—the exchange rate—we shall limit ourselves to the essentials of the institutional arrangements for exchange rate determination under which most of the world conducted its international dealings during nearly all of the post-World War II era. Then we shall move on to the first of the pair of problems: the payments system, as it functions in this environment.

EXCHANGE RATE DETERMINATION The dominant system of exchange rate determination since 1946 is generally labeled an *adjustable-peg system.* Such a system has these characteristics:[2]

1. Each national monetary unit is defined in terms of a particular commodity (usually gold). The relative gold content of any two monetary units establishes the par rate of exchange between them.
2. The monetary authorities of the various countries act to keep actual market rates of exchange within a narrow range around par rates of exchange.
3. The par value of a nation's monetary unit may be changed ("repegged") at a different level if indicated by economic circumstances.

[1] Delbert A. Snider, *International Monetary Relations* (New York: Random House, 1966), p. 4.
[2] (Based on) ibid., p. 90.

THE INTERNATIONAL MONETARY FUND The institutional heart of the international payments system is the International Monetary Fund (IMF), a supranational organization conceived at a conference of representatives of Allied nations held in Bretton Woods, New Hampshire, in 1944, near the end of World War II,[3] and was actually born two years later.

Essentially, the IMF functions as a "pool of liquidity." Each member nation initially is assigned a quota, based roughly on its national output and its volume of foreign trade. The quota determines the nation's voting rights, its "credit line," and the amount of the subscription it must pay into the fund. One-fourth of the quota must be paid in gold; the rest in the nation's own currency. These quotas have been increased several times, by membership vote, to provide the expanded liquidity necessitated by growth in the volume of international transactions. From this huge pool of gold and national money, member nations may borrow to meet shortages of foreign currency. An amount equal to the gold contribution (called the *gold tranche*) may be drawn on a no-questions-asked basis; additional amounts may be drawn, but only under prescribed conditions specifying maximum amounts, repayment terms, and interest charges.

Each member nation of the IMF also agrees to abide by the fund's rules regarding exchange rates, particularly in (1) defining the par value of its monetary unit as a certain quantity of gold, (2) maintaining the value of its monetary unit relative to gold within a specified per cent of par value, and (3) observing certain procedures when it wishes to change the par value of its monetary unit.

Concerning this last point, if a nation is persistently having difficulty in limiting its imports to an amount that it can cover by exports plus, perhaps, long-term financing, it probably would desire to devalue its currency, that is, to lower its par value relative to gold. The desired result of devaluation would be a larger volume of exports and smaller volume of imports, since its currency, hence its goods and services, would now be "cheaper" in terms of gold and foreign currencies while foreign currencies (and goods and services) would be more costly in terms of domestic money.[4]

Sometimes the opposite situation arises—a persistent tendency for a nation's international economic dealings to result in an undesirably large accumulation of foreign exchange—and the nation wishes to revalue its monetary unit upward in order to discourage exports and stimulate imports. In either set of circumstances, the nation is permitted to change the par value of its monetary unit; but, if a change greater than 10

---

[3] This extraordinarily productive conference produced not only the IMF but also the International Bank for Research and Development, which we shall meet later in this chapter.
[4] Whether or not the desired outcome would be realized would depend on a number of factors that cannot be discussed here. Consult any good recent text in international economics.

per cent is desired, the nation is supposed to obtain prior approval of the IMF.

The problem of adequacy of international reserves concerns not only individual nations but also the nations of the world collectively. Since world trade has been expanding far more rapidly than conventional international reserves—monetary gold, the IMF gold tranche, U.S. dollars, and other convertible foreign currency held as reserves—the International Monetary Fund, after careful study and extended negotiations, voted to supplement these reserves by a new instrument called *special drawing rights* (SDR's).

SDR's are issued by, but are not obligations of, the IMF. The total amount of each periodic allocation must be approved by 85 per cent of the votes in the fund, assuring a general consensus that more international reserves are needed. Of the total, the amount issued to each nation is based on the size of its quota. The first allocation of SDR's took place January 1, 1970, and, by the end of 1972, $3.4 billion of SDR's had been created.

A popular name for SDR's is "paper gold," an odd term but one that seems quite suitable because SDR's are intended to be used alongside, and on a par with, gold itself as monetary reserves. In fact, each member nation, in effect, binds itself not to discriminate against SDR's by exchanging them for gold (the fund is supposed to "deal with" any guilty nation), a fact that gives SDR's virtual "international legal tender" status. Most nations are already including SDR's in their international reserves.

So far, opinions concerning SDR's range from "they will eventually render gold obsolete" to "they merely postpone briefly the inevitable collapse of the international monetary system." However, it is much too early to render any kind of verdict on this revolutionary innovation in international finance.

This, then, is the system under which the noncommunist world has functioned most of the time since 1946. We should keep its essential properties in mind as we proceed to examine the international payments mechanism with particular reference to the United States.

Foreign Exchange Market: International Payments Facilities

The huge and increasing flow of goods, services, and claims in international trade and finance created both the necessity and the natural conditions for the development of a foreign exchange market, through which economic units offering money and short-term claims denominated in foreign monetary units can acquire domestic money or other liquid claims and through which economic units can effect the opposite kind of exchange. This country has such a market, concentrated mainly in New York, the major market institutions being twenty-five or so United States banks, a number of branches and agencies of foreign banks, and a few foreign exchange brokers.

ROLE OF THE MAJOR NEW YORK BANKS   The large participating New York banks maintain inventories of foreign exchange, mostly in the form of demand deposits denominated in the monetary units of other nations, in foreign banks. These inventories are drawn down as banks sell drafts payable in foreign money to their customers (importers, for example) and are replenished as banks purchase from their customers credit instruments payable in foreign currencies that the New York banks arrange to have credited to their deposit accounts in foreign banks.

A domestic analogy may help at this point. Suppose you have no checking account but your older brother does. If he is agreeable, you can make a $200 out-of-town payment for, say, stereo components by paying your brother $200, plus a brotherly commission, in exchange for which he would write a check for $200 payable to you, which you could then endorse over to the out-of-town company. Of course, your brother's deposit has been reduced by $200. He need only take the $200 currency that you paid him to the bank and have it credited to his account—a considerably simpler task than that of the New York bank!

OTHER INSTITUTIONS   Banks attempt to keep adequate but not excessive inventories of foreign exchange. It would be a miracle, however, if each day a particular bank would be able to buy just about the same volume of each kind of foreign money as it sold! How, then, can it adjust its shortages and overages? Fortunately, a small group of foreign exchange brokers operate among the banks, putting a bank with a shortage in a specific foreign "currency" (as foreign money and short-term liquid claims are invariably called in this context) in contact with one experiencing a surplus—for a fee, of course. Other methods of temporary adjustment to a shortage are (1) borrowing from a foreign correspondent, (2) arranging a "swap" with a foreign correspondent, through which each credits the account of the other in its own currency, and (3) arranging to buy the needed foreign exchange, from or through a foreign correspondent, in exchange for dollars.

Thus commercial banks are the key institutions in the international payments sytem, just as they are in the domestic payments system. The most important components of the domestic payments system are the banks, local clearing houses, the Federal Reserve banks, and the Interdistrict Settlement Fund, while the machinery for international payments involves mainly the banks, the foreign exchange brokers, and foreign correspondents of American banks.

SOURCES OF DEMAND AND SUPPLY   A variety of transactions give rise to demands for, and offers of, foreign exchange. Merchandise exports and imports would head most lists. An export, for example, either provides an American firm with foreign currencies or reduces the supply of dollars in the hands of foreigners. Conversely, an import either reduces our stock of foreign currencies or increases foreign holdings of dollars.

But there are also many other kinds of transactions that affect our supplies of, and demands for, foreign exchange: purchases and sales of securities between domestic and foreign economic units, tourist expenditures by Americans abroad and by foreigners here, payment of dividends on foreign stock owned by Americans or the other way around, gifts, repayment of debts, and numerous other categories.

Sometimes the combined effect of all these transactions over a given time period is a reduction of our holdings of foreign exchange and an increase of foreign holdings of dollars. The result is upward pressure on the price of foreign money relative to the dollar, perhaps setting in motion other effects as well (for example, a decrease in our imports due to the rise in their price in dollar terms). And, of course, at other times the tide moves in the other direction.

Foreign Exchange Market: Other Functions

FACILITIES FOR INTERNATIONAL FINANCE Beside providing the mechanism whereby an economic unit can acquire means of payment denominated in a monetary unit other than its own, the foreign exchange market performs two other functions.[5] First, through this market the financing of foreign trade is facilitated. Frequently in international business transactions, the arrangements for making payment to the seller on a specified date are spelled out in a formal credit instrument, the holder of which is financing the transaction. The bankers' acceptance, discussed in chapter 10, is a case in point. We recall that, through this instrument, the exporter receives payment in his own currency immediately, while the importer incurs an obligation to pay, in his own currency, on a designated future date.

FACILITIES FOR HEDGING The second additional function of foreign exchange markets is the so-called hedging function. Any economic unit that has an obligation to pay, or holds a claim to receive, an amount of money denominated in another currency is exposed to the risk that the rate of exchange between the two currencies may have changed by the due date, with the possible result that the economic unit will have to pay more, or will receive less, than originally expected. Under present conditions, the economic unit can avoid this kind of exposure by hedging.

For example (ignoring technical details), suppose that, as a part of a business transaction, you are to receive £100 in ninety days. You know *approximately* how many U.S. dollars that will represent, but not exactly, because exchange rates can fluctuate. If the rate of exchange should move against the dollar, the dollar value of your £100 may be considerably less than you had anticipated. Of course, if the dollar should rise

---

[5] Charles P. Kindleberger, *International Economics*, 4th ed. (Homewood, Ill.: R. D. Irwin, 1968), pp. 43–48.

against the pound sterling, you would be pleasantly surprised. But, like most businessmen, you would prefer not to take this risk.

In order to be sure of the dollar amount you will receive in ninety days, you can enter into a contract with another economic unit—say, a bank—under which you promise to deliver £100 in ninety days for a price in dollars agreed upon now. Then, ninety days later, you (1) receive the £100 payment and (2) deliver the £100 to the bank in exchange for the agreed-upon dollar amount. Thus regardless of any rise or fall in the exchange rate, you are protected by your hedge.

The rate of exchange on *forward* contracts, that is, contracts calling for a specified type and amount of a currency at an agreed-upon time, will probably not be the same as the *spot* (immediate delivery) rate. The difference depends on numerous factors, including relative interest rates, intervention by monetary authorities, seasonal patterns, and market expectations of supply and demand factors affecting the international economic positions of the two currencies involved.

The Dollar in World Finance

One significant aspect of the world payments system is the evolution of the United States dollar into something like a world medium of exchange in international transactions. Currently, according to one estimate, more than one-third of the total volume of international trade is financed by dollars.[6] For the world today, international finance means to a very important extent dollar financing. "This . . . role of the dollar in the world economy reflects at once the availability of dollar credits to finance just about anything anywhere, and the dollar's acceptability as a 'reserve' currency to settle imbalances in international accounts."[7]

United States dollars also serve as an international store of value, in that foreign monetary authorities, banks, and other economic units hold several billions of dollars' worth ($11.3 billion at the end of 1973)[8] of demand-deposit claims against United States banks. And the dollar as a unit of account is acquiring an important role outside our borders. As we shall discuss shortly, many bond issues floated in Europe are denominated in United States dollars, even though the issuer and most or all of the investors are non-Americans!

In short, the United States dollar has become a *key currency* or *vehicle currency*—the leading one, in fact—in the international economy. The dollar plays much the same role internationally as a national currency plays domestically.

---

[6] Joseph G. Kvasnicka, "Eurodollars—An Important Source of Funds for American Banks," *Business Conditions*, Federal Reserve Bank of Chicago (June 1969), p. 12.
[7] Ernest Bloch, "Eurodollar: An Emerging International Money Market," *The Bulletin*. C. J. Devine Institute of Finance, New York University Graduate School of Business Administration, #39 (April 1966), p. 4.
[8] *Federal Reserve Bulletin*, May 1974, p. A70.

Financial Market Relations

In this section we shall sketch briefly some of the interrelations among national financial markets. Our emphasis will be not on the market institutions of the various nations but rather on the institutions, instruments, and practices that have developed in relation to the international dealings of economic units, public and private.

In this discussion the terms *money market, capital market,* and their plurals will be used in the broad sense, comprising both negotiated and open markets.

Private Institutions in International Financial Markets

Important roles in the process of "internationalization" of the world's financial systems have been assumed by certain financial institutions: large commercial banks in particular and also investment banking houses. Others becoming more active include pension funds, insurance companies, and investment companies (mutual funds). Monetary authorities participate in some markets, in connection with their function of maintaining currency stability; and certain international and regional institutions also are participants. We shall take a broad survey of the institutional scene now before turning to the individual financial markets.

UNITED STATES BANKS AND FOREIGN BRANCHES The growth in foreign activity of U.S.-based business firms has made growth of the foreign activities of U.S.-based banks feasible and perhaps inevitable. Banks naturally have sought to serve their customers' need for new and expanded international services; and the American firms prefer to deal with American banks, with their familiar ways of doing things. Another important factor in the growth of U.S. banking abroad has been the emergence of the dollar as a key currency in international trade and finance.

The number of foreign branches of U.S. banks has grown rapidly. At the close of 1962 there were 145 foreign branches of member banks; at the end of 1972 the figure was 627 branches operating in 73 foreign countries.[9] These branches held $77.4 billion worth of assets, almost entirely financial claims, at the end of 1972.[10] Over half these totals were in branches in London, the main financial center of Europe.

Member banks are also authorized to form subsidiary corporations specifically for foreign banking and finance. Because these corporations are empowered to engage in certain activities forbidden to their parent banks but in great demand abroad—namely, holding stock in banking,[11]

---

[9] Board of Governors of the Federal Reserve System, *Annual Report, 1972* (Washington, D.C.: Board of Governors, 1973), p. 213.
[10] *Federal Reserve Bulletin*, September 1973, p. 710.
[11] Since March 1967, member banks have been authorized to purchase stock, subject to specified limits, in foreign banks.

financing, and commercial enterprises and participating in the underwriting and distribution of securities abroad—they have grown rapidly in number in recent years, reaching ninety-seven in mid-1973, up from twenty-six as recently as 1962.[12]

FOREIGN BANKS AND UNITED STATES BRANCHES There has been a similar boom in American branches of foreign-based banks, and for similar reasons. Restrictive state legislation has limited the scope of foreign banking operations in many states, but the leading "international" states, New York and California, allow full-service foreign branches.

MULTINATIONAL BANKS Of more recent origin is the formation of a number of multinational banks, each one sponsored and owned by a group of several large banks, American and/or foreign. These institutions, commonly called *consortia*, specialize in intermediate-term lending, in any monetary unit, and secure their financing partly from the parent banks, partly from deposits and bond issues. The fact that a consortium is typically owned by large banks in several countries is the source of several advantages: greater financial resource availability, a broader range of technical and other services, and business contacts in a number of countries.

OTHER PRIVATE FINANCIAL INSTITUTIONS European pension funds and insurance companies have found common stock of well-known American companies to be an attractive financial asset; and mutual funds organized to purchase American common stock have been growing rapidly. There are also several United States mutual funds that limit their portfolios largely to foreign securities.

Thus national boundaries are becoming progressively less important as barriers to financing and acquiring financing in all maturities and even for equity financing. Financial institutions, through adaptation of their policies and through establishment of cooperative relationships, are providing the financial counterpart to the internationalization of production and marketing activities.

The Export-Import Bank

An independent government agency, the Export-Import Bank (Eximbank), carries on a variety of programs in furthering its statutory objective of promoting United States exports. Eximbank both makes and guarantees loans to finance these exports. It also rediscounts export-related bank loans and makes advance commitments of financing in export transactions.

---

[12] Douglas H. Lemmonds, "Edge Corporations: A Microcosm of International Banking Trends," *Monthly Review*, Federal Reserve Bank of Richmond (September 1973), p. 15.

Most of its loans are medium-term, up to seven years, although it also grants long-term development loans that can extend up to twenty years. Such loans are always related to the purchase of American goods.

Government-Sponsored International Intermediaries

THE WORLD BANK GROUP   Three institutions, related by origin, ownership, and management, are referred to collectively as the World Bank Group. The "parent" of the group is the *International Bank for Reconstruction and Development* (IBRD), usually called the World Bank. This institution is a result of that path-breaking conference at Bretton Woods that also led to the creation of the International Monetary Fund, discussed earlier in this chapter. The other two member institutions of the World Bank Group—both of which were assisted by, and are affiliated with, the bank—are the International Finance Corporation (IFC), established in 1956, and the International Development Association (IDA), set up in 1960.

Just over 125 nations have become members of the World Bank; nearly all of them have also qualified for membership in the other two group institutions. Members are required to contribute by purchasing stock in these institutions, according to assigned quotas that are supposed to reflect their relative importance in international trade, voting rights are based on these quotas.

Each of the three group institutions has its particular specialty in lending. Briefly put, the World Bank itself was created to make loans for productive purposes to governments and to private enterprises with government guarantees. It is to operate on a "business" basis, with respect to both the kinds of projects it helps to finance and terms of the financing. About one-fourth of the bank's financing consists of capital contributed by member nations; the largest proportion of the rest is in the form of long-term bonds, about three-fourths of which are denominated in U.S. dollars.

Dissatisfaction with the narrow range of projects that the Bank was permitted to finance led to the creation of the *International Finance Corporation*.

> To supplement the work of the Bank, IFC was intended to help finance private enterprises, in association with private investors and management; to assist in developing local capital markets; and to encourage the international flow of private capital. Unlike the Bank, IFC was set up to deal exclusively with the private sector and to operate without any kind of government guarantee.[13]

---

[13] David Grenier, "IFC: An Expanded Role for Venture Capital," *Finance and Development*, V (June 1967), p. 134.

Sometimes the aid is in the form of loans or equity investment; at other times the IFC may actually underwrite (guarantee the sale of) an issue of securities. Or it may take the leadership in forming a consortium of private and government lenders to finance a particular project. The IFC also participates (along with the World Bank) in the financing of, and provides advice to, *development banks* in certain nations. They, in turn, provide financing for economically feasible private projects in those countries.

The speciality of the *International Development Association*, third and youngest member of the World Bank Group, is "soft" credits, that is, interest-free long-term credit to underdeveloped nations. The projects for which this aid is intended are those which, while not directly self-supporting, nevertheless are expected to contribute to the development of the economies involved. Examples are roads, schools, and irrigation projects.

REGIONAL AGENCIES Brief mention should be made of a number of agencies, each of which, though international, is focused on a particular region of the world. The justification for these institutions has been questioned, on grounds that they unnecessarily duplicate the functions of the World Bank Group, which (all three members taken together) can offer practically any kind of financing. Besides, it is argued that these regional institutions tend to divide the world into factional blocs, a trend not considered conducive to world peace. The answer usually given is that there are specific regional problems and interests best served by a regional financial institution.

These institutions are all comparatively young, dating from the late 1950s and 1960s. Their names are sufficient to indicate their regions. While they differ somewhat in organization, scope of activity, and method of financing, they are similar enough so that we can treat them together.

The Inter-American Development Bank, of which the United States is one of about twenty members, is the Latin American regional institution. It offers a broad array of financing services, spanning the spectrum from the World Bank to IDA-type arrangements. Others include the European Investment Bank, established by the Common Market nations to help develop less-advanced areas within its territory and also certain African countries; the African Development Bank; and the Asian Development Bank.

The foregoing discussion of private and government-sponsored financial institutions having important activities that transcend national boundaries is doubtless incomplete in terms of institutional coverage and very sketchy in its treatment of those included. Moreover, by the time these words are read, institutional details will have changed. The important point, though, is that we grasp something of the basic institutional structure of the international financial system and that we realize how the international structure, no less than the domestic structure, adapts to changing circumstances. As international trade and investment grow, there is reason to expect new financial institutions, private and government, to appear and existing ones to adapt themselves to the ever-changing financial needs of the evolving world economy.

Money Markets: Eurodollars

The past few years have witnessed the emergence of a truly new money market, the Eurodollar market. *Eurodollars* are deposits denominated in United States dollars and held in banks outside the United States, while *Eurodollar loans* are claims, again denominated in dollars, held by these banks against their customers. These arrangements hardly sound revolutionary; yet they constitute a profound change in the international payments system and in the related system of financial markets.

MECHANICS   The procedures involved in the creation of Eurodollars and in Eurodollar financing are illustrated in the following hypothetical example. Assume that a foreign firm receives, in payment of a trade debt, a $200,000 check drawn on a United States bank. This firm (step 1) turns the check over to a bank (or branch thereof) in the firm's country, in exchange for a $200,000 time-deposit claim *denominated in United States dollars* against the bank. Then (step 2) the bank makes a $200,000 loan, denominated in dollars, giving up this amount of demand-deposit claims against the American bank in exchange for a debt claim against the borrower.

TRACE 12.1

Foreign Bank			
(1) Dollar deposits in N.Y.	+$200,000	Time deposits (Eurodollar)	+$200,000
(2) Dollar deposits in N.Y. Dollar loan	−$200,000 +200,000		
(1–2) Dollar loan	+$200,000	Time deposits (Eurodollar)	+$200,000
United States Commercial Banking System			
(1)		Demand deposits (foreign bank) +$200,000 Demand deposits (other foreign) −200,000	
(2)		Demand deposits (foreign bank) −$200,000 Demand deposits (other foreign) +200,000	
(1–2)			

No increase in the United States money supply has occurred, nor has the domestic money supply increased abroad; but financing has taken place; the borrower has obtained a Eurodollar loan.

An unusual aspect of transactions involving Eurodollars is that, although neither depositor nor bank nor borrower need be an American economic unit, the medium of exchange is United States money, and the unit of account in which both the time deposit and loan were denominated is the United States dollar.

EURODOLLAR SUPPLY AND DEMAND Although the Bank for International Settlements makes regular estimates of the volume of Eurodollar deposits, such figures tell us very little about the amount of Eurodollar financing of international trade and investment. The reason is that a large and varying (but unknown) fraction of total Eurodollar deposits is of the interbank variety. For example, a foreign bank receiving dollars from a customer in exchange for a thirty-day Eurodollar deposit may, in turn, transfer this dollar claim against a U.S. bank to another bank for thirty days, at a higher interest rate. And the second bank may, in turn, deposit this claim in a third bank. At each stage a Eurodollar deposit is created, but no actual financing of international economic transactions has taken place. And we have no knowledge of the volume of such deposits contained in the published figures.

The center of the Eurodollar market is London. Perhaps five hundred or more banks, in all major and many minor trading nations, are involved in this market. Eurodollar deposits are substantial in size—$25,000 and over—and most carry maturities of one to six months. The loans range upward from $100,000; most are short-term, but some are for as long as a year or more.

Probably the main reason for the growth of the Eurodollar market is the state of European money markets; strong demand for liquid assets but comparatively small supply of suitable financial instruments has meant a constantly rising need for international money balances and for short-term financing. Thus, Eurodollars are filling a large and growing need both for a suitable liquid asset and for a convenient source of financing, denominated in a currency that has become a generally accepted medium of exchange in international transactions over most of the world.

Any economic unit holding a substantial deposit in an American bank is a potential supplier of Eurodollars. These would include foreign and American holders, both private and government. In addition, it is possible for holders of many other currencies to exchange them for dollars and deposit them in a foreign bank. Thus the potential supply of Eurodollars is enormous. The actual supply depends on such factors as transactions costs and interest rates on Eurodollar deposits as compared to alternative financial assets.

Foreign importers, of course, are leading users of Eurodollar financing, but there have been a wide assortment of other users, ranging all the way from British hire-purchase (sales finance) companies to the Belgian government.

SIGNIFICANCE   The development of the Eurodollar market is a vivid example of the growing interdependence of financial markets. One analyst has expressed it very neatly in this paragraph:

> The market has become the funnel through which temporarily unemployed funds in many parts of the world are quickly and efficiently transmitted to borrowers in need of loan accommodation. As a result, interest charges on foreign-trade loans have come under pressure in many countries and differences in local credit conditions throughout Europe have been reduced. . . . It has contributed to the emergence of an international loan market in which some banks encroach on the domain of banks in other countries, with favorable consequences for the cost of credit to commercial borrowers in Europe and elsewhere.[14]

Money Markets: Other Instruments

Despite the rapid growth and large size of the Eurodollar market and similar but far smaller markets in other currencies (Eurosterling, Euroguilder, and so on), it is still true that foreign holdings of short-term obligations of United States economic units, private and government, far exceed the total holdings of Eurodollars. The total of short-term liquid claims of foreign economic units against United States economic units on January 31, 1974, was estimated at $85.3 billion. About three-fourths of this total consisted of holdings of foreign central banks and governments; one-sixth was held by foreign commercial banks; and the remaining one-tenth by nonmonetary international and regional organizations and by nonbanking concerns and individuals.[15]

Why do these foreign economic units wish to hold such a huge amount of liquid dollar claims? The answer, as mentioned earlier, is found in the dollar's unique role as the world's leading "key currency." Related to this development is the fact that the United States has enabled foreign economic units to acquire large and growing amounts of short-term dollar claims against it by consistently running a balance-of-payments deficit, purchasing more goods, services, and securities abroad than it sold.

Table 12.1 provides a breakdown of the kinds of liquid assets held by these classes of foreign economic units. Foreign governments and monetary authorities, being concerned primarily with liquidity and safety, concentrate their liquid asset portfolios on short-term U.S. Treasury securities. In contrast, foreign commercial banks hold almost none of their liquid dollar claims in that form, concentrating instead on claims other than deposits and Treasury issues. "Other private foreign residents and unallocated" is a rather miscellaneous class whose holdings reflect the

---

[14] Fred H. Klopstock, "International Money Market: Structure, Scope, and Instruments," *Journal of Finance*, XX (May 1965), pp. 205–6.
[15] *Federal Reserve Bulletin*, May 1974, p. A68.

TABLE 12.1
Foreign Liquid Asset Holdings in the United States, by Holder and Type of Asset, December 31, 1973
(in $millions)

	Total	Demand Deposit	Time Deposit	U.S. Treasury Obligations	Other Obligations
Foreign central banks and governments	$61,919 (100.0%)	$2,119 (3.4%)	$3,916 (6.3%)	$49,623 (80.2%)	$6,261 (10.1%)
Foreign commercial banks	17,645 (100.0%)	6,968 (39.5%)	527 (3.0%)	11 (0.1%)	10,139 (57.4%)
Other private foreign residents and unallocated	6,153 (100.0%)	2,232 (36.3%)	2,487 (40.4%)	498 (8.1%)	936 (15.2%)
International and regional organizations	2,000 (100.0%)	101 (5.0%)	85 (4.3%)	344 (17.2%)	1470 (73.5%)
Total	$87,717 (100.0%)	$11,420 (13.0%)	$7,015 (8.0%)	$50,476 (57.5%)	$18,806 (21.5%)

Source: *Survey of Current Business*, March 1974, p. 51.

diverse interests of groups ranging from foreign corporations requiring some degree of liquidity for both transactions and contingency reasons to wealthy Latin Americans seeking refuge from severe domestic inflation. International and regional organizations, having highly predictable cash flows, feel but little need for substantial demand-deposit balances.

A new international financial instrument recently made its appearance: *Europaper,* or commercial paper denominated in U.S. dollars but issued in Europe by American corporations. As of this writing, only a handful of companies have floated issues; but the enthusiasm of European investors, eager for safe, liquid claims, and of American firms, eager for short-term financing, indicates that the Europaper market will probably become a viable addition to the list of international financial instruments.

Capital Markets

Many interconnections among nations in the general area of activities covered by the term *capital markets* are evident. Some we have already touched upon, such as the formation of multinational banking groups catering especially to intermediate-term financing needs, the cooperation of investment banking concerns in a number of countries in marketing a single bond issue, and the purchase of securities by individuals and institutions (such as mutual funds) in countries other than those of the issuing firms. There has also been an increase in cooperation among financial institutions across national boundaries in the areas of mortgage and real-estate financing, installment credit, and equipment leasing.

From the mid-1940s to the mid-1960s, New York was the leading source of international financing for foreign firms. Our capital-market institutions were highly developed to handle the marketing chores, government restrictions were minimal, and interest costs were low because we had been experiencing, and the Federal Reserve was battling, a rather slow rate of economic growth. However, from an international payments standpoint, the purchase of foreign securities by Americans, like imports of goods and services, tends to give rise initially to an increase in foreign short-term dollar claims against the United States, chiefly in the form of deposits in United States banks. Now, the dollar, we recall, has developed into the leading medium of exchange for international dealings, so the rest of the world welcomed *some* increase in dollars in line with the growth in world trade; but the acceptable amount of dollars was not infinite! As increases in the stock of dollars in foreign hands outpaced increased demand, one result was that foreign monetary authorities began to utilize their dollars to purchase gold from the U.S. Treasury, partly out of fear that we would devalue, that is, reduce the gold content of the dollar.

One response of the Federal government was to pass, in 1963, the so-called Interest Equalization Tax, designed to make foreign securities less attractive to U.S. investors by imposing a tax on the purchase of these securities (with some exceptions).[16] Another was to establish more or less voluntary curbs on foreign lending by American banks and other financial intermediaries.

The virtual closing of the American market to foreign issues resulted in some significant innovations in capital markets in Europe and elsewhere. It seems highly likely that some of these developments have "taken root" and will survive regardless of the future of the United States' efforts to improve its own international monetary position. By all odds the most important of these is the Eurobond market.

> The Euro-bond market, although centered in Europe, has no national boundaries. Unlike most conventional bond issues, Euro-bonds are sold simultaneously in several financial centers through multinational underwriting syndicates and purchased by an international investment clientele which extends far beyond the confines of the countries of issue.[17]

The distinctive characteristic of a Eurobond issue is that it is denominated in a monetary unit other than that of any of the nations in which it is marketed. Most often, the unit in which both principal and interest are payable is the United States dollar. Thus, although the center of the international market for long-term financing has shifted from New York to Europe, and the investors are nearly all non-United States residents (due to the Interest Equalization Tax), the currency involved is typically the U.S. dollar, again indicative of its "key currency" position.

One important result of this development is that the availability of long-term financing to an economic unit is not limited to the resources of any particular nation. This aspect of financial internationalization is favorable to economic growth, since it increases the likelihood that a particular project will be able to secure financing on the basis of probable productivity rather than availability of financial resources in the country in which it is located. One piece of evidence that capital markets are moving in this direction, incidentally, is the tendency for long-term interest rates of the various nations to move closer together in recent years.

It was perhaps inevitable that, along with Eurodollar loans, Europaper, and Eurobonds, finance people would introduce Euroequities. There have been a few tentative steps in this direction, but judgment must be deferred concerning prospects of this new international financial instrument.

---

[16] The Interest Equalization Tax was, in effect, "repealed" on January 30, 1974, by an executive order reducing the tax rate to zero. On the same day, the Federal Reserve Board removed its restraints on foreign lending.

[17] Martin Barrett, "Euro-Bonds: An Emerging International Capital Market," *Monthly Review*, Federal Reserve Bank of New York (August 1968), p. 169.

Summary

Our financial system certainly does not function in isolation from the rest of the world. For one thing, the dollar has become the most important currency in international transactions. Moreover, the financial institutions and markets of the nations are becoming ever more closely interlinked. And during the past few decades truly international financial institutions have developed, exerting a significant influence on world economic relationships. The task of understanding our financial system, therefore, obliges us to look into these institutions and their relations with our own system.

In a world of money-using economies, the foreign exchange market is prerequisite to all other international financial markets, since without arrangements for buying and selling the currencies of different nations, transactions across national boundaries would be extremely difficult and costly. Not only does the foreign exchange market furnish this service, involving both an international payments system and the means of determining exchange rates, but it also provides facilities for international finance and hedging. Large commercial banks play a vital part in the foreign exchange markets, as do central banks and the International Monetary Fund.

Large commercial banks are also important participants in the international money and capital markets, with other types of financial intermediaries becoming increasingly influential. International organizations are of considerable significance in these markets, too, notably the three institutions of the World Bank Group and various regional development banks.

KEY CONCEPTS

Rate of exchange
International monetary system
Gold tranche
Special drawing rights (SDR's)
Hedging

Key currency
Consortia
Development banks
Eurodollar
Europaper

QUESTIONS FOR REVIEW

1. If a member nation of the International Monetary Fund is experiencing difficulty in earning enough foreign exchange through exports to pay for its imports, what possible actions can it take to alleviate its problem?
2. SDR's are sometimes called "paper gold." Is this an apt description? Why or why not?

3. What are the three functions of a foreign exchange market?
4. What is the contribution of large New York banks to the functioning of the international financial markets?
5. Discuss the international monetary role of the U.S. dollar both as a unit of account and a medium of exchange.
6. Explain the term *World Bank Group*. What role does each component of the group play in international finance?
7. With the World Bank Group covering the whole range of financial risks and maturities, why have various regional development agencies been formed?
8. In what sense are Eurodollars "Euro"? In what sense, "dollars"?
9. What characteristics do Eurobonds share with Eurodollars? What differences exist?

SUGGESTIONS FOR FURTHER READING

Clarke, William M., and George Pulay. *The World's Money and How It Works*. 2d ed. New York: Praeger Publishers, 1972.

Diamond, William, ed. *Development Finance Companies: Aspects of Policy and Operations*. Baltimore: Johns Hopkins Press, 1968.

Fleming, J. Marcus. *The International Monetary Fund*. Washington, D.C.: International Monetary Fund, 1964.

Gold, Joseph. *Special Drawing Rights, Character and Uses*, 2d ed. Washington, D.C.: International Monetary Fund, 1970.

Holmes, Alan R., and Francis H. Schott. *The New York Foreign Exchange Market*. New York: Federal Reserve Bank of New York, 1965.

Horsefield, Keith, ed. *The International Monetary Fund, 1945–1965*. Washington, D.C.: International Monetary Fund, 1972.

Kindleberger, Charles, ed. *The International Corporation: A Symposium*. Cambridge: M.I.T. Press, 1970. Chapter 11.

Mason, Edward S., and Robert E. Asher. *The World Bank Since Bretton Woods*. Washington, D.C.: The Brookings Institution, 1973.

Mikesell, Raymond F. *Financing World Trade*. New York: Thomas Y. Crowell Co., 1969.

Prochnow, Herbert V., ed. *The Eurodollar*. Chicago: Rand McNally & Co., 1970.

Snider, Delbert A. *International Monetary Relations*. New York: Random House, 1966.

White, John A. *Regional Development Banks: The Asian, African and Inter-American Development Banks*. New York: Praeger Publishers, 1972.

Yeager, Leland B. *International Monetary Relations*. New York: Harper & Row, 1966.

Rationale of Government Intervention
  Magnitudes
  The Choice of Means

Government as Intermediary
  Agricultural Lending
  Housing Credit Programs
  Business Loan Credit
  *Public Facilities and
  Community Development*
  International Lending
  Other Programs
  Government Trust Funds
  *Economic Goals and
  Government Intermediation*

**Government Influences on
Private Intermediaries**
  Adequate Liquidity
  Safety
  Reallocation of Credit
  Other Purposes of Regulation
  Influencing Market Structure

Summary

The Role of Government in the Financial System 13

In the course of our discussion of financial intermediaries you have probably noticed that governments—Federal and state in particular—have been mentioned numerous times and in numerous connections. Yet our treatment of the role of government in the financial system has been deficient in (at least) two respects: (1) we have not discussed the rationale of government participation in the financial system; and (2) we have treated only certain aspects of government participation; namely, those that bear directly on the conduct of particular types of intermediaries.

This chapter attempts to deal with these two deficiencies. First, we look at the various reasons offered in support of government intervention; then we examine the various kinds of intervention: direct lending, portfolio influences, financing influences, and market-structure influences.

Rationale of Government Intervention

Government has sought to accomplish a variety of objectives by means of influencing the behavior of the financial system. For convenience, we organize these purposes under these headings: allocation of resources, distribution of income, stabilization, growth, balance-of-payments position, and certain noneconomic goals.

ALLOCATION OF RESOURCES   Economists have given much attention to the concept and criteria of an optimum allocation of resources. Very briefly stated, resources are allocated in an optimum manner when no possible reorganization of production could effect any increase in total satisfaction, given the distribution of income. Implications of a statement like this could fill (and have filled) books. But perhaps we can gain some insight into the notion of optimum allocation by describing some situations in which it does *not* exist. Whenever, for example, a firm could reduce production costs by changing its methods of production (for example, by using more capital, less labor) applied to a given volume and mix of output, or a farmer could increase sales revenue by changing his product-mix (e.g., producing more soybeans, less corn) at no change in costs, we can say that optimum allocation has not been achieved. Another kind of deviation from the optimum exists when prices of some products are continually far in excess of costs of production while prices of other products equal costs.

Sometimes the financial system functions so as to produce or perpetuate these kinds of deviation. When, for example, the price of a good is high relative to cost because existing producers are protected from competition due to the inability of potential competitors to get financing, it is possible that a genuine "credit gap" exists, one that the financial system is unwilling or unable to close. Or if a producer is unable to change to a lower-cost method of production because he cannot find suitable financing, this, too, may be an instance of inefficient resource allocation caused by improper functioning of the financial system. In both cases, we cannot be sure that the fault lies with the financial system since other factors, such as high risk or cost of extending credit, may offset likely gains in production economies.

In some cases, in order to improve resource allocation, government may form its own financing agency; in others, the decision may be to encourage private financing by such devices as a program of providing government insurance or guarantees for loans of particular kinds or by assisting in the formation of private institutions.

INCOME DISTRIBUTION   Some government actions directed toward influencing the conduct of the financial system are designed to affect income distribution. For example, the government may attempt to alleviate the plight of the poor by such means as limiting interest rates or by setting up, or providing inducements to, institutions to lend at lower rates and with more lenient standards of credit worthiness than the poor could otherwise obtain.

ECONOMIC GROWTH AND STABILITY   Government-sector activities that work through the financial system and have as their purpose an increase in the rate of economic growth or an improvement in the employment and price performance of the economy are, for the most part, limited to activities of the Federal Reserve System, which we will be discussing at some length later (Part V).

There is another approach to economic stability, however; one whose beginnings antedate the Federal Reserve by more than a century. This approach focuses attention on maintaining a "safe" banking system. By regulating the kinds of assets banks may hold, by limiting the number of banks, and through other means, government attempts to minimize the likelihood of widespread bank failures, with their accompaniment of business failures and general depression.

EXTERNAL FINANCIAL POSITION In part the government relies on the Federal Reserve System to achieve and maintain a satisfactory payments position (roughly, a balance between supply of dollars to make payments abroad and demand for dollars by foreign economic units to make payments here); but more specific means of influencing the financial system are also used, involving insurance of export loans as well as direct loans to exporters, and measures designed to influence the flow of credit and direct investment abroad.

OTHER GOALS Certain noneconomic goals have been implemented in part through government intervention in the financial system. A few of the obvious ones are (1) encouragement of individual home ownership, small business, and the cooperative form of enterprise; (2) enhancement of the international prestige of the United States; (3) an increase in family economic security through personal thrift and insurance; and (4) "fairness" in the treatment of particular kinds of institutions, financial and other.

RELATIONS AMONG GOALS In recent years we have become acutely aware of the fact that efforts to achieve one particular goal through means which involve influencing the financial system may have "side effects," favorable or unfavorable, with respect to other goals. For instance, evidence is strong that, when the Federal Reserve attempts to cool down an inflationary economy by engaging in actions that restrict the ability of the financial system to provide financing, some sectors—housing, for example—are curtailed far more than others. In part this kind of result is to be expected, but the extent of the differentials between sectors appears to be due in some degree to institutional rigidities. Thus, in this case, efforts to deal with a stabilization problem interfere with the goals of optimum resource allocation and individual home ownership.

Before we move on to the specifics of government programs, a word of warning is in order. Although we are attempting in this book to view the financial system as an interrelated whole, it has never been treated this way by the government. Rather, particular programs for affecting one or another aspect of the system are generally instituted in response to some crisis situation—war, depression, or trouble in a specific sector—with little or no regard to alternative means of accomplishing the purpose desired or to probable effects on other financial or nonfinancial sectors. In part the difficulty stems from an inadequate theoretical framework for viewing the financial system and its relations with the goods-and-services sector. In part, too, the difficulty is that the crisis environment in which many important pieces of financial legislation are passed is not conducive to careful analysis of the particular problem, of alternative means of dealing with it, and of their probable outcomes.

There is hope, however. Events and developments in the latter half of the sixties and the early seventies pointed up clearly the interrelatedness of the various segments of the financial system. We observed pressures applied on commercial banks affecting other intermediaries and even (via the Eurodollar market) money-market conditions in Europe. We have become more aware of inequities, too, resulting from our jerry-built regulatory pattern. In June 1970, President Nixon appointed a Commission on Financial Structure and Regulation to "review and study the structure, operation, and regulation of the private financial institutions in the United States, for the purpose of formulating recommendations that would improve the functioning of the private financial system."[1] The Commission's report embodies the view that public policy cannot treat particular segments of the financial system in isolation. We dare hope that this point of view will increasingly prevail in future Congressional deliberations over matters that affect the financial system.

Magnitudes

There is no continuing comprehensive statistical series on government lending, guaranteeing, and insurance programs; thus it is not always possible to get up-to-date figures on their number and size. Table 13.1, based on a study done for the House Committee on Banking and Currency, will give us some idea of the number and scope of programs at the Federal level and the dollar amounts involved as of June 30, 1962.

The government credit-program scene changes rapidly.

> [Between 1957 and 1962] new programs have been introduced to aid feeder airlines, guarantee loans to railroads for equipment purchase, establish student loan funds, help schools purchase classroom equipment, make loans on foreign currencies to private firms for trade expansion, develop small reclamation projects, lend to state and local development companies, purchase debentures in small business investment companies, lend to fisheries . . . and for several other purposes.[2]

On the other hand, a number of credit programs have been terminated or drastically curtailed, as the conditions that brought them forth ceased to exist.[3]

---

[1] *The Report of the President's Commission on Financial Structure and Regulation* (Washington, D.C.: U.S. Government Printing Office, 1971), p. 1.
[2] Warren A. Law, "The Aggregate Impact of Federal Credit Programs on the Economy," in Commission on Money and Credit, *Federal Credit Programs* (Englewood Cliffs, N. J.: Prentice-Hall, 1963), p. 310.
[3] Some formerly substantial government lending agencies and programs that have disappeared entirely are the Reconstruction Finance Corporation, Home Owners Loan Corporation, Smaller War Plants Corporation, and the joint stock land bank loan program.

TABLE 13.1
Federal Credit Programs, June 30, 1962
(dollar figures in millions)

		Volume of Loans Outstanding		
Economic Sector	Number of Programs	Total	Direct Loans	Insured or Guaranteed Loans
Housing	22	$71,049	$3,156	$67,893
Business	11	936	757	179
Agriculture	5	6,869	6,503	366
Public facilities and community development	13	1,280	427	853
Utilities and transportation	5	4,112	3,525	588
International	8	10,463	9,107	1,356
Individuals and disasters	7	908	908	
Total	71	$95,594	$24,380	$71,214
FNMA and FHLBS loans*	3	7,546	7,546	
Grand Total	74	$103,163	$31,926	$71,235

Source: U.S. Congress, House Committee on Banking Currency, *A Study of Federal Credit Programs, Volume I* (Washington, D.C.: U.S. Government Printing Office, 1964), p. 18.

* Listed separately due to double counting. The dollar figures represent the purchase of, or advances based on, mortgage loans already included under "insured or guaranteed loans" in the housing sector.

The Choice of Means

Generally the government, in seeking the accomplishment of the objectives discussed above, has a choice of means of influencing the financial system. One class of means involves direct participation through government intermediaries, which either finance a particular class of economic units directly (like farmers and exporters) or provide financing for intermediaries that behave themselves in an approved manner (for example, small business investment companies, production credit associations).

Another class of means involves government actions designed to influence the asset structures of particular private intermediaries, attempting to induce a shift toward, or away from, particular categories of finance-seekers (for example, mortgage borrowers, small businesses, securities purchasers). Included in this set are taxes and subsidies, insurance, education and examples, and even outright coercion and prohibition.

We turn now to an examination and analysis of these two classes.

Government as Intermediary

American society has a somewhat ambivalent attitude toward government intermediary activities. On the one hand, we have permitted such activities to grow rapidly in both size and scope. On the other hand, we have certain misgivings about this whole development.

One misgiving is based on the widespread conviction that "government in business" inevitably means inefficiency and corruption. Thus, in 1949 the so-called "Hoover Commission" (Commission on Organization of the Executive Branch of the Government) expressed this conviction:

> Direct lending by the Government to persons or enterprises opens up dangerous possibilities of waste and favoritism to individuals or enterprises. It invites political and private pressure, or even corruption. . . . Direct lending should be absolutely avoided except for emergencies.[4]

In 1961, the Commission on Money and Credit, in its report, strongly recommended that loan insurance or guarantee programs, rather than direct lending, be utilized by the Federal government whenever either offered promise of effectiveness.[5]

Second, there is the uneasy feeling, reinforced by the experience of certain other nations, that any increase in direct lending moves us toward control of the economy through control of the financial system. A case in point is France, where the state owns and controls about three-fourths of the nation's banking and credit institutions. "This furnishes the French government with a massive tool of financial control and influence over the whole national economy."[6]

We are certainly a long way from this condition, but there is little doubt that the trend has been in this direction. What *is* in doubt, though, is the future of the trend itself. We must not fall into the trap of blind extrapolation. As government lending programs expand, they run into increasing resistance from many sources, particularly private financial institutions with considerable influence in Congress through their national associations, especially the American Bankers Association and the United States League of Savings Associations.[7]

Third, there is the quite opposite fear that government intermediary activities are not adequately controlled by the government! While most government lending agencies are subject to budget limitations, there are five huge agencies that are not because they are entirely privately financed. The size and the rate of growth of each of them are the result of decisions of its own management, in the light of its interpretation of its Congressional mandate and of the current situation. This "big five" in-

---

[4] Commission on Organization of the Executive Branch of the Government, *Federal Business Enterprise* (Washington, D.C.: U.S. Government Printing Office, 1949), p. 22.
[5] Commission on Money and Credit, *Money and Credit: Their Influence on Jobs, Prices, and Growth* (Englewood Cliffs, N. J.: Prentice-Hall, 1961), pp. 188–98.
[6] Alfred Oxenfeldt and Vsevolod Holubnychy, *Economic Systems in Action*, 3d ed. (New York: Holt, Rinehart and Winston, 1965), p. 186. See also pp. 209–10.
[7] See Thomas B. Marvell, *The Federal Home Loan Bank Board* (New York: Frederick A. Praeger, 1969), Chapters XI–XII.

cludes two that are concerned with real estate credit and three with agricultural credit.[8]

The point is that the Federal budget is supposed to embody the judgment of the Administration and the Congress as to appropriate relative priorities in the public sector—appropriate, that is, from the standpoint of society. If, for example, Congress were convinced that exports needed encouragement, the budget allotment of the Export-Import Bank would likely be increased *by a specific amount*, considering all the competing demands on the public sector. However, once an agency is allowed to "write its own ticket," so to speak, there is no reason to believe that its size and growth will reflect the lawmakers' judgment concerning the relative social importance of, say, agricultural expansion versus expansion of higher education or antipollution activities.

Despite such misgivings, government intermediary programs have proliferated in response to a variety of demands and have taken a variety of forms. Some programs are self-supporting and even prosperous; other programs involve open or hidden subsidies. Some are financed by Treasury appropriations; others secure financing via the capital markets. Some are old and well-established; some are old but are being phased out; some are new; some are in the process of change. And so on—and on. In 1960 there were approximately fifty[9] Federal lending programs financing agriculture, housing, business in general, utilities and transportation, public facilities and community development, international operations, and the household sector. Unfortunately, we have no recent comprehensive count of lending programs, but it is certain that the number would be considerably larger because new programs continue to appear. Very recent additions include the Rural Telephone Bank, the Student Loan Marketing Association, and the United States Railway Association, which obtains financing for Amtrak.

Agricultural Lending

The first sector to qualify for a continuing Federal lending program was agriculture. A chronically credit-starved sector due to the high capital-to-output ratio and the small size of the average enterprise, as well as a sector that has long had considerable political clout, agriculture has qualified for a substantial number of government loan programs.

---

[8] These are: Federal National Mortgage Association, Federal Home Loan Bank System, and the three branches of the Farm Credit Administration.

[9] The exact number depends upon where one draws the line. As of 1958 Stewart Johnson identified fifty-one domestic programs, while a more recent compilation located only forty-nine, including five "international" lending programs. See Stewart Johnson, "Statistics on Federal Lending and Loan Insurance Programs in the United States, 1929–1958," in Commission on Money and Credit, *Federal Credit Programs* (Englewood Cliffs, N. J.: Prentice-Hall, 1963), p. 2; and House Committee on Banking and Currency, *A Study of Federal Credit Programs* (Washington, D.C.: U.S. Government Printing Office, 1964), pp. 19, 30.

The great bulk of government lending for agricultural purposes takes place through divisions of the Farm Credit Administration, an independent agency within the executive branch of the Federal government. General supervision is exercised by the *Federal Farm Credit Board.*

Although the entire Farm Credit System is now privately owned, there are good reasons for including it in this chapter. In the first place, the policy-making Federal Farm Credit Board is appointed by the President of the United States. And, second, the government lays down the rules concerning terms of lending, eligibility for loans, procedures, etc. In a real sense, then, the Farm Credit Administration is an arm of the Federal government, organized and operated to carry out a government-approved function.

Lending activities are carried out through a rather complicated system of regional "central banks." The nation is divided into twelve regions, each of which has not one but three specialized agricultural central banks: a federal land bank, an intermediate credit bank, and a central bank for cooperatives. Fortunately, in each region a single board is responsible for all three banks. These banks do not deal with farmer-borrowers directly but work through local associations and also standard financial institutions.

Credit for a wide variety of agricultural purposes, ranging from the purchase of feed, seed, and fertilizer and the storage of crops to the acquisition of farm land, is provided through local associations: land bank associations for long-term credit, and production credit associations for short-term and intermediate-term credit. The applicant must agree to purchase stock in the association equal to a minimal percentage of the amount borrowed. If the application is approved, the local association makes the loan or, in the case of a mortgage note, endorses the note and sends it on to the regional land bank, which makes the actual loan. Local associations secure financing by the sale of stock to borrowers and by discounting customers' notes with their regional intermediate credit bank.

The Farm Credit Act of 1971 enlarged the scope of lending powers of the Farm Credit System. Among the important (and controversial) provisions of the act are those authorizing mortgage and home improvement loans on nonfarm rural homes and loans to businesses that perform on-farm services (spraying, custom fertilizing, and so on) for farmers.

Most financing is obtained through open-market borrowing. In this connection, an important provision of the 1971 Act authorizes the Farm Credit Administration to issue systemwide securities, eliminating the necessity of separate issues by each of the three branches of the system. Minor amounts of financing are provided by sale of stock to local associations.

The Farm Credit Administration has achieved an excellent reputation. What its agencies do is seemingly worth doing and done well. A paragraph from the Report of the Commission on Money and Credit expresses a view that most students of agricultural credit would endorse, at least in principle:

> When the land bank system was established in 1917, maturities of farm mortgages were short, usually five years; credit was limited continuously in sparsely settled areas and generally limited during recessions; and equity requirements and interest rates were high. Because of this system owned and operated by farmers and its competitive impact on other lenders, maturities have been lengthened, up to 40 years; amortization has been introduced; interest rates are lower and interest rate differentials among regions and among loan sizes have been reduced; and funds are more readily available at all times and places. Similarly, the intermediate credit system has resulted in a more stable supply of loan funds, longer terms for loans, and lower interest rates on production credit for farmers. Finally, the banks for cooperatives have provided increased marketing credit at lower costs.
>
> In this instance a new set of institutions was probably necessary to provide a source of funds as an alternative to local unit banks in many rural communities.[10]

There are several other Federal agencies that make loans to farmers. One of these is the Farmers Home Administration, which (despite its title) includes "business"-type loans to farmers among its activities. To qualify for a loan from this agency, the applicant must show that he is unable to obtain financing on "reasonable" terms from private financial institutions and the appropriate Farm Credit Administration institution. Farmers also can obtain loans from the Commodity Credit Corporation as part of that agency's "price support" activities, with their crops in storage serving as collateral.

Housing Credit Programs

Federal government programs to aid housing totaled twenty-two by a recent count (Table 13.1). A heavy majority of these are insurance and guarantee programs rather than direct loan programs. In other words, to accomplish the purpose of stimulating housing construction and, in some cases, home ownership, the government has usually chosen to provide inducements to private lenders rather than to set up government agencies to make real estate loans to home buyers. Where there is actual government lending in this area, the borrowers are private financial intermediaries rather than the economic units—households, business firms, or public corporations—actually purchasing the housing facilities.

Direct lending programs have been established to help finance college housing and senior citizen housing and to assist veterans and farmers to finance the purchase or improvements of homes and related structures under certain circumstances. The majority of these programs

[10] Commission on Money and Credit, *Money and Credit*, p. 193.

involve some subsidy element in that interest rates are set quite low considering the risk and costs involved.

Indirect lending, that is, lending to economic units other than the ultimate borrower, is an important component of government aid to housing. The three agencies that dominate this area are the *Federal Home Loan Bank System* (FHLBS), the *Federal National Mortgage Association* (FNMA), and the *Government National Mortgage Association* (GNMA).

We were introduced to the *Federal Home Loan Bank System* in chapter 8, in connection with our discussion of the savings and loan industry. Briefly, the heart of the system is a governing board and eleven regional banks that both serve and regulate member institutions, that is, all Federally chartered and most state-chartered savings and loan associations. The particular service with which we are concerned here is, of course, the making of advances to the member associations. The volume of advances varies widely with conditions in the home mortgage market, as we would expect. During the tight-money year 1969, for example, FHLB advances outstanding rose from $5,259 billion to $9,289 billion, a 77 per cent increase. This rise continued at a slower rate, peaking in December 1970 at a level of $10,614 billion. One year later advances had declined to $7,936 billion, in the face of an increase in mortgage holdings of over $9 billion.[11]

The regional Home Loan Banks are financed through open-market borrowings, deposits of member institutions, and purchases by members of common stock in the regional banks. Short-run fluctuations in need for financing (due to changes in demand for advances by members) are met by changing the amount of open-market notes and bonds issued by the Home Loan Banks.

The Federal National Mortgage Association, another agency that assists housing by intermediation, is a rather strange hybrid. It is entirely privately owned, its stock is traded on the open market, and yet it is actually an agency of the Federal government. The securities it issues are classified as "agency securities"; it may borrow up to $2.25 billion from the United States Treasury, and the Secretary of Housing and Urban Development is charged with the responsibility of regulating FNMA in the public interest, which is interpreted as permitting a reasonable return for FNMA stockholders and as requiring a reasonable proportion of its holdings in mortgages of low- and moderate-income housing.

The function of the FNMA is to provide secondary-market facilities for home mortgage loans, that is, a means whereby existing mortgages may be bought and sold. When credit conditions are tight, the FNMA is a net buyer of such loans; when conditions ease, it tends to be a net seller. Until 1970 it was authorized to deal only in government-insured or

---

[11] *Federal Reserve Bulletin*, June 1972, p. A53.

guaranteed loans; but, under a 1970 law, the FNMA now has permission to deal in conventional mortgages, too, and has begun to do so.

Also in 1970 the establishment of the *Federal Home Loan Mortgage Corporation* was authorized as a subsidiary of the FHLBS, with the power to purchase and sell conventional and government-backed mortgages and also participations. By December 1973, this new institution held about $2.6 billion in mortgages, including $861 million of conventional mortgages.[12]

The obvious result of these secondary market provisions is increased "liquidity" of mortgages and, for builders, certainty of future financing costs on a particular project. Also, there is less likelihood that home construction will be choked off because of inability of lenders to provide financing, so long as the FNMA and FHLMC do their part by offering to purchase mortgages, thus providing the financial resources needed by lenders.

Most of the liabilities-plus-capital of the FNMA consists of open-market securities. Less than 5 per cent is equity capital. This low equity ratio is considered acceptable because the mortgages held are relatively "riskless," nearly all of them being insured or guaranteed.

The *Government National Mortgage Association* is a relatively new agency, spun off from FNMA in 1968 to handle certain "non-businesslike" operations that are considered inappropriate for FNMA. Owned entirely by the United States Government and operating within the Department of Housing and Urban Development, GNMA has been assigned the tasks of (1) liquidating certain old mortgages and (2) purchasing and holding mortgages that arise from certain government-subsidized housing projects, such as urban renewal or housing for the elderly.

We must not infer that, merely because these agencies disburse, say, $3 billion over a particular period as increases in advances and in mortgage holdings, the total flow of mortgage financing must therefore be $3 billion greater. There are several kinds of slippage involved. First, the financial institution selling the mortgages may use part or all of the proceeds to acquire other kinds of claims. This is, in fact, a common kind of portfolio switch in tight-money situations. Second, the financing obtained by the government agencies might be, to a degree, at the expense of the depository financial intermediaries themselves. This, too, seems to have happened during the tight-money periods of the late 1960s. It is generally believed that, to some extent, large economic units tended to purchase the high-yielding securities issued by FNMA and FHLBS instead of increasing their savings and loan deposits.

This situation is just one more illustration, by the way, of the interdependence of the parts of the financial system and the futility of attempting to solve a particular problem by measures that, in effect, ignore these complex interrelations.

[12] *Federal Reserve Bulletin,* May 1974, p. A49.

Business Loan Credit

There are no government lending programs for business in general. Rather, Congress has seen fit to focus on situations where there is reason to believe that private financing is unavailable or too expensive, considering the true risks and costs of lending.

The *Small Business Administration,* as its name implies, is an agency with the mission of aiding small business in a number of ways, including financing. The SBA makes both direct loans to small businesses and indirect loans through small business investment companies.

Small businesses seeking financing from the SBA must show that they cannot obtain comparable financing from private sources on reasonable terms. Often the loan is made on a participation basis, with a bank or other financial intermediary and SBA sharing in the actual loan.[13]

There are several indirect lending programs of the SBA. The largest by far is devoted to encouraging the formation and growth of small business investment companies, discussed in chapter 9. The SBA is also authorized to make loans to state and local development companies under certain circumstances.

Several other government agencies have lending programs to serve particular industries (fishing) or encourage particular economic activities (minerals exploration, urban redevelopment, rural electrification), or to alleviate hardship situations (for example, competitive pressures due to imports stimulated by tariff reductions).

Public Facilities and Community Development

A minor but rapidly growing category of government lending comprises programs directed toward financing public facilities and community development. The range of these programs—from public works planning to mass transit to irrigation distribution systems to materials for private schools—and the small aggregate dollar amount involved justify our small space allocation. Yet this is an area to watch for future growth because of our changing national priorities, shifting toward concern at the national level for urban problems, education, and control of environmental pollution.

International Lending

Government credit programs in the international sector have had a variety of objectives, including expansion of our international trade, assisting economic development abroad, and stabilization of exchange rates. Nearly all of the lending in this area is done by the *Export-Import Bank* and the *Agency for International Development,* the former having

---

[13] The SBA also offers "deferred participation," which is tantamount to a guarantee of that portion of the loan involved. This type of arrangement is discussed in the following section.

"business"-type standards for lending, the latter providing development credit on very liberal terms.

Beside making direct loans, the Export-Import Bank also will guarantee export loans and will lend to banks on the basis of their export loans, performing a sort of "central bank" function with respect to export loan paper. Both the direct and the indirect loans of the Eximbank are primarily intermediate- and long-term because loans of these maturities are relatively difficult to obtain.

Other Programs

In addition to the foregoing, the government provides loans under a variety of conditions to individuals and businesses including college students, colleges, Indians, victims of natural disaster, and holders of Veterans Administration insurance policies. We shall not bother to enumerate them because, individually and collectively, they are neither large enough nor important enough to merit detailed treatment here.

Government Trust Funds

The Federal government operates more than eight hundred trust funds, which hold many billions of dollars' worth of assets in trust for various classes of beneficiaries. In size they cover an extremely wide range.

> Some of [them] exceed America's corporate giants in assets and in the volume of "business" done, while others are more modest than the typical corner drug store.... The Social Security funds ... touch virtually every citizen at one time or another. At the other extreme, some funds serve very limited purposes.... Some of the funds have been established as independent bodies with exceedingly complex organizational structures; others operate simply as relatively incidental appendages to executive agencies whose main business has nothing to do with trust administration.[14]

The most important by any standard are the Social Security funds. These include three funds under the Old Age, Survivors, Disability, and Hospital Insurance program—one each for Federal old-age and survivors insurance, Federal disability insurance, and hospital insurance (for Medicare)—and the unemployment trust fund. These are financed by various payroll taxes. The excess of tax receipts plus investment income over disbursements from the particular fund is invested in Treasury securities.

Other personal insurance and pension plans, state and local as well as Federal, are similar to the OASDHI program. In dollar volume these

---

[14] "The Investment Role of Government Trust Funds," *Morgan Guaranty Survey*, November 1967, pp. 4–5.

funds, including the OASDHI funds, constitute by far the largest category of trust funds. Other categories include "savings institution" funds (for example, Indian tribal funds), funds to handle gifts to the government for specific purposes, and funds in which the "trust fund" form is used merely as an accounting device, to take care of tax receipts earmarked for a specific purpose until they are expended.

Economic Goals and Government Intermediation

Having looked over various government intermediary (lending and trust fund) programs, we can now cite examples of their use as means for the accomplishment of the various economic goals discussed at the beginning of the chapter. We should note, though, that some programs aim at several goals and, further, some have "side effects" that either speed or impede progress toward some goal or goals other than the primary one or ones.

RESOURCE ALLOCATION Several programs defended on resource-allocation grounds come readily to mind. In the agricultural credit area, the Farm Credit Administration programs have from the beginning been justified on grounds that lack of private credit at reasonable terms has hampered the efforts of farmers to utilize the most efficient input-mix, that is, a high capital-to-labor ratio. The fact that FCA programs have always been self-supporting despite their innovations in lending at lower rates and for longer terms than had been available from private lenders is evidence that the claim has merit. Agricultural credit programs have also contributed toward better *regional* allocation of resources in agriculture.

Government lending programs for small business are justified on similar grounds. It is often said that there is a *credit gap* at the upper end of the small business category, where the firm is too large for adequate accommodation by local sources of long-term financing yet too small to qualify for national sources.[15] Insofar as government-supplied loans provided by the Small Business Administration directly and indirectly (through small business investment companies) allow these larger small businesses to acquire productive assets that generate enough cash to pay the "true" cost of credit, the programs will have proved themselves from a resource-allocation standpoint.

Other government programs supported by the credit gap argument include intermediate- and long-term financing to develop export programs (Eximbank) and, to some extent, lending programs to aid housing, such as those of the FNMA and FHLBS.

A different kind of example is the case of loans for educational facilities. The argument here is that education confers substantial ben-

[15] James W. McKie, "Credit Gaps and Federal Credit Programs," in *Federal Credit Programs*, pp. 346–48.

efits on society as a whole as well as on the person receiving the education. So, if society provides *only* the level of education that the recipient is willing to pay for, society is denying itself the additional education that, though involving costs in excess of the expected benefits to the recipient, promises to deliver *total* benefits—to the recipient plus society as a whole—in excess of additional costs. One means of enlarging the flow of resources into education is government loans to students and to educational institutions.

Transportation loans are sometimes defended on similar grounds, as are loans to encourage hospital facilities, water conservation, and public facilities.

INCOME DISTRIBUTION Some credit programs aim primarily at "improving" the distribution of income or, perhaps more accurately, giving the lower-income members in a particular category a "break." Some of the programs that fit into this category are the programs of the Farmers Home Administration, FNMA allocation of a "reasonable" fraction of its purchases to mortgages at the lower end of the price scale, and student loan programs based on need.

ECONOMIC GROWTH AND STABILIZATION Rarely is economic growth or stabilization advanced as the primary aim of a government credit program. Of course, any program that improves resource allocation will, other things equal, be favorable to growth. The operations of FNMA and the Federal Home Loan Bank System are intended to stabilize the residential construction industry; but it has been charged that these programs tend to work against aggregate economic stability: while monetary policy makers are attempting to curb excessive aggregate spending in boom times, these housing credit agencies are pumping additional money into the construction finance market; and when times are slack, there is a tendency for mortgage lenders to buy mortgages from FNMA and for savings and loan associations to repay their FHLB advances instead of making new mortgage loans.

Whether it would be possible, or desirable, to operate government lending programs on a countercyclical basis is a debatable question. To add this objective to those of each government lending program would seem inadvisable, in view of all the difficulties that would result from the need to change lending standards, in response to changes in economic conditions, such as (1) the problems of explaining to clients why, in the face of prosperous conditions and the need for more credit, lending must be curbed, and (2) the pressures from lawmakers for special treatment for this or that industry.

In the light of all the "political," economic, and administrative difficulties that would be involved, perhaps the best we can expect is an effort to avoid intensifying the instability problem—though, even here, we must bear in mind the need to compromise among goals.

EXTERNAL ECONOMIC POSITION   There are no lending programs having as their primary goal the improvement of our external economic position. While it is true that the objective of Eximbank (to increase our exports) happens to be compatible with the objective of improving our external position under *present* conditions, there are other sets of conditions under which stimulation of exports would worsen this position. This would be the case, for example, if we were exporting far more than we were importing, and could find no better use for the surplus than piling up unneeded liquid claims against foreigners. This kind of situation would call for measures to discourage exports and/or encourage imports.

NONECONOMIC GOALS   Noneconomic considerations are important in quite a few lending programs. Our attachment to the values of independent enterprise, for example, have played and continue to play a part in justifying government lending to aid agriculture and small business. Also, home ownership is considered a fine thing, and we demonstrate our collective concern by providing a secondary market (FNMA) for mortgages insured or guaranteed by certain government agencies and by providing a supplementary source of temporary financing (FHLBS) for savings and loan associations.

Government Influences on Private Intermediaries

An alternative method of working through the financial system as a means of accomplishing public policy goals is through measures that directly influence the behavior of private intermediaries. These measures may differ in their "impact points"—some affect the choice of assets; some, the structure of liabilities and capital; and some, the number and location of branches and the scope of activities—as well as in their goals.

For the most part our interest will be in regulation: the "thou shalts" and "thou shalt nots" that have developed over the years. However, we shall also give attention to some of the devices aimed at affecting financial-intermediary behavior by making particular kinds of assets more (or less) desirable to prospective holders than they would otherwise be, since these devices are an alternative to direct regulation. We shall ignore, though, those measures whose influence on intermediary behavior is merely a byproduct of their main purpose. The tax-exempt character of municipal bonds, for example, enhances the attractiveness of such bonds to commercial banks; but we obviously did not adopt a Constitution providing for dual sovereignty, then interpret it as denying the right of the Federal government to tax the instrumentalities of the states, in order to bring about tax-exemption for municipal bonds!

Regulation of intermediaries in the United States is as old as intermediaries themselves. First to be regulated were commercial banks, both because they were the first of the intermediaries to appear and, more importantly, because we have always used bank liabilities as money—bank notes and, later, demand deposits. Then, as each new form of intermediary arrived on the scene, it was, in turn, subjected to some degree of regulation, for the protection of the small saver, or the policyholder, or the borrower, or for some other reason.

The degree or "intensity" of regulation seems to have increased in recent years. One obvious cause is the increasing complexity of our economy, which is reflected in the pressures for a wider range of financial services and arrangements. Another important reason is the growing awareness on the part of regulators of the interdependence of the elements of the financial system. A restriction imposed on one class of intermediaries may offer unexpected benefits to another class, bringing pressures to regulate *that* class. And so forth.

This very interrelatedness, however, has given rise to a strong countermovement toward a reduction in the scope and strength of government regulation. It is argued that there is less need for certain kinds of regulation now: the kinds designed to ensure competitive allocation of credit and the safety of the financial system. Effective competition in financial markets is more or less assured, thanks to the increased interpenetration of intermediaries into each others' markets. (Recall the discussion in chapter 3).

Also, it is claimed that detailed rules intended to keep financial intermediaries "safe" are no longer necessary. The Employment Act of 1946 pledged the Federal government to work toward the attainment and maintenance of high-employment stability; and this goal has been, for the most part, approximately achieved. In addition, there have been some important changes in the financial system itself—deposit insurance, improved management, and the virtually unlimited lending power of the Federal Reserve and other government agencies—which almost assure a sufficiently stable financial system.

Another argument for decreasing regulation is the observed tendency for regulations sometimes to generate more problems than they solve. A recent expression of this point of view is *The Report of the President's Commission on Financial Structure and Regulation*,[16] which argues very forcefully the case for (1) expanding the scope of permissible activities of intermediaries, that is, lending arrangements and types of obligations issued, and (2) reducing the scope of government regulation.

This is an area to watch carefully. It seems likely that the next few years will see considerable change in the regulatory environment of intermediaries in the directions indicated by the commission; but the climate of opinion *could* change in the other direction if, for example, increasing public impatience with the contribution of the financial system toward the achievement of our social goals should coincide with an administration with a strong "interventionist" philosophy.

---

[16] Washington, D.C.: U.S. Government Printing Office, 1971.

In this section we shall organize our discussion around the immediate goals of influence—liquidity, safety, reallocation of credit, and so on—bearing in mind that these are, in turn, means toward the achievement of the more general socioeconomic goals.

Adequate Liquidity

The maintenance of adequate liquidity has always been a matter for government concern and regulation in the case of depository savings intermediaries, since their liabilities have, from the beginning, consisted mainly of (1) money and (2) holdings of households' savings. Acceptability of bank notes or demand deposits on a par with other kinds of money requires that the holder be able to exchange his bank money for other forms; hence, liquidity is crucial to the maintenance of parity in a monetary system. And acceptability of savings deposits as an outlet for the savings of modest-income households depends on their ready redeemability for money. Thus, the goal of adequate liquidity of depository intermediaries is related both to the economic goal of stability and to the social goal of encouraging saving as a means, in turn, of "building character," providing personal security, and financing economic growth.

The original device to ensure liquidity was the reserve requirement, applied to commercial banks and to certain other depository intermediaries. The rationale (based on experience!) was that, without such regulations, the intermediary might be tempted to operate with as small an amount of noninterest-bearing cash (or "reserves") as possible in order to maximize earnings on assets, thus being vulnerable to an unanticipated increase in withdrawals, threatening not only that institution's ability to continue operating but others' as well, as panic would spread through the system.

This rationale no longer has much significance in the case of member banks, we know, since they may borrow from their district Reserve bank or buy Federal funds to meet any emergencies. Even nonmembers have access to additional reserves through their correspondents and other sources, as we learned in earlier chapters. And savings and loan associations have the FHLBS and the secondary mortgage facilities of FNMA as sources of additional cash. Yet the reserve requirements continue. Why?

Persistence of reserve requirements is easy to explain in the case of member banks: the Federal Reserve varies reserve requirements as part of its effort to control the money supply and credit conditions. State nonmember-bank reserve requirements seem to be based on the old "liquidity cushion" argument. In the savings and loan case, the FHLB Board varies reserve requirements in response to changing needs for mortgage credit, lowering the percentage when mortgage money is tight and raising it when conditions ease.

Another device for affecting the liquidity of a financial intermediary is to alter the terms and conditions under which it may secure additional cash through borrowing from a central bank or other government intermediary, such as the FHLBS. Third (and related), regulations affecting the right of particular classes of intermediaries to borrow on the open market have an influence on liquidity. For instance, legislation passed in 1968 gave the FHLB Board for the first time the right to issue regulations authorizing Federal savings and loans to borrow on the basis of notes and bonds.

Safety

The origins of safety regulations are as ancient as those of liquidity regulations, with the reasons about the same: (1) to safeguard the money supply for the sake of economic stability and (2) to protect and encourage household saving. The devices used, however, are considerably more numerous and varied.

Safety is sometimes sought through limitations on the kinds of assets that may be held. Particular kinds may be prohibited, or the choice of eligible assets may be limited to certain classes—which, of course, prohibits all other classes. For example, in nearly all states that permit mutual savings banks, the law specifies classes of earning assets that may be held. A national bank may not hold common or preferred stock, or even bonds that are convertible into such stock. A national bank may not accept its own stock as loan collateral.[17]

The prohibition may take the form of quality standards, which are intended to prevent the intermediary from acquiring assets of a particular type that do not measure up to certain criteria. National banks, for example, may purchase only bonds that are highly rated by the rating agencies. And almost every state has laid down standards that corporation bonds, mortgages, and other assets must meet in order to be eligible for purchase by the life insurance companies over which that state has jurisdiction.[18]

A more moderate form of regulation does not prohibit, but sets a ceiling on, certain types of assets, the ceiling being based on such magnitudes as capital, deposits, or total assets.

Interest-rate ceilings on deposits also have been defended on grounds of safety, though other reasons have been advanced as well. It has long been believed that one cause of the wave of bank failures in the late 1920s and early 1930s was that banks had been competing aggressively for deposits by offering more attractive rates and then, in order to cover these high interest costs, had turned to high-yield but higher-risk earning assets.

---

[17] There is a solid historical reason for this regulation: early in our history it was a common practice for organizers of a new bank to pay for their stock in the bank with money borrowed from the bank on a loan secured by this same stock! To the extent that this was done, the bank's capital did not represent any actual protection for the holders on demand claims (at that time, chiefly bank notes) against the bank.

[18] See Life Insurance Association of America, *Life Insurance Companies as Financial Institutions* (Englewood Cliffs, N. J.: Prentice-Hall, 1962), chapter 5 and Appendix, for details.

In this controversial area, the evidence is far from conclusive. Opponents of regulation argue that rate ceilings can create more problems than they solve. To illustrate: in 1966 interest rates rose to such an extent that the ceiling on member-bank time-deposit rates tended to result in an outflow of deposits to competing intermediaries; therefore, the latter were also placed under ceilings. But the regulators seemed not to realize that, when rates on open-market securities soar far above the deposit interest-rate ceilings, there arises the danger of "disintermediation," that is, of liquidation by households and businesses of their time-deposit accounts and use of the proceeds to purchase bonds, commercial paper, and so on. This, in fact, happened on an alarming scale.

> The result will apparently be that the flow of funds will favor lenders and borrowers who can use the open market. Other borrowers tend to be deprived of access to funds. Other suppliers of funds tend to be discriminated against by receiving interest rates below the market rate.[19]

The only way to solve these problems is to control *all* interest rates!

Another important device for increasing intermediaries' safety is deposit insurance, available to commercial banks through the Federal Deposit Insurance Corporation, to mutual savings banks through the FDIC and state insurance funds, to savings and loan associations through the Federal Savings and Loan Insurance Corporation, and (only since 1970) to credit unions through the National Credit Union Administration. Participation is voluntary—in a way—although usually it is included in a package deal, such as membership in the Federal Reserve System (for commercial banks) or qualifying for a Federal charter (for credit unions and savings and loan associations).

Regulatory agencies also stress "adequacy of capital" as a means of securing safety, although spelling this out has proved to be a knotty problem, with no really satisfactory solution as yet. Regulations imposed by the FSLIC on insured savings and loans are quite specific and detailed; those applied to commercial banks are much less so because of the greater variety of assets held by banks and, hence, the greater difficulty of assessing the asset risk involved, as we observed in chapter 4.

Reallocation of Credit

A number of goals that the government seeks to further through the financial system do not depend for their achievement on merely adequate safety and liquidity of intermediaries. They require, in addition, some alteration in the industry-mix or sector-mix of claims held by intermediaries. In some cases, the rationale for attempting thus to influence intermediaries' credit allocation is that monopoly elements, or

---

[19] Mary Ann Clements, "Deposit Interest Rate Regulation and Competition for Personal Funds," *Review* of the Federal Reserve Bank of St. Louis (November 1966), p. 20.

rigidities, or inertia distort allocation away from the competitive norm; then government intervention is needed to correct the distortion. In other cases it is not the behavior of the market that is at issue but rather the market solution itself. Social priorities demand that credit be allocated differently, favoring some classes of borrowers and downgrading others. Examples of these social priorities are military success, improvement of the economic position of certain disadvantaged groups, and the rebuilding of certain distressed areas. (Of course, sometimes the results do not gibe with the goal, but that is another matter.) Finally, sometimes the rationale is that, without intervention, the allocation of credit will tend to be destabilizing to the economy, for example, through feeding excessive speculation.

One of the most direct devices for influencing credit allocation is selective credit controls. During World War II and the Korean War, such controls were imposed in order to curb credit for the purchase of consumer durables and real estate. The Federal Reserve Board of Governors, with Congressional authorization, stipulated minimum down payments and maximum maturities on such purchases in order to reduce consumer demand for them, thus facilitating the reallocation of productive resources to war-related uses.

Usually the Federal government eschews such drastic methods of influencing allocation, preferring to rely, instead, on measures that make particular types of claims more (or less) attractive to intermediaries. One important method in this category is to guarantee the asset or insure the holder against loss in case the debtor should default. This device has been used with great success in the field of home mortgage lending by the Federal Housing Administration, beginning in 1934, and by the Veterans Administration since 1944, rendering such mortgages more acceptable to commercial and mutual savings banks and life insurance companies. Of course, the insurance or guarantee aspect is just one reason for the success of these classes of mortgages, as is brought out in this quotation:

> The genius of the underwriting programs is that they operate on both the borrowing and lending sides of the mortgage market at the same time. By enabling borrowers to acquire loans for longer periods at lower down payments and at lower interest rates than private lenders offer on conventional loans, the programs stimulate housing demand. On the lending side, the government's underwriting of default risk, its development of greater homogeneity in the security behind mortgage loans through the establishment of appraisal and construction standards, its insistence on amortization, and the development of experience records on low-down-payment loans have induced institutional lenders to supply more mortgage credit. By creating a more homogeneous and more marketable debt instrument the programs have reduced geographical differentials in rates through stimulating competition for mortgage loans among, as well as within, local markets.[20]

[20] Commission on Money and Credit, p. 190.

An interesting recent application of the guarantee idea is a new program, launched in 1968, by the Small Business Administration, in which the SBA will guarantee loans made by banks to finance the purchase by blacks of ghetto business firms as part of a broader program to increase participation of blacks in the business life of inner-city areas.[21]

A number of Federal agencies maintain insurance or guarantee programs. As of June 30, 1962, there were twenty-five Federal loan insurance or similar programs, with the volume of loans insured totaling over $71 billion.[22]

Finally, there are certain more indirect ways of influencing financial intermediaries in their credit-allocation decisions. A recent example is the "guidelines" that banks and other financial intermediaries were supposed to observe in their foreign lending and investing under the *Voluntary Foreign Credit Restraint* (VFCR) program, instituted in 1965 and managed by the Federal Reserve Board. However, use of this informal approach is not new. Banks during World War II were exhorted to watch carefully for evidence that their loans were financing excessive inventories of consumer goods. In 1950 banks were asked by the Federal Reserve to limit their lending to "essential loans" in order to facilitate defense financing. And in September 1966, member banks received a letter from the Board of Governors urging them to avoid lending for "nonproductive" purposes.

These exhortations have a certain amount of force behind them. Either explicitly or implicitly, banks can be threatened with loss of discount privilege if they fail to behave properly.[23] It is difficult to measure the success of such instances of "open-mouth policy," as it is sometimes called, but the consensus seems to be that, for short periods of time at least, they have had some degree of success.

Other Purposes of Regulation

Finally, we must mention briefly, and illustrate, several other purposes of government regulation of the financial system. One purpose, control of money and credit, we must defer until later. This is such an important topic in its own right that most of the remaining sections of this book, Parts IV and V, are directly and indirectly related to it.

INCOME DISTRIBUTION   Some regulatory measures seek to alter income distribution a bit—specifically, in favor of the lower-income part of the population—through general usury statutes, setting maximum inter-

---

[21] "Aiding Black Capitalism," *Business Week* (August 17, 1968), p. 32.
[22] *A Study of Federal Credit Programs*, pp. 18–19.
[23] For instance, the letter to member banks referred to in the preceding paragraph contained this ominous sentence: "Member banks will be expected to cooperate in the system's efforts to hold down the rate of business loan expansion—apart from seasonal needs—and to use the discount facilities of the Reserve Banks in a manner consistent with these efforts." *Federal Reserve Bulletin* (September 1966), p. 1339.

est rates on loans, and also by separate small-loan interest-rate ceilings. However, like price ceilings generally, interest-rate ceilings often have had results unanticipated by the lawgivers. In the first place, there are numerous methods of getting around the laws (for example, a multiplicity of special "charges" levied in addition to the interest itself), so the law may be ineffective in actually curbing credit cost to the poor. Second, insofar as the ceiling is effective, the very group that the law intended to aid, the lower-income group, may be "rationed out" by the lenders.

In this connection, a recent study reached the following conclusion:

> There is little doubt that usury laws and small loan laws effectively lower the finance rate to many borrowers obtaining installment loans from consumer credit lenders. But it also seems likely that the maximum rate provisions contained in small loan legislation restrict the availability of credit to marginal risk loan applicants, forcing them either to abstain from borrowing altogether or to seek credit from illegal lenders.[24]

PROVIDE INFORMATION Another set of regulatory measures is based on the premise that, in certain situations, important facts needed for rational financial decision-making are not readily available to one or the other parties to a transaction and that it is in the public interest that such information be available. Based on this premise, we have, for example, laws and numerous regulations governing the provision of information by the issuer to prospective investors in a new issue of securities.

Also in this category is the recently passed (1968) Consumer Credit Protection Act, commonly known as the Truth-in-Lending Law, as implemented by Federal Reserve Regulation Z, stipulating that any seller or lender extending consumer credit must provide the buyer-borrower with information in writing as to the actual rate of interest as well as the dollar amount of the finance charge involved.

Influencing Market Structure

Government, finally, seeks to influence the structure of markets within which financial intermediaries operate in order to make progress toward certain social goals, particularly improved resource allocation and economic stability.

One ancient device is restrictions on entry, mainly through controls of charters for new institutions and on permission for existing institutions to establish branches or other kinds of additional offices.

Commercial banks have been singled out for particular attention in this regard because of their crucial role in the monetary system (the stability goal again); but even savings and loan associations must gener-

---

[24] Maurice B. Goudzwaard, "Price Ceilings and Credit Rationing," *Journal of Finance,* XXIII (March 1968), p. 177.

ally do more than meet the criteria set up for incorporation in general. To acquire a Federal charter, for example, the applicant association must be prepared to show "the existence of a need for a federal association in the community served and the reasonable probability of the usefulness and success of a new association so located,"[25] among other things.

Entry into a particular geographical area can be curbed by other means, however, including (1) restrictions on branching and (2) rules restricting the geographic area that can be served by firms headquartered outside the area. In fact, broadening the concept of "entry" a bit further, we might state that laws or regulations forbidding a particular kind of intermediary to engage in a certain kind of financing is another device to control entry.

This broad concept of entry probably is the most meaningful from an economic standpoint. To find out how many sources of real estate credit are available in a particular area, one would not limit his search to separately incorporated banks headquartered in that area that might provide this kind of financing, nor total bank offices in that area. Rather, his concern would be with the number of financial institutions, regardless of type, location of head office, and so on, that make real estate loans in that area.

Fortunately, there is strong evidence that regulatory authorities are tending to adopt this broad view of market participation in making "entry" decisions. Federal savings and loan associations have recently been given approval to engage in several new (to them) types of lending, including mobile-home financing, loans to "equip" homes, nursing-home financing, and even Agency for International Development-guaranteed loans to finance housing projects anywhere in the world!

A measure for the Federal chartering of savings banks has been proposed in Congress a number of times, thus far without success. This measure would enable existing savings and loan associations to convert to savings bank status, enabling them to acquire a wider range of assets, that is, enter markets for claims that are now closed to them. It would permit savings banks to be established in all states, not merely the nineteen states now providing for their chartering. Entry thus would be broadened in two respects: (1) savings and loans could, through conversion, enter the market for corporation bonds and other claims now forbidden to them, and (2) savings banking could enter a large number of additional geographic areas.

The *Report* of the President's Commission on Financial Structure and Regulation, already cited several times, very vigorously advocates a loosening of restraints on entry, both in a *market* sense, permitting the various intermediaries far greater latitude in the kinds of claims they purchase, and in a *geographical* sense, allowing greater branching powers.

[25] Leon T. Kendall, *The Savings and Loan Business* (Englewood Cliffs, N. J.: Prentice-Hall, 1962), p. 30.

The probable and intended economic effect of all these developments is a better allocation of resources, since (1) financing costs would less often be assessed on a monopoloid basis and (2) the likelihood is increased that the differences in cost and availability of financing as among applicants would reflect true differences in the economic costs and risks involved. (There would be fewer "credit gaps.")

There is another kind of entry, however, that is decidedly different from the foregoing: entry into nonfinancial markets, directly or through subsidiaries. If the same firm owns both a financial intermediary—insurance or depository—and a nonfinancial business, the way is open for all sorts of "inside" dealings. The firm could easily be operated in such a way that the "business branch" of the firm would obtain easy financing, while the "financial branch" could discriminate against noncustomers of the "business branch."

The rapid rise of one-bank holding companies in the later 1960s made this kind of possibility very real. Through this device, a bank would become, in effect, a division of a holding company; and the holding company would then be free to acquire, by merger or formation, subsidiaries in any field, issuing its own securities to finance these acquisitions and formations.

> Free of Federal regulation, some one-bank holding companies acquired or established nonbank subsidiaries in order to engage in a wide variety of activities, some of which were not permitted to banks directly. In addition, a few important industrial conglomerates acquired a single commercial bank, thus mixing banking and commerce—a mixture prohibited by the 1956 [Bank Holding Company] Act to companies holding more than one bank.[26]

Congress put an end to much of the fun by passage in 1970 of a set of amendments to the Bank Holding Company Act, placing one-bank holding companies under the act and also specifically forbidding tie-in arrangements between financial and business branches, as just described. However, reflecting the somewhat more premissive regulatory climate that seems to be developing, the amendments also broadened the scope of allowable activities, subject only to the limitation that they be "so closely related to banking or managing or controlling banks as to be a proper incident thereto" and that such activities would confer net public benefits. The job of translating these general statements into specific regulations and then administering the regulations was assigned to the Federal Reserve Board of Governors. Table 13.2 summarizes the results of the board's deliberations, as of January 1973, concerning the appropriateness for bank holding companies of various nonbanking activities.

---

[26] Alfred Hayes, "The 1970 Amendments to the Bank Holding Company Act: Opportunities to Diversify," *Monthly Review*, Federal Reserve Bank of New York (February 1971), p. 23.

TABLE 13.2
Permissibility of Nonbanking Activities for Bank Holding Companies

Activities Approved by the Board:
1. Dealer in bankers' acceptances.
2. Mortgage company.
3. Finance company.
4. Credit card company.
5. Factoring company.
6. Operating an industrial bank.
7. Servicing loans.
8. Trust company.
9. Investment adviser to real estate investment trusts and to investment companies under the Investment Company Act of 1940.
10. Furnishing general economic information and advice.
11. Providing portfolio investment advice.
12. Full pay-out leasing of personal property.
13. Investments in community welfare projects.
14. Providing bookkeeping or data processing services.
15. Acting as insurance agent or broker—primarily in connection with credit extensions.
16. Underwriting credit life insurance.

Activities Denied by the Board:
1. Equity funding (the combined sale of mutual funds and insurance).
2. Underwriting general life insurance.
3. Real estate brokerage.
4. Land development.
5. Real estate syndication.
6. Management consulting.
7. Property management.

Source: Regulation Y, *Federal Reserve Bulletin*; and Robert J. Lawrence, "The Effect of Bank Holding Company Growth on the Correspondent Banking System," Table 4, in speech delivered at ABA Correspondent Banking Seminar, New Orleans, Louisiana, October 31, 1972, cited in Harvey Rosenblum, "Bank Holding Companies: An Overview," *Business Conditions*, Federal Reserve Bank of Chicago (August 1973), p. 6.

Summary

Through its activities in and through the financial system, the government has sought to influence resource allocation, income distribution, overall economic stability and growth, and our balance-of-payments position, as well as to improve our progress toward certain other economic and noneconomic goals. Despite some resistance, the role of government in this area has expanded considerably and continues to grow, utilizing a number of means—intermediation, insurance and guarantees, regulation, subsidies, and taxes—to accomplish these goals through the financial system.

Government credit (lending and insurance-type) programs have long been important in agriculture and housing but have also become more numerous (though still of minor importance) in business lending, in the financing of public facilities and certain community development projects, and in a number of other economic sectors.

Historically government regulation has gradually grown in both scope and detail. Although the ultimate goals of regulation are not different from those of government credit programs, they are sought through the more immediate objectives of adequate liquidity, safety, reallocation of credit, increased flow of information to the potential user of credit, and more competitive financial markets.

KEY CONCEPTS

Federal Farm Credit Board
Federal National Mortgage Association
Federal Home Loan Mortgage Corporation
Government National Mortgage Association
Small Business Administration
Export-Import Bank
Agency for International Development
Government trust funds
Credit gap
Truth-in-Lending Law
Voluntary Foreign Credit Restraint

QUESTIONS FOR REVIEW

1. "If the government favors a certain goal and it is known that a particular program will enable that goal to be achieved, it might nevertheless be advisable not to adopt that program." Why?
2. What arguments have been offered against increasing government participation in the financial system?
3. Why did Federal lending programs appear in agriculture prior to their appearance in other sectors of the economy?
4. Contrast the role of the Federal government in agricultural finance with its role in housing finance.
5. "If the Federal Home Loan Mortgage Association borrows $500 million in the market and uses this money to purchase $500 million of mortgages from savings and loan associations, we can be sure that housing credit will be increased by $500 million." Comment critically.
6. What economic rationale is offered in support of loans for college educational facilities?
7. Give examples of government credit programs that are justified primarily on noneconomic grounds.

8. "There is some reason to believe that the future may see diminished government regulation of financial intermediaries." Explain.
9. List some of the means used by government to enhance the liquidity and safety of financial intermediaries.

SUGGESTIONS FOR FURTHER READING

Benjamin, Gary L. "The Farm Credit System." *Business Conditions*, Chicago Federal Reserve Bank (September 1972), pp. 11–20.

Break, George F. *Federal Lending and Economic Stability.* Washington, D.C.: The Brookings Institution, 1965.

Commission on Money and Credit. *Federal Credit Agencies.* Englewood Cliffs, N.J.: Prentice-Hall, 1963.

———. *Federal Credit Programs.* Englewood Cliffs, N.J.: Prentice-Hall, 1963.

Gies, Thomas. "Portfolio Regulation and Policies." In Commission on Money and Credit, *Private Financial Institutions.* Englewood Cliffs, N.J.: Prentice-Hall, 1963.

Guttentag, Jack, and Edward S. Herman. *Banking Structure and Performance.* New York: New York University Graduate School of Business Administration, Institute of Finance, 1967.

Marvell, Thomas B. *The Federal Home Loan Bank Board.* New York: Praeger Publishers, 1969.

Report of the President's Commission on Financial Structure and Regulation. Washington, D.C.: U.S. Government Printing Office, 1971.

Robertson, Ross M. *The Comptroller and Bank Supervision.* Washington, D.C.: Office of the Comptroller of the Currency, 1968.

Saulnier, Raymond J., and Neal Jacoby. *Federal Lending and Loan Insurance.* New York: National Bureau of Economic Research, 1958.

Tax Foundation. *Federal Trust Funds: Budgeting and Other Implications.* New York: Tax Foundation, Inc., 1970.

U.S. Congress, Committee on Banking and Currency. *A Study of Federal Credit Programs.* 2 vols. Washington, D.C.: U.S. Government Printing Office, 1964.

MONETARY THEORY: THE FINANCIAL SYSTEM AND THE ECONOMY

PART IV

14

The Accounting Framework of Macroeconomic Theory

The Problem

The Accounting Framework:
The National Income
and Product Accounts
*Gross National Product (GNP)
and Its Components*
GNP: Expenditure Categories
GNP: Income Categories
*Expenditure and Income Approaches
Combined*

Summary

Most of the book thus far has been devoted to examining the structure and operations of this awesomely complicated mechanism called the financial system. However, in a treatment of the financial system from an economic viewpoint, it is not enough simply to understand institutional arrangements—the financial instruments, organizations, and practices that have evolved in relation to the goods-and-services economy—important as this is to an adequate grasp of the system. We must also examine the relations between these two closely intertwined sectors, the real and the financial, in order to perceive the economic significance of the institutions of finance and also to be able to understand and evaluate the efforts of the monetary authorities to influence the behavior of the financial system.

The branch of economics dealing with the interrelations of the financial system and the rest of the economy is generally termed *monetary theory*. Its ancestry can be traced back far beyond the birth of modern economics; even Aristotle and Saint Thomas Aquinas, for example, thought the problem worthy of their attention! However, until the fourth decade of the twentieth century, theorizing about the economic role of the financial system mainly took the form of analyzing the effects of one class of financial instruments—*money*—on one kind of economic phenomenon—*the price level*. Nonmonetary elements of the financial system were rarely accorded sustained attention, and any effects of monetary changes on the level of output and employment were generally considered temporary and insignificant.

Then, in the 1930s, the appearance of a single book, *The General Theory of Employment, Interest and Money,* by John Maynard Keynes,[1] in the midst of a catastrophic and bewildering economic depression,

[1] New York: Harcourt, Brace and World, 1936.

provided the impetus for a redirection of monetary thinking away from a narrow preoccupation with the price level and toward the problem of the level of income and employment and the influence of money (among other variables) on these magnitudes.

During and since the 1950s, however, economists have become increasingly aware of the fact that the Keynesian framework, even as amplified and amended by his successors, has too narrow a financial focus for maximum usefulness. Statistical data[2] have revealed the impressive growth of the nonbanking sectors of the financial system. The monetary authorities are stressing the need to consider not merely the money supply but also a broad spectrum of liquid assets—particularly bank time and savings deposits and the savings-type claims on the depository saving intermediaries—in attempting to trace and understand the impact of Federal Reserve and Treasury actions on the real sector. And, finally, recent attempts to develop a framework of analysis suitable for this broader approach[3] as well as econometric models incorporating more detailed financial sectors[4] encourage hope that economics is at last breaking out of this restrictive focus on money just as, three decades ago, macroeconomics evolved from its restrictive focus on price-level movements.

Unfortunately for us, monetary theory (and, hence, this book) has not yet moved fully into this third period. Whether some future Keynes will propel us rather suddenly into this period or whether financial thought will gradually evolve into it, we cannot say. For our purposes, though, the basic Keynesian framework, although not ideal, will serve quite nicely, provided that we define our problem broadly enough and keep in mind that its scope is really broader than the Keynesian model was designed for.

The Problem

Our inquiry into the determinants of the economy's aggregate performance—that is, the extent to which actual output measures up to capacity output—begins with the observation that a key role is played by aggregate spending. A high level of economic activity requires an ap-

---

[2] Particularly Raymond W. Goldsmith, *Financial Intermediaries in the American Economy Since 1900* (Princeton: Princeton University Press, 1958).

[3] Some examples: James S. Duesenberry, "The Portfolio Approach to the Demand for Money and Other Assets," *Review of Economics and Statistics*, XLV (Supplement, February 1963), pp. 9–24; John G. Gurley and Edward S. Shaw, *Money in a Theory of Finance* (Washington, D.C.: The Brookings Institution, 1960); Lyle E. Gramley and Samuel B. Chase, Jr., "Time Deposits in Monetary Analysis," *Federal Reserve Bulletin*, LI (October 1965), pp. 1380–1404.

[4] See, for example, two reports of the model recently developed cooperatively by the Federal Reserve and the Massachusetts Institute of Technology: Frank DeLeeuw and Edward Gramlich, "The Federal Reserve–MIT Econometric Model," *Federal Reserve Bulletin*, January 1968; and "The Channels of Monetary Policy: A Further Report on the Federal Reserve–MIT Model," *Journal of Finance*, XXIV (May 1969), pp. 265–90.

propriately high level of spending. Excessive spending results in a rising price level; insufficient spending means unemployment, less-than-capacity output, and perhaps falling prices.

A major part of our problem, therefore, is to relate the behavior of the financial system to total spending. Our approach will be to break total spending down into several major categories of expenditures and/or spenders and attempt to indicate (1) how changes emanating from the financial system affect the spending plans (volume and direction) of these categories of spenders and (2) how changes in spending affect, in turn, the financial system. Causation runs in both directions: we have an *interaction* problem to analyze.

To a smaller degree we shall also be watching for ways in which the financial system affects income distribution, the allocation of economic resources, the price structure, and economic growth. The financial system influences these magnitudes in part through its effects on the volume of total spending, and in part through its effect on the direction of spending. Even though the short-run impact of the financial system is probably not so important in these areas as it is for aggregate economic activity, and even though the monetary authorities do not stress these matters in defining their task, an adequate treatment of the financial system cannot completely neglect them.

The Accounting Framework: The National Income and Product Accounts

Before getting on with the analysis itself, we must familiarize ourselves with our system of national accounts. One reason is that it is largely in terms of these accounts that we record the results of monetary policy and of other developments bearing on our nation's economic performance. Second, these national accounts are almost invariably used as the framework on which economic forecasts are made and evaluated. And, third, in our discussion of monetary theory we shall be making extensive use of the terminology and concepts developed in connection with this system of accounts. These accounts will not be discussed in detail but only so far as necessary to develop the subsequent analysis.[5]

Gross National Product (GNP) and Its Components

The nation's total output of goods and services produced during a specified period of time and valued at market prices is called the *gross national product* (GNP). This concept is so important in our discussion that we must spend some time exploring its implications.

First, since the GNP is expressed in terms of dollars' worth, we cannot ascertain, without additional information, the extent to which a given

---

[5] For more extensive treatment of national income accounting, consult any standard textbook in macroeconomics.

change in GNP represents an output change or is merely the result of a change in the price level or is some combination of the two. Actually, this "additional information" is available to us: the so-called *implicit price deflator*, as developed and used by the Department of Commerce, embodies an estimate of the actual course of prices of the items comprising the GNP; and the real, or "constant dollar," GNP figures purport to record the movements in the volume of goods and services produced (see Table 14.1) as they would have appeared if prices had been the same in every recorded year as they were during a designated base period, 1958 in this example.

Second, GNP excludes certain elements of the year's "output," such as the value of the labor of the home owner who panels his basement recreation room, of the housewife who carts the kids, cleans, and cooks; of the volunteer who works without pay in behalf of the hospital, church, and United Fund; and the many other similar services that we simply cannot record or value in money terms.

Furthermore, the figures for some of the components of GNP are based on quite incomplete data. And there are differences of opinion as to whether some items not now in the GNP should be included, and similarly for items now included that some argue should be dropped.

Nevertheless, such considerations as these, while alerting us to the danger of reading too much into the recorded GNP figures, do not vitiate the figures for the uses that we have in mind for them. Our concern is

TABLE 14.1
Gross National Product Valued in Current and 1958 Prices, Selected Years, 1929–73

Gross National Product
(in $billions)

Year	Current Prices	1958 Prices
1929	103.1	203.6
1933	55.6	141.5
1939	90.5	209.4
1945	211.9	355.2
1950	284.8	355.3
1955	398.0	438.0
1958	447.3	447.3
1960	503.7	487.7
1965	684.9	617.8
1968	864.2	706.6
1969	930.3	725.6
1970	977.1	722.5
1971	1055.5	745.4
1972	1155.2	790.7
1973	1288.2	837.3

Source: *Economic Report of the President* and *Survey of Current Business*, various issues.

over short-run changes, not absolute magnitudes; and the problems of measurement and interpretation sketched above have negligible impact on year-to-year changes in GNP figures.

GNP: Expenditure Categories

It is possible to break down the aggregate GNP figure a number of ways. We shall familiarize ourselves with two classification schemes having the most direct bearing on monetary theory.

The first of these schemes analyzes GNP in terms of types of *expenditures:* personal consumption expenditures (C), gross private domestic investment (I), government purchases of goods and services (G), and net exports of goods and services (X). In algebraic shorthand, then, we may write

$$E = C + I + G + X$$

Table 14.2 presents the actual expenditure figures for a recent year, 1973. A few words about each category will clarify their meaning in this context.

Consumption expenditures comprise purchases by households of new durable goods (such as automobiles, home appliances, lawn mowers), nondurable goods (shoes, meat, stationery, gasoline for the family car), and services (haircuts, hotel accommodations, dry cleaning). Note that the purchase of a new home is not included here but is in the next category.

TABLE 14.2
Gross National Product, Expenditure Approach, 1973
(in $billions)

Personal consumption expenditures (C)		$805.0
Durable goods	$131.1	
Nondurable goods	336.3	
Services	337.6	
Gross private domestic investment (I)		201.5
Construction	$106.3	
Producers' durable equipment	87.7	
Changes in inventories	7.4	
Government purchases of goods & services (G)		277.2
Federal	$106.9	
State and local	170.3	
Net exports of goods and services (X)		4.6
Exports	$101.3	
Less: Imports	96.7	
Total GNP, Expenditures Approach (E)		$1,288.2

Source: *Economic Report of the President, 1974* (Washington, D.C.: U.S. Government Printing Office, 1974), pp. 249.

Gross private domestic investment, in the setting of the national income accounts, refers to all expenditures by business and nonprofit organizations for plant and equipment and other productive assets, including increases in inventory, and by households and businesses for new single- and multiple-family residential structures. The inventory category can carry a negative figure since busineses can, and sometimes do, experience a decline in total inventories.

The term *investment* often presents a problem to those habituated to thinking of investment in terms of buying and selling claims: bonds, shares of stock, and so on. But it should be clear that claims have no place in a classification of expenditures on our national output of goods and services.

Although we think of investment as "business spending," a varying proportion is actually household spending on new residences. Thus, our expenditure classification is not so neat as we might prefer. This need not cause alarm, however, since no conclusion we shall draw is affected by this situation.

Government purchases of goods and services by all levels of government are encompassed by this category. Observe that only government expenditures in payment for goods and for the use of productive resources (particularly labor) are included. Omitted are loans to small business, scholarship payments, interest payments on the Federal debt, payments to disabled veterans, and all other classes of payments for which there are no direct current services rendered or goods conveyed.

Exports minus imports is not really in itself a category of expenditures but is a result of subtracting our expenditures on foreign goods and services (imports) from foreigners' expenditures on our output (exports). If we were to record only our exports on the grounds that this is a category of expenditure on our output, while neglecting to subtract imports, we would be overstating the value of our output by the dollar value of our imports, since a part of our C, I, and G represents expenditures on *foreign-produced* goods and services.

GNP: Income Categories

It is also useful, for our purposes, to classify GNP in terms of *income receipts and recipients.* We use the same four categories of economic units here as we did in discussing expenditure categories: households, business, government, and the rest of the world. (See Table 14.3).

Quantitatively the most important income-receiving sector is households. Although the main source of *net disposable personal income* (Y_d)[6]

---

[6] The concept of net disposable personal income differs slightly from the standard "disposable personal income" concept employed in Department of Commerce data. We use the "net" concept for the sake of consistency. We are showing each sector's income net of double-counting and of all transfers to other sectors. This net figure is therefore the amount available during the period for expenditures and acquisition of net claims on

TABLE 14.3
Gross National Product, Income Approach, 1973
(in $billions)

Households: Net disposable income (Y_d)		$858.8
Business: Gross business saving (S_b)		134.7
Capital consumption allowance	$109.6	
Undistributed corporate profits	25.1	
Government: Taxes net of transfers (T_n)		288.8
Total tax and nontax receipts	$419.0	
Less government transfer payments	130.2	
Rest of the world: personal and government Transfer to foreigners (F)		3.6
Less: Statistical discrepancy		2.3
		$1,288.2

Source: Economic Report of the President, 1974 (Washington, D.C.: U.S. Government Printing Office, 1974), pp. 258, 259, and 355.

is factor earnings (wage and salaries, rent, and the like), an important secondary source is government transfer payments, that is payments not based on current services rendered or sale of goods to the government.

In the framework of the national income data, households have two alternatives in utilizing each dollar of net disposable personal income: they can spend it on consumption or save it. There is little possibility of misunderstanding in connection with consumption; we have already indicated the three classes of items included—durables, nondurables, and services. But the term *saving* has proved to be a source of difficulty to economics students. Actually, personal saving as used in our national accounts is a sort of residual: take net disposable personal income, subtract personal consumption expenditures, and the remaining amount is personal saving. Whether you take ten dollars of your week's income and flush it down the toilet, or pay a debt to the bank, or put it in a mutual fund, or hide it in the coffee canister, it represents current saving. Of course, the economic effects will not be the same in all cases, but that is beside the point here.

Personal saving may be negative as well as positive. Although the household sector as a whole is not likely to dissave, individual households often go through brief periods in which consumption expenditures far exceed net disposable income, as happens when the household purchases a major durable good, such as an automobile. During the quarter in which the purchase is made, if C exceeds Y_d, then saving is

---

other sectors. To obtain a Y_d figure for a particular period of time, deduct "consumer interest payments" and "personal transfer payments to foreigners" from the Department of Commerce "disposable personal income" figure.

negative, by definition, regardless of whether the purchase was financed by borrowing, by dipping into past savings (selling financial assets or drawing down deposits) or by a combination of the two. The subsequent monthly repayment of the debt, by the way, counts as "saving," since it represents a part of Y_d that is obviously not spent on current consumption.

We must take great care not to confuse saving with two related concepts: savings and hoarding. *Savings* represent the result of past saving. In popular usage, it usually comprises the household's financial assets, such as a savings account, mutual fund shares, and U.S. savings bonds. Whereas savings is a *stock*, therefore measured at a point in time, saving is a *flow*, measured over a period of time.

Hoarding is the act of accumulating money. Thus, if we earned $500 (net of taxes) and spent $450 on consumer items, keeping the remainder in the form of cash, we both saved (since Y_d exceeds C) and hoarded (increased our money holdings). If, instead, we had placed this $50 remainder in our account at a credit union, we would have saved but not hoarded. And, finally, if we had spent the entire $500 on consumer goods and services but added $200 to our cash balance by selling an old motorcycle, we would have hoarded but not saved.

Business disposable income, or *gross saving* done by corporate business (S_b), consists of capital consumption allowance and undistributed corporate profits.[7] The sum of these two categories over a given period of time comprises that portion of total business receipts not paid out either to government (mainly as taxes) or to households, in the form of wages, dividends, and other factor payments. The entire amount is utilized during the period to finance investment, to repay debt, and to acquire financial assets, including cash.

The reason we divide business disposable receipts into these two classes—undistributed corporate profits and capital consumption allowance—is that it is helpful to know how much of the total represents earnings required merely to maintain intact the nation's stock of real capital and how much is at least potentially available for expansion of this stock.

Government disposable income (T_n) is composed of total taxes *net of government transfer payments* to households and to the rest of the world. The disposable income of the "rest-of-the-world" sector (F) takes the form of transfers (gifts and grants) from our household and government sectors.

Since expenditure and income are but two sides of the same coin, we might expect to arrive at the same GNP figure regardless of our scheme of classification, so long as it is an exhaustive one. But because the GNP figures are built up in part from different sources of data in the two cases

---

[7] Plowed-back current net profits of noncorporate businesses are counted with personal saving, that is, received by owners but not spent on personal consumption.

and are based on estimates of varying quality, we must anticipate some difference in the final figures. The actual difference, included in the GNP estimate under the label *statistical discrepancy*, is very small, amounting in most recent years to less than two-tenths of 1 per cent of GNP.

Adding together the net disposable incomes of all four sectors (plus or minus the statistical discrepancy), we arrive at our GNP figure again. Algebraically:

$$Y = Y_d + S_b + T_n + F$$

That is, GNP from the standpoint of sectoral disposable incomes (Y) consists of net disposable personal income (Y_d), corporation disposable income (S_b), government disposable income, or taxes net of transfers (T_n), and disposable income acquired from us by the rest of the world, or net transfers to foreigners (F).[8]

Expenditure and Income Approaches Combined

Having examined GNP from the standpoints of both expenditures and receipts, we must now combine these approaches. The following Table (14.4) shows the relation between disposable income and expenditures for each sector for 1973.

According to this table, household net disposable income exceeded consumption expenditures in 1973 by about $54 billion. This excess, we know, is personal saving. How have households disposed of this vast sum? Part of the answer is that they have utilized a portion of their current saving in the purchase of newly constructed housing. However, this comprises but a tiny percentage of current saving because (1) the

TABLE 14.4
Relationship between Disposable Income and Expenditures, 1973
(in $billions)

Sector	Disposable Income	Expenditures	Surplus (+) or Deficit (−)
Households	Y_d = $858.8	C = $805.0	+$53.8
Business	S_b = 134.7	I = 201.5	−66.8
Government	T_n = 288.8	G = 277.2	+11.6
Rest of world	F = 3.6	X = 4.6	−1.0
Statistical discrepancy	2.3		+2.3
	Y = $1,288.2	E = $1,288.2	0

Source: Tables 14.2 and 14.3.

---

[8] We do not include *statistical discreprancy* in our equation as it occurs only because of imperfect data. Obviously it is not itself a sector having disposable income!

greater part of household expenditures on new residences is financed by borrowing, (2) even the nonborrowed part is mainly the result of *past* savings rather than saving out of the current year's income, and (3) a portion of new housing consists of apartment complexes and other rental units that are purchased by business enterprises, not households. The remainder of current personal saving was utilized to help finance, directly and indirectly, the deficits of other sectors: business and government.

Gross business saving fell far short of covering investment in 1973, even allowing for the fact that some investment was in the form of household purchases of new housing. This relation between S_b and I is the typical situation, except in years of severe depression or total war.

The government sector presents a less consistent record, years of surplus on income and product account being about as numerous as years of deficit over the post-World War II period. The foreign sector has imported more from us than it has exported to us every year since 1945, with the sole exception of 1972. In several of these years, though, private and government transfers from the United States have more than financed their deficit (our surplus), but usually these transfers have fallen short.

There is much more to the disposition of sector surpluses and financing of sector deficits than this, however. In the first place, Table 14.4 leaves out all *intra*sectoral financing, that is, the financing of an economic unit in one sector by another unit in the same sector. Examples abound, such as the granting of trade credit to one business firm by another, or a loan by the Federal government to a local housing authority.

Second, intersectoral financing does not flow only from surplus to deficit sectors. There is a considerable amount of financing of economic units in surplus sectors by economic units in deficit sectors, or between economic units in two surplus sectors or economic units in two deficit sectors. For example, some government lending agencies (deficit sector) provide financing to business firms (another deficit sector) or to households (surplus sector).

Third, and of special concern to us students of the financial system, Table 14.4 omits the entire system of financial intermediaries! In an advanced economy such as ours, by far the greatest share of financing is *indirect*, making use of at least one intermediary, sometimes several. We can illustrate this statement as applied to the household sector by means of Table 14.5. Although households acquired $130.8 billion in financial assets in 1973, they increased their (gross) claims on financial intermediaries, monetary and otherwise, by at least $112.5 billion (the first three asset categories), with their claims against nonfinancial sectors rising by only $18.4 billion.

The Federal Reserve System has developed a comprehensive system of accounts, called the flow of funds accounts, that provides a great deal of information on some of these intersectoral flows, direct and through

TABLE 14.5
Net Financial Investment of the Household Sector, 1973
(in $billions)

Claims Acquired (Net)		Obligations Incurred (Net)	
Demand deposits and currency	$13.1	Mortgage debt	$45.6
Time and savings accounts	67.7	Consumer debt	22.9
Life insurance and pension fund reserves	31.7	Security debt	− 4.6
		Other debt	5.3
Debt securities: government and private	29.5		$69.3
Corporate shares and equity in noncorporate business	− 12.6	Net financial investment	61.5
Other claims (net)	1.5		
	$130.8		$130.8

Source: Adapted from "Summary of Flow of Fund Accounts for the Year 1973," *Federal Reserve Bulletin*, October 1974, p. A.58.

intermediaries. An adequate discussion of this system would require more time and space than we can justify in this text, however.[9]

Summary

With this chapter we have begun our discussion of monetary theory: that branch of economics dealing with the interrelations of the financial system and the rest of the economy.

Our first step has been to become acquainted (or reacquainted) with our system of national accounts, because most of the discussion in subsequent chapters will utilize this system as a framework. The focus has been, and will continue to be, on the gross national product (GNP), our measure of the money value of aggregate output, and on its components, as broken down statistically into both income categories and expenditure categories of four major sectors: households, business firms, units of government, and the rest of the world (as involved in transactions that affect our GNP).

KEY CONCEPTS

Monetary theory
Gross national product
GNP implicit price deflator
Consumption expenditures

Gross private domestic investment
Net disposable personal income
Gross business saving
Government transfer payments

---

[9] See *Flow of Funds Account, 1945–1968* (Washington, D.C.: Board of Governors of the Federal Reserve System, 1970), for a full explanation, and recent issues of the *Federal Reserve Bulletin* for current data.

QUESTIONS FOR REVIEW

1. What has happened to the scope of "monetary theory" since the 1930s?
2. What is *the* problem that monetary theory attempts to analyze?
3. What are the weaknesses of "gross national product" as a measure of a nation's output?
4. Can personal saving be negative? Can gross private domestic investment? Net exports? Gross business saving?
5. Distinguish between saving and savings; saving and hoarding.
6. Why are personal transfers to *foreigners* included in the GNP (Y) while personal transfers to *persons* are not included?

SUGGESTIONS FOR FURTHER READING

Board of Governors, Federal Reserve System. *Flow of Funds Accounts, 1945–1968.* Washington, D.C.: Board of Governors. Federal Reserve System, 1970.

Denison, Edward F. "Welfare Measurement and the GNP," *Survey of Current Business,* LI (January 1971), pp. 1–8.

Office of Business Economics, U.S. Department of Commerce. "The Economic Accounts of the United States: Retrospect and Prospect," 50th Anniversary Issue of *Survey of Current Business,* LI (July 1971).

Consumption and Its Determination
Consumption and Disposable Income
Financial Factors Affecting Consumption Behavior
Other Factors Affecting Consumption Behavior
Consumption and Gross National Product

Investment
The Investment Decision
Determinants of Investment: Marginal Efficiency of Investment
The Aggregate Marginal Efficiency of Investment Schedule
Investment and Income
Determinants of Investment: Financial Factors
Housing Construction and Inventory Investment
Determinants of Investment: Some Qualifications

Government Expenditures

The Rest-of-the-World Sector

The Building Blocks of Macroeconomic Theory 15

In this chapter we begin our analysis of the economic role of the financial system, a task to occupy us for the next four chapters. Our framework is that of standard macroeconomic theory, that is, the theory of the behavior of aggregate income and output and their major components. However, we shall lay special stress on the influence of the financial system on these economic aggregates via its influences on the spending plans of households, business firms, units of government, and even of other nations with respect to their plans to purchase goods and services produced here. Also, since causation runs both ways, we shall observe the effects of changes in the behavior of these aggregates on the financial system and its components.

The system of national accounts introduced in chapter 14 provides a useful starting point. We recall from our discussion there that the total expenditures of the four above-mentioned sectors constitute the Gross National Product, or GNP. But this information, which we summarized by the identity $E = C + I + G + X$, does not help us in our efforts to understand *why* the GNP is a particular size, how the components behave, and how they are interrelated. For example, why was C $437.8 billion during a certain period? If consumers had decided to increase their spending by $10 billion the following period, would C actually have increased by this exact amount, no more and no less? Would any of the other expenditure components have been affected? If so, why, by how much, and how soon? Would an increase in G have the same aggregate impact as an increase in C of the same size? Would an increase in I? or X?

The problem is that, while our system of national accounts provides a useful framework for recording the results of economic activity over a given period in terms of income and expenditure categories, this system cannot tell us whether the figures thus recorded were in line with the plans and expectations of consumers, businessmen, and so on, or whether they were near, or very wide of, the mark.

For instance, it sometimes happens that, during a particular quarter, businessmen really want to invest considerably more than they actually succeed in doing but, because of slow deliveries, or a decrease in inventories resulting from an unexpectedly high level of sales, or even delays in obtaining financing, the actual *recorded* level of investment is far below the *planned* level. Or the opposite situation might arise. Plans by businessmen to reduce I could be temporarily thwarted by an unexpected (and unwelcome) addition to inventories as sales fell below expectations. Although a difference between planned and actual I would not show up in the national accounts, such a discrepency is of crucial importance to the economy, influencing not only future I but also (as we shall see) other expenditure components of GNP, over subsequent months and even years.

Clearly, what we need along with our system of national accounts is a theoretical framework to assist us in thinking through the effects that various events and developments will have on aggregate economic activity, total and sectoral. Fortunately for us, there exists such a framework, developed by John Maynard Keynes and his followers, as we noted in chapter 14. The present chapter and the next three will outline the elements of this approach. In this chapter and chapter 16 we plan to develop a model of the "real" sector of the economy, first outlining the determinants of each major expenditure category—C, I, G, and X—and then pulling all of them together to form a simplified yet reasonably realistic picture of the way the goods-and-services economy functions. Then, in chapter 17, we examine the behavior of the financial system on an aggregate level, that is, its response to changes in its environment. Finally, we combine the two—the real and the financial sectors—into a more comprehensive model in chapter 18 in order to gain an appreciation of the ways these sectors act on, and react to, each other as subsystems of the economic system. Chapter 18 also applies the model to the problems of inflation and growth.

One important simplifying assumption incorporated in these models (an assumption you are strongly urged to keep in mind as we go along) is a constant price level. Whenever we refer to a change in GNP, we are assuming that the entire change is in *real* GNP. This may seem remote from reality, so be assured that (1) the effects of price-level changes are introduced whenever appropriate, and (2) chapter 18 will include a discussion of the relationships between price-level changes and aggregate economic behavior.

You are hereby put on notice that, from this point on, the various concepts and symbols used to denote expenditure categories will normally be used in the *planned* sense, not in the *realized*, or recorded, sense. Thus, unless otherwise indicated, C will always refer to the amount that people *plan* to spend on consumption, I, for planned investment, and so on.

Consumption and Its Determination

By far the largest fraction of GNP consists of consumer goods and services. And by far the most important influence on consumption is income, according to both economic theory and empirical research on this subject. We all know by experience that, as our disposable income changes, we change our spending in the same direction. Also, we would probably not disagree with the statement that personal spending rises (or falls) by a smaller amount than does income, other things remaining constant. Still, it is reassuring to learn that both budget studies of individual family consumption patterns and analyses of the behavior of overall consumption support these judgments.

There are other influences on consumption, though, and the relation between consumption and income is not so simple and straightforward as we might think. A number of partially conflicting theories have been advanced to explain the nature of the response of consumption (C) to changes in net disposable personal income (Y_d) and in other factors[1] and no reconciliation appears on the horizon yet. But we need not concern ourselves with these intricacies here; the consumption-to-income relation is sufficiently strong to serve our purposes, if we keep in mind that, because of these "other factors," the relation is not exact.

First, then, we shall examine the relation between consumption and income, after which we shall consider several other influences on consumption.

Consumption and Disposable Income

Suppose that, in a particular economy, the *consumption function*—the relationship between C and Y_d—is as summarized in Table 15.1.

The table tells us several things about this consumption function. First, when Y_d changes, C changes in the same direction by 90 per cent of the change in Y_d. For example, if Y_d should increase from $420 billion

---

[1] Robert Ferber, "Consumer Economics: A Survey," *Journal of Economic Literature*, XI (December 1973), pp. 1303–42.

TABLE 15.1
**Net Disposable Personal Income,
Consumption, and Personal Saving**
(hypothetical data, in $billions)

Y_d	C	APC (C/Y_d)	MPC $(\Delta C/\Delta Y_d)$	S_p
0	9		0.9	−9
70	72	1.03	0.9	−2
140	135	0.96	0.9	5
210	198	0.94	0.9	12
280	261	0.93	0.9	19
350	324	0.93	0.9	26
420	387	0.92	0.9	33
490	450	0.92	0.9	40
560	513	0.92	0.9	47
630	576	0.91	0.9	54

to $490 billion (a rise of $70 billion), consumption would increase from $387 billion to $450 billion (a rise of $63 billion or 90 per cent of $70 billion). The ratio of the change in consumption (write ΔC) to the change in net disposable income (ΔY_d) is the *marginal propensity to consume* (MPC). In our example, the MPC is constant at .9. This assumption of a constant MPC is not completely realistic but comes close enough, over a limited range of Y_d values, to suit our needs.

Another characteristic of consumption behavior implied in Table 15.1 is that the ratio of consumption to net disposable income (C/Y_d), or the *average propensity to consume* (APC) declines somewhat as Y_d rises.

Personal saving (S_p), of course, is also tied directly to net disposable personal income. If the household sector changes its C by an amount equal to 90 per cent of a change in Y_d, it must change its S_p by an amount equal to the other 10 per cent, since it has, by definition, only these two alternatives in the disposition of its income. So, a change in Y_d from $420 billion to $490 billion will increase personal saving from $33 billion to $40 billion. Since $\Delta Y_d = \$70$ billion and $\Delta S_p = \$7$ billion, the marginal propensity to save, or $\Delta S_p/\Delta Y_d$, is .1.

The same relationships are depicted graphically in Figure 15.1. C and S are measured vertically; Y_d, horizontally. Line CC represents the consumption function and SS the personal saving function. The 45-degree line is added simply for visual orientation. Each point on this line represents a specific value of Y_d and the identical value of C. Therefore, for any given Y_d, we can determine whether, and to what extent, C exceeds or falls short of Y_d by noting the position of the CC line relative to the 45-degree line at the point representing that Y_d. Where CC crosses the 45-degree line, C equals Y_d and, therefore, S_p is zero.

Caution is needed in interpreting this information. In the first place, we may not infer that this hypothetical economy *as a whole* dissaves at

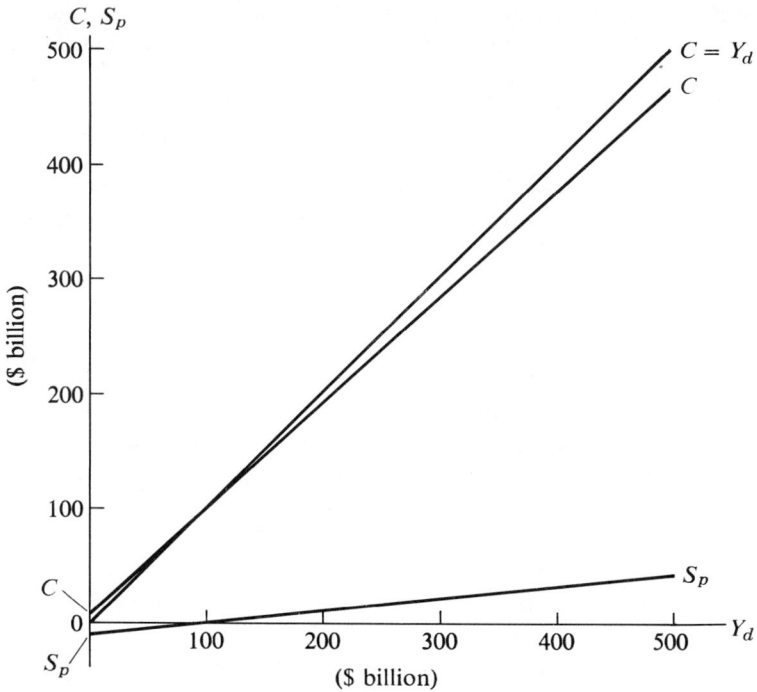

Figure 15.1
Consumption and personal saving functions.

levels of Y_d below 90. We have been considering only the household sector; we have no way of ascertaining from these figures what the budget positions of the other sectors are when households net disposable income is at any given level. Second, we cannot be sure that the relationship between C and Y_d will remain constant over time. Either gradually or suddenly this consumption function could shift in response to one or more of the financial and "other" factors affecting consumption. We now turn our attention to these factors.

Financial Factors Affecting Consumption Behavior

INNOVATIONS IN CONSUMER SAVINGS FACILITIES   The financial system is constantly evolving, as we know; and some changes have had, and are having, an impact on consumer spending practices. For example, the continually widening array of financial assets and other arrangements for committing savings makes it less likely that a person will be dissuaded from saving by the unavailability of suitable outlets for his funds. A recent study supports this conclusion. Exploring "the question of whether the presence of . . . savings and loan associations and mutual savings banks . . . increase overall liquid savings in a community," this study reached the following conclusion:

The greater the importance of near banks [that is, mutual savings banks and savings and loan associations] to commercial banks, the greater is the overall pool of savings in the area. Part of the enlarged local pool of savings may be attributed to new savings stemming from greater availability of savings facilities and increased competition among savings institutions.[2]

In particular, there has been a rapid rise in contractual saving through group life insurance, pension plans, and the like. Through arrangements such as these, families make long-term saving commitments and generally seem to build their consumption patterns around the remainder of their incomes, treating the automatic saving almost like their income-tax withholdings. These factors—a broadening choice of savings outlets and increasing use of contractual and other regular savings arrangements—in and of themselves can be expected to lead to an increase in saving out of any given level of Y_d or, in other words, should result in a higher personal saving function and a lower consumption function.

INNOVATIONS IN CONSUMER CREDIT   Also affecting consumption are innovations in consumer credit institutions and arrangements. On first thought it might seem that, since households are enabled, through borrowing and installment buying, to acquire goods (and even services) in advance of their ability to pay for them, their C out of any given Y_d would be pushed upward. But there may be offsetting influences. Suppose, for example, that the making of monthly payments develops the habit of regularly spending less than one's income, even after the debt is paid. Or suppose that buying a durable good on credit reduces the demand for costlier substitutes, thus freeing some income for spending on other things and for saving. Cases in point are home laundry equipment (substituting for laundry service) and a television set (substituting for attending the movies). On balance, therefore, we cannot be certain of the direction of the long-run effect of consumer credit on total consumer expenditures.

It seems likely that consumer credit makes consumption more unstable. When consumer incomes are growing at a rapid rate, expectations tend to be more optimistic on the part of both consumers and prospective suppliers of credit. Augmented by a larger volume of consumer credit, households will tend to spend a larger fraction of any given Y_d than they would in the absence of this factor. On the downswing, though, reluctance to enter into new installment contracts, coupled with the necessity to continue payments on previously incurred consumer debt, pushes down the C/Y_d ratio to a lower level than would have occurred without the "dead hand of debt." Consumer credit, in other words, acts to raise the consumption function when the economy is experiencing improving conditions but to lower it when the economy is slumping.

[2] George G. Kaufman and Cynthia M. Latta, "Near Banks and Local Savings," *National Banking Review*, III (June 1966), pp. 539, 541.

CHANGES IN CONSUMER CREDIT TERMS AND CONDITIONS   A related financial influence on consumption spending is the terms and conditions under which consumer credit is made available: interest rates, down payments, length of the repayment period, and standards of acceptable credit risk. Changes in these terms affect consumer demand for credit accommodation, of course, since they bear on both the number of households applying for credit and the number qualified (in the lender's eyes) for credit. But the strength of the effect of credit-term changes on aggregate consumption is very difficult to determine. An increase in consumer *credit* is not tantamount to an increase in consumer *purchases,* since a particular purchase could often have been financed by other means— sale of liquid assets, for example, or a reduction in the savings-account balance. Nevertheless, there is evidence that the interest on consumer installment loans does influence the demand for consumer durables.[3] Since durables are not perfect substitutes for other consumer expenditure categories, it is safe to conclude that the effect is felt on total consumption.

INTEREST RATES ON SAVINGS   There was a time when interest rates were considered an important determinant of the consumption *versus* saving decision. The view almost universally accepted by economists now is that changes in interest rates exert little, if any, direct effect on consumption. Both armchair theorizing and empirical research have failed to discover any significant relation, or any strong reason for expecting such a relation, between these two variables. Arguments that interest-rate rises should stimulate saving can be advanced: the incentive to accumulate is greater; and, along with the tighter general credit conditions accompanying higher rates, there is less incentive to purchase durables through credit (which involves initial dissaving). But such arguments can be countered by others: higher rates make a target estate or future income level achievable by smaller current saving, and higher rates discourage home ownership with its attendant "automatic" saving through monthly payments on the mortgage loan. Thus, there is no reason to expect changes in interest rates to have a strong effect in one direction or the other.

FINANCIAL ASSETS   Last on our list of financial influences on consumption is possession of financial assets. The reasoning here is that, other things constant (including Y_d), the greater the dollar volume of financial assets held, the greater will consumption spending be, since a cushion of financial assets provides security against adversities, thus helping to overcome resistance to spending.

The year-to-year changes in the value of holdings of some classes of financial assets, particularly common stock, can be important in this re-

---

[3] Michael J. Hamburger, "Interest Rates and the Demand for Consumer Durable Goods," *American Economic Review,* LVII (December 1967), pp. 1131–53.

gard. Even though the volume of stocks changes relatively little from one year to the next, their prices can vary substantially. A sizable drop in stock prices, such as occurred in 1970, tends to curb consumption expenditures, in the view of many analysts.

Changes in liquid asset holdings are not large from year to year and therefore probably have a negligible effect on consumption. However, the mere possession by the household sector of a large stock of such assets constitutes a potentially destabilizing factor. A recent study discovered this:

> For many families drawing on the savings account is a major alternative to the use of installment credit, although resort to a combination of both sources of funds is not infrequent. . . . These families treat their savings account as a revolving fund. . . . They intend to replace withdrawals promptly out of current income [and] . . . as a rule these "good intentions" are indeed carried out.[4]

Changes in the economic environment (such as those to be discussed below) can be expected to affect the desire of households to spend, while possession of large amounts of liquid assets enhances their ability to control their rate of spending, enabling a stronger response to economic changes, actual or expected, than would otherwise be the case.

Other Factors Affecting Consumption Behavior

A number of nonfinancial factors, attitudinal and institutional, bear on consumption, too. Although in most cases we have only the vaguest notion of their quantitative significance, these factors do throw some additional light on consumption behavior.

AGE-COMPOSITION OF THE POPULATION Given Y_d, the age-distribution of the population may affect the consumption function marginally. If the population bulge is at the lower end of the age-scale, the C/Y_d ratio will accordingly be higher because of the expenses of starting a new household and of rearing children. An increase in the proportion of the aged in the population also raises the consumption function because (1) the aged tend to be dissavers, that is, to spend more than their current income, and (2) insofar as the aged are supported by offspring, the amount saved out of the latter's income is almost inevitably reduced.

INCOME DISTRIBUTION This factor might logically be expected to affect consumption thus: the more unequal the distribution, the lower will C be out of a given Y_d because the higher-income receivers gener-

---

[4] Eva Mueller and Jane Lean, "The Savings Account as a Source for Financing Large Expenditures," *Journal of Finance*, XXII (September 1967), p. 375.

ally spend a smaller fraction of their incomes. However, economists are not so sure. On the one hand, lower-income households tend to have somewhat higher marginal propensities to consume than do higher-income households; therefore a shift in income distribution in the direction of equality would tend to raise the C/Y_d ratio. But, on the other hand, there is evidence that consumption levels result in part from efforts to emulate the living patterns of those with higher incomes.[5] Insofar as this factor is important, a reduced spread between rich and poor would tend to make it easier to "keep up with the Joneses," hence reduce the pressure to spend.

NONFINANCIAL ASSETS   Consumers hold not only financial assets but also real assets, and it is possible that these latter, too, may affect consumption. Durable goods especially have been singled out for attention by economists. On the one hand, since durables substitute to some extent for outside services, as mentioned previously, we might expect possession of these goods to reduce the pressure to spend. Countering this effect, however, is the fact that, for most durables, "it isn't the initial cost, it's the upkeep" (repairs and other maintenance, plus running costs). And there is also the factor of "planned obsolescence," which has extended its range beyond the durables category and into nondurables, particularly clothing.

No definite conclusion emerges concerning the direction of effect of real assets, particularly durables, on the consumption function. It seems safe to assert, however, that large stocks of durables in the hands of consumers will make for greater short-run instability in consumption. While a family, under pressure of declining or uncertain income, can often postpone purchase of a new automatic washer, it cannot long postpone laundering the clothes!

INSTITUTIONAL CHANGES   A number of social and economic changes seem to have an effect on people's habits in allocating income between consumption and saving; but, here again, we have two offsetting "hands," the one and the other, with no conclusive evidence as to which dominates. On the one hand, reducing the need for savings are such developments as (1) government economic stabilization policy and activities, which have reduced the likelihood of a major depression, and (2) increased coverage of various public and private insurance plans covering unemployment, illness, and disability. On the other hand, there has been a substantial rise in various forms of contractual saving, including pensions and life insurance, tending to raise the volume of household saving out of a given Y_d, as mentioned earlier.

---

[5] James Duesenberry, *Income, Saving and the Theory of Consumer Behavior* (Cambridge: Harvard University Press, 1947). This analysis is updated in Myron Ross, *Income: Analysis and Policy*, 2d ed. (New York: McGraw-Hill Book Co., 1969). pp. 73–74.

ATTITUDES AND EXPECTATIONS   To a large extent, attitudes and expectations are themselves the results of these institutional factors plus long-run and short-run developments in the economy, financial and otherwise. Thus, partly as a result of our relatively good stabilization record, consumer attitudes toward going into debt for the purchase of durables and even nondurables and services have changed radically over the past few decades, undoubtedly both reflecting and reinforcing developments in consumer credit arrangements. Also, it is conceivable that a gradual reduction of fear of another Great Depression has reduced the pressure to save for a "rainy day."

In addition, economists need to puzzle over the possible short-run effects on consumption of a wide variety of other events and developments affecting expectations. Illustrating this problem is this paragraph commenting on the situation in early 1972, when the rise in consumption was lagging behind the rise in disposable income:

> The catalog of things disturbing us includes, of course, inflation and high unemployment. Some economist-psychologists also say we're upset because the dollar no longer seems solid, the seasons have been out of sorts and the flu zapped us hard last winter. Chairman [of the Federal Reserve Board of Governors Arthur] Burns blames our condition on, among other things, "a very long and most unhappy war," the school busing controversy, the impending youth vote, the recollection of campus disorders and urban race riots, and the fact that "women also are marching in the streets."[6]

The consumption effects of changing expectations concerning inflation are far from simple to analyze. It might seem obvious that, as expectations of inflation become more widespread, we consumers would spend more out of a given income in order to beat the price increases. But what would we buy? We might increase our inventories of food a bit, and perhaps of some clothing items. But most clothing rapidly becomes obsolete because of fashion changes. Consumer durables? Again, few households would purchase, say, a new refrigerator or furnace merely because they expect a price increase.[7] Furthermore, surveys of consumer attitudes have discovered that expectations of inflation often cause a *reduction* in planned spending, as people fear that their incomes will be insufficient to cover needed expenditures in the future and as savings plans for retirement, children's education, and so on, are revised upward in line with expected increases in costs and prices.

PRICE-LEVEL CHANGES   What about the effects on consumption of actual, as distinct from expected, changes in the price level? The answer

---

[6] Sterling E. Soderlind, "Inconspicuous Disconsumption," *Wall Street Journal*, LIII (March 28, 1972), p. 14. Reprinted with permission of The Wall Street Journal, © Dow Jones & Company, Inc. 1972.

[7] There may be some inducement to buy a new home this year instead of next, but housing construction is in the *investment* category.

depends in part on the strength of the *money illusion,* that is, the extent to which consumers tend to focus on the *money* value of their incomes rather than on the *real,* or purchasing-power, value.

To illustrate, let us assume two households. Household A is free of money illusion, while in the case of Household B money illusion is complete. Each household received a net disposable income of $10,000 over a particular year. Each spent an identical $9,600 on consumer goods and services—thus having an APC of .96 and an MPC of .8. The following year the two households enjoy identical increases in Y_d of 5 per cent, raising the Y_d level to $10,500. Unfortunately, the price level also rises by 5 per cent. In real terms, therefore, their incomes have not changed. Under these circumstances, what will happen to the consumption expenditures of these two households?

Household A, without any money illusion, realizes that its real income is unchanged and therefore takes steps to maintain its real consumption at its customary level. This will require the household to increase its money expenditures on consumer items by 5 per cent, thus compensating for the price-level increase. Consumption expenditures of Household A will therefore rise by $480 (5 per cent of $9,600) to the level of $10,800. Its APC is unchanged.

Household B, having complete money illusion, treats the $500 increase in money income as though prices had not changed. With an MPC of .8, it will increase its C by $400, to $10,000. Its real consumption, however, has declined by about $76, because $10,000 now buys only as much as $9,524 would have purchased one year previously.

Generalizing, assuming that the APC exceeds the MPC (which is nearly always the case), in an inflationary situation the stronger the money illusion, the smaller will be the increase in consumer spending out of a given increase in (money) net disposable income.

Although we are not sure of the strength or duration of the money illusion effect, we do have some evidence of its existence. A recent statistical study based on the 1955–65 period indicated that "in the short run the price level has an independent effect on real consumption due to what is commonly called money illusion."[8]

OTHER FACTORS A miscellany of other influences on consumption could be passed in review, but the point has certainly been made thoroughly that consumption is subject to numerous influences, some operating quickly, some slowly. At this point it would be helpful to include a neat summary, wrapping up the entire discussion, relating all the parts to each other and to the whole. Unfortunately, this cannot be done. Take the word of Professor Siegel, who, after a thirty-five page treatment of consumption, offered this conclusion:

---

[8] William H. Branson and Alvin K. Klevorick, "Money Illusion and the Aggregate Consumption Function," *American Economic Review,* LIX (December 1969), p. 946.

The consumption function literature is rich, diversified, confusing, and unfortunately inconclusive. The various theories of the consumption function ... all have their deficiencies in explaining consumer behavior, and the effects upon consumption of variables other than income, however defined, are not yet completely understood.[9]

Yet, after all qualifications have been given their due, it remains true that, except in the most abnormal of times, consumption expenditures are fairly closely related to consumer incomes. In our analysis over the next few chapters we shall make considerable use of this relationship while, at the same time, attempting to keep in mind its limitations.

Consumption and Gross National Product

Consumption expenditures are also related to GNP, albeit less directly than to Y_d. In chapter 14 we learned that the difference between Y and Y_d is almost entirely accounted for by taxes and transfers plus corporate saving (capital consumption allowance and undistributed profits).

Taxes, net of transfer payments, (T_n) are directly related to gross national product (Y). Higher Y levels are associated with higher T_n levels because (1) some taxes, notably those on personal and corporate incomes, are highly responsive to Y levels; (2) other taxes are indirectly related to incomes (for example, sales and excise taxes, social security contributions, even property, death and gift taxes); and (3) some types of transfer payments move inversely with incomes, including unemployment compensation payments, old age assistance, and so on.

Business saving also varies with GNP. Higher GNP usually means higher profits that, because of "sticky" dividend rates in the short run, means higher retained earnings, one element of S_b. Capital consumption allowance, the other element of S_b, also varies directly with Y.

Since both net taxes (T_n) and gross business saving (S_b) are related to GNP, the remaining portion of GNP,[10] net disposable personal income (Y_d), must also be related. By way of illustration, consider this simple numerical example. Suppose that the combined effects of T_n and S_b account for 30 per cent of GNP at all levels. This being the case, Y_d must account for the remaining 70 per cent. We can express this algebraically as

$$Y_d = .7Y \tag{15.3}$$

Table 15.2 is built from the above information. Columns (1), (2), and (3) contain illustrative values of Y and the associated values of $(T_n + S_b)$ and Y_d; and the pairs of entries in columns (3) and (4) are taken from Table 15.1, depicting the relation of C and Y_d. Reading down columns (1)

---

[9] Barry N. Siegel, *Aggregate Economics and Public Policy*, 3d ed. (Homewood, Ill.: R. D. Irwin, 1970), p. 148.
[10] Ignoring a few extremely minor accounts.

TABLE 15.2
Relationship of Gross National Product,
Disposable Income, and Consumption
(in $billions)

Y (1)	$T_n + S_b$ (2)	Y_d (3)	C (4)
0	0	0	9
100	30	70	72
200	60	140	135
300	90	210	198
400	120	280	261
500	150	350	324
600	180	420	387
700	210	490	450
800	240	560	513
900	270	630	576

and (4), therefore, discloses the relation between C and Y. This relation is illustrated graphically by the CC curve in Figure 15.2.

When GNP changes by $100 billion, consumption changes by $63 billion in our model. More generally, the ratio of the change in C (ΔC) to

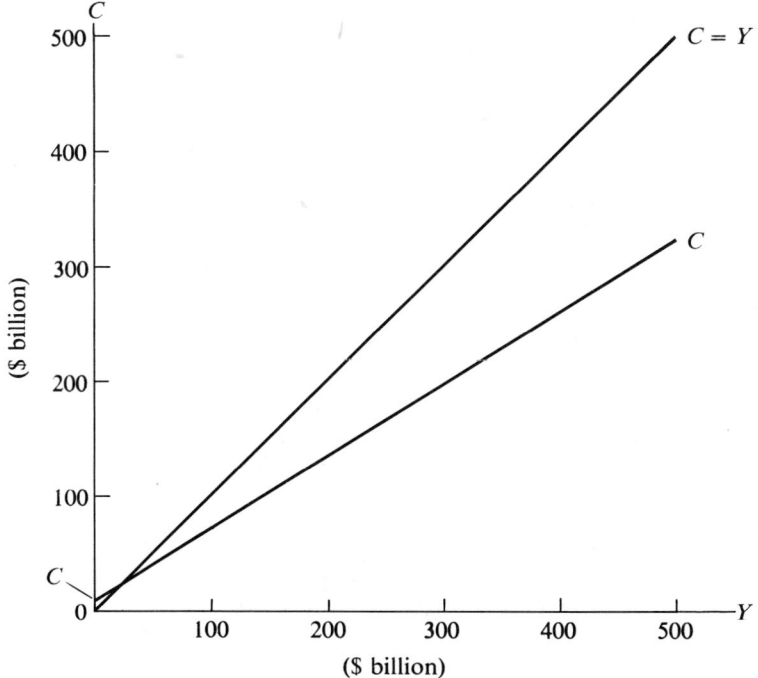

Figure 15.2
Consumption and gross national product.

the change in GNP (ΔY) is .63.[11] This relationship, $\Delta C/\Delta Y$, is labeled the *marginal propensity to consume out of GNP*.

Investment

Investment expenditures, though much smaller than consumption and even smaller than total goods-and-services expenditures by all units of government, have deservedly received much attention from economists and others concerned with forecasting and economic policy because of their variability, relative unpredictability, and influence on economic growth.

We were fortunate, in discussing consumption, to have located one variable that "explains" a great deal of the variation in consumption: net disposable personal income. Investment offers us no such single key determinant: the list of influences is long; the interconnections are many and complex. While investment is indeed related to the level of GNP, other influences tend to overshadow income as a determinant of the level of investment.

Investment, we recall, is a broad category of expenditures, including producers' durables, new construction, and inventory changes. One difficulty we face in analyzing investment determination is the differences among these classes: inventory investment is easily altered and is subject to involuntary increases and decreases as sales and production deviate from expectations; plant and equipment expenditures involve a longer planning period and a longer lag between decision and implementation; and, while intermediate-term and long-term profit expectations dominate decisions in both the foregoing categories, this factor is of much less direct influence in residential housing construction. We must be cautious, therefore, in generalizations concerning investment behavior determination.

In what follows we shall be discussing investment mainly in terms of business expenditures on plant and on producers durables, a category that has comprised about two-thirds of total gross private domestic investment during most recent years. Much of the discussion, though, will also be germane to inventory investment and to housing construction for investment purposes; but housing construction intended for owner-occupancy will require a brief separate discussion.

---

[11] The reason this particular numerical value emerged can be most easily explained algebraically. Since C changes by 90 per cent of a change in Y_d, or

$$\Delta C = .9 \Delta Y_d$$

and since Y_d changes by 70 per cent of a change in Y, or

$$\Delta Y_d = .7 \Delta Y$$

it follows that

$$\Delta C = .9\,(.7 \Delta Y)$$

which reduces to

$$C = .63 \Delta Y$$

The Investment Decision

The behavior of aggregate investment will make sense much more readily if we first examine the nature of the investment decision at the microeconomic level.

Two aspects of the investment decision are of paramount importance. Number one, the decision to invest is generally made on the basis of the expected impact of the project on long-run profits: their size and the degree of confidence with which this expectation is held. Second, every investment decision is at the same time a financing decision. Even if the financing is to be out of retained earnings, this statement is true, because in this case the decision to invest involves the decision *not* to liquidate debt or to buy CD's or to pay larger dividends. The following paragraphs will elaborate on these points.

For convenience and by custom we plan to group the determinants of investment into two categories in our discussion: (1) those that relate to the project itself, apart from its financing; and (2) those that have to do with the financing of the project.

Determinants of Investment: Marginal Efficiency of Investment

Since business capital spending by any firm is, as a rule, undertaken with the expectation that it will contribute to the profitability of the firm, the key to our gaining a comprehension of investment behavior is through identification and understanding of the factors that influence the businessman's evaluation of prospective returns from alternative investment opportunities.

The management of the firm must make judgments concerning the future course of a variety of factors, in an environment characterized by considerable uncertainty, when it decides on a given capital spending proposal. A simple listing of major factors that management must examine will have to suffice for indicating the variety of considerations involved in investment decision making. Not all of them will be applicable to every project.

Evaluation of a capital spending proposal requires, in the first place, estimates of the following:

1. The *initial cost* of the project, including such items (where appropriate) as installation costs, the costs involved in an initial testing and "debugging" period for major items, personnel costs such as recruitment, training and retraining, severance pay, and so on.
2. Changes in the pattern of the firm's *expected net cash inflows* (gross inflows less outflows) attributable to the project in operation, specified as to both timing and amount.

Notice that nearly all these factors involve some uncertainty. Even the initial cost can deviate widely from the original estimates, especially in complex projects utilizing new technologies such as computers and highly automated processes. Estimates of the other major factors, involving, as they do, projections of future conditions in output and input markets, can be extremely conjectural. What will happen to total demand for the product(s) involved? What are competitors doing in terms of production, promotion, and product development? And of what significance is the fact that a given highly specialized plant has a physical life expectancy of at least twenty-five years, in the face of the fact that technologies can be rendered obsolete almost overnight and even whole industries can disappear over a quarter-century?

Next, by comparing the anticipated net cash inflows (specified as to timing as well as amount) with the initial cost, management is able to arrive at an anticipated rate of return on the proposed project. Specifically, the anticipated rate of return on the project is that rate equating (1) the present value of expected future cash inflows associated with the project and (2) the initial cost of the project.

THE FIRM'S MARGINAL EFFICIENCY OF INVESTMENT SCHEDULE Presumably this firm has not just one but a number of possible capital projects, all of which it must evaluate in terms of anticipated rate of return. As a further step in the decision process, these projects can then be ranked according to expected rate of return, in descending order. However, this introduces a complication: the greater the firm's investment during a given time period, the higher the risk associated with an added project. To illustrate, consider a project that is estimated to have a potential rate of return over noninterest costs of 12 per cent *provided* that it is the only project to be undertaken that year by the firm. Financing, let us say, would present no big problem. Now, instead, suppose that this same project is third in priority, behind two rather costly ones that, however, show more earnings potential. In this latter case, financing costs for that same project would be higher and the firm would probably be more vulnerable to trouble were any business reverses to occur.

The point is this: when these projects are ranked by expected rate of return, it is necessary to take account, in some manner, of this increasing-risk factor. Even though the increased risk is not inherent in the project itself but in its potential impact on the firm's balance-sheet position, the decision maker will, in effect, have to treat this added burden as a negative factor in assessing the expected rate of return on this particular project.

Ranking the firm's possible investment projects according to anticipated rate of return (adjusted for risk), beginning with the highest-yielding project, gives us a schedule such as the one graphed in Figure 15.3. This schedule is called the firm's *marginal efficiency of investment*

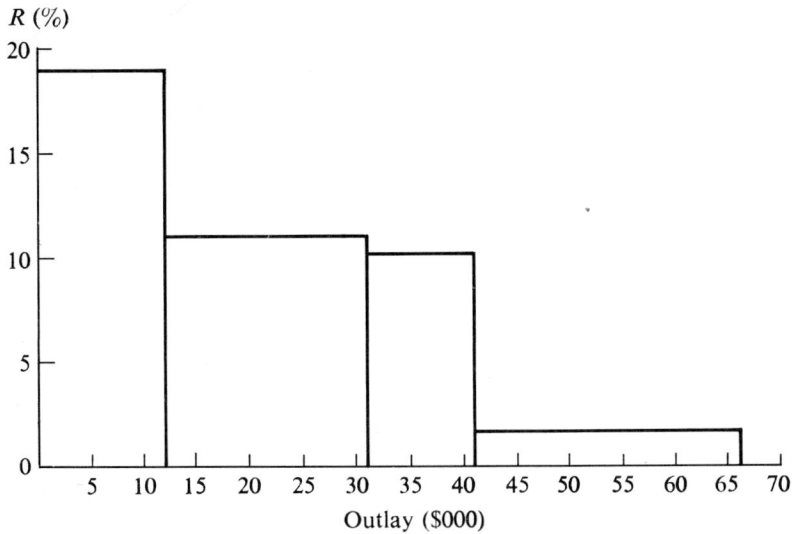

Figure 15.3
MEI schedule of the firm.

(MEI) schedule. The vertical axis records expected rates of return; the horizontal axis, the dollar outlay required.

According to the graph, there is one potential capital project that appears to promise an 18 per cent return on an investment of $12,000. Two other projects are expected to yield 12 to 10 per cent respectively, requiring outlays of $19,000 and $13,000. A poor fourth project would yield 3 per cent, it is estimated, on an investment of $22,000.

The problem is, which of these should the firm undertake and which should it postpone or reject? This is the point at which financial factors must be considered. Later in the chapter we shall analyze these factors in more detail, but for now this generalization should suffice: the lower the interest rate and the more generous are the other financing terms, the more projects will be feasible.

The Aggregate Marginal Efficiency of Investment Schedule

Now, turning to the big picture, if we were to aggregate all contemplated capital spending projects of all firms in the economy and to rank them by expected rate of return, we would obtain a graph of the type given in Figure 15.4, where curve II represents a MEI schedule for the economy as a whole. This curve can also be read as an aggregate investment demand schedule: given this array of possible capital spending projects, the lower the interest rate on new financing, the more capital spending proposals there will be that are judged economically feasible, hence the more investment that will be undertaken.

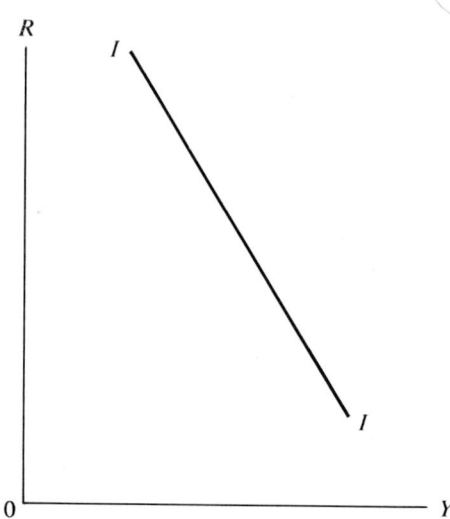

Figure 15.4
MEI schedule of the economy.

SHAPE OF THE MEI SCHEDULE   Suppose, now, that the rate of interest were to decline by one percentage point. What effect would this have on investment? Or, asking the same question in the framework of Figure 15.4, how steep is the MEI curve? Attempts to provide a quantitative answer to this question have met with much frustration and disagreement. Some researchers have asked the question (or its equivalent) of businessmen; others have examined the data on interest rates and investment in an attempt to locate consistent statistical relationships. Still others attempt to deduce the answer from assumptions of "rational" business behavior. The extent of agreement remains distressingly small.

Nearly all students of the subject would probably assent to the statement that interest rates exert *some* influence over *some* kinds of investment, while a substantial majority would probably agree that the overall effect on investment of interest rate changes of the magnitude experienced in recent decades is small. Therefore, the best answer to the original "1 per cent" question that we can come up with is "not a substantial effect."

However, this conclusion does not allow us to infer that the total influence of the financial system on investment is necessarily small. Along with higher interest rates there is usually a tightening of other credit terms, more stringent conditions attached by lenders to new loans, and increased credit rationing,[12] all of which reinforce the effects of higher interest rates on total investment. One investigator, analyzing the

---

[12] These will be discussed in chapter 17.

data from the Federal Reserve Quarterly Survey of Bank Lending, expressed his findings thus:

> The 1965–70 experience indicates that banks changed policy stringency of all loan terms closely together. They increased stringency of interest rates and non-price terms together.[13]

Even taking into account these other financial factors, however, the impact of the financial system seems to be minor, though far from negligible. The slope of the MEI curve, in other words, is probably fairly steep but not vertical.

POSITION OF THE MEI SCHEDULE   Actually, the notorious instability of investment does not stem from the shape of the MEI curve but from changes in its position. When we recall the uncertainties that surround each contemplated individual investment, we can readily accept the view that the overall MEI schedule is subject to sudden and sharp changes in position. Earlier writers, including Keynes, laid great stress on the destabilizing effects of shifts in "business psychology." Today, the time horizon of businessmen is considerably longer, and changes in short-run expectations seem to be taken in stride by managements of larger enterprises. But even though there is less reason to anticipate strong overreaction caused by economic near-sightedness, there remain *objective* changes that can bring about significant shifts in the investment demand schedule. Changes in business tax rates, for example, can affect expected sales and/or costs; technological innovations can affect the cost side of some calculations, the sales estimates of others; and changes in aggregate demand also may exert considerable impact on the pace of investment. We turn now to an explication of this last statement.

Investment and Income

Although GNP does not correlate very well statistically with the level of current investment expenditures, the two are unmistakably unrelated. To back up this statement we shall examine the influence on investment of both the *level* and the *rate of change* of GNP.

LEVEL OF AGGREGATE INCOME   First, a number of considerations suggest that it is reasonable to expect planned I to vary directly with the level of GNP.[14] Higher GNP nearly always means higher total profits (in fact, the percentage changes in the latter are usually far greater than in the former); and higher profits mean greater retained earnings, since both dividends of corporations and drawings by proprietors of noncorpo-

---

[13] Duane G. Harris, "Rationing Credit to Business: More Than Interest Rates," *Business Review*, Federal Reserve Bank of Philadelphia (August 1970), p. 5.
[14] Gardner Ackley, *Macroeconomic Theory* (New York: Macmillan Co., 1961), pp. 336–39.

rate businesses change only slowly. Because one barrier to investment, especially for smaller businesses, is inability to secure financing, a greater supply of internal funds tends to increase investment. In fact, greater profits and internal funds will often make external financing easier; the applicant can then show the prospective source of financing a more promising, lower-risk balance sheet. And smaller businesses especially, lacking the economic sophistication necessary for scientific forecasting, often base their profit projections either deliberately or unconsciously on their immediate profit experience. So higher GNP tends to shift the MEI schedule upward. For these reasons, there seems to be a logical link between current GNP and businesss investment plans.

Table 15.3 consists of an illustrative set of figures incorporating the notion that investment depends on GNP: and Figure 15.5 is a graphic rendering of this set. A given change in GNP, according to these figures, induces a change in planned investment of .1 of the GNP change. The label for this relationship, $\Delta I / \Delta Y$, is the *marginal propensity to invest* (MPI): its manifestation on Figure 15.5 is a slope of .1 in the *II* curve.

RATE OF CHANGE OF AGGREGATE INCOME Investment may be expected to vary not only with the level of GNP but also with its rate of change. The dependence of the level of investment on the rate of change of income carries the label of *acceleration principle*. The combination of a high capital/output ratio typical in American industry plus the fact that the average capital item lasts several years creates a situation in which, for the individual firm or industry, capital investment often fluctuates more widely, in percentage terms, than its sales volume.

A simple example should provide an adequate intuitive grasp of this concept.[15]

TABLE 15.3
The MPI Schedule
(in $billions)

Y	I
0	40
100	50
200	60
300	70
400	80
500	90
600	100
700	110
800	120
900	130

[15] Consult any intermediate-level macroeconomics text for a comprehensive treatment of the acceleration principle.

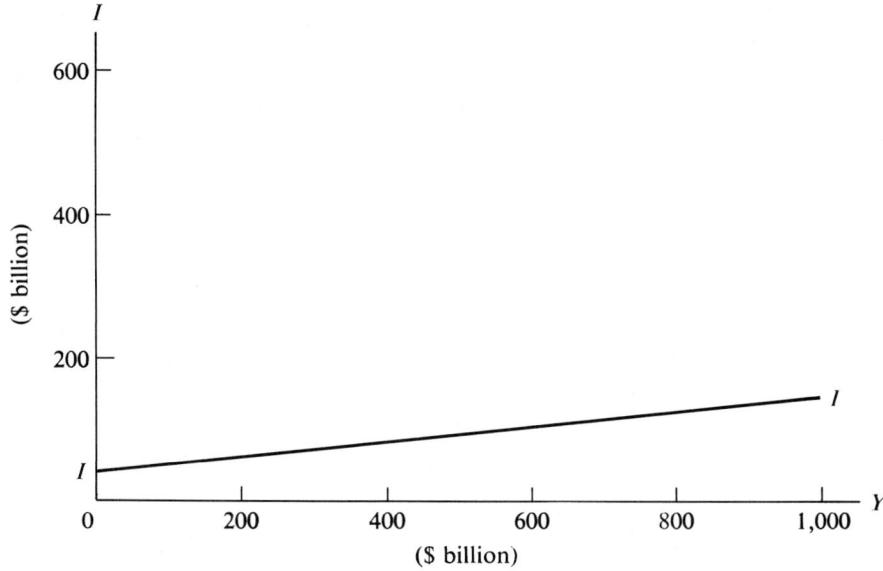

Figure 15.5
Investment and gross national product.

Suppose a company's capital equipment is maintained at half the value of its annual sales. Sales have been running at an annual volume of $1,000,000 in recent years (for example, year 0), so the company's equipment is $500,000. Suppose, further, that each item of equipment is replaced every five years, so the company's investment in equipment has been $100,000 annually.

Now conditions change: the company's physical volume of sales rises by 10 per cent, to $1,100,000 per year. To maintain the desired equipment/sales ratio of .5, the firm must increase its capital equipment by 10 per cent also, or $50,000. But this $50,000 expenditure is added to the $100,000 expenditure needed for replacement of equipment, making total equipment investment expenditures $150,000. Thus, a 10 per cent

TABLE 15.4
The Illustration of the Acceleration Principle

Year	Sales	Total Equipment	Replacement Investment	+	New Investment	=	Total Investment	Change in Sales
0	$1,000,000	$500,000	$100,000		$ 0		$100,000	—
1	1,100,000	550,000	100,000		50,000		150,000	$100,000
2	1,155,000	577,500	100,000		27,500		127,500	55,000

increase in sales (from $1 million to $1.1 million) has generated a 50 per cent increase in equipment investment!

If next year's sales were to rise again, this time by $55,000, or 5 per cent of this year's level, would investment also rise substantially? The surprising answer is no; investment would actually decline. Although replacement investment would again be $100,000, investment for expansion would be only $27,500 (half the increase in sales volume), yielding a total of only $127,500.

The point is that investment, in this illustration, depends primarily *not* on the absolute volume of sales but on the magnitude of change in sales. The first year saw a shift from constant to rising sales, so expenditures on equipment rose. Sales also increased the second year, but by a smaller amount; therefore investment in equipment declined.

For our purposes, the important question is whether we can apply this reasoning on a macroeconomic level. That is, can we expect a given change in the rate at which GNP is rising to have a determinable change on investment? Available statistical evidence tends to support a negative answer; and, in fact, there are several reasons for expecting to find that the relation between investment and the rate of change in GNP is quite loose. In the first place, whenever substantial excess capacity exists, output can usually be increased with little or no net investment. Second, some net investment is undertaken on the strength of demand projections several years into the future, not merely in response to current pressures on capacity. Third, a surge in aggregate demand will not be a strong stimulant to investment demand if the rise in demand is expected to be only temporary. Finally, capacity limits in the investment-goods industries may set a ceiling on actual investment considerably below the level of planned investment.

Yet, with all these qualifications, there remains a definite tendency for changes in final demand, whether by government, business, or households, to elicit a response in the form of revisions in planned investment by business. The longer this change is expected to endure, the stronger is investment response likely to be.[16] The acceleration principle thus constitutes one element in our explanation of investment behavior.

Determinants of Investment: Financial Factors

Having examined the important determinants of investment as they affect the shape and position of the MEI schedule, we must take a closer look now at some of the financial factors that influence investment.

As we noted earlier in this chapter, there is much more involved in the cost of financing beside the rate of interest. The firm considering a

---

[16] See Robert Eisner, "Investment: Facts and Fancy," *American Economic Review*, LIII (May 1963), pp. 237–46, for development of this point.

possible investment is, of course, concerned with the interest rate it must pay; but it also is concerned with other terms of the financing agreement as well: maturity, whether a pledge of assets is required, limitations on the distribution of earnings, penalties for violation of terms, stipulations as to compensating balances, and so on. Some of these may simply spell out accepted management practice and thus do not generally constitute a burden on the would-be borrower; others may be only mildly annoying to management, but still others may be seen as imposing excessive burdens, perhaps even as endangering the survival prospects of the firm or control by the present management of the firm.

And then there are the instances of an applicant for financing being willing, even eager, to meet the lender's credit terms—interest rate, maturity, and all the rest—but still being turned down, the victim of credit rationing. In some cases his proposition will involve an unacceptably high degree of risk (at least, as perceived by the financial institution), but in other cases the reason for rejection may simply be "tight money": the financial institution is not in a position to grant the loan—that is, to purchase the financial asset issued by the applicant—in view of its own financial position. At cyclical peaks the business press contains numerous accounts of this phenomenon.

Rejection by one institution or type of institution does not necessarily mean that the applicant will be unable to secure financing. If turned down by banks, he may be welcomed by finance companies, which accept greater risks and charge correspondingly higher rates.[17] In fact, this is a common tight-money development. Also there is a tendency for larger firms, with readier access to credit in the financial markets, to act as "lenders" to their customers and, to a lesser extent, to their smaller suppliers during periods of peak credit demand by extending credit for longer terms to them, drawing down their own holdings of liquid assets in order to be in a position to carry this increase in their receivables.[18]

THE MARGINAL COST OF FINANCING (MCF) SCHEDULE   We can incorporate much of the discussion in this section into a marginal cost of financing (MCF) schedule. For a number of reasons, this schedule will be generally upsloping, that is, will show a rising cost of obtaining additional financing during a particular time period.

---

[17] But where do finance companies get the necessary money to lend? From the banks! At first thought this might seem odd; but, due to the principle of "spreading the risk," the bank is in effect making a relatively safe loan to the finance company, which in turn makes a relatively risky loan (at an appropriately higher rate) to the would-be borrower. Rather than charge *higher* rates to buy a financial asset with a *given* risk, the bank charges *given* rates for a financial asset with *lower* risk. Either way, the bank benefits by having higher expected yields.

[18] Robert P. Hungate, *Interbusiness Financing: Economic Implications for Small Business*, Small Business Research Series No. 3 (Washington, D.C.: Small Business Administration, 1962) chapter 5; Allan Meltzer, "Monetary Policy and the Trade Credit Practices of Business Firms," in *Stabilization Policies* (Englewood Cliffs, N. J.: Prentice-Hall, 1963).

Some financing is more or less "automatic": provided that the firm is covering all costs, its depreciation allowance will provide financing for replacement investment,[19] which is nearly always the major portion of total investment. Although this source is cheap, in the sense that no negotiations are involved or payments obligations entailed, it is not "costless," since there are always alternative assets that could be purchased (or debts liquidated).

Also considered a low-cost source of financing is retained earnings. However, the more earnings retained in any time period, the greater the danger of stockholder discontent, manifesting itself in depressed stock prices and even, in extreme cases, a proxy battle against incumbent management for control of the firm.

With respect to outside financing, the greater the volume sought during a given time period, the higher will be the marginal cost of financing. The main reason is that potential suppliers of finance, realizing that more external financing means a more rapid rate of expansion and, if debt financing is involved, a higher debt-to-equity ratio, will demand a higher (anticipated) yield in exchange for assuming greater risks.

On an aggregate level, too, it seems reasonable to postulate an up-sloping MCF schedule: the more financing sought during a given period, the more business firms there will be that will encounter higher-cost sources of financing.

MEI, MCF, AND INVESTMENT A hypothetical MCF schedule is graphed in Figure 15.6 as FF. The equilibrium volume of investment, then, is that equating the aggregate MEI schedule (II) and MCF schedule (FF), illustrated in Figure 15.6 at point T, where OX investment takes place at a marginal cost and return of OR.

Any number of developments can cause one or both of these curves to shift. A rise in the interest rate, for example, will shift the MCF curve upward to, say, $F'F'$, reducing the volume of investment to OX' and raising the equilibrium MCF and marginal yield on investment to OR'. As an exercise, utilize Figure 15.6 to determine the effects on the interest rate and total investment of a development, such as an improvement in the business outlook, which raised the MEI schedule.[20]

Housing Construction and Inventory Investment

Our discussion of investment has run mainly in terms of business capital spending. What about housing construction and inventory investment? New housing intended for profit-making purposes (apartment buildings, chiefly) require no extended comment, being merely another

---

[19] Our assumption of a constant price level lets us bypass the vexing problems for depreciation accounting connected with the effects of rising prices.

[20] Both interest rate and the level of investment would rise.

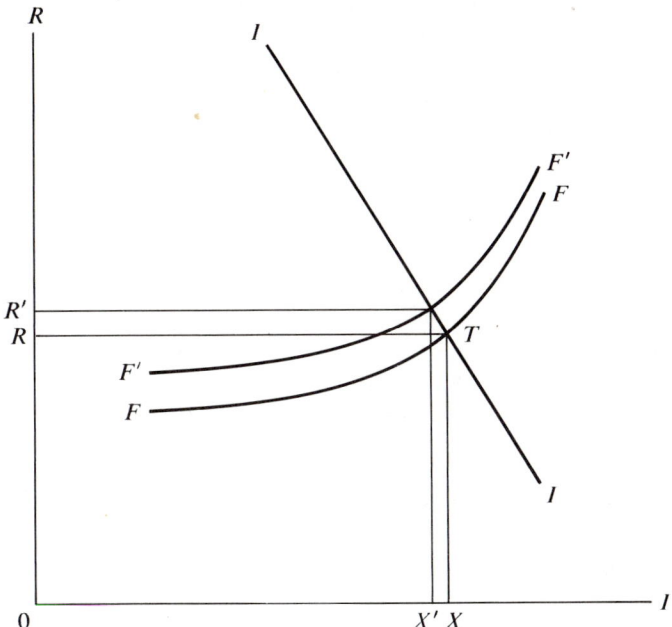

Figure 15.6
MEI and MCF schedules.

case of business investment, where yield is balanced against financing cost. For household decisions to purchase a new home there is, of course, no MEI involved. Rather, the decision on the demand side will depend on essentially the same factors that determine any major consumer durables purchase.

The fact that structures are expected to yield their satisfactions or their contributions to earnings over relatively long periods, coupled with the fact that construction investment, whether by households or by business firms, is so heavily dependent upon external financing, make this type of investment more sensitive to interest rates and other credit terms than are most or all other types of investment.

Inventory investment, although a small fraction of total investment, is the most volatile, responding to changes in sales in the manner of the acceleration principle described earlier. During tight-money periods one reads and hears about instances of inventory reduction due to credit stringency; but it is difficult to quantify this effect. However, in these days of computer-controlled inventories, it seems highly unlikely that there would be so much "slack" in inventories that an increase in cost or decline in availability of credit of the order of magnitude that we have experienced in recent years would have any pronounced effect on total investment in inventories.

Determinants of Investment: Some Qualifications

Circumstances may cause actual investment to differ (perhaps considerably) from the figure that would be obtained by combining all individual investment plans. If sales are below forecast level, inventories may pile up; conversely, unexpectedly large sales will deplete inventories or at least slow down inventory accumulation below the planned level. In fact, studies of inventory behavior show clearly that "inventories lag systematically and significantly at the cycle turning points," confirming "the theoretical notion that *unintended* inventory changes are an important component of inventory investment."[21] Moreover, if capital goods industries are operating at capacity with long order backlogs, actual investment may lag behind planned investment by a considerable period of time; and, so far as the current period figures are concerned, a delayed investment does not register at all, any more than a canceled project does.

But, in addition to the deviation of actual I from planned I, we can expect deviations of "actual planned" I from the figures that a simple model like this would predict. In the first place, profit maximization is not the only goal of management. Some writers[22] stress the desire of business managers to increase total sales even (within limits) at the expense of profits. This sort of behavior implies that investment may be deliberately extended into the range of projects in which the MCF exceeds MEI. But, on the other hand, there are some business firms that do not aggressively exploit all economic opportunities, being content with a "safe" level of profits.[23] Which type of behavior is dominant it is not possible to say; fortunately, the two counter each other. But the message again is that reality is richer and more complex than our inevitably simplified models.

A second point is that the knowledge necessary for even rough calculation of MEI and the cost of financing is beyond the capability of many firms. Instead, there is widespread reliance on "rules of thumb." The general effect is to reduce investment below what would be indicated by MEI-MCF considerations, since these rules tend to err on the side of safety.

Finally, and more technically, we might observe that MEI is not completely independent of the MCF function. If, for example, the interest rate declines, the MCF curve will shift downward. The result will be an increase in investment, as the MEI curve will now intersect the MCF

---

[21] Robert Eisner and Robert H. Strotz, "Determinants of Business Investment," in Commission on Money and Credit, *Impacts of Monetary Policy* (Englewood Cliffs, N.J.: Prentice-Hall, 1963), p. 225. The authors base this conclusion on the work of Moses Abramovitz of the National Bureau of Economic Research. See references in the bibliography of the Eisner-Strotz study.

[22] For example, William G. Baumol, *Business Behavior, Value and Growth* (New York: Macmillan Co., 1959), especially chapters 6 and 7.

[23] John R. Hicks, "Annual Survey of Economic Theory: The Theory of Monopoly," *Econometrica*, III (1935), p. 8.

curve at a point below and to the right of the original point of intersection. This same interest-rate decline may also stimulate consumer spending and even capital expenditures of state and local governments. The result is an *upward* shift in the MEI curve, in response to an increase in aggregate income, reinforcing the investment effects of the movement *along* the curve. Another instance of dependence is in the other direction, from MEI to R: a shift in the MEI curve sets in motion certain changes in income, demand for liquidity, and so on, which react back upon the interest rate, causing the MCF curve to shift. This topic will be treated in some detail in chapter 18.

In view of the foregoing qualifications, what remains of our original formulation that planned investment depends on the marginal efficiency of investment and the rate of interest? More than we might think, actually. We may, for example, *still* state with assurance that a reduction in interest rates, other things equal, will stimulate investment and that a downward shift in the MEI schedule will retard investment. We may also utilize MEI and R as convenient concepts around which to organize our thinking about the determinants of investment. What we may *not* do is to attempt to locate the actual "true" MEI or R out in the "real world." Like the supply and demand curves of microeconomics, the MEI and R concepts are useful tools for understanding, organizing our thinking about, and evaluating the behavior of, the economy; but their limitations must be appreciated along with their uses.

Government Expenditures

The statistical record shows that the growth of government expenditures on goods and services (G), the third of our four expenditure categories, has more than kept pace with the growth of GNP. However, the record also shows that short-run variations are simply too large and erratic to justify our attempting to express the relation between G and Y by any neat equation. It seems wise, instead, to treat G as *exogenous,* that is, as determined in the short run by forces other than the usual macroeconomic variables.

What this implies is that, geometrically, the relation between G and Y would be depicted as in Figure 15.7

The Rest-of-the-World Sector

Our annual balance on goods-and-services sales to, less purchases from, the rest of the world is subject to an enormous number of influences. Changes in quotas on exports and imports, tariff changes, shipping strikes, local and large-scale wars, foreign business tax and subsidy developments, changes in exchange rates, as well as all of the usual "domestic" developments, actual and expected, here and abroad—all of these and more can affect our export-import balance.

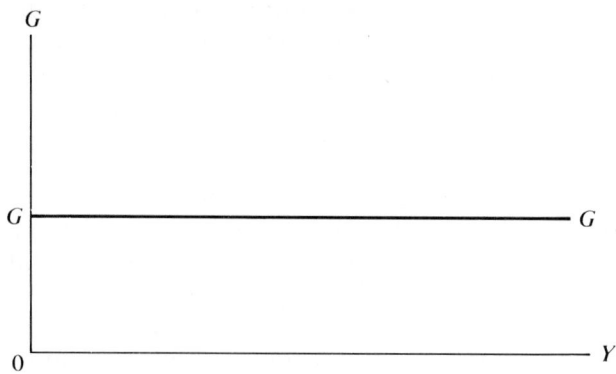

Figure 15.7
Relationship between gross national product and government expenditures for goods and services.

Most of these influences cannot be treated as determined by purely economic forces, obviously. But among the important influences on our imports is the level of our GNP: as our incomes rise, we tend to import more. Not so for exports, however, the level of which depends mainly on forces outside our direct control, as you can readily perceive by noting the factors listed in the above paragraph.

We can represent the relation between our foreign trade balance and GNP geometrically, as in Figure 15.8. This figure embodies the realistic assumptions that (1) at very low GNP levels, the economy's exports exceed imports, but (2) as GNP rises, this positive net export balance gradually diminishes and ultimately gives way to growing negative balances.

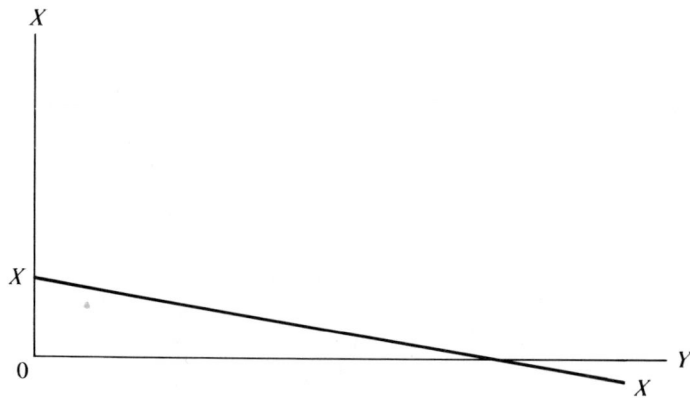

Figure 15.8
Relationship between net exports and gross national product.

Having laid out and examined separately each aggregate expenditure category and its functional relation (if any) with gross national product, what remains to be done is to put these "building blocks" of macroeconomic theory together in the form of a coherent structure. This is our agenda for chapter 16.

KEY CONCEPTS

Consumption function
Average propensity to consume
Marginal propensity to consume
Money illusion

Marginal efficiency of investment
Marginal cost of financing
Acceleration principle

QUESTIONS FOR REVIEW

1. What circumstances might result in an excess of recorded investment over planned investment? What circumstances might cause recorded investment to fall short of planned investment?
2. What financial factors influence consumption out of a given level of Y_d? Which of these seem to be long-term forces; which are mainly short-term?
3. Discuss the effects of changes in the level of GNP and interest rates on consumption, on investment, on government expenditures on goods and services.
4. How, besides through interest rate changes, might the operation of the financial system affect business investment?
5. "Total investment may be affected by both the level and the rate of change in GNP." Explain.
6. Would you expect to find a tight relationship between the level of investment and the rate of change in GNP? Why or why not?
7. "Investment will be pushed to the point at which the MEI curve intersects the MCF curve." Do you agree? Explain.

SUGGESTIONS FOR FURTHER READING. SEE END OF CHAPTER 16.

A Macroeconomic Model
Expenditure Categories and Gross National Product
The Total Expenditure Function

The Multiplier
Effects of a Change in Autonomous Expenditures
The Time Path
Why "First Approximation"?

Summary of Chapters 15 and 16

Appendix: An Algebraic Formulation
Equilibrium
Consumption
Investment
Government Expenditures and Net Exports
The Total Expenditure Function
The Multiplier

16 The Structure of Macroeconomic Theory

In chapter 14 it was shown that the level of GNP depends on total expenditures. But in chapter 15 we noted that the size of most categories of expenditures depends on the level of GNP! In this chapter we intend to reconcile these two statements.

A Macroeconomic Model

Our method will be to construct a simple numerical model of aggregate income determination, using the relationships between income and expenditures discovered in chapter 15 as building blocks.[1] Table 16.1 and Figure 16.1 will serve as the bases for our discussion. Let us look closely now at these exhibits.

Expenditure Categories and Gross National Product

CONSUMPTION[2]   Columns 1 through 4 should look familiar since they merely reproduce the corresponding columns of Table 15.2. Refreshing our memories, $T_n + S_b$ (column 2) make up 30 per cent of any level of

---

[1] The Appendix to this chapter consists of a somewhat more generalized algebraic rendering of this model.
[2] Appendix, under "Consumption."

TABLE 16.1
The Total Expenditure Function and Its Components
(in $billions)

Y (1)	$(T_n + S_b)$ (2)	Y_d (1)−(2) (3)	C (4)	I (5)	G (6)	X (7)	E (4)+(5)+(6)+(7) (8)
0	0	0	9	40	135	26	210
100	30	70	72	50	135	23	280
200	60	140	135	60	135	20	350
300	90	210	198	70	135	17	420
400	120	280	261	80	135	14	490
500	150	350	324	90	135	11	560
600	180	420	387	100	135	8	630
700	210	490	450	110	135	5	700
800	240	560	513	120	135	2	770
900	270	630	576	130	135	−1	840

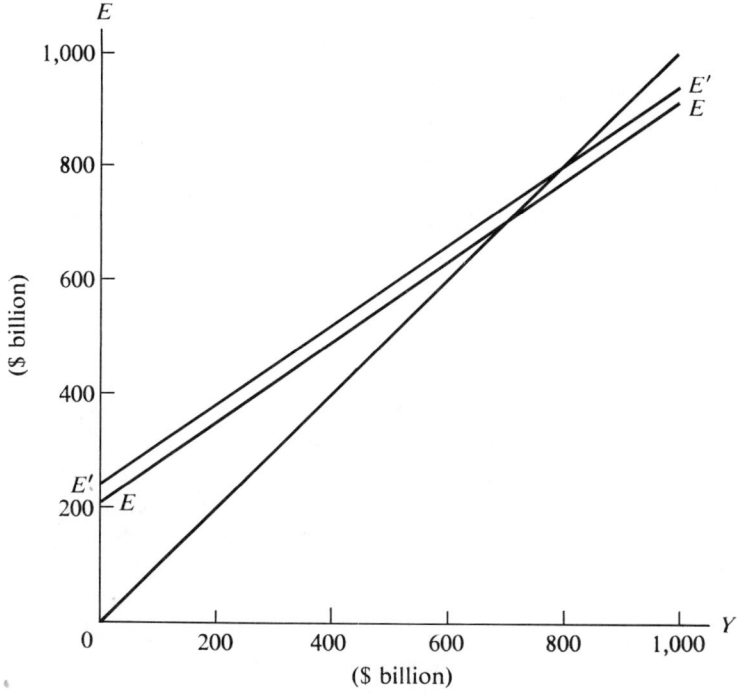

Figure 16.1
Total expenditure function.

GNP (column 1), the remaining 70 per cent being accounted for by Y_d (column 3). Columns 3 and 4 together represent the consumption function: the relation between C and Y_d. The MPC in this model, we recall, is .9. Columns 1 and 4 relate consumption to GNP, the marginal propensity to consume out of GNP being .63.

INVESTMENT[3] Columns 1 and 5 depict the assumption made in chapter 15 that the marginal propensity to invest is .1. In thus relating investment to GNP only, we are implicitly assuming that all other determinants of investment remain constant. This assumption will be dropped later.

GOVERNMENT EXPENDITURES AND NET EXPORTS[4] The level of government expenditures on goods and services (column 6), we note, is invariant with respect to the GNP level, while net exports (column 7) vary inversely with GNP.

The Total Expenditure Function

TOTAL EXPENDITURES AND GNP[5] Since an increase in the GNP level of $100 billion generates an increase of $63 billion in consumption and $10 billion in investment, plus a decrease of $3 billion in net exports (but no change in government goods and services expenditures), the rise in all expenditures combined (E) should be shown as $70 billion. A glance at columns 1 and 8 will confirm this reasoning.

The ratio of the change in total planned expenditures to the change in GNP ($\Delta E/\Delta Y$)—which we call the *marginal propensity to make expenditures,* or MPE—is evidently .7 in our model. The MPE plays a key role in the theory of GNP determination, so let us get a firm grasp on it at the outset.

Each level of GNP is thus associated with a particular level of planned expenditures. The functional relationship between the level of planned expenditures and GNP is labeled the *total expenditure function.*

Only when GNP is at $700 billion does the economy generate a volume of planned expenditures just sufficient to support the same level of income. At a higher level, say 800, planned expenditures fall short of income, inventories begin to pile up as sales fall short of projected levels, and the economy's business decision makers will adjust production plans downward, causing GNP to decline toward 700. On the other hand, if income is below 700, planned expenditures will exceed the value of the economy's output, so there will be a tendency for inventories to be depleted and shortages to develop, inducing the decision

---

[3] Appendix, under "Investment."
[4] Appendix, under "Government Expenditures and Net Exports."
[5] Appendix under "The Total Expenditure Function."

makers to revise production plans upward, pushing GNP in the direction of 700.

The same conclusion is depicted geometrically in Figure 16.1. Line *EE* is the curve of the total expenditure function, which relates total expenditures to GNP. The slope of this line measures the MPE of .7. The 45-degree line intersecting the origin is the *E-Y* line. And the point at which the two lines intersect is, of course, the equilibrium level of income, where $Y = \$700$ billion and $E = \$700$ billion.

EQUILIBRIUM GNP VERSUS FULL-EMPLOYMENT GNP Is this equilibrium level good or bad, from a macroeconomic standpoint? Actually, we have no way of answering this question without additional information about our hypothetical economy. We need to know, first of all, something about the extent of unemployment implied by this GNP. If this economy has the resources (amount and kinds) to produce a GNP of at least $900 billion, then almost certainly a GNP of $700 billion would be considered undesirable. If, on the other hand, a $700 billion level is associated with resource scarcities and bottlenecks, producing a rapid rate of inflation, this condition also would be judged unsatsifactory. The point is that it would be unwise to attach a label of "desirable" to the condition of aggregate equilibrium per se.

The Multiplier[6]

Effects of a Change in Autonomous Expenditures

Let us suppose that this economy has arrived at this equilibrium GNP level of $700 billion but that this level is far below the economy's capacity GNP. By a stroke of good fortune, however, a number of remarkable new inventions appear almost simultaneously, inventions with tremendous commercial possibilities. Businessmen respond by deciding to increase investment substantially: the aggregate amount of increase in investment involved in these individual decisions is, let us say, $30 billion. Since this increase is in *autonomous* investment (that is, investment unrelated to the current level of GNP), it raises our investment schedule by $30 billion. What effect, we wonder, will this autonomous increase in investment have on the overall behavior of our model economy?

At first thought, the answer may seem obvious—since one category of expenditures, investment, has gone up by $30 billion, total incomes also will rise by $30 billion. The flaw in this line of reasoning is that it ignores the MPE—the response of expenditure plans to changes in incomes. Thus, as a result of this increase in incomes of $30 billion, consumers and businessmen will plan to spend more and our foreign-trade balance will move slightly in a negative direction. The net effect of these re-

[6] Appendix, under "The Multiplier."

actions will be to increase incomes further, thus generating further increases in expenditures, and so on, and so on. Where will this process come to an end, or will it?

We can find the answer by means of our model, as represented in Table 16.1. First, we must record the upward shift in planned investment by raising each entry in column 5 by $30 billion. Next, we must do the same thing to column 8, since I is, after all, a component of E. In Table 16.2 we reproduce column 1 from Table 16.1, plus columns 5 and 8, both in altered form and labeled I' and E' respectively.

Inspecting columns 1 and 8, we find that the new equilibrium level of GNP, the level at which total planned expenditures equal the total value of output, is $800 billion. Evidently the increase in autonomous investment of $30 billion has resulted in a rise of $100 billion in equilibrium GNP!

To verify this result, let us check to see whether the sum of all planned expenditure changes, *induced* (that is, by the change in income) as well as autonomous, is actually $100 billion (see Table 16.3).

Figure 16.1 confirms this outcome geometrically. We redrew the EE curve $30 billion higher, labeling the new curve $E'E'$. Observe that it crosses the $E = Y$ line at $800 billion now, indicating that this is the new equilibrium GNP.

This is certainly not a "common sense" outcome, but the explanation is fairly straightforward and utilizes only facts and concepts already at hand.

1. When the economy, in response to a change in autonomous expenditures, moves from one position of equilibrium to another, the *change* in E must be equal to the *change* in Y.

TABLE 16.2
Revised Investment and Total Expenditure Function
(in $billions)

Y (1)	I' (5)	E' (8)
0	70	240
100	80	310
200	90	380
300	100	450
400	110	520
500	120	590
600	130	660
700	140	730
730	143	751
800	150	800
900	160	870

TABLE 16.3
Effects of an Increase in Autonomous Expenditures
(in $billions)

Increase in autonomous expenditures		$ 30
Induced increases in expenditures:		
C (.63 of $100 billion)	$63	
I (.1 of $100 billion)	10	
G (no response)	0	
X (−.03 of $100 billion)	− 3	70
Total increase in planned expenditures		$100

2. Since the (given) MPE is .7, any change in Y will induce a change in E equal to 70 per cent of the amount of this change.
3. With 70 per cent of the ultimate change in E explained as a response to the change in Y, it follows that the initiating change in autonomous expenditures must constitute the remaining 30 per cent.
4. Therefore, the ultimate change in equilibrium GNP will be that amount of which the autonomous expenditure change is 30 per cent. (Example: in the present case, I shifted upward by $30 billion; since $30 billion is 30 per cent of 100, the change in equilibrium GNP must be $100 billion.)

The initiating change in autonomous expenditures ($30 billion), *multiplied by 10/3*, equals the resultant change in equilibrium GNP. The ratio 10/3 is referred to as the multiplier, a key concept in macroeconomic analysis. The larger the multiplier, the more potent will be the effects on GNP of a given change in autonomous spending.

But what determines the size of the multiplier? Only one variable: the marginal propensity to make expenditures. We can easily demonstrate this by changing our assumed MPE from .7 to .8 and observing the difference this makes with respect to the new equilibrium GNP. With this greater value for the MPE, steps 3 and 4 above would read:

3. With *80* per cent of the ultimate change in E explained as a response to the change in Y, it follows that the initiating change in autonomous expenditures must constitute the remaining *20* per cent.
4. Therefore, the ultimate change in equilibrium GNP will be that amount of which the autonomous expenditure change is *20* per cent. (Example: in the present (revised) case, I shifted upward by $30 billion. Since $30 billion is 20 per cent of $150 billion, the change in equilibrium GNP must be $150 billion.)

Thus, with a MPE of .8 instead of .7, the multiplier becomes 5 (that is, 150/30) rather than 10/3 (or 100/30). The size of the multiplier, then, varies directly with the size of the MPE.

Although the autonomous change utilized in our multiplier discussion was in investment, it is worth noting that *any* autonomous change in spending sets in motion the multiplier process.

The Time Path

So far we have discussed the "before" and the "after," but we have not dealt at all with the "during." What is the time path involved? Is it slow start and then rapid acceleration, or is most of the effect in the early stages? How long do these changes take to work themselves out? While we have no definite quantitative answers to these questions, we can state and demonstrate that most of the effects will be felt early rather than late.

Assume, as we did earlier in the chapter, that autonomous expenditures have moved upward to a new level $30 billion higher than before and that the MPE is .7. For convenience, let us suppose that this amount is spread evenly through the year. Assume further that, on the average, there is a lag of four months between an increase in income and an increase in induced spending.[7] This development and these assumptions would generate the pattern described in Table 16.4.

In the first "period" of four months (period 1 in Table 16.4). GNP will rise by just $10 billion: one-third of the $30 billion increment in au-

TABLE 16.4
Multiplier: Period Analysis
(in $billions)

Time Period	Change in Autonomous Expenditures	Change in Induced Expenditures	Change in Total Expenditures	Per Cent of Ultimate Effect
0	—	—	—	—
1	$10	—	—	—
2	10	.7(10) = 7	10	30.0
3	10	.7(17) = 11.9	17	51.0
4	10	.7(21.9) = 15.3	21.9	65.7
5	10	.7(25.3) = 17.7	25.3	76.0
.	.	.	.	.
.	.	.	.	.
.	.	.	.	.
∞	10	.7(33.3) = 23.3	33.3	100.0

[7] This is within the range estimated by Gardner Ackley, "The Multiplier Time Period: Money, Inventories, and Flexibility," *American Economic Review*, XLI (June 1951), pp. 350–68.

tonomous spending. In the second period, however, GNP will be $17 billion higher because, in addition to the $10 billion of autonomous spending, there will be a $7 billion increase in expenditures *induced* by the $10 billion increment of period 1. The induced expenditure figure of period 3 is 11.9 because it is based on the $17 billion expenditure figure of period 2. Further periods can be read off the table.

If the length of each "period" is within the range of three to four months, then, with a multiplier of 10/3, more than three-quarters of the ultimate effect will have occurred within twelve to sixteen months.

Why "First Approximation"?

The process of adjustment to a new equilibrium position, as described above, may look quite definite and straightforward on paper; but we need to look at a few qualifications, relating both to the time path and to the final equilibrium position itself, in order not to leave this topic with a mistaken impression that the actual economy works in this simple fashion.

INTERACTIONS First, with reference to the time path, the reason that the process of adjustment to changes in autonomous spending proceeded so smoothly toward equilibrium in our model is that we have neglected the existence of interactions. That is, our model recognizes the dependence of each expenditure category (except G) on aggregate income but seems to imply that each of these categories is independent of all the others. In reality, it seems very likely that investment responds to the rate of change in total spending, as we discussed in chapter 15; so, rather than an uninterrupted upward or downward movement toward the new equilibrium position, we may get oscillations of various patterns—or even an explosive movement upward or downward—depending on the size of the multiplier and accelerator.[8] There may be other possible expenditure interdependencies as well.

LAGS Furthermore, we have bypassed the problem of "lags." For example, investment could conceivably respond to income changes in such a manner that 20 per cent of the reaction occurs in the quarter following the change, 40 per cent in the next quarter, 25 per cent in the third quarter following, etc. A reaction pattern like this would affect the time path toward equilibrium, too.

Obviously we had better not get involved in any such intricacies as

---

[8] The classic treatment of multiplier-accelerator interaction is Paul S. Samuelson, "Interactions Between the Multiplier Analysis and the Principle of Acceleration" *Review of Economic Statistics* XXI (May 1939), pp. 75–78, and reprinted in numerous books of readings in macroeconomics. However, all macroeconomic theory texts carry discussions, usually with numerical illustrations, of this point.

these. Merely mentioning them, however, should serve to caution us against thinking that our model embodies the *whole* truth about aggregative economic behavior.

REAL/FINANCIAL INTERRELATIONS   Finally, attainment of the new equilibrium position depends on an assumption we made in an almost offhand manner near the beginning of this chapter; namely, unchanged interest rate (or credit conditions). In so doing, we implicitly assumed either that the entire financial system bears no relation to the real (or goods-and-services) system or that the financial system adjusts, or is adjusted, so finely to changes in the real system that we can safely ignore it. Neither of these assumptions is valid. We therefore must examine rather closely the interconnections of these two subsystems of the economic system. First, though, we must investigate the ways in which the financial system affects, and is affected by, the real system. This is the subject of chapter 17. Only then, in chapter 18, do we approach the task of analyzing and integrating both systems as a single whole.

Summary of Chapters 15 and 16

Our approach to discovering the economic role of the financial system is through the framework of standard macroeconomic theory. More specifically, we attempt to identify the forces influencing macroeconomic equilibrium ($E = Y$), and then we highlight those forces relating to the financial system.

Equilibrium, in the model developed in chapters 15 and 16, is achieved when the level of planned expenditures on GNP equals the money value of GNP. When planned expenditures fall short of GNP, the economy will tend to slump; when planned expenditures exceed GNP, the economy will tend to expand.

We find that the task of understanding the influences behind the level of planned expenditures is made more manageable if we break expenditures down into the categories utilized in our national accounts; consumption expenditures, investment, government purchases of goods and services, and net exports. It turns out that GNP is itself an important influence on most kinds of expenditures, but influences operating through the financial system are far from unimportant. The level of interest rates, for example, affects consumption spending (especially on durables), investment in new housing construction and other categories, and capital spending by state and local units of government. Other credit terms, too, such as maturity and down payment requirements, influence aggregate spending. It seems probable that longer-term developments in credit institutions and arrangements for both the saver and the borrower also affect total expenditures, though we lack hard evidence bearing on this kind of influence.

KEY CONCEPTS

Total expenditure function
Marginal propensity to make expenditures (MPE)

Equilibrium GNP
Autonomous expenditures
Multiplier

QUESTIONS FOR REVIEW

1. Do changes in autonomous expenditures affect the multiplier? The multiplicand (the number multiplied by the multiplier)? equilibrium GNP?
2. Attempt to formulate an explanation of the multiplier that even your ignorant roommate can understand.
3. List several determinants of the size of the multiplier.

SUGGESTIONS FOR FURTHER READING FOR CHAPTERS 15 AND 16

Dernburg, Thomas F., and Duncan M. McDougall. *Macroeconomics*, 4th ed. New York: McGraw-Hill Book Co., 1972.

Duesenberry, James S. *Income, Saving, and the Theory of Consumer Behavior*. Cambridge: Harvard Unitersity Press, 1949.

Eisner, Robert, and Robert H. Strotz. "Determinants of Business Investment," In Commission on Money and Credit, *Impacts of Monetary Policy*. Englewood Cliffs, N.J.: Prentice-Hall, 1963, pp. 60–338.

Federal Reserve Bank of Boston. *Consumer Spending and Monetary Policy: The Linkages*. Boston: Federal Reserve Bank of Boston, 1971.

Ferber, Robert. "Consumer Economics: A Survey." *Journal of Economic Literature*, XI (December 1973), pp. 1303–42.

Friedman, Milton. *A Theory of the Consumption Function*. Princeton: Princeton University Press, 1957.

Keynes, John Maynard. *The General Theory of Employment, Interest, and Money*. New York: Harcourt, Brace and World, 1936.

Kuh, Edwin, and John R. Meyer. "Investment, Liquidity, and Monetary Policy," in Commission on Money and Credit, *Impacts of Monetary Policy*. Englewood Cliffs, N.J.: Prentice-Hall, 1963, pp. 339–474.

Siegel, Barry N. *Aggregate Economics and Public Policy*, 3d ed. Homewood, Ill.: R. D. Irwin, 1970.

Smith, Warren L. *Macroeconomics*. Homewood, Ill.: R. D. Irwin, 1970.

Suits, Daniel B. "The Determinants of Consumer Expenditures: A Review of Present Knowledge," in Commission on Money and Credit, *Impacts of Monetary Policy*. Englewood Cliffs, N.J.: Prentice-Hall, 1963, pp. 1–59.

APPENDIX: AN ALGEBRAIC FORMULATION OF THE MODEL

The concepts developed in the text of the foregoing two chapters can be developed more rigorously and succinctly in a simple algebraic formulation. Moreover, in this form, it is easier to draw implications from the relationships and also to discover the results of changing various elements in the model.

This model uses only simple linear functions. It loses a little in realism this way, but it is more readily grasped. We combine a formulation using the numerical coefficients implied in the text discussion with a more general formulation using letter coefficients. All noncoefficient numerals are assumed to be in units of $1 billion.

Equilibrium

First, we define equilibrium as a condition that exists when the level of planned expenditures (E) is equal to the nation's GNP (Y) for that period.

$$E = Y \tag{16A.1}$$

Next, we recall that, by definition

$$E = C + I + G + X \tag{16A.2}$$

From this point, the agenda will be to relate these expenditures to GNP, first individually and then collectively.

Consumption

The consumption function is represented as

$$C = 9 + .9Y_d \qquad C = C_o + aY_d \tag{16A.3}$$

where C_o is autonomous consumption, that is, that part of consumption unresponsive to changes in Y_d; a is the marginal propensity to consume.

Since our model requires us ultimately to relate C also to Y, our next step is to relate Y_d to Y. By definition,

$$Y_d = Y - (T_n + S_b) \tag{16A.4}$$

It is assumed that net taxes are 19 per cent (or t) of GNP and that gross business saving amounts to 11 per cent (or j) of GNP; so

$$T_n = .19Y \qquad T_n = tY \tag{16A.5}$$

$$S_b = .11Y \qquad S_b = jY \tag{16A.6}$$

Substituting into equation 16A.4 the values of T_n and S_b from 16A.5 and 16A.6 gives us Y_d expressed as a function of Y:

$$Y_d = Y - (.19Y + .11Y) \qquad Y_d = Y - (tY + jY)$$

which reduces to

$$Y_d = .7Y \qquad Y_d = (1 - t - j)Y \qquad (16A.7)$$

Combining equations 16A.3 and 16A.7:

$$C = 9 + .9(.7Y) \qquad C = C_o + a(1 - t - j)Y \qquad (16A.8)$$

If, for ease of handling, we let $a' = a(1 - t - j)$, we can write the right-hand equation in a shorter form (while operating on the numerical version):

$$C = 9 + .63Y \qquad C = C_o + a'Y \qquad (16A.9)$$

Investment

In this model investment (I) is functionally related to the current level of GNP (Y) as well as to "other factors," which are responsible for autonomous investment (I_o, or 40). This means that we are including credit conditions in general as a "given." Term b (or .1) represents the marginal propensity to invest. We write the investment equation as,

$$I = 40 + .1Y \qquad I = I_o + bY \qquad (16A.10)$$

Government Expenditures and Net Exports

Government expenditures (G) are treated as independent of the current level of GNP:

$$G = 135 \qquad G = G_o \qquad (16A.11)$$

and net exports (X) vary inversely with GNP, though they are strongly affected by "other" factors, as represented by X_o (or 26). Term m (or .03) is the *marginal propensity to import*.

$$X = 26 - .03Y \qquad X = X_o - mY \qquad (16A.12)$$

The Total Expenditure Function

Our next series of steps aims at expressing E as a function of Y. Taking equation 16A.2 as our basis, we substitute for C, I, G, and X their equivalents from equations 16A.9 through 16A.12:

$$E = \underbrace{9 + .63Y}_{C} + \underbrace{40 + .1Y}_{I} + \underbrace{135}_{G} + \underbrace{26 - .03Y}_{X}$$

$$E = 9 + 40 + 135 + 26 + .63Y + .1Y - .03Y$$

$$E = 210 + .7Y \qquad (16A.13)$$

$$E = \overbrace{C_o + a'Y}^{C} + \overbrace{I_o + bY}^{I} + \overbrace{G_o}^{G} + \overbrace{X_o - mY}^{X}$$
$$E = C_o + I_o + G_o + X_o + a'Y + bY - mY$$
$$E = C_o + I_o + G_o + X_o + (a' + b - m)Y \qquad (16A.13)$$

Let us introduce two more shorthand expressions:
$$A = C_o + I_o + G_o + X_o \qquad (16A.14)$$
$$e = a' + b - m \qquad (16A.15)$$

Term A signifies "autonomous expenditures," that is, that portion of total expenditures not depending on current GNP. Term e combines all of the various marginal propensities—to consume out of GNP (a'), to invest (b), and to import (m)—and therefore represents the *marginal propensity to make expenditures*. Now, we may write equation 16A.13 in the far more convenient form of:

$$E = 210 + .7Y \qquad E = A + eY \qquad (16A.16)$$

This equation—either form—is our crucially important *total expenditure function*, relating total expenditures to GNP in the same manner as equations 16A.9 through 16A.10 relate each individual expenditure category to GNP.

Finally, by combining equations 16A.1 and 16A.16 and solving as a system with two equations and two unknowns, we can determine the equilibrium value of Y. First substituting Y for E in the second of this pair of equations, we get

$$Y = 210 + .7Y \qquad Y = A + eY$$

Then, solving for Y:

$$Y - .7Y = 210 \qquad Y - eY = A$$
$$.3Y = 210 \qquad (1 - e)Y = A$$
$$Y = 700 \qquad Y = A \left(\frac{1}{1-e}\right) \qquad (16A.17)$$

The Multiplier

A change in autonomous expenditures (ΔA)—for example, 30—gives rise to a change in equilibrium GNP (ΔY). The ratio $\Delta Y/\Delta A$ we label k:

$$k = \frac{\Delta Y}{30} \qquad k = \frac{\Delta Y}{\Delta A}$$

Appendix: An Algebraic Formulation of the Model

This equation may also be written

$$\Delta Y = 30 \cdot k \qquad \Delta Y = \Delta A \cdot k \qquad (16\text{A}.18)$$

In this latter form it is evident that k is, in mathematical terminology, the *multiplier*: the number by which ΔA (in this case, 30) must be multiplied in order to arrive at the correct ΔY. So the problem of discovering the effects on Y of a change in A may be expressed as the problem of ascertaining the size of the multiplier.

To determine the value of the multiplier, we first make the observation that, for equlilibrium to be reestablished following a change in A, it is evident that the ultimate change in planned expenditures must be equal to the change in aggregate income, or GNP:

$$\Delta E = \Delta Y \qquad (16\text{A}.19)$$

We classify the expenditure changes as (1) ΔA, the autonomous change that started the whole process, and (2) ΔN, the induced changes in expenditures which follow as a consequence:

$$\Delta E = 30 + \Delta N \qquad \Delta E = \Delta A + \Delta N \qquad (16\text{A}.20)$$

These induced changes will be equal to the marginal propensity to make expenditures (.7 in our model) multiplied by the ultimate change in income.

$$\Delta N = .7 \Delta Y \qquad \Delta N = e \Delta Y \qquad (16\text{A}.21)$$

We may use equations 16A.17 through 16A.20 as our raw materials in discovering the value of the multiplier. First, substituting for ΔN in 16A.20 its equivalent from 16A.21 gives us

$$\Delta E = 30 + .7 \Delta Y \qquad \Delta E = \Delta A + e \Delta Y$$

Then, substituting for ΔE in equation 16A.20 its equivalent from 16A.19:

$$\Delta Y = 30 + .7 \Delta Y \qquad \Delta Y = \Delta A + e \Delta Y$$

Finally, solving for ΔY gives us, successively

$$\Delta Y - .7 \Delta Y = 30 \qquad \Delta Y - e \Delta Y = \Delta A$$

$$.3 \Delta Y = 30 \qquad (1 - e) \Delta Y = \Delta A$$

$$\Delta Y = 30 \left(\frac{1}{3}\right) = 100 \qquad \Delta Y = \Delta A \left(\frac{1}{1-e}\right) \qquad (16\text{A}.22)$$

Comparing equations 16A.18 and 16A.22, we discover that

$$k = \frac{10}{3} \qquad k = \frac{1}{1-e} \qquad (16\text{A}.23)$$

In words, the multiplier is equal to the reciprocal of one minus the marginal propensity to make expenditures.

In closing, it might be of interest to substitute for e its components in the multiplier formula. This gives us

$$k = \frac{1}{1 - (a' + b - m)} \qquad (16\text{A}.24)$$

Expanding further by substituting for a' its components gives us

$$k = \frac{1}{1 - [a(1 - t - j) + b - m]} \qquad (16\text{A}.25)$$

Thus, the size of the multiplier varies *directly* with a and b, *inversely* with t, j, and m.

The Concept of Liquidity
Immediate Determinants of Liquidity
General Credit Conditions and the Economic Unit

Demand for Liquidity
Elements in the Demand for Liquidity
Costs of Liquidity
Liquidity and the Financial System

Demand for, and Supply of, Money
Elements in the Demand for Money
Aggregate Income, the Interest Rate, and Money Demand
Money Demand: Conclusion
The Supply of Money

Money Demand and Supply, Income, and the Interest Rate
Adjustment to Change in Demand for Money
Adjustment to Change in Money Supply

Equilibrium in the Financial System

Summary

Appendix

The Financial Sector in Macroeconomic Theory 17

Developments in the financial sector of the economy have considerable influence on the behavior of the "real" sector. In chapter 15 we noted that consumption (of durable goods, in particular) responds to the cost and availability of credit and to changes in households' liquid asset holdings. Various categories of investment plans and government expenditure proposals, too, were seen to depend—some heavily, some only slightly—for their execution on these same conditions, which exist or originate in the financial system. But what are the determinants of these financial-sector developments; that is, what forces govern the general level of interest rates and credit availability? That is the question with which we deal in this chapter.

Probably our previous exposure to economic reasoning has conditioned us to think in terms of supply and demand factors whenever we face a situation involving price-quantity phenomena. This is helpful; but in the present situation we must first deal with this question: supply of, and demand for, what?

Different interest rate theories have come up with different answers.[1] The one that seems most suitable for our neo-Keynesian framework is the so-called *liquidity preference theory of interest,* pioneered by Lord Keynes himself and refined by more than a generation of his intellectual descendants.

The liquidity preference theory concentrates on the demand for, and the supply of, money as the immediate determinants of the equilibrium interest rate. In terms of the liquidity preference theory, our task is the discovery and understanding of the factors that influence money demand and supply.

Money, we recall, has two basic economic functions: medium of exchange (or means of payment) and liquid store of value. Although there are no perfect substitutes for money in either function, there are some classes of liquid assets that are very close substitutes as a store of value. Also there are financial arrangements that can, under some circumstances, serve the same purpose as assets held as a store of value. Moreover, there are some financial techniques used in making payments that can greatly reduce the need for money as a medium of exchange.

In view of these considerations, the question "Why hold money?" might be rephrased as, "Why not hold other liquid assets instead of all, or a part of, your money balances?" or, even more broadly, "Why hold liquid assets at all, rather than using alternative means of obtaining the services that liquid assets, including money, provide?" And that last question suggests a further one: "What are those services that liquid assets (and substitute financial arrangements) provide?"

Our approach, then, will be, first, to identify and discuss "those services"—which can be lumped together under the term *liquidity*—and then to attempt to explain demand for money within that context.

The Concept of Liquidity

Liquidity is a very tricky concept, widely used but with a number of quite different meanings and in a variety of settings—for example, the liquidity of assets, the liquidity position of a business firm or a bank, or of the banking system, or even of the economy, and international liquidity. Here our focus will be on the liquidity of a particular economic unit. In this sense, liquidity will be understood to refer to the "financial maneuverability" of the economic unit, as perceived by it, that is, the extent to which the economic unit has the power to alter the size and composition of its assets and increase the volume of services it obtains, over a (specified) brief period of time and at reasonable cost.

Some of the implications of this definition will be spelled out in the next section. But, throughout the discussion, it must be borne in mind

---

[1] See Joseph W. Conard, *An Introduction to the Theory of Interest* (Berkeley: University of California Press, 1959).

that liquidity has a *subjective* element—liquidity depends on what the economic unit *believes* to be true. If "he" feels less (or more) liquid, his behavior will reflect this conviction regardless of whether there has been any change in the objective determinants of liquidity. And, by the same token, if an actual change in these objective determinants is not perceived by the economic unit, he must feel as liquid as before; therefore, his "liquidity behavior" cannot be directly affected by the change.

Immediate Determinants of Liquidity

A number of factors affect the liquidity of an economic unit as thus understood. We naturally think of the unit's cash and noncash liquid assets; but also important to liquidity are anticipated near-term cash flow and ability to acquire, and costs of acquiring, assets and services through issuing claims. We turn briefly to each of these factors now.

At one time the *ratio of cash to total assets*, the first and most obvious of these factors, was stressed (perhaps overstressed) as *the* factor of completely overriding importance. Developments in financial institutions and markets, in types and volume of credit instruments, in government policies toward financial institutions and markets—all of which are, of course, closely interrelated—have operated to increase the relative importance of other factors affecting liquidity and thus to reduce the relative importance of cash in the total liquidity picture.

A second relevant factor is the *ratio of noncash liquid assets to total assets*. These liquid assets are assets that can be "liquidated," that is, exchanged for money, in a short period of time at reasonable cost and with minimal likelihood of reduction in value.

A noncash asset may be liquid because it has one or more of these qualities. First, its liquidity may derive from its representing a claim that is due and payable in cash at the option of the holder. Examples of this type are Series E Bonds issued by the United States Treasury, bank passbook savings accounts, and similar deposits at other depository savings intermediaries. Such an asset need not be "sold," in the conventional sense, in order for the claim holder to exchange it for money. Second, an asset may be liquid because it is scheduled to "ripen" in the near future; that is, the date is near when, according to prior agreement, the debtor is obliged to pay the holder in cash in order to extinguish the latter's claim. A third source of liquidity of an asset is a broad, active market for it and a negligible risk of substantial price change.[2] Important classes of assets in this category are United States Treasury bills, bankers' acceptances, open-market commercial paper, and bank-issued negotiable certificates of deposit.

---

[2] This source would seem to admit certain basic commodities (at least those enjoying government price support) into the liquid asset categories. We omit them, though, because they are not really considered by the managers of asset portfolios as alternatives to financial liquid assets, as a rule.

Just as money was, and sometimes still is, used as synonymous with liquidity, now one often sees the liquidity of an economic unit or a class of economic units (for example, commercial banks) measured by liquid assets, or by liquid assets as per cent of debt, or of current liabilities, or of total assets. While certainly an improvement over the "money" measure of liquidity, since liquid assets do increase the maneuverability of an economic unit, this approach still leaves out some important factors. However, sometimes, in our far-from-ideal world, measurements that rely on liquid asset ratios are the best we can do; we simply have to assume that total liquidity moves in the same direction and (hopefully) roughly in proportion with our crude measures of liquidity.

The liquidity (financial maneuverability) of an economic unit is also strongly influenced by a third factor: the *self-perceived ability of the unit to obtain goods, services, and claims and to meet due obligations through credit arrangements at reasonable cost*. This means that the liquidity position of an economic unit may be improved or impaired by a change in its ability to acquire assets and services directly "on credit" just as truly as by a change in ability to borrow money to acquire them. For example, a change in credit practices of large suppliers in the form of increased or decreased liberality in credit terms extended to their customers can have a substantial impact on the liquidity position of the customers. This also means that a debtor economic unit expecting to be able to meet a debt when due by means of, say, obtaining a loan extension or floating a new bond issue will feel more liquid, other things equal, than the poor soul who knows he will have to dig into his own cash resources to retire the obligation.

Liquidity is also affected by *the ratio of net cash flow anticipated over the near future to total assets*, since this factor plainly has a bearing on the estimation of the economic unit of the amount of assets it could acquire and debts it could liquidate, in excess of current commitments. All of us as individuals feel more liquid when we expect to receive a check within a few days. And, conversely, awareness of the need to make a substantial payment shortly will certainly reduce our financial maneuverability! The same considerations apply to businesses and other nonhousehold economic units as well as to households.

Finally, there is the *degree of confidence* that the economic unit has in its estimations of each of these factors. Any event or development either increasing or decreasing uncertainty as to the amount that the unit will be able to borrow at reasonable terms, for instance, causes a change in its perceived liquidity position. Notice: the *amount* the unit expects to be able to borrow has not changed, only the *degree of confidence* with which this expectation is held.

While these last three factors cannot be expressed readily, if at all, in quantitative terms, their importance is undeniable. This quotation, from a speech by the president of the Federal Reserve Bank of Chicago, expresses it vividly:

Liquidity is ample when an individual, business, or institution is confident that funds will be available to pay bills when they come due. Current and prospective income, the collection rate on receivables, and the extent of unused lines of credit are all important considerations. A man with a substantial bank account who thinks his job is in jeopardy is less willing to spend and assume new commitments (feels less liquid) than a man with a negative bank balance who has just been promoted.[3]

General Credit Conditions and the Economic Unit

General credit conditions affect liquidity directly, via terms on which the economic unit can borrow, that is, can issue claims to another economic unit, usually a financial intermediary, in exchange for cash. Overall credit "availability" cannot be measured directly, of course; but one indirect measure sometimes used is the ratio of bank loans to deposits, the rationale being that, in view of banks' preference for loans, the lower this ratio, the more "slack" exists in the financial system for further lending. This is no more than a very rough indicator, though, because the desired loans-to-deposits ratio may be affected by the banks' deposit-mix and various characteristics of the banks' earning-asset portfolio. Moreover, a given balance-sheet position does not accurately indicate bankers' anticipations as to availability and cost of financing to them.

Nevertheless, we have good reason to expect the liquidity of the financial system to move in the same direction as that of the rest of the economy. When banks find themselves with more reserves, or believe they can acquire additional reserves more readily and/or on more favorable terms than heretofore, this increased liquidity is transmitted to other elements of the financial system and to the other sectors of the economy as well, as those sectors enjoy (1) availability of credit on less costly, less restrictive terms and (2) larger holdings of liquid assets (deposits and otherwise). Conversely, when added reserves become more costly and less readily obtained, this situation is felt by the rest of the economy as a reduced ability to borrow and a decrease—or at least a retardation in the rate of increase—in liquid assets. Thus, the total supply of liquid assets and the availability of borrowed money and of nonfinancial assets and services "on credit" tend to move in the same direction.

Within a given set of general *credit* conditions, however, the situation facing particular economic units can vary widely, depending on such factors as its financial condition and (for a business firm) the condition of, and outlook for, the industry or industries in which it operates.

Summarizing, an economic unit will feel itself more liquid, given its total assets, (1) the larger its money holding, (2) the larger its holdings of

---

[3] Robert P. Mayo, "Rebuilding American's Liquidity," *Business Conditions*, Federal Reserve Bank of Chicago (February 1971), pp. 7–8.

noncash liquid assets, (3) the greater, in its judgment, the amount of cash it can acquire and due debts it can meet by borrowing plus the amount of other assets it can acquire on credit, at minimal cost, and in a short time, (4) the greater its anticipated net cash inflow over the near future, and (5) the more confident it is in its estimations of these factors.

Demand for Liquidity

In modern society liquidity is necessary to an economic unit for economic survival. However, an economic unit may desire and maintain a more liquid position than it absolutely needs for survival, so it makes sense to talk about the *demand* for liquidity. In other words, we can legitimately treat liquidity like an economic good or resource, relating the degree of liquidity desired by an economic unit or, for that matter, the entire economy or any sector thereof, to the "cost" of liquidity.

Elements in the Demand for Liquidity

Economic units find that there are certain advantages in being liquid. Some of the more important ones we now examine.

1. *Transactions.* Even though there may be cases where planned cash receipts of an economic unit equal planned cash payments over a designated time period, they can hardly be expected to match perfectly during each moment of the time period. There will inevitably be times during the period, therefore, when anticipated cash outflow will tend to exceed inflow in the ordinary course of events.

    This element in the total demand for liquidity—the need to have money to make required payments during periods when the anticipated cash inflow from ordinary sources falls short of the scheduled cash outflow—is labeled the *transactions demand* because it arises out of the normal course of economic transactions and payments patterns. Other things equal, the larger the volume of transactions of an economic unit (or of the entire economy), the greater the demand for liquidity for transactions purposes.

    If the time period under consideration is very short—say, for a person who is paid weekly—the appropriate way to satisfy this demand will be through money holdings, in most cases; but the longer the period, the more the advantage moves toward interest-earning liquid assets and lines of credit. Even in the case of an extremely short period, though, it may still pay to hold interest-earning liquid assets if the amount involved is large enough to offset the cost and inconvenience of undertaking the necessary transactions.

2. *Precaution.* In a world of uncertainty, it often makes sense to accumulate liquid assets and/or make arrangements for standby credit in order to be prepared for contingencies—unexpected need or desire to make expenditures or unforeseen failure of receipts. The "rainy day" motive is applicable to businesses and financial institutions as well as to households. As to which means to utilize—standby credit or liquid assets—economic units make different judgments. For example, even when borrowing would be easy, an economic unit may wish to avoid incurring (added) debt at all costs, perhaps because of personal attitudes, or tradition ("There's no reason for it; it's policy."), or fear of damaging the unit's credit rating. On the other hand, increased availability of credit cards and other forms of stand-by consumer credit have certainly reduced the demand of many a household for liquid assets as a source of "rainy day" maneuverability.

   When an economic downturn appears or is expected shortly, the urge to acquire liquid assets for precautionary reasons intensifies, of course, because of increased uncertainty of receipts (and, for financial institutions, withdrawals), plus reduced assurance concerning ability to acquire funds for expenditures by means of borrowing.

   There is another aspect to the precautionary demand in addition to the "rainy day" motive. Economic units may want to be in a flexible position to take advantage of a "good deal" in the real sector, which could be anything from a coat on sale to a company available for acquisition on favorable terms.

3. *Diversification.*[4] As a portfolio of financial assets grows, whether personal or institutional, considerations of balance demand that the liquid assets component grow, too—not necessarily in proportion to overall portfolio growth, but certainly in absolute size.

4. *Speculation.* A portion of the total demand for liquidity is based on expectations of lower future prices of assets, real and financial. If one believes that stock or bond prices are high (yields low) now relative to what they will be in the near future, he will be more inclined to "get liquid" or stay liquid. Conversely, if prices of these securities are considered too low in view of expected near-term market conditions, the portfolio manager will move toward the long end of the maturity spectrum.

   He will almost certainly not put all his financial assets into long-term securities, however, because (a) liquid assets, as we

---

[4] John G. Gurley and Edward S. Shaw, "Financial Aspects of Economic Development," *American Economic Review*, XLV (December 1955), p. 522.

know, are held for a variety of reasons, of which speculation is only one, and (b) expectations of future price and yield movements may be held with less than absolute confidence.

Costs of Liquidity

We must conclude that liquidity is a highly desirable condition, other things equal. But against the advantages of being in a liquid position, we must balance the disadvantages, in terms both of alternatives foregone and of explicit costs incurred.

For a business, the opportunity cost of increasing liquid asset holdings would involve one or more of these: (1) less fixed capital, inventory, and other nonliquid assets, (2) larger amount of debt to trade and other creditors, (3) smaller expenditures on advertising, research, and so on, and (4) smaller dividends and other payments to owners.

The first alternative would probably entail a loss of potential sales plus higher costs; the second, increased credit costs (for example, trade discounts missed); the third would involve reduced potential sales and/or loss of the potential benefits of the research foregone; and the fourth could depress the price of the company's stock.

For a household, an increase in liquid asset holdings entails a combination of these alternatives, each with its own cost: (1) curtailment of expenditures on consumption goods and services, (2) a larger amount of debt to merchants and financial institutions, and (3) a smaller quantity of nonliquid claims. The costs to governments, nonprofit organizations, and financial institutions can also be analyzed in a similar manner, by cataloging the alternatives and assessing their costs.

Availability of credit, another source of liquidity, also may involve certain costs. Often the businessman who arranges for a line of credit at his bank is assessed a charge equal to a certain percentage of the average size of the unused portion of his credit line. The household may have to pay a fixed annual fee to the issuer of certain kinds of credit cards for the privilege of this service.

We cannot pause to examine each of these costs, but it should be plain that, at the margin, the higher are yields (in terms of income and/or direct satisfaction) from these alternatives to liquidity, and the higher are the direct costs of maintaining a liquid position, the smaller will be the demand for liquidity; and the lower these yields and direct costs, the larger the demand for liquidity will be.

Liquidity and the Financial System

Liquidity is largely a product of the financial system, as influenced by the Federal government. We have only to recall quickly a few points from earlier chapters to back up this statement fully.

In the first place, liquidity is enhanced by the practice of financial intermediaries to hold the long-term liabilities of nonfinancial economic units and to issue their own short-term and demand liabilities. Thus, the surplus nonfinancial economic unit can acquire liquid assets even though the deficit nonfinancial economic unit has issued long-term obligations. The financial intermediary is enabled to perform this miracle—buying long-term assets and issuing short-term liabilities—thanks to portfolio diversification, cash reserves, a reasonably predictable cash flow, and perhaps back-up credit as well.

Second, because of the development and improvement of financial markets, the liquidity of many assets—including long-term assets such as home mortgages—has been increased.

Third, the confidence of nonfinancial economic units in their ability to acquire financing when desired, on reasonable terms, is largely dependent on the financial system. Insofar as financial intermediaries are willing and able to make and honor standby credit commitments, and insofar as businesses and households believe that they could qualify to receive credit if they would apply, their overall liquidity is to that extent increased.

Finally, many actions of the Federal government and its agencies have had effects on the liquidity positions of economic units. In some cases, the improvement in liquidity positions is through increasing the marketability of a certain category of assets, or through furnishing standby credit facilities. In other cases the effect on liquidity position is indirect. For instance, any action that demonstrates Federal government commitment to maintain reasonable economic stability or that increases public confidence in such a commitment will tend to make economic units less fearful of such bogeys of the past as "financial panics" or "liquidity crises," when many institutional arrangements that were trusted to provide liquidity failed to withstand the stress of an economic downturn.

We have been discussing developments and conditions that improve liquidity positions; but it must be obvious that reversing any of these will cause a deterioration in overall liquidity. In the long run, however, developments increasing the liquidity of assets and the ability of economic units to secure financing when they desire have clearly predominated over developments in the other direction.

Demand for, and Supply of, Money

Having looked at the reasons why economic units desire liquidity in general, we can return now to the question introduced at the beginning of the chapter: What determines the demand for the particular liquid asset known as money?

Much of what was said above concerning the demand for liquidity in general applies to money, the ultimate bearer of liquidity. Money is held for all the usual liquidity reasons, plus a few unusual ones, as we shall see.

Elements in the Demand for Money

1. *Transactions.* A portion of total liquid assets held for transaction purposes, as explained previously, must be in the form of money. If the economic unit is small and if the receipts-expenditures gap is very short, as in the case of a household of modest means relying mainly on weekly paychecks, most or all liquid assets will probably consist of money. The bother and cost of individual transactions of small magnitude would not be offset by the small monetary yield (if any) obtainable. At the other extreme, giant economic units—government and private—find it economically advantageous to "sell" surplus cash for liquid assets, even if only for a day or two. There is thus an important "scale effect" present: because of the larger sums involved and the greater financial sophistication of financial management, large economic units' transactions demands for money as a fraction of total assets may be expected to decrease as total assets increase, because the larger the size of the economic unit, the greater the opportunities to exchange money for interest-bearing liquid assets for short periods of time.[5]

For the economy as a whole, demand for money for transactions will vary with total income. Just as businessmen need to keep larger inventories of goods as the pace of business increases, so economic units generally must have larger average cash balances; in both cases the reason is the same: to minimize the cost, inconvenience, and hazards of "running out."

Transactions balances, especially those of large economic units using efficient financial management practices, also depend on interest rates. At higher rates the economic unit will have more incentive to reduce its "inventory" of money and to increase holdings of interest-earning substitutes.[6]

Improvements in business cash-management methods, stimulated in part by periods of credit stringency, coupled with institutional developments in financial markets that have made it both profitable and safe to hold interest-bearing liq-

---

[5] See Robert C. Vogel and G. S. Maddala, "Cross-Section Estimates of Liquid Asset Demand by Manufacturing Corporations," *Journal of Finance,* XXII (December 1967), pp. 557–75.

[6] William J. Baumol, "The Transactions Demand for Cash: An Inventory Theoretic Approach," *Quarterly Journal of Economics,* LXVI (November 1952), pp. 545–56.

uid assets instead of money for short periods, have enabled business to handle vastly increased sales with a much smaller rise, proportionally, in average cash balances. As evidence of this, between 1957 and 1966 the ratio of nonfinancial transactions to money holdings of nonfinancial corporations rose from about twenty-two to just under forty.[7]

Households, too, have experienced both increased opportunities and stronger inducements to reduce their transactions balances, as a fraction of their total income. Consider this list of factors:

The tendency to minimize checking account activity in order to reduce service charges, the more widespread use of charge accounts and other forms of consumer credit, the recent growth of credit-card and overdraft arrangements, and the increasing attractiveness of various kinds of thrift accounts, and more recently of consumer certificates of deposit.[8]

There are still many households that refuse to buy even major items on credit, preferring to accumulate in advance; but, even in these cases, the accumulation is seldom in the form of money but rather tends to be in savings accounts.[9]

2. *Precaution and speculation.* Little need be added to what was said on these topics in the "Demand for Liquidity" section. The amount of money demanded for precautionary reasons is generally considered dependent on the level of aggregate income and interest rates. The higher the rates, the more expensive are money holdings in terms of income foregone, of course, so the precautionary demand for money will tend to vary inversely with interest rates. Also, higher aggregate income means a larger volume of liquid assets demanded for precautionary reasons, and it seems reasonable to assume that some proportion of this desired increase in liquid assets will be in the form of money, other things equal.

Money held for so-called "speculative reasons" would be held in expectation of an early increase in interest rates (that is, fall in securities prices). At one time economists, following Keynes, laid great stress on this element in money demand. However, the dominant view now is that speculative balances will mainly take the form of nonmonetary liquid assets since (a) these assets yield an interest return and (b) speculative

---

[7] George Garvy and Martin R. Blyn, *The Velocity of Money* (New York: Federal Reserve Bank of New York, 1969), pp. 70–71. See chapters 2 and 6 on this topic.
[8] Ibid., p. 76.
[9] Eva Mueller and Jane Lean, "The Savings Account as a Source for Financing Large Expenditures," *Journal of Finance*, XXII (September 1967), pp. 375–93, especially pp. 382–85.

balances are, in the main, held by large economic units capable of more sophisticated financial management.

3. *Compensating balances.* It may come as a surprise to learn that a substantial share of all demand deposits is represented by compensating balances in banks, held to reimburse these banks for services rendered.[10] This is true, moreover, for individual as well as business accounts. Many banks, for example, base their service charges on personal checking accounts on the average (or minimum) balance as well as on the activity of the account, that is, the number of checks drawn on it during a given period. Insofar as households are induced to keep a larger demand-deposit balance than they otherwise would, in order to minimize the service charge, the cash thus held may be classified under "compensating balances."[11]

Business firms, although seldom paying service charges on checking-account activity, are commonly expected to maintain compensatory balances as a per cent of their borrowings or lines of credit, as we observed in chapter 5. Sometimes, in fact, a business firm will relate its deposit balance to the cost that in the estimation of the firm, the bank incurs in performing various services for the firm. Here again, insofar as the deposit holder is thus induced to maintain a larger demand-deposit claim against the bank, either because of the bank's requirement or on grounds of "good will," than it otherwise would for purely transactions and other normal needs, we classify this excess in the category of "compensating balances."

It is not possible to estimate the volume of demand deposits in this category, first, because we cannot know what volume businesses and households would maintain in the absence of bank stipulations and other inducements to hold larger balances and, second, because these "excess" amounts make some contribution to the total liquidity of the holder. Even a compensatory balance requirement imposed on a business is not absolute but can be drawn down in case of need (at the cost of a service charge) in most cases.

One economic implication of this behavior pattern may be noted in passing: since banks are inclined to enforce minimum balance requirements more rigidly in times of tight money, the result is an increase in total demand for money at such times, thus intensifying the condition of tightness that

---

[10] Garvy and Blyn, *The Velocity of Money*, pp. 28–32.
[11] From the standpoint of the bank, all balances are "compensating," in a sense, because it is only through the grace of the depositor that the bank has the wherewithal to purchase financial assets. Therefore, we are classifying as "compensating" only those balances held *specifically* to forestall, or replace, direct service charges by the bank.

the monetary authorities are attempting to achieve. Under opposite circumstances, relaxation of requirements in times of monetary ease reduces total demand for money, thus reinforcing the efforts of the monetary authorities in this respect.

4. *Miscellaneous.* Our list of reasons to hold money is not, nor need it be, exhaustive. Yet, there are a few minor reasons that merit brief mention.

Certain illegal activities result in a demand for currency, especially large-denomination bills. It seems probable that black-market activities were a major factor in the enormous fourfold rise in currency in circulation during World War II, both to finance and to conceal the profits from such activitites. Income tax evasion also is given as a reason for holding currency.[12] Observe that this use of currency is, in the main, not as a substitute for demand deposits, since the money is not wanted for any transaction of other purpose listed above, but only because currency is an easily concealed store of value. Its "money-ness" is incidental.

Hoarding by foreigners has also been suggested as an element in total demand for money, particularly currency. And the increased popularity of coin collecting is a factor of some importance in explaning the rapid rise in the volume of coins outstanding.

Lastly, in the case of some economic units (economically small households in particular) money is held, mostly currency, because of ignorance of the possibilities of "putting it to work" and little or no attempt to investigate possibilities. During World War II, for example, many workers who were recruited from economically poorer sections of the country to work in war-goods plants were simply at a loss to cope with the vast quantities of money in their pay envelopes. Unacquainted with banks or savings institutions, they tended to keep their savings, except for savings bond purchases, in the form of money, especially currency. At present, this factor undoubtedly explains only a small proportion of total cash holdings.

DEMAND FOR MONEY AND DEMAND FOR LIQUIDITY We have observed that the demand for money and the demand for liquid assets in general share many of the same influences; the level of GNP, the degree of uncertainty over the economic outlook, and the availability of standby credit are such influences.

---

[12] George G. Kaufman, "The Demand for Currency" (Staff Economic Studies, Board of Governors of the Federal Reserve System, 1966), p. 27.

Yet there are some factors causing the demand for liquid assets in general and the demand for money to move in opposite directions. For example, an increase in interest rates generally—including those on deposit-type and open-market liquid assets—will induce economic units to reduce their desired holdings of money relative to other liquid assets. An increase in the "liquidity" of nonmonetary liquid assets (better markets, improving their shiftability, or increased ease of cashing them in) will have a similar effect, reducing the demand for money while increasing the demand for rival liquid assets. Improvements in cash-management techniques of business and other economic units have reduced overall demand for liquid assets but, within this total, have reduced the demand for money even more.

As a result of these developments, money has declined as a per cent of total liquid assets held by nonfinancial corporations in the United States from around 70 per cent in 1953 to 39 per cent in 1972. For households, too, money represents a diminishing fraction of total liquid assets, declining from 30 per cent in 1953 to 20 per cent in 1972.[13]

Some of these developments are reversible; some are not. For instance, a decline in interest rates on nonmonetary liquid assets would reduce or, in some cases, wipe out the possible gains from switching between these assets and money. But the increased sophistication in management of liquidity positions appears to be a permanent factor affecting demand for money.

Aggregate Income, the Interest Rate, and Money Demand[14]

We observed that the quantity of money which economic units desire to hold depends on, among other factors, interest rates and the level of aggregate income. This information provides us with the raw materials for a simple model of the financial system.

In our model, there are only two financial assets: money and bonds. These bonds are all of equal quality and of the same maturity. We thus can speak of "the" interest rate and avoid the complexities of an interest-rate structure for the time being.

LEVEL OF GNP AND THE DEMAND FOR MONEY As a first step, let us treat the interest rate as given and attempt to postulate the relation between the level of GNP and the demand for money. We know that there is a relationship because of the "transactions" and "precautionary" elements in the demand for money, both of which are responsive to the level of GNP. There is good reason to believe that the relationship between changes in GNP and changes in the demand for money is approx-

---

[13] Garvy and Blyn, *The Velocity of Money*, p. 21, and *Federal Reserve Bulletin*, September 1973, pp. A71.20–A71.21.

[14] See the Appendix to this chapter for a simple algebraic treatment of this model.

Figure 17.1
Relationship between gross national product
and the demand for money.

imately proportional,[15]—in the short run, at any rate—so we may draw it as in Figure 17.1. The $L_Y L_Y$ curve incorporates these ideas. The distance OL_Y represents the demand for money for nonincome reasons (held constant), and the constant slope of the $L_Y L_Y$ curve indicates that the quantity of money demanded changes in proportion to the change in GNP.

THE INTEREST RATE AND THE DEMAND FOR MONEY   Next, let us take the level of GNP as given and develop the relationship of the rate of interest to the demand for money. In our model, the rate of interest is, of course, that which applies to bonds, the only nonmonetary financial asset. We depict the relationship of the interest rate to the demand for money as curve $L_R L_R$ in Figure 17.2.

High interest rate levels are associated with demands for relatively small quantities of money; low rate levels, with demands for relatively large quantities. More specifically, the curve embodies the assumption that (1) at very high rate levels, the $L_R L_R$ curve becomes vertical, so that higher levels do not further reduce the quantity of money demanded; and (2) as one moves lower on the interest-rate scale, the demand for money becomes increasingly elastic, that is, given percentage declines in the interest rate are associated with larger and larger percentage increases in money demanded.[16]

These properties of the LL curve just discussed are not due to a

---

[15] See, for instance, Henry A. Latané, "Cash Balances and the Interest Rate—A Pragmatic Approach," *Review of Economics and Statistics*, XXXVI (November 1954), pp. 456–60.
[16] The curve may even become horizontal; but there is considerable difference of opinion among economists on this point. In any event, the issue is not critical for us.

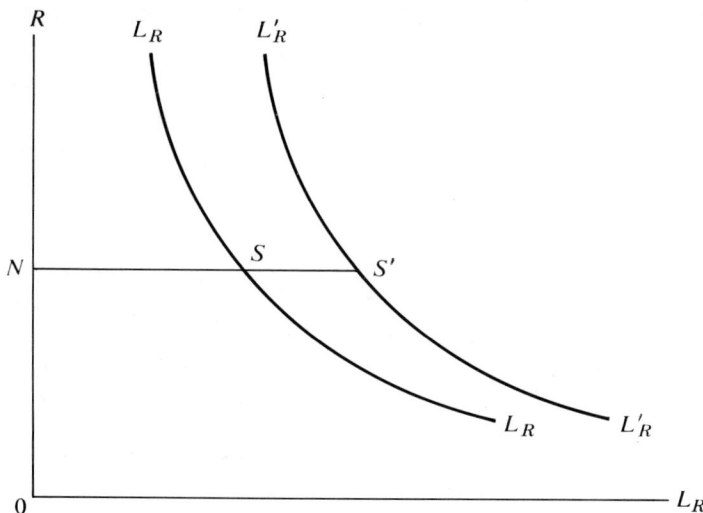

Figure 17.2
Relationship between the interest rate
and the demand for money.

draftsman's whim; they are built in deliberately to embody what most economists believe to be true about the relation between the long-term interest rate level and the demand for money. At extremely high levels, the community will be unanimous in believing that the rate can only go down, hence the more reasonable it is to hold only the bare minimum money balances required by transactions and other nonspeculative needs. But, as one moves down the interest scale, increasing numbers of economic units will be, in effect, willing to bet increasing amounts of money that the interest rate will rise, and soon. Moreover, the lower the rate of interest, the smaller the anticipated reward for assuming the risk inherent in bond holding—the risk of capital loss should the price of bonds decline—hence, the greater the incentive to shift portfolios in the direction of more money, less bonds. The quantity of money demanded will be greater than "needed" because households and financial institutions are increasingly willing to speculate on higher rates (lower securities prices). Finally, at abnormally low rates the community's virtually unanimous opinion will be that interest rates must certainly soon rise, meaning lower securities prices, therefore, it would be foolish to hold bonds. "Sell now, buy later" is the watchword.

Money Demand: Conclusion

Now we must reintroduce changes in the aggregate income level into the situation. Higher incomes, as we noted earlier, are associated with increased demand for money for transactions and other nonspeculative purposes. The effect of a rise in income on the demand for money would be depicted on Figure 17.2 as a shift on the $L_R L_R$ to the right, for example, to $L'_R L'_R$. At interest rate ON, the quantity of money demanded was NS at the original level of income, NS' at the higher level. This embodies the idea developed earlier that, given the interest rate, the demand for money varies *directly* with the level of income.

The Supply of Money

To this picture we must add the supply of money. In our simple two-financial-asset world, we assume that the money supply is whatever the monetary authorities decide it shall be. This assumption fits the facts of the real world fairly well since, as we know, the Federal Reserve authorities control member-bank reserves, which, in turn, are a major determinant of demand deposits, our chief form of money.

We draw the money supply curve, then, as a vertical line MM in Figure 17.3 because, in contrast to the money-demand case, the money supply is assumed *not* to vary automatically with the interest rate.

Money Demand and Supply, Income, and the Interest Rate

To wrap up our discussion, we combine the demand for money and the supply of money as related to the interest rate and the level of income, bringing in other aspects of the financial system as well. We start at a starkly simple level, assuming a given money supply, given level of income, given quantity of bonds, in fact, assuming everything that determines the demand for money held constant except the interest rate. Under these circumstances, equilibrium in this market exists when the

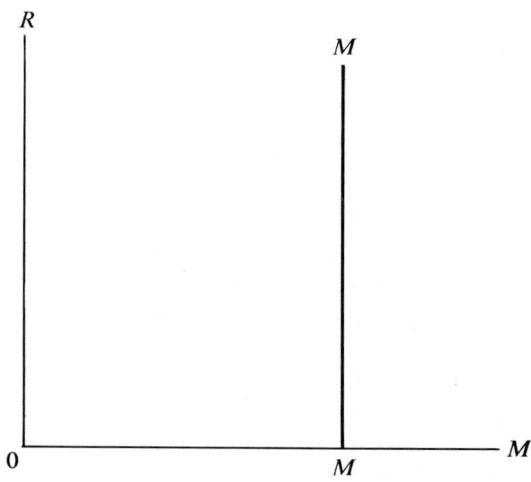

Figure 17.3
The money supply.

interest rate is at the level at which the quantity of money that economic units wish to hold equals the existing stock of money.

Figure 17.4 depicts such a situation. Curve MM is the existing stock of money; $L_R L_R$ the demand for money at the current level of GNP. (Ignore the other curves for the present.) At interest rate ON, the equilibrium rate, the public desires to hold OM dollars, which is the number of dollars in existence. At higher rates of interest, money is not so attractive an asset, for reasons already discussed, so the *desired* level of cash balances falls short of the existing money supply. At lower rates, the desired level exceeds the stock of money.

Of course, the mere fact that the quantity demanded is not equal to the quantity in existence does not in itself imply that the inequality will correct itself. The mean temperature in Orlando, Florida is higher than that of Bemidji, Minnesota, but we do not infer, from this fact, that the temperature in the two cities will move toward "equilibrium" wherein the temperatures are identical! What we must do is identify and examine a mechanism that will tend to eliminate the difference between the amount of money supplied and the amount demanded.

Adjustment to Change in Demand for Money

This mechanism of adjustment can be seen in motion if we assume that equilibrium is disturbed and then observe the process of movement to a new equilibrium.

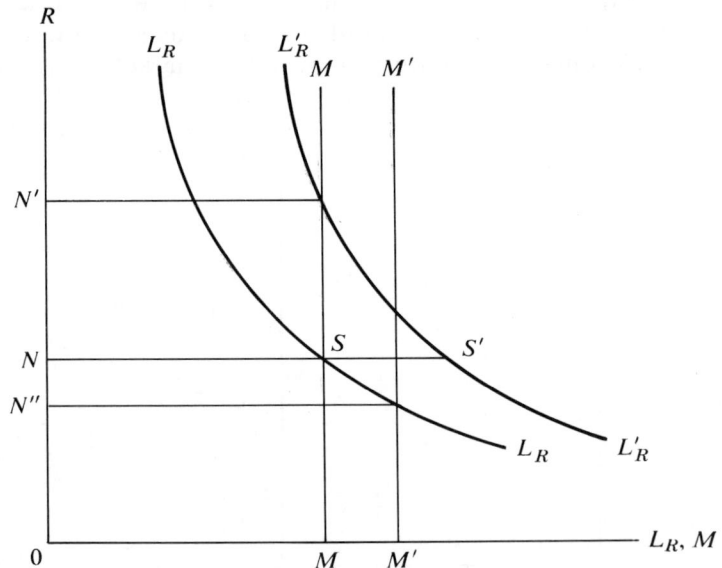

Figure 17.4
Money demand and supply.

INCREASE IN Y Let us first postulate an increase in GNP. The consequence of such an increase is a rise in demand for money for transactions purposes, shifting the $L_R L_R$ curve in Figure 17.4 to the right ($L'_R L'_R$). Now there is excess demand for money, measured by SS', at the old interest rate ON. But what actually occurs to push the rate up? This is the crucial question. To answer it, we must observe the behavior of those economic units that sense a shortage in their cash balances as a result of higher incomes.

While an individual business or household can acquire more cash by selling assets or through other means, the economy as a whole cannot do this because the stock of money is assumed fixed. Nevertheless, the effort is made. Business firms and individuals attempt to unload bonds, driving their price down. But lower bond prices mean higher yields, that is, higher interest rates. And higher interest rates result in a desire to hold less cash! The imbalance between the stock of money and the excess demand for it thus tends to correct itself; excess demand for money → unloading of bonds → lower prices (higher yields) for bonds → reduced desire to hold cash for speculative reasons. Equilibrium is restored at interest rate ON' where the quantity of money demanded (OM) once again is compatible with the existing stock of money.

One artificial element in the discussion, slipped in unannounced for the sake of simplicity, should be brought into the open now: we have been using a rather rigid time sequence, a "first this, then that" method. Actually, income does not suddenly shoot upward to a higher level, then remain there while the financial system adjusts to it. It would be more nearly accurate to state that, as income increases, there will be a rise in need for cash balances for transactions, to handle the larger volume of goods and services moving through the pipelines. This will put gradual upward pressure on interest rates, due to unloading of bonds in an effort to acquire more cash. Gradually a new equilibrium is reached, with total demand for money equal to the (unchanged) stock of money but at a higher interest rate and a higher level of aggregate income.

CHANGE IN MARKET CONDITIONS FOR OTHER LIQUID ASSETS A change originating in the financial sector also may affect equilibrium. For example, broadening our model a bit, suppose a class of nonbank intermediaries appears, issuing liabilities that are, for some purposes, good substitutes for money. The result will be a leftward shift in the $L_R L_R$ curve as the public shifts out of demand deposits and into these nonmoney liquid assets. This activity does not change the quantity of money, however; it merely transfers some of it from households and, perhaps, business firms to the aggressive nonbank intermediary. Subsequent purchases of bonds by these new institutions, in turn, acts to reduce the long-term interest rate until, once again, the demand for money is compatible with the supply.

Adjustment to Change in Money Supply

Turning to the opposite side of the market, we introduce an increase in the money supply. In order to keep it simple, the increase is assumed to take the form of a nationwide distribution of "free" money by the Treasury, authorized by the Congress, so that the supply curve shifts from MM to $M'M'$ in Figure 17.4. Under these circumstances—that is, given GNP and the interest rate—economic units feel that they hold too much money relative to bonds, so they attempt to buy more bonds. Since there is only a given number of bonds and since spending the money does not cause it to disappear, the effect of these transactions is to bid up the price of bonds and, hence, to depress the interest rate until the rate level is reached at which the public is satisfied with their present holdings of money: namely, interest rate ON''.

Equilibrium in the Financial System

Now we must broaden our perspective, from money to the financial system, in order to develop a more realistic (though less rigorous) analysis. We shall find that, although the process of adjustment to changes affecting the financial system is infinitely more complex, the nature of the process is essentially as it has already been described.

Equilibrium, for example, requires not merely that the price of "bonds," the single category of nonmonetary financial asset, bring into equality the demand for, and supply of, this asset but also that this condition be met in the market for each financial asset, regardless of maturity, riskiness, and other characteristics.

An increase in GNP sets in motion not only adjustments in "the" long-term interest rate (thus, in the price of bonds) but numerous other adjustments as well, as economic units strive to maintain liquidity in the face of increased need for transactions balances and (due to increased borrowings from banks) compensating balances. Banks, in an effort to accommodate their borrowing customers, attempt to get additional reserves by selling securities. Those nonbank purchasers will only be induced to part with money, of course, if the price of the securities is right—that is, lower—and hence, yield is greater. The outcome is a rise in interest rates and no change in either reserves[17] or money, though there may be considerable churning about as demand deposits are increasingly acquired by economic units that use them for transactions and other income-related purposes.

Our broader perspective also allows us to develop a more realistic view of the process of money creation. Assume that the Federal Reserve purchases a certain volume of securities in the open market as part of its program of achieving a more desirable set of conditions in the economy,

---

[17] Banks might increase their borrowings from the Federal Reserve, but reserves created in this manner can be offset by open-market sales.

conditions that include, or involve, an expansion of the stock of money from that represented by *MM* in Figure 17.4 to *M'M'*. The purchase of securities gives rise to an increase in bank reserves and exerts some upward pressure on securities prices and toward lower interest rates. But in order for the increase in reserves to translate itself into a multiple expansion of demand deposits, such as was described in chapter 2, there must be some inducement for the public to *want* to hold money. Something, in other words, must make them dissatisfied with their present collection of assets—its quantity and/or its mix—in order to induce them to shift toward money, despite the costs in terms of alternatives foregone, as discussed earlier.

It is not enough to respond by stating that, after all, money is created in the process of bank lending and investing and that we learned of banks' tendencies to use any additional reserves promptly by purchasing securities if not in making new loans. We need to know why this new money *remains* in existence. The initial borrowers from, or sellers of securities to, the banks had reasons to augment their cash, at least temporarily. Some sought money in order to make purchases; others for speculation or other reasons. But what about subsequent holders? Unless we make the farfetched assumption that any increase in bank lending or investing sets in motion forces automatically resulting in an immediate and permanent increase in transactions and precautionary demand for money, we can expect holders of excess cash (1) to repay loans, (2) to exchange their demand deposits for time deposits, and (3) to purchase interest-earning liquid assets.[18]

The first two of these alternatives both reduce the money supply and increase bank excess reserves. Alternative (1) reduces total deposits, hence required reserves, without affecting total reserves, and alternative (2) replaces demand deposits with time deposits, which are subject to lower reserve requirements, again without reducing total reserves. The third one, however, does not affect either the money supply or excess reserves. There has simply been an exchange of assets, money for other liquid assets and vice versa. But it holds the key to the problem of keeping the money in existence: efforts to purchase liquid assets depress interest rates, thus increasing the quantity of money people are *willing* to hold.

To recapitulate: Increased reserves → increased *potential* money supply. But interest rates must decline in order that the public might be willing to hold the increased quantity of money. Banks cannot *force* money to remain outstanding; there must be changes in the financial environment to *induce* the public to hold increased cash balances rather than alternative assets. Thus, although we are justified in assuming M to

---

[18] Remember that the increase is in money, *not* in income, so we cannot expect household recipients to spend a part of their increased money balances as though these involved income increases. Our earlier "marginal propensity to consume" discussion dealt with the effect on consumption of changes in *income,* not in the stock of money.

be under ultimate control of the monetary authorities, we discover that the mechanism is not simply (1) change in M, then (2) financial adjustments thereto, but rather a simultaneous process in which the money supply and interest rates change together. In our example, an increase in M from OM to OM' will not *cause*, but will be *associated with*, a decline in the interest rate from ON to ON''.

The process of contraction is much the same: tightened reserve position of the banks induces simultaneous decreases in demand deposits and increases in the interest rate as the economy accommodates itself to a decrease in M.

Summary

The demand for money is related to the total demand for liquidity in the same way as the demand for (say) rump roast is related to the demand for meat. The more numerous the substitutes available and the more attractive the terms under which substitutes can be acquired, the less rump roast or money will be sought. In the case of money, secular developments in the financial system have increased both the number of substitute sources of the kinds of services for which money is desired and also the attractiveness of such sources.

For expository purposes, we compress all nonmonetary financial assets into one homogeneous category, *bonds,* and all interest rates into *the* interest rate on bonds. We can then identify the equilibrium interest rate as that rate at which the demand for money is equal to the supply (or stock) of money. While the money supply is effectively under the control of the monetary authorities, the quantity of money demanded is influenced by a variety of factors, including the level of aggregate income (Y) and the interest rate (R). At any given R, the demand for money varies directly with Y; and at any given Y, the demand for money varies inversely with R. Given the money supply, then, the higher the level of GNP, the higher will R have to be to equate the quantity of money demanded with the supply. This is true in the case of a many-financial-asset economy such as ours as well as in the bonds-and-money case.

KEY CONCEPTS

Liquidity preference theory of interest

Liquidity
Compensating balances

QUESTIONS FOR REVIEW

1. What are the major determinants of the liquidity of an economic unit? How do general economic conditions affect these factors?

2. How are money and liquidity related?
3. What are the major elements in the demand for liquidity? For which of these is money usually the preferred means of providing liquidity?
4. How are liquidity and the financial system related?
5. Is money demanded for purposes other than liquidity? Explain.
6. What has happened to the relative importance of money as a provider of liquidity?
7. Under what circumstances would you expect the demand for money to move in the same direction as the demand for liquid assets in general? Under what circumstances in the opposite direction?
8. Explain the shape of the $L_R L_R$ curve. Explain its position.
9. Explain the shape of the $L_Y L_Y$ curve. Explain its position.
10. What is the justification for drawing the money-supply curve as a vertical line?
11. How will R be affected by (a) a decrease in Y? (b) an increase in the liquidity of money substitutes? (c) a decrease in the quantity of money?
12. Which is the more nearly correct statement: "An increase in Y causes an increase in R" or "An increase in Y is accompanied by an increase in R"? Why?

SUGGESTIONS FOR FURTHER READING

Burger, Albert E. *The Money Supply Process*, Belmont, Calif: Wadsworth Publishing Co., 1971.

Cagan, Phillip. *Determinants and Effects of Changes in the Stock of Money.* New York: Columbia University Press, 1965.

Conard, Joseph W. *An Introduction to the Theory of Interest.* Berkeley: University of California Press, 1959.

Duesenberry, James S. "The Portfolio Approach to the Demand for Money and Other Assets," *Review of Economics and Statistics*, XLVI (Supplement, February 1963).

Garvy, George and Martin Blyn. *The Velocity of Money.* New York: Federal Reserve Bank of New York, 1969.

Gurley, John G., and William S. Shaw. *Money in a Theory of Finance.* Washington, D.C.: The Brookings Institution, 1960.

Laidler, David E. W. *The Demand for Money: Theories and Evidence.* Scranton: International Textbook Co., 1969.

Tobin, James. "Liquidity Preference as Behavior Toward Risk," *Review of Economic Studies*, XXV (February 1958), pp. 65–86.

Wrightsman, Dwayne. *An Introduction to Monetary Theory and Policy.* New York: Free Press, 1971.

APPENDIX

Continuing with our algebraic treatment of relationships developed in the text, we learned in this chapter that the demand for money (L) depends on the rate of interest (R), the level of aggregate income (Y), and various autonomous factors (L_o). The supply of money we regard as given (recognizing that this is somewhat of an oversimplification). As in the Appendix to chapter 16, all noncoefficient numerals are in units of $1 billion.

Let us assume that each change in Y causes L to move in the same direction in an amount equal to 20 per cent (h) of the change in Y. And, to keep the model as uncomplicated as possible, let us assume that the relation between L and R also is linear, such that, when R changes by 1, L changes by 20 (or v) in the opposite direction. Further, the autonomous factors in the demand for money (L_o) account for 160, and the money supply is set at 200 (M_o). All this information yields the following system of equations, the numerical form on the left and the more general (but still linear) form on the right:

$$L = M \qquad\qquad L = M \qquad (17A.1)$$
$$M = 200 \qquad\qquad M = M_o \qquad (17A.2)$$
$$L = 160 + .2Y - 20R \qquad L = L_o + hY - vR \qquad (17A.3)$$

If we arbitrarily set $Y = 700$ (and make $L' = L_o + hY$) we can solve as follows. First, computing the value of $160 + .2(700)$ as 300, we can rewrite equation 17A.3 as follows:*

$$L = 300 - 20R \qquad L = L'_o - vR \qquad (17A.3')$$

Next, we substitute the M-value for the L-value in equation 17A.3', as authorized by 17A.1:

$$200 = 300 - 20R \qquad M_o = L'_o - vR$$

Solving for R:

$$20R = 300 - 200 = 100 \qquad vR = L'_o - M_o$$
$$R = 5 \qquad\qquad R = (L'_o - M_o)/v$$

In a similar manner, if we specify that the interest rate (R) is, say, 7 per cent, we can focus on the relation between the demand for money and the level of GNP. The procedure is as follows. First, combine the

---

*This equation yields the peculiar result that, at values of R above 15, the demand for money becomes negative! However, if we interpret this function as approximating the shape of the (actually nonlinear) L function in the range of typical values of R, we can ease ourselves out of this difficulty.

R-related demand for money with the autonomous demand in equation 17A.3, referring to $L_o - vR$ as L_o''

$$L = 20 + .2Y \qquad L = L_o'' + hY \qquad (17A.3'')$$

Next, we again substitute for L the given money supply: then we solve for Y

$$.2Y = 200 - 20 = 180 \qquad hY = M_o - L_o''$$
$$y = 900 \qquad Y = (M_o - L_o'')/h$$

Unless we specify *either R or Y*, however, we cannot identify the equilibrium position of the financial sector, because we have here three equations but four unknowns. In the appendix to chapter 18 we shall discover that, by combining this model with that of the appendix to chapter 16, a solution is possible.

A Real/Financial Model of the Economy
Real-Sector Equilibrium
Financial-Sector Equilibrium
Equilibrium: Real and Financial Sectors Combined
Some Applications of the Model

Aggregate Economic Activity and the Price Level
The Initiation of Inflation
Some Refinements and Complications

Economic Growth and the Macroeconomy

The Model World and the Real World: Final Comments

Summary

Appendix
The Real Sector
The Financial Sector
Equilibrium: Real and Financial Sectors Combined
Some Applications of the Model

18 The Real and Financial Systems: Inflation and Growth

In chapters 15 and 16 we explored, among other topics, the ways in which the financial sector acts upon the real sector, via changes in interest rates and other credit variables. This process is sometimes summarized in a form like this:

$$\Delta R \xrightarrow{\;-\;} \Delta I \xrightarrow{\;+\;} \Delta Y$$

that is, a change in credit conditions (represented by a change in *the* interest rate) causes investment to change in the opposite direction in response. The investment shift, in turn, moves equilibrium income in the same direction. As a matter of fact, the size of the response may be several times the size of the initiating change in investment.

Then we examined, in chapter 17, the impact of the real sector on the financial sector, noting that a change in aggregate income will affect the demand for money and, therefore, the interest rate:

$$\Delta Y \xrightarrow{\;+\;} \Delta L \xrightarrow{\;+\;} \Delta R$$

Now we are ready to study the interaction of the two sectors. It is tempting simply to place the two chains end to end (and this is sometimes done) like this:

$$\Delta B \xrightarrow{+} \Delta M \xrightarrow{-} \Delta R \xrightarrow{-} \Delta I \xrightarrow{+} \Delta Y \xrightarrow{+} \Delta L \xrightarrow{+} \Delta R$$

An initiating change in bank reserves (B) and the money supply was added in order to provide a "push" from outside the system.

There is something peculiar about this long chain of causation. While each individual link appears to be adequate and acceptable, the whole process described by the chain seems to imply a sort of oscillation. When reserves and the money supply increase, interest rates are driven down, stimulating I and Y. But this results in a rise in R due to higher L. Then the rise in R, in turn pushes I down again, and therefore Y will fall too, which reduces L, pulling R back down again, and so on, and so on.

A more realistic and sensible—though somewhat more difficult—way to approach the process of interaction of the two sectors is in terms of a set of interrelated developments occurring simultaneously in both sectors rather than as a sequence that switches back and forth between sectors.[1] To describe the nature of the process we employ a model incorporating various elements already introduced in the three chapters immediately preceding this one.

A Real/Financial Model of the Economy

Real-Sector Equilibrium[2]

In chapter 16 we developed a total expenditure function. Below, we reproduce as Table 18.1 columns 1 and 8 of Table 16.1, recalling that each E entry comprises $C + I + G + X$ for that level of GNP.

This schedule incorporates the assumption of a specified rate of interest, which is (let us say) 5 per cent.

We remember that in chapter 15 the idea was developed that one of the determinants of investment and also of some types of consumption expenditures and state and local expenditures is the rate of interest: higher rates (and tighter credit) tend to reduce such expenditures. Suppose, then, that, for every one percentage point increase in the interest rate, the volume of planned expenditures (given the GNP level) will decline by $15 billion. Table 18.2 depicts these relationships for several representative levels of income and interest rates (R):

Pairing any E-column with the Y-column shows the relation between E and Y at the particular rate of interest specified for that E-column. (The "5" column reproduces figures from Table 18.1 which was based on the

---

[1] Even this approach is not entirely satisfactory because it ignores "lags" in the working out of some of these developments. However, incorporating lags into our model would make it far too complex.

[2] Appendix, under "The Real Sector."

TABLE 18.1
Total Expenditure Function
(in $billions)

Y (1)	E (2)
0	210
100	280
200	350
300	420
400	490
500	560
600	630
700	700
800	770
900	840

TABLE 18.2
Relationship of Planned Expenditures (E) to Aggregate Income (Y) and the Rate of Interest (R)
(in $billions)

Y	E, when R =				
	1	3	5	7	9
0	270	240	210	180	150
.	.	.	.	.	.
.	.	.	.	.	.
500	620	590	560	530	(500)
600	690	660	630	(600)	570
700	760	730	(700)	670	640
800	830	(800)	770	740	710
900	(900)	870	840	810	780

assumption of a 5 per cent interest rate.) Then, pairing any *row* with the R-row relates total expenditures to the rate of interest, given the GNP level. For instance, if Y is $800 billion, E will be $830 billion when R = 1, $800 billion when R = 3, $770 billion when R = 5, and so on across the table.

From Table 18.2 it is evident that it is impossible to identify the equilibrium level of aggregate income—the E = Y position—until we first specify the interest rate. With a 3 per cent rate, for example, E = Y at an income level of $800 billion. At a 5 percent rate, E = Y at $700 billion. And so on. Each of these equilibrium levels has been circled for easy reference. Table 18.3 extracts the equilibrium level from each column

TABLE 18.3
Relationship between the Interest Rate and Aggregate Equilibrium
(in $billions)

R	Y at which $E = Y$
1	900
3	800
5	700
7	600
9	500

and relates it to the applicable interest rate. Figure 18.1 depicts this information graphically. Following a long tradition, we label the resulting curve *the IS curve*.[3]

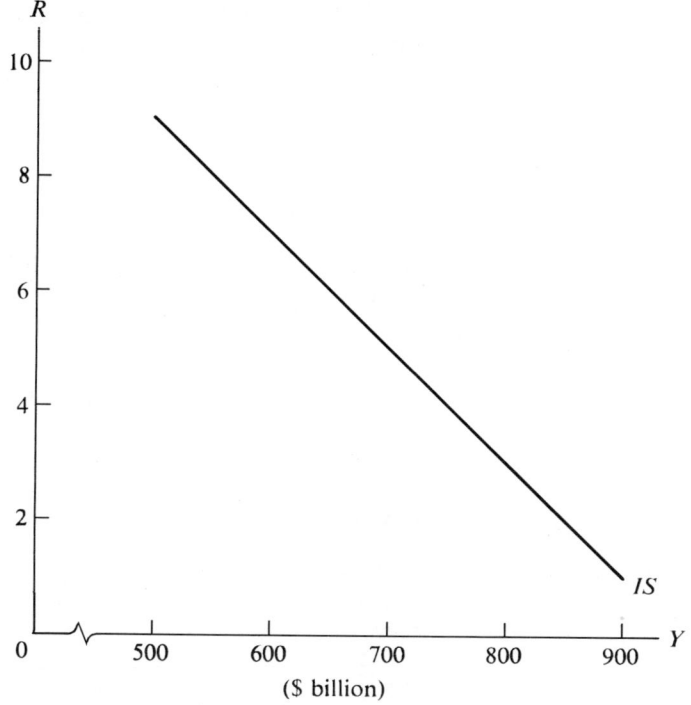

Figure 18.1
The interest rate and real-sector equilibrium.

---

[3] Actually, the term "*EY* curve" would be more appropriate, since each point on this curve represents a combination of a rate of interest and a level of GNP at which $E = Y$. However, this curve was originally labeled by Sir John Hicks in 1936, and the label has stuck. See John Hicks, "Mr. Keynes and the 'Classics': A Suggested Interpretation," *Econometrica*, V (April 1937), pp. 147–59.

Financial-Sector Equilibrium[4]

Turning now to the financial sector, we recall from our discussion in chapter 17 that the demand for money (L) depends on the level of GNP (Y) and the interest rate (R), plus a number of autonomous factors. Therefore, with any given money supply, we cannot locate the rate of interest at which total demand for money will equal this supply unless we first specify the level of income. To make this point more clearly and to help us see some of its implications, we utilize another numerical illustration (Table 18.4)

Reading across the table, we observe that a change in GNP of $100 billion will change the quantity of money demanded by $20 billion in the same direction. Reading down, we observe that a change in the interest rate of 1 per cent will cause the quantity of money demanded to move by $20 billion in the opposite direction. These characteristics are in line with our conclusions in chapter 17, that the demand for money varies directly with aggregate income and inversely with the interest rate.

If, now, we specify a money supply of $200 billion, what interest rate will bring the demand for money into equality with this supply? Answer: "It depends." We need first to know the level of GNP in order to be able to give a definite answer to the question. It is evident from Table 18.4 that, given the money supply, the higher the level of GNP, the higher the interest rate that is needed to produce monetary equilibrium, that is, equality between money demand and supply. Based on the information in the table, we can locate several equilibrium positions—combinations of Y and R that yield a demand for money equal to the given money supply of $200 billion. Again for convenience, these equilibrium positions have been encircled in Table 18.4 and recorded as Table 18.5.

This information is transferred to a graph (Figure 18.2). With the points connected, the resulting curve is called, appropriately, *the LM curve*. Each point on the curve denotes a combination of interest rate

TABLE 18.4
Relationship of the Demand for Money (L)
to Aggregate Income (Y) and the Rate of Interest (R)
(in $billions)

	L, when $Y =$				
R	500	600	700	800	900
3	(200)	220	240	260	280
4	180	(200)	220	240	260
5	160	180	(200)	220	240
6	140	160	180	(200)	220
7	120	140	160	180	(200)

[4] Appendix, under "The Financial Sector."

TABLE 18.5
Relationship Between the Interest Rate
and Monetary Equilibrium
(in $billions)

Y	R at which $L = M = 200$
500	3
600	4
700	5
800	6
900	7

and GNP at which the demand for money equals the (given) money supply.

Equilibrium: Real and Financial Sectors Combined[5]

We have learned that (1) we cannot determine equilibrium GNP in the real sector without knowing the interest rate, but (2) we cannot determine the equilibrium interest rate in the financial sector without

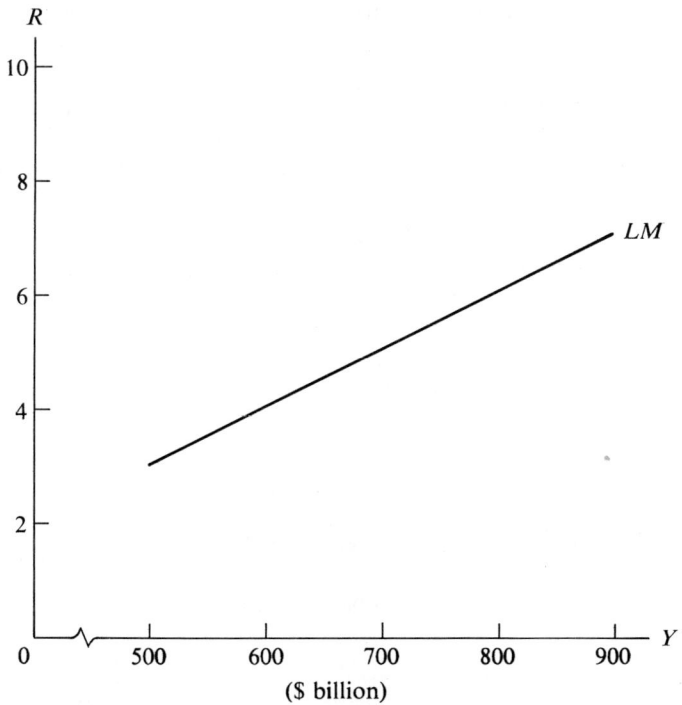

Figure 18.2
The interest rate and financial-sector equilibrium.

[5] Appendix, under "Equilibrium."

specifying the level of GNP. Evidently each sector depends on the other; so the logical way to approach the problem, as we stated at the beginning of the chapter, is to consider the two sectors simultaneously. This we are, at long last, about to do.

Fortunately, we have all the raw materials at hand, in the form of Tables 18.3 and 18.5 and Figures 18.1 and 18.2. All that remains to be done is to combine the two tables into Table 18.6 and the two figures into Figure 18.3.

From both the table and the graph, it is apparent that only one combination of GNP and interest rate—$700 billion and 5 per cent, respectively—is compatible with equilibrium in both sectors. This combination is identified in Figure 18.3 as point P_1.

Some Applications of the Model[6]

Now let us subject the model to certain changes in economic and financial circumstances—the kinds of changes that a "real world" economy encounters—and observe its reactions. This will not be mere intellectual play, by the way, because, insofar as our model embodies the main characteristics of our actual economy (a point to which we return later in the chapter), a study of the responses of the model economy will illuminate certain characteristics of real-world macroeconomic behavior.

INCREASE IN AUTONOMOUS EXPENDITURES First, let us assume that autonomous expenditures increase. The initiating force could be, say, an income-tax rate reduction, which would stimulate consumer spending

TABLE 18.6
Relationship Between the Interest Rate and GNP
at which $E = Y$ and $L = M$

R	Y, at which	
	$E = Y$	$L = M$
1	900	
2		
3	800	500
4		600
5	700	700
6		800
7	600	900
8		
9	500	

Source: Tables 18.3 and 18.5.

[6] Appendix, under "Some Applications of the Model."

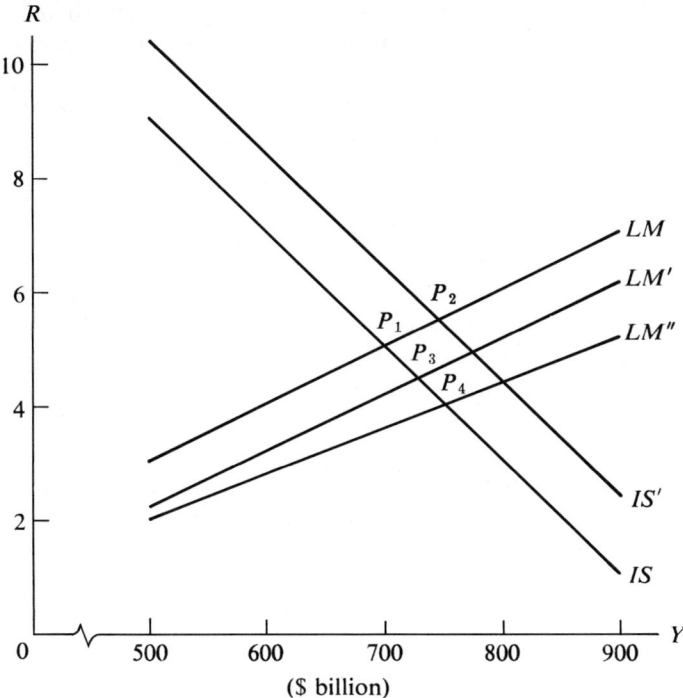

Figure 18.3
Macroeconomic equilibrium.

out of a given Y; or technological changes, which would increase business investment; or growth in state and local spending on schools; or even an economic boom abroad, increasing our exports relative to imports. In any case, as a result of this increase in autonomous spending, equilibrium GNP ($E = Y$) *at any given interest rate* will be larger than before. This we learned back in chapter 16.

With our more sophisticated chapter 18 model, however, we can move a few steps closer to reality in our analysis of the problem. The fact that equilibrium GNP will be larger at any given interest rate means that the *IS* curve in Figure 18.3 has shifted rightward—say, to *IS'*—and the new macroeconomic equilibrium position (P_2) will be characterized not only by a higher GNP level but also by a higher interest rate. Moreover, the new equilibrium GNP is not so large as it would have been if the interest rate had not risen.

That, at any rate, is what our model would lead us to conclude. Is this reasonable? Specifically, why should the interest rate rise along with the GNP increase? And why should this rise in the interest rate retard the growth in GNP? With reference to the first question, in chapter 17 we learned that an increase in GNP will generate an increase in the demand for money. This increase in demand for money, along with an unchanged money supply, will naturally produce a rise in the interest rate. No mystery there.

Then, with reference to the second question, we also learned (chapter 15) that investment and probably other categories of expenditures are somewhat sensitive to the interest rate (read: "credit conditions"). Higher rates will choke off some investment projects, some school construction, and some consumer durables purchases that would otherwise have taken place.

This conclusion requires us to qualify somewhat our earlier multiplier analysis, by the way. If we were to include the *financial* effects of an increase in autonomous spending, we would discover that the "true" multiplier is smaller than the formula $1/(1-e)$ would lead us to believe.[7]

INCREASE IN THE MONEY SUPPLY Next we consider the effects of a change originating in the financial sector; specifically, an increase of $40 billion in the money supply. The important institutional aspects of this change we bypass for now, with a warning that the arrangements through which this ΔM is accomplished can differ, with corresponding differences in economic effects.

Referring again to Table 18.4, if GNP were to remain at $700 billion, this increase in M would depress the interest rate to 3 per cent: down the "700" column, $L = \$240$ billion when $R = 3$. Translated into LM-curve terms, this implies a rightward movement of the curve. Prior to the increase in M, a GNP of $700 billion yielded monetary equilibrium ($L = M$) at an interest rate of 5 per cent (point P_1). Now, as we observed, this same GNP yields monetary equilibrium at 3 per cent. And what is true of a $700 billion GNP is true of other GNP levels as well: equilibrium interest rate has fallen by 2 per cent throughout. So, the new curve is LM' in Figure 18.3.

The importance of this example, however, is not the effects of a change in M or R but rather its effects on Y. The new equilibrium position (P_3), compared to the old (P_1), features a higher equilibrium GNP as well as a lower interest rate.

In chapters 21 and 22 we plan to devote much more attention to this link between M and Y, since it is, after all, the primary rationale for monetary policy. There is a good deal of controversy in this area at present, which we cannot get into at this point, except to note that the neo-Keynesian version of the linkage presented above, running from ΔM through ΔR (broadly understood) to ΔE, is not the only possible version. Others believe that the link running directly from ΔM to ΔE is potent. But more of that later.

[7] The Appendix to this chapter develops this idea more fully.

CHANGE IN DEMAND FOR MONEY   An increase or decrease in M is not the only type of change originating in the financial sector that can affect aggregate economic performance. Consider now a change in the demand function for money such that, at each GNP level, a smaller quantity of money is desired, as a fraction of GNP, than was the case previously. This kind of change would alter the position and shape of the LM curve in a manner represented by LM'' in Figure 18.3. The curve has moved downward, indicating that, at any given Y (and M), L will equal M at a lower interest rate than before. The slope of the curve is smaller, too, since the effect of this demand reduction would vary directly with the size of GNP.

On Figure 18.3 we locate the new equilibrium position at point P_4, the intersection of the old IS curve and the LM'' curve. The new R is, of course, lower, and Y is larger.

This kind of shift in the money demand function is by no means farfetched. Numerous institutional changes in the financial system and in the financial management practices of businesses and other kinds of economic units have had the effect of reducing considerably the "real world" L/Y over the past quarter-century. As evidence, consider the fact that the ratio of Y to M, usually called the *income velocity of money*, has risen with few interruptions since World War II, from 1.97 in 1946 to 4.59 in 1968.[8] An increase in Y now produces a smaller increase in money demand, hence a smaller rise in R, than before.

Additional examples of changes affecting the IS or LM curve could be analyzed, but it should be evident now that the process through which a change in one sector works its effects on GNP will involve both sectors simultaneously. This is easy to demonstrate in our model world; but, since the links we have postulated between the two sectors have their counterparts in the real world, we can be quite sure that this conclusion regarding the interdependence of the sectors also applies "out there."

Aggregate Economic Activity and the Price Level

Thus far in our exposition of monetary analysis we have assumed an unchanging price level. Any change in GNP has therefore been entirely a change in *real* GNP. However convenient this has been as a device to keep our discussion as elementary as possible, the constant-price-level assumption must be dropped now because failure to cope with the problem of price-level changes, particularly in an upward direction (that is what inflation is all about) would seriously limit the usefulness of our model and related discussion.

We shall assume, quite reasonably, that the rate of increase in prices is directly related to the ratio of actual GNP to *full-employment GNP*,

---

[8] George Garvy and Martin R. Blyn, *The Velocity of Money* (New York: Federal Reserve Bank of New York, 1969), p. 65.

which we define as that level of GNP incapable of being increased significantly by additions to aggregate demand. Where this ratio is quite low, inflation is unlikely; but as the ratio approaches unity, inflation becomes more likely and, finally, more intense.

It is useful to think in terms of a "zone of inflation," extending from the highest level of real GNP consistent with price-level stability to the full-employment level of real GNP. As the economy moves within this zone toward capacity, the rate of inflation increases; as the economy reverses its direction, the rate of inflation declines.[9] Note that last clause well: it is the *rate of inflation* that declines, not the price level!

The existence of a zone of inflation and its general characteristics as just described seem reasonable theoretical assumptions and have empirical confirmation as well, although attempts to put actual numbers in the picture have not been particularly successful.

The process of inflation develops something like this: As aggregate demand expands and the economy moves from outside the zone of inflation into the zone, bottlenecks begin to appear in the markets for certain raw materials and labor skills. The result inevitably is upward pressure on costs and prices in the industries affected. The farther into the zone the economy is carried by aggregate demand pressures, the larger the number of industries that will be thus affected.

There are other elements in the response of the economy to higher levels of demand that add to upward price pressures. As individual producing units approach capacity output, their unit costs of production begin to rise, and high-cost obsolescent facilities are placed in operation. Resource scarcities induce the utilization of lower-quality labor. Organized labor becomes more aggressive in wage demands, and stronger demand for output reduces management's resistance to these wage demands. Higher costs of materials and labor are experienced also by industries operating below capacity, resulting in higher price tags on their products, too.

These are not one-shot increases in costs and prices. So long as this kind of underlying conditions persists, the reactions of businesses attempting to cope with the unfavorable changes in their environment (that is, higher costs) or in a position to improve themselves economically (through raising prices) insure the continuance of inflation.

One more assumption we make is that the price level does not decline as we move out of, and away from, the zone of inflation. Rather, the entire decline in GNP is considered to be in real terms. This assumption, too, is fairly realistic under conditions that prevail in modern economies. There are strong institutional forces that resist price reductions, even in the face of shrinking demand. And labor unions, with rare exceptions, are adamant in resisting cuts in money wage rates—a factor adding to business reluctance to lower prices.

---

[9] But not necessarily quickly—a point we shall consider later in this chapter.

Before turning to our major topic in this section—the interaction of price-level changes and aggregate economic activity—we need to deal briefly with some matters of terminology. *Inflation,* in our discussion, will mean a *sustained rise in the price level.* This is an imprecise definition but a common-sense one. We could conceivably encounter some problems (How long must the price level rise be to qualify as "sustained"? How large a rise per year is required?); but, despite the possibility of some borderline cases, this definition should suffice.

We must not confuse *rising* prices with *high* prices—high, that is, with reference to those of some other period of time. What we are saying is that prices could be high in a noninflationary period or, for that matter, low in a period of inflation, since what is important as a test of inflation is not the level of prices but the rate of change in the level.

Our discussion will not deal with the fantastically rapid rates of increase in prices characteristic of hyperinflations—the type "enjoyed" within the last half-century by Germany and a few other nations[10]—because the kinds of conditions associated with hyperinflation are simply not present or likely to occur in the foreseeable future in our economy.

By *price level* we have in mind some "ideal" general price index that faithfully registers each change in average prices. There is no such index in use, of course, although the GNP implicit price deflator comes closest. However, even this index has its shortcomings, including a probable upward bias, since it does not accurately reflect quality improvements and the price declines common for products in their introductory stages.[11]

The Initiation of Inflation

Let us go back now to our real-financial model, with the "ground rules" changed to admit the possibility of inflation. We shall assume that the zone of inflation is the range of real GNP values from $750 billion to $800 billion. So long as GNP is not above $750 billion, there will be no increases in the general price level. In the region between $750 billion and $800 billion, the closer we approach $800 billion, the more rapid the rate of price-level increase. Figure 18.4 pictures this condition.

Starting from an equilibrium Y of $700 billion and R of 5 per cent (Figure 18.5), what will happen, under the circumstances now assumed, as a result of a substantial increase in autonomous spending, such that the new *IS* curve (*IS'*) intersects the *LM* curve at $800 billion. Now that we have postulated a zone of inflation above $750 billion, shall we discover that the new equilibrium will still be at $800 billion in real terms

---

[10] See P. Cagan, "The Monetary Dynamics of Hyperinflation," in Milton Friedman (ed.), *Studies in the Quantity Theory of Money* (Chicago: University of Chicago Press, 1956), pp. 25–117.
[11] George Stigler et al., *The Price Statistics of the Federal Government* (New York: National Bureau of Economic Research, 1961), pp. 35–39.

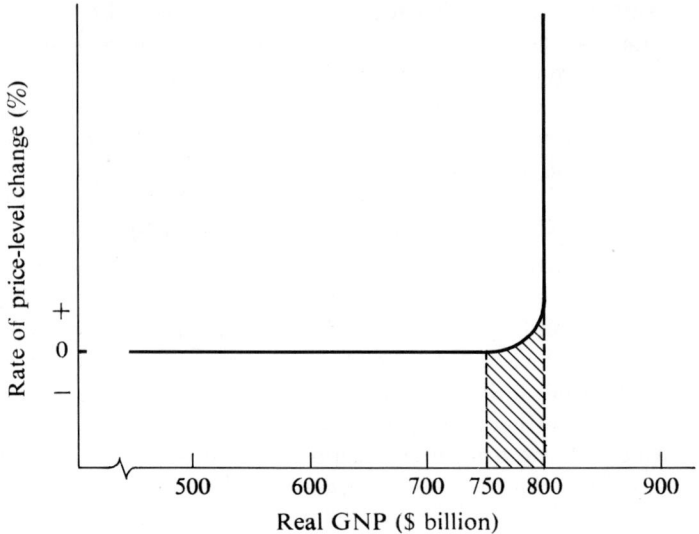

Figure 18.4
Zone of inflation.

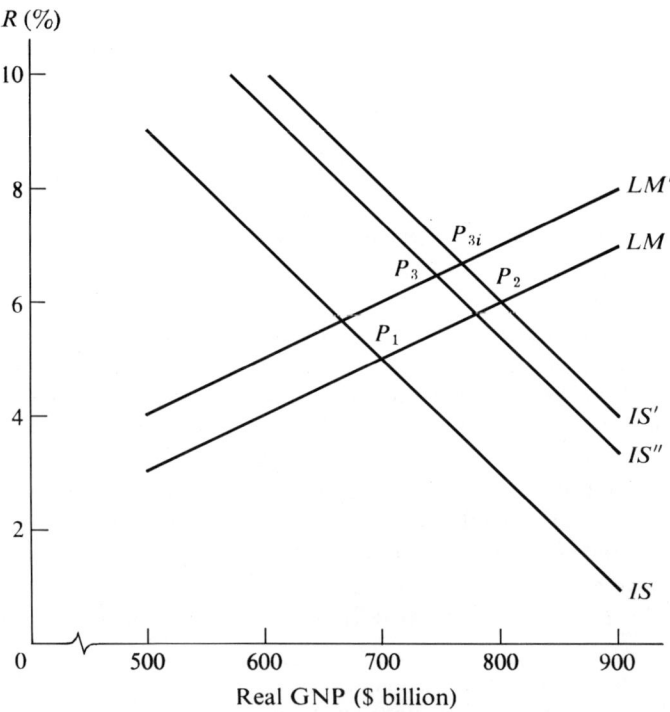

Figure 18.5
Macroeconomic equilibrium, adjusted for inflation.

but with a condition of continual inflation? The answer almost certainly is no. The rise in prices itself will have certain effects both on the *IS* curve and on the *LM* curve; these effects we must examine now.

First, consider the fact that, as the price level rises, the "real" (purchasing power) value of money shrinks. To illustrate, suppose that the money supply were to remain at $200 billion while the price index rose from 100 to 111.1—a rise of one-ninth—in response to the increased spending. The real value of the money supply will have shrunk 10 per cent, to $180 billion. Expressed another way, the purchasing power of $200 billion at the new price level is the same as that of $180 billion at the old price level.

Now observe what has happened in our model (in which we express all monetary values in real terms) as a result of a reduction of the real money supply from $200 billion to $180 billion. The reduced real stock of money will mean that, at any level of (real) GNP, the equilibrium interest rate will be higher. Thus, the *LM* curve will shift to the left— exactly the opposite of the effects of the increase in *M* discussed earlier in the chapter. This new *LM* curve (drawn as *LM'* in Figure 18.5) intersects the new *IS* curve (*IS'*, based on the increase in autonomous expenditures) at a point *within* the zone of inflation. We realize that this cannot be an equilibrium position because, in order to sustain this level of output, we must (by definition) continue to experience a rising price level, which, in turn, will further affect the *LM* curve for reasons just explained. Therefore, we label the intersection of *LM'* and *IS'* with the letter P_{2i}—the *i* standing for *interim*, since this is not the final position.

When will this process stop, then? Not until the two curves intersect at $Y = \$750$ billion. At this point the real money supply no longer suffers a continual decline due to the rising price level, therefore the *LM* curve will cease shifting leftward.

So far we have seemingly assumed that the entire process of adjustment to inflation falls on the forces that determine the LM curve. However, there is good reason to believe that inflation may also affect the *IS* curve through its influence on the real expenditure functions of the four sectors: households, business, government, and the rest of the world.

One such effect, discussed earlier (chapter 15), is the *money illusion*, the observed tendency of households to treat increases in money income as though they are increases in real income, even when part or all of the increased money income merely offsets price-level increases. This factor tends to lower the real consumption function and, therefore, the total expenditure function, of which it is a component.

Another factor often suggested as tending to lower real consumption at any given income level in consequence of inflation is the so-called *wealth effect*. As inflation continues, the real value of household debt claims (money, savings accounts, bonds, and so on) declines. Therefore, it is argued, families thus affected will be inclined to increase their saving (and, therefore, to decrease consumption) out of any given income. On the other hand, the real amount of a debtor's liabilities declines, too! The extent to which the second effect offsets the first is a controversial point; but, in any case, the impact of the wealth effect is generally considered slight.[12]

Progressive taxation also acts on the real consumption-out-of-GNP function in an inflationary situation. To illustrate, if real GNP were to remain constant over a particular time period, while prices and money incomes rose 10 per cent, personal income taxes would increase as per cent of income because the tax rate on the 10 per cent income increment would exceed the rate applicable to the former income level. With real income constant and tax revenues increased as per cent of income, it follows that real disposable income must have declined. Real consumption will also therefore decline. And what is true of the effects of progressive taxation at one level of real GNP will be true at other levels. Thus, the real consumption-out-of-GNP function will tend to move downward as inflation continues, other things unchanged.

Progressive taxation affects the after-tax profits of corporations in a similar manner. Since investment is influenced by the ability of corporations to provide financing from internal sources as well as by prospective after-tax profits, the fact that inflation, via the tax-rate effect, reduces *real* profits remaining after taxes from a given pretax level of *real* profits will, to that extent, lower the investment component of the total expenditure function.

Inflation will unquestionably have the effect of reducing the net export function, too, as higher domestic prices make foreign goods relatively less expensive to domestic economic units and domestic goods of the economy in question more costly to foreign economic units.[13]

Some of the effects of inflation of the *IS* curve come from the tendency of economic units to project past movements into the future. To the degree that this tendency exists, businesses will attempt to advance plant and equipment spending somewhat and will increase inventory investment. Both of these will raise the investment portion of the total expenditure function.

To some extent households respond similarly, especially with respect to major purchases that had been planned in advance. However, evidence based on extensive interviews conducted over a period of years by the University of Michigan Survey Research Center points to another type of household reaction:

> Asked what they would do in defense against price increases, consumers responded more often that they would reduce purchases or postpone buying than that they would buy in advance of price increases. . . .

---

[12] David E. W. Laidler, *The Demand for Money: Theories and Evidence* (Scranton: International Textbook Co., 1969), pp. 34–35.

[13] A byproduct of this development in the relation of exports to imports will be a change in the balance-of-payments position of the economy. This change may be good or bad, in any particular case, depending on the previous position of the balance of payments. We discuss this matter later, in chapter 22.

A comparison between respondents expecting only moderate price rises and respondents expecting sizeable increases showed that the group expecting sizeable increases often felt worse off and, therefore, were likely to defer purchases.[14]

It seems likely that, on balance, the forces tending to pull the total real expenditure function downward (money illusion; effects of inflation on net exports, on net wealth, on ability to finance investment internally, and on taxation as a fraction of income) outweigh the forces working in the opposite direction (the urge to beat, or take advantage of, expected price increases).[15] Based on this conclusion, we must redraw the IS curve (in Figure 18.5), shifting it downward from IS' and relabeling it IS".

You will note that, by a stroke of good fortune (or was it careful planning?), the factors influencing the IS curve plus the forces acting on the LM curve happened to be just strong enough so that the new equilibrium position (P_3) features a real income level that coincides with the left boundary of the zone of inflation. Thus we have reached a new equilibrium, achieved as the result of the effects of inflation on both the LM and IS curves.

If, instead of assuming an increase in autonomous expenditures, we had started our bout with inflation through an overexpansion of the money supply, the final outcome would be the same, so far as its effect on the nominal income level is concerned; but the equilibrium interest rate would have been lower because nearly all of the adjustment would have taken place through the LM curve. Initially, this curve would shift rightward in response to the increase in M; subsequently, rising prices would (1) move the LM curve leftward, via the effects of the price increases on the real value of the money supply, and (2) move the IS curve leftward via the various influences we have just examined, until the two curves would intersect where $Y = 750$ and R was below the initial position. The final price level obviously would be higher than it was initially.

Some Refinements and Complications

If we were to regard this model as an adequate representation of the real-world economy, our prescription for curing a case of inflation would be beautifully simple: Just keep the money supply constant (or, better, reduce it) and inflation will gradually disappear, leaving the economy in a position of equilibrium at a point where GNP is at a maximum consis-

---

[14] Charles C. Tuck, "Personal Saving and Inflation," *Business Conditions*, Federal Reserve Bank of Chicago (May 1969), pp. 15, 16. Also see Eva Mueller, "Consumer Reactions to Inflation," *Quarterly Journal of Economics*, LXXIV (May 1959), pp. 246–62.

[15] Another force tending to retard inflation is economic growth itself. Since growth acts to increase the potential supply of goods and services, it helps to offset excess demand pressure. See the following section.

tent with price-level stability. Somehow, this does not completely satisfy us, nor should it. It leaves out three important issues: (1) how long the whole process will take; (2) whether the existence of big-business firms and powerful labor unions may actually affect both the process of inflation and its final result, and (3) whether the level of unemployment implied by a GNP of 750 is socially acceptable.

Concerning the first of these, evidence is scanty. Our experience with several periods of intensified inflation since World War II suggests that the answer to the "how long" question is "it depends"—and we are not sure at this point of all the main factors determining the length of the process, let alone their relative strength and interrelations. It seems quite certain that the longer and more severe the inflation has been allowed to become before strong countermeasures are imposed, the longer it will take to reduce it to a slow crawl; but beyond that there is much disagreement.

As to whether the considerable market power of large economic units is used in a manner that aggravates inflation, we find considerable agreement that such is the case, but disagreement over how strong the effect is. In an economy such as ours, characterized by large and aggressive businesses and unions, prices of final products and of productive resources will tend to rise not only during a period of excessive aggregate demand but also sometimes, due to continued inflationary expectations, long after the excess demand conditions have been alleviated.

The sequence goes something like this: as prices begin to climb under excess-demand pressure, union wage contracts that come up for renewal will carry larger wage increases for two reasons: (1) unions will demand larger increments on grounds of higher prices and higher corporate profits;[16] and (2) management, eager to keep production at a high level and confident of its power to pass on any cost increases (plus a little bit more) in the form of higher prices, is willing to grant larger wage increases rather than risk a strike. As inflation continues, increasing numbers of labor-management agreements will extend over periods of several years and will contain a so-called "escalator clause," calling for automatic wage increases in line with increases in the consumer price index. General labor-market tightness insures that nonunion wage rates and also prices in these sectors will advance at a rapid clip, too.

The stage is thus set for continued inflation even without the support

---

[16] Quoting from a regular column, "The Outlook," by Alfred L. Malabre, Jr., in the *Wall Street Journal*, August 5, 1968, p. 1:

A glance at the economic history of the post-World War II era certainly suggests that inflation often has been just as much "profit-push" as "wage-push"....

Indeed, some analysts say that the postwar economic record suggest a chain of events that runs something like this: Profits begin to climb, first through . . . [lower] unit labor costs and then through higher prices; the rising profits finally prompt labor to attempt to "catch up" by seeking sharply higher pay . . .

(Reprinted with the permission of The Wall Street Journal, © Dow Jones & Company, Inc., 1968.)

of excess demand. As wage rates climb briskly, reflecting earlier demand conditions, business firms continue to respond to these cost increases by raising prices. This is the phenomenon called "cost-push inflation."

One set of consequences of this continued inflation, in the absence of any growth in M, would be increased monetary tightness, rising interest rates, and an inevitable decline in aggregate (real) demand and employment. In the familiar terms of Figure 18.5, the LM curve would shift leftward and the equilibrium point move upward (higher R) and to the left (lower Y).

As unemployment would thus increase, we could expect that the cost-push process would gradually lose strength. Wage demands and settlements would be more modest, and, consequently, price increases would be smaller and less frequent and the rate of advance of the overall price level would slow down, finally reaching zero. This line of reasoning thus suggests (but it does not prove) that one effect of the existence of increasing power of large economic units is to enlarge the zone of inflation (that is, price would begin to creep upward at a lower level of GNP than would otherwise be the case) and to raise the rate of inflation associated with each GNP level within the zone.

This, however, is not quite the end of the story. The previous discussion has ignored the role of the Federal government, including the monetary authorities, in this process. This is not a serious shortcoming providing we can consider government as somehow aloof and neutral toward the process. But can we? One popular view says we cannot, since the Federal government, because of its commitment to a high-employment economy, is really a part of the process of inflation. The United States economy, according to this view, is destined to be situated rather chronically in the zone of inflation because the rate of unemployment compatible with price-level stability is not socially acceptable and, therefore, not politically feasible either. In the following chapter we examine the nature and some implications of this view.

Economic Growth and the Macroeconomy

We adopted, in the foregoing exposition, the convenient device of assuming a given level of full-employment GNP and a given zone of inflation. Now we must face the fact that both the level and the zone tend to change over time, generally shifting rightward as the productive capacity of the economy increases, that is, as the economy grows. In this book we cannot deal with growth theory itself—the determinants of the rate of economic growth, the interactions among growth and other aspects of economic performance (GNP, employment, price-level movements, investment, and others)—but we can and should point up the relevance of growth to the inflation problem.

In advanced economies of the kinds that exist today on planet Earth, a positive rate of growth in real GNP is "normal" because of increases in the quantity of, and improvements in the quality of, productive resources. This gradual rightward movement of full-employment GNP is, of course, good news for inflation fighters. More and better productive resources help hold down unit costs of production in the face of increased wage rates and other factor prices. However, this same movement of full-employment GNP imposes upon society the continual burden of seeing to it that the *LM-IS* equilibrium point shifts steadily rightward as well—not too slowly, lest unemployment become serious; not too rapidly either, lest continually more severe inflation result.

The Model World and the Real World: Final Comments

We have spent several chapters attempting to understand the behavior of the economy as a whole: the real and financial sectors, their interactions, and their response to external stimuli. Much of our discussion has been built around a model of the economy, which was altered a bit here and there—expanded in a particular direction in order to highlight certain relationships or simplified in order to keep it manageable. The model was supposed to embody certain generally agreed-upon relationships (for example, consumption depends on income; demand for money depends on the interest rate) but in a form that allowed us to arrive at conclusions concerning the outcome of specified developments—conclusions sometimes next to impossible to reach by the use of words only.

Insofar as we have followed the laws of logic in our analysis, and in verbalizing about them and the theoretical relationships they portray, our model has formal, or logical, validity. But how valid is it as a representation of the real world? And to what use can we put it?

Admittedly, it is a tiny model, containing few variables and relationships, and depicting these relationships in a simple manner. Also, there are no lagged relationships; we deal explicitly with equilibrium positions only "before" and "after." This has handicapped us at several points as we tried to delve into some highly important theoretical and practical (if these can really be separated) issues, such as the acceleration effect, the time path of the multiplier process, the process of inflation, and economic growth.

Obviously, therefore, we cannot apply the model directly as a framework for economic forecasting or for advising the Federal Open Market Committee in its monetary policy decisions. But, after all, that was not our announced goal. Rather, the model and surrounding discussion will have accomplished their purpose if they have given us greater insight into the workings of the aggregate economy and the ways in which the financial system fits into it. This insight will, in turn, contribute toward our understanding of the measures, proposals, and controversies of macroeconomic policy, to which we now turn.

Summary

In order to gain a better understanding of the interrelations of the real and financial sectors of our economy we have developed and examined a model economy in which these relationships were highlighted. Our model brought out the fact that, given various expenditure functions, a demand for money function, and a stock of money, general macroeconomic equilibrium includes both a particular level of GNP and a particular interest rate. This equilibrium combination of Y and R is the one that satisfies simultaneously the requirements that $E = Y$ and $L = M$. Any change in one of the "givens" will usually change both the Y and the R values at equilibrium.

Attempting to integrate the price level into the analysis—why changes in the price level occur and how these changes affect the macroeconomy—complicates the theory considerably. Hopefully, though, we gained some insights into the problem of inflation through our discussion of some of the important factors tending to raise the price level and those tending to retard its upward movement. But, realistically, we cannot claim to have a complete answer to this complicated problem that continues to perplex the best minds in the profession.

KEY CONCEPTS

IS curve
LM curve
Income velocity of money
Full-employment zone
Inflation
Wealth effect

QUESTIONS FOR REVIEW

1. Why is the "*IS* curve" somewhat poorly named?
2. What is the reason for the name "*LM* curve"?
3. Explain to your ignorant roommate why (*a*) an increase in the money supply will tend to generate an increase in GNP; (*b*) an increase in government expenditures will tend to raise interest rates; (*c*) a fall in exports will tend to reduce imports and lower interest rates.
4. "Inflation is a period of high prices." Comment.
5. "If M grows too rapidly, the price level will rise; therefore, if the rate of increase in M is slowed down, prices will fall." Evaluate.
6. What properties of an economy will tend to slow the rate of inflation *provided* that the money supply is held to a slow growth rate?
7. What influence do "political realities" have on the process of inflation?

SUGGESTIONS FOR FURTHER READING

Bach, G. Leland. *The New Inflation.* Englewood Cliffs, N.J.: Prentice-Hall, 1973.
Ball, R. J. *Inflation and the Theory of Money.* Chicago: Aldine Publishing Co., 1964.
Commission on Money and Credit. *Inflation, Growth, and Employment.* Englewood Cliffs, N.J.: Prentice-Hall, 1964.
Dernburg, Thomas F., and Duncan M. McDougall. *Macroeconomics,* 4th ed. New York: McGraw-Hill Book Co., 1972.
Friedman, Irving S. *Inflation.* Boston: Houghton Mifflin Co., 1973.
Hicks, John. "Mr. Keynes and the Classics: A Suggested Interpretation." *Econometrica,* V (April 1937), pp. 147–59.
Laidler, David E. W. *The Demand for Money: Theories and Evidence.* Scranton: International Textbook Co., 1969.
Morley, Samuel A. *The Economics of Inflation.* Hinsdale, Ill.: Dryden Press, 1971.
Smith, Harlan. *Elementary Monetary Theory.* New York: Random House, 1968.
Smith, Warren L. *Macroeconomics.* Homewood, Ill.: R. D. Irwin, 1970.

APPENDIX

To keep our discussion on a manageable level, we shall be working with a highly simplified model of the economy. Our framework will be the following system of equations:

Real Sector

$$E = Y \qquad\qquad E = Y \qquad (18A.1)$$
$$E = 285 + .7Y - 15R \qquad E = A + eY - cR \qquad (18A.2)$$

Financial Sector

$$L = M \qquad\qquad L = M \qquad (18A.3)$$
$$M = 200 \qquad\qquad M = M_o \qquad (18A.4)$$
$$L = 160 + .2Y - 20R \qquad L = L_o + hY - vR \qquad (18A.5)$$

The Real Sector

Equation 18A.1 is, of course, the equilibrium condition for the real sector: aggregate income (Y) must equal planned expenditures (E). 18A.2 is a total expenditure function, expressing the dependence of planned expenditures on aggregate income and the rate of interest (R) as well as autonomous factors (A).

For ease of handling we are not analyzing each expenditure category separately, but it would be well to keep in mind the fact that A embodies

C_o, I_o, G_o and X_o, and that e, the marginal propensity to spend, contains all the marginal propensities discussed in chapter 15.

With two equations and three unknowns (Y, E, and R) in the real sector, no unique solution is possible. We can, however, express R as a function of Y, thusly.

First, substituting Y for E in equation 18A.2 (by authority of 18A.1) gives us

$$Y = 285 + .7Y - 15R \qquad Y = A + eY - cR$$

Next, we collect all Y-terms on the right side and move the R-term to the left:

$$15R = 285 - .3Y \qquad cR = A - (1 - e)Y$$

Then, dividing by the coefficient of R gives us

$$R = 19 - .02Y \qquad R = \left(\frac{A}{c}\right) \frac{1-e}{c} Y \qquad (18A.6)$$

Equation 18A.6 generates the *IS* curve discussed in chapter 18, relating R and equilibrium Y. A/c corresponds to the Y-intercept, and $-(1-e)/c$ is the slope of the curve. Since the slope is negative, R and Y are inversely related: other things constant (A, c, and e), a higher equilibrium Y requires a lower R.

The Financial Sector

The financial side also is a "bare bones" affairs. Equation 18A.3 states that financial-sector equilibrium requires that the demand for money (L) be equal to the stock of money (M). The stock of money is given, according to equation 18A.4. In equation 18A.5 the dependence of the demand for money on both aggregate income and the interest rate is stated.

In the financial sector, too, there are too many unknowns (L, M, Y, and R) for a solution. Again, we express R as a function of Y.

At equilibrium $L = M$. We therefore rewrite 18A.5, substituting M for L:

$$M = 160 + .2Y - 20R \qquad M = L_o + hY - vR$$

Then, substituting the "given" value of M, which is $200 billion (or M_o):

$$200 = 160 + .2Y - 20R \qquad M_o = L_o + hY - vR$$

Moving the R-term to the left side and collecting the constant terms on the right gives us:

$$20R = -40 + .2Y \qquad vR = L_o - M_o + hY$$

Finally, we divide by 20 (or v):

$$R = -2 + .01Y \qquad R = \frac{L_o - M_o}{v} + \left(\frac{h}{v}\right)Y \qquad (18A.7)$$

Equation 18A.7 generates the *LM* curve (discussed in chapter 18), each point of which depicts an interest rate and the level of GNP at which the demand for money equals the (given) money supply. $(L_o - M_o)/v$ is the Y-intercept, and h/v measures the slope.

Equilibrium: Real and Financial Sectors Combined

We now have two equations in R and Y, 18A.6 and 18A.7, so it becomes possible now to arrive at a formal solution. Since things equal to the same thing (R) are equal to each other, we may combine the two equations thusly:

$$-2 + .01Y = 19 - .02Y \qquad \frac{L_o - M_o + hY}{v} = \frac{A - (1 - e)Y}{c}$$

Next, we must cross-multiply the right-hand version:

$$c(L_o - M_o) + chY = vA - v(1 - e)Y$$

Combining the Y-terms on the left and the constant terms on the right, and collecting terms:

$$.01Y + .02Y = 19 + 2 \qquad chY + v(1 - e)Y = vA + c(M_o - L_o)$$
$$.03Y = 21 \qquad [ch + v(1 - e)]Y = vA + c(M_o - L_o)$$

Finally, we divide by the coefficient of Y

$$Y = 700 \qquad Y = \frac{1}{ch + v(1 - e)}[vA + c(M_o - L_o)]$$

We can also determine the equilibrium value of R by "plugging in" 700 in either 18A.6 or 18A.7.*

$$R = 19 - .02(700) = 19 - 14 = 5$$
$$R = -2 + .01(700) = -2 + 7 = 5$$

These solutions are, of course, the same ones as those reached by the use of the $IS - LM$ curves in chapter 18.

---

* More generally:
$$R = \frac{hA + (L_o - M_o)(1 - e)}{(1 - e)v + ch}$$

Some Applications of the Model

Our grasp of the model can be enhanced by observing its behavior in response to a change in one or another of its elements. First, assume an increase of 45 in autonomous expenditures, from 285 to 330, changing equation 18A.2 to:

$$E = 330 + .7Y - 15R \qquad (18A.2')$$

If we assumed, as we did in chapter 16, an unchanged interest rate, the new equilibrium GNP would be calculated as follows, substituting Y for E and 5 for R:

$$Y = 330 + .7Y - 15(5)$$
$$.3Y = 255$$
$$Y = 850$$

We realize now, of course, that this constant-interest-rate assumption is invalid because of the interaction of the real and financial sectors. Instead, we develop a new "IS" equation as follows, based on the revised value of A:

$$Y = 330 + .7Y - 15R$$
$$15Y = 330 - .3Y$$
$$R = 22 - .02Y \qquad (18A.6')$$

Then we combine 18A.6' with the original 18A.7 (since there has been no change in either the money supply or in the demand-for-money function), solving for Y and R as before

$$-2 + .01Y = 22 - .02Y$$
$$.01Y + .02Y = 22 + 2$$
$$.03Y = 24$$
$$Y = 800$$
$$R = 22 - .02(800) = 22 - 16 = 6$$

In chapter 16, the multiplier formula developed was

$$k = \frac{1}{1 - e}$$

In the present case, this would mean 10/3. Note, however, that ΔA of 45 gave rise to ΔY of 100, implying a multiplier of just over 2.2. The difference is, of course, due to the fact that we are now considering the effects of the initial change in autonomous expenditures on R and also the effects of an increase in R on planned expenditures.†

---

† The appropriate multiplier for a change in A is

$$\frac{v}{ch + v(1 - e)}$$

Next, consider an increase of 30 in the money supply:

$$M = 230$$

Using this new figure, we get a new equation 18A.7:

$$230 = 160 + .2Y - 20R$$
$$20R = -70 + .2Y$$
$$R = -3.5 + .01Y \qquad (18A.7')$$

Combining the old 18A.6 with 18A.7' and solving:

$$-3.5 + .01Y = 19 - .02Y$$
$$.01Y + .02Y = 19 + 3.5$$
$$.03Y = 22.5$$
$$Y = 750$$
$$R = -3.5 + .01\,(750) = -3.5 + 7.5 = 4$$

Observe that a multiplier is also involved here, relating ΔY to the initiating ΔM. Since $\Delta Y/\Delta M$ is 50/30, the value of this multiplier is evidently 10/6.‡

---

‡ The multiplier formula, again based on 18A.8, is

$$\frac{c}{ch + v(1-e)}$$

MACROECONOMIC POLICY: GOALS, MEANS, AND CURRENT ISSUES

PART V

Relation of Policy to Theory
The Goals of Macroeconomic Policy
*Full Employment
Stable Price Level
Price Stability Versus Full Employment
Adequate Rate of Growth
Balance-of-Payments Equilibrium*

Summary

Macroeconomic Policy: Goals and Means

19

Beginning with this chapter, the emphasis of our discussion shifts again. We have studied the institutions of the financial system—the classes of private and government intermediaries, the financial markets, the laws, regulations, and practices that motivate and control them—and, more recently, we have looked at the functioning of the financial system within the framework of macroeconomic theory. Our main stress from this point on will be on macroeconomic policy, particularly as it relates to the financial system. In this chapter we shall examine the relevant goals of macroeconomic policy in our society; in the remaining three chapters we shall analyze the various means utilized for their accomplishment and some of the problems and issues that have arisen in the application of macroeconomic policy to the economy.

Despite this shift in emphasis, our discussion will nevertheless be closely tied in with all that has gone before. Rational policy, after all, requires a knowledge of both the institutions of the economy and the ways in which they work and affect each other—in other words, a knowledge of facts and theory. It is for this reason, by the way, that the policy section is placed back here, at the end of the book, following our examination of institutions and our study of theory.

The term *macroeconomic policy* actually encompasses *all policies that involve the utilization of federal government powers for the purpose of influencing aggregate economic performance.* We have no single measure of "performance" in this sense, but we make use of such criteria as the rate of change of the price level, the rate of unemployment, and the rate of increase in output. The Federal government has a number of means at its disposal for influencing the aggregate economy: the tax system, the level and structure of expenditures, direct controls of various types, the cost and availability of credit extended through the Federal Reserve and other agencies, and the terms on which Federal debt obligations (Treasury and others) are offered.

Powers and responsibilities with respect to macroeconomic policy are evidently shared by several entities. Although we often refer to "the government" as though it were a single decision center, the fact is that day-to-day and even long-range policy decisions are made at various points and executed at even more points. Policy regarding the level of taxes and spending, which we label *fiscal policy*, is ultimately made by Congress, though certainly influenced by the president and the machinery of the executive branch. Policy concerning the "packages" of terms (maturities, coupon rates, eligibility for purchase, and so on) on which government securities are offered is essentially made by the Treasury and is called *debt management*. The Federal Reserve Board of Governors is entrusted by Congress with *monetary policy*, that is, policy directed toward influencing monetary and credit conditions through means that have their primary initial impact on member-bank reserve positions. And, finally, *incomes policy* is sometimes instituted by Congressional authorization as a means of influencing directly all or certain categories of wage rates, prices, and other economic magnitudes.

As befits the scope and purpose of this book, we intend to concentrate on monetary policy. We cannot, however, exclude from consideration the other branches of macroeconomic policy. For one thing, they may at times exert strong influence on the financial system; moreover, they are often alternative or complementary means of achieving a particular set of macroeconomic objectives. To illustrate the first point—the financial effects of nonmonetary-policy measures—consider the fact that a decrease in government expenditures, reducing the demands of the government on the capital and money markets, could push interest rates down and create easier credit conditions for business. And with reference to the second point, inflation control is a goal that can be sought by several means, together or individually, including increases in tax rates, direct controls on wage rates and prices, and/or restrictions on the creation of new money.

Relation of Policy to Theory

Having just (presumably) spent considerable time and effort on the elements of macroeconomic theory, we have a right to know how theory is related to policy, especially monetary policy. Is policy simply the application of theory? Not quite. Any policy measure is, to be sure, based on the view of the policy maker(s) concerning the manner in which the measure is supposed to "work" in attaining its effect, and this view *is* theory, whether based on exhaustive research or the result of an intuitive hunch. However, even complete knowledge of the eventual effects of a proposed measure would not be sufficient to tell the policy maker whether he *should* apply this particular measure. Figure 19.1 will help explain what is involved.

Theory is seen to be only one determinant of a "policy action." The decision of the policy maker will also depend on the goals that he is

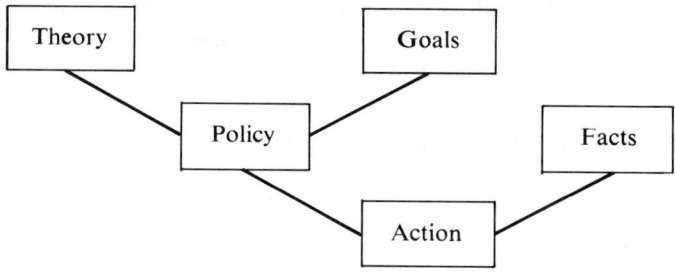

Figure 19.1
Elements in the policy process.

striving to achieve and on the facts—the current situation—as understood by the policy maker.

Utilizing Figure 19.1, we can understand why macroeconomic policy making is so agonizingly difficult. In the first place, the current state of *macroeconomic theory* leaves much to be desired. There is substantial agreement over the nature of the various macroeconomic relationships (those discussed in chapters 15 through 18, and others); but considerable differences of opinion remain over the relative importance of various elements. In chapters 21 and 22 we grapple with some of these disputes. Second, there is the question of *economic goals*—not just whether this or that would be "nice" but whether particular goals are competitive or complementary (a matter of economic theory), and, if competitive, which goal(s) should have priority and to what extent. These are extremely thorny questions that are partly economic, partly a matter of social ethics. Later in this chapter we shall examine some of the specific issues involving conflicts and priorities among goals.

Finally, there is ignorance of, uncertainty concerning, and disagreement over, *facts*. Under the heading of facts we include information regarding relevant institutions, practices, and working relationships among the parts of the system and also data on the current status of various measures of economic activity.

These considerations should help to keep students of economics— and economists—humble, a point effectively expressed by Paul Einzig in the following words. (Just prior to the quoted passage Einzig has been discussing some examples of theoreticians who had had the opportunity to serve in monetary policy-making capacities.)

> It does not necessarily mean, however, that once a monetary economist is given an opportunity to determine monetary policy either as a Finance Minister or as head of a Central Bank or as a "power behind the throne," he would necessarily set out to put his favourite monetary theory into operation. The moment he assumes a responsible post he gains access to a wealth of information which is liable to modify his views. Confronted with the responsibility for taking practical decisions that are liable to affect the lives of

many millions of people within his country and even beyond its borders, he might be inclined to reconsider his views in the light of practical considerations which he had hitherto disregarded.[1]

The Goals of Macroeconomic Policy

Look at a dozen recent lists of macroeconomic policy goals, and chances are that at least eleven of these lists will consist of the following four goals: (1) full employment, (2) price-level stability, (3) an adequate growth rate, and (4) balance-of-payments equilibrium. The lists examined must be recent, though, because our goals have been changing gradually over the past few decades, in response to a number of interrelated factors.

One of these factors shaping our goals (and the most difficult one to pin down) is our shifting *social values and attitudes.* Our ideas of the "proper" role of government have changed drastically, as have our conceptions of what constitutes equity—"fairness"—in the treatment of the unemployed and others not in a position to participate in the productive process.

Another important influence on economic policy goals is *economic theory.* As we have acquired greater knowledge of how the economic system works, we consequently have learned how alterations here and there would affect its performance. Some conditions, events, and developments that we formerly could, or had to, regard as inevitable, we now find that we know how to influence. Therefore, whether we like it or not, there are more areas in which we are required, as a society, to decide upon objectives.

Third, the existing set of *social institutions* influences our goals. For example, the fact that the Federal government has grown in economic size places it in a position to accomplish certain macroeconomic tasks that a relatively small government could not. Another illustration is the political power structure, which is inevitably an influence on the nature of, and priorities among, our macroeconomic goals.

Our discussion will be limited to the "big four" macroeconomic goals named in the first paragraph: full employment, price-level stability, an adequate growth rate, and balance-of-payments equilibrium. But we must be aware of the fact that there are other economic goals, which conceivably could receive priority over these at some future time—goals such as the break-up of giant conglomerates or a less unequal distribution of income. Further, there are noneconomic or "semi-economic" goals, which, in a sense, compete with strictly economic goals. Examples include national defense, greater personal freedom, improved social status for members of disadvantaged minority groups, and correction of conditions causing environmental pollution. The exis-

---

[1] Paul Einzig, *Monetary Policy: Ends and Means,* 2d ed. (Baltimore: Penguin Books, 1964), p. 407.

tence of these other goals must be kept in mind in any attempt to make sense out of the actual process of policy formulation.

The "big four" goals must not be thought of as some of the ultimate goals of society. Rather, each one of them is desired because of its contribution to the achievement of certain underlying social goals. This thought is well expressed by Walter Heller, former chairman of the Council of Economic Advisers:

> *Full employment* of our human and material resources. The term "full employment" stands as a proxy, as it were, for the fulfillment of the individual as a productive member of society, for the greater equality that grows out of giving every able-bodied worker access to a job, and for a national determination to demonstrate that a market economy, based on freedom of choice, *can* make full and productive use of its great potential.
>
> *Rapid economic growth,* our proxy for a rising standard and quality of life at home, and an ever-broadening base for our economic and political leadership abroad.
>
> *Price stability,* our proxy for equity between fixed and variable income recipients and, in today's outward-looking economy, a vital condition for maintaining our competitive position in world markets without trade restrictions.
>
> *Balance-of-payments equilibrium,* our proxy for promoting an international economic setting in which there will be free movement of people, commerce, and finance across national boundaries, and free scope for expansionary domestic policies.[2]

Full Employment

Our first goal to be discussed is full employment, which we shall define as *that level of employment which cannot be raised appreciably in the short run by increasing aggregate demand.* Such unemployment as remains at this point is, by definition, nearly all of a frictional nature, a byproduct or side effect of the operation of a dynamic, free-market economy.

Frictional unemployment exists in a full-employment economy because of a variety of factors, each one minor in itself but of considerable importance when taken together. Examples are the decline or failure of an individual firm, the exhaustion of a mineral deposit, the completion of a construction project, the obsolescence of a skill, the introduction of an automated process, resignation from a job for personal reasons, and the end of a particular harvest. However, even though the immediate cause of a person's loss of a job may have nothing to do with aggregate demand, the length of his unemployment obviously does, since, the stronger is aggregate demand, the more quickly, on the average, a person will ac-

---

[2] Walter W. Heller, *New Dimensions of Political Economy* (New York: W. W. Norton & Co., 1967), pp. 59–60.

quire new employment. It is no wonder, then, that estimates of frictional unemployment vary, although they generally run between 3 and 5 per cent of the labor force.

A number of measures have been proposed, and some have been adopted, for dealing with one or another type of frictional unemployment—job retraining, improved publicity on job openings, and assistance with relocation expenses are examples. However, since this topic really lies outside the realm of macroeconomic policy, we can mention these measures only in passing.

Except for employment agencies, almost no one benefits from unemployment. Obviously, the unemployed people themselves and their dependents are nearly always worse off than before.[3] But all society suffers from unemployment, too. Economically, the short-run cost is in goods that could have been produced by the human and capital resources forced into idleness; the long-run cost is in lost skills and in psychological unemployability of persons, caused by their experience of long idleness. Socially, severe unemployment can produce unrest and even violence on the part of those elements of society most seriously affected. Finally, there is a moral case for maximizing employment opportunities because in our society it is difficult for a person, especially the male breadwinner, to maintain self-respect and status without a job.

Full employment (actually, "maximum employment") is the only goal that is specifically recognized by statute. The Declaration of Policy (Section 2) of the Employment Act of 1946 (Public Law 304, 79th Congress) reads as follows:

> The Congress hereby declares that it is the continuing policy and responsibility of the Federal Government to use all practicable means consistent with its needs and obligations and other essential considerations of national policy . . . to coordinate and utilize all its plans, functions, and resources for the purpose of creating and maintaining, in a manner calculated to foster and promote free competitive enterprise and the general welfare, conditions under which there will be afforded useful employment opportunities, including self-employment, for those able, willing, and seeking to work, and to promote maximum employment, production, and purchasing power.

Although on the surface this hardly appears revolutionary, it represented a significant milestone both in the "official" acceptance of macroeconomic theory and in attitudes toward the proper economic role of government. By 1946, a decade after publication of Keynes's *General Theory*, the nation's leaders had become convinced that depressions are not "Acts of God," like earthquakes, to be borne as best we can, but are

---

[3] There are exceptions. For example, some who are "officially" counted as unemployed are housewives and semiretired people who accept seasonal employment, expecting to be laid off in slack season and to draw unemployment compensation for a period of time thereafter.

capable of being dealt with by application of the available tools of economic policy. Moreover, the view that the Federal government can best deal with deprssions by keeping its hands off the economy had given way to the conviction that the government not only *can* alleviate unemployment but *should* do so, by using all its powers to that end.

Interpreted literally, the first sentence of the Declaration of Policy would imply that the maximum-employment goal is completely subordinate to other "needs and obligations and other essential considerations of national policy," in that this goal is to be pursued only if doing so would be "consistent with" these other considerations. However, in practice this language has not interfered with the effective application of the act.

> Two decades have brought widespread acceptance of the spirit of the act, both inside the government and out, whatever the letter of the law. This is evidenced by a long series of Economic Reports of the President, by many statements by congressmen and high government officials, and by sweeping acceptance of the spirit of the act by observers outside the government—from newspaper writers to corporation presidents.[4]

Stable Price Level

Although not explicitly declared by statute to be one of our macroeconomic goals, there is no doubt of its status as such, based on statements by presidents, Congressional leaders, and Federal Reserve officials, reports of the Council of Economic Advisers, and arguments used in Congressional hearings.

The case for a stable price level would seem to be self-evident: the "evils of inflation" have been the subject of countless articles and books at all levels of sophistication. The indictment generally covers most or all of these points: inflation distorts production, destroys the real value of financial savings, discourages capital formation, and tends to feed on itself, becoming progressively worse. It also is said to produce social unrest and strife. While not denying the *existence* of the first three of these effects, most students of this subject are inclined to question their seriousness, in cases of mild inflation. The really drastic and socially disruptive effects of inflation that have been observed have occurred during, and as a result of, hyperinflation. As to whether inflation really "feeds on itself," we cannot be completely sure. If it is any comfort, though, there have been no observed instances of an economically advanced country which, although having no serious external problems or internal disturbances, simply inflated at a gradually increasing rate until its price-level movements were out of control.

There are certain effects of mild inflations, however, that are well

---

[4] G. L. Bach, *Making Monetary and Fiscal Policy* (Washington, D.C.: The Brookings Institution, 1971), p. 22.

documented.[5] One is that inflation arbitrarily "taxes" people on fixed incomes, inmates of institutions, and certain other groups. Secondly, inflation puts a nation's exports at a competitive disadvantage in world markets. Whether this result is considered beneficial or harmful will depend on the country's external position, though. If it is experiencing a substantial and continuing surplus in its balance of payments, an inflation would be most helpful in this regard. Under deficit conditions in the balance, however, inflation would intensify the problem.[6]

Price Stability Versus Full Employment

There are both theoretical and empirical reasons to believe that these first two goals—full employment and price-level stability—are not likely to be fully compatible. The theoretical basis was explained in chapter 18: lower rates of unemployment imply tighter labor market conditions, which are associated with stronger, upward pressure on wage rates and prices. Now we shall look at some results of statistical studies of the relationship between the rate of unemployment and the rate of change in the price level. Some possible courses of action in response to this situation are mentioned, too.

A growing number of studies have attempted to spell out quantitatively the "trade-off" between inflation and unemployment. This relationship is commonly depicted diagramatically as a curve in which rates of unemployment are paired with rates of price level change (Figure 19.2). The curve is generally called a modified Phillips curve, named after A. W. Phillips, in whose pioneering study of the relationship between wage-rate changes and unemployment this type of diagram first appeared,[7] but as "modified" to relate price-level changes to unemployment.

Figure 19.2 was taken from a recent study of this relationship by Jerome C. Darnell. We are not presenting it as *the* correct curve but merely as an illustration. According to Darnell,

> The curve shows that to have 4% unemployment on an annual basis we must be willing to accept at least 3% annual rise in the [Consumer Price] Index. ... If a 1.5% annual rise in the CPI is an acceptable definition of "reasonable price stability" we are not likely to see stable prices until the unemployment rate rises above 5%. ... If full employment is assumed to be in the range of 3.5 to 4% unemployment and as price stability is currently viewed, then we must conclude that these two goals are incompatible.[8]

---

[5] Joseph W. Conard, "The Causes and Consequences of Inflation," in Commission on Money and Credit, *Inflation, Growth, and Employment* (Englewood Cliffs, N.J.: Prentice-Hall, 1964), pp. 75–82.

[6] Chapter 22 contains an elaboration of this point.

[7] A. W. Phillips, "The Relation between Unemployment and the Rate of Change of Money Wage Rates in the United Kingdom, 1861–1957," *Economica*, XXV (November 1958), pp. 283–99.

[8] Jerome C. Darnell, "Another Look at the Trade-Off between Inflation and Unemployment," *The Conference Board Record* (January 1970), p. 20.

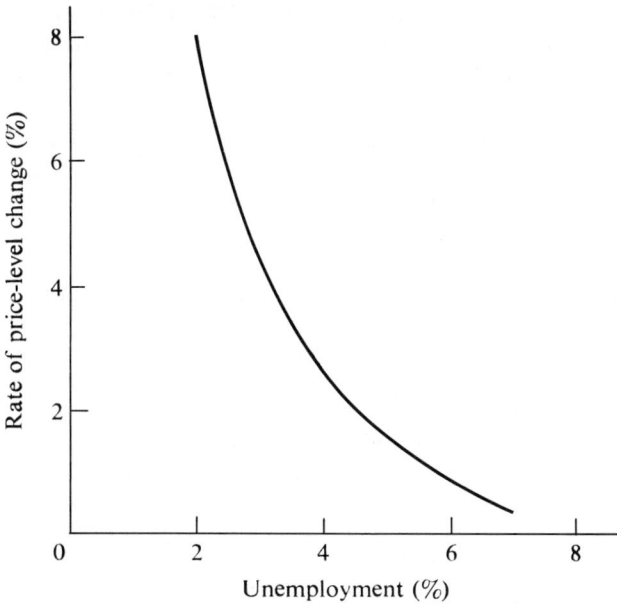

Figure 19.2
Modified Phillips curve.

Source: Jerome C. Darnell, "Another Look at the Trade-Off Between Inflation and Unemployment," *The Conference Board Record* (January 1970), p. 21.

The functional relationship depicted in this figure, even if accurate for the late 1960s, is not necessarily correct today. The curve has probably shifted rightward, in fact, indicating a worsened trade-off situation. That is, any given rate of unemployment will involve tighter labor market conditions, hence stronger upward pressure on wages and prices, than this same rate would have involved a few years ago. The primary reason for this view is that the labor force has undergone a profound change in composition. Women and teenagers constitute a much larger fraction of the total now, and these groups have chronically high unemployment rates.

Some economists are skeptical of the whole idea of a "trade-off" between inflation and unemployment. Milton Friedman,[9] for example, believes in a *"natural" rate of unemployment,* toward which the economy tends. His argument is that, if the economy is overstimulated by a one-shot inflationary increase in the money supply, the actual rate of unemployment may very well fall below this natural rate. However, money wage rates will then rise faster to catch up with rising prices, as continued inflation comes to be anticipated; and so, with labor becoming

---

[9] Milton Friedman, "The Role of Monetary Policy," *American Economic Review,* LVIII (March 1968), pp. 7–11. Also see Edmund S. Phelps, "Money-Wage Dynamics and Labor Market Equilibrium," *Journal of Political Economy,* LXXVII (July–August, 1968, Part 2), pp. 678–701.

more costly to employ, unemployment will gradually rise to its natural rate—but at a higher rate of inflation. The only way to keep the unemployment rate below the natural rate is by a continual *increase* in the rate of inflation.

A recent econometric study of the inflation process supports this view—the *"accelerationist" position*—in some respects and the Phillips curve analysis in others. A quotation from the Summary of Conclusions will explain:

> We find that the wage-price mechanism gradually becomes explosive once unemployment falls below a critical level, a level with the current structure of the economy in the range of 4 to 4.5 per cent. The initially incomplete and delayed reflection in wage claims of deteriorating price behavior keeps the rate of inflation from moving up quickly. But as inflation persists and the wage claims increasingly respond to the price factor, the wage-price spiral accelerates until it reaches an explosive condition. . . . Thus our findings support an "accelerationist" . . . view of the inflationary process if the unemployment rate is kept below its critical level. But at higher levels of unemployment the traditional Phillips Curve analysis remains valid. Thus, there is a similarity in our findings with the monetarist [that is, Friedman et al.] position under conditions of full employment, but a rejection of this view under slack circumstances.[10]

The authors of this study further emphasize that, in the short run (a year or so), the Phillips curve is nearly horizontal: the economy responds to policy changes mainly through changes in the unemployment rate rather than through changes in the rate of inflation. However, in the long run (a period long enough to allow the economy to adjust to a given initial rate of unemployment, which they estimate to be about four years), the Phillips curve for the United States probably looks like that in Figure 19.3.[11]

If the Eckstein-Brinner conclusions are approximately correct in principle—and there would probably be wide agreement that they are—what alternatives are open to policy makers facing this seeming dilemma: inability to maintain simultaneously both full employment and stable prices? Actually, several options are available. One is to "define the problem away." We could aim at something called "reasonably full employment," which we would define as that level compatible with price-level stability. But, based on Darnell's study, price-level stability would require a level of unemployment in excess of 7 per cent! To call this a condition of "reasonably full employment" is hardly likely to satisfy most of us. Another option is to hold, mainly on faith, the view that the two goals are naturally compatible and that, therefore, failure to

---

[10] Otto Eckstein and Roger Brinner, *The Inflation Process in the United States: A Study Prepared for the Use of the Joint Economic Committee, Congress of the United States* (Washington, D.C.: U. S. Government Printing Office, 1972), p. 1.
[11] Ibid., pp. 35–36.

Figure 19.3
The Eckstein-Brinner long-run Phillips curve.

Source: Adapted from Otto Eckstein and Roger Brinner, *The Inflation Process in the United States* (Washington, D.C.: U.S. Government Printing Office, 1972), p. 39.

achieve both goals must be due to unions, big business, government meddling, or the Communist conspiracy.

A third option is to aim at one of the two goals, in effect ignoring the other. For instance, to those who believe that we must have a "sound dollar," otherwise all is lost, the substantial unemployment that results is simply "the price we must pay." Others tend to stress full employment at all costs. A fourth option is to compromise, accepting less-than-desired average rates of unemployment and more-than-desired rates of inflation, perhaps by stressing first the one goal, then the other, depending on which one has deviated farthest from an acceptable position. This seems to be our usual pattern.

The fifth option, one that is compatible with any of the others, is to work on the conditions underlying the curve itself, through measures directed toward reducing the market power of organized labor and big business, improving the geographic and occupational mobility of labor, and lowering international trade barriers. Studies of the unemployment-inflation dilemma generally stress the fifth option as worth pursuing aggressively,[12] and recent Federal budgets reflect a small beginning in this respect. We cannot develop this topic further here, though, because it involves areas of economic policy—manpower, antitrust, and international trade—that are far beyond the scope of our study.

[12] See, for example, ibid., p. 44, and the references cited therein.

Adequate Rate of Growth

Full employment and price-level stability can be defined *fairly* well as policy goals, even though measurement problems are thorny. But the idea of an "adequate" rate of growth, besides involving difficulties of measurement, is also troublesome conceptually. Perhaps the best we can do is to specify as "adequate" that rate which does not generate strong pressures for an increase.

A relative latecomer in the list of macroeconomic policy objectives, economic growth has almost attained the status of an equal, in the company of the two goals just discussed. Growth became an issue in the presidential campaign of 1960, in the famous television debates between candidates John F Kennedy and Richard M. Nixon. Statements by national leaders, reports by research groups, and developments in economic theory—all have contributed to the rise of concern over our national rate of growth. However, it is no coincidence that the emergence of interest in growth occurred during a period when unemployment was abnormally high. Once the unemployment rate was reduced to an acceptable level, our rate of growth also seemed generally satisfactory, in the sense that there were no strong pressures to institute changes in macroeconomic policy solely or mainly in order to increase the growth rate.

These statements do not imply a lack of interest in growth and its results. Rather, it seems that the goal of full employment and the goal of adequate growth fortunately happen to have been complementary—so far. If we should ever arrive at a point where, even at (nearly) full employment, our rate of growth is considered inadequate, then we would have to face up to some very hard choices as a society, since most measures to influence growth involve certain sacrifices, such as a smaller output of consumer goods in order to increase capital-goods output, and higher taxes in order to increase resources devoted to education (investment in human capital).[13]

The goal of economic growth is still quite controversial, though. Strong arguments are offered on both sides of the question of whether we should have a national growth objective in the same sense as a national employment or price level objective. A positive growth policy is advocated for these reasons:

1. To strengthen us for competing in the international "arms race" without undue sacrifice with respect to other goals.
2. To enable us to provide assistance to developing nations.
3. To demonstrate to uncommitted nations the superiority of the free economy over controlled economies as a source of progress.

---

[13] An interesting nontechnical treatment of this topic is Edward F. Denison's paper, "How to Raise the High-Employment Growth Rate by One Percentage Point," *American Economic Review*, LII (May 1962), pp. 67–75.

4. To provide steadily rising (material) levels of living in the face of a rising population.
5. To furnish the means of meeting urgent social needs without any decline in private levels of living.

On the other side are several kinds of arguments. One is ideological, based on a wholehearted belief in a free-market economy, in which government plays a minimal role. Acceptance of this view binds one to a number of corollaries, including the notion that whatever rate of growth a free-market economy (such as ours approximates) generates is to be accepted and not tampered with. Harry Johnson, for example, argues thus:

> Growth, as such, is not self-evidently an object of policy in a free-enterprise economy; and the recent emphasis on the desirability of a high rate of growth seems to me to involve grafting on to a free enterprise system standards appropriate to a planned economy with military and political ambitions.[14]

A sociological-ethical argument is given by Kenneth Boulding, who, although generally in favor of growth, yet feels uneasy about it:

> The records are full of people who have been damned by a sudden increase in riches; whose wants were of such an undesirable character that, while they did not have the power to satisfy them, they got along fairly well, but as soon as the power to satisfy these undesirable wants was granted, licentiousness, debauchery, and ruin followed.... The same may even be true of nations and societies. Indeed, one may question whether it is not true of our own society; whether the tremendous increase in riches that has occurred in the last hundred years or so has not actually perverted out taste, debauched our cultural life, and permitted us to indulge in wars of a scale and extravagance that poorer ages never dreamed of.[15]

Moreover, there is currently a protest movement opposing economic growth on grounds that the social harm resulting from the increased environmental pollution accompanying growth will more than outweigh any benefits from the increase in the production of goods and services.

Balance-of-Payments Equilibrium

The final macroeconomic objective, equilibrium in our balance of payments, is of quite a different sort from the other three. It might even be called a *constraint*, something that can be an obstacle to the achievement of goals. This is a complex issue, even to define, in the case of a

---

[14] Harry G. Johnson, "Objectives, Monetary Standards, and Potentialities," *Journal of Political Economy*, XLV (Supplement; February 1963), p. 137.
[15] Kenneth E. Boulding, *Principles of Economic Policy* (Englewood Cliffs, N.J.: Prentice-Hall, 1958), p. 23.

"key-currency" country such as the United States, though we return to it in chapter 22.

Essentially, the problem is that, in attempting to raise or maintain employment, some of our desired measures would tend to jeopardize our financial position with reference to the rest of the world. As employment and GNP rise, we import more, thus reducing our net export figure. If this rise in GNP is also accompanied by an increase in the price level, our net export position will deteriorate even more. Also, if our attempts to increase domestic economic activity involve reducing interest rates, Americans will tend to look elsewhere for higher returns and will therefore import foreign securities. All of these developments increase the dollar holdings of foreign economic units while reducing our holdings of their money and short-term claims.

Summary

The "big four" macroeconomic goals—full employment, price-level stability, adequate economic growth, and balance-of-payments equilibrium—have gradually emerged in response to several interrelated factors: (1) improvements in the quantity and quality of economic data, increasing the public's awareness of economic conditions, (2) developments in economic theory, enabling better prediction of the consequences of particular policy measures; and (3) experience and familiarity with government stabilization policies, raising public expectations of government performance in the macroeconomic sphere.

These goals have a number of interrelations, some competitive, some complementary. The relation between price-level stability and full employment, in particular, has received much attention and thought at both theory and policy levels and appears to be a true case of incompatibility. Other combinations, too, may involve conflicts: full employment versus balance-of-payments equilibrium, for example, at least under circumstances that are all too likely. Illustrations of complementary relations (again, under certain circumstances) are (1) full employment and adequate growth and (2) price-level stability and balance-of-payments equilibrium.

Decisions concerning relative priorities of these goals—and other, nonmacroeconomic goals—at any particular time are, of course, hammered out through the political process. It is encouraging to observe that these decisions are to an increasing extent being made in consideration of arguments that are economically respectable, though we still have a long way to go in this direction.

Given these goals, how do we get there from here? This is the question that occupies our attention for the remainder of the book, as we turn now to a consideration and evaluation of the means used in the furtherance of our macroeconomic goals.

KEY CONCEPTS

Macroeconomic policy
Full employment
Modified Phillips curve

Accelerationist position
"Natural" rate of unemployment

QUESTIONS FOR REVIEW

1. "Economic policy may be defined simply as the application of economic theory." Evaluate.
2. List the "big four" macroeconomic goals. How are they related to more fundamental social goals?
3. What is the legal standing of these macroeconomic goals?
4. In cases of conflicts among macroeconomic goals (for example, full employment versus price-level stability), does Federal law provide guidance as to priorities?
5. "Full employment can be precisely identified as a situation in which 4 per cent or less of the labor force are unemployed." Comment.
6. If there is indeed an irreconcilable conflict between the goals of full employment and price-level stability, what options are open to government policy makers in attempting to deal with the situation?
7. To what extent are full employment and adequate growth complementary? If we attain a satisfactory level with respect to one of the two goals, are we necessarily doing the same with respect to the other? Why or why not?
8. List the pros and cons of economic growth as a macroeconomic goal.
9. To what extent are the goals of full employment and balance-of-payments equilibrium compatible? Under what circumstances might they be competitive?

SUGGESTIONS FOR FURTHER READING

Boulding, Kenneth E. *Principles of Economic Policy.* Englewood Cliffs, N.J.: Prentice-Hall, 1958.
Commission on Money and Credit. *Inflation, Growth, and Employment.* Englewood Cliffs, N.J.: Prentice-Hall, 1964.
Eckstein, Otto, and Roger Brinner. *The Inflation Process in the United States.* Washington, D.C.: U.S. Government Printing Office, 1972.
Friedman, Milton. "The Role of Monetary Policy." *American Economic Review,* LVIII (March 1968), pp. 1–17.
Mishan, E. J. *The Cost of Economic Growth.* New York: Praeger Publishers, 1967.

Monetary Policy

Fiscal Policy
Fiscal Macroeconomics
The "Full Employment Surplus" Analysis

Debt Management
Mechanics of Treasury Financing
Disposal of Surplus
Refunding
Debt Management Policy

Macroeconomic Role of Incomes Policy
The "Guideposts" Experiment
The "Freezes" and "Phases" of the 1970s

Summary

The Means: Fiscal Policy, Debt Management, and Incomes Policy — 20

The means utilized to accomplish the macroeconomic objectives discussed in chapter 19 are conventionally divided into four categories—monetary policy, fiscal policy, debt management, and incomes policy—each of which will be given our attention in the remainder of this book. As is the case with respect to goals, the question of which means are appropriate for which task has received different answers, depending on social values, the state of economic theory, and the particular set of conditions that exists in the society at a given time.

Illustrating the effect of our social values on the means question is the conflict between price stability and full employment. To solve the problem, all we need to do is (1) pass a law declaring that raising a price, or advocating such an action, is a Federal crime, punishable by death; and (2) establish a nationwide system of Federal work camps, in which all unemployed persons would be confined until employment could be found "outside." Thus we could obtain simultaneously stable prices and zero unemployment.

We also have the means to achieve a much more rapid rate of growth. For example, Congress could enact a flat 20 per cent tax on consumption, earmarking the proceeds for the construction of factories, roads, terminals, and other types of capital investment.

These two examples show clearly that our failure to achieve our macroeconomic goals is not due to economic factors—we have the resources and know-how to do the job. Rather, the obstacles are essentially ethical: society's values are such that we simply do not feel that the use of certain means is right.

The state of economic theory and the stage of development of the economy are two other important determinants of society's choice of means. Classical economics taught that an increase in government spending unmatched by an increase in tax revenue could not be depended on to stimulate the economy because the money obtained by government to fill the gap would come largely out of that which would have financed business investment. Now, with improved understanding of the economic process, we realize that this view is not valid: that the outcome of increased government spending depends on such factors as (1) the source of financing and (2) the rate of unemployment.[1] For this reason (and perhaps others), most of us have come to consider fiscal policy an appropriate means to fight economic slumps.

As an example of the influence of the stage of economic development on the means choice, consider the difficulties standing in the way of any attempt to use open-market operations in government securities to regulate bank reserves—our chief monetary policy weapon—in a country that has no government securities market and scarcely any commercial banking system!

These considerations should help explain the fact that the "mix" of macroeconomic policy tools changes over time and should lead us to expect changes in the future in response to developments in our social values, our economic understanding, and the size and other characteristics of our economy.

Monetary Policy

Since we shall devote all of chapters 21 and 22 to monetary policy, we need only introduce the topic here. We define monetary policy as *the branch of economic policy that seeks to accomplish macroeconomic goals primarily through influence over financial variables.*

In practice, the formulation and execution of monetary policy have been delegated by Congress to the Federal Reserve System's Board of Governors and, to a much smaller degree, the United States Treasury Department. Over the years since its establishment in 1914, the Federal Reserve has developed a kit of powerful tools that it uses to influence such financial variables as member-bank reserves, money-market interest rates, the money supply, and bank credit, thereby affecting the level and rate of change of GNP, the price level, and the balance-of-payments position of the United States.

The adjective *monetary* in monetary policy is admittedly too narrow to indicate the scope of this area of policy, but it is universally used in discussions such as this, so we may as well retain it.

---

[1] Roger W. Spencer and William P. Yohe, "The 'Crowding-Out' of Private Expenditures by Fiscal Policy Action," *Review*, Federal Reserve Bank of St. Louis (October 1970), pp. 12–24.

Fiscal Policy

Our definition of fiscal policy is *the branch of economic policy that seeks to accomplish macroeconomic goals through taxation, government expenditures on goods and services, and transfer payments.* Fiscal policy and monetary policy are considered the two most important categories of macroeconomic policy in the United States and most other Western nations. We have chosen to consider fiscal policy first because monetary policy, in practice, must accommodate itself to fiscal policy. The reason is that fiscal policy measures generally are subject to the ponderous process of legislation, a process simply not geared to prompt response to rapidly changing situations, whereas monetary policy decisions are quickly made and executed—and easily reversed.

One implication of this definition of fiscal policy is that a country can operate without a "fiscal policy." This would be the case when decisions concerning the level and structure of taxes and government expenditures are made without regard to their effect on aggregate economic behavior. In that sense, our Federal government operated virtually without a fiscal policy until recently.

Here, again, increased knowledge has brought increased responsibility. We can, in retrospect, excuse the government for pushing the economy into the sharp recession of 1937 by reducing government expenditures and simultaneously increasing taxes.[2] Today, this same action, under similar economic circumstances, would rightly be considered completely inexcusable, in view of the government's assumption of responsibility for working toward high employment, through the Employment Act of 1946, along with our improved grasp of macroeconomics.

The Employment Act of 1946 represented the birth of fiscal policy in the United States. Although it is true that, prior to this event, there had been laws passed and executive orders issued that were based primarily on macroeconomic considerations, these were rare occasions and also were not based on any underlying philosophy or statement of principles, such as the 1946 Act provided.

On the other hand, the mere fact that this act is now "on the books" does not imply that macroeconomic considerations have, since that date, received priority over all others. Any student of the legislative process would know better. Congress simply is not organized for efficient fiscal policy. In fact, the only committee of Congress specifically instructed to consider these broad macroeconomic issues is the Joint Economic Committee, established by this same Employment Act of 1946; and even this committee has no power to initiate legislation. However, it has had considerable effect on the level of economic thinking of Congress in two

---

[2] Monetary policy must share the blame for the slump. Despite continued rather high unemployment, the Federal Reserve raised reserve requirements because prices had begun to rise slightly.

ways: (1) It conducts hearings and makes published reports receiving wide circulation among influential people who, in turn, express their ideas—supported by the committee's publications—to Congressmen, (2) Membership of JEC members on important committees dealing with taxation, appropriations, and related matters, and circulation of JEC publications among Congressmen increase considerably the likelihood that macroeconomic aspects of legislative proposals will be introduced into the discussion.[3]

The president, too, is obliged to take macroeconomic factors into account in his taxing and spending proposals. In fact, he is expected to take the leadership in this regard. "Congress is not a program-making agency; no legislature is. Its job is not to act, but to react."[4]

Undoubtedly the Great Breakthrough in fiscal policy legislation took place in 1963–64. In January of 1963 President Kennedy proposed a substantial income tax cut, despite the fact that the Federal budget was already in a deficit position and Federal expenditures were rising. Admittedly, a tax cut would increase the deficit. Against these strong "political" disadvantages there were two selling points: first, tax cuts always feel good; and, second, the tax cut was designed to increase aggregate demand, thus stimulating the nation's output of goods and services and reducing the level of unemployment. Fortunately, Congress overcame its traditional misgivings concerning deficits and, partly due to the assurances of the president's economic advisers that the tax reduction would indeed stimulate the economy and generate additional tax revenues, passed the *Revenue Act of 1964.*

Unfortunately, President Johnson and Congress neglected the principle that fiscal policy works both ways; failure to counteract the stimulation of increased military spending by enacting tax increases to curb private spending was an important factor in initiating the long, frustrating inflationary period that began in 1965–66 and still continues.

Fiscal Macroeconomics

We should readily recall that government activities loom large in our national accounts and are an important determinant of the level of GNP. In this section we discuss taxation and government spending from a fiscal policy standpoint. It is important to keep in mind, however, that we do not label every change in government spending or tax receipts an alteration in fiscal policy. Only if a change—or, for that matter, a nonchange—of this kind is the result of a decision made in consideration of macroeconomic goals does it involve fiscal policy.

---

[3] Ralph K. Huitt, "Congressional Organization and Operations in the Field of Money and Credit," in Commission on Money and Credit, *Fiscal and Debt Management Policies* (Englewood Cliffs, N.J.: Prentice-Hall, 1963), pp. 480–82.
[4] Ibid, p. 494.

AUTOMATIC STABILIZERS Actual shifts in government taxing and spending schedules obviously affect the macroeconomic behavior of the economy. But the government also exerts a strong influence on this behavior even when its tax schedule and expenditure programs remain unchanged. There are a number of important so-called *automatic fiscal stabilizers* affecting the response of the economy to autonomous shifts in expenditure schedules. We may consider as an automatic fiscal stabilizer *any tax or expenditure program that moderates the effects of an autonomous change in expenditures on equilibrium GNP.*

The personal income tax is a good example. Suppose that planned investment were to rise substantially. The result would be to stimulate personal income. This increase in income would, in turn, give rise to increased consumption spending. The higher the effective tax rate on the increment in personal income, the greater the retarding effect of the tax on disposable income, therefore on consumption. However, the effect works both ways: in the case of a decline in incomes, the fact that tax liability also declines helps to sustain expenditures.

The personal income tax is one of the largest and most important automatic stabilizers; but nearly all our major taxes—state and local as well as Federal, incidentally—have a stabilizing effect, but of varying degrees. A number of programs involving transfer payments also qualify, including unemployment compensation and agricultural price supports. An increase in unemployment automatically triggers a rise in unemployment benefit payments, cushioning the decline in disposable income and, hence, helping to sustain the level of consumption expenditures. Conversely, as unemployment declines, the fact that a reduction in benefit payments partially offsets the increase in wage payments limits the speed and size of the increase in consumer expenditures. Thus, while we praise these stabilizers for their sustaining effect in an economic downturn, we curse them for their restraining effect in an upturn.

We can construct a useful illustration of automatic stabilization out of some of the "building blocks" of our chapter 16 model, adding another block or two as needed. You may recall that we used a marginal propensity to consume there of .9.

Now let us assume that we are moving from a situation where T_n (taxes, net of transfer payments) does not change with Y to one where T_n changes by 20 per cent of any change in Y. To keep it simple, let $Y_d = Y - T_n$, that is, gross business saving is zero. Under the old tax system, a rise in Y of $100 billion would generate an increase in C of $90 billion, due to the MPC of .9. Under the new system, however, this same rise in Y of $100 billion would cause T_n to rise by 20 per cent of this amount ($20 billion), thus limiting the rise in Y_d to $80 billion, and the resulting increase in C to $72 billion. The marginal propensity to consumer *out of GNP* has declined from .9 to .72.

Since the size of the multiplier depends directly on the MPE, which includes the MPC out of GNP, it is apparent that the multiplier will be considerably smaller under the new tax system than under the old one. Generalizing, the larger the ratio of the change in net taxes to the change in GNP, the smaller will be the multiplier, other things equal, hence the less responsive the economy will be to changes in autonomous expenditures.

There have been some attempts to quantify the built-in stabilizer concept. One such study, for example, reached the conclusion that the "present" (1966) Federal taxation and transfer structure will prevent 35–50 per cent of a cyclical decline in national income and 25–40 per cent of a cyclical advance, the exact amount depending on the numerical values of certain marginal propensities to spend.[5]

There is another automatic effect of the macroeconomic behavior of our tax-transfer system. Over the long run it exerts a *fiscal drag* on the economy.

> As the economy moves along the potential output path (that is, at a rate of growth of 3½–4 per cent per year), with reasonably stable prices, the Federal tax system generates an increase in revenues of about 6 percent a year. Unless this revenue growth is offset by reductions in taxes or increases in expenditures, it acts as a "fiscal drag" by siphoning off income. Actions by the private sector can conceivably offset this effect if businesses increase investment expenditures faster than the growth of internal funds, or if households reduce their rate of saving. But under normal conditions needed expansion may be prevented.[6]

Under certain circumstances, as the quotation suggests, this characteristic of our tax-transfer system can be harmful to the economy. When, however, society's demands for government-furnished services are expanding at a rapid rate, the enormous revenue-generating power of our fiscal system can be of great value in that it automatically provides money for a substantial annual increase in expenditures without the need for tax legislation or debt financing.

The other side of this coin, though, is the fact that this same automatic increase in revenues constitutes a powerful temptation to legislators to enlarge government spending regardless of its merits relative to private expenditures.

DISCRETIONARY FISCAL ACTION   Because of the "fiscal drag" effect and also because achievement of our macroeconomic goals may on occasion require stronger medicine than that provided "automatically," much attention has been devoted to the possibility of *discretionary fiscal actions*, that is, *fiscal measures intended to influence one or more of the determinants of the total expenditures function.* These measures may

---
[5] Peter Eilbott, "The Effectiveness of Automatic Stabilizers," *American Economic Review*, LVI (June 1966), pp. 450–65.
[6] Council of Economic Advisers, *Annual Report, 1969* (Washington, D.C.: U.S. Government Printing Office, 1969), p. 73.

take the form of changes in the tax structure (taxes and tax rate schedules) or in the volume of government expenditures on goods and services and/or transfer payments.

Previous discussion showed that an increase in tax rates (government expenditures assumed constant) would involve a decline in the total expenditure function, that is, a reduction in the level of planned expenditures (E) associated with each level of income (Y), therefore decreasing the equilibrium level of GNP, given the rate of interest (R). In terms of our *IS-LM* analysis, this tax rate increase will affect the *IS* function, moving the *IS* curve downward to a position such as that illustrated by *IS'* in Figure 20.1, so that it intersects the (unchanged) *LM* curve at a point designating a lower equilibrium GNP and a lower R, the latter result due to the reduced demand for money at the smaller GNP. A decrease in tax rates will, of course, produce the opposite set of results, as private expenditures are stimulated and the rate of interest rises in response to the increase in demand for money.

The same effects are produced on GNP by changes in the level of government spending. An increase in G shifts the total expenditure function to the right. In other words, at any given R, the real sector will reach equilibrium $(E = Y)$ at a higher Y than before.[7]

In practice, true discretionary fiscal policy has not exactly swept the field. A comprehensive study by Wilfred Lewis, Jr., of the fiscal actions of the Federal government during the first four postwar recessions

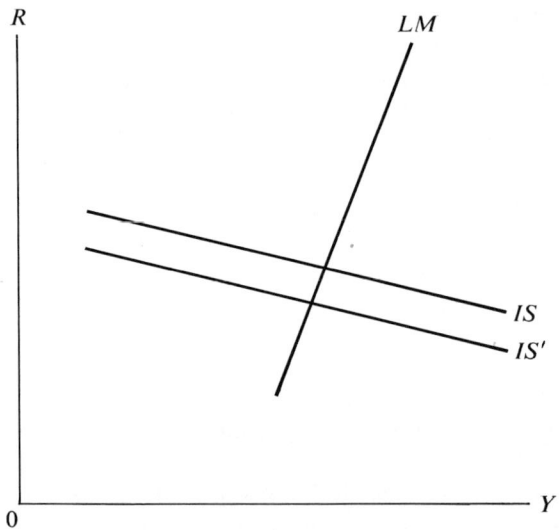

Figure 20.1
Effects of fiscal measures.

---

[7] Of course, the GNP is allocated differently in the two cases: in the second case a larger fraction of the GNP goes to the public sector.

turned up mostly negative results.[8] Perhaps the main reason for the failure of discretionary fiscal action to make a significant contribution to recoveries was the fact that, the political process being what it is, macroeconomic considerations are often far down the list of priorities.

Among the specific considerations cited by Lewis as interfering with fiscal policy considerations are prior commitments and long-term goals, concern over "balancing the budget," trust fund financing and earmarked revenues (linking expenditure levels in a given program to receipts from particular taxes), and uncertainty over the economic outlook. Where a fiscal action was taken mainly on antirecession grounds, it was generally an increase in expenditures rather than a tax cut, because the former could be justified on other grounds (defense, social need, and so on) while a tax cut was feared by lawmakers because it might be interpreted as a signal of real trouble.

In this respect, the Revenue Act of 1964, mentioned a few pages ago, probably constituted a major turning point. This was the first time Congress had passed a tax reduction measure on mainly macroeconomic grounds to sustain the pace of the economy—this despite the fact that the Treasury was already running a deficit and the tax reduction would increase it. Although there has been some backsliding in the years that followed, the corner was definitely turned in 1964.

> By the time the tax cut of 1964 was enacted, budget-balancing had ceased to have an important influence on fiscal decisions and compensatory finance had taken its place as standard doctrine and major, though by no means exclusive, determinant of action. This change was confirmed by experience in the years that followed. . . .
>
> The experience of 1966–68 confirmed the evidence of 1962–64 that fiscal decisions would not be dominated by considerations of functional finance exclusively. . . . Nevertheless, the 1966–68 experience did not alter the fact that by the 1960s compensatory finance had become the standard doctrine of fiscal policy to which action would approximate.[9]

The "Full Employment Surplus" Analysis

Based on the foregoing discussion, we can see that the Federal budget could move into a (deeper) deficit for two quite different reasons:

1. If the economy were to slump, the automatic stabilizers would reduce tax receipts and increase transfer payments. This we can call a *passive deficit*.

---

[8] Wilfred Lewis, Jr., *Federal Fiscal Policy in the Postwar Recessions* (Washington, D.C.: The Brookings Institution, 1962).
[9] Herbert Stein, *The Fiscal Revolution in America* (Chicago: University of Chicago Press, 1969), pp. 454, 457.

2. If the government wanted to stimulate the economy, it might enact a program of tax reduction and/or expenditure increases. The resultant deficit (or increase thereof) can be labeled an *active deficit*.

In an attempt to enable a clear distinction to be made between these two causes of a change in the budget position, the concept of the full employment surplus[10] was developed[11] and has gained considerably in popularity and usage. Briefly, the idea is that two (or more) alternative fiscal programs can be compared as to their macroeconomic effects by calculating the position of the Federal budget at "full employment" under each program. The smaller the full-employment surplus generated, the more stimulative is the program.

Consider the hypothetical fiscal program represented in Table 20.1 and by curve *FES* in Figure 20.2. Note that this model embodies the assumptions that (1) for every $100 billion change in GNP, the tax structure generates a $24 billion change in revenue and (2) government expenditures on goods and services are unaffected by GNP changes.

If $1,000 billion represents the economy's full-employment position, then the full-employment surplus (*FES*) is $10 billion, or 1 per cent of full-employment GNP.

There are several possible ways of increasing the *FES*, of course: (1) increase tax rates or the number of taxes, (2) decrease transfer payments, and (3) decrease government goods and services expenditures. The first two of these would increase the numbers in column 2; the third would decrease those in column 3, in all cases increasing the entries in column 4. But would it be advisable to attempt to increase the *FES*? It depends!

One factor on which "it depends" is the level of planned expenditures in the other sectors of the economy at full employment. If total

TABLE 20.1
Relationship of GNP and Federal Budget Position
(in $billions)

Possible GNP Levels (1)	Federal Net Taxes (2)	Federal Expenditures on Goods and Services (3)	Surplus (+) or Deficit (−) (4)
500	80	190	−110
600	104	190	−86
700	128	190	−62
800	152	190	−38
900	176	190	−14
1,000	200	190	+10

[10] Sometimes called the "high-employment budget surplus."
[11] See Arthur M. Okun and Nancy H. Teeters, "The Full Employment Surplus Revisited," *Brookings Papers on Economic Activity* (1:1970), pp. 78–79, for a brief account of the origin and evolution of the concept.

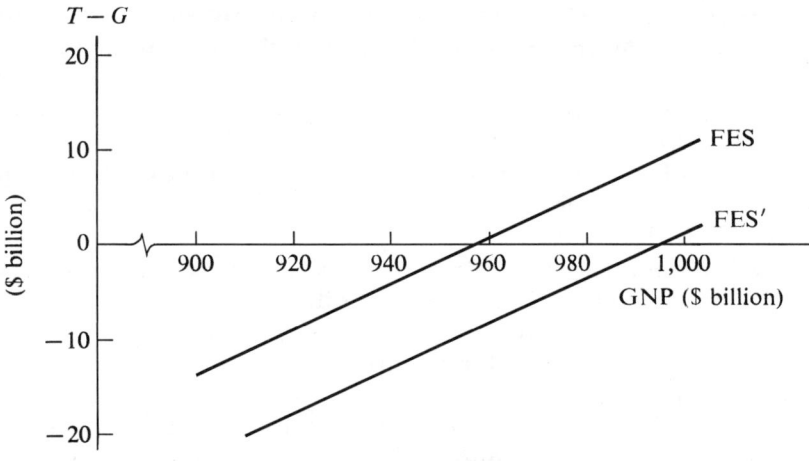

Figure 20.2
Full-employment surplus under alternative fiscal programs.

planned consumption plus gross investment plus state and local government expenditures plus net exports add up to $840 billion, then, by all means, let us consider using one or more of these methods of increasing the *FES*, because when $840 billion is added to the $190 billion of planned Federal government expenditures, the resultant figure—$1,030 billion—exceeds full-employment GNP. But if total planned expenditures of all sectors except the Federal Government is $780 billion, this figure, added to the $190 billion of planned Federal expenditures, totals only $970 billion, which falls $30 billion short of the full-employment GNP of $1,000 billion. In this kind of situation, the *FES* should be reduced, if anything, since any of the three means of doing so—tax reduction, transfer increase, or "real" expenditures increase—will raise the total expenditure function.

A second determinant of the desired *FES* gets us into the issue of the "mix" of macroeconomic policies. Let us say that the economy is in equilibrium at full employment and we have an *FES* of $10 billion. Theoretically, we could increase this *FES* without at the same time depressing the economy by increasing taxes and/or reducing government spending and simultaneously easing monetary and credit conditions through monetary policy, thus balancing a fiscal depressant with a monetary stimulus. The issue, then, is between a relatively larger *FES* and easier money conditions or a relatively smaller *FES* and tighter money. This is a difficult issue, one which we must defer until chapter 22, by which time we will have more background in monetary policy determination.

USES OF FULL EMPLOYMENT SURPLUS ANALYSIS   This analytical device is useful in a number of ways. First, it can help us distinguish clearly between the effects of automatic stabilizers and the effects of discretionary action. The potency of the automatic stabilizers is measured by the slope of the curve in Figure 20.2: the steeper the slope, the more powerful the stabilizing effect. Discretionary fiscal actions alter the position, or both the position and the slope, of the curve. A stimulative change (tax rate reduction or spending increase) will lower the curve, registering the fact that, at each GNP level there will be smaller surplus than before. A change designed to contract or restrain the economy will, of course, raise the curve.

These last sentences suggest a second use of this device; namely, as a means of describing the macroeconomic effects of alternative fiscal programs. By comparing the full employment surplus that would be generated by two fiscal programs (for example, the present program and one incorporating a specified change), one can determine which of the two is the more expansionary or contractionary and by how much. As a matter of fact, this was its original purpose.[12] However, used in this way, the device is vulnerable to the criticism that it does not allow for the financial implications of the change. It fails to take explicit account of the fact that an expansionary fiscal action, given the money supply, will tend to generate tightening credit conditions, causing a scaling-down or postponement of certain spending projects. Putting it another way, *FES* analysis implies a chapter 16-type model, not a chapter 18-type! Therefore, it is probable that the device tends to exaggerate the potential effects of a fiscal change.

A third way in which this device is helpful is in depicting the "fiscal drag" concept. With reference to Figure 20.2, as the level of full-employment GNP moves rightward year by year, the full-employment government surplus rises automatically. In other words—given the level of government expenditures on goods and services—the excess of the revenues that the government receives from the private sector over the government's expenditures, which constitute the return flow to the private sector, increases. As we saw a few pages ago, the difficulties of maintaining full employment grow accordingly.

Finally, this device helps us to solve a seeming contradiction between fact and theory in fiscal economics. The *fact* that in periods of recession the Federal government generally experiences sizable deficits seems to contradict the *theory* that fiscal programs of tax reductions and increased government spending, which increase the government deficit, are expansionary. Let us suggest the solution through an illustration, again using the figures from our model. Suppose GNP should slide from $900 billion to $800 billion. According to the model, the deficit will increase automatically by $24 billion—from $14 billion to $38 billion—as the government stands idly by. This is the often-observed real-world fact: the big deficit in recession.

On the other hand, suppose that the economy is at $900 billion and

[12] See Council of Economic Advisers, *Annual Report, 1962* (Washington, D.C.: U.S. Government Printing Office, 1963), pp. 77–78.

the government institutes a fiscal program to raise GNP to $930 billion by means of an increase in G. Assume that the required increase is $9 billion. This change in G is a true discretionary action; and we now have a different fiscal program. The entries in column 3 of Table 20.1 should be changed to $199 billion and all the entries in column 4 reduced by $9 billion. Also, the new curve on Figure 20.1 (FES') should be lower by $9 billion than the FES curve, indicating a reduction in surplus (or increase in deficit) of $9 billion at each GNP level.

The actual deficit, however, will not rise by $9 billion but by $1.8 billion (ignoring financial implications), because the $30 billion increment in GNP will bring in $7.2 billion in added tax revenues, thus offsetting most of the $9 billion increase in G.

Thus, in the first case, the increased deficit was the result of a decline in GNP—this is the "observed" case, the passive deficit. In the second case, the increased deficit was, in a sense, the *cause* of an increase in GNP, since the larger deficit was a consequence of an expansionary fiscal program. It is the latter situation, the active deficit, that the fiscal economists have in mind when they advocate "deficit finance" for a lethargic economy.

Debt Management

Fiscal policy, we have learned, calls for government deficits under certain circumstances and surpluses under others. Debt management picks up the story at that point. While Congress is responsible for fiscal policy, the United States Treasury Department has the responsibility for debt management. Its twin concerns are (1) arranging for the financing of current deficits and the disposal of current surpluses and (2) controlling the composition of the (previously incurred) national debt.

Debt management is a continuous process. Deficits and surpluses do not suddenly appear at the end of a time period; they gradually accrue during the period. There is even a seasonal pattern to the government's cash needs, as we saw in chapter 11, so that in the fiscal year the Treasury could be running at a surplus part of the time and at a deficit the rest. Moreover, individual debt issues are continually coming due, requiring decisions to be made as to the most appropriate type of securities to issue in their place. Sometimes, in fact, the Treasury decides to replace an outstanding issue with a new one before the old one matures, an action called advance refunding.

We can get some idea of the dollar magnitudes involved by looking at Table 20.2. Of the $270.2 billion of marketable securities outstanding at the end of November 1973, just over half ($139.4 billion) were scheduled to mature within one year. In fact, at least one issue matures each week.

Tables 20.2 and 20.3 bring out another point clearly: the "national debt" is not just one big undifferentiated mass of securities but is made up of a number of different categories, in most of which there are several

TABLE 20.2
Ownership and Maturity Composition of Marketable Treasury Securities, November 30, 1973
(in $billions)

Held by	Total	Maturity				
		Within 1 Yr.	1–5 Yrs.	5–10 Yrs.	10–20 Yrs.	20 Yrs.
All holders	$270.5	$140.9	$80.6	$27.0	$16.0	$6.0
U.S. gov't. agencies and trust funds	21.3	2.5	7.5	4.5	5.2	1.6
Federal Reserve banks	80.0	47.3	22.8	8.0	1.7	0.2
Private investors	169.1	91.1	50.3	14.5	9.1	4.2
Commercial banks	(43.0)	(13.5)	(23.1)	(5.2)	(1.0)	(0.3)
Other fin. institutions	(8.7)	(1.6)	(2.8)	(1.9)	(1.8)	(0.6)
Nonfinancial corporations	(4.5)	(2.8)	(1.3)	(0.3)	(0.1)	(*)
State and local governments	(10.2)	(6.4)	(1.8)	(0.7)	(1.0)	(0.3)
All other	(102.7)	(66.8)	(21.2)	(6.4)	(5.3)	(2.9)

Source: Adapted from *Federal Reserve Bulletin*, June 1974, P. A43.
* Less than $0.5 billion.

individual issues, and is held by the widest possible array of investors, individual and institutional. A substantial portion of the gross debt is not even owned by the public but is held *within* the Federal government itself by some agencies (mostly the Federal Reserve banks and the Social Security trust fund) against another (the Treasury). At the end of 1973, 44 per cent of the gross debt—$204.2 billion out of $464.0 billion—was internally held.[13]

Mechanics of Treasury Financing

Let us follow the balance-sheet traces of some illustrative debt management transactions now, in order to observe their effects on bank reserves and other monetary aggregates. We must simplify and also break up into separate steps what is almost a continuous process, but the end results are not thereby affected.

FINANCING A DEFICIT   First, consider this case: because of a reduction in tax rates, the Treasury's budget position moves from balance to a deficit of $1 billion during a given period. To "pay the bills" (step 1), the

[13] *Federal Reserve Bulletin*, January 1974, p. A42.

TABLE 20.3
Composition of the Public Debt, Selected Years,
1941–73
(in $billions)

End of Year	Gross Public Debt	Marketable Securities					Other Securities		
		Total	Bills	Certi- ficates	Notes	Bonds	Savings Bonds and Notes	Special Issues	Other
1941	57.9	41.6	2.0	—	6.0	33.6	6.1	7.0	3.2
1946	259.1	176.6	17.0	30.0	10.1	119.5	49.8	24.6	8.1
1962	303.5	203.0	48.3	22.7	53.7	78.4	47.5	43.4	9.6
1969	368.2	235.9	80.6	—	85.4	69.9	52.2	71.0	9.1
1973	469.9	370.2	107.8	—	124.6	37.8	60.8	107.1	31.8

Source: Adapted from *Federal Reserve Bulletin*, May 1972, p. A44, and January 1974, p. A42.

Treasury draws down its balances at the Federal Reserve banks, thus returning to the public $1 billion more than it (the Treasury) had received in taxes. We may take it for granted that this $1 billion is deposited in the banks, all of which, for simplicity's sake, are assumed to be member banks. The money supply increases by $1 billion, in the form of new demand deposits. Since the form that these payments took was checks on the Federal Reserve banks, the receiving banks also experience an increase of $1 billion in reserves. The effects on the balance sheets of the participants are shown below. (All figures in this and subsequent balance-sheet traces in this chapter are in billions of dollars.)

TRACE 20.1

Treasury		Federal Reserve	
(1) Deposit at Federal Reserve −$1		Treasury deposit Member bank reserve deposits	−$1 +1

Banking System			
Reserves with Federal Reserve	+$1	Demand deposits	+$1

Probably the Treasury, in order to replenish its cash balances, will seek to borrow $1 billion.[14] But what terms shall it offer? Numerous decisions must be made regarding the various characteristics of the security issue or issues to be offered. Some of these are quite technical and of little concern to us now; but one characteristic, maturity, is important because the shorter the maturity, the more liquid is the security, and different classes of investors have different maturity preferences. Although it is generally agreed that changes in the maturity structure of the national debt are of decidedly less importance than equal changes in its size, the matter of maturity structure cannot be neglected.

Suppose, first, that the purchaser of the newly issued securities is none other than the Federal Reserve banks. Below, we repeat step 1 (the Treasury's reduction of its Federal Reserve deposit) and add the results of step 2 (the issuance of securities).

TRACE 20.2

Treasury		Federal Reserve	
(1) Deposit at Federal Reserve −$1		Treasury deposit Member-bank reserve deposits	−$1 +1
(2) Deposit at Federal Reserve +$1	Securities outstanding −$1	U.S. government securities +$1	Treasury deposit +$1
(1–2)	Securities outstanding +$1	U.S. government securities +$1	Member-bank reserve deposits +$1

[14] Actually, of course, the Treasury might take care of its needs for "new money" along with its need to refinance one or more maturing issues; but, to keep our illustration as simple as possible, we are focusing on only one aspect of debt management here: the need for new financing.

Banking System			
(1) Reserves with Federal Reserve	+$1	Demand deposits	+$1
(2)			
(1–2) Reserves with Federal Reserve	+$1	Demand deposits	+$1

Financing the deficit in this manner (steps 1 and 2) results in an increase in member-bank reserves and a potential expansion of the money supply equal to several times the size of the Federal deficit. Good or bad? It depends. If the economy is in the throes of a severe recession, this method has much to recommend it, since it does not involve competition with efforts to secure financing for private projects. But if the economy is already in or near the zone of inflation, the evaluation is more difficult. The expansion of bank reserves and money paves the way for increased bank lending at easier terms and thus a larger volume of expanded private expenditures, resulting in both accelerated inflation (bad) and higher real GNP (good). So an evaluation should take into account both (1) the probable extent of inflation and expansion of real output that would result and (2) society's preferences among possible sets of values for goal-variables, as perceived by the policy makers.

Now consider the case of commercial banks' purchases of the newly issued government securities. If the banks had no excess reserves at the outset, the purchase of the entire $1 billion worth of newly issued Treasury securities would cause the banks to experience a reserve deficiency, since the demand deposits added in step 1 would have lost their reserve "backing" in step 2. The banks would therefore have to cut back on their credit to the private sector.

TRACE 20.3

Treasury		Federal Reserve	
(1) Deposit at Federal Reserve −$1		Treasury deposit −$1 Member-bank reserve deposits +1	
(2) Deposit at Federal Reserve +$1	Securities outstanding +$1	Treasury deposit +$1 Member-bank reserve deposits −1	
(1–2)	Securities outstanding +$1		

Banking System			
(1) Reserves with Federal Reserve	+$1	Demand deposits	+$1
(2) Reserves with Federal Reserve U.S. government securities	−$1 +1		
(1–2) U.S. government securities	+$1	Demand deposits	+$1

If the above illustration seemed highly unrealistic to you, that is encouraging! Based on what we learned earlier about bank behavior, it is inconceivable that a bank would deliberately overbuy government securities and then curtail lending to its household and business customers. Rather, what commonly happens is that the Federal Reserve, in order to assure the success of the Treasury's financing operation, will temporarily supply additional reserves to the banking system.

> While the Treasury could officially decide what securities it would issue at what rates, it has consistently counted on the help of Federal Reserve open market operations to keep the markets on "even keel" during large Treasury financing. In essence, the Federal Reserve has underwritten the success of Treasury issues by putting adequate funds into the market to assure generally stable interest rates at the agreed level.[15]

Thus, the banking system will find itself with increased reserves as a result of Federal Reserve open-market purchases of government securities and will thereby be encouraged to purchase the newly issued securities (among others).

Finally, if the entire $1 billion issue is purchased by that heterogeneous collection of business firms, state and local governments, individuals, foreign economic units, nonbank financial intermediaries, and so on, known as the "nonbank public," the effect of steps 1 and 2 on bank reserves and the money supply is zero:

TRACE 20.4

Treasury		Federal Reserve	
(1) Deposit at Federal Reserve −$1		Treasury deposit −$1 Member-bank reserve deposits +1	
(2) Deposit at Federal Reserve +$1	Securities outstanding +$1	Treasury deposit +$1 Member-bank reserve deposits −1	
(1–2)	Securities outstanding +$1		

Banking System			
(1) Reserves with Federal Reserve	+$1	Demand deposits	+$1
(2) Reserves with Federal Reserve	−$1	Demand deposits	−$1
(1–2)			

However, we would not be justified in concluding that, therefore, the total economic effect of a government deficit financed in this manner is also zero. The initial reduction in taxes that gave rise to the deficit consti-

---

[15] G. L. Bach, *Making Monetary Policy*, (Washington, D.C.: The Brookings Institution, 1971), p. 171.

tuted an increase in disposable income to the fortunate economic units involved, and we know that a goodly proportion of this increment will be used for increased expenditures. But in all probability the economic units that purchased the securities did *not*, for the most part, curtail expenditures on goods and services by an equivalent amount. Rather, the decisions to purchase these particular securities were probably *portfolio* decisions, involving simultaneous decisions (1) to reduce cash balances, (2) to sell other securities, or (3) to borrow to finance the purchase.

The initial effects of the $1 billion securities' offering are to be found in the financial sector: a fall in the prices of competing securities, hence a rise in their yields. The rise in yields results in reduced demand for money and also, in the real sector, the possibility of some curtailment of expenditures in categories that are sensitive to interest rates and susceptible to wide swings in credit availability, for example, construction.

We might mention, too, that the private sector now holds more wealth (the government securities) than would have been the case in the absence of the tax reduction. But, in the aggregate, the anticipation of added *yield* from these securities may be offset by the expectation of added *taxes* to pay the interest on them. The combined influence of these two offsetting factors on economic behavior is a disputed point at present.

Disposal of Surplus

The Treasury frequently faces the problem of disposing of a surplus, sometimes because of seasonal patterns, sometimes because of booming economic conditions, and sometimes because of a change in the fiscal program. The analysis of the effects of different dispositions of a surplus is very similar to the analysis of deficit financing, so we can be brief.

If the Treasury "impounds" the surplus—keeps it on deposit at the Federal Reserve banks (step 1 only)—or uses it to retire Federal Reserve-held Treasury securities (steps 1 and 2), the result is a reduction of bank reserves and demand deposits. The loss of bank reserves is especially contractionary, of course, since it could result in a severalfold decline in demand deposits.

Treasury		Federal Reserve		TRACE 20.5
(1) Deposit at Federal Reserve +$1			Treasury deposit +$1 Member-bank reserve deposits −1	
(2) Deposit at Federal Reserve −$1	Securities outstanding −$1	U.S. government securities −$1	Treasury deposit −$1	
(1–2)	Securities outstanding −$1	U.S. government securities −$1	Member-bank reserve deposits −$1	

Banking System

(1) Reserves with Federal Reserve	−$1	Demand deposits	−$1
(2)			
(1–2) Reserves with Federal Reserve	−$1	Demand deposits	−$1

If bank-held government securities are retired, bank reserves lost as a result of the Treasury's accumulation of the surplus are restored in step 2. Demand deposits have declined, but, since reserves are unchanged, we can expect the banking system to restore demand deposits to their initial level via the deposit expansion process.

TRACE 20.6

Treasury

(1) Deposit at Federal Reserve +$1		
(2) Deposit at Federal Reserve −$1	Securities outstanding −$1	
(1–2)	Securities outstanding −$1	

Federal Reserve

	Treasury deposit +$1
	Member-bank reserve deposits −1
	Treasury deposit −$1
	Member-bank reserve deposits +1

Banking System

(1) Reserves with Federal Reserve	−$1	Demand deposits	−$1
(2) Reserves with Federal Reserve U.S. government securities	+$1 −1		
(1–2) U.S. government securities	−$1	Demand deposits	−$1

Finally, the effects of the Treasury's accumulation of a surplus and its use of the proceeds to retire debt held by the public are (1) no change in reserves or the money supply but (2) a less liquid and wealthy condition on the part of the public than before.

TRACE 20.7

Treasury

(1) Deposit at Federal Reserve +$1		
(2) Deposit at Federal Reserve −$1	Securities outstanding −$1	
(1–2)	Securities outstanding −$1	

Federal Reserve

	Treasury deposit +$1
	Member-bank reserve deposits −1
	Treasury deposit −$1
	Member-bank reserve deposits +1

Banking System			
(1) Reserves with Federal Reserve	−$1	Demand deposits	−$1
(2) Reserves with Federal Reserve	+$1	Demand deposits	+$1
(1–2)			

Refunding

Sometimes Treasury debt operations result in some shifting of government securities among the three categories of holders. By rights, each type of shift should be analyzed as (1) a purchase of U.S. government securities by one or two classes of holders and (2) retirement of U.S. government securities held by the other one or two categories. However, because of the number of possible shifts, this procedure would be very tedious. Let us, instead, demonstrate the effects of one such shift and rely on Table 20.4 for information as to the outcome of other two-sector shifts. Our example will be (1) sale of $1 billion of securities to the nonbank public and (2) use of the proceeds to retire $1 billion of securities held by the Federal Reserve System (the upper right cell in Table 20.4).

The first step, purchase of Treasury securities by the nonbank public, reduces bank reserves and deposits: the purchasers pay by means of checks drawn on their bank accounts, and these checks are utilized by the Treasury to build up their Federal Reserve deposit accounts in preparation for the next step.

TRACE 20.8

Treasury		Federal Reserve	
(1) Deposit at Federal Reserve +$1	Securities outstanding +$1		Treasury deposit +$1
			Member-bank reserve deposits −1
(2) Deposit at Federal Reserve −$1	Securities outstanding −$1	U.S. government securities −$1	Treasury deposit −$1
(1–2)		U.S. government securities −$1	Member-bank reserve deposits −$1

Banking System			
(1) Reserves with Federal Reserve	−$1	Demand deposits	−$1
(2)			
(1–2) Reserves with Federal Reserve	−$1	Demand deposits	−$1

Step 2, the Treasury's utilization of its Federal Reserve deposit in retiring the Federal Reserve-held government securities, cancels out $1 billion of claims that each party has on the other but has no effect on the

TABLE 20.4
Effects of Shifts of Government Securities Among Classes of Holders

	To:		
FROM:	Federal Reserve System	Commercial Banking System	Nonbank Public
Federal Reserve System		Reserves − Demand dep. 0	Reserves − Demand dep. −
Commercial Banking System	Reserves + Demand dep. 0		Reserves 0 Demand dep. −
Nonbank Public	Reserves + Demand dep. +	Reserves 0 Demand dep. +	

banking system. The combined effects of steps 1 and 2, however, are a reduction in member-bank reserves and deposits, as Table 20.4 shows.

Shifts to or from the Federal system are the most potent of the six possible shifts, since they involve changes in bank reserves. Shifts to or from the nonbank public involve a reverse change in demand deposits in every case, since the public is exchanging government securities for demand deposits and vice versa. The importance of these changes should not be exaggerated; any such shift considered undesirable by the monetary authorities could be promptly offset by means of open-market operations.

Debt Management Policy

Debt management and monetary management are closely related in some of their aspects. For example, when the Federal Reserve sells from its holdings Treasury securities on the open market, the effect is to increase the public's holdings of these securities just as truly as if the Treasury had done the selling directly. In fact, the effects on bank reserves and the money supply are the same, too. When the nonbank public buys, paying by check, the ultimate[16] result is a decline in bank reserves and demand deposits. When commercial banks buy the securities, an equivalent amount of reserves (deposits at the Federal Reserve) is given up in exchange. Of course, the significant difference lies in the fact that, when the Federal Reserve sells, it does so in order to wipe out the reserves, whereas when the Treasury sells, its purpose is to provide the wherewithal for making expenditures (or to replenish its cash, drawn down as a result of past expenditures in excess of receipts—which, considered over a longer period, merges into the original reason).

Although the Treasury, along with other agencies of the Federal gov-

---

[16] Allowing time for the Treasury to withdraw the proceeds from the banks to the Federal Reserve banks.

ernment, is bound by the Employment Act of 1946 at least to take into account the macroeconomic effects of debt management activities, its concerns, like those of Congress, go beyond these considerations. Spokesmen for the Treasury have indicated their feeling that they must consider the interest costs of the debt and the need to "tailor the debt to the market," as well as the need to give due attention to macroeconomic policy goals.

For example, a debt management policy pursuing single-mindedly the goals of high employment and price stability would seek to keep long-term interest rates down during slumps, lest business investment be discouraged, and to push these rates upward during times of actual or threatened inflation. This would call for the Treasury to refinance maturing obligations and to finance any new deficits through the sale of (short-term) bills in recession and long-term securities in peak times. There would be little difficulty in carrying out the first half of the recipe—short-term financing is usually cheap and abundant for qualified borrowers in slack times. But for the Treasury to attempt to go into the market for billions of dollars of long-term financing near the peak of the boom would be to risk total demoralization of the market, because interest rates are already high and credit tight at such times.

As far as long-term Treasury financing is concerned, the moral is: "you can't win." Considerations of stabilization oppose sale of long-term bonds in recession; market considerations get in the way at the peak. This is the reason that some experts on the subject have (sometimes reluctantly) concluded that the proper debt-management policy for the Treasury to pursue is to strive to be neutral with respect to economic conditions, that is, to develop a balanced maturity structure of debt and attempt to adhere to it.[17] The job of carrying out policies to achieve macroeconomic objectives, then, would fall primarily on the fiscal and monetary policy makers.

Macroeconomic Role of Incomes Policy

Our final category of macroeconomic policy tools to be discussed in this chapter is *incomes policy,* which we define as *the branch of economic policy that seeks to accomplish macroeconomic goals through programs that influence the nonmarket determinants of wage and price decisions.*

In the United States, the use of incomes policy in the macroeconomic area has been aimed at two of the four goals—price-level stability and, indirectly, balance-of-payments equilibrium—though in several other nations incomes policy has been, and is being, used to foster more rapid economic growth as well. The measures employed in incomes policy

---

[17] See Tilford C. Gaines, *Techniques of Treasury Debt Management,* (New York: Free Press, 1962), chapter VIII, "Conclusions"; and Warren L. Smith, *Debt Management in the United States,* Study Paper No. 19 for the Joint Economic Committee (Washington, D.C.: U.S. Government Printing Office, 1960), especially Chapter VI.

range all the way from the gentlest appeals for voluntary restraint to the strictest and most detailed restrictions on price and wage changes.

Historically, the role of incomes policy has not been large in our nation, mainly because of our strong ideological preference for broad monetary and fiscal measures that do not bear directly on individual industries and markets and because these measures have generally produced satisfactory results. However, under certain conditions these broad policy measures have been considered inadequate to the task. In times of war, for example, we accept the argument that monetary and fiscal measures cannot cope with the awesomely large and complex task of placing the national economic machine on a war footing. Even under peacetime conditions we are coming to place increasing reliance on incomes policy measures to supplement monetary and fiscal policy. In the early 1960s, the purpose was mainly to prevent serious inflation; but in the early 1970s, the purpose was to cure, or at least alleviate, a stubborn case of chronic inflation.

The "Guideposts" Experiment

During the early 1960s, the Federal government experimented with an extremely mild form of incomes policy called *guideposts.* Introduced by the Council of Economic Advisers in their January 1962 *Economic Report,* the guideposts attempted to lay down the principles of responsible price and wage behavior. Essentially, they defined noninflationary wage settlements as those in which the increase in wage rates (including fringe benefits) equaled the *overall* rate of increase in productivity for the economy over the previous five years (specified as 3.2 per cent in the 1964 *Report*). Certain exceptions were provided for: higher wage increases when necessitated by difficulties of recruitment; lower, when there was evidence of surplus labor.

Price behavior was supposed to reflect *relative* productivity changes: in industries experiencing higher than average improvement in productivity, prices should decline accordingly, while prices in lagging industries should rise. Assuming on-target wage increases in each case, the price rise or fall should then enable profit margins to be maintained. There were other qualifications, but these were the basic elements in the scheme.

Several research attempts have been made to estimate the impact of the guideposts.[18] The general conclusion seems to be that the effect on price and wage increases was substantial, especially during the three-year period 1964–66. If this is the case, it certainly is a point in favor of guideposts. Other advantages are their noncoercive nature and their usefulness in fighting inflations that have strong nondemand-pull elements.

[18] For instance, G. L. Perry, *Unemployment, Money Wage Rates, and Inflation* (Cambridge: MIT Press, 1966); John Sheehan, *The Wage-Price Guideposts* (Washington, D.C.: The Brookings Institution, 1967).

Objections to the guideposts approach to inflation control center around two supposed characteristics: (1) the inevitable tendency of pressures for compliance to increase over time and (2) their unfair incidence. For example, in 1966 a group of Congressmen of the House Government Operations Committee pointed out that

> the guideposts that were only rhetoric in the President's 1962 Economic Report somehow became a specific numerical formula in the 1964 report.... They progressed all the way from mere enunciation to exhortation to extra-legal enforcement against price increases in certain industries, indifferently applied against wage demands in other cases, or ignored altogether when considered expedient.[19]

What would have happened had "normal" conditions continued after 1965 we do not know. With the heating up of the Viet Nam conflict and our failure to apply monetary and fiscal policy effectively, inflation began to accelerate. It hardly made sense to continue to call for 3.2 per cent wage increases when prices were advancing at that rate or more rapidly. Thus, the guideposts idea was allowed to expire quietly.

The "Freezes" and "Phases" of the 1970s

Although stricter forms of incomes policy have been employed in several other countries, until 1971 our experience with strict controls on wages and prices was limited to war conditions. There are a number of reasons why the United States shied away from them. On both ideological and "practical" grounds, business and organized labor dislike intensely this kind of interference with their freedom. Moreover, by preventing changes in relative prices in response to shifting cost and demand conditions, such controls interfere with the resource-allocation function of price in a private-enterprise economy. Administration of strict price and wage controls tends to be costly; the collection of information necessary for administrative decisions on wages and prices, plus the manpower and other facilities needed to enforce these decisions, would require a small army of civil servants in an economy as large and diversified as ours. And our experience with controls in wartime supports the conviction that, the longer such controls are continued, the larger the number of developing inequities and the greater the antagonism toward the system.

Yet the experiences of certain European countries with various kinds of incomes policies under various sets of circumstances teach us that, under certain conditions, incomes policy can be a useful tool of mac-

---

[19] Excerpted from the *Forty-first Report of the House Government Operations Committee: 1966*, reprinted in *The Wage-Price Issue: the Need for Guideposts, Hearings before the Joint Economic Committee* (Washington, D.C.: U.S. Government Printing Office, 1968), p. 31.

roeconomic policy.[20] One condition favorable to the chances of success of incomes policy is the absence of full employment. This condition implies that the existing inflation is not a matter of "too much money chasing too few goods" (although that may well have been the initiating factor) but a matter of "cost-push," that is, of powerful businesses "passing along" wage increases in the form of higher prices and powerful unions demanding and getting large wage increases based on price rises. Experience suggests that an incomes policy can sometimes break this kind of spiral.

Another favorable circumstance is appropriate monetary and fiscal policies, designed to avoid overstimulation during the crucial period in which the public is becoming accustomed to a lower rate of inflation.

Third, the support of the public, particularly the economic block such as big business and organized labor, is crucial to the success of incomes policy. And, finally, rising productivity is of great help. The more rapidly productivity increases, the more rapidly wage and other labor costs can rise without upward pressure on prices or downward pressure on profits.

On August 15, 1971, despite a strong ideological commitment to free-market ideals, the Nixon administration decided that the then-existing set of economic conditions called for the imposition of rather strong price and wage controls. The economy was not responding in a satisfactory manner to the conventional medicine of restrictive monetary and fiscal policy. Unemployment, to be sure, was hovering around 6 per cent, but the price level continued to rise rapidly. Whether or not persistence in monetary-fiscal tightness would eventually reduce price-level increases to a tolerable rate was a question to which the administration felt it could not afford to wait for an answer.

As seen by the President's Council of Economic Advisers, the situation was this:

> As the months of spring and early summer 1971 passed it became increasingly clear that the economy was not meeting the . . . goals of the Administration. . . . The rate of increase of real GNP fell to 3.4 percent in the second quarter—not enough to reduce the unemployment rate. . . . By May the unemployment rate had returned to its December level of 6.1 percent. The decline in the rate of increase of the consumer price index had not continued, nor had the slowdown of inflation been confirmed by other measures. . . . The second quarter also brought a rapid deterioration in the U.S. balance of payments position. . . .
>
> This combination of problems created a dilemma for economic policy. A rate of expansion and a level of unemployment less favorable than policy had projected could have been remedied by more expansive fiscal and monetary measures. But this remedy would have made the other problems worse. It

---

[20] Robert H. Floyd, "Incomes Policy: A Quick Critique," *Monthly Review*, Federal Reserve Bank of Atlanta (December 1970), pp. 176–81.

would have stimulated the still lively expectations of continuing or ever accelerating inflation and it would have speeded up the flight from the dollar. *The problems had to be dealt with simultaneously.*[21]

One element in the response of the Administration to the situation (as thus perceived by the executive leadership, at any rate) was to impose a ninety-day wage-price freeze.[22] This was succeeded by a less-severe program known as Phase II, which was supposed to bring about, in combination with other appropriate macroeconomic policies, the weakening of the public's inflation psychology—its conviction that prices will continue to rise at a rapid clip—thus making general price and wage controls unnecessary.

Very briefly, Phase II established mandatory controls on most prices and wages. Administrative machinery was set up to develop guidelines and procedures, to hear and decide requests for wage and price increases, and to handle other tasks in connection with the program. The target for the average increase in wages was 5.5 per cent, a figure obtained by adding the estimated rate of growth of 3 per cent to an interim target rate of inflation of between 2 and 3 per cent.

Phase II, which remained in effect from November 1971 to January 1973, seems to have succeeded reasonably well, although this verdict is not unanimous. Two early statistical studies of this period concluded that the controls did, in fact, reduce inflation to a rate well below what it otherwise would have been.[23]

On January 11, 1973, President Nixon instituted Phase III. This new phase was far more lenient with respect to the enforcement of standards; and the rate of inflation rose rapidly. It is impossible to judge the extent to which Phase III was responsible for the resurgence of inflation, though, because several powerful inflationary factors were operating on the economy at the same time, including (1) some "catch-up" price increases that had been suppressed during Phase II; (2) a belief on the part of many businessmen that a stricter Phase IV would soon be imposed, hence this could be the last chance for some time to obtain "needed" price increases; (3) the devaluation of the dollar, which stimulated exports and discouraged imports while raising their costs; (4) a cyclical expansion in aggregate demand, foreign as well as domestic; (5) fairly rapid growth in the money supply; and (6) tight conditions in world food markets due to poor harvests and rising world demands.

---

[21] *Economic Report of the President* (Washington, D.C.: U.S. Government Printing Office, 1972), p. 22. Emphasis added.

[22] The other elements, which we will not discuss at this point, were (1) a 10 per cent import surcharge, (2) a suspension of the gold convertibility of the dollar, and (3) a package of fiscal proposals.

[23] Barry Bosworth, "Phase II: The U.S. Experiment with an Income Policy," *Brookings Papers on Economic Activity*, (II: 1972), pp. 343–83; and Robert J. Gordon, "Wage-Price Controls and the Shifting Phillips Curve," ibid., pp. 385–421.

Then, on June 13, 1973, the President imposed another freeze on prices, which was succeeded sixty days later by Phase IV, a period of gradual decontrol of prices and wages, as particular industries were deemed "ready" for freedom. The months since then have seen no abatement in the rate of inflation; but the effects of the recent Arab oil embargo and other aspects of the "energy crisis" that the nation is undergoing, superimposed on the continuing influences of the factors listed in the previous paragraph, render any attempt to assess incomes policy on the basis of our 1970s experience extremely hazardous, if not downright foolhardy.

Summary

Monetary policy is the macroeconomic "policy of last resort"; that is, monetary policy makers must take into account developments in the public sector, involving policies other than monetary policy, as well as developments originating in the private sector, in making their decisions. Therefore, before we focus on monetary policy, we must first become familiar with the other major means for accomplishing macroeconomic goals: fiscal policy, debt management, and incomes policy.

1. Fiscal policy, involving the use of tax and expenditure programs for macroeconomic purposes, has not been with us very long. Probably the first major clear fiscal policy measure was the Revenue Act of 1964, which provided for reduction in tax rates in the face of budget deficits in order to stimlate the economy. Fiscal policy affects the behavior of the economy largely through changing sectoral expenditure functions: the G-function directly through changes in government expenditures on goods and services, and private-sector functions indirectly through changes in tax and transfer programs.
2. *Debt management* is the Treasury's task, a continuous one. Every week one or more individual debt issues come due. Moreover, because the debt fluctuates seasonally and has increased secularly, decisions must be made as to terms on new securities, disposal of surpluses, and so on. The effects on bank reserves and on the nation's money supply resulting from a deficit or surplus will depend on which classes of economic units purchase the new issues or replace retired issues with cash: changes in Federal Reserve-held debt have the largest impact; changes in debt held by the public, the smallest. Experts consider the potential role of debt management in stabilization policy to be relatively modest.
3. *Incomes policy*, though not widely accepted on a continuing basis in the United States, was utilized in the early 1960s (the "guideposts" program) and again in the early 1970s. The

major purpose of the latter episode was to reduce inflationary expectations that had been generated by the experience of several years of rising price levels. Such expectations, built into the cost-price structure, tended to result in price and wage increases that were not "justified" by current supply-demand conditions. The efficacy of these attempts is still the subject of intense disagreement.

KEY CONCEPTS

Monetary policy
Fiscal policy
Employment Act of 1946
Revenue Act of 1964
Automatic fiscal stabilizers
Fiscal drag
Discretionary fiscal action

Passive deficit
Active deficit
Full employment surplus analysis
Debt management
Refunding
Incomes policy
Wage-price "guideposts"

QUESTIONS FOR REVIEW

1. What factors influence society's choice of means for achieving its macroeconomic goals? Would you expect this choice to change over time? Why?
2. Can a country operate without a "fiscal policy"? Explain.
3. "In macroeconomic policy, increased knowledge brings increased responsibility." Explain and illustrate.
4. Two milestones in fiscal policy were (a) the Employment Act of 1946 and (b) the Revenue Act of 1964. What was the significance of each of these?
5. In what way does the personal income tax act as an automatic stabilizer? Do such stabilizers speed or retard progress from a recession to full employment?
6. Is "fiscal drag" more closely related to automatic stabilizers or to discretionary fiscal action?
7. Do increases in tax rates exert their primary effects on the IS curve or the LM curve?
8. "The higher the full employment surplus, the better." Do you agree? Explain.
9. To what uses has the full employment surplus analysis been put? What possible hazards are involved in its use?
10. What government agency or agencies actually make fiscal policy? What agency or agencies manage the Federal debt?
11. If the Treasury must obtain financing for a deficit and wishes to help the economy recover from an inflation, should it tailor the terms of

its new securities to appeal to banks (which, we assume, have ample excess reserves) or to the public? Why?
12. If the Treasury accumulates a surplus and is attempting to alleviate inflation, should it retire debt held by the public or by the Federal Reserve? Why?
13. What are some of the disadvantages of incomes policy? Under what conditions might it work?

SUGGESTIONS FOR FURTHER READING

Bach, G. Leland *Making Monetary Policy*. Washington, D.C.: The Brookings Institution, 1971.
Beard, Thomas. *U.S. Treasury Advance Refunding*. Washington, D.C.: Board of Governors, Federal Reserve System, 1966.
Commission on Money and Credit. *Fiscal and Debt Management Policies*. Englewood Cliffs, N.J : Prentice-Hall. 1963.
———. *Stabilization Policies*. Englewood Cliffs, N.J.: Prentice-Hall, 1963.
Floyd, Robert H. "Incomes Policy: A Quick Critique," *Monthly Review*, Federal Reserve Bank of Atlanta (December 1970), pp. 174–81.
Gaines, Tilford C. *Techniques of Treasury Debt Management*. New York: Free Press, 1962.
Lewis, Wilfred, Jr. *Federal Fiscal Policy in the Postwar Recessions*. Washington, D.C.: The Brookings Institution, 1962.
Okun, Arthur, and Nancy H. Teeters. "The Full Employment Surplus Revisited." *Brookings Papers on Economic Activity* 1 (1970) pp. 77–110.
Schultz, George P., and Robert Z. Aliber (eds.). *Guidelines, Informal Controls and the Market Place*. Chicago: University of Chicago Press, 1969.
Sheehan, John. *The Wage-Price Guideposts*. Washington, D.C.: The Brookings Institution, 1967.
Stein, Herbert. *The Fiscal Revolution in America*. Chicago: University of Chicago Press, 1969.
Weber, Arnold R. *In Pursuit of Price Stability: The Wage-Price Freeze of 1971*. Washington, D.C.: The Brookings Institution, 1974.

Monetary Policy Formation
Ultimate Goals and Intermediate Indicators
The Inside Lag

Federal Reserve Actions: Alternatives and Evaluation
Open-Market Operations
The Discount Mechanism
Reserve Requirements
The General Weapons: A Comparison
Other Monetary Control Weapons: Selective Credit Controls
Moral Suasion

Federal Reserve Actions and the Economy's Response
Effect on Financial and Real Sectors
Monetarist Challenge to Keynesian Orthodoxy
The "Outside Lag"
Monetary Policy as Automatic Stabilizer

Summary

The Means: Monetary Policy

21

Most economists would agree that fiscal policy is a potent weapon of macroeconomic policy,[1] but it is subject to one serious deficiency. Because the machinery for its implementation works ponderously and uncertainly (so much so that for much of our history it is doubtful that there really *was* a fiscal policy, in our sense of the term), it cannot be relied on as a consistent weapon of macroeconomic policy. Debt management policy is generally considered to be of limited usefulness, partly because moderate shifts in the structure of the debt do not seem effective in influencing aggregate expenditures, partly because the Treasury sometimes experiences a conflict of goals, preventing it from concentrating entirely on macroeconomic policy goals. And incomes policy is probably not acceptable to most Americans as a continuing means of accomplishing macroeconomic objectives.

Thus we finally come now to the last of the macroeconomic policy categories: monetary policy. Alone among these categories, monetary policy is conducted consciously and continually with a view to affecting the aggregate economy. For this reason, and also because it operates primarily through the financial system, we are devoting far more space to it than to any of the other categories.

---
[1] An important dissenting view, that of the monetarists, will be examined later in the chapter.

Monetary policy is, for all practical purposes, the responsibility of the Federal Reserve Board of Governors. In its conduct of monetary policy, the Board is *almost* free to pursue single-mindedly the macroeconomic goals discussed in chapter 19. The only qualifications are its responsibilities to prevent disorderly conditions in the financial markets and to maintain an "even keel" in the markets during periods of major Treasury financing operations. Because of the relative freedom of the Federal Reserve from conflicts between macroeconomic goals and other goals and constraints and because of the flexibility and quick reversibility of Federal Reserve actions, the Federal Reserve has the de facto responsibility to be the "policy maker of last resort," so to speak, adjusting not only to developments in the private economy but also to Congressional and Treasury actions that have macroeconomic implications.

The Federal Reserve authorities cannot affect the economy by increasing or decreasing the system's purchases of goods and services by billions of dollars. Nor do they have the power to coerce households and businesses directly to raise or lower their expenditures. Yet it is generally agreed by economists that the Federal Reserve is able to exert a powerful influence on macroeconomic variables—GNP, employment, and the price level. The process through which this influence works is quite complex and, not surprisingly, controversial at several points; but its importance more than justifies our efforts to comprehend it.

Fortunately, we have already examined nearly all the individual elements of this process—in chapters 2, 7, and 14 through 18. Virtually all that remains is to put them together now. Following a brief summary of the process through which monetary policy decisions are made and a glance at some of the issues involved, we shall examine the means by which the Federal Reserve influences the financial system and the channels through which these financial effects spill over into the real sector, influencing the behavior of economic aggregates. Then, in chapter 22, we turn to two other important aspects of the effects of monetary policy—its international impact and its sectoral incidence—concluding with a recapitulation of our entire macroeconomic policy discussion.

Monetary Policy Formation

By law, the Board of Governors is the policy-making authority of the Federal Reserve System. Changes in reserve requirements of member banks originate with the board; and proposals for changes in the discount rate, although "on paper" initiated by the individual Reserve banks, must be approved by the board. Sometimes even the proposals themselves are prompted by the board's suggestion. However, as we learned in chapter 7, decisions regarding open-market policy—the key weapon of the system—are made not directly by the board but by the

Federal Open Market Committee (FOMC), consisting of the seven members of the board and five presidents of the Reserve banks.

Since the FOMC meets frequently—approximately every four weeks, with telephone contacts between meetings—and since the entire board is represented at these meetings, the FOMC has evolved into *the* forum at which economic intelligence is presented and discussed and monetary policy decisions are debated and made.

These policy makers take into account a substantial number of economic time series—with recent past, estimated present, and projected values. A quotation from an "insider" brings this out:

> In reaching policy decisions, the Open Market Committee not only pays attention to the real economy—GNP and the balance of payments—but it also considers a broad range of interest rates and monetary measures. Among the monetary measures, there are the various reserve measures—total reserves, nonborrowed reserves, excess reserves, and free or net borrowed reserves. Next are the measures of money. . . . Finally, there are the credit measures . . . ranging on out to total credit in the economy and the flow of funds.[2]

Forecasts are of particular importance because of the lags in the effects of monetary policy actions on the behavior of the macroeconomic aggregates.

Ultimate Goals and Intermediate Indicators

The ultimate goals of the Federal Reserve in its conduct of monetary policy are those macroeconomic goals discussed in chapter 19: price-level stability, full employment, adequate growth, and balance-of-payments equilibrium. The Federal Reserve has acknowledged this repeatedly in its publications, in testimony by board members before Congressional committees, and on other occasions.

A common view of students of macroeconomic policy is that the Federal Reserve tends to stress price-level stability relative to full employment and rapid growth more than do other governmental agencies. Yet no study of Federal Reserve policy making has found evidence to support this view. An examination of studies bearing on this subject led one investigator to this conclusion:

> These studies suggest that the Federal Reserve does in fact pursue multiple goals, but that the goals of full employment and rapid growth are of primary importance, suggesting further that a policy trade-off exists between full employment and growth, on the one hand, and stable prices and external equilibrium on the other.[3]

[2] Alan R. Holmes, "Operational Constraints on the Stabilization of Money Supply Growth," in *Controlling Monetary Aggregates* (Boston: Federal Reserve Bank of Boston, 1969), p. 66.
[3] Dwayne Wrightsman, *An Introduction to Monetary Theory and Policy* (New York: Free Press, 1971), p. 188. See references given there.

At any given time, the Federal Reserve tends to concentrate on that goal from which the economy's actual position deviates most. Thus, when inflation seems the most serious problem, Federal Reserve policy tends to be uncompromisingly restrictive; "but all studies agree that substantial and rising unemployment dominated policy actions, when it appeared, albeit with a lag in some cases.[4]

The tools of monetary policy at the disposal of the Federal Reserve operate highly indirectly on the real sector, as we know, through a lengthy "chain of causation." Some of the major links in this chain are indicated in this diagram:

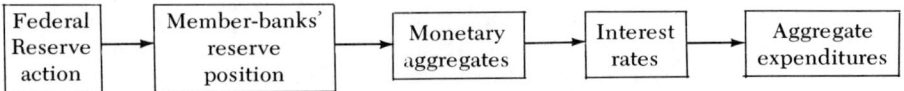

If the reserve authorities move to increase bank reserves, the result will almost certainly be an increase in the size of the *monetary aggregates* (the money supply, or money plus bank time deposits, or bank credit, and so on) and a decrease in interest rates (and an easing of other credit terms and conditions), which will induce an opposite movement—an increase—in planned expenditures.

Actually, the linkages are a good deal more numerous and complex than this,[5] but this scheme will suffice for now. The point is that the monetary policy decision makers require far more than a knowledge of the *direction* of the effects of their actions. Ideally, they also should know the *strength* and *time pattern* of these effects as well. But monetary theory is not that highly developed. Therefore, in utilizing its available tools in order to move the economy closer to the achievement of the macroeconomic goals, the Federal Reserve must rely on certain *indicators* to enable it to monitor the effects of policy so that "midcourse corrections" can be taken in case the Federal Reserve's actions turn out to be stronger or weaker than anticipated.

Ideally, an indicator should have the following characteristics:[6]

1. It should be an important link in the "chain of causation."
2. It should be positioned near the beginning of the chain.
3. Information on its magnitude should be available frequently and promptly.
4. The primary influence on it should be Federal Reserve actions.
5. There should be minimum feedback on it from the "real" sector.

[4] G. L. Bach, *Making Monetary Policy*, (Washington, D.C.: The Brookings Institution, 1971), p. 166, n. 8.
[5] See "Open Market Operations and the Monetary and Credit Aggregates—1971." *Monthly Review*, Federal Reserve Bank of New York, (April 1972), pp. 79–94.
[6] This list was adapted from George G. Kaufman, "Indicators of Monetary Policy: Theory and Evidence," *National Banking Review*, IV (June 1967), pp. 482–83.

If we look at the "chain of causation" depicted earlier, we can see that there are three possible kinds of indicators: (1) measures of member-bank reserve position, (2) measures of money or bank credit, and (3) measures of interest rates. In each category there are several possibilities; most of these have their defenders and detractors on theoretical and/or empirical grounds.

There is no lack of indicator candidates that meet the first three criteria. We have excellent, prompt, and frequent information available on a wide variety of interest rates, monetary aggregates, and measures of bank reserves (total reserves, net free reserves, nonborrowed reserves, and member-bank reserves plus currency—the so-called "monetary base").

The difficulties come with criteria (4) and (5). *All* indicators are subject, to a greater or lesser degree, to non-Federal Reserve influences; and feedback from the real sector, never entirely absent, is especially important in the case of interest rates. As a result, two indicators may, and sometimes do, give conflicting signals. In fact, a recent study, in which eight frequently used indicators were compared, by pairs, over the 1965–69 period reached this conclusion:

> Most of the indicator pairs agreed in 35 to 45 of the 60 months. . . . Moreover, separate calculations for each of the five years show that the degree of agreement for each pair of indicators varies considerably from year to year.[7]

In case of conflicting signals, which indicator should the monetary authorities rely on? Consider this hypothetical case. For several months the Federal Reserve has been pursuing an expansionary policy, pumping reserves into the system at a more rapid rate than usual; and the indicators have been reflecting this policy: falling interest rates, money supply expanding at a 6 per cent annual rate, and so on. But the just-available figures for last month show short-term interest rates *rising*, even though the money supply is continuing to expand at a 6 per cent rate!

Clearly we have a problem. If the Federal Reserve interprets the rising interest rates as evidence of a tightening of credit conditions, it would respond by increasing bank reserves at a still more rapid rate. If, on the other hand, the Federal Reserve would focus on the money supply change as the key indicator, it would likely conclude that monetary policy is about "on target."

Until recently, the Federal Open Market Committee would have placed relatively greater weight on the interest-rate movement. However, beginning in the early 1960s, there has been a gradual shift in the views of the men at the top. In response both to events and to developments in economic analysis, the monetary policy makers have

---

[7] William N. Cox, III, "Measuring Monetary Policy," *Monthly Review*, Federal Reserve Bank of Atlanta (December 1970), p. 184.

come to realize that interest rate movements can at times give misleading signals for two reasons: (1) The very success of monetary policy in stimulating the economy results in increased demand for money (recall chapters 17 and 18), putting upward pressure on rates. (2) When inflationary expectations are becoming stronger, even extreme monetary ease can be accompanied by rising interest rates, as lenders and borrowers build this factor into their estimations of the "real" yield of financial assets.

In 1966 the Federal Open Market Committee for the first time gave evidence that it considered monetary aggregates an important class of indicators of the effects of monetary policy. In its directives to the Manager of the System Open Market Account, issued at each meeting, the committee initiated the practice of including a clause instructing the Account Management to alter its money-market targets from the levels initially specified by the committee if bank credit growth was found to be deviating significantly from the path projected at the meeting. Money-market conditions were still clearly the dominant consideration, both explicitly and as the Account Management interpreted their assignment.

Early in 1970 the FOMC took another step toward assigning a significant role to movements in monetary aggregates when it adopted explicit goals for the growth rates of one or more of these aggregates. But in February of 1972 the committee turned to another magnitude, which it calls RPD's, or "reserves available to support private deposits."

RPD's have several advantages over monetary aggregates as indicators. In terms of the five criteria listed earlier, RPD's are nearer the beginning of the "chain of causation," and information is available on the size of this magnitude with a shorter lag. Moreover, it is less subject to outside influences than are the monetary aggregates.[8]

The FOMC does not believe it has found the ultimate indicator, though. Spokesmen for the Federal Reserve continue to emphasize that, while the primary focus is currently (early 1975) on RPD's, careful attention is also given to the behavior of various monetary aggregates, to conditions in the domestic money and capital markets, and also to international financial markets. There is little or no acceptance by Federal Reserve policy makers of the idea that the FOMC should follow a single indicator, come what may.

The Inside Lag

One crucial question with respect to the monetary policy decision process is the so-called *inside lag* of monetary policy, that is, the length of time elapsing between the need for action and the actual response by the Federal Reserve. This lag can be further divided into the *recognition*

---

[8] Frank E. Morris, "RPD's as the Target," in *Controlling Monetary Aggregates II: The Implementation* (Boston: Federal Reserve Bank of Boston, 1973), pp. 9–23.

lag (from the need for action to the awareness by the Federal Reserve of the need for action), and the *action lag* (from awareness to response). Attempts have been made to measure the lengths of these lags, by observing the relationship between turning points of the business cycle and apparent reversals of Federal Reserve policy. The results are generally quite optimistic concerning the record of the recent past and the outlook for the future. As measured by Willes,[9] the combined length of both inside lags in recent turning points has ranged from minus two quarters to plus three quarters. The negative figures are due to the Federal Reserve's reversal of policy well in advance of the turning point of the cycle.

Federal Reserve Actions: Alternatives and Evaluation

The only monetary magnitude that the Federal Reserve authorities can affect directly is member-bank reserves. Earlier, in chapter 7, we studied the "accounting trace" aspects of Federal Reserve actions, so we shall only summarize them here—though you are strongly urged to review those earlier pages at this point. In this section we examine the major control weapons of the Federal Reserve: open-market operations, the discount mechanism, and reserve requirements.

Open-Market Operations

Assume a decision by FOMC that, under current and anticipated conditions, a somewhat more rapid increase in RPD's is desirable. This judgment would be communicated to the Manager of the System Open Market Account (although he probably was present at the meeting at which the decision was reached), and he and his staff would then be responsible for taking appropriate steps to achieve this condition. Implementation would almost certainly involve the purchase of United States government securities on the open market, the immediate effect of which would be an increase in member-bank reserves and demand deposits as the sellers deposited checks from the Reserve banks in their own banks. Under our fractional-reserve banking system, only a small per cent of these new reserves are required by virtue of the increased deposits; the major part of the new reserves is excess. The banks generally utilize these excess reserves quickly by making loans and purchasing securities, the result in either case being a further expansion of demand deposits.

If, instead, the system's judgment dictated the sale of some of its holdings of United States government securities, the result would be a reduction in bank reserves; and we would expect a negative change in

---

[9] Mark H. Willes, "The Inside Lags of Monetary Policy: 1952–1960," *Journal of Finance*, XXII (December 1967), pp. 591–93.

the quantity of demand deposits, via the money creation and destruction mechanism, equal to a multiple of the reserve reduction.

The task of changing the money supply by $X billion is far more than a matter of merely increasing or decreasing reserves by some appropriate fraction of that amount. Recall, again from chapter 7, the major nonpolicy factors affecting bank reserves: changes in the gold stock, the movement of currency into and out of circulation, changes in the Treasury's cash position, and variations in the size of the Federal Reserve float. While the Federal Reserve has developed quite effective forecasting techniques. enabling the FOMC generally to foresee and adjust to these developments, these techniques yield results that are still far from perfect, so the money managers are forced to make decisions under conditions of considerable uncertainty. Fortunately, open-market operations are instantly reversible; therefore, if new information indicates that an action just taken was inappropriate, a counteraction can immediately offset it.

ADVANTAGES AND DISADVANTAGES   The gradual rise of Federal Reserve open-market operations to its present position of number one monetary control weapon testifies to its advantages, the following in particular:

1. They are conducted with no "fanfare," so these operations are less likely to upset financial markets.
2. The initiative lies completely with the monetary authorities.
3. Open-market operations are extremely flexible in amount, timing, and reversibility.

Against these advantages may be set certain problems and disadvantages that, however, do not appear to be serious in the eyes of most observers of monetary policy:

1. The fact that the manager of the open-market account must attempt to reconcile two sometimes-conflicting considerations—those relating to financial markets ("defensive") and economic conditions ("dynamic")—not only makes his job arduous but also imposes difficulties on those who must interpret Federal Reserve policy.
2. Open-market operations can exert a nonneutral impact on the structure of interest rates; for example, if the Federal Reserve would buy only, or chiefly, short-term securities, short-term rates would tend to be forced down relative to the long rates.

In connection with the response of the banking system to a Federal Reserve action, we again face a "lag" problem. A recent study of this question by William R. Bryan concluded that the lag between the action and the response ranges from one to ten weeks. Other researchers earlier had concluded that this kind of lag was considerably longer; but, according to Bryan, the reasons for this result in the earlier studies were lack of weekly data and the fact that these studies used aggregate banking statistics while Bryan's study was based on observations of individual banks.[10]

The Discount Mechanism

Although, as was stated, the Federal Reserve relies mainly on open-market operations for the conduct of monetary policy, it does have at its disposal two other general weapons: the discount mechanism and reserve requirements.

The discount mechanism refers to the arrangements through which member banks can borrow from their district Federal Reserve banks. This privilege is utilized for several reasons—unexpected reserve loss and seasonal needs being the most common. As related to monetary policy, the discount mechanism constitutes a "safety valve," permitting banks which are hard-hit by, say, an open-market sale by the Federal Reserve to acquire reserves temporarily, pending other portfolio adjustments.

"Seasonal needs" received official approval as a legitimate reason for borrowing from the Federal Reserve by an amendment to Federal Reserve Regulation A, effective April 1973. A qualified member bank, by making advance arrangements with its district bank, may be granted credit for periods up to ninety days, if needed, with the possibility of renewal. This privilege is intended for the two thousand or so member banks, mostly small in size and located in agricultural or resort areas, having a regularly recurring period of at least eight weeks at about the same time each year, during which there is a heavy deposit outflow and/or increase in loan demand.

The Reserve authorities rely somewhat on a *"tradition against borrowing"* to prevent abuse of the privilege. However, they are also on guard against any possible tendency on the part of some banks to stay in debt to the Federal Reserve more or less continuously, especially when there is an opportunity for the banks to profit by taking advantage of a substantial spread between the cost of borrowing from the Federal Reserve and the income from lending. Despite this reluctance to borrow, reinforced by Federal Reserve vigilance, the record shows that, when money is tight, the level of borrowing by member banks from the Reserve banks is higher than under other circumstances. The reason is that, even though individual banks repay their indebtedness promptly in nearly all cases, many more banks than usual face reserve deficiencies and decide to borrow.

---

[10] William R. Bryan, "Bank Adjustments to Monetary Policy: Alternative Estimates of the Lag," *American Economic Review*, LVII (September 1967), p. 864.

The discount rate (the rate paid by member banks on their borrowings from the Reserve banks) is raised or lowered in reflection of developments in money-market rates—which developments are themselves strongly influenced by Federal Reserve open-market operations. Although a change in the discount rate does not in itself tighten or ease credit conditions significantly, it is widely regarded as a means used by the Federal Reserve to signal the financial community that the direction in which money-market rates are moving is in accord with the Reserve's intentions. Thus, for example, a rise in the discount rate charged by the Reserve banks, following a period in which money-market rates had been rising, would serve notice that the movement in money-market rates was no fluke but was a result of the Federal Reserve's policy of tightening, or permitting a tightening in, credit conditions.

WEAKNESSES AND SOME REFORM PROPOSALS Despite the undoubted benefits of the "safety valve" function of the discount mechanism, this weapon of the system's, as now administered, has come in for some severe criticism. For one thing, a change in the discount rate, since it is so very visible, is cited as a potentially upsetting influence on the financial markets. Ideally, the psychological impact should increase the effectiveness of the Federal Reserve's action. For example, a drop in the rate should be interpreted as confirming a trend toward easier credit, thus encouraging lending, borrowing, and spending. However, a drop could have exactly the opposite effect just as reasonably: people could interpret the reduction as a signal that the Federal Reserve expects further deterioration of economic conditions. Acting on the basis of this interpretation, they would adjust their planned expenditures downward.

In recent years a number of monetary economists have proposed changes in the discount mechanism. One of the least drastic is the proposal to tie the discount rate to the Treasury bill rate, that is, to change the discount rate frequently so that it is positioned at a more or less constant distance above the bill rate. This would eliminate the ambiguous "announcement effect" described in the paragraph just above and would also prevent any inducement for banks to borrow in order to profit from an increased spread between discount rate and their lending rates.

Other proposals run the gamut from complete abolition of the discount mechanism[11] to making certain changes in it in order to convert it into a major Federal Reserve control weapon.[12] We cannot pause to examine the underlying premises of these and other schemes nor their details, advantages, and drawbacks.[13] However, we can see the point:

---

[11] Milton Friedman, *A Program for Monetary Stability* (New York: Fordham University Press, 1960), pp. 35–45.
[12] James Tobin, "Toward Improving the Efficiency of the Monetary Mechanism," *Review of Economics and Statistics,* XLII (August 1960), pp. 276–79.
[13] See Warren Smith, "The Discount Rate as a Credit-Control Weapon," *Journal of Political Economy,* LXVI (April 1958), pp. 171–77.

the number and variety of reform plans testifies to a rather widespread conviction that there are flaws in the discount mechanism as presently structured; but the lack of real pressure toward reform on the part of the Board of Governors, Congressional policymakers, or any organized or disorganized group testifies to the conviction that the mechanism is working at least tolerably well.

The discount mechanism does introduce some slippage into the monetary policy process. Although the FOMC has the power to counteract the effect on member-bank reserves of any increase or decrease in borrowing from the Federal Reserve, the amount of increased discounting that will result from a given open-market sale cannot be foreseen accurately. This does not, however, appear to be a serious problem in the implementation of monetary policy.

Reserve Requirements

Our final general weapon of monetary control is the reserve requirement: the requirement that a member bank maintain legal reserves at least equal to a stipulated percentage of particular categories of deposits. Recalling the discussion in chapter 7, the percentage required depends on (1) the *type* of deposit, being higher for demand than time deposits, and (2) the *volume* of deposits in each category, varying directly with volume.

ADVANTAGES AND DISADVANTAGES   We also noted in chapter 7 that changing the reserve requirement is a potent weapon of monetary control, one that can instantly transmute hundreds of millions of dollars from excess to required reserves or the other way around. This characteristic is of particular usefulness when the monetary authorities must immobilize large amounts of excess reserves in a hurry, as sometimes happens in connection with the debt financing of government expenditures in time of war. Another advantage is its broad and immediate geographic coverage.

Against these advantages are certain drawbacks, some of which have already been suggested. One is the fact that frequent use of this weapon is a nuisance to bankers. When credit conditions during a boom are tightened through open-market sales by the Federal Reserve, the effects are not quite so obvious for most banks as is a tightening through raising reserve requirements, which seems like a personal attack, especially frustrating because it usually occurs when loan demand is strong and advance commitments must be honored.

Of course, it can well be argued that monetary policy is not conducted for the convenience of bankers. However, so long as banks have the option of pulling out of the system—quite a live option for many smaller member banks—it behooves the Federal Reserve authorities not to antagonize them needlessly, and frequent use of this weapon, in view of the availability of an effective alternative weapon, would indeed be needless.

A second weakness is the clumsiness of reserve-requirement changes. Even a one-half per cent change has a large impact on reserve positions. There are two means of alleviating this lumpiness, neither of which is really satisfactory. First, the Federal Reserve can counterbalance any excessive effect on reserves with open-market operations working in the opposite direction. However, there would still have to be a great deal of churning about because it is not at all certain that the banks experiencing the greatest change in reserve positions will also be most affected by the open-market operation. Second, the Federal Reserve can make very small changes in reserve requirements— conceivably on the order of .01 per cent or even less. However, there would then have to be frequent changes; and we are back to the first objection: frequent changes are a real burden on banks, especially small banks.

Another problem is that changes in reserve requirements are so obvious. Although often considered an advantage ("You can *see* that the Federal Reserve is acting!"), the problem, as we mentioned earlier in connection with changes of the discount rates, is that the direction of impact of this kind of communication (let alone its strength) is uncertain.

FEDERAL RESERVE USE OF RESERVE-REQUIREMENT CHANGES How, in fact, has the Board of Governors used this particular weapon of control? Very sparingly, especially for increases. From 1949 to 1958 most of the growth in member-bank deposits was supported by reductions in reserve requirements. Since that period, however, the Federal Reserve has provided for increases in member-bank deposits mainly by increasing reserves through open-market operations.

The reason for this pattern seems to lie in the Federal Reserve's belief that (1) the level of reserve requirements had been abnormally high and needed to be reduced, but (2) other weapons are more efficient in smoothing out cyclical fluctuations and in providing for the growth in the money supply appropriate to the growth in real GNP.

A COMPARISON OF OPEN-MARKET OPERATIONS AND RESERVE-REQUIREMENT CHANGES Since both open-market operations and changes in reserve requirements are means whereby the Federal Reserve authorities can change bank reserve positions *directly*, it would be instructive to compare these two weapons as alternative means of accomplishing a given objective. Let us assume that the objective is to increase demand deposits by $6 billion. Using the reserve-requirement weapon, we reduce the required percentage by just the amount necessary to enable the banking system to add $6 billion to its demand-deposit liabilities without requiring any addition to system reserves. For simplicity, all banks are assumed to be member banks. The accounting trace (with figures in $billions) will be:

	Banking System		
Earning assets	+$6.0	Demand deposits	+$6.0

TRACE 21.1

If the same goal were sought via open-market purchases, the Federal Reserve would have to pump in enough reserves to support $6 billion in new demand deposits. Assuming the reserve requirements to be 15 per cent, this expansion in demand deposits would necessitate $900 million in additional reserves. In this case, the accounting trace (again, with figures in $billions) would be:

Banking System				Federal Reserve Banks			
Reserves	+$0.9	Demand deposits	+$6.0	Earning assets	+$0.9	Member-bank reserve deposits	+$0.9
Earning assets	+5.1						

TRACE 21.2

In the first case, the banking system increased its earning assets by $6 billion, an amount equal to the entire increment in demand deposits, since no additional reserves were involved. However, in the open-market case, the addition of $900 million of (required) reserves means that earning-assets can expand by only $5.1 billion, or 85 per cent of the deposit increment.

Little wonder, therefore, that the American Bankers Association has for years been recommending on every possible occasion the reduction of reserve requirements!

PROPOSALS FOR CHANGE IN THE RESERVE-REQUIREMENT WEAPON There is no lack of suggestions for changes in the rules concerning reserve requirements. Hardly a single aspect of this weapon has escaped attention. The variety and complexity of the issues involved render impossible a really adequate discussion of all of the various proposals: their characteristics, advantages, and disadvantages.

Some schemes advocate a change in *institutional coverage*, with Federal Reserve authority to impose reserve requirements being extended to cover all commercial banks or all insured commercial banks, not merely member banks.

The Federal Reserve authorities are vigorously advocating this kind of reform currently. The main thrust of the argument is that the present system limits the ability of the Federal Reserve to control the money supply. In the first place, the fact that member banks have the option of dropping their affiliation with the Federal Reserve System tends to restrain the Board of Governors from increasing reserve requirements when this move would be advisable from a monetary policy standpoint. Second, the fact that a substantial and increasing percentage of total deposits are obligations of banks *outside* the system loosens the control of the Federal Reserve over the money supply. The reason is that shifts of deposits between member banks and nonmember banks can drastically change the potential expansibility of each dollar of reserve deposits, and the larger the nonmember-bank sector, the more serious is this effect.

Assume, for example, that depositors of member banks send $100,000 of checks to depositors of nonmember banks, who deposit the checks in their own banks. These banks then send the checks to their big-city correspondents, which are all member banks, for deposit credit. (In all but five states nonmember banks may count such deposits as part of their legal reserves.) All this is recorded as step 1 in the balance-sheet trace below:

TRACE 21.3		Member Banks			Nonmember Banks	
	(1)	Demand deposits (nonbank) Demand deposits (bank)	−$100 +100	(1) Reserves (correspondent balances)	+$100	Demand deposits +$100
	(2)			(2) Loans	+$85	Demand deposits +$85
	(3)	Demand deposits (nonbank) Demand deposits (bank)	+$85 −85	(3) Reserves (correspondent balances)	−$85	Demand deposits −$85
	(1–3)	Demand deposits (nonbank) Demand deposits (bank)	−$15 +15	(1–3) Reserves (correspondent balances) Loans	+$15 +85	Demand deposits +$100

So far, the money supply has not changed, since bank balances in other banks are not included as part of the money supply; but the nonmember banks now have excess reserves. If we assume reserve requirements of 15 per cent, then these nonmember banks can increase their earning assets by $85,000. Step 2 records the initial results of an increase in loans of $85,000. Even if we make the extreme assumption that this entire amount is withdrawn as borrowers write checks on it and all these checks are deposited in member banks (step 3), the money supply can still increase by $100,000, since (1) nonmember bank demand deposits have increased by $100,000 while (2) member banks, not having lost any reserves, can reexpand their demand deposits to their original level. If the nonmember bank sector retains a portion of these reserves, the expansion will, of course, be larger.

When the nonmember bank sector is extremely small relative to the member-bank sector, these movements can be shrugged off as minor deviations from perfection. But the nonmember bank sector has been growing relative to the member-bank sector, both in numbers and in demand deposits. Nonmember banks account for nearly one-fourth of total private demand deposits now, up from less than 15 per cent in 1947. Thus, the problem of slippage has become increasingly serious. In the words of one Federal Reserve official,

The Federal Reserve's control, if this trend continues, would be as poor as that of a fisherman trying to reel in a tuna on a line that was alternately as unyielding as an anchor chain and as elastic as a rubber band.[14]

Another class of proposals for reform of reserve requirements relates to the *basis for differentiation among banks* as to the percentage of the base required as reserves. One suggestion is to differentiate according to the asset-mix, with loans, for example, requiring more reserves per dollar than investments, or a higher percentage per dollar of private securities compared to, say, United States government securities.

The *base* on which the reserves are required has also come in for attention. Some plans specify bank assets instead of deposits as the base. Another possible base is the turnover, rather than the quantity, of deposits. Yet another proposal is to limit the base to demand deposits alone.

Proposals for change are also distinguishable on the basis of the *form* in which they stipulate that reserves can be held. Some would permit short-term United States securities to be included in legal reserves. Others would impose a secondary reserve requirement in addition to the conventional one. This latter was seriously discussed during and after World War II when it seemed to offer an ideal method of "freezing" part of the government debt rather permanently in the portfolios of banks, debt that the banks might otherwise be tempted to sell in order to make loans, thus pushing government securities prices down and yields up. This possibility was much dreaded at that time since a decline in the prices of these securities might give the impression that the Federal government's financial position was shaky.

Finally, there are several proposals relating to the actual per cent requirement itself. At one extreme is the idea that the level should be zero;[15] at the other, that the level (relative to demand deposits) should be set at 100 percent.[16] The latter proposal would entail the abolition of fractional-reserve banking as applied to demand deposits. With respect to the zero–per cent proposal, although probably not many economists would support complete abolition of reserve requirements, a fair number advocate their abolition as applied to time deposits.

The General Weapons: A Comparison

In summarizing this discussion of the general instruments of monetary control, it might be interesting to make a comparison of the three instruments by a number of criteria. Table 21.1, worked out by Thomas

---

[14] Thomas O. Waage, "The Need for Uniform Reserve Requirements," *Monthly Review,* Federal Reserve Bank of New York (December 1973), p. 305.

[15] Deane Carson, "Is the Federal Reserve System Really Necessary?" *Journal of Finance,* XIX (December 1964), pp. 652–61.

[16] A recent discussion of this idea is George Tolley, "100 Percent Reserve Banking," in Leland B. Yeager (ed.), *In Search of a Monetary Constitution* (Cambridge: Harvard University Press, 1962), pp. 275–304.

TABLE 21.1
Relative Advantages of Various Monetary Tools for Countercyclical Actions
Comparing:

	Discount-Rate Changes	Open-Market Operations	Discount-Rate Changes	Reserve-Requirement Changes	Reserve-Requirement Changes	Open-Market Operations
Strength		X		X	$-^1$	$-^1$
Flexibility		X	$?^2$	$?^2$		X
Precision		X	$?^3$	$?^3$		X
Faster geographic spread	X			—	X	
Willingness of banks to change assets	—	—	—	—	X	
Good relations with commercial banks	—	—	X^4	—		X^4
Relative strength of announcement effect	X^5		—	—	X^5	

Source: From *Monetary Policy in the United States*, by Thomas Mayer. Copyright © 1968 by Random House, Inc. Reprinted by permission of the publisher.

X denotes superiority. —denotes approximate equality.

[1] Both have more than adequate strength.
[2] The relative flexibility of these two tools is uncertain; the Federal Reserve appears to believe that discount-rate changes are the more flexible tool and, hence, uses this tool more flexibly.
[3] The relative precision of these two tools is uncertain. Given present Federal Reserve practices, discount-rate changes are probably more precise. With a different Federal Reserve policy, reserve-requirement changes may be more precise.
[4] Applies to increases on reserve requirements, not to decreases.
[5] Whether a strong announcement effect is desirable is uncertain. The check mark may be undeserved.

Mayer, does just that. It is easy to see why open-market operation has emerged as the dominant instrument since it is superior, or at least adequate, with respect to all of the criteria generally ranked as most important: strength, flexibility, and precision.

Other Monetary Control Weapons: Selective Credit Controls

The "big three" instruments of control work their magic primarily through their effect on member-bank reserve positions—quantity of reserves and their expansibility. In addition, the Federal Reserve has in its arsenal certain other weapons that we shall inspect now.

One such weapon—actually a category of weapons—is called *selective credit controls*. As the title implies, controls of this type are aimed at particular industries or sectors of the economy. In the broadest sense, programs to stimulate certain kinds of financing should probably be included, as well as programs to curb them.[17] Common practice, however, limits usage of the term to the latter type.

In the United States, this category is far from crowded: the only kind of selective control on the books at present is that which the Federal Reserve Board of Governors exercises over margin requirements on the purchase of stock and securities convertible into stock. "Margin" is jargon for "down payment." The Board is authorized to specify the minimum percentage of the price that would-be stock purchasers must put down—or, what is the same thing, the maximum percentage that lenders may advance when the securities purchased are to serve as collateral for the loan. The purpose is to limit speculation: the higher the margin requirement, the less "leverage" one has in buying these securities. For example, with a margin requirement of 25 per cent, the borrower could buy $40,000 worth of stock with only $10,000 of his own money as margin while, with an 80 per cent requirement, he could buy only $12,500 worth.

The Federal Reserve has had and has utilized this authority since 1934, but the consensus of experts seems to be that the influence of margin requirements is (dare we say it?) marginal. There is no clearly discernible relation between stock price movements and changes in margin requirements.[18]

Although control over margin requirements is the only instance of selective credit controls in effect now, there have been others in the past. During certain emergencies the Board of Governors has been made responsible for the administration of controls over real estate credit and consumer credit, setting maximum maturities and minimum percentage

[17] Arthur Smithies, "Uses of Selective Credit Controls," in The American Assembly, *United States Monetary Policy* (New York: The American Assembly, Columbia University, 1958), p. 74.
[18] Harry L. Johnson, "Margin Requirements and Stock Market Credit," *Business and Government Review*, VI (November–December, 1965), pp. 5–10.

down payments in each case. The former was instituted in 1950 during the Korean conflict and was allowed to expire in 1952; the latter was in effect during and after World War II, from 1941 to 1947, then briefly from September 1948 to June 1949, and most recently during the Korean conflict, terminating in 1952.

THE CASE FOR SELECTIVE CONTROLS Several arguments have been advanced in defense of selective controls. These arguments mostly relate to one idea—that the market does not do an adequate job of allocating credit—but there are several aspects to the arguments.

First, it is observed that the so-called "general instruments" are really selective in their effects. When the Federal Reserve attempts to exercise restraint, some types of credit are hardly affected while others are severely restricted. The rebuttal is that this is the way it ought to be; credit should flow where it is most in demand; and, if manufacturers see prospects of high returns from additional investment, they will be able to outbid households seeking financing for new homes. The problem with this kind of allocation is that it could involve a great deal of unemployment and numerous business failures in one sector while the other is running into inflation-producing bottlenecks. If somehow the white-hot sector could be cooled down via a selective credit control device, perhaps the investment boom could be prolonged and proceed at a less inflationary pace. At least, that is the argument.

Another reason general controls can be selective in their impact is that financial markets are less than perfect. Sometimes the ability of an economic unit to obtain financing will depend on the economic power of the applicant or on the market organization of the economic unit's traditional sources of financing.

Second, it can be argued that selective credit controls are really "negative credit programs." Just as government credit programs can help to achieve certain high-priority social goals by spurring particular kinds of economic activities or favoring particular classes of borrowers, so selective controls can discourage or impede certain activities or borrowers. So the arguments advanced in chapter 13 in support of the idea of government credit programs are equally applicable to nonquantitative credit controls.

Third, selective controls can help in reallocating resources during wartime or mobilization periods. The government, rather than attempting to outbid would-be purchasers of autos and appliances to obtain productive resources that it needs to utilize to turn out military goods, can impose stringent controls on the use of credit for private purchase of durables, a move that, in our credit-oriented society, would remove many potential auto and appliance purchasers from the market.

Finally, if useful in war, the argument goes, why not in peace? If we want to increase our rate of economic growth, we should use selective credit controls to aid in shifting resources out of consumer goods and services industries into capital goods and other growth-producing industries.

THE CASE AGAINST SELECTIVE CONTROLS Against these arguments, opponents of selective controls raise some powerful counterarguments, both philosophical and economic. One we have already introduced: ours is a free-market economy, and no abridgement of the market principle should be permitted without ample justification. Second, it is counterargued that if we do a good job with general instruments of monetary control, there will be less likelihood of a rapid change in the autonomous planned expenditures of any sector or subsector, therefore less likelihood of need for selective measures.

Third, selective credit control programs are often difficult and costly to administer. They require the establishment of a new bureaucracy or the expansion of an existing one in order to set up, publicize, administer, and enforce the program. Moreover, compliance costs, which can be substantial, are imposed on the economic units being regulated.

Fourth, such programs often operate at the expense of the poorer households and newer businesses, since these are more likely to need financing in order to make a substantial expenditure, while the wealthier households and old-established businesses are more likely to have adequate internal resources: chances are greater that these latter can meet the down payment and maturity requirements.

Finally, selective credit-control programs are often less effective than anticipated because the economic units affected can frequently discover or develop ways of circumventing the intent of the controls. A case in point is the so-called margin requirement. At first (1934) covering only credit extended by securities brokers and dealers to customers for buying or carrying equities, this control has experienced an extension of coverage numerous times in order to plug loopholes that continue to be opened up by resourceful investors and lenders and discovered by vigilant regulators. As early as 1936, margin controls were applied to banks. Then in 1968 coverage was widened to include *all* domestic lenders having securities lending as an important part of their business. Finally (?), in 1970 the margin requirement was extended to cover credit provided to U.S. economic units by foreign lending institutions because these lenders tended to secure their financing, in turn, from United States sources![19]

Whether our society will move toward greater use of selective credit controls cannot, of course, be predicted confidently. Barring any substantial shift in ideology, though, it seems likely that only highly unsat-

---

[19] For a sketch of these and other developments, see James M. O'Brien, "Can Credit Controls Be Controlled?" *Business Review*, Federal Reserve Bank of Philadelphia (January 1972), pp. 5–7.

isfactory performance of our economy, in terms of attainment of our economic goals, will induce us to accept any significant expansion of selective credit controls.

Moral Suasion

A final weapon of the Federal Reserve System, hardly a "control" in the usual sense but yet not without potency, is usually referred to by the old-fashioned title of moral suasion or, with less dignity, "open-mouth policy." This weapon consists of efforts of the Reserve authorities to induce or pressure member banks to alter their asset portfolios in directions desired by the Federal Reserve. The actual method may vary: a letter of exhortation to all member banks, perhaps, or the establishment of "guidelines" or standards as to which loan categories are acceptable for increase, which ones are not. Examples of the guidelines type are (1) the Voluntary Credit Restraint program, of the Korean conflict era, through which banks and other financial intermediaries were encouraged to channel their lending into defense-related purposes and away from speculation, and (2) the Voluntary Foreign Credit Restraint program which, beginning in 1965, sought to curtail the growth of foreign lending by American financial institutions. Both of these seem to have been reasonably successful; however, there are some severe limitations on the usefulness of this method in a highly decentralized financial system such as ours. Frictions tend to build up: some institutions break away, and resentment at the restraints on freedom develops, as does a feeling that certain classes of institutions are being treated unfairly.

Federal Reserve Actions and the Economy's Response

In chapter 18 we discussed the interrelation of the real sector and the financial sector in terms of a highly simplified model of the economy. Perhaps we can make sense out of the effects of the Federal Reserve's monetary actions on the economy by utilizing the concepts developed there. Let us begin with an open-market purchase by the Federal Reserve Bank of New York and trace the everwidening circles of influence of this action. Just to pick a convenient amount, assume that the volume of securities purchased is $500 million.

Effects on Financial and Real Sectors

The first problem we face is that our macromodel has no term for member-bank reserves. One possible way out might be to assume that the increase in reserves created by the open-market purchase results, through bank lending and investing, in an increase in the money supply equal to some multiple of the reserves increment. Then we could apply our chapter 18 analysis of the effects of a rise in M on equilibrium GNP. However, this "bare bones" approach, while useful for identifying some crucial macroeconomic relationships, misses a wealth of real-world institutional details, some of which are important for an adequate understanding of the actual process.

Examining first the initial set of transactions, we note that, in the course of purchasing the securities, the Federal Reserve has simultaneously (1) increased the liquidity of the portfolios of the sellers, who received cash for the securities, and (2) nudged interest rates down and securities prices up a bit, since purchases of this magnitude in a short time period would be strongly felt on sensitive money markets.

Now disequilibria appear in various places. The original sellers to the Federal Reserve—government securities dealers and their clients—probably feel excessively cash-heavy and attempt to shift their portfolios, adding to the demand for securities that are close substitutes for those that they were induced to sell to the Federal Reserve. Banks have unwanted excess reserves, which they utilize by purchasing securities and/or granting loans. Associated with these activities we would also observe (1) a further downward pressure on interest rates and upward pressure on securities prices, (2) increased availability of loan credit to would-be borrowers at more generous terms, and (3) an expansion of the money supply through the banks' acquisition of earning assets.

In the framework of our chapter 18 model, we could depict these three developments (Figure 21.1) as a downward shift of the LM curve to say, LM'; meaning that, at any given Y level, the interest rate equating the supply of, and demand for, money is lower than before, due to the increase in M. From an (assumed) equilibrium position, designated as (1), the initial reaction of the economy is summarized as a decline in

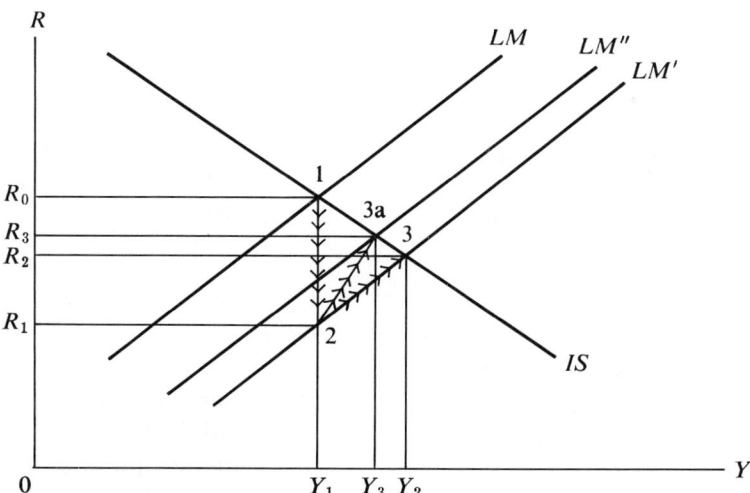

Figure 21.1
Macroeconomic effects of a Federal Reserve open-market purchase.

"the" interest rate (R) from OR_0 to OR_1. At that interest rate, given level of income OY_1, the demand for money is compatible with the expanded money supply.

All these developments inevitably affect the real sector. As a result of increases in financial asset prices, declines in yields, and easier financing terms generally, the disequilibria spread to business and household expenditure flows. In response to lower-cost and less-restrictive financing, the business sector will increase its investment expenditures—this, after all, is the likely purpose of at least a portion of those new bank loans—and the household sector, in response to (1) increases in wealth (due to higher securities prices) and (2) easier credit, will probably raise expenditures out of a given disposable income.

What this means, in the language of *IS-LM* analysis, is a movement along the new *LM* curve from point 2 to point 3. As aggregate income expands in response to monetary ease, the economy begins to experience some tightening of credit conditions: the demand for money for transactions purposes grows. Increased demands for financing on the part of businesses and households also puts demand pressures on interest rates. The new equilibrium position, at point 3, is that combination of Y (OY_2) and R (OR_2) simultaneously satisfying the condition that $L = M$ and that $E = Y$.

If we also include in our analysis the possibility that the Federal Reserve's action may induce or intensify an inflationary development, raising the *LM* curve to *LM"*, in our illustration, the final equilibrium, at 3a, is characterized by a higher (nominal) R (OR_3) and a lower (real) (OY_3) than at 3. The reason we should recall from chapter 18: given the nominal money supply, a higher price level implies a lower (real) money supply, hence a leftward shift of the *LM* curve, thus the new equilibrium must be above and to the left of the old one, at the edge of the zone of inflation.

Obscured in this aggregative type of analysis are the effects of Federal Reserve actions on the allocation of credit. A portion of chapter 22 will be devoted to this topic; but we should mention here that the financial system is far from neutral in its effects on allocation of credit among the sectors of the economy.

Monetarist Challenge to Keynesian Orthodoxy

Most economists would agree with the substance of the foregoing paragraphs; but there is currently a good deal of controversy over the relative importance of each of these relationships. Unfortunately, this is not one of those cases in which the rest of us—including policy makers—can simply dismiss the disputes between the learned doctors of economics as "merely theoretical arguments," because the alternative views have quite different implications for macroeconomic policy. In other words, if theory A is correct, policy X is called for; but if theory B is valid, then policy X would have highly unfavorable economic consequences while policy Y would lead us to prosperity.

There are two major schools of thought in this connection. One school, adherents of which are called *monetarists*, originated at the University of Chicago and owes much of its intellectual stimulus to the work of Milton Friedman. The other school, far less easy to identify, has been labeled variously as Keynesian, Neo-Keynesian, Fiscalist, and even the Establishment! However, since it is largely built on the Keynesian foundation, we shall refer to it simply as Keynesian. The analysis in chapters 15 through 18 is definitely in this tradition. Within each school there is a broad spectrum of opinion. Nevertheless we can detect and discuss certain general characteristics of the two approaches.

The literature turned out by the disputants in recent years is overwhelming. Not only are there journal articles almost without number exploring one or another aspect of monetary theory and policy from one or another viewpoint and presenting or attacking a snippet of evidence bearing on the case, but it has become the "in" thing to hold a symposium at which representatives of the two major camps are invited to air their views, and then to publish the papers and comments presented there. As the battle rages, one can discern subtle changes in position, too, so it becomes difficult to be certain whether the statement of Professor N, made in 1966, really represents his *current* thinking. All of which means that any attempt to discuss the dispute in a few paragraphs is bound to produce distortions and oversimplifications—just as is the case for any other kind of battlefield reporting in which the battle is still in progress and the reporter is more sympathetic with one side than with the other!

THE MONETARIST POSITION[20]   There seems to be a common core of beliefs and emphases that characterize the monetarist position. First of all, as the monetarists' world is one in which full or nearly full employment is the normal condition, their analyses are generally built on this assumption. Accordingly, the monetarists lay greater stress on the price-level effects of policy measures than traditional Keynesians are inclined to do (or, at least, *were* inclined to do until recently). This weakness of the traditional Keynesian analysis undoubtedly reflects the fact that the theory was conceived and born in the 1930s depression, when inflation

---

[20] Some useful references on this topic are: (1) Leonall C. Anderson, "The State of the Monetarist Debate," *Review*, Federal Reserve Bank of St. Louis (September 1973), pp. 2–14; (2) Leonall C. Anderson and Keith M. Carlson, "A Monetarist Model for Economic Stabilization," ibid., (April 1970), pp. 7–15; (3) David I. Fand, "A Monetarist Model of the Monetary Process," *Journal of Finance*, XXV (May 1970), pp. 275–89; (4) Milton Friedman, "A Theoretical Framework for Monetary Analysis," *Journal of Political Economy*, LXXVIII (March–April 1970), pp. 193–238. Two illuminating commentaries on monetarism are (1) Harry G. Johnson, "The Keynesian Revolution and the Monetarist Counter-Revolution," *American Economic Review*, LXI (May 1971), pp. 1–14; and (2) Ronald Teigen, "A Critical Look at Monetarist Economics," *Review*, Federal Reserve Bank of St. Louis, (January 1972), pp. 10–23.

was a very minor worry of most economists. By confusing real and nominal changes in aggregate magnitudes such as GNP, say the monetarists, Keynesians arrive at erroneous conclusions, as will shortly be illustrated.

Second, changes in the money supply are considered to have effects on the level of nominal GNP that are both powerful and predictable, though working with a lag that is long and of varying length.

Third, the *transmission mechanism* of monetary policy emphasizes a direct link between money and aggregate expenditures. When the money supply is increased, asset portfolios are generally thrown out of balance, generating efforts to get rid of excess money by purchasing not only financial assets but real assets as well. This belief of monetarists in the existence of a strong direct link between M and E differentiates them sharply from Keynesians, who hold that the linkage is more complex and indirect, as we studied earlier.

This rise in the demand for goods and services increases sales and puts upward pressure on prices, stimulating producers to increase output, insofar as the economy has excess capacity.

Several implications of monetarism can be noted. First, according to the monetarists, although the Federal Reserve can control the *nominal* money supply, it cannot control the *real* money supply. No matter how much money the monetary authorities cause to be created, "they will ultimately fail [to bring about an increase in real balances] and serve only to raise prices, unless there is a substantial volume of unused resources."[21]

Second, monetarism leads to the conclusion that fiscal policy is almost useless as a macroeconomic policy weapon. Assuming an unchanged money supply, an expansion of government spending, although initially stimulative, will cause a shortage of money, because the equilibrium relationship between M and Y will have been upset. Economic units will attempt to acquire additional money by increasing their sales of goods and services—but, alas, since M is (we assumed) constant, their efforts are thwarted in the aggregate. The only result will be reduced prices (increased interest rates) on securities and depressed prices and sales—and, therefore, production—of commodities, including capital goods in the private sector. Therefore, in the final analysis, increased government expenditures will have no impact on the level of real GNP but will cause a shift in the output-mix: more G and less $C + I$.

The third implication, closely related to the second, is the relatively minor role played by any change in autonomous spending. If, for example, an important technological breakthrough were to stimulate investment tremendously, this would not excite a thoroughgoing monetarist. Just as happened in the fiscal policy case, the rise in one type of autonomous spending—investment, in this case—would set in motion

---

[21] Fand, "A Monetarist Model," p. 280. Professor Fand's paper was a helpful source for this discussion.

forces that would largely cancel out any short-run gains:[22] reduced consumption, curtailed state and local construction, and a decline in housing construction.

As the fourth implication in the monetarist view, efforts of the Federal Reserve to control the nominal interest rate are futile and self-defeating. Although the initial impact of an increase in M would be to reduce R, this is only transitory and will be *more than offset* eventually by the combined effects of (1) higher GNP and (2) expectation of higher future prices. And if the monetary authorities persist in attempting to keep R down, misreading the rise in R as a tightening of credit conditions, they will have to expand the money supply—and prices—at an ever-increasing rate.

Finally, this analysis leads monetarists to the conclusion that the correct monetary policy to follow, assuming the desirability of stable economic growth, is a stable growth of the money supply at approximately the same rate as the feasible growth rate of the economy,[23] rather than attempting to smooth out all the little ups and downs in money-market rates. In view of these characteristics of monetarist thought, it is little wonder that this position is so difficult for traditional macroeconomic theory and policy to digest.

RESULTS OF THE CONTROVERSY   The work of the monetarists has had some worthwhile results thus far. First, a greater appreciation has developed among economists for the economic role of the money supply and, hence, the power of monetary policy, and for the crucial distinction between real and nominal income and between real and nominal interest rates. Although these points are all perfectly compatible with a Keynesian framework, Keynesian economists have not always kept them in mind in their analyses and policy recommendations.

A second result has been the stimulation of "counterresearch" by Keynesian defenders of the faith, eager to point out weaknesses in the monetarist position. A third result has been in the area of monetary policy: the Federal Open Market Committee, after years of policy directives phrased in terms of money-market conditions, in January of 1970 changed its instructions toward focusing on money and bank credit. The contrast in the following quotations (one just before and the other just after the change) is quite revealing. The first one is taken from the report of the meeting of December 16, 1969:

---

[22] The more rapid growth made possible by the reallocation of resources to investment might be counted as a *long-run* gain, other things equal.

[23] This conclusion is even stronger when supported by the common belief of monetarists (and others) that monetary policy works only with quite long lags. If the lags are long, measures taken during a boom that are designed to slow the economy may well have their major impact during the subsequent slump, when the slowdown effect is definitely not needed; and the main result of antirecession monetary measures will be to stimulate the boom.

> To implement this policy [described earlier in the Committee's report], System open market operations until the next meeting of the Committee shall be conducted with a view to maintain the prevailing firm conditions in the money market; provided, however, that operations shall be modified if bank credit appears to be deviating significantly from current projections or if unusual liquidity pressures should develop.

In contrast, this paragraph from the report of the March 10, 1970 meeting:

> To implement this policy, the Committee desires to see moderate growth in money and bank credit over the months ahead. System open market operations until the next meeting of the Committee shall be conducted with a view to maintaining money market conditions consistent with that objective.[24]

The monetarist challenge was probably not the sole reason for this change, but that it was a factor in inducing the change seems fairly obvious and is generally conceded. Moreover, as we noted earlier in the chapter, this increased emphasis on monetary aggregates by monetary policy makers has continued.

It is frustrating for writer and reader alike to have to leave so many loose ends; but this reflects the actual situation in the theory of monetary policy. It would be misleading to pretend otherwise. The author's personal opinion is that, after the din of battle has quieted, the traditional analytical framework will have proved adequate to assimilate the valid aspects of the monetarist position and that macroeconomic analysis will have been considerably enriched in the process.

The "Outside Lag"

The final issue concerning the economic effects of monetary policy to be discussed in this chapter is the so-called "outside lag," that is, the length of time that this whole process takes, from Federal Reserve action to the economic effects of the action. This is one of those empirical problems that are difficult to formulate; and, once the calculations are made, they yield results that are difficult to interpret.

When we refer to the period between policy action and economic effect, we realize, of course, that these effects do not occur at a particular point in time but rather extend over a considerable period, as was brought out in our discussion of the multiplier. The length of the lag, therefore, is usually thought of as the number of months or quarters between the policy action and the month or quarter by which most (or over half) of the total effect has taken place. Sometimes, though, the lag is measured by the distance in time between the turning points in two

---

[24] "Record of the Policy Actions of the Federal Open Market Committee," *Federal Reserve Bulletin*, March 1970, p. 278; and June 1970, p. 512.

series, for example, rate of change in the money supply and the business cycle turning point.[25]

A number of estimates have been made, covering different time periods and using different variables in measuring the lag. Predictably, the length of the lag discovered varies widely, from one or two quarters[26] to four quarters at cycle troughs and six at peaks.[27] Professor Thomas Mayer, who himself has done considerable work analyzing these lags, reaches this conclusion after surveying a number of studies:

> The fact that [all but one of] the studies found a lag of two quarters or more provides strong evidence that the lag is at least two quarters. This is so because these studies used a wide variety of different approaches so that even if *some* of the studies contain errors the overall result would still hold.[28]

On the other hand, a Federal Reserve bank staff economists replies:

> The consistency with which long [outside] lags have been found, even in areas where we would expect them to be short, arouses suspicion regarding estimating procedures. The estimates of long lags are based on a narrow range of variation in monetary policy. Evidence from the 1966–67 period suggests that sharp and substantial shifts in monetary policy can precipitate dramatic changes in the economy in a very short period of time.[29]

Much remains to be done in obtaining reliable information not only on the length of the outside lag but on its variability as well. But this issue is of far more than academic interest to monetary policy makers. The danger is that the outside lag might be so long that stimulative actions taken to combat a slump would not take effect until an upswing is well under way, or that monetary tightening to fight a boom might only intensify a subsequent slump.

Monetary Policy as Automatic Stabilizer

The foregoing discussion of "lags," with its stress on Federal Reserve action, neglects the fact that monetary policy affects the economy even when it is passive. To illustrate, suppose that the Federal Reserve maintains unchanged the discount rate, reserve requirements, and ceiling interest rates on bank time deposits (Regulation Q). Suppose, further, that it conducts its open-market operations with the aim of holding the banking system's unborrowed reserves constant.

---

[25] For example, Milton Friedman and Anna Schwartz, "Money and Business Cycles," *Review of Economics and Statistics,* XLV (Supplement: February 1963), pp. 34–38.
[26] J. Ernest Tanner, "Lags in the Effects of Monetary Policy: A Statistical Investigation," *American Economic Review,* LIX (December 1969), pp. 794–805.
[27] Friedman and Schwartz, "Money and Business Cycles," pp. 37–38.
[28] Thomas Mayer, *Monetary Policy in the United States* (New York: Random House, 1968), p. 183. This reference contains citations of most lag studies made up to that date.
[29] Maurice Mann, "How Does Monetary Policy Affect the Economy?" *Federal Reserve Bulletin,* (October 1968), p. 806.

Now assume an increase in autonomous expenditures, shifting the *IS* curve rightward. The inevitable result will be a rise in interest rates. Very likely there will also be a slight increase in the money supply as a result of (1) a reduction in excess reserves, (2) increased use by the banks of the Federal Reserve's discount facilities, which raises total bank reserves, and (3) perhaps a decline in time deposits, if the Regulation Q interest ceiling induces some time-deposit holders to shift to other liquid assets. However, on balance the net result will be tightened credit conditions, credit rationing, and a slowing down of the rate of increase in aggregate demand—all without the Federal Reserve's "doing" anything!

We could illustrate the same process at work in a slump: declining aggregate demand due to a leftward shift of the *IS* curve resulting in reduced interest rates and a general relaxation of credit terms and conditions, thus cushioning the decline. The point is that we have here a mechanism much like that which we observed in the case of fiscal policy, a mechanism acting as a brake on both downward and upward movements of the economy. And, just as increased tax revenue does not necessarily mean "tighter" fiscal policy—it could be the natural result of a booming economy, with an unchanged tax structure—so a rise in interest rates does not necessarily mean that the Federal Reserve is "tightening the screws." Perhaps it is merely *permitting* the screws to tighten.

Summary

Monetary policy is the responsibility of the Federal Reserve. Although this responsibility is centered ultimately in the Board of Governors, for practical reasons policy decisions are actually hammered out at meetings of the Federal Open Market Committee. Assisted by the staff, members of the committee monitor the course of monetary policy as revealed by certain indicators (money supply, RPD's, and so on) and issue instructions to the system's open-market account management in the light of these indicators plus other economic and financial data and forecasts.

By far the most important monetary policy tool is open-market operations because of its advantages of potency, flexibility, and lack of fanfare. The other general weapons of control are the discount mechanism and reserve requirements, both of which have been subject to considerable criticism but are not generally considered to be seriously defective. Selective controls and moral suasion have been advocated as supplements to the three general weapons but have not been extensively used in the United States.

It is generally believed that monetary policy measures have potent effects on the behavior of the economy, but there is sharp disagreement between Keynesians and monetarists over the actual mechanism through which these effects are transmitted. The "standard" Keynesian view is that monetary policy should attempt to compensate for destabilizing influences in the economy (dynamic monetary policy) and in the money markets (defensive monetary policy). In contrast, the views of the monetarists about the way the economy functions lead them to conclude that monetary policy should be directed toward the accomplishment of one objective: a steady expansion of the money supply at a predetermined rate.

KEY CONCEPTS

Monetary aggregates
Indicators (of monetary policy)
RPD's
Inside lag
Recognition lag

Action lag
"Tradition against borrowing"
Selective credit controls
Moral suasion
Monetarists

QUESTIONS FOR REVIEW

1. Why is the Federal Reserve characterized as the "policy maker of last resort"?
2. What is a monetary policy "indicator" supposed to do? What are the criteria of an "ideal" indicator?
3. Why is the so-called RPD considered a superior indicator to, say, the money supply (M_1)?
4. What are some advantages and disadvantages of open-market operations as a tool of monetary policy?
5. Under what circumstances may a member bank legitimately borrow from its district Reserve bank for a few days? for several months?
6. How might the discount mechanism be improved, in the opinion of some students of the subject?
7. What are the major advantages and drawbacks of reserve requirements as a monetary policy weapon?
8. Of the two methods of easing money—reductions in reserve requirements and open-market purchases—which would bankers be likely to prefer? Why?
9. Give the case for selective credit controls. Why are they not widely used in the United States?
10. What are the major monetarist criticisms of Keynesian "orthodoxy"? What impact has monetarism had on monetary theory and policy?

SUGGESTIONS FOR FURTHER READING

Ahearn, Daniel S. *Federal Reserve Policy Reappraised, 1951–1959.* New York: Columbia University Press, 1963.
Anderson, Leonall, and Keith M. Carlson. "A Monetarist Model of Economic Stabilization." *Review,* Federal Reserve Bank of St. Louis. April 1970, pp. 7–25.

Aschheim, Joseph. *Techniques of Monetary Control.* Baltimore: Johns Hopkins Press, 1963.

Bach, G. Leland. *Making Monetary and Fiscal Policy* Washington, D.C.: The Brookings Institution, 1971.

Brunner, Karl (ed.). *Targets and Indicators of Monetary Policy.* San Francisco: Chandler Publishing Co., 1969.

Cagan, Phillip. *Recent Monetary Policy,* Washington, D.C.: American Enterprise Association, 1971.

Commission on Money and Credit, *Impacts of Monetary Policy.* Englewood Cliffs, N.J.: Prentice-Hall, 1963.

———, *Monetary Management.* Englewood Cliffs, N.J.: Prentice-Hall, 1963.

———. *Stabilization Policies.* Englewood Cliffs, N.J.: Prentice-Hall, 1963.

Cox, William N. "Measuring Monetary Policy." *Monthly Review,* Federal Reserve Bank of Atlanta, December 1970, pp. 182–187.

De Leeuw, Frank, and Edward M. Gramlich. "The Channels of Monetary Policy," *Federal Reserve Bulletin,* LV (June 1969), pp. 472–91.

Fand, David I. "A Monetarist Model of the Monetary Process." *Journal of Finance,* XXV (May 1970), pp. 1275–89.

Federal Reserve Bank of Boston *Controlling Monetary Aggregates.* Boston: Federal Reserve Bank of Boston, 1969.

———. *Controlling Monetary Aggregates II: The Implementation.* Boston: Federal Reserve Bank of Boston, 1973.

Friedman, Milton. *A Theoretical Framework for Monetary Analysis.* New York: Columbia University Press/National Bureau of Economic Research, 1971.

———, and Anna J. Schwartz. *A Monetary History of the United States: 1867–1960.* Princeton: National Bureau of Economic Research, 1963.

Hamovitch, William, ed., *Monetary Policy: The Argument from Keynes' Treatise to Friedman.* Lexington, Mass.: D. C. Heath and Co., 1966.

Johnson, Harry G. "The Keynesian Revolution and the Monetarist Counterrevolution." *American Economic Review,* LXI (May 1971), pp. 1–14.

Kaufman, George C. *Current Issues in Monetary Economics and Policy: A Review.* New York: Institute of Finance, New York University, 1969.

Maisel, Sherman J. *Managing the Dollar.* New York: W. W. Norton, 1973.

Mayer, Thomas. *Monetary Policy in the United States.* New York: Random House, 1968.

Meek, Paul. *Discount Policy and Open Market Operations.* Washington, D.C.: Board of Governors, Federal Reserve System, 1968.

Meigs, A. James. *Money Matters.* New York: Harper & Row, 1972.

Shull, Bernard. *Reappraisal of the Federal Reserve Discount Mechanism.* Washington. D.C.: Board of Governors, Federal Reserve System, 1968.

Smith, Warren L. "The Instruments of General Monetary Control." *National Banking Review,* I (September 1963), pp. 47–76.

Teigen, Ronald. "A Critical Look at Monetarist Economics." *Review,* Federal Reserve Bank of St. Louis, January 1972, pp. 10–23.

Willes, Mark H. "Lags in Monetary and Fiscal Policy." *Business Review,* Federal Reserve Bank of Philadelphia, March 1968, pp. 3–10.

Wrightsman, Dwayne. *An Introduction to Monetary Theory and Policy.* New York: Free Press, 1971.

International Aspects of Monetary Policy
The Balance of Payments
Complications for Federal Reserve Policy Making
The Federal Reserve and the International Monetary System

The Incidence of Monetary Policy
Housing Construction
State and Local Capital Expenditures
Possible Remedial Actions

Recapitulation of Macroeconomic Policy
Multiple Goals
Multiple Decision Centers
Multiple Means
Relations Among Types of Macroeconomic Policy

Summary

Monetary Policy: Further Considerations

The basic analysis of monetary policy presented in chapter 21 must be qualified and amplified in several respects. First, we have to explore the implications for monetary policy of the fact that the United States exists in a world economy. Next, we examine the relations of monetary policy to other types of macroeconomic policy. Finally, we consider some of the unsolved problems and unresolved issues relating to monetary policy.

International Aspects of Monetary Policy

In chapter 19 we included "balance-of-payments equilibrium" as one of the macroeconomic goals of our American society. Our concern since that point, however, has been almost exclusively with the effects of monetary and other macroeconomic policy measures on the domestic economy: income and employment, the price level, and the rate of economic growth. Yet, in striving toward achievement of our domestic macroeconomic goals, the policy makers must bear in mind the interrelations between our economy—the real and financial sectors—and those of other nations. Sometimes progress with respect to domestic objectives can be impeded by our need to attain or to maintain a satisfactory external financial position. In this section we plan to explore this problem.

The Balance of Payments[1]

In order to understand the goal of balance-of-payments equilibrium, we obviously must first acquaint ourselves with the type of financial statement known as the balance of payments. An essential tool for studying a nation's position vis-à-vis other nations, it summarizes in a small number of general categories the results of all transactions between the nation and the rest of the world over a given period of time.

Table 22.1 presents a simplified balance-of-payments statement for the United States for the year 1973. The figures themselves are not especially important at this point. The year 1973 was far from a normal one with respect to international monetary matters, and the balance-of-payments figures reflect these stresses. Rather, what we are concerned with are the basic concepts and terminology used in discussions of balance-of-payments matters.

Several characteristics of this statement should be noted and kept in mind. First, the statement records *flows*, not stocks. It tells us the dollar volume of goods and services and also the flow of financial claims[2] of all kinds moving between (in this case) the United States and the rest of the world. Second, the statement is based on double-entry bookkeeping. Thus, for example, to record an export of farm machinery temporarily financed by a short-term loan to the importer by the exporter's bank, we would *debit* an account representing short-term credit extended abroad and *credit* exports. Naturally, therefore, the total on the debit side will be equal to the credit total—or would be, if every transaction were actually recorded. However, since there are gaps in our information system and some transactions are not reported, an entry labeled "errors and omissions" must be included.

The first two accounts listed and described in Table 22.1, exports and imports, are considerably broader in scope than is generally realized. Although merchandise comprises by far the largest share of both exports and imports—roughly two-thirds of each in recent years—the size of the remainder, the other third, indicates that we ought not think of exports and imports as synonymous with merchandise. *The balance on goods and services* is another name for "net exports," (X_n), which we encountered several times in Part IV.

The *balance on current account* records the outcome of the inflow and outflow of goods, services, and unilateral transfers, both private and government. All the remaining items, with the exceptions of "errors and omissions" and gold, record the changes in various categories of debt and equity claims on, and obligations to, the rest of the world. Because the outflow exceeded the inflow of long-term capital in 1973, the *balance*

---

[1] A helpful elementary treatment of this topic is John Pippenger, "Balance-of-Payments Definitions: Measurement and Interpretation," *Review*, Federal Reserve Bank of St. Louis, (November 1973), pp. 6–14.

[2] For some categories of claims we recorded only the *net* flow in or out. The reader interested in the details should consult the source of Table 22.1.

TABLE 22.1
Balance of Payments of the United States, 1973
(in $millions)

Category	Debits (−)	Credits (+)	Balance
Exports (merchandise; military sales; transportation, travel, and other services rendered; income from foreign investments)		$102,744	
Imports (merchandise; military expenditures; transportation, travel, and other services received; investment income payments)	$95,844		
BALANCE ON GOODS AND SERVICES			$6,900
Remittances, pensions, and other transfers	1,913		
U.S. government grants (excluding military).	1,947		
BALANCE ON CURRENT ACCOUNT			3,041
U.S. government capital flows (net) and nonliquid liabilities to other than foreign official reserve agencies	1,469		
U.S. long-term private capital flows (net)	7,023		
Foreign long-term private capital flows (net)		6,666	
BALANCE ON CURRENT ACCOUNT AND LONG-TERM CAPITAL			1,214
Nonliquid short-term private capital flows (net)	4,210		
Errors and omissions, net	4,793		
NET LIQUIDITY BALANCE			−7,789
U.S. liquid private capital flows (net)	1,933		
Foreign liquid private capital flows (net)		4,436	
OFFICIAL RESERVE TRANSACTIONS BALANCE			−5,286
financed by changes in:			
Liabilitis to foreign official agencies		5,077	
U.S. official reserve assets		209	
Gold		(0)	
SDR's		(9)	
Convertible currencies		(233)	
Gold tranche position in IMF	(33)		

Source: Adapted from *Survey of Current Business*, December 1973, pp. 35, 43–44.

on current account and long-term capital was about $1.8 billion smaller than the current-account balance.

The *net liquidity balance* shows the effects of the year's foreign transactions on our international liquidity position. The $7.8 billion deficit in this balance records for 1973 the amount of liquid assets we parted with plus liquid liabilities we incurred as a nation in excess of the liquid assets we acquired, plus any reduction in our liquid liabilities to foreigners. An examination of the items below this balance reveals that most of this amount, about $5.1 billion, consisted of additions to our "liabilities to foreign official agencies," with the remaining $2.7 billion represented by (1) the addition to our liquid obligations to private foreign economic units net of the addition of our stock of claims against them (about $2.5 billion) and (2) a decline in our official reserve assets ($.2 billion).

This balance is one of the two most commonly used in discussions of the nation's balance-of-payments position, the other being the *official reserve transactions balance*. There is no unanimity among analysts as to which one is the more meaningful from the standpoint of monetary policy; and the Department of Commerce publishes both balances on a regular basis. Regardless of the specific balance used, the balance-of-payments figures must be supplemented by a great deal of information concerning real and financial conditions here and in the other major nations. Even then, experts often differ in their interpretations of the data and in their policy recommendations.

Every year since 1960 the United States has incurred a balance-of-payments deficit, using the net liquidity balance; and in ten of these fourteen years our official reserve transactions balance also showed a deficit.[3]

One financial manifestation of our balance-of-payments deficits is a net increase of short-term claims against us. Such claims initially take the form mainly of increases in foreign deposits in American banks (and decreases in our deposits abroad). However, dollar deposits in excess of actual working-balances needs are generally utilized to purchase short-term dollar claims, particularly Treasury bills but also bankers' acceptances, commercial paper, and other safe liquid securities. Thus, at the end of 1973 foreign economic units had accumulated more than $87.7 billion in liquid claims against United States economic units. (Table 22.2. For more details, see Table 12.1)

With all the pressing needs for economic development at home, why are foreign economic units (private and government) willing to hold this immense volume of liquid claims against us? In large part the answer is related to the international monetary role of the dollar as the leading reserve currency and international medium of exchange, which we dis-

---

[3] *Economic Report of the President, 1974* (Washington, D. C.: U.S. Government Printing Office, 1974), p. 351.

TABLE 22.2
United States Liquid Liabilities to Foreigners,
December 31, 1973
(in $millions)

Claim Holder	Amount of Claim
Central banks and government	$61,919
Foreign commercial banks	17,645
Other private foreign residents and unallocated	6,153
Nonmonetary international and interregional organizations	2,000
Total	$87,717

Source: *Survey of Current Business*, March 1974, p. 51.

cussed in chapter 12. Nations—or, more exactly, public and private economic units within nations—hold international monetary reserves for essentially the same reasons as those for which they hold domestic liquid assets: mainly for transactions, precaution, and (at times) speculation. As the volume of world trade and other international transactions increases, there is a corresponding growth in demand for international reserves for transactions and contingency purposes.

Nevertheless, there is always the danger that, if the United States incurs excessively large deficits, the dollar's acceptability will deteriorate, gradually or suddenly. This is one reason—the main reason— for concern over our balance-of-payments position. The problem, however, is: how large is "too large"? We have pointed out that the world needs an ever-increasing volume of international reserves and that the dollar is one widely used type of reserve. Since world monetary gold reserves are not capable of "automatic" increases in response to increased need, we could argue that our deficits have served world trade by providing the needed liquidity.

This brings us to the question of the relationship between the deficit in the balance of payments and *equilibrium* in the balance of payments. What the above suggests is that equilibrium may not necessarily imply "absence of a surplus or deficit in the balance of payments," at least with respect to the United States, so long as foreigners desire to hold an increasing volume of liquid claims against us to serve as part of their monetary reserves. Unfortunately, there is no known indicator that will tell us unambiguously whether our deficits are, or have been, too large or too small, regardless of which basis we use to measure them.

As this is an extremely complex and unsettled area of analysis, there would be no point in attempting to wrap it all up with a few simple conclusions. Seeing that the world's monetary experts disagree—or simply do not venture an answer—we shall not be so foolhardy as to take sides.

Complications for Federal Reserve Policy Making

The Federal Reserve, however, cannot take this easy way out. It must conduct monetary policy with a view not only to meeting domestic goals but also to maintaining our international financial position. Besides being alert to the effects of its actions on our international economic and financial position, the Federal Reserve must note the implications of foreign economic and financial developments for the performance of our domestic economy—as measured by employment, prices, and the rate of growth—and on our balance-of-payments position. Therefore, we are not surprised to learn that a part of the briefing session at each meeting of the Open Market Committee consists of an analysis of such variables as our recent and projected trade surplus or deficit and balance-of-payments position as well as developments in foreign exchange markets.

To refresh our memories, let us recall briefly some of the connections between domestic economic developments and our position with respect to the rest of the world. First, and perhaps most obviously, domestic price movements affect our net exports (exports minus imports). An inflation domestically reduces our net export balance in two related ways: (1) our goods and services become costlier, so exports tend to decline, and (2) foreign goods and services become relatively less expensive, so imports tend to increase. All this, of course, assumes other things, including technology, foreign prices, import duties, and so on, unchanged.

A change in domestic income is another source of shift in our international position. Higher incomes, as we learned in chapter 15, result in a higher level of consumption, part of which consists of purchases of foreign-made goods. Also, it is conceivable that higher corporate profits—which usually accompany higher incomes—will encourage and enable an increase in overseas investment by domestic firms.

Third, our international position is affected by interest rates and credit availability. When short-term rates decline and credit becomes generally easier here, financial institutions and other economic units with large portfolios of short-term claims tend to purchase foreign claims instead of domestic, while their foreign counterparts tend to liquidate some of their short-term dollar claims.

Thus there is no question but that the actions of the Federal Reserve directed primarily toward influencing the domestic economy—its price level, income and employment, and growth—have effects on our economic and financial relations with the rest of the world. And, in a similar manner, economic and financial developments abroad often have a noticeable effect here. In fact, it is necessary to carry the analysis a step further: the Federal Reserve must take into account the likely effects of its actions on our economy *via their effects on financial markets elsewhere*! In other words, our understanding of the channels of monetary policy must be broadened to take in the financial institutions and markets of other nations as well as our own.

Here is a vivid illustration of this point:

> Before 1966, most U.S. banks regarded the Eurodollar market as a borrowing source of "last resort," only to be tapped in times of stress or when the cost of borrowing was exceptionally attractive. However . . . U.S. banks now regard the market as simply another source of funds to be tapped whenever the interest rates are appropriate. . . .
>
> Thus, as a result of these developments, changes in U.S. domestic monetary conditions are reflected more quickly than ever before in world monetary conditions. . . . The Eurodollar market has become, to all intents and purposes, an extension of the New York money market. The most important implication of these developments is that the Federal Reserve will presumably be forced in the future to take even greater account of the international effects of its policies than it has in the past.[4]

With this background let us now consider several possible combinations of domestic and balance-of-payments conditions and observe the way in which this additional responsibility affects the Federal Reserve's task in each case.[5] It is assumed in every instance that the condition described is both persistent and substantial.

DOMESTIC UNEMPLOYMENT AND BALANCE-OF-PAYMENTS SURPLUS
This combination tells the Federal Reserve to pursue an expansionary policy. Domestically, the result of this kind of policy should be higher income and employment. In *IS-LM* terms, the *LM* curve shifts rightward, signifying a higher equilibrium GNP and a lower equilibrium rate of interest.

We recall that the net exports curve slopes downward, that is, at higher levels of GNP the net export balance is lower. So an expansionary monetary policy should reduce the current-account surplus.

What about capital flows? Lower interest rates will encourage an outflow of capital as domestic financial intermediaries and other economic units are encouraged by the decline in domestic interest rates to seek relatively more favorable yields elsewhere. This development, too, tends to reduce our payments surplus. A factor working in the opposite direction is the improved domestic profit picture, which will tend to discourage the outward flow of equity investment.

---

[4] Geoffrey L. Bell, "Comment: The Effects of Monetary Policy on Specific Sectors of the Economy," *Journal of Political Economy*, LXXVI (July–August 1968), Part II, "Issues in Monetary Research, 1967," pp. 818–19.

[5] The subsequent discussion is built on the framework used in J. Herbert Furth, "International Developments and Monetary Policy," *Business Conditions*, Federal Reserve Bank of Chicago (October 1964), pp. 5–12.

DOMESTIC INFLATION PLUS BALANCE-OF-PAYMENTS DEFICIT Here the correct policy is just the opposite: tighten up. The result should be an eventual slowdown (perhaps even a halt) in inflation and an improvement in the balance-of-payments position.

DOMESTIC INFLATION PLUS BALANCE-OF-PAYMENTS SURPLUS From a monetary policy standpoint, this case presents problems. Efforts to curb inflation tend to increase our export surplus. The problem of the surplus, however, can be handled by fiscal measures: a reduction in tariff rates and in other barriers to imports.[6]

DOMESTIC UNEMPLOYMENT PLUS BALANCE-OF-PAYMENTS DEFICIT This is the only combination for which there is no satisfactory set of remedial measures. The heart of the problem is that domestic policy considerations demand low interest rates and easy monetary conditions, to facilitate expansion of income and employment, while the deficit condition in the balance of payments calls for high interest rates and tight money.

At first thought it might seem logical to utilize the same measures as in number 3 above, except in the opposite direction: impose or increase tariffs and other import barriers. But this is undesirable not only on resource-allocation grounds—since it impedes international specialization on the basis of comparative advantage—but also in generating ill will on the part of other nations and inviting retaliatory increases in their import barriers against us.

Another suggested remedy is to keep long-term interest rates low, encouraging domestic investment, while pushing up short-term rates, discouraging portfolio managers from purchasing (importing) foreign short-term claims. This possibility is of more than theoretical interest, by the way. The Federal Reserve and Treasury attempted for a time, beginning in 1961, to "twist" the interest rate structure in this direction. The Treasury issued mainly bills, thus increasing the supply of short-term claims on the market; and the Federal Reserve increased its holdings of non-short-term Treasury securities, thus putting upward pressure on prices (downward pressure on yields) of these latter securities and opposite pressures on the prices and yields of short-term claims.

The fact that this policy was not pursued consistently and vigorously and the overwhelming pressures of other factors make it impossible to obtain a clear-cut verdict on this policy.[7] However, on a theoretical level, insofar as securities in neighboring maturity categories are feasible substitutes in portfolios, we can expect that attempts to maintain a rate structure "artificially" will take an enormous amount of offsetting

---

[6] Some nations could impose, or increase, a tax on exports, but the Constitution of the United States (Article I, section 8) expressly forbids use of this device by our government.

[7] Representing two opposing views of the results are (1) favorable: Gary Fromm, "Recent Monetary Policy: An Econometric View," *National Banking Review* (March 1966), especially p. 304; (2) unfavorable: Myron H. Ross, "Operation Twist: A Mistaken Policy," *Journal of Political Economy*, LXXIV (April 1966), pp. 195–99.

open-market operations. On the other hand, if the "market segmentation" theories are more nearly correct, the monetary authorities will be able to exert a continuing and powerful influence on the maturity structure of yields.[8]

A third approach to this difficult situation is to utilize a combination of "tight" monetary policy and "easy" fiscal policy—which, in turn, requires a knowledgeable and cooperative Congress. The monetary authorities must utilize restrictive measures in order to raise interest rates, thus lowering the inducement to purchase foreign short-term claims. On the *IS-LM* diagram, this would be represented by a leftward (upward) movement of the *LM* curve, for example, from *LM"* to *LM* in Figure 22.1. Fiscal policy, in turn, must be expansive, stimulating private demand through tax policy and/or increasing government spending, thus shifting the *IS* curve rightward.

If the policy makers are sufficiently astute (or lucky) so that this plan is successful, the result will be an improvement in our balance-of-payments position (because of the rise in R) plus an increase in our equilibrium GNP. However, the cost of continued monetary restraint will be reduced business investment, hence a probable retardation in the rate of economic growth.

This is not merely an abstract theoretical dilemma, either; the United States faced just this kind of situation in the 1960s. Among the measures adopted by the Federal government to deal with the situation were the Interest Equalization Tax in 1964, as mentioned earlier, and the Volun-

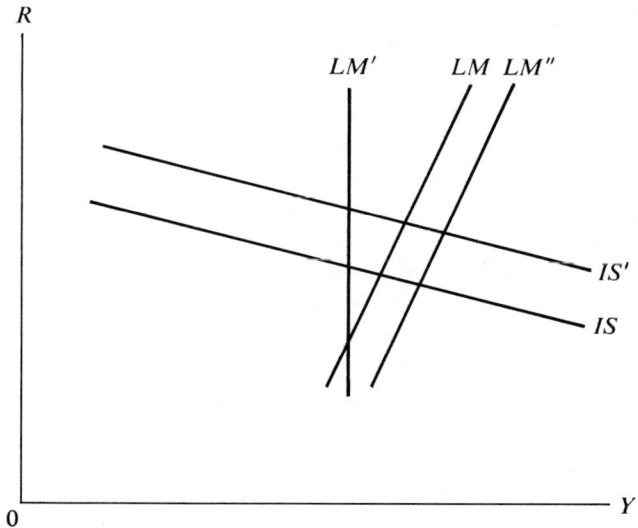

Figure 22.1
Effects of monetary and fiscal policy on aggregate equilibrium.

[8] Recall the discussion of the interest rate structure in chapter 11.

tary Foreign Credit Program (VFCP), begun in 1965, designed to discourage financial and nonfinancial firms from making foreign investments and from other activities that would aggravate our balance-of-payments deficit.[9]

Dealing with the problem in this manner, that is, attempting to cure a balance-of-payments deficit through artificial limitations on private capital movements, does not get high marks from economists. If condition 4 were to prove our "normal" state of affairs, the measures utilized would be of doubtful value as elements in a long-run solution.

> First, it inhibits the operation of market forces in allocating resources in an efficient manner. Second, it retards the development of integrated capital markets. . . . Third, its balance-of-payments effects are transitory. Once the movement of capital is reduced, room for further reduction is limited. Moreover, after a few years, foreign loans and investments begin to yield a return flow of interest and dividends which may be much larger than the initial capital outlay.[10]

The Federal Reserve and the International Monetary System

Thus far in the discussion we have taken a strictly domestic point of view regarding international monetary matters, analyzing them as they relate to *our* economy, *our* balance-of-payments problem, and *our* central bank's monetary policy task, treating the international monetary system as a "given." However, we must also recognize that the Federal Reserve has certain responsibilities with respect to the development and conduct of the international monetary system. These responsibilities are related to domestic monetary policy, but they go far beyond it, since an effectively functioning international monetary system affects the pattern and volume of world trade, economic growth of both advanced and less-developed nations, and international political relations as well.

A well-functioning international monetary system requires three elements: (1) adequate international liquidity, (2) an effective adjustment process, and (3) confidence among the participating nations in the stability of exchange rates. *Liquidity* is a matter of international reserves (gold, convertible foreign currencies, the IMF "gold tranche," and the recently instituted Special Drawing Rights)[11] and credit facilities provided by the IMF and other agencies. *Adjustment* to balance-of-payments disequilibria can take place through measures affecting net exports via domestic price and income changes and through changing exchange rates. *Confidence* is a product of the many and often elusive factors influencing expectations of exchange rate stability. When confidence deteriorates, holders of claims denominated in the monetary unit that is expected to be devalued attempt to liquidate them and to acquire claims in monetary units that they trust.

---

[9] The VFCP was made mandatory beginning in 1968.
[10] Delbert A. Snider, *International Monetary Relations* (New York: Random House, 1966), p. 116.
[11] Recall chapter 12.

Obviously, these three requirements are interrelated. For example, the amount of liquidity needed depends in part on the effectiveness of the adjustment mechanism; and, conversely, the greater the volume of international reserves and credit resources, the less pressure on the adjustment mechanism. Also, the more effective the adjustment mechanism and the larger the volume of international reserves, the less likelihood there is of destabilizing flows of short-term funds.

Now, how does the Federal Reserve fit into this picture? In several ways. The Federal Reserve contributes to liquidity through an ingenious set of bilateral "swap" arrangements with other central banks. These arrangements might be termed *mutual lines of credit,* each one of which is a pact whereby either party agrees that it will grant credit automatically to the other party in case of temporary balance-of-payments pressures. While this does not increase international reserves, it does expand the network of credit arrangements working to reduce the need for international reserves.

The Federal Reserve contributes to the adjustments process, too, in a number of ways: (1) during slumps it attempts, within the limitations imposed by domestic economic policy needs, to keep short-term interest rates from falling so low as to induce an outflow of short-term funds; (2) it administers the program of restraints on investment abroad; and (3) it keeps the policy makers in Congress and in the executive branch apprised of international financial needs.

Finally, although the primary consideration behind Federal Reserve actions designed to affect the international financial environment is our own balance-of-payments position, an important byproduct is an improvement in international financial conditions—which, in turn, contributes to a higher level of confidence in the viability of the system.

The Incidence of Monetary Policy

We have been considering the effects of monetary policy almost as though they were confined to the big economic aggregates: consumption, investment, exports, and so on. It is time now to narrow our focus: to investigate the impact of monetary policy *within* these aggregates, in recognition of the fact that these aggregate effects come about only because individual economic units are induced to change their spending decisions as a result of monetary policy measures. This shift may come either because the financing terms available to the economic unit have changed or, more indirectly, because the economic situation (as it appears to the economic unit) has been altered, changing profit prospects, price or income expectations, or some other variable influencing the decision to spend.

There was a time when monetary policy was advocated on grounds that its effects were neutral because, in contrast to fiscal policy—which necessarily utilizes changes in *particular* taxes or *particular* expenditure programs—monetary policy measures involve changes in the stock of that most widely used of all financial assets: money. This point of view is no longer tenable—we know too much! As a result of intensive studies of the effects of monetary policy on various sectors of the economy, particularly during tight-money periods, we have begun to acquire some idea of the incidence of monetary policy, that is, of the pattern of its effects on particular industries and expenditure categories. We want to know which groups or sectors are especially hard-hit by monetary measures, why this situation exists, and what can or should be done about it.

Our discussion will deal mainly with the differential effects of *tight* money. When credit conditions are easy, we do not worry particularly about the incidence of monetary policy; but when money is tight, the cry of "discrimination" is heard in the land.[12]

Housing Construction

One sector in particular that shows severe effects of monetary tightness is residential construction. This should not surprise us. The purchase of new housing depends heavily on credit, but, as interest rates rise, the traditional suppliers of housing credit (savings and loan associations, mutual savings banks, and commercial banks) often experience difficulties in obtaining financing due to ceilings on the rates that they may pay on thrift deposits. Moreover, VA and FHA interest-rate ceilings may effectively limit yields on these types of mortgages, and usury laws sometimes curb the interest rates that may be charged on conventional mortgages; thus, other long-term financial assets, such as corporate bonds, begin to look more attractive to these lenders.

Even apart from these artificial constraints, however, is the fact that mortgage borrowers, especially those financing the purchase of their own homes, are more sensitive to interest-rate shifts than are most classes of borrowers. A small interest-rate change means a relatively large change in the all-important monthly payment, as does any reduction in the maturity of the loan. Business demand for financing is relatively sensitive to economic conditions, and firms willingly pay higher interest rates for accommodation when the outlook is favorable; but household demand for financing for new construction does not exhibit this kind of pattern at all since personal incomes fluctuate much less than do business profits.

State and Local Capital Expenditures

State and local government capital expenditures also show above-average sensitivity to changes in credit conditions.[13] In this case, too, an important reason is that costs of borrowing fluctuate far more than ex-

---

[12] Incidentally, we are concerned here only with possible discriminatory effects of monetary policy, not with discrimination arising from monopoly monetary conditions, "credit gaps," and other market imperfections for which monetary policy can hardly be blamed.

[13] John E. Peterson, "Response of State and Local Governments to Varying Credit Conditions," *Federal Reserve Bulletin* (March 1971), pp. 209–24.

pected yields from the projects. By the same token, though, capital spending by states and municipal units of government should increase by more than average percentages during easy-money periods. While this might seem "discriminatory" in that this kind of expenditure is affected more than average, consider this:

> The contracyclical fluctuations of state and local bond sales, contract awards and construction work, although relatively small in amplitude, have made a substantial contribution to the stabilization of the economy since 1952. The most ardent advocate of compensatory monetary policy could hardly have hoped for a better performance.[14]

Possible Remedial Actions

Perhaps there are other groups as well which are, or may be, affected disproportionately strongly by tight money.[15] But, in any case, what action ought to be taken to even out the effects of monetary policy?[16] One alternative is—no action. That is, after considering the possible benefits and costs of intervention, it might possibly be better to tolerate the existing imperfect situation than to attempt to change it through monetary policy. For example (accepting the position that housing construction is strongly affected by tight money), if considered desirable on other grounds (social urgency of housing, sustaining construction employment, and so on) to avoid this large reduction in home building, the problem might be dealt with through direct subsidies. Fluctuations in state and local capital expenditures could be reduced through similar measures.

Another approach to the problem is to work toward the elimination of market imperfections and other barriers to free-market allocation of credit. Obvious illustrations of barriers are interest-rate ceilings on mortgage loans and on thrift deposits. Regulations and other actions to deal with particular problem situations with which the general instruments of monetary policy are incapable of dealing make up the third approach. This one has been, and is being, used by the Federal Reserve in a number of ways. Familiar examples are margin requirements on securities purchases, moral suasion to curb less desirable forms of bank

---

[14] Frank Morris, "Impact of Monetary Policy on State and Local Governments: An Empirical Study," *Journal of Finance*, XV (May 1960), p. 249.

[15] Small businesses and lower-income households are sometimes mentioned in this connection, but the evidence is not clear-cut. See George L. Bach and Clarence J. Huizenga, "The Differential Effects of Tight Money," *American Economic Review*, LI (March 1961), pp. 52–80; William L. Silber and Murray E. Polakoff, "The Differential Effects of Tight Money: An Econometric Study," *Journal of Finance*, XXV (March 1970), pp. 83–97; and Oswald Brownlee and Alfred Conrad, "Effects upon the Distribution of Income of a Tight-Money Policy," in Commission on Money and Credit, *Stabilization Policies* (Englewood Cliffs, N.J.: Prentice-Hall, 1963), pp. 499–558.

[16] The following paragraphs are based on David P. Eastburn, "Uneven Impacts of Monetary Policy: What to Do about Them?" *Business Review*, Federal Reserve Bank of Philadelphia (January 1967), pp. 2, 21–23.

lending, and regulations limiting real estate and consumer installment credit during war periods.

These three approaches to altering the incidence of monetary policy are not mutually exclusive, of course. In any particular case, the appropriate alternative would depend on (1) the seriousness of the effect of tight money or, stating it differently, the gain from correction of the situation; (2) available remedies, if any; and (3) their relative cost, in terms of both economic and noneconomic considerations.

Recapitulation of Macroeconomic Policy

Let us attempt to pull together the various aspects of macroeconomic policy so that, hopefully, we leave the topic with a clear impression of the forest after having spent much time and effort on the individual trees.

Multiple Goals

We identified four major goals of macroeconomic policy: price-level stability, full employment, an adequate rate of economic growth, and a sustainable position with respect to our balance of payments. As there are both complementary and competitive relationships among these goals, an attempt to make more progress toward achieving one of them may simultaneously move us closer to one or two of them and farther from the other(s).

It would be completely futile to attempt to identify the one particular combination out of all feasible combinations of values for all four goal-variables (price level, rate of unemployment, rate of growth, and balance-of-payments position) that would be most desired by our society. In the first place, economic theory has not advanced enough so that we can determine which combinations are possible and which are not. Second, even if we could solve that problem, we still would not have the slightest idea of how to ascertain the one possible combination that would be "most desired." And, third, even if we could discover a way to identify *the* best combination, by the time we could put into effect the necessary policies and these policies worked their magic, a completely different array of economic possibilities and a changed social attitude toward goals and priorities might have emerged.

Probably a much more realistic approach would be in terms of *acceptability* of combinations. If our position with respect to economic growth, level of employment, and balance of payments were tolerable but we were experiencing an excessive rate of inflation—10 per cent, for instance—this would constitute an unacceptable combination. Social pressures on the policy makers would be set in motion to induce them to take corrective action.

Sometimes we may experience a combination that is unacceptable in terms of more than one goal—say, the rate of change of the price level and the level of unemployment—correction of which calls for incompatible actions. (This kind of situation has, in fact, happened recently, both in the late 1950s and again in the period beginning in 1969.) Then the policy makers must attempt to follow policies that, in their judgment, will minimize pressures. However, the policy makers themselves are often subject to conflicting pressures, the lags involved in the process may be long and variable, the information system is far from ideal, and knowledge of what to do with the information is deficient—all of which makes the task of economic policy making exceedingly difficult.

Multiple Decision Centers

One characteristic of the policy-making machinery itself that raises some problems is the existence of several more or less separate policy decision centers. Although the policy mandate of the Congress, the Federal Reserve Board of Governors, the U.S. President, and the Secretary of the Treasury is the same with respect to macroeconomic policy, there are often differences both in judgment concerning goal priorities and in pressures experienced. Thus, while the Reserve Board is reasonably free to follow its convictions with respect to monetary policy, the Congress may hesitate to legislate an increase in tax rates in an election year, even though considerations of fiscal policy might call for such action. Largely for this reason—conflicting pressures—we treated monetary policy as the "last resort" policy, which is expected to respond to the conditions of the economy and also to the stance of fiscal and debt management policies.

Multiple Means

Finally, both fiscal policy and monetary policy may be implemented through a number of combinations of means, or "weapons." While it is conceivable that any one of several of these weapons could be employed to achieve the same *direct* effect on a particular goal-variable, there is a strong probability that each of them would have different effects on other goal-variables and an even stronger probability that they would differ in their incidence. Therefore, policy makers (even Federal Reserve authorities) must take into account other economic goals of society beside those relating strictly to the aggregate economy.

Relations Among Types of Macroeconomic Policy

We can illustrate many of the foregoing points, and do a bit of reviewing as well, by following a hypothetical situation in which the relations among these three types of macroeconomic policy may be observed.

Assume that our economy has been neither declining nor advancing appreciably for several quarters. We can take it for granted that, as a result, the rate of unemployment has gone up, since (1) technological progress and increased capital (assuming positive net investment) enables the same aggregate output to be produced with fewer workers, and (2) the labor force has (probably) continued to grow. Thus our position is unsatisfactory relative to two goals: full employment and adequate growth. Assume further that the rate of price increase is tolerable and that our balance of payments is in excellent shape.

Now, in order to move the economy upward, and because it happens to be an election year, Congress decides to reduce tax rates on both personal and corporate incomes. It is anticipated that (1) consumption will increase because of the resultant rise in disposable incomes and (2) investment also will rise because of increased after-tax profitability of capital spending projects and increased ability of corporations to finance their own investment spending. If Congress is greatly concerned about our economic growth rate, it will stress tax reductions that will stimulate investment. If the main concern is happy prospective voters, perhaps the stress will be on measures to raise household disposable incomes. In any case, in terms of our *IS-LM* analysis, we have an increase in autonomous expenditures, shifting the *IS* curve rightward to *IS'* (Figure 22.1).

Unfortunately, we seem to have forgotten something. The Treasury must obtain money from somewhere to fill the gap in revenues left by the tax reduction, in order to maintain its (unchanged) expenditure level. Several possible sources come to mind. First, it could sell securities to nonbank investors—insurance companies, individuals, pension funds, savings banks, and so on—by offering attractive terms. This, however, would mean reduced availability of financing and also higher financing costs to other economic units (including business firms and prospective buyers of new homes), tending to counteract the effects on investment of reduced tax rates.

Or, the Treasury might attempt to make the issue of securities attractive to commercial banks. Unless we make the farfetched assumption that the banks just happen to have large amounts of unwanted excess reserves, the only way they can make room in their portfolios for more Treasury securities is by reducing their credit extended to other sectors. Result: some would-be household and business borrowers that would have been accommodated must be turned away.

In both these cases we are assuming that the Federal Reserve is pursuing a passive, "hands off" policy; yet money is tightening and interest rates are moving upward because of the increased Federal demands for financing superimposed on existing private and non-Federal government demands. This situation illustrates the "automatic stabilizer" stance of monetary policy.

Will this tightening effect completely offset the stimulation of reduced taxes as an influence on aggregate spending? In other words, is the LM curve completely vertical over the relevant range (like LM' in Figure 22.1), so that the rising IS curve merely pushes R up? Probably not. As interest rates rise, businesses and financial institutions have a stronger incentive to economize on cash balances. In some instances, this means handling a larger volume of business without increasing the average cash balance; in others, it means utilizing idle cash to purchase earning assets. But the result is that a constant money supply can accommodate a larger GNP, though at a higher interest-rate level.

It would be the height of irresponsibility for the Federal Reserve to remain inactive in the situation described, unless, in the judgment of the Board of Governors, fiscal policy alone would provide enough upward thrust—"enough," that is, so far as the Federal Reserve was concerned, with the possibility remaining that other decision centers might not agree. Normally, though, conditions are such that the Federal Reserve will pitch in, so that monetary policy will contribute in a positive manner.

If the Federal Reserve were to reduce reserve requirements, the banking system could absorb additional government securities, adding to the money supply besides. The Federal Reserve could also contribute either by purchasing the newly issued securities directly from the Treasury or by purchasing other government securities from banks or nonbank portfolios. In either case, bank reserves would be increased; and, through bank lending and investing, the money supply would grow by an amount several times the reserves increment. Thus, the economic effects of the rightward shift of the IS curve caused by fiscal action would be supplemented by the rightward shift of the LM curve (LM'' in Figure 22.1) due to monetary policy action.

* * *

If you were to reread the last section, writing down the numbers of the chapter or chapters in this book in which each idea, concept, or term first appeared, you would discover that all or nearly all the chapters would be represented. Why not reread it anyway, with that thought in mind?

This idea underlines the essential unity of the financial system in its three aspects: structure, functions, and policy. To a point, one can study structure apart from function, and vice versa, or both of these without policy. Yet all three are parts of a complete system, though, of course, even this system is only a subsystem of a still larger system—the economic system—which is, in turn, part of a larger system, ad infinitum.

We come now to the parting of the ways, having gone through many experiences together since we met in the Overview. Hopefully, you have found the whole venture interesting, on balance. But assuredly, the venture will provide returns, in numerous ways, over the years to come.

Summary

The fact that the United States is but one nation, albeit a powerful one, in the world economy entails certain problems for monetary policy. External events and developments at times impose strains on our domestic economy, but our policy response may, under certain circumstances, be hampered by balance-of-payments considerations. Moreover, since the dollar is the leading "key currency" of the world, the Federal Reserve has certain duties and responsibilities related to the maintenance of a viable international monetary system.

Another important aspect of monetary policy is its incidence, that is, its nonuniform effects on different sectors of the economy. The housing construction sector has been found to be particularly sensitive to changes in overall credit conditions, with state and local capital expenditures, small business, and low-income households also sometimes included as hard-hit sectors. As to what should be done about these differential effects, suggestions vary from "do nothing" to quite elaborate regulatory schemes.

KEY CONCEPTS

Balance of payments
Balance on goods and services
Balance on current account
Balance on current account and long-term capital
Net liquidity balance
Official reserve transactions balance
Incidence of monetary policy

QUESTIONS FOR REVIEW

1. Why is it so difficult to identify *equilibrium* in a nation's balance of payments?
2. What is the relationship between our balance-of-payments deficit and foreign holdings of short-term claims against us?
3. Why do foreigners hold such a huge volume of short-term liquid dollar claims? Does this imply that foreigners might actually favor deficits in our balance of payments? Explain.
4. How does each of the following tend to affect our balance-of-payments position: (*a*) rising domestic prices, (*b*) a decline in our GNP, (*c*) an increase in short-term rates in U.S. money markets?
5. Which combination of conditions is easier to handle, from the standpoint of monetary policy: domestic unemployment plus a balance-of-payments surplus, or domestic unemployment plus a balance-of-payments deficit? Why? What, then, might be done to cope with the more difficult combination?
6. What are the three criteria of a well-functioning international mon-

etary system? How can the Federal Reserve contribute to their attainment?
7. What public policies might be pursued with respect to the problem of wide swings in credit availability for housing construction?

SUGGESTIONS FOR FURTHER READING

Aliber, Robert Z. *The Future of the Dollar as an International Currency*. New York: Praeger Publishers, 1966.

Brownlee, Oswald, and Alfred Conrad. "Effects upon the Distribution of Income of a Tight Money Policy," in Commission on Money and Credit, *Stabilization Policies*. Englewood Cliffs, N.J.: Prentice-Hall, 1963.

Federal Reserve Bank of Boston. *Housing and Monetary Policy*. Boston: Federal Reserve Bank of Boston, 1970.

Furth, J. Herbert. "International Developments and Monetary Policy," *Business Conditions*. Federal Reserve Bank of Chicago, October, 1964, pp. 5–12.

Kaufman, George G. *Current Issues in Monetary Economics and Policy: A Review*. New York: Institute of Finance, New York Universiy, 1969.

Petersen, John E. "Response of State and Local Governments to Varying Credit Conditions." *Federal Reserve Bulletin*, LVII (March 1971), pp. 209–32.

Index

Acceleration principle, 350–52
Acceptances (*see* Bankers' acceptances)
Ackley, Gardner, 349*n*, 366*n*
Action lag, 477
Active deficit, 450
Adequate rate of economic growth, 438–39
Adjustable-peg system (exchange rates), 270
African Development Bank, 279
Agency for International Development, 299–300
Agency securities, 241–42
Agricultural credit: government role, 294–97
Ahearn, Daniel S., 499
Alhadeff, David A., 79
Aliber, Robert Z., 470, 519
Anderson, Leonall C., 493*n*, 499
Anderson, William M., 210*n*
Anticipated income theory of liquidity, 108
Aschheim, Joseph, 500
Asher, Robert E., 287
Asian Development Bank, 279
Auerbach, Irving, 43*n*, 173*n*, 179*n*
Aufricht, Hans, 147*nn*, 148*n*, 164
Automatic fiscal stabilizers, 446–47
Autonomous expenditures
 effects of change on macroeconomic equilibrium, 406–408
 macroeconomic significance of changes: Keynesian vs. monetarist views, 494–95
Average propensity to consume, 334

Bach, G.L., 153*n*, 155*n*, 420, 433*n*, 458*n*, 470, 474*n*, 500, 513*n*
Balance of payments
 characteristics, 502–505
 United States, 503*t*
Balance-of-payments deficits
 financial system and, 504
 United States, 504–505
Balance-of-payments equilibrium
 goal of macroeconomic policy, 439–440
 related to balance-of-payments deficit, 505
Balance on current account, 502–504
Balance-sheet trace statement, 3
Ball, R.J., 420
Bank holding companies, 53, 249–250
 nonbanking activities permitted, 313*t*
Bank Holding Company Act, 312
Bankers' acceptances
 Federal Reserve holdings, 167
 member-bank reserves and, 175
 as money-market instruments, 246–48
Bankers' bank
 central banking function, 146–47
 Federal Reserve services as, 158
Banking system

branch banking, 51, 52*t*, 53
 correspondent banking, 54–55
 group banking, 53
 holding companies, 53
 interbank relations, 53–55
 links with rest of financial system, 104–105
 monetary role, 47–78
 size distribution of commercial banks, 51*t*
 structure, 50–53
Banks (*see* Commercial banks; Federal Reserve banks; Member banks)
Barger, Harold, 36*n*, 65*n*
Barrett, Martin, 285*n*
Barter economy, 8
Baumol, William G., 356*n*, 384*n*
Baxter, Nevins D., 248*n*, 267
Bearc, Thomas, 470
Beckhart, Benjamin H., 164
Bell, Geoffrey L., 507*n*
Benjamin, Gary L., 315
Benston, George J., 230
Bimetallic standard, 29–31
 Gresham's Law and, 29–30
Black, Robert P., 230
Bloch, Ernest, 275*n*
Blyn, Martin R., 103, 385*n*, 386*n*, 388*n*, 397, 409
Board of Governors, Federal Reserve System
 coordination with other agencies, 153–54
 "independence" issue, 152–53
 membership, 151–52
 monetary policy role, 472, 482–83, 487
 powers and duties, 152
Boatwright, H. Lee, 74*n*
Bopp, Karl R., 86*n*
Borrowing intermediaries, 97, 218–223
 characteristics, 218
 classes, 218
Bosworth, Barry, 467*n*
Boulding, Kenneth, 439, 441
Branch banking, 51, 52*t*, 53
Branching
 commercial banks, 51, 52*t*, 53
 mutual savings banks, 194
 savings and loan associations, 196–98
Branson, William H., 341*n*
Break, George F., 315
Breimyer, Frederick S., 248*n*, 250*n*
Brill, Daniel, 207*n*
Brinner, Roger, 436*n*, 437*n*, 441
Brownlee, Oswald, 513*n*, 519
Brunner, Karl, 500
Bryan, William R., 479*n*
Burger, Albert E., 79, 397
Burke, William, 30*n*
Business credit: role of government, 299

Cagan, Philip, 79, 397, 411, 500
Cameron, Rondo, 103
Capital markets, 252–58
　instruments, 253–58
　international aspects, 284–86
　related to money markets, 258
Capital-market instruments, 253–58
　contrasted with money-market instruments, 252–53
Carlson, Keith M., 493n, 499
Carson, Deane, 15, 485n
CDs (*see* Certificates of deposit)
Central banking
　central banks and, 148–49
　characteristic functions, 145–49
　in United States prior to 1914, 149–150
Central banks, 144–49 (*see also* Federal Reserve System)
　central banking and, 148–49
Certificates of deposit, 117–121
　example of liability management banking, 121
　as money-market instrument, 244–46
　variants of, 121
Chairnoff, Hugh, 131n
Chase, Samuel B., 320n
Checks
　clearing and collection, 74–76
　monetary status, 37
Claims
　creation, 3–5
　debts and equities, 3
　related to finance, 3
　related to money, 5–6
Clarke, John J., 79
Clarke, William M., 287
Clearing and collection of checks, 74–76
Clearing house, 55
Clements, Mary Ann, 307n
Cloos, George W., 212n
Cochran, James S., 256n
Cohan, Avery B., 261n
Colean, Miles L., 230
Commercial bank, 47–50
　capital adequacy, 110–111
　liquidity goal, 107–109
　nonfinancial firm and, 48–50
　other financial firms and, 72–73
Commercial banking (*see also* Commercial banks)
　evolution in United States, 87, 88–89, 92–93
　government regulation, 121–23, 124, 136–37
Commercial banking system (*see* Banking system)
Commercial banks, 50–55, 104–143
　balance-sheet management, 137–141
　　criteria, 137–39
　　external influences, 139–140
　borrowing by, 123–24
　capital accounts, 109–111
　combined balance sheet, 105t, 106
　demand deposits, 113–15

　deposits, 112t
　earning assets, 132–37, 133t
　foreign operations in United States, 277
　government regulation, 115–121, 124, 136–37
　investments, 66, 134–36
　loans, 132–34
　money-market participation, 239t, 241, 242–48, 249–250
　relations with financial system, 198–207 210, 216, 221, 223, 225
　reserve policies, 129–131
　role in foreign exchange market, 273
　role in international finance, 276–77
　service charges, 115
　sources of financing, 109–124
　time deposits, 115–123
Commercial paper, 248–252
Commission on Money and Credit, 293–96
Commodity Credit Corporation, 296
Commodity standards, 27–31
　bimetallism, 29–31
　gold, 27–29
Compensating balances, 67–68
　element in demand for money, 386–87
Conard, Joseph W., 376n, 397, 434n
Conrad, Alfred, 513n, 519
Consortia (in international finance), 277
Consumer credit
　consumption and, 336–37
　extended by nonfinancial firms, 229
　selective controls, 487–88
Consumer Credit and Protection Act, 310
Consumer finance: evolution in United States, 90–92
Consumption, 323, 333–344, 360
　financial influences, 335–38
　GNP and, 342, 343t
　inflation as an influence, 340–41, 414–15
　interest rates as an influence, 337
Consumption function, 333–34, 334t
Contractual savings intermediaries, 96, 201–212
　contrasted with depository savings intermediaries, 201
　distinguishing characteristics, 201–202
Corporate bond market, 254–56
Corporate securities, 254–58
Corporate stock, 256–58
Correspondent banking, 54–55
"Cost-push" inflation, 416–17
Cox, Jack W., 129n, 184n
Cox, William N., III, 475n, 500
Creation of demand deposits (*see* Demand deposits)
Credit allocation: government influence, 307–308
Credit standards, 31–33
　in history, 31–32
　relation to precious metal, 31
Credit unions, 200–201
　characteristics, 200
　financial assets and liabilities, 193t

Credit unions (*cont.*)
  relations with financial system, 221
Crosse, Howard D., 48*n*, 143
Croteau, John T., 91*n*, 92*n*, 230
CUNA International, 201
Currency
  demand deposits and, 38
  determinants of volume, 37–39
  outstanding and in circulation, 33*t*
  types, in United States, 33–35
Currency in circulation, 33*t*
  member-bank reserves and, 172–73

Darnell, Jerome C., 434*n*
Davis, Richard G., 117*n*
Davis, Thomas E., 134*n*
Debt management, 453–463
  defined, 453
  disposal of surplus, 459–461
  financing a deficit, 454–59
  policy, 462–63
  refunding process, 461–62
  related to fiscal policy, 453
Defensive aspects of Federal Reserve actions, 183–84
DeLeeuw, Frank, 320*n*, 500
Demand-deposit creation, 56–73
  characteristics, 61–62
  empirical investigations, 64
  limits, 62–63
Demand-deposit destruction, 69
Demand deposits
  adjusted, as money, 35–36
  currency and, 38
  foreign holdings, in United States, 275
  implicit return on, 114, 115
  ownership of, 112*t*, 113–115
Denison, Edward F., 330, 438*n*
Depository savings intermediaries, 191–201, 216
  characteristics, 95–96, 191
  contrasted with contractual savings intermediaries, 201
Deposits
  insurance, 307
  interest-rate ceilings, 306–307
Dernburg, Thomas F., 369, 420
Development credit corporations, 221, 223
Dewald, William G., 149*n*
Diamond, William, 287
Dill, Arnold, 143
Direct finance, 10
Direct placement (bond issues), 255
  life-insurance companies and, 206
Discount mechanism (Federal Reserve)
  defined, 479
  reform proposals, 480–81
  weaknesses, 480
Discount rate, 480
Discretionary fiscal action, 447–49
Diversification, 11

influence on demand for liquidity, 381
Doenges, R. Conrad, 15
Dougall, Herbert E., 267
Dublin, Jack, 230
Duesenberry, James S., 320*n*, 339*n*, 369, 397
Dynamic aspects of Federal Reserve actions, 185–86

Earning assets, commercial bank, 132–37, 133*t*
Eckstein, Otto, 436*n*, 437*n*, 441
Ehrlich, Edna E., 226*n*
Eilbott, Peter, 447*n*
Einzig, Paul, 5*n*, 46, 430*n*
Eisner, Robert, 352*n*, 356*n*, 369
Elasticity (monetary), 43
Employment Act of 1946, 153
  influence on fiscal policy, 444–45
Entine, Alan, 15
Equilibrium
  balance-of-payments (*see* Balance-of-payments equilibrium)
  financial sector, 404–405
  macroeconomic, 405–406, 406*t*
  real sector, 401–403
Equilibrium GNP, 363
Equilibrium: money demand and supply, 392–94
  effects of change in GNP, 393
  effects of change in liquid-asset markets, 393
  effects of change in money supply, 394
Ettin, Edward C., 86*n*, 103
Eurobond market, 285
Eurodollars, 280–82
  financing, 280–81
  market, 281–82
Euroequities, 285
Europaper market, 284
European Investment Bank, 279
Excess reserves, 131
Exchange rates, 270–71, 275, 510
  determination of, 270–71
Eximbank (*see* Export-Import Bank)
Expectations hypothesis, 264–65
Export-Import Bank, 277, 299, 301

Fand, David I., 493*n*, 494*n*, 500
Farm Credit Act of 1971, 295–96
Farm Credit Administration, 295–96, 301
Farmers Home Administration, 296, 302
FDIC (*see* Federal Deposit Insurance Corporation)
Federal Advisory Council, 151*n*
Federal Financing Bank, 242
Federal funds, 129
  as money-market instrument, 242–44
  related to monetary policy, 244
Federal Home Loan Bank System
  advances to member associations, 200
  housing credit and, 297
  membership, 197*t*, 199
  organization, 199–200

Federal Home Loan Bank System (*cont.*)
  sources of financing, 200
Federal Home Loan Mortgage Corporation, 298
Federal Housing Administration, 308
Federal National Mortgage Association, 297–98, 301, 302
Federal Open Market Committee
  controversial aspects, 154–55
  international financial considerations, 506–507
  membership, 154
  monetary policy role, 472–73
Federal Reserve Act, 150
Federal Reserve balance sheet, 166–68, 167*t*
Federal Reserve bank credit (*see* Reserve bank credit)
Federal Reserve Bank of New York, 161, 170
Federal Reserve banks, 156–162
  boards of directors, 156–57
  controversy over board composition, 157
  earnings and expenses, 157–58, 159*t*
  functions of board, 157
  organization, 155–58
  ownership, 157
  presidents, 157
  services, 158–162
  size (assets), 157, 159*t*
Federal Reserve discount mechanism (*see* Discount mechanism)
Federal Reserve discount rate, 480
Federal Reserve districts, map, 156
Federal Reserve notes, 34
Federal Reserve system, 149–162
  historical background, 149–150
  monetary role, 41–43, 471–499, 501–518
  structure, 150–58
Federal Savings and Loan Insurance Corporation, 196
  membership, 197*t*
Ferber, Robert, 333*n*, 369
FHLBS (*see* Federal Home Loan Bank System)
Finance, 2
  direct, 10
  indirect, 11
  "price" of, 6
Finance companies, 219–221
  financial assets and liabilities, 220*t*
  participation in money market, 237, 249
  portfolio composition, 219
  relations with financial system, 221, 223
  sources of financing, 220–21
  structure of industry, 219
Financial claims (*see* Claims)
Financial development related to economic development, 2
Financial institutions, 6–7 (*see also* Financial intermediaries)
  system of in United States, 93–98, 94*t*
Financial intermediaries, 6–7
  assets, total, 192*t*
  in developing West (U.S.), 88–89
  economic role, 10–12
  evolution and recent trends (U.S.) 86–93
  government influences, 303–304
  influence on liquidity, 383
  nonintermediation activities, 85–86
  regulation of entry, 311
Financial intermediary
  nature, 98–101
  primary objectives, 99–101
Financial markets, 7, 232–267 (*see also* Money markets; Capital markets)
  categories, 233–34
  elements, 232
  influence on liquidity, 383
Financial system
  elements, 3
  equilibrium, 394–96
  influence on liquidity, 382–83
  influence on resource allocation, 289
  international aspects, 269–286
  "real" system and, 8
  reasons for studying, 13
  role of financial markets, 232
  role of government, 288–314
Fiscal agency
  Federal Reserve services as, 158, 160–61
  function of central bank, 147–48
"Fiscal drag," 447
Fiscal macroeconomics, 445–49
Fiscal policy, 444–453
  automatic stabilizers, 446–47
  defined, 444
  discretionary fiscal action, 447–49
  evaluation: Keynesian vs. monetarist, 494
Fischer, Gerald C., 79
Fleming, J. Marcus, 287
Float
  on Federal Reserve balance sheet, 168
  influences on size of, 179–180
  member-bank reserves and, 178–180
Floyd, Robert H., 466*n*, 470
Foreign exchange brokers, 273
Foreign exchange market, 272–74
  demand and supply, 273–74
Fousek, Peter G., 164, 188, 236*n*
Frictional unemployment, 431–32
Friedman, Irving S., 420
Friedman, Milton, 32*n*, 46, 369, 435, 441, 480*n*, 493*n*, 497*n*, 500
Friend, Irwin, 230
Fromm, Gary, 508*n*
FSLIC (*see* Federal Savings and Loan Insurance Corporation)
Full employment
  goal of macroeconomic policy, 431–33
  price-level stability versus, 434–37
"Full-employment surplus" analysis, 449–453
  uses, 451–53
Furth, J. Herbert, 507*n*, 519

Gaines, Tilford C., 463*n*, 470
Garvy, George, 385*n*, 386*n*, 388*n*, 397, 409

524 Index

General instruments of monetary policy,
    477–487 (*see also* Open-market policy,
    discount mechanism; Member-bank
    reserve requirement)
  comparison, 485–87
  reform proposals, 480–81, 483–85
Gies, Thomas G., 143, 215*n*, 219*n*, 315
GNP (*see* Gross national product)
Gold
  present domestic monetary role, 33–34
  production, 28*n*
Gold, Joseph, 287
Gold certificates, 166–67
Gold standard, 27–29
Gold stock, related to member-bank
    reserves, 170–71
Goldsmith, Raymond W., 2*n*, 103, 203*n*,
    108*n*, 214*n*, 230, 320*n*
Goldsmiths, monetary role, 21–24, 41
Gordon, Robert J., 467*n*
Goudzwaard, Maurice B., 310*n*
Government and financial intermediaries,
    303–313
  trends, 303–304
Government expenditures on goods and
    services, 357–58
Government intermediary activities
  effects on resource allocation, 301–302
  social attitudes toward, 292–94
Government National Mortgage Association,
    298
Government role in the financial system
  dollar magnitudes, 291, 292*t*
  means employed, 292
  rationale, 288–291
Government securities dealers, 240–41
Government trust funds, 300–301
Gramley, Lyle E., 320*n*
Gramlich, Edward B., 320*n*, 500
Grebler, Leo, 230
Grenier, David, 278*n*
Gresham, Sir Thomas, 29–31
Gresham's Law, 29–31
  bimetallism and, 29–30
  Greenbacks and, 30
  silver coins and, 30
Gross national product, 321–29
  equilibrium versus full-employment, 363
  expenditure categories, 323*t*
  implicit price deflator, 322
  income categories, 325*t*
Gross private domestic investment (*see*
    Investment)
Group banking, 53
Guideposts (1960s), 464–65
Gurley, John G., 8*n*, 320*n*, 381*n*, 397
Guttentag, Jack M., 117*n*, 315

Haines, Walter, W., 158*n*
Hamburger, Michael J., 337*n*
Hammond, Bray, 103

Hamovitch, William, 500
Harless, Doris, 230
Harris, Duane, 349*n*
Hayes, Alfred, 312*n*
Hayes, Douglas, A., 143
Hedging (foreign exchange), 274–75
Heller, Walter W., 431*n*
Herman, Edward S., 315
Hicks, Sir John, 25, 26*n*, 356*n*, 403, 420
Hoarding, 326
  element in demand for money, 387
Hodgman, Donald R., 143
Holmes, Alan R., 287, 473*n*
Holubnychy, Vsevolod, 293*n*
Homer, Sidney, 267
Horsefield, J. Keith, 145*n*, 287
Horwich, George, 64*n*
Housing and Urban Development Act of 1968,
    198
Housing credit: government role, 296–98
Housing investment, 354–55
Huitt, Ralph K., 445*n*
Huizenga, Clarence J., 513*n*
Hungate, Robert P., 85*n*, 103, 268, 353*n*
Hurley, Evelyn M., 219*n*, 220*n*
Hyperinflation, 411

Incidence of monetary policy, 513–14
Income velocity of money, 409
Incomes policy
  defined, 463
  "freezes" and "phases" of 1970s, 465–68
  guideposts (1960s), 464–65
  macroeconomic role, 463–68
Indicators (monetary policy), 472–76
  desirable characteristics, 474–75
  interest rate movements, 475–76
  monetary aggregates, 476
  RPDs, 476
Indirect finance, 11
Inflation, 409–417, 433–37
  "cost-push," 416–17
  defined, 411
  duration, 416
  effects of market concentration, 416–17
  harmful effects, 33–34
  initiation, 411
  process, 411–17
  trade-off between unemployment and,
    434–37
Inside lag of monetary policy, 476
Institutional trustees, 206, 226–27
Insurance companies (*see also* Life insurance
    companies; Property and liability in-
    surance companies)
  in capital markets, 255
  foreign in U.S. capital markets, 277
  in U.S. financial history, 90
Inter-American Development Bank, 279
Interbank deposits, 113–14
Interbank relations, 53–55

Index 525

Interbusiness financing, 85, 228–29
Interest equalization tax (1964), 509
Interest rate
   demand for money related to, 389–390
   liquidity preference theory, 376
Interest-rate ceilings: loan, 137, 309–310
Interest-rate structure, 258–266
   dimensions, 261–63
   pattern, 263t
Intermediaries (see Financial intermediaries)
Intermediation, 84–86
   financial intermediaries and, 84–86
   by nonintermediaries, 84–85
International Bank for Reconstruction and Development, 278
International Development Association, 279
International finance, 269–286
   government role, 299–300
International Finance Corporation, 278–79
International financial relations and central banking, 148
International financial-market relations, 276–285
International Monetary Fund, 271–72
International monetary relations, 270–75
International payments system, 270–72
Inventory investment, 355
Investment, 324, 344–357
   financial factors, 352–54
   GNP and, 349–352
Investment banking houses, 244, 255–56
Investment companies, 96–97, 213–16
   characteristics, 192, 213
   classes, 213–14
   financial assets and liabilities, 213t
   portfolio policies, 214–15
   relation to financial system, 204, 206, 212
Investment counselors and advisers, 227
Investment decision, 345–47, 352–53
Investments, commercial bank, 66–67, 134–36
   money creation and, 66–67
IS curve
   derived, 401–403
   inflation and, 413

Jacobs, Donald P., 103, 214n, 230
Jacoby, Neil H., 141n, 315
Jessup, Paul F., 143
Johnson, Harry G., 154n, 439n, 493n, 500
Johnson, Harry L., 487n, 500
Johnson, Stewart, 294n
Joint Economic Committee, 444

Kahler, C. P., 74n
Kaufman, George G., 336n, 387n, 474n, 500, 519
Kendall, Leon T., 89n, 230, 311
Key currency: role of U.S. dollar, 275
Keynes, J. M., 257, 319, 369, 376
Kindleberger, Charles, P., 274n, 287

Klaman, Saul B., 225n
Klevorick, Alvin K., 341
Klopstock, Fred H., 282n
Knight, Robert E., 124n
Kreps, Clifton H., Jr., 112n
Kroos, Herman E., 46, 103
Kuh, Edwin, 369
Kvasnicka, Joseph G., 275n

Laffer, Arthur, 40n
Lags of monetary policy, 476–77, 478–79, 496–97
Laidler, David E. W., 397, 414n, 420
Lash, Nicholas, 46, 164
Latane, Henry, A., 389n
Latta, Cynthia, 336n
Laurent, Robert D., 38n
Law, Warren A., 291n
Lean, Jane, 338n, 385n
Legal reserves, 128
Lemmond, Douglas H., 277n
Levy, Yvonne, 30n
Lewis, Wilfred, Jr., 449n, 470
Liability management banking, 108–109
   certificates of deposit and, 121
   federal funds and, 243
Life insurance companies, 202–207
   activities other than life insurance, 204
   financial assets and liabilities, 205t
   portfolio policy and management, 204–206
   relations with financial system, 198, 206–207, 212
   sources of financing, 203–204
   structure of the industry, 203
Lindow, Wesley, 230, 268
Line of credit, 67
Liquid assets
   as factor in liquidity, 377
   foreign holdings in U.S., 283t
Liquidity
   objective of financial intermediary, 101
   theories of (bank), 107–109
Liquidity (economic unit)
   costs, 382
   defined, 376–77
   of financial intermediaries: government influence, 305
   general credit conditions and, 379–380
   immediate determinants, 377–79
Liquidity, demand for, 380–82
   related to demand for money, 387–88
Liquidity preference
   term structure of interest rates and, 265
   theory of the interest rate, 376
LM curve
   derived, 404–405
   inflation and, 413
Loans, commercial bank, 132–34
Loans, Federal Reserve, and member-bank reserves, 174–75
Ludtke, James B., 231

Macroeconomic equilibrium, 405–406, 406t
  effects of fiscal actions, 448–49
  effects of open-market operations, 491–92
Macroeconomic model
  "first approximation," 360–68
  real/financial, 400–409
Macroeconomic policy
  alternative means, 428, 442–43
  defined, 427
  goals, 430–440
  recapitulation, 514–17
  related to macroeconomic theory, 428–430
Macroeconomic theory
  defined, 331
  influence on choice of policy means, 443
  influence on macroeconomic policy goals, 430
  related to macroeconomic policy, 428–430
Maddala, G. S., 384n
Madden, Carl H., 236n, 268
Maisel, Sherman J., 188, 500
Malabre, Alfred L., Jr., 416n
Malkiel, Burton G., 265n, 268
Manager of the System Open Market Account, 476, 477
Mann, Maurice, 497n
Margin requirements, 487
  U.S. experience, 489
Marginal cost of financing schedule, 353–54
Marginal efficiency of investment, 345–49
Marginal propensity to consume, 334
  out of GNP, 344
Marginal propensity to invest, 350, 350t
Marginal propensity to make expenditures, 362
  related to multiplier, 363–66
Marginal propensity to save, 334
Market-segmentation theory, 264, 509
Marvell, Thomas B., 293n, 315
Mason, Edward S., 287
Mason, Will E., 46
Mayer, Thomas, 486n, 497n, 500
Mayo, Robert P., 379n
McDougall, Duncan M., 369, 420
McKie, James W., 301n
McKinnon, Ronald I., 12n, 46
Meek, Paul W., 129n, 184n, 188, 500
Meigs, A. James, 141n, 500
Meiselman, David, 268
Meltzer, Allan, 353n
Member-bank reserve requirements, 181–82, 481–85, 486–88, 486t
  on commercial paper, 250
Member-bank reserves
  calculation of required reserves, 181–82
  effect of government deficit or surplus, 454–461
  factors supplying, 170–72, 173–180
  Federal Reserve and, 168–186
  Federal Reserve control over, 180–86
  "pooling of reserves" fallacy, 158

  sources of change, 185t
Mendelsohn, M. S., 91n
Mergers
  commercial banks, 51, 53
  finance companies, 219
  savings and loan associations, 198
Meyer, John R., 369
Mikesell, Raymond F., 287
Minsky, Hyman P., 12n
Mints, Lloyd W., 107n
Mishan, E. G., 441
Mitchell, George W., 114n
Monetarist approach to macroeconomics, 492–96
  compared to Keynesian approach, 493–95
Monetary aggregates
  as indicators of monetary policy, 476
  in transmission mechanism of monetary policy, 474
Monetary policy
  automatic stabilizer role, 497–98
  defined, 443
  effects on housing construction, 512
  effects on state-local capital spending, 512–13
  formation, 472–77
  general instruments, 477–487
  goal priorities of Federal Reserve, 473–74
  incidence, 511–14
  indicators, 473–76
  international aspects, 501–511
  as "policy of last resort," 472
  role of Federal Open Market Committee, 472–73
  selective controls, 388, 487–490
  transmission mechanism: Keynesian vs. monetarist, 494
Monetary standards, 27–33
  commodity standards, 27–31
  credit standards, 31–33
Monetary system, 26–44
  elements, 26
  performance criteria, 43–44
Monetary theory, 319–424
  defined, 319
  evolution, 319–320
Money
  as claim, 5, 24–25
  control of supply, 41–43, 145–46
  definitions and concepts, 19, 39–40
  demand for, 383–391
    interest rate and, 389–390
    level of GNP and, 388–390
    related to demand for liquidity, 387–88
  evolution, 21–26
    early role of banks, 21–24
    financial system and, 25
    future, 25
    as process of decommoditization, 44
  general acceptability, 20–21
  irredeemable paper, 24

Money (cont.)
  issuance, 40–43
Money demand, 70, 383–391
  effects of change on macroeconomic equilibrium, 409
Money economy, 9
Money illusion related to consumption, 341, 413
Money markets, 234–351
  participants, 236–38
Money-market instruments, 238–251, 238t
  contrasted with capital-market instruments, 252–53
  criteria for open-market status, 235
  economic role, 235–36
  financial functions, 235
  foreign holdings, in U.S., 282–84, 283t
Money supply, 391
  agencies of control (U.S.), 41–43
  effect of government deficit or surplus, 454–461
  effects of change on macroeconomic equilibrium, 408–409
  management of as central banking function, 145–46
Monhollon, Jinnie, 145n, 147n
Moral suasion, 490
Morley, Samuel A., 420
Morris, Frank E., 476n, 513n
Morrison, George R., 143
Mortgage companies, 225–26
  compared with investment bankers, 225
  relations with financial system, 207
Mueller, Eva, 338n, 385n, 415n
Multinational banks, 277
Multiplier, 363–67
  autonomous expenditure change and, 363–64
  effect of including financial system in model, 408
  marginal propensity to make expenditures and, 363–66
  time path, 366–67, 366t
Murphy, Neil G., 143
Murray, Roger F., 231
Mutual funds, 196, 213–14
Mutual savings banking evolution, 87–88, 93
Mutual savings banks
  asset structure, 194–95
  financial assets and liabilities, 193t
  nonbanking activities of, 196
  sources of financing, 195–96
  structure of industry, 193–94
Mutual Savings Central Fund, Inc., 194

Nadler, Paul S., 113n, 118n, 143
National Credit Union Administration, 201
National Monetary Commission, 150
"Natural" rate of unemployment, 435–36
Negotiable order of withdrawal, 195–96
Net disposable personal income, 325–26

Net exports
  GNP and, 357–58
  effect of inflation on, 414
Net income as an objective of financial intermediary, 99–100
Net liquidity balance, 504
Nichols, Dorothy M., 268
Nonbank financial intermediaries: economic role, 191
Nonfinancial corporations
  issuers of securities, 254–58
  participants in money market, 237, 240, 245, 250
Nonintermediary financial firms, 97, 223–27
NOW accounts (see Negotiable order of withdrawal)
Noyes, Guy E., 66
Nussbaum, A. A., 46

O'Brien, James M., 489n
Official reserve transactions balance, 504
Okun, Arthur M., 450n, 470
One-bank holding company, 312
Open-market operations, 175–78, 477–79, 482–83, 486–87, 486t
  advantages and disadvantages, 478–79
  macroeconomic effects, 490–92
Open-market policy: procedures, 477–78
"Open-mouth" policy (see Moral suasion)
Outside lag of monetary policy, 496–97
Over-the-counter market, 256
Oxenfeldt, Alfred, 293n

Parity (monetary), 43, 146
Passive deficit, 449
Payments system, 53–54, 73–77
  evaluation, 76–77
  innovations, 76–77
Pension funds, 210–12
  distinguishing characteristics, 210
  European, in U.S. capital markets, 277
  financial assets and liabilities, 211t, 212t
  investment policies, 210–12
  relations with financial system, 204, 207, 212, 216
Perry, G. L., 464n
Personal saving, 325–26
  hoarding versus, 326
Peterson, John E., 512n, 519
Phelps, Edmund S., 435n
Phillips, A. W., 434
Phillips curve, 434–37
  means to improve position, 436–37
Pierce, James L., 138n
Pippenger, John, 502n
Polakoff, Murray, 231, 268, 513n
Prather, Charles F., 138n
Precaution
  influence on demand for liquidity, 381
  influence on demand for money, 385
Price, 9

Price level
  changes, related to consumption, 340–41
  defined, 411
  related to aggregate economic activity, 409–419
Price-level stability
  full employment versus, 434–37
  macroeconomic policy goal, 433–34
Primary reserves, 126–27
Pritchard, Leland J., 34n, 95n
Prochnow, Harold, V., 108n, 143, 287
Property and liability insurance companies, 207–210
  contrasted with life insurance companies, 207
  financial assets and liabilities of, 209t
  portfolio policy and management, 208–209
  relation to financial system, 210, 212, 216
  sources of financing, 208
  structure of industry, 208
Pulay, George, 287
Purchase-lease-back arrangements, 206

Rangarajan, C., 64n
Rasminsky, Louis, 145, 164
Ratchford, B. U., 145n, 147n, 164
Reagan, Michael D., 152n, 155n, 157n, 164
Real estate credit: selective credit controls on, 487–88
Real estate investment trusts, 215–16
  financial assets and liabilities, 216t
  relations with financial system, 216
Recognition lag, 476–77
Regulation J, 169n
Regulation Q, 121–23
  large CDs and, 246
Regulation Z, 310
Repurchase agreement, 177, 241
Reserve bank credit
  components, 167–68
  and Federal Reserve balance sheet, 167–68
  Federal Reserve control over, 180–81
  member-bank reserves and, 173–180
Reserve equation, 169t
Reserve requirements
  members of FHLBS, 200
  rationale, 128, 305–306
Reserve requirements: member banks, 55–56
  advantages and disadvantages, 481–82
  current pattern, 182t
  effects of change, 182
  reform proposals, 483–85
  utilization as credit-control instrument, 482
Reserves: commercial bank, 126–131
  legal and working, 128
  primary and secondary, 126–28
Reserves available to support private deposits (RPDs), 476
Revenue Act of 1964, 445
  discretionary fiscal policy and, 449
Richardson, Dennis W., 46
Ritter, Lawrence S., 15, 28n
Robertson, Ross M., 315
Robinson, Roland I., 138n, 143, 211n, 233n, 258n, 268
Roosa, Robert V., 183, 188
Ross, Myron, 339n, 508n
Rothwell, Jack C., 135n
Rozen, Marvin, 87n
RPDs, 476
Ruebling, Charlotte E., 121

Safety
  financial intermediaries: government influence, 306–307
  objective of the financial intermediary, 100–101
Samuelson, Paul A., 367n
Saulnier, Raymond J., 141n, 315
Savings and loan associations
  asset-mix, 198
  effects of Housing and Urban Development Act of 1968, 198
  evolution, in U.S., 89–90, 93
  financial assets and liabilities, 193t
  membership in FHLBS, 199–200
  relations with financial system, 206
  sources of financing, 198–99
  structure of industry, 196–98, 197t
Savings Bank Trust Company, 194
Savings deposits, commercial bank, 116–17
Sayers, R. S., 145n, 164, 165n, 188
Schadrack, Frederick C., 248n, 250n
Scheld, Karl A., 141n
Schulkin, Peter A., 215n
Schultz, George P., 470
Schwartz, Anna J., 46, 497n
Scott, Ira O., Jr., 268
SDR (see Special drawing rights)
Secondary market
  agency securities, 242
  bankers' acceptances, 248
  certificates of deposit, 245
  corporate bonds, 256
  corporate stock, 257–58
  state and local short-term debt, 242
  Treasury bills, 240–41
Secondary reserves, 127
Securities brokers and dealers, 224–25
Selective credit controls, 308
  case against, 489–490
  case for, 488–89
  defined, 487
  United States experience, 487–88
Self-liquidating theory of (bank) liquidity, 107–108
Severn, Alan K., 64n
Shapiro, Eli, 65n, 147n
Shaw, Edward S., 8n, 320n, 381n, 397
Sheehan, John, 464n, 470
Shiftability approach to (bank) liquidity, 108

Shull, Bernard, 500
Siegel, Barry N., 342n, 369
Silber, William L., 513n
Slesinger, Reuben E., 153n
Small Business Administration, 299, 301
Small business investment companies, 221–23
  relations with financial system, 221, 223
Smith, Harlan, 420
Smith, Warren L., 15, 95n, 154n, 188, 369, 420, 463n, 480n, 500
Smithies, Arthur, 487n
Snider, Delbert A., 270n, 287, 510n
Social Security funds, 300–301
Soderlind, Sterling, E., 340n
Spahr, Walter, 28n
Special drawing rights, 272
Special drawing rights certificate account
  Federal Reserve balance sheet, 167
  member-bank reserves and, 171
Speculation
  influence on demand for liquidity, 381–82
  influence on demand for money, 385
Spencer, Roger W., 443n
Staats, William F., 110n
Stein, Herbert, 449n, 470
Stigler, George, 411n
Stock exchanges, 257–58
Stock market, 257–58
Stockton, John S., 148n
Stone, R. W., 268
Strotz, Robert H., 356n, 369
Struble, Frederick M., 268
Studenski, Paul, 46, 103
Suits, Daniel B., 369
Syndicate, 224

Talley, Ronald J., 241n
Tanner, J. Ernest, 497n
Taxation, progressive, and inflation, 414
Teck, Alan, 231
Teeters, Nancy H., 450n, 470
Teigen, Ronald L., 15, 154n, 493n, 500
Term structure of interest rates, 263–66
  theories, 264–66
Thompson, F. P., 25, 46
Time deposit interest rate regulation, 121–23, 122t
Time deposits, commercial bank, 115–123
  ownership, 112t
Tobin, James, 72n, 79, 397, 480n
Tolley, George, 485n
Total expenditure function, 362–63, 364t
Trade credit, 228–29
  as form of intermediation, 85
"Tradition against borrowing," 479
Transactions
  influence on demand for liquidity, 380–381
  influence on demand for money, 384–85
Treasury of the United States (*see* United States Treasury)
Treasury bills, 239–241
Treasury currency outstanding: member-bank reserves and, 171–72
Trescott, Paul B., 103
Truth-in-lending law, 310
Tuck, Charles C., 415n

Unemployment, 431–33
  frictional, 431–32
  trade-off between inflation and, 434–37
Unemployment compensation, 446
Unit of account, 20
  related to money, 20
United States government debt: composition, 455t
United States government securities
  book-entry system, 241
  in capital markets, 253–54
  holders, short-term, 239t
  Federal Reserve holdings, 168
    member-bank reserves and, 175–76
  ownership and maturity structure, 454t
  tax-anticipation bills, 240
United States notes ("greenbacks"), 30, 35
United States Treasury
  debt management function, 453–463
  deposits in commercial banks, 36, 113, 154
  deposits in Federal Reserve banks, 168, 173
  influence on member-bank reserves, 170, 171–73
  monetary role, 40–41
  pattern of cash receipts and payments, 240t

Van Horne, James C., 265n, 268
Vehicle currency: role of U.S. dollar, 275
Vogel, Robert C., 384n
Voluntary Foreign Credit Restraint program, 309, 509–510

Waage, Thomas O., 485n
Ward, Richard A., 15
Wealth effect: related to inflation, 413
Weber, Arnold, 470
Welfling, Weldon, 231
White, John A., 287
Whittlesey, Charles R., 86n
Willes, Mark H., 477n, 500
Willis, Parker B., 238n, 244n, 268
Wolf, Harold A., 15
Woodworth, G. Walter, 234n, 268
Working reserves, 128
World Bank, 278
World Bank Group, 278–79
Wrightsman, Dwayne, 397, 473n, 500

Yeager, Leland B., 287, 485*n*
Yield (of a claim): computation, 259–261
Yohe, William P., 443*n*

Zone of inflation, 410–11
  influence of economic growth, 417–18